CLASSIC READINGS IN PSYCHOLOGY

CLASSIC READINGS IN PSYCHOLOGY

Edited by

James V. McConnell, Ph.D.

and

Daniel W. Gorenflo, Ph.D.

Holt, Rinehart and Winston, Inc.

Fort Worth   Chicago   San Francisco
Philadelphia   Montreal   Toronto
London   Sydney   Tokyo

Acquisitions Editor: Eve Howard
Developmental Editor: Tod Gross
Project Editor: Michele Tomiak
Production Manager: Kathy Ferguson
Design Supervisor: Guy Jacobs

Copyright © 1989 by Holt, Rinehart and Winston, Inc.

All rights reserved. No part of this publication may be reproduced or transmitted in any form or by any means, electronic or mechanical, including photocopy, recording or any information storage and retrieval system, without permission in writing from the publisher.

Requests for permission to make copies of any part of the work should be mailed to: Copyrights and Permissions Department, Holt, Rinehart and Winston, Inc., Orlando, Florida 32887.

Photographs in Chapter 14 reproduced courtesy of William Vandivert and *Scientific American.*

Statement of copyright and permission to reprint for each of the 22 articles reprinted in this book can be found in the footnotes at the end of each chapter.

Printed in the United States of America

ISBN 0-03-027614-4

9 0 1 2 066 9 8 7 6 5 4 3 2 1

PREFACE

This book of readings is unique in at least three ways: the manner in which the articles were *selected*, the way in which the articles are *presented*, and the technology involved in *publishing* the book. In order to describe what this book is like, therefore, we need to discuss all three of these unique features.

SELECTING THE ARTICLES

Most editors of "readers" use rather arbitrary criteria to select the journal articles that they include in their books. While this approach has its strengths, it also has one glaring weakness: The editors typically screen the literature for papers *they* think are important. Whether or not the editors' selections are those that most *instructors* of introductory classes want to assign their students, therefore, is a matter of chance.

We approached the task of selecting articles for our reader from rather a different viewpoint. We assumed that most instructors would prefer to have a reader contain papers that *almost all psychology teachers* would agree are important. The problem then became how to determine which articles might meet that criterion.

Our solution was simple-minded in concept, but fairly difficult in execution. We assumed that the authors of most introductory psychology texts survey the behavioral literature rather thoroughly. Obviously, the authors of these texts have their own sets of biases. But, we decided, if we collated the bibliographies of a substantial number of introductory texts, the overlap *across* texts would compensate for idiosyncracies *within* any single book. So this is the approach we took.

First, we selected 24 of the best-known introductory psychology texts presently on the market. The list of these texts appears at the end of this Preface.

Next, we used an optical scanner to "read" the bibliographies of each of the 24 texts onto the hard disk of a computer. All in all, we ended up with more than 37,000 different entries. Then we "sorted" this massive list of references alphabetically and checked to see which journal articles appeared on the list most frequently. The results of our labors were as follows:

Cited in 22 of 24 Textbooks

Miller, G.A. (1956). The magical number seven, plus or minus two: Some limits on our capacity for processing information. *Psychological Review*, **63**, 81-97.

Schachter, S., & Singer, J.E. (1962). Cognitive, social, and physiological determinants of emotional state. *Psychological Review*, **69**, 379-399.

Sperling, G. (1960) The information available in brief visual presentations. *Psychological Monographs*, **74**, 1-29.

Cited in 21 of 24 Textbooks

Holmes, T.H., Rahe, R.H. (1967). The social readjustment rating scale. *Journal of Psychosomatic Research*, **11**, 213-218.

Peterson, L.R., & Peterson, M.J. (1959). Short-term retention of individual verbal items. *Journal of Experimental Psychology*, **58**, 193-198.

Cited in 19 of 24 Textbooks

Bem, D.J., & Allen, A. (1974). On predicting some of the people some of the time: The search for cross-situational consistencies in behavior. *Psychological Review*, **81**, 506-520.

Bower, G.H.. (1981). Mood and memory. *American Psychologist*, **36**, 129-148.

Brown, R.W., & McNeil, D. (1966). The "tip of the tongue" phenomenon. *Journal of Verbal Learning and Verbal Behavior*, **5**, 325-337.

Hobson, J.A., & McCarley, R.W. (1977). The brain as a dream state generator: An activation-synthesis hypothesis of the dream process. *American Journal of Psychiatry*, **134**, 1335-1348.

Rosenhan, D.L. (1973). On being sane in insane places. *Science*, **179**, 250-258.

Scarr, S., & Weinberg, R.A. (1976). IQ test performance of black children adopted by white families. *American Psychologist*, **31**, 726-739.

Cited in 18 of 24 Textbooks

Asch, S.E. (1951). Effects of group pressure upon the modification and distortion of judgments. In K.S. Guetzkow (Ed.), *Groups, leadership, and men*. Pittsburgh: Carnegie Press.

Eysenck, H.J. (1952). The effects of psychotherapy: An evaluation. *Journal of Consulting Psychology*, **16**, 319-324.

Jensen, A.R. (1969). How much can we boost I.Q. and scholastic achievement? *Harvard Educational Review*, **39**, 1-123.

Watson, J.B., & Rayner, R. (1920). Conditioned emotional reactions. *Journal of Experimental Psychology*, **3**, 1-14.

Cited in 17 of 24 Textbooks

Cannon, W.B. (1927). The James-Lange theory of emotions: A critical examination and an alternative theory. *American Journal of Psychology*, **39**, 106-124.

Craik, F.I.M., & Lockhart, R.S. (1972). Levels of processing: A framework for memory research. *Journal of Verbal Learning and Verbal Behavior*, **11**, 671-684.

Ekman, P., Levenson, R.W., & Friesen, W.V. (1983). Autonomic nervous system activity distinguishes among emotions. *Science*, **221**, 1208-1210.

Festinger, L.A., & Carlsmith, J.M. (1959). Cognitive consequences of forced compliance. *Journal of Abnormal and Social Psychology*, **58**, 203-210.

Gibson, E.J., & Walk, R.D. (1960). The "visual cliff." *Scientific American*, **202**, 64-71.

Milgram, S. (1963). Behavioral study of obedience. *Journal of Abnormal and Social Psychology*, **67**, 371-378.

Rodin, J. (1981). Current status of the internal-external hypothesis for obesity: What went wrong? *American Psychologist*, **36**, 361-372.

Cited in 16 of 24 Textbooks

Bandura, A., Ross, D., & Ross, S. (1963). Imitation of film-mediated aggressive models. *Journal of Abnormal and Social Psychology*, **66**, 3-11.

Tolman, E.C., & Honzik, C.H. (1930). Introduction and removal of reward, and maze performance in rats. *University of California Publications in Psychology*, **4**, 257-275.

This book of readings includes 22 of the 24 articles on the above list. We did not include the article by Gordon Bower since, in recent publications, he states that his early work on "mood and memory" (described in the article listed above) cannot be replicated reliably even in his own laboratory. Nor did we include the article on "racial differences in IQ" by Arthur Jensen since it ran to 123 pages in length and would have taken up almost half the pages in *this* book.

Analyzing the Articles

Several points of interest emerge from an analysis of these 24 articles:

1. In terms of content, the articles cover almost the entire field of psychology. Perhaps that isn't surprising, given the fact that introductory texts are presumed to range across psychology from its biological underpinnings to its sociological strivings. Given that fact, however, we find it somewhat surprising that there wasn't *more* overlap among the bibliographies of the 24 introductory texts. How can it be, we asked ourselves, that not one article was cited by *all* the texts, and that only three articles in *all of the psychological literature* were important enough to merit mention in at least 22 of these texts? The answer seems to be that there was tremendous overlap among the texts as far as *authors cited* was concerned, but far less agreement as to which of the authors' *works* were cited.

2. There are surprisingly few *recent* articles on the list. Only two are from the 1980s, and the oldest (by Watson and Rayner) was published in 1920. Most of the articles, in fact, were published in the 1960s and 1970s. These, then, really are *classic* readings in psychology.

3. There is considerable overlap as far as the source of the articles is concerned: Three appeared in the *Psychological Review*, another three were in the *American Psychologist*, and three more were published in the *Journal of Abnormal and Social Psychology*. Two articles on the list appeared in *Science*, and another two were taken from the *Journal of Verbal Learning and Verbal Behavior*. Thus, some 60 percent of the articles came from just five journals.

4. Despite the fact that all of the authors of these 24 journal articles are well known, there are some rather famous psychologists whose names are missing: Skinner, Freud, and Piaget, to name but three. An inspection of the textbook bibliographies suggests, however, that

psychologists of this exalted stature primarily appear as authors of *books,* not as authors of *journal articles.*

As far as the content of the articles is concerned, there were few surprises. Given the fact that the majority of articles come from the 1960s and 1970s, when classical "learning theory" still was dominant, we might expect this topic to appear frequently. And it does. At least 10 of the 24 articles touch on this subject. Social psychology comes in second, being the main topic in at least eight of the articles. However, given the emphasis in modern-day psychology on child and developmental psychology, it strikes us as odd that only two articles on the list focus on this area. Clinical psychology and personality theory also appear to be under-represented.

Overall, however, we believe that our "collating" technique snared 24 of the most important journal articles ever published in the field of psychology.

PRESENTING THE ARTICLES

We believe, as do many other instructors who have taught the introductory course, that reading the primary literature is an excellent way to help beginning students discover what our field is all about. Unfortunately, most of these students have neither the experience to make much sense of the average journal article, nor do they typically find digging into articles a very rewarding endeavor. We have tried to solve both these problems in this reader.

First, in the introductory chapter, we attempt to explain to the students in very simple terms what science is all about, why scientists publish their data, and why anyone who takes an introductory course should learn something about experimental design. In addition, we give the students some helpful hints on *how to read a journal article.*

Second, we have written comments that appear at the start of each chapter in which we attempt to explain why this particular article is "classic." We also attempt to put the published material into historical context and explain what prompted the author(s) to conduct the research (or write the article). Whenever possible, we have tried to discuss the relationships that exist *across articles.*

Third, there is the matter of *definitions.* Most beginning students simply don't comprehend the complex terminology used in most journal articles. They are perfectly capable of *learning* these terms, but are unlikely to do so unless given a fair amount of assistance. In our experience, students simply don't look words up in the dictionary, nor do they make much use of a glossary if it appears at the end of the book. However, they *will* learn new terms if the definitions appear close to where the students actually encounter the terms themselves. Therefore, we have included a *running glossary* with each article. We have printed in **boldface** each term the student might have difficulties with in the article. We then give a rough pronunciation for the term, as well as a working definition, in the lower right-hand corner of even-numbered pages throughout the reader.

As far as we know, the first use of a "running glossary" in any text was in the first edition of the senior editor's book *Understanding Human Behavior* (McConnell, 1974). Since that date, feedback gathered from thousands of students suggests that they greatly value the "running glossary." We believe that use of this pedagogical device is even more important in a book of readings than in an introductory text. Given that fact, we are surprised that no one seems to have used a page-by-page glossary before in a reader.

Finally, we have included quotations from William James at the end of many chapters. Most of these quotes come from his monumental text, *The Principles of Psychology*, which was published almost exactly 100 years ago. We selected the quotations to shed new light and understanding on the material covered in the chapter the student has just read. We were surprised--as we think the students themselves will be--at how "current" much of what James said a century ago turns out to be.

All things considered, we hope we have made it as easy and as rewarding as possible for the beginning student to discover the exciting world of information contained in the primary scientific literature.

PUBLISHING THE BOOK

Years ago, when the editors of a book of readings were ready to publish their selections, they would simply send to the publisher copies of the materials they had chosen. The production department at the publisher would then reset the journal articles in type, redraw the graphic materials, and redo the tables and graphs. This process was not only slow and laborious, but quite expensive as well.

These days, publishers are beginning to demand that authors and editors provide the publisher with *camera-ready copy*. With the growing availability of computers and optical scanners, that demand has recently become easier for authors and editors to meet.

Desktop Publishing

This book was prepared in final form by employing techniques that are now known as "desktop publishing." For those people with an interest in modern technology, we used both an IBM PS/2 Model 80 and an IBM PC AT computer as our primary devices. Optical scanning was accomplished with a Kurzweil Discover Model 30 optical scanner. We printed the final draft of the manuscript using a Hewlett-Packard Laserjet Series II laser printer.

For initial preparation of the text, we used two word-processing software packages, High-Style and WordPerfect 5.0. To prepare some of the graphics, we made use of Harvard Graphics. The final step in preparing the manuscript involved gathering all the materials together and laying out the pages using a powerful software package called Ventura Publisher (version 2.0).

Use of the Kurzweil optical scanner allowed us to "read" the text of many of the articles onto the computer straight from the pages of the journals themselves. Using a very complicated algorithm and a built-in dictionary, the scanning software attempts to "interpret" what it sees on each page as English language. It then files each page on the computer's memory disk as text, not merely as a "picture." We then could edit and rearrange the scanned text according to our own needs, just as if we had typed the article into the computer by hand. The scanning process is far from perfect, but can save enormous amounts of effort when it works. We retrieved the text itself from bound journals borrowed from the University of Michigan and Eastern Michigan University libraries. Unfortunately, as we soon found out, many of the journal articles had been so marked up by generations of students that the scanner was hard-pressed to "read through" the underlining, the yellow highlighting, and the cryptic hand-written comments that covered the pages. In some cases, then, we did have to type the articles directly into the computer the old-fashioned way. We also used the Kurzweil to copy some graphics and artwork onto the computer, and then (using Ventura Publisher) we simply "plugged" the artwork into the text at the "appropriate" places.

Whether, overall, computers actually "save time" is still something that hasn't been precisely determined. However, it is apparent that these marvelous machines allow us to do things we couldn't (or wouldn't) have done before. Take, for example, the matter of determining which articles to include in this reader. As noted, we scanned the bibliographies of the 24 introductory texts into a single file on the computer using the Kurzweil. The file itself was huge: The 37,000+ entries took up 6 million bytes on the computer's hard disk. Putting this many references into alphabetical order by hand would have been a formidable task. However, a software package called Opt-Tech Sort alphabetized all 37,000 entries in less than five minutes. We had hoped to create a software program that would scan the 37,000 entries for redundancy. However, there was so little stylistic consistency across the 24 texts that we soon gave up hope. Fewer than half the textbook authors followed APA style when preparing their bibliographies. The sorting program we used is excellent, but it cannot tell that an entry under "Watson, J.B." is the same as one under "Watson, John B." Nor does the sorting software recognize that an article by "Watson *and* Rayner" is the same as an article by "Watson & Rayner." There still are some tasks that the human brain accomplishes better than today's computers do!

Finally, and in the same vein, we ask the reader's indulgence. Since we scanned most of the articles from the journal pages into the computer, we have left them (for the most part) *as is*. Which is to say that the authors of the journal articles too used different styles, particularly when preparing their bibliographies. We have maintained consistency in such matters within, but not across, the articles.

We believe that the use of desktop publishing techniques will become more widespread in the near future, and we anticipate that instructors will soon use this technology to "custom-tailor" the materials they use in class. We note, though, that the process remains laborious, and simply tracking down long-out-of-print journals (such as the *University of California Publications in Psychology*) can be a major chore.

FINAL THOUGHTS

Despite the many obstacles we had to overcome using the new technology described above, we have thoroughly enjoyed the process of putting together this book of readings. Editing the articles reprinted herein--some read for the first time, we reluctantly admit--has given us new respect for the wisdom of our peers. We continue to be convinced that the *science* of psychology is a robust discipline with much to offer students in any field.

We hope too that the pedagogical devices we have employed in this book will make it easier for students to learn what our discipline is all about, and perhaps encourage them to become involved in creative activities in the behavioral sciences.

Finally, it is our sincerest wish that both the instructors and the students who read this book will find it a rewarding experience.

REFERENCES

Atkinson, R.L., Atkinson, R.C., Smith, E.E., & Hilgard, E.R. (1987). *Introduction to psychology*, 9e. San Diego, CA: Harcourt Brace Jovanovich.

Benjamin, Jr., L.T., Hopkins, J.R., & Nation, J.R. (1987). *Psychology*. New York: Macmillan.

Bernstein, D.A., Roy, E.J., Srull, T.K., & Wickens, C.D. (1988). Boston, MA: Houghton Mifflin.

Bootzin, R.R., Bower, G.H., Zajonc, R.B., & Hall, E. (1986). *Psychology today: An introduction*. New York: Random House.

Coon, D. (1986). *Introduction to psychology: Exploration and application*, 4e. St. Paul, MN: West.

Crider, A.B., Goethals, G.R., Kavanaugh, R.D., & Solomon, P.R. (1986). *Psychology*, 2e. Glenview, IL: Scott, Foresman.

Crooks, R.L., & Stein, J. (1988). *Psychology: Science, behavior and life*. New York: Holt, Rinehart and Winston.

Feldman, R.S. (1987). *Understanding psychology*. New York: McGraw-Hill.

Gleitman, H. (1987). *Basic psychology*, 2e. New York: W.W. Norton.

Kalat, J.W. (1986). *Introduction to psychology*. Belmont, CA: Wadsworth.

Krebs, D., & Blackman, R. (1988). *Psychology: A first encounter*. San Diego, CA: Harcourt Brace Jovanovich.

Lahey, B.B. (1986). *Psychology: An introduction*, 2e. Dubuque, IA: Wm. C. Brown.

Lefton, L.A. (1985). *Psychology*, 3e. Boston, MA: Allyn and Bacon.

McConnell, J.V. (1989). *Understanding human behavior*, 6e. New York: Holt, Rinehart and Winston.

Morgan, C.T., King, R.A., Weisz, J.R., & Schopler, J. (1986). *Introduction to psychology*, 7e. New York: McGraw-Hill.

Morris, C.G. (1988). *Psychology: An introduction*, 6e. Englewood Cliffs, NJ: Prentice-Hall.

Myers, D.G. (1986). *Psychology*. New York: Worth.

Papilia, D.E., & Olds, S.W. (1985). *Psychology*. New York: McGraw-Hill.

Rathus, S.A. (1987). *Psychology*, 3e. New York: Holt, Rinehart and Winston.

Rubin, Z., & McNeil, E.B. (1985). *Psychology: Being human*, 4e. New York: Harper & Row.

Santrock, J.W. (1986). *Psychology: The science of mind and behavior*. Dubuque, IA: Wm. C. Brown.

Smith, R.E., Sarason, I.G., & Sarason, B.R. (1986). *Psychology: The frontiers of behavior*, 3e. New York: Harper & Row.

Wade, C., & Tavris, C. (1987). *Psychology*. New York: Harper & Row.

Wortman, C.B., Loftus, E.F., & Marshall, M.E. (1988). *Psychology*, 3e. New York: Knopf.

Contents

Chapter	Title and Author	Page
	Preface James V. McConnell and Daniel W. Gorenflo	v
1	*Compulsory Introduction: Please Read This Chapter First!* James V. McConnell and Daniel W. Gorenflo	1
2	*Conditioned Emotional Reactions* John B. Watson and Rosalie Rayner	12
3	*Introduction and Removal of Reward, and Maze Performance in Rats* E. C. Tolman and C.H. Honzik	20
4	*The James-Lange Theory of Emotions: A Critical Examination and an Alternative Theory* Walter B. Cannon	30
5	*Autonomic Nervous System Activity Distinguishes Among Emotions* Paul Ekman, Robert W. Levenson, and Wallace V. Friesen	42
6	*Cognitive, Social, and Physiological Determinants of Emotional State* Stanley Schachter and J. E. Singer	48
7	*Current status of the internal-external hypothesis for obesity: What Went Wrong?* Judith Rodin	66
8	*The Magical Number Seven, Plus or Minus Two: Some Limits on Our Capacity for Processing Information* George A. Miller	80
9	*The Information Available in Brief Visual Presentations* George Sperling	94
10	*Short-term Retention of Individual Verbal Items* Lloyd R. Peterson and Margaret Jean Peterson	120
11	*Levels of Processing: A Framework for Memory Research* Fergis I. M. Craik and Robert S. Lockhart	128
12	*The "Tip of the Tongue" Phenomenon* Roger W. Brown and David McNeil	142
13	*The Brain as a Dream State Generator: An Activation-Synthesis Hypothesis of the Dream Process* J. A. Hobson and R. W. McCarley	156
14	*The "Visual Cliff"* Eleanor J. Gibson and Richard D. Walk	174
15	*IQ Test Performance of Black Children Adopted by White Families* Sandra Scarr and R. A. Weinberg	184
16	*Imitation of film-mediated aggressive Models* Albert Bandura, Dorothea Ross, and Sheila A. Ross	200
17	*On Predicting Some of the People Some of the Time: The Search for Cross-situational Consistencies in Behavior* Daryl J. Bem and Andrea Allen	210

18	*The Social Readjustment Rating Scale*	224
	Thomas H. Holmes and Richard H. Rahe	
19	*Effects of Group Pressure upon the Modification and Distortion of Judgments*	232
	Solomon E. Asch	
20	*Behavioral Study of Obedience*	242
	Stanley Milgram	
21	*Cognitive Consequences of Forced Compliance*	252
	Leon A. Festinger and James M. Carlsmith	
22	*The Effects of Psychotherapy*	260
	Hans J. Eysenck	
23	*On Being Sane in Insane Places*	268
	David L. Rosenhan	

CHAPTER 1

Compulsory Introduction: Please Read This Chapter First!

James V. McConnell and Daniel W. Gorenflo[1]

THE PILFERING PROBLEM

Suppose that you are the manager of a large department store. One day, as you check the quarterly sales figures, you notice that shop-lifting has increased dramatically in the last several months. Some of your customers (or maybe even some of your own employees) are stealing you blind. You ask yourself, what should you do to stop this "pilfering problem?"

First off, you call a friend who manages a similar store. She tells you that when she had the same difficulty, she "used psychology." That is, she hired a company that installed public address loudspeakers throughout the store. A high-powered stereo set played background music through the speakers all day long. But "hidden" in the music were *subliminal messages* that whispered, "Don't steal," over and over again. She claims that shoplifting decreased by 50 percent in her store immediately thereafter.

You ask her what *subliminal messages* are. She informs you that they are commands spoken so softly that you can't consciously hear them. "How can they work?" you ask her. "Psychologists have found that subliminal messages 'speak directly to the subconscious mind,'" she replies. "You don't know they're there, so you can't guard against them. The thieves respond to the messages unconsciously and stop stealing without knowing why they're doing so. It's really neat," she says. "And not only is it highly scientific, it actually works! How else can you explain the fact that shoplifting went down by 50 percent?"

Subliminal Stimulation

As it happens, there *are* such things as "subliminal messages." They are stimulus inputs which are so weak they function *below the threshold of conscious awareness* (*limen* is the Latin word for "threshold"). And, under very stringent laboratory conditions, these very weak stimuli *can* have a "just detectable" influence on behavior. However, study after study has shown that subliminal stimulation has *no measurable effect* in real-life situations (McConnell, 1966; McConnell, Cutler, & McNeil, 1958).

But didn't shoplifting *decrease* after your friend installed all that fancy equipment to broadcast the subliminal commands? Doesn't that fact *prove* that the hidden messages worked, no matter what the scientific data show? No, not at all. But if you are to understand why this is the case--and what actually did occur in your friend's store--you first must learn something about the *science of psychology*. And that, of course, is the major goal of this book.

THE SCIENCE OF PSYCHOLOGY

Psychology is a *science*. It came into being as a separate academic discipline some 100 years ago. Medicine had already shown the benefits that could come from studying the workings of the human body from an objective point of view. And psychology got its start when a number of American and European philosophers, physicists, and physiologists decided to study the mind in the same scientific manner.

Because psychology *is* a science, its theories and conclusions are based primarily on *experimental evidence*. That is, the scientific study of human behavior is based on findings obtained from laboratory studies and other types of objective observations. For the most part, these findings are published in scientific journals. If you want to become a psychologist--or if you want to learn more about human behavior from an objective point of view--then you *must* become acquainted with the scientific literature. This book is designed to help you do just that.

Why Science?

What is the major difference between a "witch doctor" who attempts to cure sick people in primitive cultures, and a "medical doctor" who attempts to cure sick people in America? The answer--as you know quite well--is *scientific knowledge*. The witch doctor's techniques are based on superstition and casual observations; the techniques the medical doctor uses are based on evidence gathered from thousands and thousands of experiments conducted in scientific laboratories.

Make no mistake: Some of the witch doctors' patients do get better; and some medical patients get worse (or even die) despite being treated with the best techniques modern technology can offer. But *overall*, your chances of being cured of a serious disease are far better if you go to see an M.D. than if you put yourself in the hands of a witch doctor.

Why do some sick people treated by witch doctors get better? There are several reasons. First, your body is a marvelous biological machine with great powers to cure itself. Many medical doctors will tell you that about half the patients they see would get better whether they were treated or not--an effect known as "spontaneous recovery." (Both witch doctors and medical doctors have been known to take credit for these "natural cures," of course.) But second, the very act of *seeing a doctor* or *taking a pill* can have a profound effect on the way your body mobilizes its natural defenses--something we call the "placebo effect." For example, if you have a headache and take a placebo (sugar pill) rather than an aspirin, your body may well (1) produce an increased amount of its natural painkillers, the endorphins; and/or (2) produce an increased amount of the "arousal hormones," adrenalin and nor-adrenalin. Thus, taking a placebo can not only reduce pain, but increase activity levels as well. Little wonder, then, that placebos have an honored place in both witch doctoring and in medicine. However, consider also the following facts: Medical studies show that about 60 percent of the people who take placebos for their headaches report relief--and about half those individuals report *as much relief* as if they had taken aspirin (McConnell, 1989). But some 90 percent of the patients who take aspirin report relief. Given the data, which pill would *you* prefer to take if you had a headache?

Furthermore, if a witch doctor gives you a pill for your heachache, and you *don't* get better, the witch doctor may well say that the fault is *yours*--you don't have the "right attitude," or you have "bad karma," or you are "being punished for your sins." If the treatment prescribed by your physician doesn't work, he or she will probably put you on a different medication--or even suggest a series of tests (including a brain scan) to determine whether there might be something seriously wrong with you. One of the major differences between the two approaches, therefore, is the *extensiveness of the data base* on which the techniques are based.

Why Journal Articles?

If a "conjure woman" living in a remote area discovers through experience that chewing the bark of the willow tree seems to "cure headaches," she has no way of communicating her findings with witch doctors and conjure women elsewhere in the world. However, if a group of medical scientists discovers through experimentation that chemicals extracted from the bark of the willow tree alleviate the pain associated with headaches, they can communicate their findings with other physicians throughout the world in rather short order. They do so by publishing the results of their research in a scientific journal. Other researchers can then attempt to *replicate* the original findings in their own laboratories and clinics. If the original results "held up" under further tests--which is what "replication" is all about--physicians everywhere might well begin prescribing willow bark extracts for headaches. Other medical scientists who had read the reports might then be motivated to determine how the bark extracts actually brought about pain relief. Eventually--because of the worldwide communication that scientific journals allow--some smart experimenter might discover a way to synthesize the important ingredient in willow bark extracts (which is how aspirin was actually developed).

If the results of the first study *didn't* hold up under replication, of course, that fact would be reported in the literature as well. And medical doctors who *read the literature* would soon learn that was the case and probably would stop prescribing willow bark.

THE SCIENTIFIC METHOD

At its simplest, the scientific method (as practiced both in psychology and in medicine) is little more than a *set of controlled observations* that can be *repeated by other scientists*. However, scientific discoveries often begin with "hunches," or *uncontrolled observations*.

For instance, suppose you were the first person to notice that giving willow bark extracts to people with headaches helped ease their pain. Is the fact that you gave the extracts to 50 people--and discovered that almost all of them reported relief--a *controlled* observation? No, as you will see, it's an *uncontrolled* observation. But it does give you the notion that willow bark might contain a natural pain-killer. In science, we call this kind of notion a "hypothesis." But you haven't really tested this hypothesis scientifically yet. As we've already noted, the mere act of giving a "pill" to people often acts to relieve their pain.

So, what next? To *prove* the willow bark extract really works, you must perform a set of *controlled* observations. Which is to say, you'd need to undertake a scientific experiment.

In psychology, almost all scientific studies are based on comparisons of performance--comparisons made either *across groups*, or comparisons made on the same group of subjects *across time*. We call the former "between-subjects" comparisons, and the latter "within-subjects" comparisons. If you wanted to test the power of willow bark extract to cure headaches, you could use either approach.

Within-subjects Comparisons

Let's assume you have 60 patients who frequently suffer from heachaches. You might well decide to give each of the 60 patients the willow bark extract the *first* time one of them came to you for help. But the *second* time the same patient had a headache, you'd give the person a placebo (or "sugar pill") instead. The third time the patient asked for help, you'd give her or him the willow bark again, but the fourth time the patient would again receive a placebo medicaton. If the patients reported far greater pain relief after taking the willow bark than after taking the placebo, you'd have *compared the same subjects across time*. Put more technically, since you'd have taken repeated measures on the same people, you would have used a "within-subjects comparison," since you would have compared the performance of each subject at *one point in time* with his or her performance at *another point in time*. And, given the fact that the subjects showed greater improvement after taking the willow bark, you'd have scientific evidence to support your hypothesis that willow bark extracts are helpful.

Of course, you'd also want to control for a few other aspects of the experimental situation, as well. For one thing, you'd want to make sure that the two types of pills looked (and tasted) the same. Otherwise, your results might be due to the look or taste of the pill, not to what was in it. (For obvious reasons, we call this "running the experiment blind.") Second, you'd have the same person who gave out the pills the first time give them out the second, third, and fourth times too. Third, you'd make certain that the person distributing the two types of pills (and the person who recorded whether the patients felt any pain relief) *didn't know which pill was which*. (Can you guess why this is called "using a double-blind control?") Fourth, you'd probably want to give half the subjects the willow bark extract first, and the placebo second. The other half would receive the pills in reverse order. (We use this technique to control for what are called "order effects.")

Between-subjects Comparisons

When you make "within-subjects" comparisons, you systematically *vary* what you do to each subject, and note how each person responds. When you make "between-subjects" comparisons, however, you first divide the subjects into various groups, and then vary the conditions *across groups*. For instance, if you started with 60 patients, you might divide them into three groups of 20 patients each. The first group--which technically is known as the *experimental group*--would receive the willow bark extract. The second and third sets of patients would act as *controls*, thus would be called "control groups." One of these control groups would receive no pill at all--and thus would "control for" the fact that most people who get headaches recover rather rapidly even if they *don't* take medications. The other control group would, of course, receive the placebo--a control for the effects of "just taking a pill." Here, you're comparing performance *between* various groups of subjects.

At the end of the study, if the patients in the experimental group reported far greater relief than did the patients in either of the two control groups, you'd have scientific evidence to support your hypothesis that willow bark extracts reduced the pain associated with headaches.

Of course, you'd run this type of experiment using "double-blind" controls. But you'd also want to be very careful that you selected the patients for each group in truly *random* fashion. It might be, for example, that young people respond to placebos more frequently (or in stronger fashion) than do older people. Thus, if you put all the young patients in the "placebo control" group, you'd surely bias your results.

To summarize: In the "within-subjects design," you test each subject more than once and use each subject as her or his own control. In the "between-subjects design," you typically test each subject but once and use different groups of subjects as controls.

Generally speaking, the *more control groups you use, the more reliable your results are likely to be*. That's why we call science "a set of controlled observations."

Statistics

There's probably nothing that "turns off" students to psychology more than the thought that, somewhere down the line, they'll have to learn a little something about *statistics*. In fact, statistical devices are merely tools to help you describe sets of data and to determine what is likely to be true, and what isn't. You "use statistics" every time you play a game of chance (such as poker, bridge, or the lottery), or figure out a baseball player's batting average, or calculate your chances of getting into graduate school.

Unless you actually *conduct* psychological research yourself, you don't really need to learn much about most types of statistical techniques. There are three important points you should understand, though.

First, there are two types of statistics. We call them *descriptive* and *inferential* statistics. Descriptive statistics help you "describe" something, such as a distribution of scores. A "bell-shaped curve" is a descriptive statistic that tells you the distribution of scores on some set of data (such as the scores on an intelligence test). Whenever you calculate your grade point average, you're "figuring the mean of a distribution," which is also a descriptive statistic. However, you use inferential statistics to help you *draw conclusions*. And usually the conclusion that you wish to draw is that the responses you observed in your experimental group subjects were somehow *conclusively different* from those you observed in your control group subjects. Put another way, inferential statistics let you decide whether the results of your study were "for real," or whether they probably were due to chance effects.

Second, behavioral scientists typically report their data in terms of *probabilities*, which they calculate using such inferential statistics as "T-tests," "U-tests," and "correlation coefficients." By convention, if the results of a study probably wouldn't have occurred "by chance alone" more than one time in 20--which is usually written as $p < .05$, or $p = .05$--we assume the differences between the groups were *statistically significant*. If the statistical test shows that the differences were *not* significant "at the .05 level or better," then the hypothesis being tested wasn't confirmed.

Third, and perhaps most important, the first law of scientific research is as follows: Your statistical inferences are never better than the design of your experiment will allow. Picking the right sort of control groups in a given study is, practically speaking, far more important than is picking the "proper" statistical tool to use. For, if you fail to control for obvious sources of variability in a study (such as not running "blind" controls, or not using a "placebo control"), your results will be garbage no matter how elegant your statistics happen to be. In brief, the old saying, "garbage in, garbage out" applies to scientific research as it does to many other aspects of life. Let's show you why that's the case by taking a closer look at how psychologists discovered "the facts" about those "subliminal messages" that supposedly reduce pilfering in department stores.

SUBLIMINAL PERCEPTION

First, some history. More than a century ago, a middle-European experimenter named Suslowa made a remarkable discovery. As you surely know, the *sensitivity* of the receptors in your skin varies from one part of the body to another: The skin on your lips, on the tip of your tongue, and on your fingertips is much more sensitive than is the skin on your stomach or on the small of your back. Suslowa was one of the early experimenters who "mapped out" the human skin in terms of its sensitivity. He did so by measuring what is called the "two-point threshold" on various areas of the body.

The Two-point Threshold

Suslowa used an instrument that had two adjustable, needle-like points on it. He blindfolded his subjects and then touched the instrument to the subject's skin. Sometimes he touched the skin with both points, but sometimes he used just one point. When the points were far apart, the subjects could almost always discriminate them as being two. However, when the points were close together, the subjects often couldn't tell whether Suslowa had touched them with two points, or just one. By varying the distance between the two points, Suslowa determined how far apart the points had to be for the subjects to guess correctly exactly 50 percent of the time. By definition, that's what we call a *threshold* (or "limen")--a stimulus just strong enough to be perceived correctly 50 percent of the time.

When Suslowa did this sort of research a century ago, he discovered that the skin on the small of the back was very insensitive: The two-point threshold (limen) on the back is about 2 inches for most people. Which is to say that, when the points were 2 inches apart, Suslowa's subjects perceived them as "two" 50 percent of the time. Having made this discovery, Suslowa then did rather an odd thing. He adjusted the points so they were only half an inch apart. At this distance, his subjects *almost never* consciously perceived them as being "two." However, when Suslowa *absolutely demanded* that they guess whether the stimulus was one point or two, their guesses were significantly above the chance level. Don't misunderstand: The subjects' couldn't *perceive* the points as being one or two; but *if forced to guess*, their guesses were in the right direction. Put more properly, the subjects were responding correctly to what were below-threshold (sub-liminal) stimuli.

When Subliminal Stimulation Works

There have been hundreds of similar studies since Suslowa's. In almost all cases, subjects in these experiments could make "above chance level" guesses about subliminal stimuli. But they only did so under rather special conditions:

(1) The effect occurred only in laboratory settings where the subject could be *forced* to focus closely on the stimulus input.

(2) The effect occurred only if the subjects were *highly motivated* to guess correctly, usually because they were rewarded for giving right answers or were punished for being wrong.

Unless *both* these conditions occurred, the subjects simply *ignored* the subliminal inputs. There is not one study in the scientific literature showing that people pay any attention to subliminal messages *outside the laboratory* (McConnell, 1989; McConnell, Cutler, & McNeil, 1958). (This fact alone should tell you why it's important to read the scientific literature. Suppose someone tells you that "hidden messages" reduce shoplifting. If the effect is "for real," a search of the literature will turn up lots of experiments supporting the "realness" of the phenomenon. But if you search the literature and can't find any support, the effect is probably a fake of some kind.)

Now, how do we get from Suslowa's laboratory to the department store you're supposedly manager of? We do so by looking at what happened in a movie theater in New Jersey some 30 years ago.

Subliminal Advertising

Back in 1956, an advertising executive named James Vicary shocked the world by reporting that he had conducted a "scientific study" in a movie theater in Fort Dix, New Jersey. He claimed that when he projected "subliminal messages" on the screen (during the movie), the audience responded in surprising fashion. The messages Vicary said he projected were "Eat Popcorn" and "Drink Coca-Cola." Vicary announced that popcorn sales rose some 50 percent and Coca-Cola sales went up about 18 percent over the previous week.

As soon as Vicary announced his results, the news media went into a frenzy about this new method of "mind control." Distinguished members of Congress made eloquent speeches denouncing Vicary and introduced bills designed to outlaw the use of subliminal advertising. And the radio and television networks announced that they would *never* allow the use of subliminal messages on their networks.

Behavioral scientists, however, took rather a different approach. First, they asked Vicary what variables he had *controlled for* in his so-called study. Vicary refused to answer. (What sorts of things would *you* have tried to control for? For instance, what influence on cola sales or popcorn purchases might the *type of movie* being shown have had?) When Vicary refused to describe his work in detail, or publish it in a scientific journal, many psychologists tried to *replicate* his results under controlled conditions. Unfortunately for Vicary, they failed to do so (McConnell, 1958). As a result of this failure, there presently is no law against the use of subliminal advertising in the US. There doesn't have to be: It just doesn't work. (If it did, the government would probably be bombarding you right now with such "hidden" announcements as "Pay your taxes" and "Vote Republican," and General Motors would have long ago taken over the entire automobile industry.)

But people seem to love magical solutions to difficult problems. And little wonder. For, at times, magic not only is cheaper and easier to use than is scientific investigation, it also sometimes seems to work.

Being Right for the Wrong Reason

There's a crucial difference between subliminal advertising and the "subliminal messages" used to reduce pilfering in department stores: Subliminal advertising simply isn't effective under any known conditions. Oddly enough, though, some department stores did report significant (short-term) reductions in shop-lifting after they began playing subliminal "Don't steal" messages over their public address systems. And that fact *proves* that the subliminal messages *worked*, right?

No, it merely proves how necessary it is to understand what the scientific method is *really* all about. For, unless you base your opinions on *controlled* observations, you risk the chance of getting good (if temporary) results, but not for the reason you think.

Correlations and Causes

Perhaps the most important point to remember about scientific experiments is this one: *Correlations don't prove causes*. Most humans grow up believing that if Event A *precedes* Event B, then A must have *caused* B to occur. We are particularly likely to *apply causality* in such situations if we have some *logical explanation* that seems to link Events A and B (Dasser, Ulback, & Premack, 1989; Michotte, 1963).

One of the major purposes of using control groups in scientific studies is to determine what actually *causes* the results we get in our experiments. Generally speaking, the more control groups we use, the more likely it is that we will discover the real causal factors in any given situation.

Some Limitations

Make no mistake about it: The scientific approach to studying human behavior is neither perfect nor is it complete. For example, art, literature, music, religion, and many other viewpoints have important things to tell us about why we think, feel, and act as we do.

It's also true that not all studies that appear in the literature stand up under the test of time. Occasionally, one group of scientists will perform an experiment and neglect certain important controls. However, because researchers publish their results for everyone to see, science tends to be *self-correcting*. Chances are that another group of experimenters will discover what's wrong about the original study and point out this fact in print.

Finally, there's the problem of *narrow theoretical viewpoints*. Many scientists get so caught up in the importance of their own theories that they fail to see alternative explanations to the data they're trying to explain. For example, the first article in this book (Chapter 2) is by John B. Watson and Rosalie Rayner. Watson is often called "the father of behavioral psychology." He believed that people were little more than "biological machines," and often asserted that psychologists should look at what organisms *did*, not at what "went on inside their minds." As far as Watson was concerned, therefore, *learning* was merely a matter of "acquiring stimulus-response connections." Taking this constricted view allowed the behaviorists to make significant discoveries about human psychology, particularly in the field of learning. However, the narrowness of their theory limited the extent of their contributions.

By demonstrating that rats (and other organisms) not only "acquire stimulus-response connections," they also "create cognitive maps" when they learn a task, E. C. Tolman (Chapter 3) demonstrated that behavior is far more complex than Watson thought it was. However, Tolman (and other cognitive psychologists) tended to over-emphasize the importance of *internal variables* (such as thoughts and feelings) in explaining human behavior, and ignored genetic (biological) and social influences on our feelings and actions. Thus, while the cognitive viewpoint adds to our comprehension of psychology, it too is limited in its scope.

Some psychologists--such as Stanley Schachter (Chapter 6) and Leon Festinger (Chapter 21)--are famous for emphasizing the strong effects that the social environment has on what we do and feel. However, in so doing, these social psychologists tend to ignore the importance of biological and cognitive variables.

If you read articles *just* by the behaviorists, or *just* by biological psychologists, or *just* by cognitive or social psychologists, you might well get the wrong notion of "what makes people tick." For, as Judith Rodin (Chapter 7) and Daryl Bem and Andrea Allen (Chapter 17) note, it is the *interaction* among biological, behavioral, cognitive, and social influences that actually determines most of the complexities of your thoughts, feelings, and actions. It will help you considerably if you remember that point as you read the articles in this book.

Now that we've pointed out some of the limitations of the scientific method, let's turn again to discussing its many strengths.

The Hidden Aspects of Using Hidden Messages

As we noted earlier, scientific experimentation typically involves making a series of *controlled observations*. If you merely start broadcasting "hidden messages" over a store's public address loudspeakers, and then note a decrease in shop-lifting, all you've shown is that *something* about the situation apparently led to less stealing. Just as if you give someone who has a headache a "sugar pill," and the person reports pain relief, all you've shown is that *something* about taking a pill can reduce pain. Put more precisely, what you've demonstrated is that Event A was followed by Event B--but you haven't yet discovered *what* the causal connection between the two events is. And *that's* what you use control groups for.

First, let's consider the types of "placebo-type" controls we might use to help us determine what caused the reduction in shop-lifting in a given department store. If the *hidden messages* were really responsible for the reduction in pilfering, then what would happen if you did the following: You install the loudspeakers with great pomp and circumstance, and tell your employees that you're going to broadcast "hidden messages." But, in fact, you then *don't* play any subliminal commands over the loudspeakers. Would you be surprised if thievery decreased? (This would, as you can see, be a sort of "placebo control" situation.) And if it's the subliminal command "Don't steal" that supposedly is responsible for the good results, what would happen if you played the subliminal command "Steal more merchandise" over the loudspeakers? If shop-lifting still *decreased*, what would you conclude?

In truth, if you were testing this effect scientifically, you'd surely want to use either the "between-subjects" or the "across-subjects" design. For example, you might install the "subliminal machine" in several stores. Then, using *blind controls* (so no one at any store knew *which* message was being used), you'd play "Don't steal" in some stores, "Steal more merchandise" in other stores, and no message at all in still other stores. Or you could use all three messages *at different times* in the same store, and see what happened. If you got a reduction in shop-lifting under all conditions, as likely would be the case, what would you conclude?

Why might shop-lifting decrease under these "placebo conditions?" Well, ask yourself the following question: If you were a sales person at a department store, and the boss installed this new gadget that (according to rumor) was supposed to reduce shop-lifting, how would you behave? Would you be more likely to watch your customers very carefully after the machine was installed than before? And if *you* had perhaps been "borrowing a few items" from the store yourself, how would you react?

Of course, you could also save yourself a lot of time by checking the literature before you spent all that money performing the study. As we mentioned, there simply aren't any *controlled* studies in the scientific journals showing that "subliminal messages" have any effect in department stores or other real-world settings. So that's your first clue.

But second, you might ask the people who sell this type of equipment to *prove scientifically* that their equipment works (as psychologists asked James Vicary to prove that subliminal messages increased popcorn sales). Ask them, for instance, what control they used in testing their techniques. If you did, you'd probably get rather an odd response. For the people who sell this equipment typically say that since shoplifting decreases after the machines are installed, they don't *need* to use controlled experiments to prove their techniques work. What do you think?

You can save yourself a lot of money if you demand that witch doctors and other people who offer you "magic cures" also show you the *published scientific data* proving that their techniques are effective. Otherwise, keep your wallet in your pocket.

HOW TO FIND THE SCIENTIFIC LITERATURE

Okay, suppose you're convinced that the scientific method actually works, and that it's important to keep up with what's being published in a field like psychology. The problem then becomes, how do you find out what's been published on a certain topic you're interested in?

The obvious answer is, look for books and journal articles that contain information about your interests. However, that's easier said than done. For each year there probably are at least 50 books and a thousand journal articles published that you should look at. Presuming you could *find* all these books and journals, you'd suffer from a severe case of input overload if you tried to read them all. So, what to do?

For most students, the best thing to do is to *go to the library*. You can check the card catalogue to track down books that might be pertinent to your interests. And since most of the cards in the catalogues have a brief explanation of what the book is about, you can often weed out non-relevant materials rather quickly.

Another thing you can do is to read *Contemporary Psychology*, a monthly publication of the American Psychological Association that can be found in almost every college library in the US and Canada. This journal contains reviews of recent books. Each review is about a page long, and gives you an overview of what the book is all about. If you discover a book you might wish to read, the library will probably have it available by the time its review appears in *Contemporary Psychology*. However, just *reading* this journal monthly will help keep you current with the entire field.

But what about journal articles? There are more than 100 journals whose contents are devoted entirely to the field of psychology alone, not to mention such publications as *Science, Nature, Scientific American*, and the *American Scientist*, which sometimes contain articles on the behavioral sciences. And magazines such as *Psychology Today*, *OMNI*, and *Discover* frequently print brief excerpts of scientific discoveries, including descriptions of psychological experiments. Can you read them all? Obviously not. But again, there are solutions you can adopt. The simplest way out, perhaps, is to read *Science News*, a weekly magazine that does an excellent job of summarizing the recent literature in almost all fields of science. If you can spare a bit more time, look for a monthly publication by the American Psychological Association called *Psychological Abstracts,* which contains brief summaries of almost every article published anywhere in the world that touches on the field of psychology.

If you have to write a term paper on a given topic--or if you want to look more deeply into something that interests you--you can probably get your local friendly librarian to help out. Most college libraries can provide you with *computerized* searches of the scientific literature. Scattered across the US are several "on-line databases," which consist of huge computers whose files contain abstracts of all the medical and scientific literature (including books). You give the librarian a set of "key terms" that describe the range of topics you're interested in. The librarian then "plugs into" one of the databases (using the library's computer) and calls up all the recent material on those topics. Since most of these databases contain *Psychological Abstracts*, a computer search is by far the easiest way to look through the literature. (If you have your own computer, a modem, and lots of money to pay the fees, you can search the databases on your own.)

Once you've found a journal article you're interested in, of course, you still must *read* it.

HOW TO READ AN ARTICLE IN A SCIENTIFIC JOURNAL

The authors of most journal articles follow a fairly specific form in reporting their results. The actual style the authors use is determined in part by the requirements of the journal itself, and these requirements vary from one journal to another. However, many scientific articles begin with an *abstract* (or summary) of what the authors did and why they did it. You should *always* read this abstract carefully, if only to discover whether you're really interested in reading the rest of the article.

Immediately following the abstract is (in most cases) the *introduction* to the article. In this part of the article, the authors "lay out the problem." That is, they tell you the historical background of the problem and briefly discuss other research on the topic. At the end of their introductory comments, the authors will probably *state the hypothesis* they plan to test with their research.

Following the introductory comments, there typically is a section called "Methods and Procedure." (Some articles have two such sections, one for "methods" and the other for "prodecures.") In the Methods section of the article, the authors describe such things as (1) the subjects they used in the study (animals or humans, the number of subjects in each group, and the age and other special characteristics of the subjects), and (2) the apparatus, psychological tests, or other materials employed in conduct of the research. In the Procedures section, the researchers describe in fairly precise terms what was done to each subject (or group of subjects), how the data were gathered, the "blind controls" that were employed, and so forth.

Next comes the Results section. Here the authors will present the actual data they gathered during the study. This information is often presented in the form of tables or graphs. Next, the authors describe whatever statistical analyses they made of the data, and often will give their justification for treating the data in the manner that they did.

The Discussion section usually is next. Here the authors describe their findings in words (rather than in figures), and try to show why their results are worthy of your attention. The authors will also note whether their data supported their original hypothesis, and often will state what they might have done to improve their study and what they plan to do next.

Some journal articles contain a Conclusions section, or a Summary and Conclusions section, in which the authors briefly describe their findings again and state what conclusions they've drawn from their research. However, the authors' conclusions sometimes appear as the last part of the Discussion section, and articles that begin with a lengthy Abstract often omit the Summary section.

Most journal articles end with two sections: one called "Footnotes" (which contains comments by the authors on the material they've presented), the other called "References" (which is a list of the books and articles they've mentioned in the article). In some journals--such as *Science*--these two sections are combined.

Given the massive amount of material that appears in each journal article, how in the world do you make sense of it?

Why Journal Articles Are Often Difficult to Read

Let's be honest. Most students--particularly those in introductory classes--approach the reading of a journal article with the same amount of eagerness with which they approach a lengthy session in a dentist's chair. There are several good reasons why this is so.

To begin with, journal articles are written for *experts in the field*, not for beginning students. Therefore, journal articles are often filled with scientific terms that experts use daily but which most undergraduates can't even pronounce, much less define.

Second, to be absolutely frank, many scientists who are top-notch researchers are not all that good at communicating their findings. Only one psychologist, Sigmund Freud, was ever a serious contender for the Nobel Prize in literature--and he never quite made the grade. As far as their literacy levels go, therefore, journal articles are seldom an "easy read." However, you typically will get about as much out of an article as you are willing to put into trying to understand it.

Despite these problems, the scientific literature offers a wealth of exciting material, and you can't expect to be a very good scientist if you don't keep up with your field. It's often the case, too, that your teacher may *require* you to read (and comprehend) an article or two, whether you're personally interested in doing so or not. Therefore, here are some tips on how to make the procedure more rewarding.

Overview First; Details Second

When you pick up a scientific article, the first thing to do (after reading the title and the names of the authors) is to *read the abstract*. If no abstract is provided, turn to the end of the article and see if there's a summary of some kind. Scientific studies suggest that you'll almost always do better if you get an overview of the article *before* you dig into the details (Walter & Siebert, 1987).

Next, read the introduction, or the first few paragraphs. Doing so will not only give you some notion of what the study is all about, but also will tell you *why* it was done. Then you might wish to skip over the main part of the article and read the Discussion section. Again, the purpose of doing so is to help you comprehend *why* the article was written, what the author(s) concluded, and what conclusions the author(s) drew from having performed the study.

To be truthful, many readers will stop at this point, for all they may wish is a quick overview of the experiment. And, at the start of your career in any field, you may simply find yourself overwhelmed by the detail that is packed into the Methods, Procedures, and Results sections of most articles and thus skip over the "gory details." As you gain experience and knowledge, though, you might well begin to enjoy wading through all this information. For it is here that most of the controversy (and lots of the fun) associated with reading scientific articles can be found. You will soon find yourself asking such questions as: Did the experimenters design the study properly? Did they run enough subjects, and did they select these subjects in unbiased fashion? Did the researchers figure out the right sorts of control groups to employ? Did they perhaps pick the wrong statistics to use? These are important scientific questions to ask as you read an article. And we assure you that even a beginning student in psychology may be wise enough to figure out that the experimenters should have run an additional control group (or two!) in a particular study. (Most of the time, of course, the experimenters will have realized this was the case themselves, and will offer a good reason for omitting a specific control.)

It will also be helpful to your cause if you take the time to *outline* each article as you read it. However, we have a favor to ask: Make your outline on a separate piece of paper, not in the journal itself. In similar fashion, if you are reading an article in the library, please resist the urge to mark it up, to write comments in the margins, or even to highlight certain parts. If you absolutely *must* mark up a journal article in some fashion, make a photocopy of it first, take the *copy* home, and then you can mark it up to your heart's content without ruining it for other readers.

How We've Made Things Simple for You

In this book, we've tried to make what may be your first venture into the scientific literature as rewarding as possible.

First, we've *selected* 22 of the most cited (and most famous) journal articles for you. Many journal articles are, to be truthful, of little lasting significance except, perhaps, to a very limited audience. The articles in this book, though, are of prime importance to anyone interested in psychology. (Read the Preface if you're interested in why we picked the articles we've included in this book.)

Second, we've *gathered* the articles together in one place--this book--so you don't have to look for them in the stacks of your local library.

Third, we've begun each article with a *summary statement* we call "Editors' Comments." In this part of each chapter, we try to put the article itself into perspective--to give you some background on the problem(s) the authors were attempting to solve. We also try to point out why most psychologists believe each article is worthy of your attention.

Last, but surely not least, we've provided you with a *running glossary* in which we define some of the complex terms that the authors use. We also give you a notion of how to pronounce each word (or term) that we've included. You will find this "running glossary" in the lower right-hand column of the odd-numbered pages in this book. Each time you encounter a **boldfaced term** in the article itself, you can immediately look up its meaning in the running glossary (without having to turn to the end of the book, where glossaries traditionally have been printed).

The running glossary contains those words or phrases we believe the *average* introductory student might not have a ready definition for. If you already know some of the terms we define, that simply means you have a good head start on understanding the psychological literature. However, the person sitting next to you in class may not be so fortunate. This book is for everybody--those with big vocabularies, and those people who are just beginning to learn what psychology is all about.

Words are tools. The sooner you learn to use scientific terms properly, the sooner you will be able to *think* scientifically. And we assure you that it's far easier if you learn to "think science" before you try to "do science".

Final Thoughts

Most people who become psychologists find reading the scientific literature a fascinating experience. But even the most famous of behavioral scientists had to start their journeys just where you are now--at the very beginning. Don't despair if the going is sometimes a little rough. The rewards down the line are rich indeed.

We wish you a very enjoyable journey indeed.

FOOTNOTES

[1]James V. McConnell is Professor Emeritus of Psychology at the University of Michigan, Ann Arbor. Daniel W. Gorenflo is supervisor of research for a large corporation in Ann Arbor, Michigan.

REFERENCES

Dasser, V., Ulbaek, I., & Premack, D. (1989). The perception of intention. *Science*, **243**, 365-357.

McConnell, J.V. (1958). Subliminal stimulation: An appraisal of recent developments. Paper presented at Amer. Psychol. Assoc., Washington, D.C., September 1958.

McConnell, J.V. (1966). Persuasion and behavioral change. In *The art of persuasion in litigation handbook*. West Palm Beach, FL: Amer. Trial Lawyers Assoc.

McConnell, J.V. (1989). *Understanding human behavior*, 6e. New York: Holt, Rinehart and Winston.

McConnell, J.V., Cutler, R.L., & McNeil, E.B. (1958). Sublimination stimulation: An overview. *American Psychologist*, **13**, 229-242.

Michotte, A. (1963). *The perception of causality*. London: Metheun.

Walter, T., & Siebert, L.A. (1987). *Student success: How to do well in college and still have time for your friends*, 4e. New York: Holt, Rinehart and Winston.

Classic Quotations from William James

I wished, by treating Psychology *like* a natural science, to help her to become one.
    (*A Plea for Psychology as a Natural Science* [1892].)

Introspective Observation is what we have to rely on first and foremost and always. The word introspection need hardly be defined--it means, of course, the looking into our own minds and reporting what we there discover. Every one agrees that we there discover states of consciousness. So far as I know, the existence of such states has never been doubted by any critic, however sceptical [sic] in other respects he may have been.
    (*The Principles of Psychology* [1890], ch. 1.)

CHAPTER 2

"Conditioned Emotional Reactions"

John B. Watson and Rosalie Rayner[1]

EDITORS' COMMENTS. There's an old saying that "the burnt child dreads the fire." And once burned, the child dreads not only the fire, but also the stove, the kitchen, and perhaps pictures of fires as well. That's only to be expected, you say? Maybe. But when we try to analyze the situation in scientific terms, this type of emotional conditioning turns out to be surprisingly complex. Why should we bother analyzing such things? Because a knowledge of how fear and other emotional reactions are *acquired* might give us important insights into how best we might help people who suffer from a variety of emotional problems, such as phobias.

Let's begin with a child named Mary who's never experienced fire before. The pretty blue and orange flames look attractive, so Mary leans forward and tries to touch them. Almost immediately she experiences intense pain and jerks back her hand. The next time she sees dancing flames, presumably, she will avoid touching them. That's what *conditioning* is all about. But once conditioned to avoid fire, why should the child also avoid (dread?) pictures of the fire as well? Surely the child can *discriminate* the difference between a real flame and a photograph.

Cognitive psychologists would probably say that the child avoids the picture of the fire because it *reminds* her of a painful experience. However, John B. Watson refused to use such "mentalistic" terms as "dread" and "reminds." Instead, he assumed that the sight of a fire is a highly complex visual pattern, made up of many different stimulus elements. Each of these elements (and everything else physically present when the child was burnt) presumably becomes associated with the fear/withdrawal response. Since the picture of the fire contains some of the same visual stimuli present in the fire itself, we would expect the picture to elicit a similar (but weaker) avoidance reaction as does the flame itself. Indeed, if we could somehow *measure* what the "visual stimuli" were, we could determine how many of the stimulus elements in the fire itself were also found in the picture and thus could predict how much of the avoidance reaction would *generalize* from the actual flame to the picture. And that, to some extent, is what Watson and Rayner actually did some 70 years ago.

The Watson and Rayner article is important not only for the details it gave us about how fears are acquired and how they generalize, but also because Watson and Rayner understood that what can be *learned* through conditioning can obviously be *unlearned* using similar techniques. Four years after the publication of this research, Mary Cover Jones (a student of Watson's, and Rayner's best friend) used what we now call "counter conditioning" to extinguish an animal phobia in a small child. She presented the animal at great distance to the child while he was eating, then brought it closer step by step. At the start of the study, the animal never got close enough to the child to evoke the avoidance response, and the pleasure associated with eating soon *generalized* to the animal, just as the "dread" of the animal "generalized" to the Santa Claus mask in the present study.

Many psychologists today still prefer to try to treat phobias by dealing with the "dread," rather than the behavioral responses themselves. These clinicians encourage their patients "talk out their fears," and sometimes this approach does help. However, the experimental data suggest that simple phobias are often best handled with counter conditioning, not with "talk therapy." We must thank Watson, Rayner, and Jones for pointing us in the right direction so many years ago.

One final but important point: The American Psychological Association's Code of Ethics now prohibits psychologists from conducting research such as that described in this article.

In recent literature various speculations have been entered into concerning the possibility of conditioning various types of emotional response, but direct experimental evidence in support of such a view has been lacking. If the theory advanced by Watson and Morgan[2] to the effect that in infancy the original emotional reaction patterns are few, consisting so far as observed of fear, rage and love, then there must be some simple method by means of which the range of stimuli which can call out these emotions and their compounds is greatly increased. Otherwise, complexity in adult response could not be accounted for. These authors without adequate experimental evidence advanced the view that this range was increased by means of conditioned reflex factors. It was suggested there that the early home life of the child furnishes a laboratory situation for establishing conditioned emotional responses. The present authors have recently put the whole matter to an experimental test.

Experimental work has been done so far on only one child, Albert B. This infant was reared almost from birth in a hospital environment; his mother was a **wet nurse** in the Harriet Lane Home for Invalid Children. Albert's life was normal: he was healthy from birth and one of the best developed youngsters ever brought to the hospital, weighing twenty-one pounds at nine months of age. He was on the whole **stolid** and unemotional. His stability was one of the principal reasons for using him as a subject in this test. We felt that we could do him relatively little harm by carrying out such experiments as those outlined below.

At approximately nine months of age we ran him through the emotional tests that have become a part of our regular routine in determining whether fear reactions can be called out by other stimuli than sharp noises and the sudden removal of support. Tests of this type have been described by the senior author in another place.[3] In brief, the infant was confronted suddenly and for the first time successively with a white rat, a rabbit, a dog, a monkey, with masks with and without hair, cotton wool, burning newspapers, etc. A permanent record of Albert's reactions to these objects and situations has been preserved in a motion picture study. Manipulation was the most usual reaction called out. *At no time did this infant ever show fear in any situation.* These experimental records were confirmed by the casual observations of the mother and hospital attendants. No one had ever seen him in a state of fear and rage. The infant practically never cried.

Up to approximately nine months of age we had not tested him with loud sounds. The test to determine whether a fear reaction could be called out by a loud sound was made when he was eight months, twenty-six days of age. The sound was that made by striking a hammer upon a suspended steel bar four feet in length and three-fourths of an inch in diameter. The laboratory notes are as follows:

One of the two experimenters caused the child to turn its head and fixate her moving hand; the other, stationed back of the child, struck the steel bar a sharp blow. The child started violently, his breathing was checked and the arms were raised in a characteristic manner. On the second stimulation the same thing occurred, and in addition the lips began to pucker and tremble. On the third stimulation the child broke into a sudden crying fit. This is the first time an emotional situation in the laboratory has produced any fear or even crying in Albert.

We had expected just these results on account of our work with other infants brought up under similar conditions. It is worth while to call attention to the fact that removal of support (dropping and jerking the blanket upon which the infant was lying) was tried exhaustively upon this infant on the same occasion. It was not effective in producing the fear response. This stimulus is effective in younger children. At what age such stimuli lose their potency in producing fear is not known. Nor is it known whether less placid children ever lose their fear of them. This probably depends upon the training the child gets. It is well known that children eagerly run to be tossed into the air and caught. On the other hand it is equally well known that in the adult fear responses are called out quite clearly by the sudden removal of support, if the individual is walking across a bridge, walking out upon a beam, etc. There is a wide field of study here which is aside from our present point.

The sound stimulus, thus, at nine months of age, gives us the means of testing several important factors. I. Can we condition fear of an animal, e.g., a white rat, by visually presenting it and simultaneously striking a steel bar? II. If such a conditioned emotional response can be established, will there be a **transfer** to other animals or other objects? III. What is the effect of time upon such conditioned emotional responses? IV. If after a reasonable period such emotional responses have not died out, what laboratory methods can be devised for their removal?

Wet nurse. Not all mothers are capable of (or wish to) nurse their newborn infants. A wet nurse is a woman hired to breast-feed someone else's infant.

Stolid (STOLL-id). To be unemotional.

Transfer. Modern psychologists use the term *stimulus generalization* to refer to the type of "transfer" that Watson and Rayner tested for. If a subject who has been conditioned to fear a rat subsequently fears fur coats and beards, we say that "stimulus generalization" has occurred: That is, the fear response has *generalized* or *transferred* to a similar stimulus.

I. *The establishment of conditioned emotional responses.* At first there was considerable hesitation upon our part in making the attempt to set up fear reactions experimentally. A certain responsibility attaches to such a procedure. We decided finally to make the attempt, comforting ourselves by the reflection that such attachments would arise anyway as soon as the child left the sheltered environment of the nursery for the rough and tumble of the home. We did not begin this work until Albert was eleven months, three days of age. Before attempting to set up a conditioned response we, as before, put him through all of the regular emotional tests. *Not the slightest sign of a fear response was obtained in any situation.*

The steps taken to condition emotional responses are shown in our laboratory notes.

11 Months 3 Days

1. White rat suddenly taken from the basket and presented to Albert. He began to reach for rat with left hand. Just as his hand touched the animal the bar was struck immediately behind his head. The infant jumped violently and fell forward, burying his face in the mattress. He did not cry, however.

2. Just as the right hand touched the rat the bar was again struck. Again the infant jumped violently, fell forward and began to whimper.

In order not to disturb the child too seriously no further tests were given for one week.

11 Months 10 Days

1. Rat presented suddenly without sound. There was steady fixation but no tendency at first to reach for it. The rat was then placed nearer, whereupon tentative reaching movements began with the right hand. When the rat nosed the infant's left hand, the hand was immediately withdrawn. He started to reach for the head of the animal with the forefinger of the left hand, but withdrew it suddenly before contact. It is thus seen that the two joint stimulations given the previous week were not without effect. He was tested with his blocks immediately afterwards to see if they shared in the process of conditioning. He began immediately to pick them up, dropping them, pounding them, etc. In the remainder of the tests the blocks were given frequently to quiet him and to test his general emotional state. They were always removed from sight when the process of conditioning was under way.

2. Joint stimulation with rat and sound. Started, then fell over immediately to right side. No crying.

3. Joint stimulation. Fell to right side and rested upon hands, with head turned away from rat. No crying.

4. Joint stimulation. Same reaction.

5. Rat suddenly presented alone. Puckered face, whimpered and withdrew body sharply to the left.

6. Joint stimulation. Fell over immediately to right side and began to whimper.

7. Joint stimulation. Started violently and cried, but did not fall over.

8. Rat alone. *The instant the rat was shown the baby began to cry. Almost instantly he turned sharply to the left, fell over on left side, raised himself on all fours and began to crawl away so rapidly that he was caught with difficulty before reaching the edge of the table.*

This was as convincing a case of a completed conditioned fear response as could have been theoretically pictured. In all seven joint stimulations were given to bring about the complete reaction. It is not unlikely had the sound been of greater intensity or of a more complex clang character that the number of joint stimulations might have been materially reduced. Experiments designed to define the nature of the sounds that will serve best as emotional stimuli are under way.

II. *When a conditioned emotional response has been established for one object, is there a transfer?* Five days later Albert was again brought back into the laboratory and tested as follows:

11 Months 15 Days

1. Tested first with blocks. He reached readily for them, playing with them as usual. This shows that there has been no general transfer to the room, table, blocks, etc.

2. Rat alone. Whimpered immediately, withdrew right hand and turned head and trunk away.

3. Blocks again offered. Played readily with them, smiling and gurgling.

4. Rat alone. Leaned over to the left side as far away from the rat as possible, then fell over, getting up on all fours and scurrying away as rapidly as possible.

5. Blocks again offered. Reached immediately for them, smiling and laughing as before.

The above preliminary test shows that the conditioned response to the rat had carried over completely for the five days in which no tests were given. The question as to whether or not there is a transfer was next taken up.

6. Rabbit alone. The rabbit was suddenly placed on the mattress in front of him. The reaction was pronounced. Negative responses began at once. He leaned as far away from the animal as possible,

whimpered, then burst into tears. When the rabbit was placed in contact with him he buried his face in the mattress, then got up on all fours and crawled away, crying as he went. This was a most convincing test.

7. The blocks were next given him, after an interval. He played with them as before. It was observed by four people that he played far more energetically with them than ever before. The blocks were raised high over his head and slammed down with a great deal of force.

8. Dog alone. The dog did not produce as violent a reaction as the rabbit. The moment fixation occurred the child shrank back and as the animal came nearer he attempted to get on all fours but did not cry at first. As soon as the dog passed out of his range of vision he became quiet. The dog was then made to approach the infant's head (he was lying down at the moment). Albert straightened up immediately, fell over to the opposite side and turned his head away. He then began to cry.

9. The blocks were again presented. He began immediately to play with them.

10. Fur coat (seal). Withdrew immediately to the left side and began to fret. Coat put close to him on the left side, he turned immediately, began to cry and tried to crawl away on all fours.

11. Cotton wool. The wool was presented in a paper package. At the end the cotton was not covered by the paper. It was placed first on his feet. He kicked it away but did not touch it with his hands. When his hand was laid on the wool he immediately withdrew it but did not show the shock that the animals or fur coat produced in him. He then began to play with the paper, avoiding contact with the wool itself. He finally, under the impulse of the manipulative instinct, lost some of his negativism to the wool.

12. Just in play W. put his head down to see if Albert would play with his hair. Albert was completely negative. Two other observers did the same thing. He began immediately to play with their hair. W. then brought the Santa Claus mask and presented it to Albert. He was again pronouncedly negative.

11 Months 20 Days

1. Blocks alone. Played with them as usual.

2. Rat alone. Withdrawal of the whole body, bending over to left side, no crying. Fixation and following with eyes. The response was much less marked than on first presentation the previous week. It was thought best to freshen up the reaction by another joint stimulation.

3. Just as the rat was placed on his hand the rod was struck. Reaction violent.

4. Rat alone. Fell over at once to left side. Reaction practically as strong as on former occasion but no crying.

5. Rat alone. Fell over to left side, got up on all fours and started to crawl away. On this occasion there was no crying, but strange to say, as he started away he began to gurgle and coo, even while leaning far over to the left side to avoid the rat.

6. Rabbit alone. Leaned over to left side as far as possible. Did not fall over. Began to whimper but reaction not so violent as on former occasions.

7. Blocks again offered. He reached for them immediately and began to play.

All of the tests so far discussed were carried out upon a table supplied with a mattress, located in a small, well-lighted dark-room. We wished to test next whether conditioned fear responses so set up would appear if the situation were markedly altered. We thought it best before making this test to freshen the reaction both to the rabbit and to the dog by showing them at the moment the steel bar was struck. It will be recalled that this was the first time any effort had been made to directly condition response to the dog and rabbit. The experimental notes are as follows:

8. The rabbit at first was given alone. The reaction was exactly as given in test (6) above. When the rabbit was left on Albert's knees for a long time he began tentatively to reach out and manipulate its fur with fore-fingers. While doing this the steel rod was struck. A violent fear reaction resulted.

9. Rabbit alone. Reaction wholly similar to that on trial (6) above.

10. Rabbit alone. Started immediately to whimper, holding hands far up, but did not cry. Conflicting tendency to manipulate very evident.

11. Dog alone. Began to whimper, shaking head from side to side, holding hands as far away from the animal as possible.

12. Dog and sound. The rod was struck just as the animal touched him. A violent negative reaction appeared. He began to whimper, turned to one side, fell over and started to get up on all fours.

13. Blocks. Played with them immediately and readily.

On this same day and immediately after the above experiment Albert was taken into the large well-lighted lecture room belonging to the laboratory. He was placed on a table in the center of the room immediately under the skylight. Four people were present. The situation was thus very different from that which obtained in the small dark room.

1. Rat alone. No sudden fear reaction appeared at first. The hands, however, were held up and away from the animal. No positive manipulatory reactions appeared.

2. Rabbit alone. Fear reaction slight. Turned to left and kept face away from the animal but the reaction was never pronounced.

3. Dog alone. Turned away but did not fall over. Cried. Hands moved as far away from the animal as possible. Whimpered as long as the dog was present.

4. Rat alone. Slight negative reaction.

5. Rat and sound. It was thought best to freshen the reaction to the rat. The sound was given just as the rat was presented. Albert jumped violently but did not cry.

6. Rat alone. At first he did not show any negative reaction. When rat was placed nearer he began to show negative reaction by drawing back his body, raising his hands, whimpering, etc.

7. Blocks. Played with them immediately.

8. Rat alone. Pronounced withdrawal of body and whimpering.

9. Blocks. Played with them as before.

10. Rabbit alone. Pronounced reaction. Whimpered with arms held high, fell over backward and had to be caught.

11. Dog alone. At first the dog did not produce the pronounced reaction. The hands were held high over the head, breathing was checked, but there was no crying. Just at this moment the dog, which had not barked before, barked three times loudly when only about six inches from the baby's face. Albert immediately fell over and broke into a wail that continued until the dog was removed. The sudden barking of the hitherto quiet dog produced a marked fear response in the adult observers!

From the above results it would seem that emotional transfers do take place. Furthermore it would seem that the number of transfers resulting from an experimentally produced conditioned emotional reaction may be very large. In our observations we had no means of testing the complete number of transfers which may have resulted.

III. *The effect of time upon conditioned emotional responses.* We have already shown that the conditioned emotional response will continue for a period of one week. It was desired to make the time test longer. In view of the imminence of Albert's departure from the hospital we could not make the interval longer than one month. Accordingly no further emotional experimentation was entered into for thirty-one days after the above test. During the month however, Albert was brought weekly to the laboratory for tests upon right and left-handedness, imitation, general development, etc. No emotional tests whatever were given and during the whole month his regular nursery routine was maintained in the Harriet Lane Home. The notes on the test given at the end of this period are as follows:

1 Year 21 Days

1. Santa Claus mask. Withdrawal, gurgling, then slapped at it without touching. When his hand was forced to touch it, he whimpered and cried. His hand was forced to touch it two more times. He whimpered and cried on both tests. He finally cried at the mere visual stimulus of the mask.

2. Fur coat. Wrinkled his nose and withdrew both hands, drew back his whole body and began to whimper as the coat was put nearer. Again there was the strife between withdrawal and the tendency to manipulate. Reached tentatively with left hand but drew back before contact had been made. In moving his body to one side his hand accidentally touched the coat. He began to cry at once, nodding his head in a very peculiar manner (this reaction was an entirely new one). Both hands were withdrawn as far as possible from the coat. The coat was then laid on his lap and he continued nodding his head and whimpering, withdrawing his body as far as possible, pushing the while at the coat with his feet but never touching it with his hands.

3. Fur coat. The coat was taken out of his sight and presented again at the end of a minute. He began immediately to fret, withdrawing his body and nodding his head as before.

4. Blocks. He began to play with them as usual.

5. The rat. He allowed the rat to crawl towards him without withdrawing. He sat very still and fixated it intently. Rat then touched his hand. Albert withdrew it immediately, then leaned back as far as possible but did not cry. When the rat was placed on his arm he withdrew his body and began to fret, nodding his head. The rat was then allowed to crawl against his chest. He first began to fret and then covered his eyes with both hands.

6. Blocks. Reaction normal.

7. The rabbit. The animal was placed directly in front of him. It was very quiet. Albert showed no avoiding reactions at first. After a few seconds he puckered up his face, began to nod his head and to look intently at the experimenter. He next began to push the rabbit away with his feet, withdrawing his body at the same time. Then as the rabbit came nearer he began pulling his feet away, nodding his head, and wailing "da da." After about a minute he reached out tentatively and slowly and touched the rabbit's ear with his right hand, finally manipulating it. The rabbit was again placed in

his lap. Again he began to fret and withdrew his hands. He reached out tentatively with his left hand and touched the animal, shuddered and withdrew the whole body. The experimenter then took hold of his left hand and laid it on the rabbit's back. Albert immediately withdrew his hand and began to suck his thumb. Again the rabbit was laid in his lap. He began to cry, covering his face with both hands.

8. Dog. The dog was very active. Albert fixated it intensely for a few seconds, sitting very still. He began to cry but did not fall over backwards as on his last contact with the dog. When the dog was pushed closer to him he at first sat motionless, then began to cry, putting both hands over his face.

These experiments would seem to show conclusively that directly conditioned emotional responses as well as those conditioned by transfer persist, although with a certain loss in the intensity of the reaction, for a longer period than one month. Our view is that they persist and modify personality throughout life. It should be recalled again that Albert was of an extremely phlegmatic type. Had he been emotionally unstable probably both the directly conditioned response and those transferred would have persisted throughout the month unchanged in form.

IV. *"Detachment" or removal of conditioned emotional responses.* Unfortunately Albert was taken from the hospital the day the above tests were made. Hence the opportunity of building up an experimental technique by means of which we could remove the conditioned emotional responses was denied us. Our own view, expressed above, which is possibly not very well grounded, is that these responses in the home environment are likely to persist indefinitely, unless an accidental method for removing them is hit upon. The importance of establishing some method must be apparent to all. Had the opportunity been at hand we should have tried out several methods, some of which we may mention. (1) Constantly confronting the child with those stimuli which called out the responses in the hopes that habituation would come in corresponding to "fatigue" of reflex when differential reactions are to be set up. (2) By trying to " recondition" by showing objects calling out fear responses (visual) and simultaneously stimulating the **erogenous** zones (tactual). We should try first the lips, then the nipples and as a final resort the sex organs. (3) By trying to "recondition" by feeding the subject candy or other food just as the animal is shown. This method calls for the food control of the subject. (4) By building up "constructive" activities around the object by imitation and by putting the hand through the motions of manipulation. At this age imitation of overt motor activity is strong, as our present but unpublished experimentation has shown.

Incidental Observations

(a) Thumb sucking as a compensatory device for blocking fear and noxious stimuli. During the course of these experiments, especially in the final test, it was noticed that whenever Albert was on the verge of tears or emotionally upset generally he would continually thrust his thumb into his mouth. The moment the hand reached the mouth he became impervious to the stimuli producing fear. Again and again while the motion pictures were being made at the end of the thirty-day rest period, we had to remove the thumb from his mouth before the conditioned response could be obtained. This method of blocking noxious and emotional stimuli (fear and rage) through erogenous stimulation seems to persist from birth onward. Very often in our experiments upon the **work adders** with infants under ten days of age the same reaction appeared. When at work upon the adders both of the infants arms are under slight restraint. Often rage appears. They begin to cry, thrashing their arms and legs about. If the finger gets into the mouth crying ceases at once. The organism thus apparently from birth, when under the influence of love stimuli is blocked to all others.[4] This resort to sex stimulation when under the influence of noxious and emotional situations, or when the individual is restless and idle, persists throughout adolescent and adult life. Albert, at any rate, did not resort to thumb sucking except in the presence of such stimuli. Thumb sucking could immediately be checked by offering him his blocks. These invariably called out active manipulation instincts. It is worth while here to call attention to the fact that Freud's conception of the stimulation of erogenous zones as being the expression of an original "pleasure" seeking principle may be turned about and possibly better described as a compensatory (and often conditioned) device for the blockage of noxious and fear and rage producing stimuli.

(b) Equal primacy of fear, love and possibly rage. While in general the results of our experiment offer no particular points of conflict with Freudian concepts, one fact out of harmony with them should be emphasized. According to proper Freudians sex (or in our terminology, love) is the principal emotion in which conditioned responses arise which later limit and distort personality. We wish to take sharp issue with this view on the basis

Erogenous (air-RODGE-en-us). Eros was the Greek god of love. "Erogenous" means to *generate Eros*, or "create erotic sensations." The "erogenous zones" of your body are those parts (such as the genitals) that generate erotic sensations when stroked or caressed.

Work adders. A "work adder" was a device used early in this century to test the responsiveness of infants.

of the experimental evidence we have gathered. Fear is as primal a factor as love in influencing personality. Fear does not gather its potency in any derived manner from love. It belongs to the original and inherited nature of man. Probably the same may be true of rage although at present we are not so sure of this.

The Freudians twenty years from now, unless their hypotheses change, when they come to analyze Albert's fear of a seal skin coat--assuming that he comes to analysis at that age--will probably tease from him the recital of a dream which upon their analysis will show that Albert at three years of age attempted to play with the pubic hair of the mother and was scolded violently for it. (We are by no means denying that this might in some other case condition it). If the analyst has sufficiently prepared Albert to accept such a dream when found as an explanation of his avoiding tendencies, and if the analyst has the authority and personality to put it over, Albert may be fully convinced that the dream was a true revealer of the factors which brought about the fear.

It is probable that many of the phobias in psychopathology are true conditioned emotional reactions either of the direct or the transferred type. One may possibly have to believe that such persistence of early conditioned responses will be found only in persons who are constitutionally inferior. Our argument is meant to be constructive. Emotional disturbances in adults cannot be traced back to sex alone. They must be retraced along at least three collateral lines — to conditioned and transferred responses set up in infancy and early youth in all three of the fundamental human emotions.

FOOTNOTES

[1] Reprinted by permission of the authors' estate and the publisher from the *Journal of Experimental Psychology*, 1920, **3** (No. 1), 1-14. Copyright 1920 by the American Psychological Association.

[2] Emotional Reactions and Psychological Experimentation. *American Journal of Psychology*, **28**, 163-174, 1917.

[3] Psychology from the Standpoint of a Behaviorist, p. 202.

[4] The stimulus to love in infants according to our view is stroking of the skin, lips, nipples and sex organs, patting and rocking, picking up, etc. Patting and rocking (when not conditioned) are probably equivalent to actual stimulation of the sex organs. In adults of course, as every lover knows, vision, audition and olfaction soon become conditioned by joint stimulation with contact and kinesthetic stimuli.

Classic Quotations from William James

For the entire nervous system *is* nothing but a system of paths between a sensory [stimulus] and a muscular, glandular, or other [response]. A path once traversed by a nerve-current might be expected to follow the law of most of the paths we know, and to be scooped out and made more permeable than before; and this ought to be repeated with each new passage of the current.
(*The Principles of Psychology* [1890], ch. 4.)

Habit simplifies the movements required to achieve a given result, makes them more accurate and diminishes fatigue.
(*The Principles of Psychology* [1890], ch. 4.)

Man is born with a tendency to do more things than he has ready-made arrangements for in his nerve-centers. Most of the performances of other animals are automatic. But in him the number of them is so enormous, that most of them must be the fruit of painful study. If practice did not make perfect, nor habit economize the expense of nervous and muscular energy, he would therefore be in a sorry plight.
(*The Principles of Psychology* [1890], ch. 4.)

CHAPTER 3

"Introduction and Removal of Reward, and Maze Performance in Rats"

E.C. Tolman and C.H. Honzik[1]

EDITORS' COMMENTS. From 1920 to 1960, the dominant force in American psychology was *learning theory*--that is, the attempt to determine the "laws of learning," usually by studying how rats learned mazes. Following the lead of such early behaviorists as E.L. Thorndike and John B. Watson, Yale psychologist C.L. Hull and his student, Kenneth Spence, created elaborate equations that purported to describe *mathematically* how maze learning proceded. Hull and Spence believed that a rat "acquired a maze habit" by learning which way to turn at each choice point in the maze. The "learning equations," therefore, merely stated the *behavioral tendency* of the rat to turn left or right at each choice point. This tendency presumably was influenced by such factors as motivation (or drive), and by the strength of the connection between the stimuli at the choice point (S) and the correct response (R). The S-R bond at each choice point was said to be strengthened by *reinforcement*, or reward. At no time, from the behaviorist viewpoint, did the rat learn such "cognitive" things as the *spatial relationships* of the various parts of the maze. Nor would the animal have learned *anything at all* had it not found a food reward in the goal box at the end of the maze.

As is often the case in such matters, the first equations derived by Hull and Spence were rather simple: $B = f(H \times D)$, or "*B*ehavior is a function of *H*abit strength times *D*rive." The more experiments Hull and Spence ran, however, the more factors they discovered that could influence maze behavior, and the more complicated their formulas became: $_sE_r = V_2 \times D \times K \times J \times {_sH_r} - {_sI_r} - I_r - {_sO_r} - {_sL_r}$, whose terms we won't bother to define. Finally--to the great relief of millions of psychology students who had been forced to memorize the equations--the formulas became so complex that this rather simple-minded approach sank of its own dead weight.

Although Hull and Spence dominated experimental psychology for many years, they were vigorously opposed by a small group of *cognitive* theorists who insisted that rats were not mere "behavioral machines," limited to the mere acquisition of behavioral tendencies at choice points in the maze. Rather, said E.C. Tolman and his students at Berkeley, rats create *cognitive maps* of where things are in the maze--and then perform accordingly. As evidence this was the case, Tolman noted the following: Hull and Spence claimed that reward was necessary for *learning*, because of its effect on "habit strength." But rats couldn't survive in the wild, Tolman said, if they weren't constantly learning things about their environments--and in the wild they didn't have a behaviorist standing over them to give them a piece of food each time they did something right. Learning occurs "on its own," Tolman claimed. Reward merely affects the rat's eagerness to *perform*. As evidence this was the case, Tolman and his students ran many experiments in which rats were put into mazes and allowed to explore. They showed no evidence of learning. However, if after exploratory trials, the rat suddenly found food at the end of the maze, the *next* time the animal was put in the maze it would race through the apparatus, making few if any errors. The learning was *latent* in this case, Tolman said. The addition of the food reward merely made the learning *visible*. (Hull and Spence added "K"--for "Incentive"--to their elaborate equation to account for Tolman's results.)

In Chapter 1, we urged you to read the Summary of an article before plowing into the details. It is particularly important that you do so with this paper. There is little that is inherently exciting about this study, unless you understand its background. However, it is a "classic" because it was one of the most important of several similar experiments whose publication led to the downfall of the Hull-Spence theory of learning.

INTRODUCTION

Experiments by Blodgett (1), Simmons (5), Szymanski (6), Williams (9), and Elliott (3) have shown that, if rats begin the learning of a maze with no reward, or with only a slightly effective reward, and then at a later stage a more effective reward is introduced, sudden drops in the error and time curves appear. These drops seem to testify to *a latent learning* acquired during the non-reward or poorly rewarded period, a learning which is made manifest only after the introduction of the more effective reward.

A reverse phenomenon has also been recently demonstrated. Elliott (3) obtained a sudden rise in the performance curves when an originally effective reward was removed, and a less effective one substituted. Since the completion of the experiments to be reported here, Bruce (2) and Sharp (4) have also presented findings similar to those of Elliott. They all found a disintegration in the performance directly subsequent to the removal of an initial reward.

The present experiment was designed to examine both types of phenomena, and especially to analyze them with respect to entrances into food-(exit)-pointing and into non-food-(non-exit)-pointing **blinds**, considered separately.

APPARATUS AND METHODS

Maze.--The maze was a 14-unit T-maze, used in the previous study (8) (See fig. 1). The arrangement of the blinds is shown in figure 1a.

General procedure.--Eighty-two male rats, divided into two groups of 41 rats each, were run in the maze. One group was called the Hungry Reward-Non-reward (HR-NR) Group, the other, the Hungry Non-reward-Reward (HNR-R) Group.

Preliminary training.--This accustomed the rats to being **handled**, and taught them to manipulate the gates and curtains before being run in the maze itself. It involved the use of a straightaway and a single T-unit for five days and was in every way identical with that of the previous study (8).

Training proper.--This consisted, for the two groups, of one run a day in the 14-unit maze for 22 days. For the *Hungry Reward-Non-reward (HR-NR) Group* a food reward was given at the end of each run from the first to the tenth day, inclusive. On the eleventh day of training food was withdrawn, and the rats ran into end boxes that had never contained food of any sort but were in all physical aspects like the real food boxes. It should be noted that this eleventh day, although no food was in

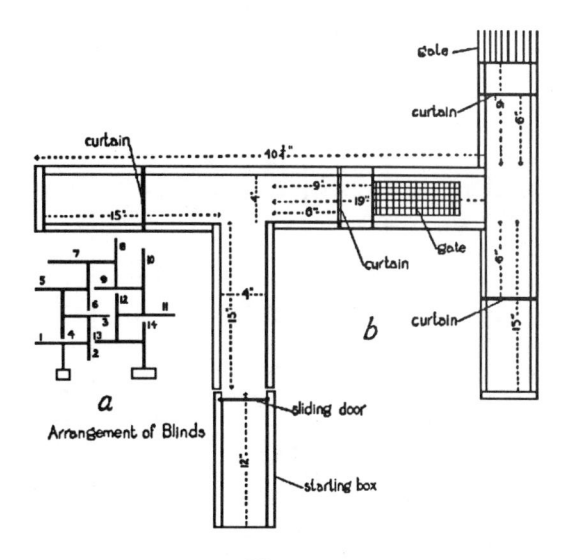

Figure 1.

the end box, belongs with the first ten days, i.e., in the reward period, since the rats did not know, when they started this day's run, that no food was to be had. The non-reward period extended, then, from the twelfth to the twenty-second day, inclusive. During this period the rats were fed in their living cages (one rat in a cage) not less than three hours nor more than four hours after the completion of the day's run. The amount of the daily food ration during the total 22-day period was adjusted to the weight of the rat and was such that the rats lost weight in various degrees (i.e., from 10 to 32 grams), depending somewhat on initial weight. (Table 1.)

For the *Hungry Non-reward-Reward (HNR-R) Group* no food was given in the end boxes from the first to the tenth day inclusive. The rats were fed during this period, in their living cages, not less than three hours after the day's run, as in the non-reward period of the other group. On the eleventh day food was placed in the end boxes. Again it should be noted that this eleventh day belongs with the first ten days, since the rats did not know at the beginning of the run that they would be rewarded. The reward period extended therefore from

Blinds. What Tolman and Honzik call "blinds," today's learning theorists would call "blind alleys." As Figure 1 shows, each arm of the T-shaped maze had a curtain blocking the animal's view. The curtain therefore "blinded" the animal, so that it couldn't merely *look* down the alley and tell which was the correct arm to enter.

Handled. Surprisingly enough, you can't merely "buy" a rat at a pet shop, take it home, and expect it to run a maze immediately. Rather, you must "handle" the animal for several days, as gently as possible, so that it becomes accustomed to being used as a subject in an experiment. Put more bluntly, the rat has to learn a lot about you (and the apparatus) before you can test its "learning" in the maze. Today, we use the term "gentling the animals" to refer to the act of *habituating* the animal to the experimental conditions.

TABLE 1
INITIAL WEIGHTS AND LOSSES IN WEIGHT IN GRAMS DURING TRAINING

\multicolumn{3}{c	}{Hungry Reward–Non-reward}	\multicolumn{3}{c	}{Hungry Non-reward–Reward}	\multicolumn{3}{c	}{Hungry Reward–Non-reward}	\multicolumn{3}{c}{Hungry Non-reward–Reward}
Rat No.	In. Wt.	Loss	Rat No.	In. Wt.	Loss	Rat No.	In. Wt.	Loss	Rat No.	In. Wt.	Loss
W 26	110	10	W 27	110	8	H 4	150	20	H 3	145	20
W 49	110	10	W 34	120	15	W 50	152	22	H 13	146	28
G 7	110	12	W 23	120	12	W 48	154	21	G 3	150	18
H 15	112	14	W 22	120	15	G 2	158	18	H 11	150	25
W 21	118	8	H 5	122	12	B 13	160	30	W 36	150	21
W 63	120	20	W 33	122	14	W 30	160	28	W 32	154	24
W 42	125	16	W 57	130	20	W 65	170	30	G 6	156	26
H 7	125	15	W 54	132	19	W 73	170	31	W 46	160	18
B 4	128	20	W 31	132	20	B 12	170	28	B 7	160	15
W 56	130	20	W 55	133	16	W 70	182	30	B 9	164	18
W 61	132	21	B 3	133	12	W 25	184	24	W 24	164	24
W 60	135	16	W 21	134	14	H 20	184	25	H 9	165	19
H 12	136	25	H 8	135	16	H 21	190	32	H 14	174	30
H 6	138	26	W 35	140	20	W 28	190	26	H 16	174	29
W 43	140	20	W 45	142	16	W 67	200	25	W 64	175	28
W 40	142	18	W 44	142	17	W 71	200	27	W 58	178	30
W 62	143	23	H 10	142	12	W 66	214	32	B 11	190	29
W 41	144	18	W 59	145	20	W 72	214	28	B 10	196	28
W 39	150	20	G 1	145	22	W 68	230	30	H 17	196	32
W 47	150	24	W 53	145	15	——	——	—	——	——	—

the twelfth to the twenty-second day inclusive. Throughout the total 22-day period the rats were fed in proportion to their weight so as to keep them hungry. (Table 1.)

The daily runs were given as nearly at the same hour of the day as was possible; actually fluctuations in this respect, when they occurred, did not extend beyond one hour. Small sections of both groups were run concurrently. This assured that improvements in technique, or other changes, if any, would affect both groups equally.

The rats.--The rats of the two groups were males 3 1/2 to 5 months old, without any previous training, and of mixed coat-color, some being hooded, others black, but most being white. The coat-colors were fairly equally distributed by chance between the two groups. The rats at the beginning of the experiment were all healthy and in good condition. As against the 82 rats that completed the training four were discarded because of illness and three were discarded because for unknown reasons they refused to run.

Scoring.--Time and error records were kept. An entrance into a blind the full body-length (not including the tail) was considered an error. No attempt was made to record degrees of entrance. A second or third entrance into a blind during the same run was also considered an error and included in the records. Returns into units just traversed were prevented by the gates; thus this type of error is not presented in our maze.

The blinds in the maze were numbered in order from the first to the fourteenth, and each error was recorded by the number of the blind in which it was made. A convex mirror over the maze made it possible to see the movements of the rat in any part of the maze.

GROSS QUANTITATIVE RESULTS

Hungry Reward-Non-reward Group.--Figure 2 presents the **learning curves** based on error scores of the HR-NR Group as compared with two other groups, namely, a Hungry Reward (HR) Group, and a Hungry Non-reward (HNR) Group. The two latter groups were parts of the previous experiment (8) in which the same maze was used and other conditions were the same, save that these other groups were run at an earlier time. Each of the latter two groups consisted of 36 (instead of 41) rats, but the three curves of figure 2 are comparable since they are in terms of average numbers of errors.

Examination of the three curves brings out the following points: First, the rate of learning of the HR-NR Group during the reward period was approximately equal to that of the HR Group during the same eleven-day period. If anything, the HR-NR Group learned a

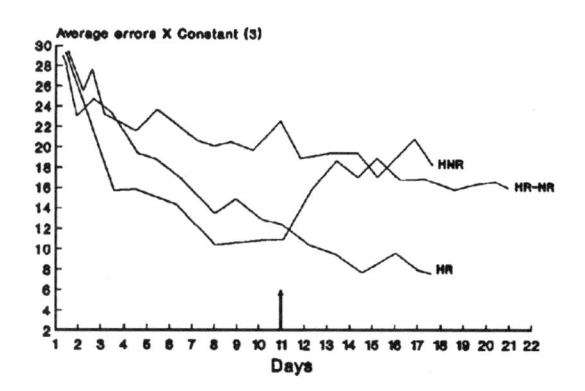

Figure 2. Error curves for HR, HNR, and HR-NR.

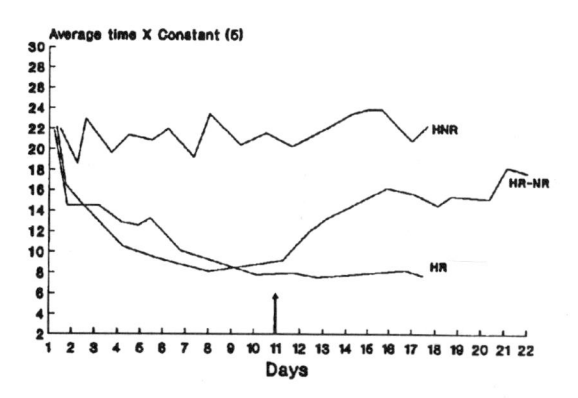

Figure 3. Time curves for HR, HNR, and HR-NR.

little more rapidly from the third to the eighth day. Secondly, on the day following the removal of reward, that is, the twelfth day, there is a sudden rise in the curve. This rise is continued on the thirteenth day. Thirdly, the level reached by this sudden rise corresponds closely to the level of the HNR Group at the same stage of the training.

Figure 3 presents the time curves of the three groups. The same three points are to be noted but with certain modifications. First, the rise in the time curve of the HR-NR Group, when reward was removed, does not appear to be so sudden. Secondly, the time curve, after removal of reward, does not reach that of the HNR Group.

TABLE 2
Mean Errors

	Mean rise in errors	Difference between the two rises	S.D. of Difference	Critical ratio
HR Days 14-15	.4166	.8761	.3931	2.23
HR-NR Days 11-12	1.2927			

With regard to the error curves of the HR-NR Group it is to be noted that the sudden increase in number of errors on the day following removal of reward is equal to 53 errors, or an average increase per rat of 1.3 error. The increase on the next day equals 32 errors, an average of about .75 error per rat. During the *reward* period of this group there were slight rises in the curve on the fifth, ninth, and tenth days. But in each case the rise was equal to only one error, or an average per rat of .25 error. There are, however, larger upward jumps in the HR Group on the third, ninth, and fifteen days. Of these the largest is that of the fifteenth day, and amounts to 15 errors (average, .42 error). To show that the average rise on the twelfth day in the HR-NR curve

is significantly larger than the average jump of the HR curve we must compare the two jumps as to their standard deviations. These comparisons are given in table 2.

A critical ratio of 2.23, interpreted in terms of probability, means that a difference between the two upward jumps as large as that obtained would occur by chance about 1.4 times in 100 times, or slightly less than one-seventieth of the time. It is therefore fairly certain that the rise on the twelfth day of the HR-NR error curve was due to the removal of reward and not to ordinary chance factors such as produce occasional rises in the curve for the HR Group.

Although a full day intervened between the time the rats made their first non-rewarded runs and the next succeeding runs, there was evidently a decided memorial effect of the previous foodless run twenty-four hours before, as was evidenced by the searching of blind alleys normally avoided; and hence the increase in number of errors.

In the time curve of the HR-NR Group the *average* upward jumps on the twelfth, thirteenth, fourteenth, and fifteenth days were equal (using whole numbers) to 37 seconds, 13 seconds, 18 seconds, and 4 seconds, respectively. During the *reward* period of this group there were also *average* rises on the tenth and eleventh days equal to 6.6 and 6.0 seconds, respectively. To show that the upward jump on the twelfth day was larger than can be accounted for by chance factors, it is necessary to compare this jump with the largest, i.e., the 6.6-second jump, in the reward period, or with the largest

Learning curves. How do you measure learning in a maze situation? For the most part, early psychologists recorded the *speed* at which the animal rushed through the apparatus, and the *number of errors* the rat made while doing so. The assumption was that, the more the animal learned, the faster it would run and the fewer errors it would make. We now know, however, that both variables are affected by such factors as how hungry the animal is, the quality of the reward offered, the animal's prior experiences, the barometric pressure, the time of day the animal is trained, how gently the animal is handled, and so forth. In brief, what we call "learning curves" really are *performance* curves.

rise in the curve of the control HR Group. The largest rise in the HR curve, however, is less than the largest jump in the reward period of the HR-NR Group, and we have therefore taken for comparison the 6.6-second rise of the HR-NR Group, reward period. The results of the comparison are given in table 3.

TABLE 3
Mean Time Scores

	Mean rise in seconds	Difference between the two rises	S.D. of Difference	Critical ratio
HR-NR Days 9-10	6.6	30.25	10.65	2.94
HR-NR Days 11-12	36.85			

TABLE 4
Mean Errors

	Mean drop in seconds	Difference between the two drops	S.D. of Difference	Critical ratio
HNR-Days 1-2	1.1	1.0	.416	2.40
HNR-R Days 11-12	2.1			

The critical ratio of 2.84 indicates that the difference obtained would occur by chance about .26 times in 100. We are therefore safe in concluding that the rise in time on the twelfth day was due to the removal of food and not to chance factors.

Hungry Non-reward-Reward (HNR-R) Group.--Figure 4 shows the error curves of the HNR-R Group as compared with the same two control groups used with the HR-NR Group. It will be noted first that during the non-reward period of the HNR-R Group, there is a downward trend of the curve similar to that of the HNR Group. Secondly, on the twelfth day there is a large drop. And thirdly, this drop, plus the one on the thirteenth day, brings the curve considerably below that of the HR Group at the same stage of the training. This drop in the HNR-R curve *below* the HR curve raises an interesting question.

The non-reward period of the HNR-R Group was undoubtedly a period of latent learning. Does the drop of the HNR-R curve *below* the HR curve, when reward is introduced, mean that this latent learning was more effective than the overt learning of the HR Group during the same period of time? To get some statistical information on the reliability of the difference between the two curves *from the twelfth day on,* the error scores for the two groups (HR and HNR-R) were taken and the critical ratio between the two computed. It was found to amount to 2.205. It would therefore appear that the difference was a statistically significant one. We are not ready, however, to state with any certainty that this was due to the greater efficiency of the latent learning. Other factors may have influenced the situation. It may have been that the rats of the HNR-R Group were brighter as regards maze learning than the HR Group. But the possibility that it was due to the greater efficiency of latent learning remains.

We turn next to a comparison of the drop in the HNR-R *error* curve on the twelfth day with the largest drop either in the non-reward period in the HNR-R curve or in the HNR curve. The largest drop happens to be on the second day of the HNR Group. Table 4 gives the results of this comparison.

A difference between the two drops in the error curves as large as that found here would occur by chance around about .8 times in 100. We may conclude that the drop in the error scores was due to the introduction of reward.

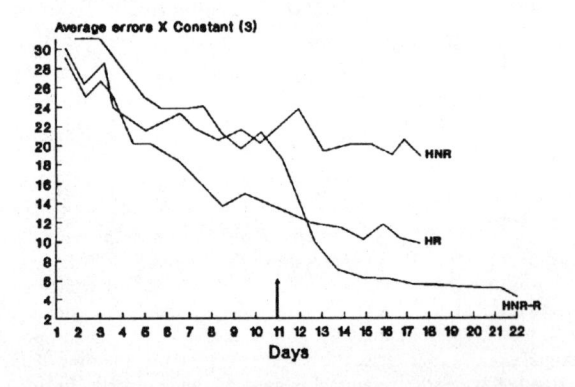

Figure 4. Error Curves for HR, HRN, and HNR-R.

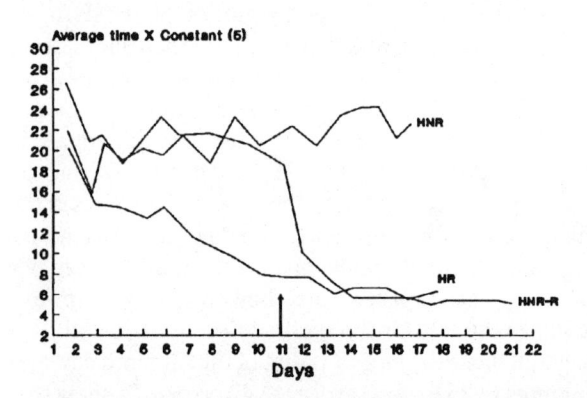

Figure 5. Time curves for HR, HNR, and HRN-R.

TABLE 5
Mean Time Scores

	Mean drop in time	Difference between the two drops	S.D. of Difference	Critical ratio
HNR-Days 1-2	54 sec.	37 sec.	13.07	2.83
HNR-R-Days 11-12	91 sec.			

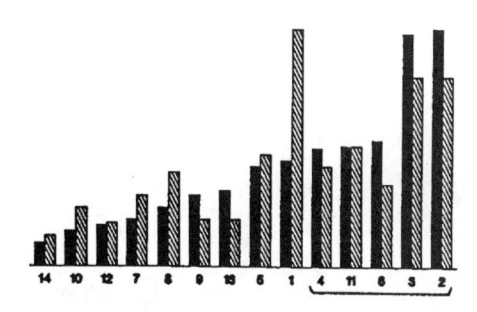

Figure 6. Showing relative difficulty of blinds in reward and non-reward periods.

Turning now to the time curve of the HNR-R group (fig. 5), we note again the large drop in time on the twelfth day. During the non-reward period the HNR-R curve was approximately on the same level with the HNR Group. But the drop in time on the introduction of reward did not bring the curve significantly *below* the HR curve, as was the case with the error curve of the HNR-R Group.

Table 5 gives the comparisons between the twelfth day drop of the HNR-R curve and the drop on the second day of the HNR curve, which happens to be larger than any other drop in the HNR-R curve during the non-reward period.

The critical ratio of 2.83 warrants the statement that the twelfth-day drop in the HNR-R curve was undoubtedly due to the introduction of reward.

RESULTS FOR INDIVIDUAL BLINDS

The second question set for the the present experiment was in regard to the effects in individual blinds. Stated in other words, the question is, does the introduction or removal of reward change the difficulty of some blinds more than other?

Hungry Reward-Non-reward Group.--Figure 6 is a bar diagram representing the relative difficulty of the fourteen blinds of the maze. The height of each bar is based on the per cent of total errors made in the blind represented by the bar. The blinds (solid bars) are arranged in increasing order of difficulty from left to right as this order was determined during the *reward period*. It will be noted that the last five blinds to the right of the figure are the most difficult. These five blinds point either down or to the right, that is, in the general **direction** of food (see fig. 1a). These same five blinds were found to be the most difficult in the previous study; and it was there concluded that, of the factors determining the order of difficulty of blinds, the direction in which the blind points is one of the more influential.

Besides the solid bars, cross-hatched ones are given. These show the relative difficulty of blinds during the *non-reward period* and indicate the changes in difficulty produced by the change from reward to non-reward. Three points are to be noted: *First,* blind 1 appears to have increased in difficulty more than any other. *Secondly,* all the food-pointing blinds, i.e., the last five blinds in the figure, except blind 11, decreased in difficulty. *Thirdly,* all the non-food-pointing blinds, except blinds 9 and 13, increased in difficulty.

These three points are subject to interpretation which unfortunately must be largely **anthropomorphic**. Our general experience with maze learning by rats has convinced us that the first blind in the maze is always quite difficult; it is always above the average in difficulty. Observation of the rat's behavior in the maze indicates that the difficulty of the first blind, i.e., the large number of entrances into this blind, is due largely to the nervous behavior of the rat when he first enters the maze--a behavior often present even in the later stages of learning and characterized by slow or rapid exploration of the first unit as if the rat were seeking his bearings. Even rats that run through the remainder of the maze with great speed and few errors very often make this preliminary exploration. It would seem probable, therefore, that the large increase in difficulty of blind 1 on the removal of reward may have been due merely to an increased cautiousness and hence to a greater explora-

Direction. The major bone of contention between Tolman and C.L. Hull was whether an rat in a maze learned *more* than just a set of discrete stimulus-response connections. Hull said no; Tolman proved that rats typically learned a lot about the *spatial orientation* of the various elements of the maze. Tolman called this "the creation of a cognitive map" of the apparatus. In this study, Tolman and Honzik showed that the animals were more likely to enter a "blind alley" (which was scored as an error) if it pointed in the direction of the goal box than if it didn't. This finding suggests the rats "knew" which direction the goal box was when they were inside the maze, and tried to "move in that direction" whenever possible. Hull found it very difficult to explain such findings as this one.

Anthropomorphic (an-throw-poh-MOR-fick). The act of attributing human characteristics to animals. Most pet owners--and many psychologists--are guilty of assuming that if *they* like something, their *animals* will like it too. The best animal trainers, however, take the time to discover what their subjects are *really like,* without imposing human values on the animals' behaviors.

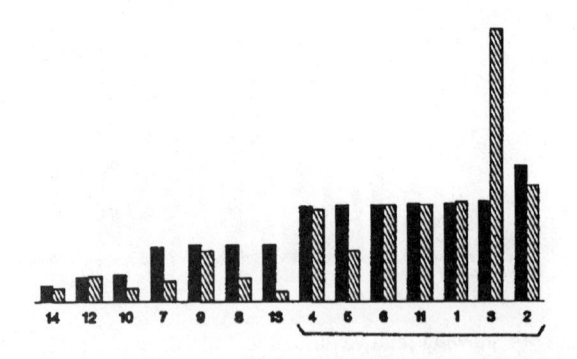

Figure 7. Showing relative difficulty of blinds in reward and non-reward periods.

tion of the first unit. The non-rewarded run on the previous day would appear to make the rat more anxious to get started correctly.

The second fact, that the blinds that were difficult during the reward period become less difficult on the removal of reward, again, must be interpreted somewhat anthropomorphically. These blinds no longer point toward food since the food has been removed. There is no longer the drive toward a goal which was in a definite position. There is on the contrary a tendency to seek in other directions.

Finally, the third fact of the increase in difficulty of the blinds which were previously non-food-pointing would be a corollary of the above second fact. The rats now begin hunting in these other blinds. Such a positive hunting was also discovered by Bruce (2).

Hungry Non-reward-Reward Group.--Figure 7 indicates graphically the relative difficulty of the blinds during the non-reward and reward periods of the HNR-R group. Here the blinds (solid bars) are arranged in ascending order of difficulty as this was determined during the period of *non-reward*. It will be noted that with no reward the blinds have approximately the same order as was obtained during the *reward period* of the HR-NR Group. The food-pointing--in this case the exit pointing--blinds are again the most difficult ones, except for blinds 1 and 5 which have become more difficult and are in this respect like the food-pointing group. Aside from this exception, it appears that blinds may be divided into two classes, as regards difficulty, on the basis of the direction in which they point. But since in the non-reward period the blinds do not point to food, we must postulate an exit-seeking as well as a food-seeking maze learning, as was also done in the previous study.

Two other points are to be noted. First, there was no increase of entrances into food-pointing blinds when reward was introduced, except for blind 3, which shows an enormous increase. Secondly, all the non-food-pointing blinds, except 1 and 12, show decrease in difficulty, i.e., in number of entrances. In the case of blinds 10 and 13 this decrease is particularly striking.

The great increase of entrances into blind 3 on the introduction of reward may reasonably be accounted for by the increased drive in the direction of the exit which now provides not only escape from the maze but food besides. But why was there no similar increase in the other food-pointing blinds? The present data do not furnish any clear answer.

The large decreases in difficulty of non-food-pointing blinds may be accounted for by the same assumption mentioned above, namely, that introduction of reward increases the strength of the drive toward food so that there is less tendency to enter blinds pointing away from food.

Table 6 shows the *changes* in percentages of total errors made in the two classes of blinds when a change is made from reward to non-reward, and from non-reward to reward. Thus, for the HR-NR group, the five food-pointing blinds had 61 per cent of the errors during the reward period, while during the non-reward period the per cent was 49. For the HNR-R Group, the errors in the five food-pointing blinds were 56 per cent during the non-reward period, and rose during the reward period to 75 per cent.

TABLE 6

PERCENTAGE OF TOTAL ERRORS MADE IN THE FOOD-POINTING AND THE NON-FOOD-POINTING BLINDS DURING REWARD AND NON-REWARD PERIODS

Hungry Non-reward-Reward Group				Hungry Reward-Non-reward Group			
Food-pointing blinds	Non-food-pointing blinds	Food-pointing blinds	Non-food-pointing blinds	Food-pointing blinds	Non-food-pointing blinds	Food-pointing blinds	Non-food-pointing blinds
.56 ± .006	.44 ± .006	.75 ± .013	.25 ± .013	.61 ± .007	.39 ± .007	.49 ± .007	.51 ± .007

RELIABILITY COEFFICIENTS OF THE MAZE FOR REWARD AND NON-REWARD PERIODS

To get some idea of the reliability of the maze under reward and non-reward conditions, we have computed the reliability coefficients based on odd-day versus even-day scores for both error and time scores. These are given in table 7.

It will be noticed that the **reliability coefficients** both for error scores and time scores are, with one exception, higher for the reward period than for the non-reward period. The differences between r's in two cases, namely, between the r's of the NR and R periods of the HNR-R Group for error scores, and between the r's of the R and NR periods of HR-NR Group for time scores, are large enough to be significant. It may be concluded that under reward conditions the maze is a more reliable instrument for the measuring of learning ability than under non-reward conditions. But it must be pointed out that in the previous study a hungry rewarded group of rats had a reliability coefficient for errors slightly lower than that of a hungry non-rewarded group.

TABLE 7
RELIABILITY COEFFICIENTS BASED ON EVEN-DAY versus ODD-DAY SCORES IN ERRORS AND TIME

Group	Reliability coefficients for error scores	Reliability coefficients for time scores
HR-NR (Reward period)	.962 ± .008	.965 ± .007
HR-NR (Non-reward period)	.937 ± .013	.876 ± .024
HNR-R (Non-reward period)	.894 ± .021	.954 ± .011
HNR-R (Reward period)	.956 ± .009	.903 ± .019

SUMMARY

1. Rats run with food reward at the end of the maze showed, when reward was removed, large increases in both time scores and error scores, which could not be accounted for by chance factors alone.

2. Rats run without reward, when reward was introduced, showed large decreases in both time scores and error scores, which also could not be accounted for by chance factors alone.

3. The drop in the error curve for the group of rats that were rewarded on the eleventh day brought the curve significantly below the curve of a control group of rats that had been rewarded from the first. This suggests that latent learning may be more effective than overt learning.

4. Removal of reward after a period of reward changed the relative difficulty of blinds.

(a) The first blind become especially difficult.

(b) Non-food-pointing blinds became relatively more difficult than they were during the reward period.

(c) Food-pointing blinds became relatively less difficult than they were during the reward period.

5. Introduction of reward after a period of non-reward likewise changed the relative difficulty of blinds.

(a) Non-food-pointing blinds became relatively less difficult during the reward period.

(b) Food-pointing blinds changed very little in difficulty when reward was introduced. But one food-pointing blind, number 3, increased very greatly in difficulty.

6. Reliability coefficients based on even-day versus odd-day scores in errors and time indicate that the maze is a more reliable instrument under reward conditions. But even under non-reward conditions the reliability coefficients were surprisingly high.

FOOTNOTES

[1] Reprinted by permission of the authors and the publisher from *University of California Publications in Psychology*, 1930, **4**, 257-275. Copyright 1930 by the University of California Press.

REFERENCES

1. Blodgett, H. C. 1929. The effect of introduction of reward upon the maze performance of rats. *Univ. Calif. Publ. Psychol.*, **4**:115-134.
2. Bruce, R. H. 1930. The effect of removal of reward on the maze performance of rats. *Univ. Calif. Publ. Psychol.*, **4**:203-214.
3. Elliott, M. H. 1928. The effect of change of reward on the maze performance of rats. *Univ. Calif. Publ. Psychol.*, **4**:19-30.
4. Sharp, W. S. 1929. Disintegrative effects of continuous running and removal of the food incentive upon the maze habit of albino rats. *Jour. Comp. Psychol.*, **9**:405-423.
5. Simmons, R. 1924. The relative effectiveness of certain incentives in animal learning. *Comp. Psych. Mon.*, **2**:no. 7.
6. Szymanski, J. S. 1918. Ein experimenteller Beitrag zur Analyse der bei Entstehung neuer Gewohnheiten mitwirkenden Faktoren. *Pfluger's Arch. f. d. ges. Physiol.*, **170**:197-220.
7. Tolman, E. C., Honzik, C. H., and Robinson, E. W. 1930.

Reliability coefficients (koh-ee-FISH-ents). Similar to "correlation coefficients." A correlation coefficient is a statistical measure that tells you how similar two sets of data are.

Effects of different degrees of hunger and of reward and non-reward on time and error elimination in maze learning by the rat. *Univ. Calif. Publ. Psychol.,* **4**:189-202.

8. Tolman, E. C., and Honzik, C. H. 1930. Degrees of hunger, reward and non-reward in maze performance of rats. *Univ. Calif. Publ. Psychol.,* **4**:

9. Williams, K. A. 1927. The reward value of a conditioned stimulus. *Univ. Calif. Publ. Psychol.,* **4**:31-55.

Classic Quotations from William James

The mind's relations to other objects than the brain are *cognitive and emotional* relations exclusively, so far as we know. It knows them, and it inwardly *welcomes or rejects them*, but it has no other dealings with them.
(*The Principles of Psychology* [1890], ch. 8.)

The psychologist's attitude towards cognition will be so important in the sequel that we must not leave it until it is made perfectly clear. *It is a thoroughgoing dualism.* It supposes two elements, mind knowing and thing known, and treats them as irreducible. Neither gets out of itself or into the other, neither in any way *is* the other, neither *makes* the other. They just stand face to face in a common world, and one simply knows, or is known until, its counterpart... Some sort of *signal* must be given by the thing to the mind's brain, or the knowing will not occur... it must strike the brain in some way, as well as be there, to be known... The thing remains the same whether known or not. And when once there, the knowledge may remain there, whatever becomes of the thing.
(*The Principles of Psychology* [1890], ch. 8.)

CHAPTER 4

"The James-Lange Theory of Emotions: A Critical Examination and an Alternative Theory"

Walter B. Cannon[1]

EDITORS' COMMENTS. There are many different controversies in psychology, but none of them is more important--or more pervasive--than the "infamous" mind-body problem. For, at its heart, it asks, "What are people really like?" Are we mere biological machines, programmed by our genes and past experiences to respond mechanically to whatever environmental stimuli come our ways? Or are we capable, even in small part, of *choosing* our responses to whatever environment we find ourselves in? One way or another, almost every article in this book touches on the mind-body problem.

For example, consider the question we asked in our discussion of the Watson and Rayner article. What happens when a "burnt child" experiences fire for the second time? According to the *mind* position, she sees the fire, experiences fear (dread), and then moves away because she *knows* that "fire hurts." This is the position that cognitive psychologists such as Tolman (Chapter 3) took, of course. More than a century ago, however, William James offered quite a different point of view.

William James was the father of American psychology. As far as emotional arousal was concerned, he took a strong "body" position. According to James, when a "burnt child" subsequently sees a fire, the child *first* becomes physically aroused, then moves away (reflexively). Only afterward does she experience "dread." Put in simpler terms, James held that, in dangerous situations, "you are afraid because you run away, rather than running away because you are afraid." In 1885, the noted Danish scientist Karl G. Lange independently proposed much the same sort of explanation of emotional behavior. For that reason, this viewpoint is often called the James-Lange theory of emotions.

Walter B. Cannon was one of America's greatest neuroscientists. In this article--first published some 40 years after James and Lange presented their viewpoint--Cannon offered three important objections to the James-Lange theory: (1) James assumed that your feelings are dependent on (and follow from) arousal in your sympathetic nervous system. However, Cannon noted, people who have lost their sympathetic nervous systems still experience emotional feelings. (2) The physical changes associated with emotion generally occur *after* the "feelings" have started, not before (as James would have to predict). And (3) the *same* physical changes tend to occur in very *different* emotional states--and in non-emotional states as well.

According to Cannon, your feelings are mediated (controlled) by a lower center of the brain called the thalamus, while another lower center called the hypothalamus controls your bodily reactions in emotional situations. These two emotional systems operate independently, Cannon said, but typically interact with each other to produce emotions. P. Bard advanced almost the same viewpoint in 1927. For that reason, we often refer to this position as the Cannon-Bard theory of emotions.

In 1960, Karl Lashley (who worked with John B. Watson while a graduate student) pointed out a fatal flaw in the Cannon-Bard theory: People with a damaged thalamus still experience emotional feelings, and people with a damaged hypothalamus still show emotional arousal. Thus, as we will see in several subsequent articles in this book, the question of whether emotions are primarily a product of the mind or of the body is far from settled. However, Cannon was one of the first to suggest that it is, really, the joint *interaction* of mind and body that leads to a full-fledged emotional experience.

In his introduction to the reprinting of the classic papers by James and Lange, Dunlap[2] declares that their theory of emotions as organic processes "has not only become so strongly entrenched in scientific thought that it is practically assumed today as the basis for the study of the emotional life, but has also led to the development of the hypothesis of reaction or response as the basis of all mental life." And Perry[3] has written, "This famous doctrine is so strongly fortified by proof and so repeatedly confirmed by experience that it cannot be denied substantial truth. In spite of elaborate refutation it shows no signs of **obsolescence**." With some **trepidation**, therefore, one ventures to criticise a view of the nature of emotions which has proved so satisfactory as a means of interpreting affective experience and which has commended itself so generally to psychologists. There are now at hand, however, pertinent physiological facts which were not available when James and Lange developed their ideas and which should be brought to bear on those ideas, and there are alternative explanations of **affective** experience which should be considered, before the James-Lange theory is granted **basal** claims in this realm of psychology.

James first presented his view in 1884, Lange's monograph appeared in Danish in 1885. The cardinal points in their respective ideas of the nature of emotions are so well known that for purposes of comment only brief references need be made to them. James' theory may be summarized, in nearly his own terms, as follows. An object stimulates one or more sense organs; **afferent** impulses pass to the cortex and the object is perceived; thereupon currents run down to muscles and viscera and alter them in complex ways; afferent impulses from these disturbed organs course back to the cortex and when there perceived transform the "object-simply-apprehended" to the "object-emotionally-felt." In other words, "the feeling of the bodily changes as they occur is the emotion—the common sensational, associational and motor elements explain all."[4] The main evidence cited for the theory is that we are aware of the tensions, throbs, flushes, pangs, suffocations—we feel them, indeed, the moment they occur—and that if we should take away from the picture of a fancied emotion these bodily symptoms, nothing would be left.

According to Lange[5] stimulation of the **vasomotor center** is "the root of the causes of the affections, however else they may be constituted." "We owe all the emotional side of our mental life," he wrote, "our joys and sorrows, our happy and unhappy hours, to our vasomotor system. If the impressions which fall upon our senses did not possess the power of stimulating it, we would wander through life unsympathetic and passionless, all impressions of the outer world would only enrich our experience, increase our knowledge, but would arouse neither joy nor anger, would give us neither care nor fear." Since we are unable to differentiate subjectively between feelings of a central and **peripheral** origin, subjective evidence is unreliable. But because wine, certain mushrooms, hashish, opium, a cold shower, and other agencies cause physiological effects which are accompanied by altered states of feeling, and because abstraction of the bodily manifestations from a frightened individual leaves nothing of his fear, the emotion is only a perception of changes in the body. It is clear that Lange had the same conception as James, but elaborated it on a much narrower basis—on changes in the circulatory system alone.

A CONSIDERATION OF THE VISCERAL FACTORS

The backflow of impulses from the periphery, on which James relied to account for the richness and variety of emotional feeling, was assumed to arise from all parts of the organism, from the muscles and skin as well as the **viscera**. To the latter, however, he inclined to attribute the major role—on "the visceral and organic part of the expression," he wrote, "it is probable that the chief part of the felt emotion depends."[6] We may distinguish, therefore, his two sources of the afferent stream. We shall first consider critically the visceral source. In connection therewith we shall comment on Lange's idea that the vasomotor center holds the explanation of emotional experience.

(1) *Total separation of the viscera from the central nervous system does not alter emotional behavior.* Sher-

---

Obsolescence (ob-so-LESS-ence). The act of going out of date or going out of style.

Trepidation (trep-ih-DAY-shun). Fearfulness.

Affective. The psychological side of an emotional experience, as opposed to the physiological reactions that occur during arousal. The "affective disorders" are those that involve unusual emotional reactions, such as mania and depression.

Basal (BAY-sal). The *base* or foundation of a house is its "basal level."

Afferent (AFF-er-ent). The "input" side of the nervous system, that is, those sensory nerves that run from the receptor organs to the spinal cord and brain.

Vasomotor center (VASS-oh-motor). The part of the brain that controls the expansion and contraction of the blood vessels.

Peripheral (Per-IF-er-al). The "periphery" (per-IF-er-ee) of any space or object is that area that lies far from the center, along the object's outer edge. The human nervous system has two major divisions—the central nervous system (brain and spinal cord, often abbreviated CNS), and the peripheral nervous system, composed of all the nerves (such as those in the skin and muscles) that lie outside the CNS.

Viscera (VISS-sir-ah). The internal organs of the body—such as the heart, liver, kidneys, and stomach—that lie in the central cavity of the body.

rington[7] transected the spinal cord and the **vagus nerves** of dogs so as to destroy any connection of the brain with the heart, the lungs, the stomach and the bowels, the spleen, the liver and other abdominal organs—indeed, to isolate all the structures in which formerly feelings were supposed to reside. Recently Cannon, Lewis and Britton[8] have succeeded in keeping cats in a healthy state for many months after removal of the entire **sympathetic division** of the **autonomic system**, the division which operates in great excitement. Thus all vascular reactions controlled by the vasomotor center were abolished; secretion from the **adrenal medulla** could no longer be evoked; the action of the stomach and intestines could not be inhibited, the hairs could not be erected, and the liver could not be called upon to liberate sugar into the blood stream. These extensively disturbing operations had little if any effect on the emotional responses of the animals. In one of Sherrington's dogs, having a "markedly emotional temperament," the surgical reduction of the sensory field caused no obvious change in her emotional behavior; "her anger, her joy, her disgust, and when provocation arose, her fear, remained as evident as ever." And in the **sympathectomized** cats all superficial signs of rage were manifested in the presence of a barking dog—hissing, growling, retraction of the ears, showing of the teeth, lifting of the paw to strike—*except* erection of the hairs. Both sets of animals behaved with full emotional expression in all the organs still connected with the brain; the only failure was in organs disconnected. The absence of reverberation from the viscera did not alter in any respect the appropriate emotional display; its only abbreviation was surgical.

As Sherrington has remarked, with reference to his head-and-shoulder dogs, it is difficult to think that the perception initiating the wrathful expression should bring in sequel angry conduct and yet have been impotent to produce "angry feeling."

At this point interpretations differ. Angell[9] has argued that Sherrington's experiments afford no evidence that visceral sensation plays no part in the emotional psychosis, and further that they do not prove that the psychic state, "emotion," precedes its "expression." And Perry[10] has declared that whether in the absence of sensations from the organs surgically isolated, the emotion is *felt* remains quite undecided.

It must be admitted, of course, that we have no real basis for either affirming or denying the presence of "felt emotion" in these reduced animals. We have a basis, however, for judging their relation to the James-Lange theory. James attributed the chief part of the felt emotion to sensations from the viscera, Lange attributed it wholly to sensations from the circulatory system. Both affirmed that if these organic sensations are removed *imaginatively* from an emotional experience nothing is left. Sherrington and Cannon and his collaborators varied this procedure by removing the sensations *surgically*. In their animals all visceral disturbances through sympathetic channels—the channels for nervous discharge in great excitement—were abolished. The possibility of return impulses by these channels, and in Sherrington's animals by vagus channels as well, were likewise abolished. According to James's statement of the theory the felt emotion should have very largely disappeared, and according to Lange's statement it should have wholly disappeared (without stimulation of our vasomotor system, it will be recalled, impressions of the outer world "would arouse neither joy nor anger, would give us neither care nor fear"). The animals *acted*, however, insofar as nervous connections permitted, with no lessening of the intensity of emotional display. In other words, operations which, in terms of the theory, largely or completely destroy emotional feeling, nevertheless leave the animals behaving as angrily, as joyfully, as fearfully as ever.

(2) *The same visceral changes occur in very different emotional states and in non-emotional states.* The **preganglionic** fibers of the sympathetic division of the autonomic system are so related to the outlying neurones that the resulting innervation of smooth muscles and glands throughout the body is not particular but diffuse.[11] At the same time with the diffuse emission of sympathetic impulses **adrenin** is poured into the blood. Since it is thereby generally distributed to all parts and has the same effects as the sympathetic impulses wherever it acts, the humoral and the neural agents cooperate in producing diffuse effects. In consequence of these arrangements the sympathetic system goes into action as a unit—there may be minor variations as, for example, the presence or absence of sweating, but in the main features integration is characteristic.

The visceral changes wrought by sympathetic stimulation may be listed as follows: acceleration of the heart, contraction of **arterioles**, dilatation of **bronchioles**, increase of blood sugar, inhibition of activity of the digestive glands, inhibition of gastro-intestinal **peristalsis**, sweating, discharge of adrenin, widening of the pupils and erection of hairs. These changes are seen in great excitement under any circumstances. They occur in such readily distinguishable emotional states as fear and rage.[12] Fever[13] and also exposure to cold[14] are known to induce most of the changes—certainly a faster heart rate, **vasoconstriction**, increased blood sugar, discharge of adrenin and erection of the hairs. **Asphyxia** at the stimulating stage evokes all the changes enumerated above, with the possible exception of sweating. A too great reduction of blood sugar by insulin provokes the "hypoglycemic reaction" characterized by pallor, rapid heart, dilated pupils, discharge of adrenin, increase of blood sugar and profuse sweating.[15]

In this group of conditions which bring about in the viscera changes which are typical of sympathetic discharge are such intense and distinct emotions as fear and rage, such relatively mild affective states as those attending chilliness, hypoglycemia and difficult respiration, and such a markedly different experience as that attending the onset of fever. As pointed out earlier by Cannon[16] the responses in the viscera seem too uniform to offer a satisfactory means of distinguishing emotions which are very different in subjective quality. Furthermore, if the emotions were due to afferent impulses from the viscera, we should expect not only that fear and rage would feel alike but that chilliness, hypoglycemia, asphyxia, and fever should feel like them. Such is not the case.

In commenting on this criticism of the James-Lange theory Angell[17] admits that there may be a considerable **matrix** of substantially identical visceral excitement for some emotions, but urges that the differential features may be found in the extra-visceral disturbances, particularly in the differences of tone in skeletal muscles. Perry[18] likewise falls back on the conformation of the **proprioceptive** patterns, on the "motor set" of the expression, to provide the distinctive elements of the various affective states. The possible contribution of skeletal muscles to the genesis of the felt emotion will be considered later. At present the fact may be emphasized that Lange derived no part of the emotional psychosis from that source; and James attributed to it a minor role — the chief part of the felt emotion depended on the visceral and organic part of the expression.

(3) *The viscera are relatively insensitive structures.* There is a common belief that the more deeply the body is penetrated the more sensitive does it become. Such is not the fact. Whereas in a spinal nerve trunk the sensory nerve fibers are probably always more numerous than the motor, in the nerves distributed to the viscera the afferent (sensory) fibers may be only one-tenth as numerous as the **efferent**.[19] We are unaware of the contractions and relaxations of the stomach and intestines during digestion, of the rubbing of the stomach against the diaphragm, of the squeezing motions of the spleen, of the processes in the liver — only after long search have we learned what is occurring in these organs. Surgeons have found that the alimentary tract can be cut, torn, crushed or burned in operations on the unanesthetized human subject without evoking any feeling of discomfort. We can feel the thumping of the heart because it presses against the chest wall, we can also feel the throbbing of blood vessels because they pass through tissues well supplied with sensory nerves, and we may have abdominal pains but apparently because there are pulls on the **parietal peritoneum**.[20] Normally the visceral processes are extraordinarily undemonstrative. And even when the most marked changes are induced in them, as when adrenalin acts, the results, as we shall see, are sensations mainly attributable to effects on the cardiovascular system.

Vagus nerves (VAY-gus). The nerves that connect the viscera with the brain.

Sympathetic division (sym-pah-THET-tick). The autonomic nervous system (see below) has two main divisions, the sympathetic and the parasympathetic (PAIR-ah-sym-pah-THET-tick). Activity in the sympathetic nervous system arouses the organism; activity in the parasympathetic system slows down bodily processes.

Autonomic system (aw-toh-NOM-ick). That part of the nervous system which controls those "automatic" bodily processes, such as emotional reactions, digestion, sexual arousal, and so forth.

Adrenal medulla (add-DREE-nal med-DULL-ah). The adrenal glands, which sit atop the kidneys, secrete some 20 hormones that affect bodily processes. The top section of the gland is called the adrenal cortex; the bottom section is the medulla. The medulla secretes two hormones—adrenalin (add-DREN-ah-lin) and nor-adrenalin, sometimes called epinephrin (epp-ee-NEFF-rin) and nor-epinephrin—which arouse the body in the same fashion that activity in the sympathetic nervous system does.

Sympathectomized (sim-pah-THECK-toh-mized). The medical term *ectomy* means "to remove, usually by surgery". An appendectomy is an operation involving the removal of the appendix. A sympathectomy is an operation involving the removal of part or all of the sympathetic nervous system.

Preganglionic (pre-gang-lee-AHN-ick). A *ganglion* is a mass of nerve tissue that lies outside the brain or spinal cord (CNS) and that functions as a primitive "processing center". Almost all of the nerve tracts in the sympathetic and parasympathetic systems have ganglia (GANG-lee-ah) associated with them. Preganglionic fibers are those that run to the ganglia; postganglionic fibers are those that run out from the ganglia.

Adrenin (ad-DREN-in). An older name for adrenalin.

Arterioles (ar-TEER-ee-ohls). Small branches at the ends of the arteries that lead to the capillaries (CAP-ih-lair-ees).

Bronchioles (BRONK-ee-ohls). Air goes into the lungs by way of the large bronchial tubes, which branch into smaller tubes called "bronchioles."

Peristalsis (pair-ee-STALL-sis). Successive waves of involuntary muscular contraction that pass along the walls of the intestine and push food onward. Peristalsis is controlled (in large part) by activity in the parasympathetic nervous system.

Vasoconstriction (VASS-oh-con-STRICT-shun). Constriction of the blood vessels, which leads to higher blood pressure.

Asphyxia (ass-FIX-ee-ah). The state that occurs when your breathing is interrupted, and that usually leads to loss of consciousness.

Matrix (MAY-tricks). From the Latin word for "womb." A matrix is something within which something else originates or develops.

Proprioceptive (pro-pree-oh-SEPT-ive). Your internal organs all send "neural messages" to your brain telling the brain what is going on in the organs (and the rest of your body). *Proprioceptive* inputs are those that originate within the body rather than coming from outside the body.

Efferent (EFF-er-ent, or sometimes EE-fer-ent). The output side of the nervous system, that is, nerves that run from the CNS out to the muscles and glands.

Parietal peritoneum (pair-EYE-ih-tal pair-it-toh-KNEE-um). The peritoneum is the membrane that lines the abdomen, or body cavity, and thus encloses the viscera. The parietal peritoneum is the upper or outer layer of the peritoneum.

(4) *Visceral changes are too slow to be a source of emotional feeling.* The viscera are composed of smooth muscle and glands—except the heart, which is modified **striate muscle**. The motions of the body with which we are familiar result from quick-acting striate muscle, having a true latent period of less than 0.001 sec. Notions of the speed of bodily processes acquired by observing the action of skeletal muscle we should not apply to other structures. Smooth muscle and glands respond with relative sluggishness. Although Stewart[21] found that the latent period of smooth muscle of the cat was about 0.25 sec., Sertoli[22] observed that it lasted for 0.85 sec. in the dog and 0.8 sec. in the horse. Langley[23] reported a latent period of 2 to 4 secs. on stimulating the *chorda tympani* nerve supply to the **submaxillary** salivary gland; and Pawlow[24] a latent period of about 6 *minutes* on stimulating the vagus, the secretory nerve of the gastric glands. Again, Wells and Forbes[25] noted that the latent period of the **psychogalvanic reflex** (in man), which appears to be a glandular phenomenon, was about 3 secs.

In contrast to these long delays before peripheral action in visceral structures barely starts are the observations of Wells;[26] he found that the latent period of affective reactions to pictures of men and women ended not uncommonly within 0.8 sec. More recent studies with odors as stimuli have yielded a similar figure (personal communication). According to the James-Lange theory, however, these affective reactions result from reverberations from the viscera. But how is that possible? To the long latent periods of smooth muscles and glands, cited above, there must be added the time required for the nerve impulses to pass from the brain to the periphery and thence back to the brain again. It is clear that the organic changes could not occur soon enough to be the occasion for the appearance of affective states, certainly not the affective states studied by Wells.

(5) *Artificial induction of the visceral changes typical of strong emotions does not produce them.* That adrenin, or the commercial extract of the adrenal glands, "adrenalin," acts in the body so as to mimic the action of sympathetic nerve impulses has already been mentioned. When injected directly into the blood stream or under the skin it induces dilatation of the bronchioles, constriction of blood vessels, liberation of sugar from the liver, stoppage of gastrointestinal functions, and other changes such as are characteristic of intense emotions. If the emotions are the consequence of the visceral changes we should reasonably expect them, in accordance with the postulates of the James-Lange theory, to follow these changes in all cases. Incidental observations on students who received injections of adrenalin sufficiently large to produce general bodily effects have brought out the fact that no specific emotion was experienced by them—a few who had been in athletic competitions testified to feeling "on edge," "keyed up," just as before a race.[27] In a careful study of the effects of adrenalin on a large number of normal and abnormal persons Marañon[28] has reported that the subjective experiences included sensations of precardial or **epigastric palpitation**, of diffuse arterial throbbing, of oppression in the chest and tightness in the throat, of trembling, of chilliness, of dryness of the mouth, of nervousness, malaise and weakness. Associated with these sensations there was *in certain cases* an indefinite affective state coldly appreciated, and without real emotion. The subjects remarked, "I feel as if afraid," "as if awaiting a great joy," "as if moved," "as if I were going to weep without knowing why," "as if I had a great fright yet am calm," "as if they are about to do something to me." In other words, as Marañon remarks, a clear distinction is drawn "between the perception of the peripheral phenomena of vegetative emotion (i.e. the bodily changes) and the psychical emotion proper, which does not exist and which permits the subjects to report on the vegetative syndrome with serenity, without true feeling." In a smaller number of the affected cases a real emotion developed, usually that of sorrow, with tears, sobs and sighings. This occurs, however, "only when the emotional predisposition of the patient is very marked," notably in **hyperthyroid** cases. In some instances Marañon found that this state supervened only when the adrenalin was injected after a talk with the patients concerning their sick children or their dead parents. In short, only when an emotional mood already exists does adrenalin have a supporting effect.

From the evidence adduced by Marañon we may conclude that adrenalin induces in human beings typical bodily changes which are reported as sensations, that in some cases these sensations are reminiscent of previous emotional experiences but do not renew or revive those experiences, that in exceptional cases of preparatory emotional sensitization the bodily changes may tip the scales towards a true affective disturbance. These last cases are exceptional, however, and are not the usual phenomena as James and Lange supposed. In normal conditions the bodily changes, though well marked, do not provoke emotion.

The numerous events occurring in the viscera in consequence of great excitement, as detailed by Cannon,[29] have been interpreted as supporting the James-Lange theory.[30] From the evidence presented under the five headings above it should be clear that that interpretation is unwarranted. Since visceral processes are fortunately not a considerable source of sensation, since even extreme disturbances in them yield no noteworthy emotional experience, we can further understand now why these disturbances cannot serve as a means for discriminating between such pronounced emotions as fear and rage, why chilliness, asphyxia, hyperglycemia and fever, though attended by these disturbances, are not attended by emotion, and also why total exclusion of visceral factors from emotional expression makes no difference in emotional behavior. It is because the returns from the thoracic and abdominal "sounding-board," to use James' word, are very faint indeed, that they play such a minor role in the affective complex. The processes going on in the thoracic and abdominal organs are truly remarkable and various; their value to the organism, however, is not to add richness and flavor to experience, but rather to adapt the internal economy so that in spite of shifts of outer circumstance the even tenor of the inner life will not be profoundly disturbed.

A CONSIDERATION OF THE POSTURAL FACTORS

In his discussion of the cerebral processes accompanying emotion, James[31] argued that either there were special centers for them or they occurred in the ordinary motor and sensory centers of the cortex. And if in the ordinary centers, according to his postulate, the processes would resemble the ordinary processes attending sensation. Only that and full representation of each part of the body in the cortex would be needed to provide a scheme capable of representing the modus operandi of the emotions. Object—sense organ—cortical excitation—perception—reflexes to muscle, skin and viscus—disturbances in them—cortical excitation by these disturbances—perceptions of them added to the original perceptions; such are the occurrences which result in the "object-emotionally-felt." The strict alternative, however, of cortical processes *or* special centers we need not accept. There may be cortical processes *and* special centers. Whether such is the arrangement we may now consider.

(1) *Emotional expression results from action of subcortical centers.* In a paper published in 1887 Bechterev[32] argued that emotional expression must be independent of the cortex because at times the expression cannot be inhibited (e.g. laughing from tickle, grinding the teeth and crying from pain), because visceral changes occur which are beyond control, and because it is seen just after birth before cortical management is important. Furthermore, he reported that after removing the cerebral hemispheres from various kinds of animals appropriate stimulations would evoke corresponding responses of an affective character. Noxious stimuli would cause the hemisphereless cats to snarl, the dogs to whine, to show their teeth and to bark; gentle stimuli (stroking the back) would cause the cats to purr and the dogs to wag their tails. Since these effects disappeared when the optic thalamus was removed, he drew the conclusion that it plays a predominant role in emotional expression.

In 1904 Woodworth and Sherrington[33] proved that many of the physiological phenomena of great excitement would appear in cats from which the thalamus had been wholly removed by section of the brain stem at the mesencephalon. Strong stimulation of an afferent nerve was required to evoke the "pseudaffective" responses. Although these observations tended to lessen the importance of the thalamus as a center, recent experiments have again emphasized its dominance. In 1925 Cannon and Britton[34] described a pseudaffective preparation—a cat decorticated under ether anesthesia—which on recovery displayed spontaneously the complete picture of intense fury. Further study by Bard (work still unpublished) showed that this sham rage

---

Striate muscle (STRY-ate). *Striate* means "striped." There are two main types of muscle—smooth muscle (which lines the digestive tract, for example) and striate muscle (which has a "striped" appearance and which is found in the arms and legs, among other places). You can control most striate muscle voluntarily, but smooth muscle generally is not under your voluntary control.

Submaxillary (sub-MAX-ih-lair-ee). The *maxilla* is the technical term for the jawbone. The submaxillary saliva gland is one that lies just below the jawbone.

Psychogalvanic reflex (SIGN-koh-gal-VAN-ick). Emotional arousal often leads to reflexive sweating—particularly in the skin on the fingers and toes. This sweat changes the electrical resistance of the skin, which can be measured using an instrument called a galvanometer (gal-van-OHM-eter). The so-called "lie detector" actually measures the psychogalvanic reflex, which is associated with *any* type of emotional arousal, not just with guilt or lying.

Epigastric palpitation (EPP-ih-GAS-trick pal-pih-TAY-shun). When your heart beats rapidly, it "palpitates." The epigastric muscles are those lying on or over the stomach. When your "gut clenches up" you experience epigastric palpitation.

Hyperthyroid (HIGH-per-THIGH-roid). The thyroid gland lies at the base of the neck and secretes a hormone that stimulates the sympathetic nervous system. If the gland secretes too much of the hormone (hyperthyroidism), the person will be abnormally aroused or active much of the time.

Thoracic (thor-ASS-sick). Having to do with the chest.

Postulate (POSS-tew-late). To postulate is to assume, or to propose a theoretical explanation for something.

Modus operandi (MOH-dus op-er-AN-die). A Latin term meaning "method of operation."

Noxious (KNOCKS-shush). Unpleasant, or painful.

Thalamus (THALL-ah-muss). A subcenter of the brain that acts as a "central relay station" for most incoming sensory messages. The optic thalamus is that part of the thalamus involved in processing visual inputs.

Mesencephalon (MEES-en-seff-ah-lon). The Latin term *meso* means "middle," while *cephalon* means "brain." Thus, the mesencephalon is the middle division of the brain.

Pseudaffective (SOOD-aff-FECK-tive). Literally, "false emotional" or "sham emotional" response.

continued after ablation of all the brain anterior to the **diencephalon**. Only when the lower posterior portion of the thalamic region was removed did the extraordinary activities of the preparation subside. These results clearly point to the thalamus as a region from which, in the absence of cortical government, impulses are discharged which evoke an extreme degree of "emotional" activity, both muscular and visceral.

The evidence just cited is confirmed by observations on human beings. As has been pointed out elsewhere[35] when the cortical processes are abolished by anesthesia, emotional display may be most remarkable. During the early (excitement) stage of ether anesthesia, for example, there may be sobbing as in grief, or laughter as in joy, or lively and energetic aggressive actions as in rage. The surgeon may open the chest or perform other operations of equal gravity, while the patient is pushing, pulling, shouting and muttering; a few minutes later the conscious patient will testify that he has been wholly unaware of what has happened. It is when "laughing gas" has set aside the cortical functions that the subjects laugh and weep. Similar release of the mechanisms for emotional expression is indicated in the depression of cortical activity during acute alcoholism. In all these conditions the drug acts first as a depressant on the highly sensitive cells of the cortex, and thus lessens or temporarily destroys their control of lower centers; only when the drug becomes more concentrated does it depress also the lower centers; but before that stage is reached the lower centers, released from the cortical dominance as in the surgically decorticated animals, show forth their functions in free play.

Consistent with the experimental and pharmacological evidence is the evidence derived from pathological cases. In certain forms of **hemiplegia** the patients may be incapable of moving the face on the paralyzed side; if suddenly they are affected by a sorrowful or joyous emotion, however, the muscles, unresponsive to voluntary control, spring into action and give both sides of the face the expression of sadness or gaiety.[36] These cases occur when the motor tract is interrupted subcortically and the optic thalamus is left intact. The opposite of this condition is seen in unilateral injury of the thalamus. A patient described by Kirilzev[37] moved symmetrically both sides of his face at will, but when he laughed in fun or made a grimace in pain the right side remained motionless; at autopsy a tumor was found in the center of the left optic thalamus. This localization of the central neural apparatus for the expressions of pleasure and pain has interesting relations to emotive phenomena commonly seen in so-called "**pseudo-bulbar palsy**." In such cases there is usually a bilateral facial paralysis, with one side slightly more involved than the other. Voluntary pursing of the lips as in whistling, or wrinkling of the forehead, or making a grimace may be impossible. The intractable facial muscles, however, function normally in laughing or crying, scowling or frowning. These well-executed expressions come in fits and are uncontrollable and prolonged. One patient is described who started laughing at 10:00 o'clock in the morning and continued with few pauses until 2:00 in the afternoon! Tilney and Morrison,[38] who have reported on 173 recorded cases of the disease, found such fits of crying and laughing in seventeen percent of the cases, crying alone in sixteen percent, and laughing alone in fifteen percent. The fits appear as a rule without any of the usual provocations and most frequently are inopportune. The patient may have all the appearances of being convulsed with laughter, yet may not experience any of the feeling which the motions of face and body indicate. Such cases are attributed by Brissaud[39] to lesions of a special part of the cortico-thalamic tract which free a portion of the thalamus from the cortical check. It seems probable, as later evidence will suggest, that afferent thalamo-cortical tracts are also defective. Finally, cases of "**narcolepsy**" are known in which emotional expression is nearly nil; **gibes** and insults which enrage or infuriate the normal person are usually quite without effect. In some of these cases, examined **post-mortem**, were found tumors on the under side of the diencephalon, often affecting the whole hypothalamus.

All these observations, experimental and clinical, consistently point to the optic thalamus as a region in which resides the neural organization for the different emotional expressions. The section of James' discussion, headed "No Special Brain Centres for Emotion" must be modified in the light of this accumulated information. The cortex at one end of the nerve paths as a reflex surface and the peripheral organs at the other end as a source of return impulses make too simple an arrangement. Between the cortex and the periphery lies the diencephalon, an integrating organ on the emotive level, a receiving and discharging station, that on proper stimulation is capable of establishing in stereotyped forms the **facies** and bodily postures typical of the various affective states. That all afferent paths leading towards the cortex have relays in the diencephalon is a fact of great significance in explaining the nature of emotions.

(2) *Thalamic processes are a source of affective experience.* The relaying of all sensory neurones in some part of the optic thalamus has been stressed by Head[40] in his important clinical studies. He and Holmes[41] attributed to this region a sort of consciousness, an "awareness." The effect of anesthesia in abolishing consciousness while leaving emotional expression (thalamic in origin) undisturbed would seem to con-

tradict this view. But even if consciousness is associated only with events in cortical neurones, the important part played by thalamic processes is little disturbed thereby. The relays of sensory channels in the thalamus and the evidence that disturbances in that region are the occasion for intensely affective sensations are all that we need for understanding its relation to the nature of emotions.

Head[42] has cited numerous cases of unilateral lesions in the thalamic region in which there is a marked tendency to react excessively to affective stimuli; pin pricks, painful pressure, excessive heat or cold, all produce more distress on the damaged than on the normal side of the body. Agreeable stimuli also are felt keenly on the damaged side; warmth stimuli may evoke intense pleasure, attended by signs of enjoyment on the face and exclamations of delight. Again, affective stimuli, such as the playing of music and the singing of hymns, may arouse such increased emotional feeling on the damaged side that they may be intolerable. Affective conscious states have an influence on the damaged side similar to stimuli from the surface receptors. This extravagant influence of affective stimuli, whether from above or below, Head attributed to release of the thalamus from cortical inhibition. It is not an irritative effect, he argued, because it persists for long periods, well after all the disturbances due to the injury have subsided. And since the affective states are increased when the thalamus is freed from cortical control, Head's conclusion is that the essential thalamic center is mainly occupied with the affective side of sensation.

We are now in a position to consider the evidence that the positions and tensions of skeletal muscle make the **differentia** of emotion. It will be recalled that, although James belittled this element in his theory, his supporters have stressed it, especially since the visceral element proved inadequate. The thalamic cases provide a means of testing the contribution from skeletal muscles, for the feeling-tone of a sensation is a product of thalamic activity, and the fact that a sensation is devoid of feeling-tone shows that the impulses which underlie its production make no thalamic appeal.

Head found that his patients reported marked differences in the feeling-tone of different sensations. A tuning fork may have no effect, whereas patriotic music is felt intensely on the damaged side. All thermal stimuli make a double appeal, to the cortex and to the thalamus. Unselected **tactile** stimuli act similarly. On the other hand, *sensations which underlie the appreciation of posture are entirely lacking in feeling-tone*. Precisely those afferent impulses from muscles and joints which James and his supporters have relied upon to provide the extra-visceral-part of the felt-motion are the impulses which lack the necessary quality to serve the purpose!

The quality of emotions is to be found, therefore, neither in returns from the viscera nor in returns from the innervated muscles.

A THEORY OF EMOTION BASED ON THALAMIC PROCESSES

The foregoing discussion has disclosed the fact that the neural arrangements for emotional expression reside in subcortical centers, and that these centers are ready for instant and vigorous discharge when they are released from cortical restraint and are properly stimulated. Furthermore, the evidence is clear that when these centers are released the processes aroused in them become a source of vivid affective experience. That this experience is felt on only one side in hemiplegic cases is a peculiarly happy circumstance, for in the same individual the influence of the same affective stimulus can be observed under normal conditions and compared with its influence when given free rein.

The neural organization for an emotion which is suggested by the foregoing observations is as follows. An external situation stimulates receptors and the consequent excitation starts impulses towards the cortex. Arrival of the impulses in the cortex is associated with conditioned processes which determine the direction of the response. Either because the response is initiated in a certain mode or figure and the cortical neurones therefore stimulate the thalamic processes, or because

---

Diencephalon (DIE-en-seff-ah-lon). The forward or front region of the brain has two major parts, of which the diencephalon is the posterior or rear subdivision.

Hemiplegia (HEM-ee-PLEE-gee-ah). *Hemi* means "half," and *plegia* means "paralysis." A hemiplegia is a paralysis of the left or the right half of the body.

Pseudo-bulbar palsy (SOO-doh-BULB-ar PAHL-see). The medulla (med-DULL-ah) is a neural structure in the brain stem. Damage to a bulb-shaped area of the medulla leads to a paralysis of, or to an uncontrollable trembling of, part or all of the body. "Pseudo-bulbar palsy" is a similar condition that is not, in fact, caused by damage to the medulla itself.

Narcolepsy (NARK-koh-LEP-see). A sleep disorder in which the person falls asleep involuntarily, usually just after a strong emotional experience.

Gibes (rhymes with "vibes"). Gibes are teasing or taunting words, that is, "put-downs."

Post-mortem (post-MORE-tem). A medical examination aimed at determining the cause of the "mortem," or death.

Facies (FAH-sheeze). Facial expressions that are characteristic of a given condition.

Differentia (diff-er-EN-she-ah). The elements or features that distinguish one state or class from another.

Tactile (TACK-tile). Having to do with the sense of touch. Tactile inputs are those that come from the receptors in the skin and muscles.

on their **centripetal** course the impulses from the receptors excite thalamic processes, they are roused and ready for discharge. That the thalamic neurones act in a special combination in a given emotional expression is proved by the reaction patterns typical of the several affective states. These neurones do not require detailed innervation from above in order to be driven into action. Being *released* for action is a primary condition for their service to the body—they then discharge precipitately and intensely. Within and near the thalamus the neurones concerned in an emotional expression lie close to the relay in the sensory path from periphery to cortex. We may assume that when these neurones discharge in a particular combination, they not only innervate muscles and viscera but also excite afferent paths to the cortex by direct connection or by irradiation. The theory which naturally presents itself is that the *peculiar quality of the emotion is added to simple sensation when the thalamic processes are roused.*

The theory just suggested appears to fit all the known facts. Its service in explaining these facts may be briefly summarized.

When the thalamic discharge occurs, the bodily changes occur almost simultaneously with the emotional experience. This coincidence of disturbances in muscles and viscera with thrills, excitements or depressions was naturally misleading, for, with the role of the thalamus omitted from consideration, the obvious inference was that the peculiar quality of the emotion arose from the peripheral changes. Indeed, that inference is the heart of the James-Lange theory. The evidence presented in the foregoing pages shows that the inference is ill-founded; the sensations from the peripheral changes, contrary to James' view, are "pale, colorless and destitute of emotional warmth," whereas the thalamic disturbances contribute glow and color to otherwise simply cognitive states. The theory now proposed explains how James and Lange could reasonably make the suggestion which they made. The lack of factual support for their suggestion requires another account of emotional origins. This is provided by the evidence that thalamic processes can add to sensation an aura of feeling.

One of the strongest arguments advanced for the James-Lange theory is that the assumption of an attitude does in fact help to establish the emotional state which the attitude expresses. "Sit all day in a moping posture, sigh, and reply to everything with a dismal voice, and your melancholy lingers." On the contrary, "smooth the brow, brighten the eye, contract the **dorsal** rather than the **ventral** aspect of the frame, and speak in a major key, pass the genial compliment, and your heart must be frigid indeed if you do not gradually thaw!" Persons who have tried this advice have testified to its soundness, and have been convinced, therefore, of the truth of the claim that the moods have followed the assumed attitudes. Not all agree, however, that mimicking the outward appearance of an emotion results in the emotion itself. James suggested that the explanation of the discrepancy lay in variations of involvement of the viscera in the artificial expression. As shown above, however, the visceral changes offer only unreliable support for that idea. Again the processes in the thalamus offer a reasonable and simple explanation. As the cases reported by Head have shown, emotions originating from memories and imagination affect more intensely the half-thalamus that has been released from motor control than they affect the normal half. This shows that cortical processes may start thalamic processes and thus arouse an affective return from that portion of the brain. And if in addition a typical emotional attitude is assumed the cortical inhibition of the thalamic neurones with reference to that attitude is abolished so that they have complete release. Under such circumstances the enacted emotion would have reality. On the other band a purely cortical mimicry of emotional expression without thalamic involvement would be as cold and unaffective as some actors have declared it to be. Whether the emotion results or not, the thalamic theory of the source of feeling offers a more satisfactory explanation of the effects of assumed postures than does the James-Lange theory.

The cases of release of the thalamus from cortical control on one side, with accompanying **ipsilateral** intensification of emotional tone, present an insurmountable obstacle to the James-Lange theory. Neither the thoracic nor the abdominal viscera can function by halves, the vasomotor center is a unity, and the patients certainly do not engage in right- or left-sided laughter and weeping. The impulses sent back from the disturbed peripheral organs, therefore, must be bilaterally equal. For explanation of the unsymmetrical feeling we are driven to the organ which is functioning unsymmetrically—*i.e.* the thalamus. It is there that the suggested theory places the source of the emotions.

Another serious difficulty for the James-Lange theory is the evidence that the emotion increases in intensity although the expression is checked. Indeed, there are psychologists who maintain that the emotional state lasts only so long as there is inner conflict between the impulse to act and the hesitant or **prudential** check on that impulse. So long as the check prevails, however, the organic changes supposed to be the source of the feeling are suppressed. How then can there be felt-emotion? Two answers to this question may be found in James' argument. First he denies the objection. "Refuse to express a passion," he wrote, "and it dies." "Count ten before venting your anger, and its occasion seems ridiculous." On the other hand, he appears to admit that a pent emotion may operate disastrously. "If tears or anger are simply suppressed, whilst the object of grief or rage remains unchanged before the mind, the current which would have invaded the normal channels turns into others, for it must find some outlet of escape. It may then work different and worse effects later on. Thus vengeful brooding may replace a burst of indignation; a dry heat may consume the frame of one who **fain** would weep, or he may, as Dante says, turn to stone within." There is no intimation that vengeful brooding, being consumed by a dry heat, and turning to stone within are not emotional experiences. Instead of recognizing them as such, however, James stressed the importance of training for repression of emotional display. These rather equivocal and indecisive comments leave untouched the common testimony that intense fear, for example, may be felt, with a pathetic sense of helplessness, before any overt act occurs, and that scarcely does the appropriate behavior start than the inner **tumult** begins to subside and the bodily forces are directed vigorously and effectively to serviceable ends. The difficulties of the James-Lange theory in meeting this situation are obvious. If there is a double control of behavior, however, both the inner conflict with its keen emotional accompaniment and the later partial subsidence of feeling are readily explicable. The thalamic patterned processes are inherent in the nervous organization, they are like reflexes in being instantly ready to seize control of the motor responses, and when they do so they operate with great power. They can be controlled, however, by the processes in the cerebral cortex, by processes conditioned by all sorts of previous impressions. The cortex also can control all the peripheral machinery except the viscera. The inhibited processes in the thalamus cannot set the organism in action, except the parts not under voluntary control, but the turmoil there can produce emotions in the usual manner, and possibly with greater violence because of the inhibition. And when the cortical check is released, suddenly the conflict is resolved. The two controls formerly in opposition, are now cooperative. The thalamic neurones, so long as they continue energetically active, provide the condition for the emotion to persist, as James claimed it does, *during* the manifestation. The new theory, therefore, not only avoids the difficulty of the James-Lange theory, but accounts satisfactorily for the **poignancy** of feeling in the period of paralyzed inaction.

In relation to the double control of the response there is another point that may be emphasized. McDougall[43] has objected to the James-Lange theory on the ground that it is admittedly concerned with the *sensory* aspect of emotion; it pays little or no attention to the always present and sometimes overwhelming *impulsive* aspect of the experience. The localization of the reaction patterns for emotional expression in the thalamus — in a region which, like the spinal cord, works directly by simple automatisms unless held in check — not only accounts for the "sensory side," the "felt emotion," but also for the impulsive side, the tendency of the thalamic neurones to discharge. These powerful impulses originating in a region of the brain not associated with cognitive consciousness and arousing therefore in an *obscure* and *unrelated* manner the strong feelings of emotional excitement, explain the sense of being seized, possessed, of being controlled by an outside force and made to act without weighing of the consequences.

Finally, the view that thalamic processes add feeling-tone to sensation meets satisfactorily a difficulty which the James-Lange theory encountered in explaining the "subtler emotions." James had to assume indefinite and hypothetical bodily reverberations in order to account for mild feelings of pleasure and satisfaction. If a warm test tube, however, is capable of yielding keen delight on the damaged side in a case of thalamic injury, it is clear that almost any object or situation which can rouse thalamic processes can add affective quality to sensation. And just as a stimulus can become conditioned for a certain motor or glandular response, so likewise a stimulus can be conditioned for the patterns of neurone action in the thalamus. When that stimulus recurs the emotion recurs because the pattern is activated. In such manner we may consider that richness and variety of our emotional life are elaborated.

Centripetal (sen-TRIP-ih-tal). In physics, centripetal forces are those that tend to move an object in toward the center of rotation. In neurophysiology, centripetal forces are those which push inputs from the receptors toward the brain.

Dorsal, Ventral. (DOOR-sal, VEN-tral). *Dorsal* means "back" or "posterior," while *ventral* means "front," or "anterior."

Ipsilateral (IPP-see-LATT-er-al). From the Latin words meaning "same side." Although the left half of the brain controls the right side of the body, and the right side of the brain controls the left half of the body, damage to one side of the thalamus sometimes leads to intensification of emotional expression on the ispilateral, or the same side, of the body.

Prudential (pru-DENT-shall). A prudent man is a cautious man.

Fain (rhymes with "rain"). If you "fain would weep," you feel compelled to weep.

Tumult (TOO-mult). A confused and often noisy situation.

Poignancy (POYN-yan-see). A poignant (POYN-yant) experience is one that deeply affects the emotions.

FOOTNOTES AND REFERENCES

[1] Reprinted by permission of the American Psychological Association from the *American Journal of Psychology*, 1927, **39**, 106-124. Copyright 1927 by the American Journal of Psychology.

[2] W. James and C. G. Lange, *The Emotions*, 1922.

[3] R.B. Perry, *General Theory of Value*, 1926, 295.

[4] James, *op. cit.*, 123.

[5] Lange, *op. cit.*, 73.

[6] James, *op. cit.*, 116.

[7] C.S. Sherrington, Experiments on the value of vascular and visceral factors for the genesis of emotion, *Proc. Roy. Soc.*, **66**, 1900, 397.

[8] W.B. Cannon, J. T. Lewis and S. W. Britton, The dispensability of the sympathetic division of the autonomic system, *Bost. Med. and Surg. J.*, **197**, 1927, 514.

[9] J.R. Angell, A reconsideration of James's theory of emotion in the light of recent criticisms, *Psychol. Rev.*, **23**, 1916, 259.

[10] Perry, *op. cit.*, 298.

[11] Cannon, *Bodily Changes in Pain, Hunger, Fear and Rage*, 1915, 26.

[12] Cannon, *op. cit.*, 277.

[13] Cannon and J. R. Pereira, Increase of adrenal secretion in fever, *Proc. Nat. Acad. Sci.*, **10**, 1924, 247.

[14] Cannon, A. Querido, S. W. Britton and E. M. Bright, The role of adrenal secretion in the chemical control of body temperature, *Amer. J. Physiol.*, **79**, 1927, 466.

[15] Cannon, M. A. McIver and S. W. Bliss, A sympathetic and adrenal mechanism for mobilizing sugar in hypoglycemia, *Amer. J. Physiol.*, **69**, 1924, 46.

[16] Cannon, *op. cit.*, 280.

[17] Angell, *op. cit.*, 260.

[18] Perry, *op. cit.*, 300.

[19] J.N Langley and H.K. Anderson, The constituents of the hypogastric nerves, *J. Physiol.*, **17**, 1894, 185.

[20] K. G. Lennander *et al*, Abdominal pains, especially in ileus, *J. Amer. Med. Assoc.*, **49**, 1907, 836 (see also p. 1015).

[21] C. C. Stewart, Mammalian smooth muscle--the cat's bladder, *Amer. J. Physiol.*, **4**, 1900, 192.

[22] E. Sertoli, Contribution à la physiologie général des muscles lisses, *Arch. ital. de biol.*, **3**, 1883, 86.

[23] J. N. Langley, On the physiology of the salivary secretion, *J. Physiol.*, **10**, 1889, 300.

[24] J. P. Pawlow and E. O. Schumowa-Simanowskaja, Die Innervation der Magendrüsen beim Hunde, *Arch. f. Physiol.*, 1895, 66.

[25] F. L. Wells and A. Forbes, On certain electrical processes in the human body and their relations to emotional reactions, *Arch. Psychol.*, **2**, 1911, No. 16, p. 8.

[26] Wells, Reactions to visual stimuli in affective settings, *J. Exper. Psychol.*, **8**, 1925, 64.

[27] F. W. Peabody, C. C. Sturgis, E. M. Tompkins and J. T. Wearn, Epinephrin hypersensitiveness and its relation to hyperthyroidism, *Amer. J. Med. Sci.*, **161**, 1921, 508, (also personal communication from J. T. Wearn).

[28] G. Marañon, Contribution à l'étude de l'action émotive de l'adrenaline, *Rev. franç. d'endocrinol.*, **2**, 1924, 301.

[29] Cannon, *op. cit.*, 184.

[30] G. Humphrey, *The Story of Man's Mind*, 1923, 211.

[31] James, *op. cit.*, 123.

[32] W. Bechterev, Die Bedeutung der Sehhugel auf Grund von experimentellen und pathologischen Daten, *Virchow's Archiv*, **110**, 1887, 102, 322.

[33] R. S. Woodworth and C. S. Sherrington, A pseudaffective reflex and its spinal path, *J. Physiol.*, **31**, 1904, 234.

[34] Cannon and S. W. Britten, Pseudaffective medulliadrenal secretion, *Amer. J. Physiol.*, **72**, 1925, 283.

[35] Cannon, Neural basis for emotion expression, *Wittenberg Symposium on Feelings and Emotions*, 1927.

[36] G. Roussy, *La couche optique*, 1907, 31.

[37] Kirilzev, Cases of affections of the optic thalamus (Russian). Reviewed in *Neurologisches Centralblatt*, **10**, 1891, 310.

[38] F. Tilney and J. F. Morrison, Pseudo-bulbar palsy clinically and pathologically considered, *J. Ment. and Nerv. Diseases*, **39**, 1912, 505.

[39] E. Brissaud, *Leçons Cliniques*, 1894.

[40] H. Head, Release of function in the nervous system, *Proc. Roy. Soc.*, **92B**, 1921, 184.

[41] Head and G. Holmes, Sensory disturbances from cerebral lesions, *Brain*, **34**, 1911, 109.

[42] Head, *Studies in Neurology*, 1920, II, 620.

[43] W. McDougall, *Outline of Psychology*, 1923, 328.

Classic Quotations from William James

Our natural way of thinking about these coarser emotions is that the mental perception of some fact excites the mental affection called the emotion, and that this latter state of mind gives rise to the bodily expression. My theory, on the contrary, is that *the bodily changes follow directly the perception of the exciting fact, and that our feeling of the same changes as they occur* IS *the emotion*. Common-sense says, we lose our fortune, are sorry and weep; we meet a bear, are frightened and run; we are insulted by a rival, are angry and strike. The hypothesis here to be defended says that this order of sequence is incorrect, that the one mental state is not immediately induced by the other, that the bodily manifestations must first be interposed between, and that the more rational statement is that we feel sorry because we cry, angry because we strike, afraid because we tremble, and not that we cry, strike, or tremble, because we are sorry, angry, or fearful, as the case may be. Without the bodily states following on the perception, the latter would be purely cognitive in form, pale, colorless, destitute of emotional warmth.

(*The Principles of Psychology* [1890], ch. 25.)

CHAPTER 5

"Autonomic Nervous System Activity Distinguishes Among Emotions"

Paul Ekman, Robert W. Levenson, and Wallace V. Friesen[1]

EDITORS' COMMENTS. In 1872, the noted naturalist Charles Darwin published a book entitled *The Expression of Emotions in Man and Animals*. According to Darwin, emotions have two major purposes, both of which increase an organism's ability to survive. First, inner feelings *motivate* an organism to approach pleasurable inputs and to avoid painful inputs. The survival value of "proper motivation" is obvious. But second, the *expression* of emotions allows one animal to communicate its feelings to other animals. For example, when a lion bares its teeth, other (smaller) animals can increase their chances of surviving by running away. When a female chimpanzee smiles at an approaching male to let him know that she is sexually receptive, she is more likely to "capture" him (for mating purposes) than if she snarls and spits at him. The importance of *communicating* subjective feelings seemed obvious to Darwin.

Judging from what he says in his 1872 book, Darwin apparently believed that facial expressions (and bodily postures) *mirrored*, and hence were *caused by*, the animal's inner feelings. But the James-Lange position that subjective feelings *follow*, and hence are *caused by*, physical reactions, still dominates some areas of modern-day psychology. For example, in 1962, S.S. Tomkins modified Darwin's views by stating that the facial muscles respond *innately* to certain types of emotional situations. Tomkins noted that, worldwide, people have similar facial expressions when expressing joy, sadness, or anger. Therefore, Tomkins said, these facial responses must be coded for in the genes. But you don't use these facial reactions to communicate your "inner states" to others, as Darwin believed. Rather, Tomkins claimed, you smile or frown innately as a reaction to a stimulus input. Feedback from your muscles then triggers off *both* the autonomic arousal and subjective "feelings" associated with the emotion. Following James-Lange, then, Tomkins held that your body reacts *innately*, and your mind *interprets* these innate responses--particularly the reactions of your facial muscles--as "emotions."

The objections that Cannon raised to the James-Lange position apply to much of Tomkins' theorizing as well (see Chapter 3). For instance, people whose facial muscles are paralyzed still experience normal emotions subjectively, as do people with damage to the right hemisphere that keeps them from expressing those emotions either with their facial muscles or by laughing or crying. So the matter is far from settled. However, in this article, Paul Ekman, R.W. Levenson, and W.V. Friesen do offer rather interesting data that seem to support Tomkins' theory. Particularly important is their finding that specific facial expressions lead to fairly specific patterns of physical arousal, as well as to subjective feelings typically associated with those facial expressions.

Which viewpoint is right? Are your emotions *primarily* a set of physiological reactions, determined almost entirely by your genes and your past conditioning? In short, does your body rule your mind? Or does your mind *interpret* what's happening to you and then order your body to respond appropriate? Or is there, perhaps, a third factor we've neglected, namely, the social environment? For example, if you painfully whack your thumb while your mother is watching, do you express your feelings in precisely the same language as you might if no one were around? Are you more likely to blush--and to *feel* shame or guilt--if someone of the opposite sex accidentally sees you in the nude than if someone of the same sex catches you in a state of undress? How would Tomkins explain your differing reactions in these two situations?

We will have more to say about this fascinating set of affairs at the beginning of the next chapter. Meanwhile, relax, paint a smile on your face, and consider the interesting data in the present article.

Fig. 1. Frames from the videotape of one of the actor's performance of the fear prototype instructions: (A) "raise your brows and pull them together." (B) "now raise your upper eyelids," (C) "now also stretch your lips horizontally, back toward your ears."

Abstract. Emotion-specific activity in the autonomic nervous system was generated by constructing facial prototypes of emotion muscle by muscle and by reliving past emotional experiences. The autonomic activity produced distinguished not only between positive and negative emotions, but also among negative emotions. This finding challenges emotion theories that have proposed autonomic activity to be undifferentiated or that have failed to address the implications of autonomic differentiation in emotion.

For almost a century scientists have argued about whether or not activity in the **autonomic nervous system** (ANS) is emotion-specific. Some of the most influential cognitive theories of emotion(1, 2) presume undifferentiated autonomic arousal despite a number of reports of emotion-specific autonomic activity (3-5). We now report evidence of such specificity in an experiment designed to remedy methodological problems that have lessened the impact of previous studies: (i) A broad sample of six emotions was studied, rather than the two or three that are typical. (ii) Verification procedures were instituted to maximize the likelihood that each sample contained only the single target emotion and no other. (iii) A sufficiently broad sample of autonomic measures was obtained to enable differentiation of multiple emotions, with appropriate statistical protection against spurious findings due to multiple dependent measures. (iv) Autonomic measures were taken from the onset of emotion production continuously until it was terminated. More typical measures taken before and after production of an emotion may completely miss short-lived target emotions. (v) Multiple eliciting tasks were used with the same subjects. (vi) Professional actors (N = 12) and scientists who study the face (N = 4) served as subjects to minimize contamination of emotion samples by extraneous affect associated with frustration or embarrassment.

We studied six target emotions (surprise, disgust, sadness, anger, fear, and happiness) elicited by two tasks (directed facial action and relived emotion), with emotion ordering **counterbalanced** within tasks. During both tasks, facial behavior was recorded on videotape, and second-by-second averages were obtained for five **physiological** measures: (i) heart rate--measured with **bipolar chest leads** with Redux paste; (ii) left- and (iii) right-hand temperatures--measured with **thermistors** taped to the palmar surface of the first **phalanges** of the middle finger of each hand; (iv) skin resistance--measured with **Ag-AgCl electrodes** with Beckman paste attached to the palmar surface of the middle phalanges of the first and third fingers of the nondominant hand; and (v) forearm flexor muscle tension--measured with Ag-AgCl electrodes with Redux paste and electronic integration of the **electromyogram**.

Autonomic nervous system (aw-toh-NOM-ick). That part of the nervous system which controls involuntary activities such as breathing, heart rate, digestion, and so forth.

Counterbalanced. A research technique in which the order of treatments is rotated. For instance, suppose you wanted to determine whether subjects respond to kittens in the same (emotional) way that they respond to puppies. In a counterbalanced design, you would present the kittens first to half the subjects, and then the puppies. The other half of the subjects would experience the puppies first.

Physiological (FIZZ-ih-oh-LODGE-ih-kal). Having to do with the body rather than with the mind.

Bipolar chest leads. Disk-shaped electrodes that are "glued to the chest" with special paste in order to measure electrical activity in the region of the heart.

Thermistors (THERM-is-tors). Electrodes that respond electrically to temperature changes.

Phalanges (fal-LAN-jes). The bone segments in your fingers.

Ag-AgCl electrodes. Electrodes containing a mixture of silver (Ag) and silver chloride (AgCl) that are used to detect changes in the electrical resistance of the skin.

Electromyogram (ee-leck-troh-MY-oh-gram). A device used to record electrical activity in the muscles.

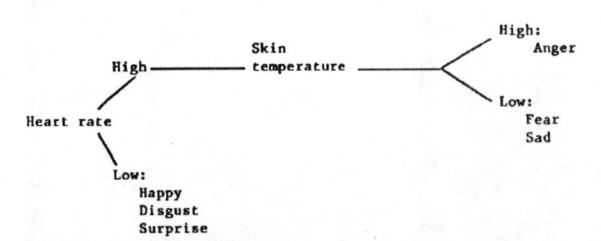

Fig. 2. Decision tree for discriminating emotions in direction facial action task.

The directed facial action task comprised six trials; in each a nonemotional expression was performed and followed by an emotion-prototypic expression, that is, an expression that theory and evidence indicate universally signals one of the target emotions (6). Subjects were not asked to produce an emotional expression but instead were told precisely which muscles to contract (Fig. 1). Their attempts to follow these instructions were aided by a mirror and coaching (by P.E.). The nonemotional expression comprised two actions not included in any of the emotional expressions to control for ANS changes associated with making any facial movement. Expressions were held for 10 seconds. This task resembles a traditional emotion posing task (in which, for example, subjects are asked to look fearful), but improves on it by precisely specifying for the subject, and for the experimenter's subsequent verification, the exact set of muscle movements that is required. Video records of facial expressions were measured (7) to ensure that autonomic data would be included in the analyses only if the instructed set of actions had been made; 86.5 percent of the data were used.

In the relived emotion task, subjects were asked to experience each of the six emotions (in counterbalanced orders) by reliving a past emotional experience for 30 seconds. This task resembles traditional imagery tasks, but more specifically focuses on reliving a past emotional experience. After each trial, subjects rated the intensity of any felt emotion on a scale from 0 to 8. Autonomic data were used only when the relived emotion was felt at the midpoint of the scale or greater and when no other emotion was reported at a similar strength; 55.8 percent of the data were used.

Change scores were computed for each emotion on each task (directed facial action: averaged data during emotional face minus that during nonemotional face; relived emotion: averaged data during relived emotion minus that during the preceding 10-second rest period). The experiment was analyzed in a 2 by 2 by 6 (actors versus scientists by task by emotion) **multivariate analysis of variance**. Our hypothesis that there are autonomic differences among the six emotions was supported [emotion main effect, $F(25,317) = 2.51$, $P < 0.001$]. There were differences in emotion-specific autonomic patterns between the two eliciting tasks [task by emotion interaction, $F(25, 62) = 2.0$, $P = 0.014$].

The nature of the emotion-specific ANS activity was explored with t-tests within significant **univariate** effects. Two findings were consistent across tasks: (i) Heart rate increased more in anger (mean calculated across tasks ± standard error, +8.0 ± 1.8 beats per minute) and fear (+8.0 ± 1.6 beats per minute) than in happiness (+2.6 ±1.0 beats per minute). (ii) Left and right finger temperatures increased more in anger (left, +0.10°C ± 0.009°; right, +0.08°C ± 0.008°)than in happiness (left, -0.07° ± 0.002°; right, -0.03°C ± 0.002°).

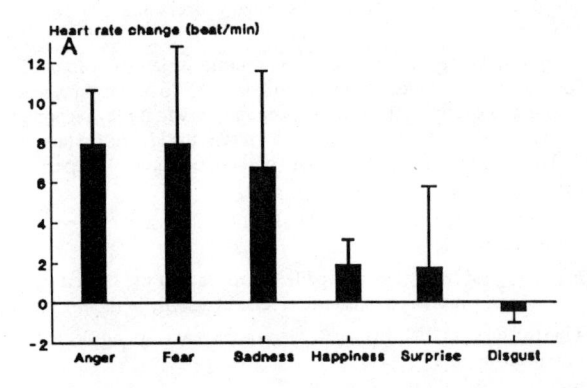

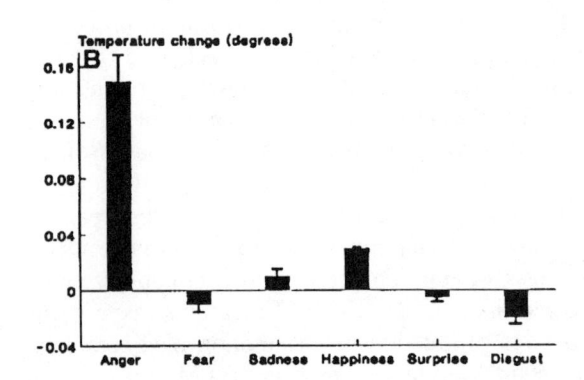

EMOTIONS

Fig. 3. Changes in (A) heart rate and (B) right finger temperature during the directed facial action task. Values are means ± standard errors. For heart rate, the changes associated with anger, fear, and sadness were all significantly greater ($P < 0.05$) than those for happiness, surprise, and disgust. For finger temperature,

In addition to these differences between the negative emotions of anger and fear and the positive emotion of happiness, there were important differences among negative emotions. In the directed facial action task we were able to distinguish three subgroups of emotions (Fig. 2) on the basis of heart rate and finger temperature differences (Fig. 3). Additional differentiation in the relived emotions task enabled distinction between sadness and other negative emotions on the basis of significantly larger decreases in skin resistance in sadness [-12.6 ± 164.6 kilohm (8)] than in the others (fear, -0.37 ± 1.0 kilohm; anger, -2.1 ± 3.7 kilohm; and disgust, +4.4 ± 6.6 kilohm).

There were also three negative findings of note. No significant differences were found between emotions on the forearm flexor measure, thus indicating that heart rate effects were not artifacts of fist clenching or other related muscle activity. No statistically significant differences were found between actors and scientists studying facial expression, indicating that the findings generalized to both of these populations. Finally, when the major analyses were rerun including all ANS data without regard to whether verification criteria were met, only the negative versus positive emotional distinctions remained; all distinctions among negative emotions were lost. We interpret this finding as supporting the importance of verification of emotional state and as indicating one reason previous studies that failed to include verification procedures have been unable to distinguish so many negative emotions.

Combining the results from the two tasks, this experiment provides the first evidence (to our knowledge) of autonomic differences among four negative emotions (disgust and anger distinguished from each other and from fear or sadness in the directed facial action task; sadness distinguished from disgust, anger, or fear in the relived emotion task) as well as showing general distinctions between positive and negative emotions in both tasks. In addition to this new evidence, we **replicated** with the directed facial action task the single most reliable finding from past studies: anger and fear show similar heart rate increases but differ in peripheral vascular function (indicated by our finding of colder fingers in fear than in anger). The magnitude of these heart rate increases, both mean (Fig. 3) and maximum (fear, +21.7; anger, +25.3 beats per minute) are comparable to other such findings (9).

Further research is needed to choose between two alternative explanations of the differences in the results we obtained with the two eliciting tasks: (i) the tasks involve different neural substrates, which generate different patterns of emotion-specific autonomic activity; or (ii) the tasks differ in the extent of emotion blending they produce. Further work is also needed to demonstrate that emotion-specific autonomic activity is not unique to actors and scientists, although the possibility that training in either profession would have such a profound effect on autonomic patterning in emotion seems unlikely.

Our finding of emotion-differentiated autonomic activity, albeit important in its own right, begets the question of how that activity was generated. Particularly intriguing is our discovery that producing the emotion-prototypic patterns of facial muscle action resulted in autonomic changes of large magnitude that were more clear-cut than those produced by reliving emotions (a more naturalistic process). With this experiment we cannot rule out the possibility that knowledge of the emotion labels derived from the facial movement instructions or seeing one's own or the coach's face was directly or indirectly responsible for the effect. We find this unlikely since it would indicate either (i) that just viewing an emotional face directly produced autonomic patterning or (ii) that subjects inferred the "correct" set of autonomic changes from the label and then somehow produced these complex patterns. The biofeedback literature (10) suggests that people cannot voluntarily produce such complex patterns of autonomic activity.

We propose instead that it was contracting the facial muscles into the universal emotion signals which brought forth the emotion-specific autonomic activity. This might occur either through peripheral feedback from making the facial movements, or by a direct connection between the motor cortex and **hypothalamus** that translates between emotion-prototypic expression in the face and emotion-specific patterning in the ANS. Although further studies are needed to verify this hypothesis and to determine the pathways involved, the fact that emotion-specific autonomic activity occurred is of fundamental theoretical importance, no matter what the underlying mechanisms may turn out to be. It raises the questions of how such complex patterns of autonomic activity relate to changes in the central nervous system, cognitive processes, motor behaviors, and the subjective experience of emotion; it also underscores the centrality of the face in emotion as Darwin (11) and Tomkins (12) suggested.

Multivariate analysis of variance (mul-tee-VAIR-ih-at). A statistical technique used to determine whether a given set of variables has a significant effect on some other variable.

Univariate (YOU-knee-VAIR-ih-at). Univariate means *one* variable. A univariate analysis would examine the effects of one variable on another.

Replicated (REP-lee-kate-ed). To *replicate* means to "reproduce the findings" from a previous experiment.

Hypothalamus (HIGH-poh-THALL-ah-muss). A very important neural center lying just under the thalamus. The hypothalamus influences many types of motivated or emotional behavior, including eating or drinking.

FOOTNOTES

[1] Reprinted by permission of the authors and the publisher from *Science*, 1983, **221**, 1208-1210. Copyright 1983 by the American Association for the Advancement of Science. Dr. Ekman is at the University of California, San Francisco.

REFERENCES AND NOTES

1. S. Schachter and J. E. Singer, *Psychol. Rev.* **69**, 379 (1962).
2. G. Mandler, *Mind and Emotion* (Wiley, New York, 1975).
3. A. F. Ax, *Psychosom. Med.* **15**, 433, (1953).
4. D. H. Funkenstein, S. H. King, M. Drolette. *ibid.* **16**, 404 (1954); R. A. Sternbach, *J. Psychosom. Res.* **6**, 87 (1962).
5. R. J. Roberts and T. C. Weerts, *Psychol. Rep.* **50**, 219 (1982).
6. P. Ekman and H. Oster, *Annu. Rev. Psychol.* **30**, 527, (1979).
7. P. Ekman and W. V. Friesen, *The Facial Action Coding System* (Consulting Psychologists Press, Palo Alto, Calif., 1978). To avoid directly suggesting emotional labels, we did not obtain emotion ratings, relying instead on facial measurement for verification in this task.
8. This large value reflects the influence of one outlying subject.
9. Distinctions between fear and anger were based on changes in heart rate and diastolic blood pressure and on the magnitude of heart rate change (*3, 5*). Increases were also comparable to heart rate change in Schachter and Singer's (*1*) anger-epinephrine condition.
10. G.E. Schwartz [*Science* **175**, 90(1972)] reported one of the few instances in which biofeedback produced complex patterns of two ANS functions-heart rate and blood pressure. There are a few reports of different patterns of one autonomic and one somatic function (for example, heart rate and respiration rate) [D. Newlin and R. Levenson, *Biol. Psychol.* **7**, 277 (1978)].
11. C. Darwin, *The Expression of the Emotions in Man and Animals* (Univ. of Chicago Press, Chicago, 1965).
12. S. S. Tomkins, Affect, Imagery, and Consciousness (Springer, New York, 1962).
13. We thank E. Callaway, R. Lazarus, P. Tannenbaum, and S. Tomkins for their comments on this report; the John D. and Catherine T. MacArthur Foundation for research funding; and L. Temoshok, J. Kamiya, and L. Zegans for the use of equipment.

Classic Quotations from William James

If we fancy some strong emotion, and then try to abstract from our consciousness of it all the feelings of its bodily symptoms, we find we have nothing left behind, no 'mind-stuff' out of which the emotion can be constituted, and that a cold and neutral state of intellectual perception is all that remains.
(*The Principles of Psychology* [1890], ch. 25.)

In its widest possible sense, however, a man's Self is the sum total of all that he can call his, not only his body and his psychic powers, but his clothes and his house, his wife and children, his ancestors and friends, his reputation and works, his lands and horses, and yacht and bank account. All these things give him the same emotions. If they wax and prosper, he feels triumphant; if they dwindle and die away, he feels cast down.
(*The Principles of Psychology* [1890], ch. 10.)

A purely disembodied human emotion is a nonentity.
(*The Principles of Psychology* [1890], ch.25.)

CHAPTER 6

"Cognitive, Social, and Physiological Determinants of Emotional State"

Stanley Schachter and J.E. Singer[1,2]

EDITORS' COMMENTS. Imagine the following situation: Two college football teams--traditional rivals--are fighting it out during the last game of the season. Late in the fourth quarter, the Blue team moves down the field and, after a long pass, has the ball on the Red team's 5-yard line. With just a few seconds left on the game clock, the Blue team's quarterback hands the ball to the running back, who dives over the line into the end zone for the winning touchdown. The Blue team players dance about on the field, and their fans go into an emotional frenzy. The running back starts to "spike" the ball in victory, but just as he does so, someone hits him hard on his back. Now, how does he react to this rather painful stimulus?

If you've watched football on television, you probably know the answer. First comes an anger response, quite visible in both the player's face and posture. However, this reaction is almost immediately "frozen in place" as the runner quickly looks to see who it was who hit him. Was it a teammate, or one of the opposing players? If it was a teammate, the "frozen" anger response is terminated, the running back will probably smile broadly, spike the ball, and then give his teammate a jubilant "high five." However, if the person who hit him was a member of the opposing team, the full fury of the anger response is unleashed, and the runner might well throw the football at the other player rather than at the ground.

Here, the stimulus (the blow to the player's back) evokes quite a different emotional reaction *depending on the social situation*. The response *begins* in rather automatic fashion, but then is suspended until the runner has time to *interpret* the meaning of the stimulus. The emotional reaction then continues in one of many different ways depending on the player's *cognitive interpretion* of the stimulus.

How can the James-Lange theory of emotions--or that of Cannon and Bard, or Tomkins--explain the sudden shift in direction that this emotional response can take? The answer is, not very well. As Stanley Schachter and Jerome Singer point out in this article, your emotions are more than arousal of your autonomic nervous system, the release of adrenalin and nor-adrenalin, your facial responses, and your subjective feelings: Emotions are reactions that are *guided by the interaction between your past experiences and your present cognitive activities*. And the "guiding force" for most of your cognitive reactions is your present environment.

In this provocative article, Schachter and Singer report what happened when they injected subjects with adrenalin (epinephrine), an "arousal hormone" almost always released by the adrenal glands in highly emotional situations. They report that both the *subjective quality* and the *extent of physical arousal* varied according to the person's interpretation of the situation. Those subjects given the arousal hormone *without any psychological reason to feel aroused* reported little in the way of "emotional feelings," nor were their autonomic nervous systems as "activated" as were subjects who had a psychosocial reason for being elated or angry.

Mind, or body, or social situation? In truth, emotional behavior--as all other human actions--are *multi-determined*. We can no more reduce all of human experience to neural firings and glandular secretions than we can ignore the importance of those physical reactions. And behavior *always* takes place in an environment that subtly shapes on-going responses. As Schachter and Singer note, our responses are simply too complicated for *any* simplistic psychological theory to account for.

The problem of which cues, internal or external, permit a person to label and identify his own emotional state has been with us since the days that James (1890) first tendered his doctrine that "the bodily changes follow directly the perception of the exciting fact, and that our feeling of the same changes as they occur *is* the emotion" (p. 449). Since we are aware of a variety of feeling and emotion states, it should follow from James' proposition that the various emotions will be accompanied by a variety of differentiable bodily states. Following James' pronouncement, a formidable number of studies were undertaken in search of the physiological differentiators of the emotions. The results, in these early days, were almost uniformly negative. All of the emotional states experimentally manipulated were characterized by a general pattern of excitation of the sympathetic nervous system but there appeared to be no clear-cut physiological discriminators of the various emotions. This pattern of results was so consistent from experiment to experiment that Cannon (1929) offered, as one of the crucial criticisms of the James-Lange theory, the fact that "the same visceral changes occur in very different emotional states and in non-emotional states" (p. 351).

More recent work, however, has given some indication that there may be differentiators. Ax (1953) and Schachter (1957) studied fear and anger. On a large number of indices both of these states were characterized by a similarly high level of **autonomic** activation but on several indices they did differ in the degree of activation. Wolf and Wolff (1947) studied a subject with a **gastric fistula** and were able to distinguish two patterns in the physiological responses of the stomach wall. It should be noted, though, that for many months they studied their subject during and following a great variety of moods and emotions and were able to distinguish only two patterns.

Whether or not there are physiological distinctions among the various emotional states must be considered an open question. Recent work might be taken to indicate that such differences are at best rather subtle and that the variety of emotion, mood, and feeling states are by no means matched by an equal variety of visceral patterns.

This rather ambiguous situation has led Ruckmick (1936), Hunt, Cole, and Reis (1958), Schachter (1959) and others to suggest that cognitive factors may be major determinants of emotional states. Granted a general pattern of sympathetic excitation as characteristic of emotional states, granted that there may be some differences in pattern from state to state, it is suggested that one labels, interprets, and identifies this stirred-up state in terms of the characteristics of the precipitating situation and one's apperceptive mass.

This suggests, then, that an emotional state may be considered a function of a state of physiological arousal[3] and of a cognition appropriate to this state of arousal. The cognition, in a sense, exerts a steering function. Cognitions arising from the immediate situation as interpreted by past experience provide the framework within which one understands and labels his feelings. It is the cognition which determines whether the state of physiological arousal will be labeled as "anger," "joy," "fear," or whatever.

In order to examine the implications of this formulation let us consider the fashion in which these two elements, a state of physiological arousal and cognitive factors, would interact in a variety of situations. In most emotion inducing situations, of course, the two factors are completely interrelated. Imagine a man walking alone down a dark alley, a figure with a gun suddenly appears. The perception-cognition "figure with a gun" in some fashion initiates a state of physiological arousal; this state of arousal is interpreted in terms of knowledge about dark alleys and guns and the state of arousal is labeled "fear." Similarly a student who unexpectedly learns that he has made Phi Beta Kappa may experience a state of arousal which he will label "joy."

Let us now consider circumstances in which these two elements, the physiological and the cognitive, are, to some extent, independent. First, is the state of physiological arousal alone sufficient to induce an emotion? Best evidence indicates that it is not. Marañon[4] (1924), in a fascinating study, (which was replicated by Cantril & Hunt, 1932, and Landis & Hunt, 1932) injected 210 of his patients with the **sympathomimetic** agent **adrenalin** and then simply asked them to introspect. Seventy-one percent of his subjects simply reported their physical symptoms with no emotional overtones; 29% of the subjects responded in an apparently emotional fashion. Of these the great majority described their feelings in a fashion that Marañon labeled "cold" or "as if" emotions, that is, they made statements such as "I feel *as if* I were afraid" or "*as if* I were awaiting a great happiness." This is a sort of

---

Autonomic (aw-toh-NOM-ick). That part of the nervous system which controls involuntary activities such as breathing, heart rate, digestion, and so forth. Its two major divisions are the sympathetic and the parasympathetic nervous systems. Activity in the sympathetic nervous system tends to arouse the organism, while activity in the parasympathetic tends to depress the organism.

Gastric fistula (GAS-trick FISS-tew-lah). A hole or opening in the wall of the digestive system.

Sympathomimetic (sim-PATH-oh-mih-METT-ick). Anything that "mimics" activity in the sympathetic nervous system. Adrenalin has the same effect on physical arousal as does arousal of the sympathetic nervous system.

Adrenalin (add-DREN-ah-linn). One of two "arousal" hormones secreted by the kidneys. Also called ephinephrin (epp-ee-NEFF-rin).

emotional "déjà vu" experience; these subjects are neither happy nor afraid, they feel "as if" they were. Finally a very few cases apparently reported a genuine emotional experience. However, in order to produce this reaction in most of these few cases, Marañon (1924) points out:

> One must suggest a memory with strong affective force but not so strong as to produce an emotion in the normal state. For example, in several cases we spoke to our patients before the injection of their sick children or dead parents and they responded calmly to this topic. The same topic presented later, during the adrenal commotion, was sufficient to trigger emotion. This adrenal commotion places the subject in a situation of 'affective imminence' (pp. 307-308).

Apparently, then, to produce a genuinely emotional reaction to adrenalin, Marañon was forced to provide such subjects with an appropriate cognition.

Though Marañon (1924) is not explicit on his procedure, it is clear that his subjects knew that they were receiving an injection and in all likelihood knew that they were receiving adrenalin and probably had some order of familiarity with its effects. In short, though they underwent the pattern of sympathetic discharge common to strong emotional states, at the same time they had a completely appropriate cognition or explanation as to why they felt this way. This, we would suggest, is the reason so few of Marañon's subjects reported any emotional experience.

Consider now a person in a state of physiological arousal for which no immediately explanatory or appropriate cognitions are available. Such a state could result were one covertly to inject a subject with adrenalin or, unknown to him, feed the subject a sympathomimetic drug such as ephedrine. Under such conditions a subject would be aware of palpitations, tremor, face flushing, and most of the battery of symptoms associated with a discharge of the sympathetic nervous system. In contrast to Marañon's (1924) subjects he would, at the same time, be utterly unaware of why he felt this way. What would be the consequence of such a state?

Schachter (1959) has suggested that precisely such a state would lead to the arousal of "evaluative needs" (Festinger, 1954), that is, pressures would act on an individual in such a state to understand and label his bodily feelings. His bodily state grossly resembles the condition in which it has been at times of emotional excitement. How would he label his present feelings? It is suggested, of course, that he will label his feelings in terms of his knowledge of the immediate situation.[5] Should he at the time be with a beautiful woman he might decide that he was wildly in love or sexually excited. Should he be at a gay party, he might, by comparing himself to others, decide that he was extremely happy and euphoric. Should he be arguing with his wife, he might explode in fury and hatred. Or, should the situation be completely inappropriate he could decide that he was excited about something that had recently happened to him or, simply, that he was sick. In any case, it is our basic assumption that emotional states are a function of the interaction of such cognitive factors with a state of physiological arousal.

This line of thought, then, leads to the following propositions:

1. Given a state of physiological arousal for which an individual has no immediate explanation, he will "label" this state and describe his feelings in terms of the cognitions available to him. To the extent that cognitive factors are potent determiners of emotional states, it could be anticipated that precisely the same state of physiological arousal could be labeled "joy" or "fury" or "jealousy" or any of a great diversity of emotional labels depending on the cognitive aspects of the situation.

2. Given a state of physiological arousal for which an individual has a completely appropriate explanation (e.g., "I feel this way because I have just received an injection of adrenalin") no evaluative needs will arise and the individual is unlikely to label his feelings in terms of the alternative cognitions available.

Finally, consider a condition in which emotion inducing cognitions are present but there is no state of physiological arousal. For example, an individual might be completely aware that he is in great danger but for some reason (drug or surgical) remain in a state of physiological quiescence. Does he experience the emotion "fear"? Our formulation of emotion as a joint function of a state of physiological arousal and an appropriate cognition, would, of course, suggest that he does not, which leads to our final proposition.

3. Given the same cognitive circumstances, the individual will react emotionally or describe his feelings as emotions only to the extent that he experiences a state of physiological arousal.[6]

PROCEDURE

The experimental test of these propositions requires (a) the experimental manipulation of a state of physiological arousal, (b) the manipulation of the extent to which the subject has an appropriate or proper explanation of his bodily state, and (c) the creation of situations from which explanatory cognitions may be derived.

In order to satisfy the first two experimental requirements, the experiment was cast in the framework of a study of the effects of vitamin supplements on vision. As soon as a subject arrived, he was taken to a private room and told by the experimenter:

> In this experiment we would like to make various tests of your vision. We are particularly interested in how certain vitamin compounds and vitamin supplements affect the visual skills. In particular, we want to find out how the vitamin compound called 'Suproxin' affects your vision.
>
> What we would like to do, then, if we can get your permission, is to give you a small injection of Suproxin. The injection itself is mild and harmless; however, since some people do object to being injected we don't want to talk you into anything. Would you mind receiving a Suproxin injection?

If the subject agrees to the injection (and all but 1 of 185 subjects did) the experimenter continues with instructions we shall describe shortly, then leaves the room. In a few minutes a physician enters the room, briefly repeats the experimenter's instructions, takes the subject's pulse and then injects him with Suproxin.

Depending upon condition, the subject receives one of two forms of Suproxin-epinephrine or a placebo.

Epinephrine or adrenalin is a sympathomimetic drug whose effects, with minor exceptions, are almost a perfect mimicry of a discharge of the sympathetic nervous system. Shortly after injection systolic blood pressure increases markedly, heart rate increases somewhat, cutaneous blood flow decreases, while muscle and cerebral blood flow increase, blood sugar and lactic acid concentration increase, and respiration rate increases slightly. As far as the subject is concerned the major subjective symptoms are palpitation, tremor, and sometimes a feeling of flushing and accelerated breathing. With a subcutaneous injection (in the dosage administered to our subjects), such effects usually begin within 3-5 minutes of injection and last anywhere from 10 minutes to an hour. For most subjects these effects are dissipated within 15-20 minutes after injection.

Subjects receiving epinephrine received a subcutaneous injection of 1/2 cubic centimeter of a 1:1000 solution of Winthrop Laboratory's Suprarenin, a saline solution of epinephrine bitartrate.

Subjects in the placebo condition received a subcutaneous injection of 1/2 cubic centimeter of saline solution. This is, of course, completely neutral material with no side effects at all.

Manipulating an Appropriate Explanation

By "appropriate" we refer to the extent to which the subject has an authoritative, unequivocal explanation of his bodily condition. Thus, a subject who had been informed by the physician that as a direct consequence of the injection he would feel palpitations, tremor, etc. would be considered to have a completely appropriate explanation. A subject who had been informed only that the injection would have no side effects would have no appropriate explanation of his state. This dimension of appropriateness was manipulated in three experimental conditions which shall be called: Epinephrine Informed (Epi Inf), Epinephrine Ignorant (Epi Ign), and Epinephrine Misinformed (Epi Mis). Immediately after the subject had agreed to the injection and before the physician entered the room, the experimenter's spiel in each of these conditions went as follows:

Epinephrine Informed. I should also tell you that some of our subjects have experienced side effects from the Suproxin. These side effects are transitory, that is, they will only last for about 15 or 20 minutes. What will probably happen is that your hand will start to shake, your heart will start to pound, and your face may get warm and flushed. Again these are side effects lasting about 15 or 20 minutes.

While the physician was giving the injection, she told the subject that the injection was mild and harmless and repeated this description of the symptoms that the subject could expect as a consequence of the shot. In this condition, then, subjects have a completely appropriate explanation of their bodily state. They know precisely what they will feel and why.

Epinephrine Ignorant. In this condition, when the subject agreed to the injection, the experimenter said nothing more relevant to side effects and simply left the room. While the physician was giving the injection, she told the subject that the injection was mild and harmless and would have no side effects. In this condition, then, the subject has no experimentally provided explanation for his bodily state.

Epinephrine Misinformed. I should also tell you that some of our subjects have experienced side effects from the Suproxin. These side effects are transitory, that is, they will only last for about 15 or 20 minutes. What will probably happen is that your feet will feel numb, you will have an

---

Déjà vu (day-zha-voo). The feeling that you have previously experienced what you are presently experiencing.
Quiescence (kwee-ESS-ent, or kwy-ESS-ent). The state of physical rest.
Suproxin (supp-ROCKS-in). An imaginary drug.
Placebo (plah-SEE-bo). From a Latin word meaning "to please." A harmless drug given for its psychological effect, especially to satisy the patient or to act as a control in an experiment.

itching sensation over parts of your body, and you may get a slight headache. Again these are side effects lasting 15 or 20 minutes.

And again, the physician repeated these symptoms while injecting the subject.

None of these symptoms, of course, are consequences of an injection of epinephrine and, in effect, these instructions provide the subject with a completely inappropriate explanation of his bodily feelings. This condition was introduced as a control condition of sorts. It seemed possible that the description of side effects in the Epi Inf condition might turn the subject introspective, self-examining, possibly slightly troubled. Differences on the dependent variable between the Epi Inf and Epi Ign conditions might, then, be due to such factors rather than to differences in appropriateness. The false symptoms in the Epi Mis condition should similarly turn the subject introspective, etc., but the instructions in this condition do not provide an appropriate explanation of the subject's state.

Subjects in all of the above conditions were injected with epinephrine.

Finally, there was a placebo condition in which subjects, who were injected with saline solution, were given precisely the same treatment as subjects in the Epi Ign condition.

Producing an Emotion Inducing Cognition

Our initial hypothesis has suggested that given a state of physiological arousal for which the individual has no adequate explanation, cognitive factors can lead the individual to describe his feelings with any of a diversity of emotional labels. In order to test this hypothesis, it was decided to manipulate emotional states which can be considered quite different— **euphoria** and anger.

There are, of course, many ways to induce such states. In our own program of research, we have concentrated on social determinants of emotional states and have been able to demonstrate in other studies that people do evaluate their own feelings by comparing themselves with others around them (Schachter 1959; Wrightsman 1960). In this experiment we have attempted again to manipulate emotional state by social means. In one set of conditions, the subject is placed together with a stooge who has been trained to act euphorically. In a second set of conditions the subject is with a stooge trained to act in an angry fashion.

Euphoria

Immediately[9] after the subject had been injected, the physician left the room and the experimenter returned with a stooge whom he introduced as another subject, then said:

Both of you have had the Suproxin shot and you'll both be taking the same tests of vision. What I ask you to do now is just wait for 20 minutes. The reason for this is simply that we have to allow 20 minutes for the Suproxin to get from the injection site into the bloodstream. At the end of 20 minutes when we are certain that most of the Suproxin has been absorbed into the bloodstream, we'll begin the tests of vision.

The room in which this was said had been deliberately put into a state of mild disarray. As he was leaving, the experimenter apologetically added:

The only other thing I should do is to apologize for the condition of the room. I just didn't have time to clean it up. So, if you need any scratch paper or rubber bands or pencils, help yourself. I'll be back in 20 minutes to begin the vision tests.

As soon as the experimenter had left, the stooge introduced himself again, made a series of standard icebreaker comments, and then launched his routine. For observation purposes, the stooge's act was broken into a series of standard units, demarcated by a change in activity or a standard comment. In sequence, the units of the stooge's routine were the following:

1. Stooge reaches for a piece of paper and starts doodling saying, "They said we could use this for scratch, didn't they?" He doodles a fish for some 30 seconds, then says:
2. "This scrap paper isn't even much good for doodling" and crumples paper and attempts to throw it into wastebasket in far corner of the room. He misses but this leads him into a "basketball game." He crumples up other sheets of paper, shoots a few baskets, says "Two points" occasionally. He gets up and does a jump shot saying, "The old jump shot is really on today."
3. If the subject has not joined in, the stooge throws a paper basketball to the subject saying, "Here, you try it."
4. Stooge continues his game saying, "The trouble with paper basketballs is that you don't really have any control."
5. Stooge continues basketball, then gives it up saying, "This is one of my good days. I feel like a kid again. I think I'll make a plane." He makes a paper airplane saying, "I guess I'll make one of the longer ones."
6. Stooge flies plane. Gets up and retrieves plane. Flies again, etc.
7. Stooge throws plane at subject.
8. Stooge, flying plane, says, "Even when I was a kid, I was never much good at this."
9. Stooge tears off part of plane saying, "Maybe this plane can't fly but at least it's good for something." He wads up

paper and making a slingshot of a rubber band begins to shoot the paper.

10. Shooting, the stooge says, "They [paper ammunition] really go better if you make them long. They don't work right if you wad them up."

11. While shooting, stooge notices a sloppy pile of manila folders on a table. He builds a tower of these folders, then goes to the opposite end of the room to shoot at the tower.

12. He misses several times, then hits and cheers as the tower falls. He goes over to pick up the folders.

13. While picking up, he notices, behind a portable blackboard, a pair of hula hoops which have been covered with black tape with a few wires sticking out of the tape. He reaches for these, taking one for himself and putting the other aside but within reaching distance of the subject. The stooge tries the hula hoop, saying, "This isn't as easy as it looks."

14. Stooge twirls hoop wildly on arm, saying, "Hey, look at this--this is great."

15. Stooge replaces the hula hoop and sits down with his feet on the table. Shortly thereafter the experimenter returns to the room.

This routine was completely standard, though its pace, of course, varied depending upon the subject's reaction, the extent to which he entered into this bedlam and the extent to which he initiated activities of his own. The only variations from this standard routine were those forced by the subject. Should the subject originate some nonsense of his own and request the stooge to join in, he would do so. And, he would, of course, respond to any comments initiated by the subject.

Subjects in each of the three "appropriateness" conditions and in the placebo condition were submitted to this setup. The stooge, of course, never knew in which condition any particular subject fell.

Anger

Immediately after the injection, the experimenter brought a stooge into the subject's room, introduced the two and after explaining the necessity for a 20 minute delay for "the Suproxin to get from the injection site into the bloodstream" he continued, "We would like you to use these 20 minutes to answer these questionnaires." Then handing out the questionnaires, he concludes with, "I'll be back in 20 minutes to pick up the questionnaires and begin the tests of vision."

Before looking at the questionnaire, the stooge says to the subject,

I really wanted to come for an experiment today, but I think it's unfair for them to give you shots. At least, they should have told us about the shots when they called us; you hate to refuse, once you're here already.

The questionnaires, five pages long, start off innocently requesting face sheet information and then grow increasingly personal and insulting. The stooge, sitting directly opposite the subject, paces his own answers so that at all times subject and stooge are working on the same question. At regular points in the questionnaire, the stooge makes a series of standardized comments about the questions. His comments start off innocently enough, grow increasingly querulous, and finally he ends up in a rage. In sequence, he makes the following comments.

1. Before answering any items, he leafs quickly through the questionnaire saying, "Boy, this is a long one."

2. Question 7 on the questionnaire requests, "List the foods that you would eat in a typical day." The stooge comments, "Oh for Pete's sake, what did I have for breakfast this morning?"

3. Question 9 asks, "Do you ever hear bells?_____. How often?_____." The stooge remarks, "Look at Question 9. How ridiculous can you get? I hear bells every time I change classes."

4. Question 13 requests, "List the childhood diseases you have had and the age at which you had them" to which the stooge remarks, "I get annoyed at this childhood disease question. I can't remember what childhood diseases I had, and especially at what age. Can you?"

5. Question 17 asks "What is your father's average annual income?" and the stooge says, "This really irritates me. It's none of their business what my father makes. I'm leaving that blank."

6. Question 25 presents a long series of items such as "Does not bathe or wash regularly,' "Seems to need psychiatric care," etc., and requests the respondent to write down for which member of his immediate family each item seems most applicable. The question specifically prohibits the answer "None" and each item must be answered. The stooge says, "I'll be damned if I'll fill out Number 25. 'Does not bathe or wash regularly'--that's a real insult." He then angrily crosses out the entire item.

7. Question 28 reads: "How many times each week do you have sexual intercourse?" 0-1_____ 2-3_____ 4-6_____ 7 and over_____. The stooge bites out, "The hell with it! I don't have to tell them all this."

8. The stooge sits sullenly for a few moments then he rips up his questionnaire, crumples the pieces and hurls them to the floor, saying, "I'm not wasting any more time. I'm getting my books and leaving" and he stamps out of the room.

9. The questionnaire continues for eight more questions ending with: "With how many men (other than your father) has your mother had extramarital relationships?" 4 and under_____ 5-9_____ 10 and over_____.

Subjects in the Epi Ign, Epi Inf and Placebo conditions were run through this "anger" inducing sequence.

<u>Euphoria</u> (you-FOR-ee-ah). From the Greek word meaning "good feeling," hence a rush of pleasure.

The stooge, again, did not know to which condition the subject had been assigned.

In summary, this is a seven condition experiment which, for two different emotional states, allows us (a) to evaluate the effects of "appropriateness" on emotional inducibility and (b) to begin to evaluate the effects of sympathetic activation on emotional inducibility. In schematic form the conditions are the following:

EUPHORIA	ANGER
Epi Inf	Epi Inf
Epi Ign	Epi Ign
Epi Mis	Placebo
Placebo	

The Epi Mis condition was not run in the Anger sequence. This was originally conceived as a control condition and it was felt that its inclusion in the Euphoria conditions alone would suffice as a means of evaluating the possible **artifactual** effect of the Epi Inf instructions.

Measurement

Two types of measures of emotional state were obtained. Standardized observation through a one-way mirror was the technique used to assess the subject's behavior. To what extent did he act euphoric or angry? Such behavior can be considered in a way as a "semi-private" index of mood for as far as the subject was concerned, his emotional behavior could be known only to the other person in the room--presumably another student. The second type of measure was self-report in which, on a variety of scales, the subject indicated his mood of the moment. Such measures can be considered "public" indices of mood for they would, of course, be available to the experimenter and his associates.

Observation

Euphoria. For each of the first 14 units of the stooge's standardized routine an observer kept a running chronicle of what the subject did and said. For each unit the observer coded the subject's behavior in one or more of the following categories:

Category 1: Joins in activity. If the subject entered into the stooge's activities, e.g., if he made or flew airplanes, threw paper basketballs, hula hooped, etc., his behavior was coded in this category.

Category 2: Initiates new activity. A subject was so coded if he gave indications of creative euphoria, that is, if, on his own, he initiated behavior outside of the stooge's routine. Instances of such behavior would be the subject who threw open the window and, laughing, hurled paper basketballs at passersby; or, the subject who jumped on a table and spun one hula hoop on his leg and the other on his neck.

Categories 3 and 4: Ignores or watches stooge. Subjects who paid flatly no attention to the stooge or who, with or without comment, simply watched the stooge without joining in his activity were coded in these categories.

For any particular unit of behavior, the subject's behavior was coded in one or more of these categories. To test **reliability** of coding two observers independently coded two experimental sessions. The observers agreed completely on the coding of 88% of the units.

Anger. For each of the units of stooge behavior, an observer recorded the subject's responses and coded them according to the following category scheme:

Category 1: Agrees. In response to the stooge the subject makes a comment indicating that he agrees with the stooge's standardized comment or that he, too, is irked by a particular item on the questionnaire. For example, a subject who responded to the stooge's comment on the "father's income" question by saying, "I don't like that kind of personal question either" would be so coded (scored +2).

Category 2: Disagrees. In response to the stooge's comment, the subject makes a comment which indicates that he disagrees with the stooge's meaning or mood; e.g., in response to the stooge's comment on the "father's income" question, such a subject might say, "Take it easy, they probably have a good reason for wanting the information" (scored -2).

Category 3: Neutral. A noncommittal or irrelevant response to the stooge's remark (scored 0).

Category 4: Initiates agreement or disagreement. With no instigation by the stooge, a subject, so coded, would have volunteered a remark indicating that he felt the same way or, alternatively, quite differently than the stooge. Examples would be "Boy I hate this kind of thing" or "I'm enjoying this" (scored +2 or -2).

Category 5: Watches. The subject makes no verbal response to the stooge's comment but simply looks directly at him (scored 0).

Category 6: Ignores. The subject makes no verbal response to the stooge's comment nor does he look at him; the subject, paying no attention at all to the stooge, simply works at his own questionnaire (scored -1).

A subject was scored in one or more of these categories for each unit of stooge behavior. To test reliability, two observers independently coded three experimental sessions. In order to get a behavioral index of anger, observation protocol was scored according to the values presented in parentheses after each of the above definitions of categories. In a unit-by-unit comparison, the two observers agreed completely on the scoring of 71% of the units jointly observed. The scores of the two observers differed by a value of 1 or less for 88% of the units coded and in not a single case did the two observers differ in the direction of their scoring of a unit.

Self Report of Mood and Physical Condition

When the subject's session with the stooge was completed, the experimenter returned to the room, took pulses and said:

Before we proceed with the vision tests, there is one other kind of information which we must have. We have found, as you can probably imagine, that there are many things beside Suproxin that affect how well you see in our tests. How hungry you are, how tired you are, and even the mood you're in at the time — whether you feel happy or irritated at the time of testing will affect how well you see. To understand the data we collect on you, then, we must be able to figure out which effects are due to causes such as these and which are caused by Suproxin.

The only way we can get such information about your physical and emotional state is to have you tell us. I'll hand out these questionnaires and ask you to answer them as accurately as possible. Obviously, our data on the vision tests will only be as accurate as your description of your mental and physical state.

In keeping with this spiel, the questionnaire that the experimenter passed out contained a number of mock questions about hunger, fatigue, etc., as well as questions of more immediate relevance to the experiment. To measure mood or emotional state the following two were the crucial questions:

1. How irritated, angry or annoyed would you say you feel at present?

I don't feel at all irritated or angry	I feel a little irritated or angry	I feel quite irritated or angry	I feel very irritated or angry	I feel extremely irritated or angry
(0)	(1)	(2)	(3)	(4)

2. How good or happy would you say you feel at present?

I don't feel at all happy or good	I feel a little happy and good	I feel quite happy and good	I feel very happy and good	I feel extremely happy and good
(0)	(1)	(2)	(3)	(4)

To measure the physical effects of epinephrine and determine whether or not the injection had been successful in producing the necessary bodily state, the following questions were asked:

1. Have you experienced any palpitation (consciousness of your own heart beat)?

Not at all	A slight amount	A moderate amount	An intense amount
(0)	(1)	(2)	(3)

2. Did you feel any tremor (involuntary shaking of the hands, arms or legs)?

Not at all	A slight amount	A moderate amount	An intense amount
(0)	(1)	(2)	(3)

To measure possible effects of the instructions in the Epi Mis condition, the following questions were asked:
1. Did you feel any numbness in your feet?
2. Did you feel any itching sensation?
3. Did you experience any feeling of headache?

To all three of these questions was attached a four-point scale running from "Not at all" to "An intense amount."

In addition to these scales, the subjects were asked to answer two open-end questions on other physical or emotional sensations they may have experienced during the experimental session. A final measure of bodily state was pulse rate which was taken by the physician or the experimenter at two times — immediately before the injection and immediately after the session with the stooge.

When the subjects had completed these questionnaires, the experimenter announced that the experiment was over, explained the deception and its necessity in detail, answered any questions, and swore the subjects to secrecy. Finally, the subjects answered a brief questionnaire about their experiences, if any, with adrenalin and their previous knowledge or suspicion of the experimental setup. There was no indication that any of the subjects had known about the experiment

Artifactual (art-ih-FACT-you-al). Results in an experiment which are caused by something which the experimenter did not control or account for.

Reliability. A reliable friend is someone you can depend on, someone who treats you the same way day in and day out. In psychological research, reliability means that a test will yield the same results no matter how frequently you give it.

beforehand but 11 subjects were so extremely suspicious of some crucial feature of the experiment that their data were automatically discarded.

Subjects

The subjects were all male, college students taking classes in introductory psychology at the University of Minnesota. Some 90% of the students in these classes volunteer for a subject pool for which they receive two extra points on their final exam for every hour that they serve as experimental subjects. For this study the records of all potential subjects were cleared with the Student Health Service in order to insure that no harmful effects would result from the injections.

Evaluation of the Experimental Design

The ideal test of our propositions would require circumstances which our experiment is far from realizing. First, the proposition that: "A state of physiological arousal for which an individual has no immediate explanation will lead him to label this state in terms of the cognitions available to him" obviously requires conditions under which the subject does not and cannot have a proper explanation of his bodily state. Though we toyed with such fantasies as ventilating the experimental room with vaporized adrenalin, reality forced us to rely on the disguised injection of Suproxin—a technique which was far from ideal for no matter what the experimenter told them, some subjects would inevitably attribute their feelings to the injection. To the extent that subjects did so, differences between the several appropriateness conditions should be attenuated.

Second, the proposition that: "Given the same cognitive circumstances the individual will react emotionally only to the extent that he experiences a state of physiological arousal" requires for its ideal test the manipulation of states of physiological arousal and of physiological quiescence. Though there is no question that epinephrine effectively produces a state of arousal, there is also no question that a placebo does not prevent physiological arousal. To the extent that the experimental situation effectively produces sympathetic stimulation in placebo subjects, the proposition is difficult to test, for such a factor would attenuate differences between epinephrine and placebo subjects.

Both of these factors, then, can be expected to interfere with the test of our several propositions. In presenting the results of this study, we shall first present condition by condition results and then evaluate the effect of these two factors on experimental differences.

RESULTS

Effects of the Injections on Bodily State

Let us examine first the success of the injections at producing the bodily state required to examine the propositions at test. Does the injection of epinephrine produce symptoms of sympathetic discharge as compared with the placebo injection? Relevant data are presented in Table 1 where it can be immediately seen

TABLE 1
THE EFFECTS OF THE INJECTIONS ON BODILY STATE

Condition	N	Pulse Pre	Pulse Post	Palpitation	Tremor	Numbness	Itching	Headache
Euphoria								
Epi Inf	27	85.7	88.6	1.20	1.43	0	0.16	0.32
Epi Ign	26	84.6	85.6	1.83	1.76	0.15	0	0.55
Epi Mis	26	82.9	86.0	1.27	2.00	0.06	0.08	0.23
Placebo	26	80.4	77.1	0.29	0.21	0.09	0	0.27
Anger								
Epi Inf	23	85.9	92.4	1.26	1.41	0.17	0	0.11
Epi Ign	23	85.0	96.8	1.44	1.78	0	0.06	0.21
Placebo	23	84.5	79.6	0.59	0.24	0.14	0.06	0.06

that on all items subjects who were in epinephrine conditions show considerably more evidence of sympathetic activation than do subjects in placebo conditions. In all epinephrine conditions pulse rate increases significantly when compared with the decrease characteristic of the placebo conditions. On the scales it is clear that epinephrine subjects experience considerably more palpitation and tremor than do placebo subjects. In all possible comparisons on these symptoms, the mean scores of subjects in any of the epinephrine conditions are greater than the corresponding scores in the placebo conditions at better than the .001 level of significance. Examination of the absolute values of these scores makes it quite clear that subjects in epinephrine conditions were, indeed, in a state of physiological arousal, while most subjects in placebo conditions were in a relative state of physiological quiescence.

The epinephrine injection, of course, did not work with equal effectiveness for all subjects; indeed for a few subjects it did not work at all. Such subjects reported almost no palpitation or tremor, showed no increase in pulse and described no other relevant physical symptoms. Since for such subjects the necessary experimental conditions were not established, they were automatically excluded from the data and all further tabular presentations will not include such subjects. Table 1, however, does include the data of these subjects. There were four such subjects in euphoria conditions and one of them in anger conditions.

In order to evaluate further data on Epi Mis subjects it is necessary to note the results of the "numbness," "itching," and "headache" scales also presented in Table 1. Clearly the subjects in the Epi Mis condition do not differ on these scales from subjects in any of the other experimental conditions.

Effects of the Manipulations on Emotional State

Euphoria: Self-report. The effects of the several manipulations on emotional state in the euphoria conditions are presented in Table 2. The scores recorded in this table are derived, for each subject, by subtracting the value of the point he checks on the irritation scale from the value of the point he checks on the happiness scale. Thus, if a subject were to check the point "I feel a little irritated and angry" on the irritation scale and the point "I feel very happy and good" on the happiness scale, his score would be +2. The higher the positive value, the happier and better the subject reports himself as feeling. Though we employ an index for expositional simplicity, it should be noted that the two components of the index each yield results completely consistent with those obtained by use of this index.

TABLE 2

SELF-REPORT OF EMOTIONAL STATE IN THE EUPHORIA CONDITIONS

Condition	N	Self-Report scales	Comparison	p[a]
Epi Inf	25	0.98	Epi Inf vs. Epi Mis	<.01
Epi Ign	25	1.78	Epi Inf vs. Epi Ign	.02
Epi Mis	25	1.90	Placebo vs. Epi Mis,	ns
Placebo	26	1.61	Ign, or Inf	

All *p* values reported throughout paper are two-tailed.

Let us examine first the effects of the appropriateness instructions. Comparison of the scores for the Epi Mis and Epi Inf conditions makes it immediately clear that the experimental differences are not due to artifacts resulting from the informed instructions. In both conditions the subject was warned to expect a variety of symptoms as a consequence of the injection. In the Epi Mis condition, where the symptoms were inappropriate to the subject's bodily state the self-report score is almost twice that in the Epi Inf condition where the symptoms were completely appropriate to the subject's bodily state. It is reasonable, then, to attribute differences between informed subjects and those in other conditions to differences in manipulated appropriateness rather than to artifacts such as introspectiveness or self-examination.

It is clear that, consistent with expectations, subjects were more susceptible to the stooge's mood and consequently more euphoric when they had no explanation of their own bodily states than when they did. The means of both the Epi Ign and Epi Mis conditions are considerably greater than the mean of the Epi Inf condition. It is of interest to note that Epi Mis subjects are somewhat more euphoric than are Epi Ign subjects. This pattern repeats itself in other data shortly to be presented. We would attribute this difference to differences in the appropriateness dimension. Though, as in the Epi Ign condition, a subject is not provided with an explanation of his bodily state, it is, of course, possible that he will provide one for himself which is not derived from his interaction with the stooge. Most reasonably he could decide for himself that he feels this way because of the injection. To the extent that he does so he should be less susceptible to the stooge. It seems probable that he would be less likely to hit on such an explanation in the Epi Mis condition than in the Epi Ign condition for in the Epi Mis condition both the experimenter and the doctor have told him that the effects of the injection would be quite different from what he actually feels. The effect of such instructions is probably to make it more difficult for the subject himself to hit on the alternative explanation described above. There is some evidence to support this analysis. In open-end questions in which subjects described their own mood and state, 28% of the subjects in the Epi Ign condition made some connection between the injection and their bodily state compared with the 16% of subjects in the Epi Mis condition who did so. It could be considered, then, that these three conditions fall along a dimension of appropriateness, with the Epi Inf condition at one extreme and the Epi Mis condition at the other.

Comparing the placebo to the epinephrine conditions, we note a pattern which will repeat itself throughout the data. Placebo subjects are less euphoric than either Epi Mis or Epi Ign subjects but somewhat more euphoric than Epi Inf subjects. These differences are not, however, statistically significant. We shall consider the epinephrine-placebo comparisons in detail in a later section of this paper following the presentation of additional relevant data. For the moment, it is clear that, by self-report manipulating appropriateness has had a very strong effect on euphoria.

Behavior. Let us next examine the extent to which the subject's behavior was affected by the experimental manipulations. To the extent that his mood has been affected, one should expect that the subject will join in the stooge's whirl of manic activity and initiate similar activities of his own. The relevant data are presented in Table 3. The column labeled "Activity index" presents summary figures on the extent to which the subject joined in the stooge's activity. This is a weighted index which reflects both the nature of the activities in which the subject engaged and the amount of time he was active. The index was devised by assigning the following weights to the subject's activities: 5-hula hooping; 4-shooting with slingshot; 3-paper airplanes; 2-paper basketballs; 1-doodling; 0-does nothing. Pretest scaling on 15 college students ordered these activities with respect to the degree of euphoria they represented. Arbitrary weights were assigned so that the wilder the activity, the heavier the weight. These weights are multiplied by an estimate of the amount of time the subject spent in each activity and the summed products make up the activity index for each subject. This index may be considered a measure of behavioral euphoria. It should be noted that the same between-condition relationships hold for the two components of this index as for the index itself.

The column labeled "Mean number of acts initiated" presents the data on the extent to which the subject deviates from the stooge's routine and initiates euphoric activities of his own.

On both behavioral indices, we find precisely the same pattern of relationships as those obtained with self-reports. Epi Mis subjects behave somewhat more

TABLE 3

BEHAVIORAL INDICATIONS OF EMOTIONAL STATE IN THE EUPHORIA CONDITIONS

Condition	N	Activity index	Mean number of acts initiated
Epi Inf	25	12.72	.20
Epi Ign	25	18.28	.56
Epi Mis	25	22.56	.84
Placebo	26	16.00	.54

p value

Comparison	Activity index	Initiates
Epi Inf vs. Epi Mis	.05	.03
Epi Inf vs. Epi Ign	ns	.08
Plac vs. Epi Mis, Ign, or Inf	ns	ns

* Tested by X^2 comparison of the proportion of subjects in each condition initiating new acts.

euphorically than do Epi Ign subjects who in turn behave more euphorically than do Epi Inf subjects. On all measures, then, there is consistent evidence that a subject will take over the stooge's euphoric mood to the extent that he has no other explanation of his bodily state.

Again it should be noted that on these behavioral indices, Epi Ign and Epi Mis subjects are somewhat more euphoric than placebo subjects but not significantly so.

Anger: Self-report. Before presenting data for the anger conditions, one point must be made about the anger manipulation. In the situation devised, anger, if manifested, is most likely to be directed at the experimenter and his annoyingly personal questionnaire. As we subsequently discovered, this was rather unfortunate, for the subjects, who had volunteered for the experiment for extra points on their final exam, simply refused to endanger these points by publicly blowing up, admitting their irritation to the experimenter's face or spoiling the questionnaire. Though as the reader will see, the subjects were quite willing to manifest anger when they were alone with the stooge, they hesitated to do so on material (self-ratings of mood and questionnaire) that the experimenter might see and only after the purposes of the experiment had been revealed were many of these subjects willing to admit to the experimenter that they had been irked or irritated.

This experimentally unfortunate situation pretty much forces us to rely on the behavioral indices derived from observation of the subject's presumably private interaction with the stooge. We do, however, present data on the self-report scales in Table 4. These figures are derived in the same way as the figures presented in Table 2 for the euphoria conditions, that is, the value checked on the irritation scale is subtracted from the

TABLE 4

SELF-REPORT OF EMOTIONAL STATE IN THE ANGER CONDITIONS

Condition	N	Self-Report scales	Comparison	p
Epi Inf	22	1.91	Epi Inf vs. Epi Ign	.08
Epi Ign	23	1.39	Placebo vs. Epi Ign or Inf	ns
Placebo	23	1.63		

value checked on the happiness scale. Though, for the reasons stated above, the absolute magnitude of these figures (all positive) is relatively meaningless, we can, of course, compare condition means within the set of anger conditions. With the happiness-irritation index employed, we should, of course, anticipate precisely the reverse results from those obtained in the euphoria conditions; that is, the Epi Inf subjects in the anger conditions should again be less susceptible to the stooge's mood and should, therefore, describe themselves as in a somewhat happier frame of mind than subjects in the Epi Ign condition. This is the case; the Epi Inf subjects average 1.91 on the self-report scales while the Epi Ign subjects average 1.39.

Evaluating the effects of the injections, we note again that, as anticipated, Epi Ign subjects are somewhat less happy than Placebo subjects but, once more, this is not a significant difference.

Behavior. The subject's responses to the stooge, during the period when both were filling out their questionnaires, were systematically coded to provide a behavioral index of anger. The coding scheme and the numerical values attached to each of the categories have been described in the methodology section. To arrive at an "Anger index" the numerical value assigned to a subject's responses to the stooge is summed together for the several units of stooge behavior. In the coding scheme used, a positive value to this index indicates that the subject agrees with the stooge's comment and is growing angry. A negative value indicates that the subject either disagrees with the stooge or ignores him.

The relevant data are presented in Table 5. For this analysis, the stooge's routine has been divided into two phases—the first two units of his behavior (the "long" questionnaire and "What did I have for breakfast?") are considered essentially neutral, revealing nothing of the stooge's mood; all of the following units are considered "angry" units for they begin with an irritated remark about the "bells" question and end with the stooge's fury as he rips up his questionnaire and stomps out of the room. For the neutral units, agreement or disagreement with the stooge's remarks is, of course, meaningless as an index of mood and we should anticipate no difference between conditions. As can be seen in Table 5, this is the case.

For the angry units, we must, of course, anticipate that subjects in the Epi Ign condition will be angrier than subjects in the Epi Inf condition. This is indeed the case. The Anger index for the Epi Ign condition is positive and large, indicating that these subjects have become angry, while in the Epi Inf condition the Anger index is slightly negative in value indicating that these subjects have failed to catch the stooge's mood at all. It seems clear that providing the subject with an appropriate explanation of his bodily state greatly reduces his tendency to interpret his state in terms of the cognitions provided by the stooge's angry behavior.

Finally, on this behavioral index, it can be seen that subjects in the Epi Ign condition are significantly angrier than subjects in the Placebo condition. Behaviorally, at least, the injection of epinephrine appears to have led subjects to an angrier state than comparable subjects who received placebo shots.

Conformation of Data to Theoretical Expectations

Now that the basic data of this study have been presented, let us examine closely the extent to which they conform to theoretical expectations. If our hypotheses are correct and if this experimental design provided a perfect test for these hypotheses, it should be anticipated that in the euphoria conditions the degree of experimentally produced euphoria should vary in the following fashion:

Epi Mis = or > Epi Ign > Epi Inf = Placebo

TABLE 5

BEHAVIORAL INDICATIONS OF EMOTIONAL STATE IN THE ANGER CONDITIONS

Condition	N	Neutral units	Anger units
Epi Inf	22	+0.07	−0.18
Epi Ign	23	+0.30	+2.28
Placebo	22*	−0.09	+0.79

Comparison for anger units	p
Epi Inf vs. Epi Ign	<.01
Epi Ign vs. Placebo	<.05
Placebo vs. Epi Inf	ns

* For one subject in this condition the sound system went dead and the observer could not, of course, code his reactions.

And in the anger conditions, anger should conform to the following pattern:

Epi Ign > Epi Inf = Placebo

In both sets of conditions, it is the case that emotional level in the Epi Mis and Epi Ign conditions is considerably greater than that achieved in the corresponding Epi Inf conditions. The results for the Placebo condition, however, are ambiguous for consistently the Placebo subjects fall between the Epi Ign and the Epi Inf subjects. This is a particularly troubling pattern for it makes it impossible to evaluate unequivocally the effects of the state of physiological arousal and indeed raises serious questions about our entire theoretical structure. Though the emotional level is consistently greater in the Epi Mis and Epi Ign conditions than in the Placebo condition, this difference is significant at acceptable probability levels only in the anger conditions.

In order to explore the problem further, let us examine the experimental factors identified earlier, which might have acted to restrain the emotional level in the Epi Ign and Epi Mis conditions. As was pointed out earlier, the ideal test of our first two hypotheses requires an experimental setup in which the subject has flatly no way of evaluating his state of physiological arousal other than by means of the experimentally provided cognitions. Had it been possible to physiologically produce a state of sympathetic activation by means other than injection, one could have approached this experimental ideal more closely than in the present setup. As it stands, however, there is always a reasonable alternative cognition available to the aroused subject--he feels the way he does because of the injection. To the extent that the subject seizes on such an explanation of his bodily state, we should expect that he will be uninfluenced by the stooge. Evidence presented in Table 6 for the anger condition and in Table 7 for the euphoria conditions indicates that this is, indeed, the case.

As mentioned earlier, some of the Epi Ign and Epi Mis subjects in their answers to the open-end questions

TABLE 6
THE EFFECTS OF ATTRIBUTING BODILY STATE TO THE INJECTION ON ANGER IN THE ANGER EPI IGN CONDITION

Condition	N	Anger index	p
Self-informed subjects	3	−1.67	ns
Others	20	+2.88	ns
Self-informed vs. Others			.05

TABLE 7
THE EFFECTS OF ATTRIBUTING BODILY STATE TO THE INJECTION ON EUPHORIA IN THE EUPHORIA EPI IGN AND EPI MIS CONDITIONS

Epi Ign

	N	Activity Index	p
Self-informed subjects	8	11.63	ns
Others	17	21.14	ns
Self-informed vs. Others			.05

Epi Mis

	N	Activity Index	p
Self-informed subjects	5	12.40	ns
Others	20	25.10	ns
Self-informed vs. Others			.10

clearly attributed their physical state to the injection, e.g., "the shot gave me the shivers." In Tables 6 and 7 such subjects are labeled "Self-informed." In Table 6 it can be seen that the self-informed subjects are considerably less angry than are the remaining subjects; indeed, they are not angry at all. With these self-informed subjects eliminated the difference between the Epi Ign and the Placebo conditions is significant at the 0.01 level of significance.

Precisely the same pattern is evident in Table 7 for the euphoria conditions. In both the Epi Mis and the Epi Ign conditions, the self-informed subjects have considerably lower activity indices than do the remaining subjects. Eliminating self-informed subjects, comparison of both of these conditions with the Placebo condition yields a difference significant at the 0.03 level of significance. It should be noted, too, that the self-informed subjects have much the same score on the activity index as do the experimental Epi Inf subjects (Table 3).

It would appear, then, that the experimental procedure of injecting the subjects, by providing an alternative cognition, has, to some extent, obscured the effects of epinephrine. When account is taken of this artifact, the evidence is good that the state of physiological arousal is a necessary component of an emotional experience for when self-informed subjects are removed, epinephrine subjects give consistent indications of greater emotionality than do placebo subjects.

Let us examine next the fact that consistently the emotional level, both reported and behavioral, in Placebo conditions is greater than that in the Epi Inf conditions. Theoretically, of course, it should be ex-

TABLE 8
SYMPATHETIC ACTIVATION AND EUPHORIA IN THE EUPHORIA PLACEBO CONDITION

Subjects whose:	N	Activity index	p
Pulse decreased	14	10.67	ns
Pulse increased or remained same	12	23.17	ns
Pulse decrease vs. pulse increase or same			.02

pected that the two conditions will be equally low, for by assuming that emotional state is a joint function of a state of physiological arousal and of the appropriateness of a cognition we are, in effect, assuming a multiplicative function, so that if either component is at zero, emotional level is at zero. As noted earlier this expectation should hold if we can be sure that there is no sympathetic activation in the Placebo conditions. This assumption, of course, is completely unrealistic for the injection of placebo does not prevent sympathetic activation. The experimental situations were fairly dramatic and certainly some of the placebo subjects gave indications of physiological arousal. If our general line of reasoning is correct, it should be anticipated that the emotional level of subjects who give indications of sympathetic activity will be greater than that of subjects who do not. The relevant evidence is presented in Tables 8 and 9.

As an index of sympathetic activation we shall use the most direct and unequivocal measure available—change in pulse rate. It can be seen in Table 1 that the predominant pattern in the Placebo condition is a decrease in pulse rate. We shall assume, therefore, that

TABLE 9
SYMPATHETIC ACTIVATION AND ANGER IN ANGER PLACEBO CONDITION

Subjects whose:	N[a]	Anger index	p
Pulse decreased	13	+0.15	ns
Pulse increased or remained same	8	+1.69	ns
Pusle decrease vs. pulse increase or same			.01

[a] N reduced by two cases owing to failure of sound system in one case and experimenter's failure to take pulse in another.

these subjects whose pulse increases or remains the same give indications of sympathetic activity while those subjects whose pulse decreases do not. In Table 8, for the euphoria condition, it is immediately clear that subjects who give indications of sympathetic activity are considerably more euphoric than are subjects who show no sympathetic activity. This relationship is, of course, confounded by the fact that euphoric subjects are considerably more active than noneuphoric subjects—a factor which independent of mood could elevate pulse rate. However, no such factor operates in the anger condition where angry subjects are neither more active nor talkative than calm subjects. It can be seen in Table 9 that Placebo subjects who show signs of sympathetic activation give indications of considerably more anger than do subjects who show no such signs. Conforming to expectations, sympathetic activation accompanies an increase in emotional level.

It should be noted, too, that the emotional levels of subjects showing no signs of sympathetic activity are quite comparable to the emotional level of subjects in the parallel Epi Inf conditions (see Tables 3 and 5). The similarity of these sets of scores and their uniformly low level of indicated emotionality would certainly make it appear that both factors are essential to an emotional state. When either the level of sympathetic arousal is low or a completely appropriate cognition is available, the level of emotionality is low.

DISCUSSION

Let us summarize the major findings of this experiment and examine the extent to which they support the propositions offered in the introduction of this paper. It has been suggested, first, that given a state of physiological arousal for which an individual has no explanation, he will label this state in terms of the cognitions available to him. This implies, of course, that by manipulating the cognitions of an individual in such a state we can manipulate his feelings in diverse directions. Experimental results support this proposition for, following the injection of epinephrine, those subjects who had no explanation for the bodily state thus produced gave behavioral and self-report indications that they had been readily manipulable into the disparate feeling states of euphoria and anger.

From this first proposition, it must follow that given a state of physiological arousal for which the individual has a completely satisfactory explanation he will not label this state in terms of the alternative cognitions available. Experimental evidence strongly supports this expectation. In those conditions in which subjects were injected with epinephrine and told precisely what they would feel and why, they proved relatively immune to any effects of the manipulated cognitions. In the anger condition, such subjects did not report or show anger; in the euphoria condition, such subjects reported themselves as far less happy than subjects with an identical bodily state but no adequate knowledge of why they felt the way they did.

Finally, it has been suggested that given constant cognitive circumstances, an individual will react emotionally only to the extent that he experiences a state of physiological arousal. Without taking account of experimental artifacts, the evidence in support of this proposition is consistent but tentative. When the effects of "self-informing" tendencies in epinephrine subjects and of "self-arousing" tendencies in placebo subjects are partialed out, the evidence strongly supports the proposition.

The pattern of data, then, falls neatly in line with theoretical expectations. However, the fact that we were forced, to some extent, to rely on internal analyses in order to partial out the effects of experimental artifacts inevitably makes our conclusions somewhat tentative. In order to further test these propositions on the interaction of cognitive and physiological determinants of emotional state, a series of additional experiments, published elsewhere, was designed to rule out or overcome the operation of these artifacts. In the first of these, Schachter and Wheeler (1962) extended the range of manipulated sympathetic activation by employing three experimental groups—epinephrine, placebo, and a group injected with the **sympatholytic** agent, chlorpromazine. Laughter at a slap-stick movie was the dependent variable and the evidence is good that amusement is a direct function of manipulated sympathetic activation.

In order to make the epinephrine-placebo comparison under conditions which would rule out the operation of any self-informing tendency, two experiments were conducted on rats. In one of these Singer (1961) demonstrated that under fear inducing conditions, manipulated by the simultaneous presentation of a loud bell, a buzzer, and a bright flashing light, rats injected with epinephrine were considerably more frightened than rats injected with a placebo. Epinephrine-injected rats defecated, urinated, and trembled more than did placebo-injected rats. In nonfear control conditions, there were no differences between epinephrine and placebo groups, neither group giving any indication of fear. In another study, Latané and Schachter (1962) demonstrated that rats injected with epinephrine were notably more capable of avoidance learning than were rats injected with a placebo. Using a modified Miller-Mowrer **shuttlebox**, these investigators found that during an experimental period involving 200 massed trials, 15 rats injected with epinephrine avoided shock an average of 101.2 trials while 15 placebo-injected rats averaged only 37.3 avoidances.

Taken together, this body of studies does give strong support to the propositions which generated these experimental tests. Given a state of sympathetic activation, for which no immediately appropriate explanation is available, human subjects can be readily manipulated into states of euphoria, anger, and amusement. Varying the intensity of sympathetic activation serves to vary the intensity of a variety of emotional states in both rats and human subjects.

Let us examine the implications of these findings and of this line of thought for problems in the general area of the physiology of the emotions. We have noted in the introduction that the numerous studies on physiological differentiators of emotional states have, viewed en masse, yielded quite inconclusive results. Most, though not all, of these studies have indicated no differences among the various emotional states. Since as human beings, rather than as scientists, we have no difficulty identifying, labeling, and distinguishing among our feelings, the results of these studies have long seemed rather puzzling and paradoxical. Perhaps because of this, there has been a persistent tendency to discount such results as due to ignorance or methodological inadequacy and to pay far more attention to the very few studies which demonstrate *some* sort of physiological differences among emotional states than to the very many studies which indicate no differences at all. It is conceivable, however, that these results should be taken at face value and that emotional states may, indeed, be generally characterized by a high level of sympathetic activation with few if any physiological distinguishers among the many emotional states. If this is correct, the findings of the present study may help to resolve the problem. Obviously this study does *not* rule out the possibility of physiological differences among the emotional states. It is the case, however, that given precisely the same state of epinephrine-induced sympathetic activation, we have, by means of cognitive manipulations, been able to produce in our subjects the very disparate states of euphoria and anger. It may indeed be the case that cognitive factors are major determiners of the emotional labels we apply to a common state of sympathetic arousal.

Let us ask next whether our results are specific to the state of sympathetic activation or if they are generalizable to other states of physiological arousal. It is clear that from our experiments proper, it is impossible to answer the question for our studies have been concerned largely with the effects of an epinephrine created state of sympathetic arousal. We would suggest, however, that our conclusions are generalizable to almost any pronounced internal state for which no appropriate explanation is available. This suggestion receives some support from the experiences of Nowlis and Nowlis (1956) in their program of research on the effects of drugs on mood. In their work the Nowlises typically administer a drug to groups of four subjects who are physically in one another's presence and free to interact. The Nowlises describe some of their results with these groups as follows:

> At first we used the same drug for all 4 men. In those sessions **seconal**, when compared with placebo, increased the checking of such words as expansive, forceful, courageous, daring, elated, and impulsive. In our first statistical analysis we were confronted with the stubborn fact that when the same drug is given to all 4 men in a group, the N that has to be entered into the analysis is 1, not 4. This increases the cost of an already expensive experiment by a considerable factor, but it cannot be denied that the effects of these drugs may be and often are quite contagious. Our first attempted solution was to run tests on groups in which each man had a different drug during the same session, such as 1 on seconal, 1 on **benzedrine**, 1 on **dramamine**, and 1 on placebo [lactose, a milk sugar]. What does seconal do? Cooped up with, say, the egotistical benzedrine partner, the withdrawn, indifferent dramamine partner, and the slightly bored lactose man, the seconal subject reports that he is distractible, dizzy, drifting, glum, defiant, languid, sluggish, discouraged, dull, gloomy, lazy, and slow! This is not the report of mood that we got when all 4 men were on seconal. It thus appears that the moods of the partners do definitely influence the effect of seconal (p. 350).

It is not completely clear from this description whether this "contagion" of mood is more marked in drug than in placebo groups, but should this be the case, these results would certainly support the suggestion that our findings are generalizable to internal states other than that produced by an injection of epinephrine.

Finally, let us consider the implications of our formulation and data for alternative conceptualizations of emotion. Perhaps the most popular current conception of emotion is in terms of "activation theory" in the sense employed by Lindsley (1951) and Woodworth and Schlosberg (1958). As we understand this theory, it suggests that emotional states should be considered as at one end of a continuum of activation which is defined in terms of degree of autonomic arousal and of electroencephalographic measures of activation. The results of the experiment described in this paper do, of course, suggest that such a formulation is not completely adequate. It is possible to have very high degrees of activation without a subject either appearing to be or describing himself as "emotional." Cognitive factors appear to be indispensable elements in any formulation of emotion.

SUMMARY

It is suggested that emotional states may be considered a function of a state of physiological arousal and of a cognition appropriate to this state of arousal. From this follows these propositions:

1. Given a state of physiological arousal for which an individual has no immediate explanation, he will label this state and describe his feelings in terms of the cognitions available to him. To the extent that cognitive factors are potent determiners of emotional states, it should be anticipated that precisely the same state of physiological arousal could be labeled "joy" or "fury" or "jealousy" or any of a great diversity of emotional labels depending on the cognitive aspects of the situation.

2. Given a state of physiological arousal for which an individual has a completely appropriate explanation, no evaluative needs will arise and the individual is unlikely to label his feelings in terms of the alternative cognitions available.

3. Given the same cognitive circumstances, the individual will react emotionally or describe his feelings as emotions only to the extent that he experiences a state of physiological arousal.

An experiment is described which, together with the results of other studies, supports these propositions.

FOOTNOTES

[1] Reprinted by permission of the authors and the publisher from the *Psychological Review*, 1962, 69, 379-399. Copyright 1962 by the American Psychological Association.

[2] This experiment is part of a program of research on cognitive and physiological determinants of emotional state which is being conducted at the Department of Social Psychology at Columbia University under PHS Research Grant M-2584 from the National Institute of Mental Health, United States Public Health Service. This experiment was conducted at the Laboratory for Research in Social Relations at the University of Minnesota.

Sympatholytic (sim-path-oh-LITT-tic). A chemical that destroys or reduces sympathetic arousal.

Shuttlebox. An experimental apparatus in which the animal is forced to jump (or shuttle) from one side to another by jumping over a hurdle of some kind.

Seconal (SEE-koh-nal). A type of barbituate; a drug that reduces physical activity and/or brings on sleep.

Benzedrine (BEN-zeh-dreen). An "upper."

Dramamine (DRAM-ah-meen). A seasickness remedy.

The authors wish to thank Jean Carlin and Ruth Hase, the physicians in the study, and Bibb Latané and Leonard Weller who were the paid participants.

[3] Though our experiments are concerned exclusively with the physiological changes produced by the injection of adrenalin, which appear to be primarily the result of sympathetic excitation, the term physiological arousal is used in preference to the more specific excitation of the sympathetic nervous system because there are indications, to be discussed later, that this formulation is applicable to a variety of bodily states.

[4] Translated copies of Marañon's (1924) paper may be obtained by writing to the senior author.

[5] This suggestion is not new for several psychologists have suggested that situational factors should be considered the chief differentiators of the emotions. Hunt, Cole, and Reis (1958) probably make this point most explicitly in their study distinguishing among fear, anger, and sorrow in terms of situational characteristics.

[6] In his critique of the James-Lange theory of emotion, Cannon (1929) also makes the point that sympathectomized animals and patients do seem to manifest emotional behavior. This criticism is, of course, as applicable to the above proposition as it was to the James-Lange formulation. We shall discuss the issues involved in later papers.

[7] It was, of course, imperative that the sequence with the stooge begin before the subject felt his first symptoms for otherwise the subject would be virtually forced to interpret his feelings in terms of events preceding the stooge's entrance. Pretests had indicated that, for most subjects, epinphrine-caused symptoms began within 3-5 minutes after injection. A deliberate attempt was made then to bring in the stooge within 1 minute after the subject's injection.

REFERENCES

Ax, A. F. Physiological differentiation of emotional states. *Psychosom. Med.,* 1953, **15,** 433-442.

Cannon, W. B. *Bodily changes in pain, hunger, fear and rage.* (2nd ed.) New York: Appleton, 1929.

Cantril, H., & Hunt, W. A. Emotional effects produced by the injection of adrenalin. *Amer. J. Psychol.,* 1932, **44,** 300-307.

Festinger, L. A theory of social comparison processes. *Hum. Relat.,* 1954, **7,** 114-140.

Hunt, J. McV., Cole, M. W., & Reis, E. E. Situational cues distinguishing anger, fear, and sorrow. *Amer. J. Psychol.,* 1958, **71,** 136-151.

James, W. *The principles of psychology.* New York: Holt, 1890.

Landis, C., & Hunt, W. A. Adrenalin and emotion. *Psychol. Rev.,* 1932, **39,** 467-485.

Latané, B., & Schachter, S. Adrenalin and avoidance learning. *J. comp. physiol. Psychol.,* 1962, **65,** 369-372.

Lindsley, D. B. Emotion. In S. S. Stevens (Ed.), *Handbook of experimental psychology.* New York: Wiley, 1951. Pp. 473-516.

Marañon, G. Contribution a l'étude de l'action emotive de l'adrenaline. *Rev. Francaise Endocrinol.,* 1924, **2,** 301-325.

Nowlis, V., & Nowlis, H. H. The description and analysis of mood. *Ann. N. Y. Acad. Sci.,* 1956, 345-355.

Ruckmick, C. A. *The psychology of feeling and emotion.* New York: McGraw-Hill, 1936.

Schachter, J. Pain, fear, and anger in hypertensives and normotensives: A psychophysiologic study. *Psychosom. Med.,* 1957, **19,** 17-29.

Schachter, S. *The psychology of affiliation.* Stanford, Calif.: Stanford Univer. Press, 1959.

Schachter, S., & Wheeler, L. Epinephrine, chlorpromazine, and amusement. *J. abnorm. soc. Psychol.,* 1962, **65,** 121-128.

Singer, J. E. The effects of epinephrine, chlorpromazine and dibenzyline upon the fright responses of rats under stress and non-stress conditions. Unpublished doctoral dissertation, University of Minnesota, 1961.

Wolf, S., & Wolff, H. G. *Human gastric function.* New York: Oxford Univer. Press, 1947.

Woodworth, R. S., & Schlosberg, H. *Experimental psychology.* New York: Holt, 1958.

Wrightsman, L. S. Effects of waiting with others on changes in level of felt anxiety. *J. abnorm. soc. Psychol.,* 1960, **61,** 216-222..

Classic Quotations from William James

Let anyone try, I will not say to arrest, but to notice or attend to, the *present* moment of time. One of the most baffling experiences occurs. Where is it, this present? It has melted in our grasp, fled ere we could touch it, gone in the instant of becoming.
        (*The Principles of Psychology* [1890], ch. 15.)

Consciousness... does not appear to itself chopped up in bits... A "river" or a "stream" are the metaphors by which it is most naturally described. In talking of it hereafter, let us call it the stream of thought, of consciousness, or of subjective life.
        (*The Principles of Psychology* [1890], ch. 9.)

CHAPTER 7

"Current Status of the Internal-External Hypothesis for Obesity: What Went Wrong?"

Judith Rodin[1,2]

> **EDITORS' COMMENTS.** The study by Schachter and Singer (Chapter 6) showing that emotional reactions were "guided" to a great extent by psychological variables and by cues from the external environment came as a shock to many physiologically-oriented behavioral scientists, who believed that the "body" dominates the "mind" in almost all situations. Schachter's early success in taking this approach to studying emotionality led him to continue looking for situations im which "mind over matter" might be the rule. He soon became fascinated with *obesity* and, during the 1960's and 1970's, undertook an extensive research program on the various cues that prompt people to overeat.
>
> Early on, some of Schachter's studies suggested that people of normal weight tend to control their caloric intake by paying attention primarily to *internal stimuli*. That is, they eat when their bodies tell them it's time to do so, and they eat only as much as their body tells them they need. Schachter called these people "internalizers." People who were overweight, however, often seemed to consume food primarily in response to external (often social) cues. They ate when the clock said it was lunch time even if they weren't experiencing "hunger pangs," and they ate whatever amount seemed appropriate to the situation. Schachter called these individuals "externalizers." In a fascinating series of experiments, Schachter found that fat people tended to be "plate cleaners" who ate everything set before them. Internalizers, however, often "left a little something on the plate" if they weren't particularly hungry. He also reported that obese externalizers were more affected by the *taste* of food than were normal-weight internalizers. That is, obese individuals were more likely to "pig out" when offered rich foods (and to refuse poor-tasting foods), while people of normal weight ate what they physically needed whether the food was a huge slice of chocolate cake or a bowl of bland oatmeal. Fat externalizers were also more likely to work for good-tasting than for poor-tasting food, and more willing to perform physical labor or suffer mild amounts of pain to get to eat, than were people of normal weight. By the early 1970's, Schachter concluded that his "external-internal" theory could explain almost all obesity.
>
> One of Schachter's brightest students while doing this work was Judith Rodin, now a distinguished researcher on her own. By the late 1970's, her own studies had convinced her that Schachter had overemphasized the importance of cognitive variables (and social cues) as far as being overweight was concerned. As she put it in a recent interview, being fat is "determined by a combination of genetic, metabolic, psychological, and environmental events." In a recent article[3], Schachter has apparently concluded that Rodin is right, and that obesity is a *multi-determined problem*. The following article contains the data that helped convince Schachter to change his position.
>
> As is often the case in all fields of human endeavor, the pendulum in psychology first had swung too far toward the "body" explanation of emotional reactions (including overeating), then had swung too far back toward the "mind" point of view. Thanks to the work of Rodin (and many other behavioral scientists), however, we now realize that emotionally-influenced behaviors such as overeating have physiological components, cognitive components, and are affected by on-going events in the social environment. It is the fascinating *interaction* of these variables that determines how we will react in any given situation, no matter how unusual. To emphasize any one of the many components that affect our actions is to do injustice to the exquisite complexities of human experience.

ABSTRACT: Though the consequences of obesity that maintain fatness can be specified, the causes of obesity are far less clear. The internal-external distinction is a widely held and cited framework used to explain differences between overweight and average weight persons, but this article challenges that application. Externality appears in persons of all weight categories and can lead to overeating in these individuals under specifiable conditions. But degree of weight gain and level of obesity depend on a variety of other factors. Moreover, the data suggest that internal sensitivity is not a unique characteristic of normal weight persons. Finally, the extreme separation of external and internal cues in the regulation of eating is not empirically supported. External stimuli can be shown to directly influence internal physiological state, and a hypothesis regarding ways in which short-term internal signals may influence external cue salience can be tested. Thus, there is now considerable evidence challenging a simplistic internal-external dichotomy.

Almost any overweight person can lose weight; few can keep it off. It is this fact that makes the study and treatment of obesity so intriguing. What makes obesity unique, unlike many other disorders? First, heavy people are forced to wear the consequences of their affliction on their body and have probably built up a whole **armamentarium** of defenses to deal with that circumstance. No other physical characteristic except skin color is so stigmatized in our society (Allon, 1975; Cahnman, 1968). Second is the delightful but problematic fact that food is a positive and **reinforcing** stimulus for most of us. Since we have to eat to survive, the problem behavior can never be eliminated completely. Third, and probably most unfair of all, obesity is unusual because being fat is one of the factors that may keep one fat (Rodin, in press; Rodin, Note 1). Indeed, we have all heard the familiar refrain of many an overweight person who complains, "But I eat so little." Despite the disbelieving and reproachful looks of their lean friends, the perverse fact is that it often does take fewer calories to keep people fat than it did to get them fat in the first place. This occurs because obesity itself changes the fat cells and body chemistry and alters level of energy expenditure. Each of these factors operates to maintain obesity once it has developed.

SOME CONSEQUENCES OF OBESITY

First, people's **metabolic** machinery is constituted in such a way that the fatter they are, the fatter they are primed to become. This unfortunate state of affairs occurs because the larger a fat cell gets, the greater its capacity to store fat and become still larger (Salans, Knittle, & Hirsch, 1968). In addition, overweight people tend to have higher basal levels of **insulin** than people of normal weight (Rabinowitz & Zierler, 1962). This condition, which is called **hyperinsulinemia**, enhances fat storage because it accelerates the entry of sugar into the fat cell and actually speeds the conversion of sugar into fat. Humans in a state of natural or induced hyperinsulinemia report hunger (Crain & Thorn, 1949; Grossman & Stein, 1948; Janowitz & Ivy, 1949; Williams, 1960). Thus, the enlarged fat cells found in all overweight individuals, and the hyperinsulinemia found in most, may make them hungrier and prime their metabolic apparatus to make and store more fat.

Second, obesity also affects the degree of energy expenditure the overweight person is capable of. This occurs through its impact on activity level and resting metabolism. But metabolism is actually more interesting because metabolic processes use two thirds of all the energy expenditure of an individual. Even if one did nothing but lie in bed basal metabolism (which keeps the internal life maintenance systems going) would account for an expenditure of about one calorie a minute. Fat tissue is more metabolically inert than lean tissue, so fatness itself can directly lower metabolic rate if fat tissue begins to replace lean tissue. This may be one of the reasons why some overweight people seem to need fewer calories to maintain a high level of body weight than people who are overeating for the first time to achieve the same weight (Sims et al., 1973). Metabolic rate also decreases during food deprivation, so when overweight people are dieting, their basal metabolism and thus their overall level of energy expenditure may slow down, making dieting both difficult and frustrating (Apfelbaum, 1975; Garrow, 1978). This fact suggests that dieting itself may be a critical factor in promoting the maintenance of overweight. In addition, this energy-saving slowdown of metabolism becomes more pronounced with each weight loss attempt (S.C. Wooley, Wooley, & Dyrenforth, 1979). It is as if the body has learned from earlier periods of deprivation and begins to slow down and decrease energy expenditure

---

Armamentarium (ar-mah-men-TAIR-ih-um). A large collection of things, such as all the weapons a country has for engaging in warfare.

Reinforcing. Rewarding. Any event that occurs after a given response tends to strengthen or "reinforce" that response.

Metabolic (met-ah-BOLL-ick). Metabolisim is the sum of internal processes that provide the energy to keep your body going.

Insulin (IN-sull-in). A hormone secreted by the pancreas, which is a small organ near the stomach. Insulin makes it easier for the cells in your body to take in sugar molecules.

Hyperinsulinemia (HIGH-per-in-sull-in-E-me-ah). The presence of excess insulin in the body.

sooner and more efficiently after still another diet is begun.

The remaining third of a person's energy expenditure, the part not used for metabolism, is used for physical activity and exercise. Ever since Jean Mayer and his colleagues documented the popular assumption that obese people are less active than slender ones (Bullen, Reed, & Mayer, 1964), most people have concluded that laziness breeds plumpness. But actually, this process, too, may have occurred in reverse. Obesity makes physical activity more difficult and probably less pleasurable than average weight does, and it may encourage people to be **sedentary**. With less exercise, overweight people burn fewer calories. Moreover, inactivity can lead to a lowering of metabolic rate (Garrow, 1978).

It thus seems clear that a variety of factors serve to maintain and enhance obesity once it has developed. But the elements that cause obesity in the first place remain the subject of considerable current debate.

CAUSES OF OBESITY

What is certain is that obesity is a complex disorder with multiple levels of metabolic and behavioral characteristics which interact with one another. Getting fat involves some combination of food intake, energy expenditure, and the cellular tissue in which fat is stored, but the nature of the contribution of each and the way that they are involved vary greatly. The plump baby, the chubby adolescent boy, the woman who gets fatter after pregnancy, the overweight business executive--all have fatness in common--but it is doubtful that the cause or natural history of their fatness is the same (Bray, 1979). This is hardly surprising because our current views of eating generally see food-relevant behavior as a multiply-regulated process that is influenced by interactions among physiological, cognitive, social, and cultural variables in a control system to which they are all essential, even in the disordered state of obesity (Booth, Toates, & Platt, 1976; Lytle, 1977; Rodin, Note 1). Thus, attempts to provide simplistic explanations of obesity or descriptions of the characteristics of all obese people may often be misleading. Unfortunately, this is the state of affairs in current applications of the "**internal-external**" hypothesis for obesity.

The Internal-External Distinction

This formulation developed in the late 1960s, when Schachter, Nisbett, and their associates reported a provocative series of studies suggesting that the eating behavior of their overweight subjects was greatly influenced by the apparent passage of time, the taste and sight of food, and the number of highly palatable food cues present (Nisbett, 1968a, 1968b; Schachter & Gross, 1968). These studies implied a **dichotomy** between internal and external control of feeding, suggesting that the eating behavior of normal weight people was responsive to internal stimuli (cf. Schachter, Goldman, & Gordon, 1968) and that, in contrast, the eating behavior of overweight people was unresponsive to internal stimuli and instead was primarily controlled by external cues.

The internal-external distinction is a widely held and cited framework. It appears, for example, in almost every introductory psychology textbook published in the last eight years. Because of its elegance and simplicity, it also attracted a considerable number of researchers to the area of human eating behavior and obesity. Yet, many investigators who pursued this dichotomy after Schachter seem to have greatly overextended its applicability. Indeed, it now appears that the injunction of extreme **discontinuity** between internal-physiological and external-environmental stimuli is wrong, especially for eating behavior. In addition, there are now many indications that the internal versus external view is far too simple a description of differences between different weight groups.

USE OF THE INTERNAL-EXTERNAL DISTINCTION TO EXPLAIN DIFFERENCES BETWEEN OBESE AND NORMAL WEIGHT PEOPLE

First, consider the argument that obese individuals are more responsive to environmental cues than are people of average weight. Although Schachter and I reported that many overweight subjects are highly responsive to external food and nonfood stimuli (Schachter & Rodin, 1974), these studies have not always been easy to replicate. Many experiments have failed to demonstrate that overweight individuals are more responsive to external food and nonfood cues than are their normal weight peers (e.g., Goldman, 1969; Nisbett & Storms, 1975; Nisbett & Temoshok, 1976; Shaw, 1973; Stunkard & Levitz [cited in Levitz, 1975]; S. Wooley, 1972).

The inconsistency of these results is not surprising for several reasons. First, it would be most unusual if the wide variety of manipulations of external cues that have been used were shown to have uniform effects. The seeming inconsistencies also arise from a failure to have developed a very good definition of external responsiveness. It now seems clear that external responsiveness is most easily defined as the extent to which a greater magnitude response (e.g., increased eating, increased emotionality, increased attention) is evoked by highly **salient** cues, as compared with cues of low salience, in the external environment. In other words, it should be calculated as the difference score for each subject between his or her response to a high- versus a low-intensity cue, with intensity determined on the basis of independent criteria (e.g., *number* of food cues, **decibels** of noise, *degree* of proximity of food) and not the subject's response. Comparing responses when there are no cues versus when there are some cues would not be a reasonable test in this case.

A second reason for these inconsistent findings relates to issues of sampling. My own early studies with colleagues were among those that failed to show reliable overweight/normal weight differences consistently from subject population to subject population, or even from study to study within the same population (Rodin, 1975; Rodin, Moskowitz, & Bray, 1976; Rodin, Slochower, & Fleming, 1977). The evidence is now quite clear, however, that *all* overweight individuals are not externally responsive; neither are *all* normal weight individuals internally sensitive. Therefore, mean differences in any single study depend on how many individuals of each type wind up in samples divided according to weight. This assertion comes from experiments in which the internal or external responsiveness of several hundred individuals who also varied in degree of overweight was tested. These studies found that in every weight category there were people who were externally responsive and people who were not (e.g., Nisbett & Storms, 1975; Nisbett & Temoshok, 1976; Rodin & Slochower, 1976; Tom & Rucker, 1975). The same was true for internal responsiveness (e.g., Hibscher & Herman, 1977; Price & Grinker, 1973; Speigel, 1973; S. Wooley, 1972). Moreover, across all weight groups, degree of overweight was not strongly related to the degree of external or internal responsiveness demonstrated in these studies (Nisbett, 1972; Price & Grinker, 1973; Rodin et al., 1977). In fact, at extreme degrees of obesity, some individuals showed very little responsiveness to external cues. Later in this article, I attempt to explain this outcome, but to continue historically, these findings in the early 1970s raised the question of whether there really was a relationship between obesity and externality.

Alternative Explanations Based on Set Point

Nisbett (1972) has suggested that the association between overweight and cue responsiveness is an artifact. He argues that extremely obese people have eaten so much that they are at their biologically-determined set point for body weight. By contrast, many less obese overweight individuals remain below their set point by dieting and so exist at a level of chronic deprivation. It is this deprivation, Nisbett suggests, that produces responsiveness to external food cues. His arguments are based on data from between-subjects comparisons, but subsequent studies using within-subjects designs have not borne them out. For example, my colleagues and I conducted a series of studies that tested individuals for their responsiveness to food- and non-food-related external cues before and after they lost considerable amounts of weight through strenuous dieting. These studies tested adolescent girls at weight reduction summer camps where they underwent severe **caloric** restriction (eating only 500 calories per day) in order to lose weight. The campers' deprivation is attested to by the fact that counselors stood guard duty at night on the road leading to a nearby diner. We also tested women attending outpatient obesity clinics for weight reduction. The results indicated that the subjects' degree of responsiveness to external or cognitive cues, such as the sight or thought of food, did not reliably change, a conclusion based on the difference scores in response to conditions of high versus low food cue salience (Rodin et al., 1977). In none of these studies did subjects significantly *increase* their responsiveness to environmental cues after weight loss, as the Nisbett hypothesis would require.

Sedentary (SED-en-tair-ee). A lack of movement, or the act of sitting rather than running about.

Internal-external. According to one theory, some people are "externalizers," which is to say that their behavior is determined primarily by the external environment. Other people are said to be "internalizers," which is to say that their actions are determined primarily by biological and psychological factors inside the person. According to this theory, people who are overweight are supposed to be "externalizers."

Dichotomy (die-KOT-oh-me). A division into two mutually exclusive or contradictory groups.

Discontinuity. A discontinuity is a sharp break in an otherwise continuous curve or distribution. If you cut something in half--as when you divide all the people in the world into two separate classes or personality types--you have created a discontinuity.

Salient (SAY-lih-ent). A salient feature is something that is noticeable, or something that stands out.

Decibels (DESS-ih-bells). Units for expressing the intensity of sounds. Abbreviated db.

Caloric (KAL-or-ick). The caloric content of anything is the amount of heat it will generate when burned. Your body "burns" food when it converts what you eat into energy to keep you alive.

Alternative Explanations Based on Conscious Restraint of Eating

A different effort to explain the poor results of attempts to replicate the relationship between obesity and externality came from the studies of Herman and Polivy and their co-workers (Herman & Mack, 1975; Herman, Polivy, & Silver, 1979; Hibscher & Herman, 1977). They suggested, like Nisbett, that the obesity-externality correlation was an **epiphenomenon** of the fact that the obese were always dieting. But they asserted that it was conscious restraint which was the correlate of externality, rather than obesity or deprivation. While this suggestion has a good deal of intuitive appeal and some empirical support, it should be noted that restraint, too, is only a descriptive term and not a mechanism. Restraint is what some people do if they feel compelled by external cues. In other words, it is external responsiveness that appears to lead to restraint in some people, to overeating when restraint is not exercised in others, and often to alternating periods of both restraint and overeating in still others. This line of reasoning suggests that external responsiveness is the primary mechanism leading to conscious restraint of eating in some people and to overeating in others. But this means, as the data have shown, that there can be externally responsive people in all weight categories. Indeed, a variety of studies have shown that there are people in all weight categories who are *highly* responsive to external cues (Levitz, 1975; Nisbett & Temoshok, 1976; Price & Grinker, 1973; Rodin et al., 1977).

Tests of the Assumption that Externality Is Not Determined by Body Weight

To explore the hypothesis that external responsiveness is not caused by obesity, deprivation, or restraint, but is primary and therefore could lead to overeating and contribute to weight gain given a plentiful food environment, we observed children at an eight-week summer camp for normal weight girls (Rodin & Slochower, 1976). It was a place where food was abundant and freely available. Parents sent candy and sweets to their children, a canteen selling food was open every afternoon and evening, and the meals were tasty and served family style. In short, as far as eating was concerned, it was a land of milk and honey. The girls who were hyperresponsive to all kinds of external cues--as determined in a pretest at the beginning of the summer--were those who gained the most weight when exposed to a major change in their food-relevant environment. The significance of this result lies in the fact that these subjects were normal weight children with no prior history of overweight.

The data are also important in pointing out that degree of external responsiveness, while strongly influential in determining short-term regulation of eating and weight gain, is not the only factor which determines the *levels* of body weight that are maintained over the long term. Of the externally responsive, normal weight campers who gained weight during the summer, 70% reached their highest weights before the final week of the eight-week summer program and then began to lose some weight. While the final weighing showed that they still weighed more at the end of the summer than they had at the beginning, these data suggest that other factors may become more important than external responsiveness in influencing the final levels of body weight attained. These variables could be physiological, for example, metabolic or **adipose** tissue parameters, or psychological, for example, body image.

It is likely that some features of responsiveness to external cues can be learned or modified during early childhood, and animal data suggest that **neonatal** feeding experiences related to the unpredictable availability of food lead to the development of an animal analogue of external responsiveness (Gross, 1968). In addition, it is possible that responsiveness to external cues also has some inherited component and can be identified at birth. Many anthropologists have argued for a genetic adaptation such as this, since the largest segment of human history covers a time when food was scarce and was acquired in unpredictable amounts and by dint of tremendous caloric expenditure (Beller, 1978). For this reason, people might have developed the capacity to store food in fat tissue so that it would be possible, if necessary, to eat only periodically and withstand times of starvation.

The long history of food scarcity and its persistence in much of the world could not have gone unnoticed by such an adaptive species as the human race. In those circumstances, it would have been biologically useful for organisms to overeat whenever external cues representing food were accessible in the environment. The genetic makeup of individuals who showed this trait to the extreme would therefore have been "selected" for continued contribution to the gene pool of the species. However, now that food is abundantly available in much of the world, this tendency has become **dysfunctional**.

If feeding is influenced by the infant's inherited responsivity to attractive food cues, and if abundant and relatively good-tasting food is available, then the more responsive infant may overeat and gain weight. A key question is whether the perceptual differences that characterize high external responsiveness could be found at birth and to what characteristics of parents or infants such differences would be related.

A study, conducted by Milstein (1980), tested infants who were selected on the basis of the weight of their parents. The sample included only children who had either two overweight parents or two normal weight parents. Two different tests were used: One involved sucking response (a measure of avidity) to sweet solutions versus water solutions, and the other involved external responsiveness, in this case visual responsiveness to presentation of stripes of light of different intensity against a dark background.

The study showed first that the children of overweight and normal weight parents did not differ on a variety of developmental measures such as **gestational** age, birth weight, skinfold thickness, and body mass index. The number of decisions to breast- or bottle-feed was also similar for both groups. There were striking differences between the two groups, however, in their responses to the manipulated stimuli. The infants of overweight parents were significantly more responsive to differences between the taste of water and the taste of sweet solution and were more active in shifting their direction of gaze as a function of stimulus intensity in visual fields containing pairs of stripes.

Children of overweight parents rejected the water solution after sucking the glucose solution more than did the children of normal weight parents, although both groups sucked rather avidly for the sweet solution. Their visual responses, measured by the degree of eye shift during a period when two stripes of different intensities were presented simultaneously in the visual field, revealed that babies of overweight parents shifted their gaze more often and with greater magnitude than did babies of normal weight parents. The scanning patterns of the babies of the overweight parents did not appear to be random or eccentric, but were constrained by the location of the stripes in the field. This measure seems a direct analog in infants of the distractibility observed in externally responsive adults faced with competing prominent cues (Rodin, 1973). These infants are now part of a longitudinal study, and in-home feeding observations are under way to determine the relationship between infant external responsiveness, later feeding behavior, and the development of obesity.

To compare his findings with previous research (e.g., Desor, Mailer, & Turner, 1973; Engen, Lipsitt, & Robinson, 1978; Nisbett & Gurwitz, 1970), Milstein looked further at the possible relations of heaviness, maturity, and fatness to infant responsiveness. He grouped babies according to their birth weight, gestational age, skinfold thickness (SFT), and weight/length^2 or body mass index (BMI). None of the indicators was significantly related to the effects obtained for visual shift--the measure of external responsiveness. On the other hand, classifications by both SFT and BMI did show reliably different patterns in babies' responses to the taste solutions. Essentially, both of these measures revealed an increasing sweet preference with increasing glucose concentration for medium and fat babies and a decreased preference at the highest concentrations for the thinner babies. In a similar study using food *intake* as the measure, Grinker (1978) also found that the thinner infants preferred the less sweet solutions to those that were more intensely sweet, although in her study maternal weight did not correlate with infant's food intake.

Based on these findings, Milstein proposed that the thin babies of normal weight parents would be at less risk for obesity, all other things being equal, because they both were less responsive to environmental cues and found sweet-tasting solutions relatively aversive. The infants at greatest risk, again all other things being equal, would be those who had overweight parents and were themselves of moderate or greater fatness, since they both were highly responsive to external cues and showed a greater preference for the sweeter solutions.

Because of the limitations imposed by subject selection procedures in the Milstein study, it is not yet known what characteristics of which parent were most important in the findings of a relationship between parental weight and infant external responsiveness. Moreover, the role of each parent alone could not be assessed, since there were no groups in which just the mother or the father was overweight. Current studies are under way to address these issues.

The Rodin and Slochower (1976) and Milstein (1980) studies suggest that external responsiveness is evident even in normal weight persons and can lead to overeating and weight gain in such people. Indeed, it may be an individual-difference characteristic that is identifiable at birth. But not all externally responsive people become fat, and the degree of obesity they attain,

Epiphenomenon (EPP-ih-fee-NOM-ee-non). A secondary event accompanying another and caused by it. For instance, when you turn on a lamp so you can read, the light generated by the electric bulb is the primary phenomenon (or event) that occurs. However, the heat generated by the bulb is an epiphenomenon.

Adipose (ADD-ih-pohs). Fat, or fatty.

Neonatal (KNEE-oh-nat-al). *Neonate* means "newborn."

Dysfunctional (dis-FUNK-shun-al). Impaired or abnormal functioning.

Gestational (jess-TAY-shun-al). The development of a child from conception to birth. Since some children are born after spending seven months in the womb, while other children are born after spending 9 to 10 months in the womb, some newborn infants have a greater gestational age at birth than do others.

if they do gain weight, is not determined by external responsiveness alone. To assume this to be true is to fail to recognize that obesity also depends on genetic factors, on fat cell number, and on individual differences in **endocrine** function and metabolic efficiency. These factors make it likely that up to some limit, even with equal externality-induced overeating, some people will simply get fatter than others. For example, Rose and Williams (1961) matched pairs of individuals who were maintaining identical weights, which varied very little over several weeks, who had comparable levels of activity, and who were approximately the same age and height. Yet, one of the pair often ate twice as many calories as the other. Extraordinary as this may seem, this finding suggests that in different individuals an identical type and quantity of food eaten is not necessarily or even likely to be stored or expended in the same way, even given equal activity levels. Studies such as these help to explain the lack of a strong correlation between degree of obesity and degree of responsiveness to external food cues.

A further reason for the lack of the expected high correlation is statistical. Given that there are mediating variables between external responsiveness, on the one hand, and obesity, on the other, the final correlation between these two factors is the multiplicative value of each of them with the intervening variables. To take a simple example, if

external responsiveness ----> increased fat cell number via overeating---->

obesity

and the correlation of each factor with the mediator was .5 (i.e., correlation of external responsiveness and fat cell number was .5 and correlation of fat cell number and obesity was .5), the correlation between externality and obesity would be only .25.

The lack of a strong relationship between externality and obesity per se also supports the finding that there is no single obese eating style which derives from being hyperresponsive to external cues. In fact, it has become increasingly hard to identify any aspect of eating behavior that is uniquely characteristic of all or even a large proportion of the overweight population (Mahoney, 1975; Wilson, 1980; S. C. Wooley et al., 1979; Rodin & Spitzer, Note 2). Thus, treatments for obesity that use behavior modification techniques must focus on assessing whether or not individuals are externally responsive before working to change this presumed tendency of all overweight people.

Internal Responsiveness and Body Weight

It now seems clear that the opposite component of the internal-external hypothesis is also not easily demonstrated. The original evidence for a lack of internal responsiveness in the obese came from studies showing their failure to regulate their intake as accurately as normal weight people did (Nisbett, 1968b; Pliner, 1973; Schachter et al., 1968). These studies are widely cited, although the greater number of studies has failed to find obese-normal differences in response to manipulations that varied the caloric value of a preload given prior to the test meal (Herman & Mack, 1975; Hibscher & Herman, 1977; Hill & McCutcheon, 1975; Nisbet & Storms, 1975; Price & Grinker, 1973; Ruderman & Wilson, 1979; Singh, 1973). These inconsistent findings are readily explained, since there is now a great deal of evidence that even normal weight people show poor regulation when they only have internal signals to go on (Jordan, 1975; Speigel, 1973; S. Wooley, 1972). It is simply not true that people who are of average weight can interpret hunger pangs, low blood sugar, and other physiological signals which tell them when they are hungry and that overweight people cannot, and that this is why they are fat. In fact, most people are pretty inadequate at knowing how many calories they have consumed or how much food their bodies really need on the basis of internal cues alone. Studies using disguised caloric dilution have shown that only some normal weight subjects are able to compensate over several days for changes in the caloric density of their diets, and in nearly all cases compensation is incomplete (Campbell, Hashim, & Van Itallie, 1971; Jordan, 1969; Speigel, 1973; O. Wooley, 1971).

The problem is that there are as yet no clear-cut measures of internal sensitivity, in part because it has not been possible to identify **unequivocally** the unconditioned stimuli for hunger and satiety, although there are currently some interesting leads (cf. Booth et al., 1976; Friedman & Stricker, 1976). Vast individual differences exist in the bodily cues that people use as signals of hunger and satiety, and much of the relevant data suggest strongly that these differences are not at all correlated with overweight (Leon & Roth, 1977; O. W. Wooley & Wooley, 1975; Rodin, Note 1). No doubt they have to do more with learning histories than with any characteristic related to weight per se.

This discussion was intended to outline some of the reasons why the internal versus external control dichotomy does not relate simply or directly to differences between overweight and normal weight people. Further understanding of the multiple mechanisms involved in the regulation of eating and body weight is needed before the specific sets of characteristics and array of causal factors that relate to fatness can be detailed more precisely. The present state of the literature demands a shift of orientation to understanding the **etiology** of obesity or, indeed, the several obesities that all have fatness as their common observable characteristic. It is not possible to divide samples sensibly without these data, and even current characterizations relying on juvenile versus adult-onset obesity, degree of restraint, number of fat cells, and degree of external responsiveness are presently insufficient, although they hold promise. What all this means is that it is no longer very useful, or valid, to conduct research that simply divides individuals on the basis of their degree of overweight and then looks for the external- or internal-sensitivity characteristics on which they differ. While any single study may indeed find an effect, the next replication, even by the same investigators, may not. This is because the extent to which people are responsive to internal and external stimuli seems to be an individual-difference characteristic that is related, but only meagerly, to *current* levels of body weight. Sometimes a normal weight sample contains many subjects who are highly insensitive to internal stimuli, and sometimes it contains individuals who are responsive in the extreme to external cues. Overweight samples may contain the same types of individuals.

INTERACTION OF EXTERNAL AND INTERNAL SIGNALS

The second point that changes one's view about the internal versus external hypothesis is that internal and external cues interact in the regulation of eating. For example, external cues may exert some of their effects by triggering internal, physiological signals that motivate the individual to eat. In this way, salient external cues could affect internal state, doing so even before food enters the mouth.

Arousal

External food cues such as the smell and sight of food are arousing. Many investigators have argued that this physiological arousal plays a crucial role in the control of feeding in both people and animals (Marshall, 1976; Rowland & Antelman, 1976; Wolgin, Cytawa, & Teitelbaum, 1976; Rodin, Note 1). Hyperarousal in response to external stimuli appears to be related to overeating in **ventromedial-hypothalamic-lesioned** animals and in many people (e.g., Marshall, 1975; White, 1973). In each of these groups, heightened responsiveness to external stimuli can be shown to produce physiological arousal, which leads to overeating and weight gain over time. An external stimulus can thus be seen as having two effects: a specific one that elicits some appropriate motivational state and a nonspecific one that arouses the organism and thereby permits the responses to occur (Stricker & Zigmond, 1976). Organisms could literally be turned on by an external stimulus, and at the same time, this arousal would make them even more likely to eat, perhaps because arousal reciprocally increases responsiveness to external cues. The neurochemical link among responsivity, arousal, and feeding systems that has been so beautifully worked out for animals in the past few years (Antelman, Szechtman, Chin, & Fisher, 1975; Marshall, 1976) has exciting implications for the study of external responsiveness in human obesity.

At present, it does not appear appropriate to argue for the underlying anatomical or neurochemical dysfunction of these responses in humans. However, many investigators have proposed that there are large individual differences both in rate of activation and in basal levels of arousal in humans (Maddi, 1968; Thayer, 1967). These individual differences may be the basis for differences in external responsiveness and are therefore important for the understanding of factors involved in overeating and obesity. Recently, we have obtained data suggesting a relationship between individual differences in arousability in response to external non-food-related stimuli and subsequent overeating and weight gain when the subjects lived in an abundant food environment (Spitzer & Rodin, Note 3). This line of reasoning nicely explains arousal-related overeating without relying on psychodynamic factors.

Metabolic Factors

In addition to general arousal, a second interaction of external cues and internal factors may arise from the effects of the external cues on metabolic events or digestive processes. Here one's own experience can validate what has now been demonstrated in the laboratory. Tempted by external stimuli, people tend to salivate, which is the first internal response in the digestive process. The Wooleys and their co-workers have shown

---

Endocrine (EN-doh-krin). An endocrine is a hormone produced by a ductless gland, such as the thyroid or the pituitary.

Unequivocally (un-ee-KWIV-oh-kal-lee). Without doubt or exception.

Etiology (ee-tee-OLL-oh-gee). The cause of something, or the search for why it happened.

Ventromedial-hypothalamic-lesioned (ven-tro-ME-dih-al high-poh-thal-AM-ick LEE-shunnd). Literally, animals that have sustained a lesion (or cut) in the front-middle part of the hypothalamus.

that salivation is much greater when subjects are presented with a food as opposed to a nonfood stimulus in their visual field and that these salivary responses to food stimuli vary as a function of the imagined **palatability** of the food and whether or not it will be available for subsequent ingestion (O. Wooley, Wooley, & Dunham, 1976; S. Wooley & Wooley, 1973).

Insulin release is another major candidate for an intervening physiological mechanism that might be responsive to external stimuli. As indicated earlier, insulin is involved in promoting increased **ingestion** and in increased storage of nutrients as fat. It is thus a critical internal response in the digestive and fat-storing process. The important role of insulin responses to the sight and taste of food in animals has been explored by Powley (1977) and Woods et al. (1977), who have showed that rats develop the tendency to secrete insulin in the presence of stimuli which reliably predict the opportunity to eat (time of day or odor). The relationship of increased insulin to overeating and weight gain (Lovett & Booth, 1970; MacKay, Calloway, & Barnes, 1940; Steffens, 1975) appears to hold despite the fact that insulin is secreted by the **pancreas** following the intestinal absorption of **glucose** (McIntyre, Holdsworth, & Turner, 1965), suggesting that increased insulin levels should actually correlate with satiety.

In several studies, my co-workers and I tested subjects who had not eaten for 18 hours (Rodin, 1978). To accomplish this level of deprivation we asked them to come to the laboratory at lunchtime after having eaten nothing since the end of dinner on the preceding evening. While blood samples were being drawn a steak was brought in and placed in front of them, the steak grilling and crackling in a frying pan to provide rich visual, auditory, and olfactory food cues.

We had previously determined subjects' degree of external responsiveness using a battery of non-eating measures (cf. Rodin et al., 1977). The externally responsive subjects, whether they were normal weight or overweight, showed the greatest insulin response to the sight, smell, and sound of the grilling steak, although there was considerable within-group variability.

In none of these studies were there significant changes in blood glucose levels, but preliminary data examining subjects' **glucagon** suggest that their glucose levels were not being maintained by **gluconeogenesis**. Comparable studies of Sjostrom, Krotkiewski, Garrelick, and Luyckx (1980) found no changes in plasma glucose, glucagon or **cortisol** in subjects showing insulin release in response to visual food stimuli. They and Parra-Covarrubias, Rivera-Rodriquez, and Almarez-Ugalde (1971) also reported greater **biphasic** insulin release in response to visual food stimuli in some obese individuals than in normal weight people. Sjostrom et al. (1980), however, found no correlation between the extent of this insulin response and body weight, body fat, or mean fat cell weight.

Another study (Rodin, 1978) explored whether the insulin response would increase as a function of the palatability of the food stimulus, especially for the most externally responsive subjects. S. Wooley and Wooley (1973) had found that degree of salivation to food stimuli varied directly with their subject-rated appeal, and we anticipated the same sort of relationship for insulin release. For externally responsive subjects, the magnitude of the hormonal response that did occur was indeed correlated with the subject-rated appeal of the food. Remember that all of these effects occur before food has entered the mouth, so these are not physiological responses to the presence of food in the digestive tract. If externally responsive people oversecrete insulin in the presence of compelling food cues, they might eat more calories in order to balance this hormonal and metabolic output. Here external cues trigger internal stimuli that might also signal increased eating. Thus, appetite could be stimulated and overeating might result as a consequence of increased physiological responsiveness to potent, palatable external stimuli.

Effects of Internal Signals on External Cues

Having considered how external cues trigger internal physiological events, it is important to look at whether internal signals can affect external cues. Certainly, there are animal data suggesting that arousal, induced, for example, by a mild tail pinch, increases overall responsiveness to external stimuli (Antelman, Rowland, & Fisher, 1976). One possibility in humans, then, is that arousal or other "internal" factors make external cues of a given level of intensity more salient or push people, regardless of their chronic, dispositional level of external responsiveness, further up on the response scale. Here the overall level would be raised, but the individual's difference score between a high- versus low-intensity cue would not change, since arousal would presumably make both the high- and the low-intensity cue equally more salient.

This speculation is not inconsistent with the hypothesis advanced in the first section of the article, namely, that there are individual differences in degree of responsiveness to external cues which are not a function of body weight per se and which are not changed by weight loss (and the reduction of adipose tissue stores with which considerable weight loss is associated). Since these long-term energy state signals related to fat stores may be different from short-term signals related to the ready availability of metabolic fuels (Van Itallie, Smith, & Quartermain, 1977), it is possible that the latter, but not the former, could feed back to influence the salience of the cues themselves. Whether or not short-term internal signals do in fact influence external changes remains to be specified by future research. Such findings are important to our understanding of the regulation of feeding in general, as well as to the study of obesity in particular.

CLARIFYING WHAT CONSTITUTES AN EXTERNAL CUE

The more precise definition of external cue responsiveness suggested here, which focuses on differential responsiveness to high- versus low-intensity stimuli, should be useful in further research endeavors. But the notion of what constitutes an external cue itself has to be reconsidered. Manipulations of **putative** external cues for eating have even included whether or not the experimenter was dressed as a scientist (Stalling & Friedman, Note 4) or variations of the color of the granulated sugar glaze on the top of cookies (Cheung, Barnes, & Barnes, 1980). There is also reason to argue that responsiveness to taste and other **oropharyngeal** stimuli should be different from responsiveness to visual or cognitive cues. First, the receptor sites of stimulation by taste and smell are quite different from those of visual cues (Pfaffmann, 1960). In the hypothalamic region, Rolls (1976) found specific and different neurons firing to the sight of food and to the taste of food in deprived animals. Second, taste can serve as an unconditioned stimulus for learning and appears to have more direct biological significance for the organism (Garcia & Hankins, 1974; Rozin & Kalat, 1971).

There exists **empirical** support for the assertion that responsiveness to taste and responsiveness to external visual cues are linked to different factors. Milstein (1980) found increased taste responsiveness to be associated with greater body mass index and skinfold thickness in newborn infants, but neither of these indices related to visual cue responsiveness. Rodin et al. (1977) found that overweight subjects were more responsive to differences between good- and bad-tasting ice milk than were normal weight subjects prior to weight loss, and the former became even more so following weight reduction. By contrast, weight loss in the overweight subjects did not reliably change the degree of responsiveness to manipulations of high versus low *visual* salience of food cues. Thus, long-term factors related to energy reserves do appear to influence **hedonic** responsiveness to taste but not responsiveness to visual cues.

Other internal signals, like the state of the gastrointestinal tract, also directly affect responsiveness to taste but not responsiveness to external visual cues. We recently studied patients who had undergone intestinal bypass surgery, which creates a greatly shortened intestinal tract (Bray, Barry, Benfield, Castelnuovo-Tedesco, & Rodin, 1976). This surgery results in malabsorption of ingested food and extensive weight loss. The patients showed a dramatic change in responsiveness to sweet taste following surgery, and the change was in a direction identical to the **nonmonotonic** preference curves obtained for normal weight individuals (Rodin et al., 1976). Comparable normalization of preference curves did not occur for obese people who lost relatively similar amounts of weight by dieting (Rodin et al., 1976). These data suggest that local changes in the intestinal tract itself--for example, the small percentage of absorptive surface left intact or the reduced number of glucose receptors along the intestinal wall--may actually influence perceived palatability. The bypass patients showed no changes, however, in response to the visual salience of external cues following surgery (Rodin, 1980).

Palatability (pal-ah-tah-BILL-it-tee). A food is said to be "palatable" (PAL-ah-tah-bill) if it tastes good, or is easy to eat.

Ingestion (in-JEST-shun). To take something in. When you eat you ingest food.

Pancreas (PAN-kree-us). A large gland near your stomach that secretes disgestive enzymes and the hormone insulin.

Glucose (GLUH-koz). A type of sugar.

Glucagon (GLUH-kah-gon). A hormone that increases the content of sugar in the blood by increasing the rate of breakdown of sugar in the liver.

Gluconeogenesis (gluh-kon-ee-oh-JEN-ee-sis). The formation of glucose with the body. Specifically, the process by which the liver uses fats and proteins to produce glucose.

Cortisol (KORT-ih-sol). A hormone from the adrenal cortex that is used in the treatment of arthritis.

Biphasic (by-FAZE-ick). Something that has two phases, or which occurs in two parts.

Putative (PEW-tah-tive). Commonly accepted or supposed.

Oropharyngeal (OR-oh-fair-en-GEE-al). Having to do with the area between the lips and the pharynx (the back of the throat).

Empirical (em-PEER-ih-cal). To be "empirical" is to rely on data or experimentation rather than on theory or guess.

Hedonic (he-DON-ick). Pleasurable, or related somehow to pleasure.

Nonmonotonic (non-mon-oh-TONN-ick). A variable is said to be "monotonic" if it never increases or decreases. A variable is said to be "nonmonotonic" if it changes over time.

CONCLUSION

To conclude I would like to reiterate that onset and degree of overweight are determined by a combination of genetic, metabolic, psychological, and environmental events. Considerable data arguing against the simplistic notion that all overweight people are externally responsive and lack internal sensitivity, and that people of average weight show the opposite pattern, have been reviewed. It may never be possible to find the "magic bullet," since obesity is not a single syndrome, has no single cause, and therefore probably does not have a single cure. Medicine is frequently condemned by behavioral scientists because it usually focuses on changing the body--the internal processes--and forgets the role of the environment. With this I agree. However, some behavioral scientists are trying to change responses to the environment without examining its effects on internal processes. This too is one-sided. I believe the answers must come from a model that appreciates the integration of these processes, and psychology may now be approaching it.

REFERENCE NOTES

1. Rodin, J. *Obesity: Why the losing battle?* Master Lecture on Brain-Behavior Relationships presented at the meeting of the American Psychological Association, San Francisco, August 1977.

2. Rodin, J., & Spitzer, L. *A prospective study of the relationship among eating habits, prior weight history and energy regulation in college undergraduates.* Manuscript in preparation, Yale University, 1980.

3. Spitzer, L., & Rodin, J. *Individual differences in arousability: Its relationship to eating.* Manuscript in preparation, Yale University, 1980.

4. Stalling, R. B., & Friedman, L. *Effect of fictitious food ratings and experimenter's attire on eating behavior of obese and normal people.* Unpublished manuscript, Bradley University, 1978.

FOOTNOTES

[1] Reprinted by permission of the author and the publisher from *American Psychologist*, 1981, **36**, 361-372. Copyright 1981 by the American Psychological Association.

[2] This article is based on a Division 8 invited address at a session to honor the author as recipient of an APA Early Career Award, at the meeting of the American Psychological Association, New York City, September 1979. The author's work reported here was supported by National Science Foundation Grants GS-37953 and BNS 76-81126.

[3] Schachter, S. (1982). Don't sell habit-breakers short. *Psychology Today*, **16**(8), 18.

REFERENCES

Allon, N. The stigma of overweight in everyday life. In G. A. Bray et al. (Eds.), *Obesity in perspective* (Vol. 2, DHEW Publication No. NIH 75-708). Washington, D.C: U.S. Government Printing Office, 1975.

Antelman, S. M., Rowland, N. E., & Fisher, A. E. Stimulation bound ingestive behavior: A view from the tail. *Physiology and Behavior*, 1976, **17**, 743-748.

Antelman, S. M., Szechtman, H., Chin, P., & Fisher, A. E. Tail pinch-induced eating, gnawing and licking behavior in rats: Dependence on the nigrostriatal dopamine system. *Brain Research*, 1975, **99**, 319-337.

Apfelbaum, M. Influence of level of energy intake on energy expenditure in man: Effects of spontaneous intake, experimental starvation and experimental overeating. In G. A. Bray et al. (Eds.), *Obesity in perspective* (Vol. 2, DHEW Publication No. NIH 75-708). Washington, D.C.: U.S. Government Printing Office, 1975.

Beller, A. S. *Fat and thin: A natural history of obesity*. New York: McGraw-Hill, 1978.

Booth, D. A., Toates, F. M., & Platt, S. V. Control system for hunger and its implications in animals and man. In D. Novin, W. Wyrwicka, & G. A. Bray (Eds.), *Hunger: Basic mechanisms and clinical implications*. New York: Raven Press, 1976.

Bray, G. A. (Ed.). *Obesity in America* (DHEW Publication No. NIH 79-359). Washington, D.C.: U.S. Government Printing Office, 1979.

Bray, G. A., Barry, R. W., Benfield, J., Castelnuovo-Tedesco, P., & Rodin, J. Intestinal bypass surgery for obesity decreases food intake and taste preferences. *Journal of Clinical Nutrition*, 1976, **29**, 779-783.

Bullen, B. A., Reed, R. B., & Mayer, J. Physical activity of obese and nonobese adolescent girls, appraised by motion picture sampling. *American Journal of Clinical Nutrition*, 1964, **14**, 211-223.

Cahnman, W. J. The stigma of obesity. *Sociological Quarterly*, 1968, **9**, 283-299.

Campbell, R. G., Hashim, S. A., & Van Itallie, T. B. Studies of food-intake regulation in man: Responses to variations in nutritive density in lean and obese subjects. *New England Journal of Medicine*, 1971, **285**, 1402-1407.

'Cheung, R. C., Barnes, T. R., & Barnes, M. J. Relationship between visually based food preference and amount eaten. *Perceptual and Motor Skills*, 1980, **50**, 780-782.

Crain, E. L., Jr., & Thorn, G. W. Functioning pancreatic islet cell adenomas. *Medicine*, 1949, **28**, 427-447.

Desor, J. A., Maller, O., & Turner, R. E. Taste in acceptance of sugars by human infants. *Journal of Comparative and Physiological Psychology*, 1973, **58**, 63-67.

Engen, T., Lipsitt, L. P., & Robinson, D. O. Birthweight and maternal weight as factors in the newborn infant's response to sapid fluids. *Infant Behavior and Development*, 1978, *1*, 118-121.

Friedman, M. I., & Stricker, E. M. The physiological psychology of hunger: A physiological perspective. *Psychological Review*, 1976, *83*, 409-431.

Garcia, J., & Hankins, W. G. The evolution of bitter and the acquisition of toxaphobia. In D. Denton (Ed.), *Fifth International Symposium on Olfaction and Taste* (DHEW Publication No. NIH 74-563). Washington, D.C.: U.S. Government Printing Office, 1974.

Garrow, J. The regulation of energy expenditure. In G. A. Bray (Ed.), *Recent advances in obesity research* (Vol. 2). London: Newman, 1978.

Goldman, R. L. The effects of the manipulation of the visibility of food on the eating behavior of obese and normal subjects (Doctoral dissertation, Columbia University, 1968). *Dissertation Abstracts International*, 1969, *30*, 807A.

Grinker, J. Infant taste responses are correlated with birthweight and unrelated to indices of obesity. *Pediatric Research*, 1978, *12*, 371. (Abstract)

Gross, L. The effects of early feeding experience on external responsiveness. Unpublished doctoral dissertation, Columbia University, 1968.

Grossman, M. I., & Stein, I. F. The effect of vagotomy on the hunger producing action of insulin in man. *Journal of Applied Physiology*, 1948, *1*, 263-269.

Herman, C. P., & Mack, D. Restrained and unrestrained eating. *Journal of Personality*, 1975, *43*, 647-660.

Herman, C. P., Polivy, J., & Silver, R. Effects of an observer on eating behavior: The induction of "sensible" eating. *Journal of Personality*, 1979, *47*, 85-99.

Hibscher, J. A., & Herman, C. P. Obesity, dieting, and the expression of "obese" characteristics. *Journal of Comparative and Physiological Psychology*, 1977, *91*, 374-380.

Hill, S., & McCutcheon, N. Eating responses of obese and non-obese humans during dinner meals. *Psychosomatic Medicine*, 1975, *37*, 395-401.

Janowitz, H. D., & Ivy, A. C. Role of blood sugar levels in spontaneous and insulin-induced hunger in man. *Journal of Applied Physiology*, 1949, *2*, 643-645.

Jordan, H. Voluntary intragastric feeding: Oral and gastric contributions to food intake and hunger in man. *Journal of Comparative and Physiological Psychology*, 1969, *68*, 498-506.

Jordan, H. A. Physiological control of food intake in man. In G. A. Bray et al. (Eds.), *Obesity in perspective* (Vol. 2, DHEW Publication No. NIH 75-708). Washington, D.C.: U.S. Government Printing Office, 1975.

Leon, G. R., & Roth, L. Obesity: Psychological causes, correlations, and speculations. *Psychological Bulletin*, 1977, *84*, 117-139.

Levitz, L. The susceptibility of human feeding to external controls. In G. A. Bray et al. (Eds.), *Obesity in perspective* (Vol. 2, DHEW Publication No. NIH 75-708). Washington, D.C.: U.S. Government Printing Office, 1975.

Lovett, D., & Booth, D. A. Four effects of exogenous insulin on food intake. *Quarterly Journal of Experimental Psychology*, 1970, *22*, 406-419.

Lytle, L. D. Control of eating behavior. In R. J. Wurtman & J. J. Wurtman (Eds.), *Nutrition and the brain* (Vol.2). New York: Raven Press, 1977.

MacKay, E. M., Calloway, J. W., & Barnes, R. H: Hyperalimentation in normal animals produced by protamine insulin. *Journal of Nutrition*, 1940, *20*, 59-66.

Maddi, S. *Personality theories: A comparative analysis*. Homewood, Ill.: Dorsey Press, 1968.

Mahoney, M. J. The obese eating style: Bites, beliefs and behavior modification. *Addictive Behavior*, 1975, *1*, 47-53.

Marshall, J. Increased orientation to sensory stimuli following medial hypothalamic damage in rats. *Brain Research*, 1975, *86*, 373-387.

Marshall, J. Neurochemistry of central monoamine systems as related to food intake. In T. Silverstone (Ed.), *Appetite and food intake*. Braunschweig, West Germany: Pergamon Press, 1976.

McIntyre, N., Holdsworth, C. D., & Turner, D. S. *Journal of Clinical Endocrinology*, 1965, *25*, 1317.

Milstein, R. M. Responsiveness in newborn infants of overweight and normal weight parents. *Appetite*, 1980, *1*, 65-74.

Nisbett, R. E. Determinants of food intake in human obesity. *Science*, 1968, *159*, 1254-1255. (a)

Nisbett, R. E. Taste, deprivation and weight determinants of eating behavior. *Journal of Personality and Social Psychology*, 1968, *10*, 107-116. (b)

Nisbett, R. E. Hunger, obesity, and the ventromedial hypothalamus. *Psychological Review*, 1972, *79*, 433-453.

Nisbett, R. E., & Gurwitz, S. B. Weight, sex, and the eating behavior of human newborns. *Journal of Comparative and Physiological Psychology*, 1970, *73*, 245-253.

Nisbett, R. E., & Storms, M. D. Cognitive, social, psychological determinants of food intake. In H. London & R. E. Nisbett (Eds.), *Cognitive modification of emotional behavior*. Chicago: Aldine, 1975.

Nisbett, R. E., & Temoshok, L. Is there an external cognitive style? *Journal of Personality and Social Psychology*, 1976, *33*, 36-47.

Parra-Covarrubias, A., Rivera-Rodriguez, I., & Almarez-Ugalde, A. Cephalic phase of insulin secretion in obese adolescents. *Diabetes*, 1971, *20*, 800-802.

Pfaffmann, C. The pleasures of sensation. *Psychological Review*, 1960, *65*, 253-268.

Pliner, P. L. Effect of liquid and solid preloads on eating behavior of obese and normal persons. *Physiology and Behavior*, 1973, *11*, 285-290.

Powley, T. The ventromedial hypothalamic syndrome, satiety, and a cephalic phase hypothesis. *Psychological Review*, 1977, *84*, 89.

Price, J. M., & Grinker, J. Effects of degree of obesity, food deprivation, and palatability on eating behavior of humans. *Journal of Comparative and Physiological Psychology*, 1973, *85*, 265-271.

Rabinowitz, D., & Zierler, K. L. Forearm metabolism in obesity and its response to intra-arterial insulin: Characterization of insulin resistance and evidence for adaptive hyperinsulinism, *Journal of Clinical Investigation*, 1962, **41**, 2173-2181.

Rodin, J. Effects of distraction on the performance of obese and normal subjects. *Journal of Comparative and Physiological Psychology*, 1973, **83**, 68-78.

Rodin, J. The effects of obesity and set point on taste responsiveness and intake in humans. *Journal of Comparative and Physiological Psychology*, 1975, **89**, 1003-1009.

Rodin, J. Has the distinction between internal versus external control of feeding outlived its usefulness? In G. A. Bray (Ed.), *Recent advances in obesity research* (Vol. 2). London: Newman, 1978.

Rodin, J. Changes in perceptual responsiveness following jejunoileostomy: Their potential role in reducing. *American Journal of Clinical Nutrition*, 1980, **33**, 457-464.

Rodin, J. *Exploding the obesity myth*. London: Multimedia, in press.

Rodin, J., Moskowitz, H. R., & Bray, G. A. Relationship between obesity, weight loss, and taste responsiveness. *Physiology & Behavior*, 1976, **17**, 591-597.

Rodin, J., & Slochower, J. Externality in the non-obese: The effects of environmental responsiveness on weight. *Journal of Personality and Social Psychology*, 1976, **29**, 557-565.

Rodin, J., Slochower, J., & Fleming, B. The effects of degree of obesity, age of onset, and energy deficit on external responsiveness. *Journal of Comparative and Physiological Psychology*, 1977, **91**, 586-597,

Rolls, E. T. Neurophysiology of feeding. In T. Silverstone (Ed.), *Appetite and food intake*. Braunschweig, West Germany: Pergamon Press, 1976.

Rose, G. A., & Williams, R. T. Metabolic studies of large and small eaters. *British Journal of Nutrition*, 1961, **15**, 1-9.

Rowland, N., & Antelman, S. Stress-induced hyperphagia and obesity in rats: A possible model for understanding human obesity. *Science*, 1976, **191**, 310-312.

Rozin, P., & Kalat, J. W. Specific hungers and poison avoidance as adaptive specializations of learning. *Psychological Review*, 1971, **78**, 459-486.

Ruderman, A. J., & Wilson, G. T. Weight restraint, cognitions and counterregulation. *Behaviour Research and Therapy*, 1979, **17**, 581-590.

Salans, L. B., Knittle, J. L., & Hirsch, J. The role of adipose cell size and adipose tissue insulin sensitivity in the carbohydrate intolerance of human obesity. *Journal of Clinical Investigation*, 1968, **47**, 153-165.

Schachter, S., Goldman, R., & Gordon, A. Effects of fear, food deprivation, and obesity on eating. *Journal of Personality and Social Psychology*, 1968, **10**, 91-97.

Schachter, S., & Gross, L. Manipulated time and eating behavior. *Journal of Personality and Social Psychology*, 1968, **10**, 98-106.

Schachter, S., & Rodin, J. *Obese humans and rats*. Washington, D.C.: Erlbaum/Halsted, 1974.

Shaw, J. C. *The influence of food type and method of presentation on human ingestive behavior*. Unpublished doctoral dissertation, University of Pennsylvania. 1973.

Sims, E., Danforth, E., Horton, E., Bray, G., Glennon, J., & Salans, L. Endocrine and metabolic effects of experimental obesity in man. *Recent Progress in Hormonal Research*, 1973, **29**, 457-496.

Singh, D. Role of response habits and cognitive factors in determination of behavior of obese humans. *Journal of Personality and Social Psychology*, 1973, **27**, 220-238.

Sjostrom, L., Krotkiewski, M., Garrelick, G., & Luyckx, A. Peripheral insulin in response to the sight and smell of food. *Metabolism*, 1980, **29**, 901-909.

Speigel, T. A. Caloric regulation of food intake in man. *Journal of Comparative and Physiological Psychology*, 1973, **84**, 24-37.

Steffens, A. B. Influence of reversible obesity on eating behavior, blood glucose. and insulin in the rat. *American Journal of Physiology*, 1975, **228**, 1738-1744.

Stricker, E., & Zigmond, M. Brain catecholamines and the lateral hypothalamic syndrome. In D. Novin, W. Wyrwicka, & G. A. Bray (Eds.), *Hunger: Basic mechanisms and clinical implications*. New York: Raven Press, 1976.

Thayer, R. Measurement of activation through self-report. *Psychological Reports*, 1967, **20**, 663-678.

Tom, G., & Rucker, M. Fat, full, and happy. *Journal of Personality and Social Psychology*, 1975, **32**, 761-766.

Van Itallie, T. B., Smith, N. S., & Quartermain, D. Short-term and long-term components in the regulation of food intake: Evidence for a modulatory role of carbohydrate status. *American Journal of Clinical Nutrition*, 1977, **30**, 742-757.

White, C. The effects of viewing film of different arousal content on the eating behavior of obese and normal weight subjects (Doctoral dissertation, University of Miami, 1973). *Dissertation Abstracts International*, 1973, **34**, 2324B.

Williams, R. H. Hypoglycemosis. In R. H. Williams (Ed.), *Diabetes*. New York: Hoeber, 1960.

Wilson, G. T. Behavior therapy and the treatment of obesity. In W. R. Miller (Ed.), *Addictive disorders*. New York: Pergamon Press, 1980.

Wolgin, D., Cytawa, J., & Teitelbaum, P. The role of activation in the regulation of food intake. In D. Novin, W. Wyrvicka, & G. A. Bray (Eds.), *Hunger: Basic mechanisms and clinical implications*. New York: Raven Press, 1976.

Woods, S. C., Vaselli, J. R., Kaestner, E., Szakmary, G. A., Milburn, P., & Vitiello, M. V. Conditioned insulin secretion and meal feeding in rats. *Journal of Comparative and Physiological Psychology*, 1977, **91**, 128-133.

Wooley, O. Long-term food regulation in the obese and non-obese. *Psychosomatic Medicine*, 1971, **33**, 436.

Wooley, O., Wooley, S., & Dunham, R. Deprivation, expectation and threat: Effects on salivation in the obese and non-obese. *Physiology & Behavior*, 1976, **17**, 187-193.

Wooley, O. W., & Wooley, S. C. The experimental psychology of obesity. In T. Silverstone & J. Findham (Eds.), *Obesity: Its pathogenesis and management*. Lancaster, England: Medical and Technical Publishing, 1975.

Wooley, S. Physiologic versus cognitive factors in short-term food regulation in the obese and non-obese. *Psychosomatic Medicine*, 1972, **34**, 62.

Wooley, S., & Wooley, O. Salivation to the sight and thought of food: A new measure of appetite. *Psychosomatic Medicine*, 1973, **35**, 136.

Wooley, S. C., Wooley, O. W., & Dyrenforth, S. R. Theoretical, practical, and social issues in behavioral treatments of obesity. *Journal of Applied Behavior Analysis*, 1979, **12**, 3-25.

CHAPTER 8

"The Magical Number Seven, Plus or Minus Two: Some Limits on Our Capacity for Processing Information"

George A. Miller[1,2]

EDITORS' COMMENTS. As we noted in Chapter 1, when psychology first appeared on the scene about 100 years ago, it was an odd mixture of medicine (physiology), physics (sensory psychology), and philosophy. With the exception of the physiologists, most early psychologists were "mentalists" or, as we might call them today, *cognitive* in their orientation. Although William James emphasized "bodily reactions" in his theory of emotions, he did so because he really didn't think very highly of what he considered to be "mere animal passions." At heart, James was a cognitive psychologist. In his famous 1890 textbook, *Principles of Psychology*, he defined *psychology* as "the science of mind." And he defined *mind* as "the sum total of human experience." At about the same time, Wilhelm Wundt (the father of European psychology) stated that the goal of psychology was to determine "the atoms of conscious experience." To determine what these "basic units" of consciousness were, Wundt used a technique called *introspection*, which involved having trained observers try to analyze their own perceptual (or cognitive) processes. James soon adopted introspection too.

By the early 1900's, however, the behaviorists came into power. E. L. Thorndike began using animal subjects in his studies of the learning process, and of course, animals can't "introspect." As we noted in our introduction to Chapter 2, John B. Watson even took the radical step of throwing the concept of *mind* out of psychology entirely. Behaviorists ruled the roost in American psychology until the 1960's, when cognitive psychology slowly began coming back into fashion. But today's "mentalists" are quite a different breed than were Wundt and James. For, instead of using physics as their guide, many cognitive psychologists (such as George Miller) have adopted the *computer* as "a model of the mind." And rather than using introspection as a way of dissecting mental processes, today's "mentalists" make use of *information theory*. William James spoke of *stimuli and responses*, and explained mental activities in terms of "thinking" and "reasoning." Miller speaks in terms of *inputs* and *outputs*. And rather than talking about *thinking*, Miller discusses *bits of information*, *channel capacity*, and *information processing*.

Because computers are physical devices, there are *limits* to how much information they can process during any brief period of time. Presuming the mind can be likened to a computer, there must be a physical limit to the mind's capacity to process information as well, since all mental activities are a reflection of neural (physical) activity in the brain. After surveying the literature, Miller suggests that the mind/brain can store only *seven* items in Short-term Memory at once.

As computers have "wormed their way" into daily life in America, cognitive psychology has gained strength and respectability. Indeed, it is now at least as dominant a force as it was during the era of Wundt and James. Whether or not the comparison of the "mind" to a "computer" is a valid one, however, remains to be seen. Radical behaviorists (such as B.F. Skinner) tend to dismiss such theorizing out of hand, and many psychologists believe the comparison of the mind to an "information processing system" robs humans of their special dignity. But by emphasizing the importance of the *interaction* of biological, intra-psychic, and environmental factors, information theory does offer a more useful solution to the mind-body problem than do older approaches.

Whatever the case, there is little doubt that Miller's article "The magical number seven plus or minus two" is one of the main foundations on which modern-day cognitive psychology was built.

My problem is that I have been persecuted by an integer. For seven years this number has followed me around, has intruded in my most private data, and has assaulted me from the pages of our most public journals. This number assumes a variety of disguises, being sometimes a little larger and sometimes a little smaller than usual, but never changing so much as to be unrecognizable. The persistence with which this number plagues me is far more than a random accident. There is, to quote a famous senator, a design behind it, some pattern governing its appearances. Either there really is something unusual about the number or else I am suffering from delusions of persecution.

I shall begin my case history by telling you about some experiments that tested how accurately people can assign numbers to the magnitudes of various aspects of a stimulus. In the traditional language of psychology these would be called experiments in absolute judgment. Historical accident, however, has decreed that they should have another name. We now call them experiments on the capacity of people to transmit information. Since these experiments would not have been done without the appearance of **information theory** on the psychological scene, and since the results are analyzed in terms of the concepts of information theory, I shall have to preface my discussion with a few remarks about this theory.

INFORMATION MEASUREMENT

The "amount of information" is exactly the same concept that we have talked about for years under the name of "variance." The equations are different, but if we hold tight to the idea that anything that increases the variance also increases the amount of information we cannot go far astray.

The advantages of this new way of talking about variance are simple enough. Variance is always stated in terms of the unit of measurement—inches, pounds, volts, etc.—whereas the amount of information is a dimensionless quantity. Since the information in a **discrete statistical distribution** does not depend upon the unit of measurement, we can extend the concept to situations where we have no **metric** and we would not ordinarily think of using the variance. And it also enables us to compare results obtained in quite different experimental situations where it would be meaningless to compare variances based on different metrics. So there are some good reasons for adopting the newer concept.

The similarity of variance and amount of information might be explained this way: When we have a large variance, we are very ignorant about what is going to happen. If we are very ignorant, then when we make the observation it gives us a lot of information. On the other hand, if the variance is very small, we know in advance how our observations must come out, so we get little information from making the observation.

If you will now imagine a communication system, you will realize that there is a great deal of variability about what goes into the system and also a great deal of variability about what comes out. The input and the output can therefore be described in terms of their variance (or their information). If it is a good communication system, however, there must be some systematic relation between what goes in and what comes out. That is to say, the output will depend upon the input, or will be correlated with the input. If we measure this correlation, then we can say how much of the output variance is attributable to the input and how much is due to random fluctuations or "noise" introduced by the system during transmission. So we see that the measure of transmitted information is simply a measure of the input-output correlation.

There are two simple rules to follow. Whenever I refer to "amount of information," you will understand "variance." And whenever I refer to "amount of transmitted information," you will understand "**covariance**" or "correlation."

The situation can be described graphically by two partially overlapping circles. Then the left circle can be taken to represent the variance of the input, the right circle the variance of the output, and the overlap the covariance of input and output. I shall speak of the left circle as the amount of input information, the right circle as the amount of output information, and the overlap as the amount of transmitted information.

Information theory. There are several different psychological theories that attempt to explain how human beings *perceive* the world, one of which is called *information theory*. According to this viewpoint, the nervous system receives sensory information (called "inputs") from the outside world, processes this information, and then produces "outputs," usually in the form of behavioral responses. Information itself is often measured in terms of *bits*. A "bit" is the amount of information needed to reduce uncertainty by 50 percent. When you flip a coin, your uncertainty is 50 percent, because there are two equally-likely outcomes: heads, or tails. Therefore, by definition, once the coin lands, your uncertainty has been reduced by 50 percent. A coin-flipping situation then contains one bit of information; so does an on-off switch.

Discrete statistical distribution. A distribution of real scores, such as the heights of all the students at a particular school. The *shape* of the distribution of heights (i.e., the "curve") would be the same whether you measured the students in inches, centimeters, or "hands" (the metric often used to measure the height of horses).

Metric. A system of measurement, such as feet and inches or meters and centimeters.

Covariance (KOH-vair-ee-ants). Literally, *correlated variance*, or two sets of scores that tend to vary in a related manner. For example, in humans height and weight have a high covariance, because taller people tend to weigh more than do shorter people.

In the experiments on absolute judgment, the observer is considered to be a communication channel. Then the left circle would represent the amount of information in the stimuli, the right circle the amount of information in his responses, and the overlap the stimulus-response correlation as measured by the amount of transmitted information. The experimental problem is to increase the amount of input information and to measure the amount of transmitted information. If the observer's absolute judgments are quite accurate, then nearly all of the input information will be transmitted and will be recoverable from his responses. If he makes errors, then the transmitted information may be considered less than the input. We expect that, as we increase the amount of input information, the observer will begin to make more and more errors; we can test the limits of accuracy of his absolute judgments. If the human observer is a reasonable kind of communication system, then when we increase the amount of input information the transmitted information will increase at first and will eventually level off at some **asymptotic** value. This asymptotic value we take to be the *channel capacity* of the observer: it represents the greatest amount of information that he can give us about the stimulus on the basis of an absolute judgment. The channel capacity is the upper limit on the extent to which the observer can match his responses to the stimuli we give him.

Now just a brief word about the *bit* and we can begin to look at some data. One bit of information is the amount of information that we need to make a decision between two equally likely alternatives. If we must decide whether a man is less than six feet tall or more than six feet tall and if we know that the chances are 50-50, then we need one bit of information. Notice that this unit of information does not refer in any way to the unit of length that we use—feet, inches, centimeters, etc. However you measure the man's height, we still need just one bit of information.

Two bits of information enable us to decide among four equally likely alternatives. Three bits of information enable us to decide among eight equally likely alternatives. Four bits of information decide among 16 alternatives, five among 32, and so on. That is to say, if there are 32 equally likely alternatives, we must make five successive binary decisions, worth one bit each, before we know which alternative is correct. So the general rule is simple: every time the number of alternatives is increased by a factor of two, one bit of information is added.

There are two ways we might increase the amount of input information. We could increase the rate at which we give information to the observer, so that the amount of information per unit of time would increase.

Or we could ignore the time variable completely and increase the amount of input information by increasing the number of alternative stimuli. In the absolute judgment experiment we are interested in the second alternative. We give the observer as much time as he wants to make his response; we simply increase the number of alternative stimuli among which he must discriminate and look to see where confusions begin to occur. Confusions will appear near the point that we are calling his "channel capacity."

ABSOLUTE JUDGMENTS OF UNIDIMENSIONAL STIMULI

Now let us consider what happens when we make absolute judgments of tones. Pollack (17) asked listeners to identify tones by assigning numerals to them. The tones were different with respect to frequency, and covered the range from 100 to 8000 **cps** in equal **logarithmic** steps. A tone was sounded and the listener responded by giving a numeral. After the listener had made his response he was told the correct identification of the tone.

When only two or three tones were used the listeners never confused them. With four different tones confusions were quite rare, but with five or more tones confusions were frequent. With fourteen different tones the listeners made many mistakes.

These data are plotted in Fig. 1. Along the bottom is the amount of input information in bits per stimulus. As the number of alternative tones was increased from 2 to 14, the input information increased from 1 to 3.8 bits. On the **ordinate** is plotted the amount of transmitted information. The transmitted information be-

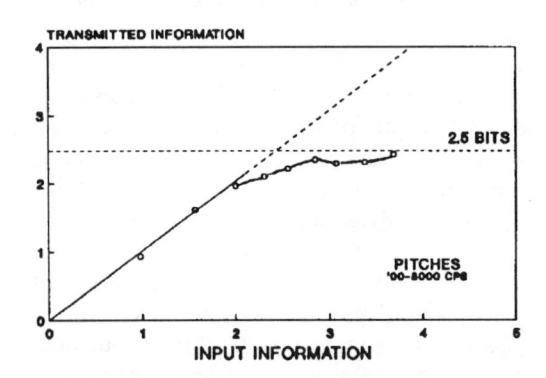

Fig. 1. Data from Pollack (17, 18) on the amount of information that is transmitted by listeners who make absolute judgments of auditory pitch. As the amount of input information is increased by increasing from 2 to 14 the number of different pitches to be judged, the amount of transmitted information approaches as its upper limit a channel capacity of about 2.5 bits per judgment.

haves in much the same way we would expect a communication channel to behave; the transmitted information increases linearly up to about 2 bits and then bends off toward an asymptote at about 2.5 bits. This value, 2.5 bits, therefore, is what we are calling the channel capacity of the listener for absolute judgments of **pitch**.

So now we have the number 2.5 bits. What does it mean? First, note that 2.5 bits corresponds to about six equally likely alternatives. The results mean that we cannot pick more than six different pitches that the listener will never confuse. Or, stated slightly differently, no matter how many alternative tones we ask him to judge, the best we can expect him to do is to assign them to about six different classes without error. Or, again, if we know that there were N alternative stimuli, then his judgment enables us to narrow down the particular stimulus to one out of N/6.

Most people are surprised that the number is as small as six. Of course, there is evidence that a musically sophisticated person with absolute pitch can identify accurately any one of 50 to 60 different pitches. Fortunately, I do not have time to discuss these remarkable exceptions. I say it is fortunate because I do not know how to explain their superior performance. So I shall stick to the more pedestrian fact that most of us can identify about one out of only five or six pitches before we begin to get confused.

It is interesting to consider that psychologists have been using seven-point rating scales for a long time, on the intuitive basis that trying to rate into finer categories does not really add much to the usefulness of the ratings. Pollack's results indicate that, at least for pitches, this intuition is fairly sound,

Next you can ask how reproducible this result is. Does it depend on the spacing of the tones or the various conditions of judgment? Pollack varied these conditions in a number of ways. The range of frequencies can be changed by a factor of about 20 without changing the amount of information transmitted more than a small percentage. Different groupings of the pitches decreased the transmission, but the loss was small. For example, if you can discriminate five high-pitched tones in one series and five low-pitched tones in another series, it is reasonable to expect that you could combine all ten into a single series and still tell them all apart without error. When you try it, however, it does not work. The channel capacity for pitch seems to be about six and that is the best you can do.

While we are on tones, let us look next at Garner's (7) work on loudness. Garner's data for loudness are summarized in Fig. 2. Garner went to some trouble to get the best possible spacing of his tones over the intensity range from 15 to 110 **db**. He used 4, 5, 6, 7, 10, and

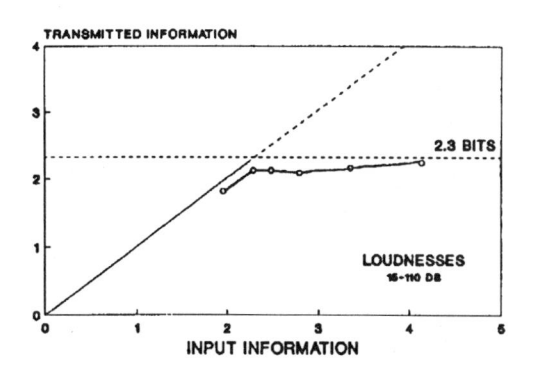

Fig. 2. Data from Garner (7) on the channel capacity for absolute judgments of auditory loudness.

20 different stimulus intensities. The results shown in Fig. 2 take into account the differences among subjects and the sequential influence of the immediately preceding judgment. Again we find that there seems to be a limit. The channel capacity for absolute judgments of loudness is 2.3 bits, or about five perfectly discriminable alternatives.

Since these two studies were done in different laboratories with slightly different techniques and methods of analysis, we are not in a good position to argue whether five loudnesses is significantly different from six pitches. Probably the difference is in the right direction, and absolute judgments of pitch are slightly more accurate than absolute judgments of loudness. The important point, however, is that the two answers are of the same order of magnitude.

The experiment has also been done for taste intensities. In Fig. 3 are the results obtained by Beebe-Center, Rogers, and O'Connell (1) for absolute judgments of the concentration of salt solutions. The concentrations ranged from 0.3 to 34.7 **gm.** **NaCl** per 100 **cc.** tap water in equal subjective steps. They used 3, 5, 9, and 17

Asymptotic (ass-sim-TOT-ick, or A-sim-tot-ick). Consider what happens when you step on the gas in an automobile. The curve describing how fast the car is going at any instant in time rises rapidly at first. However the *increase* in speed tends to flatten out fairly quickly as you approach the fastest speed at which the car can go. Technically speaking, you have now reached the *asymptote* (ASS-sim-tote) of the speed curve.

Cps. Cycles per second, now called Hertz (abbreviated Hz.).

Logarithmic (log-ah-ryth-mick). A way of plotting an exponential curve as a straight line.

Ordinate (OR-dih-nate). The Y-axis of a graph.

Pitch. The apparent "highness" or "lowness" of a musical tone.

Db. The abbreviation for a decibel (DESS-ih-bel). A decibel is a unit for expressing the relative loudness of sounds.

Gm. The abbreviation for a gram. A gram is a unit of weight.

NaCl. The chemical symbol for table salt.

Cc. Cubic centimeters, a measure of volume.

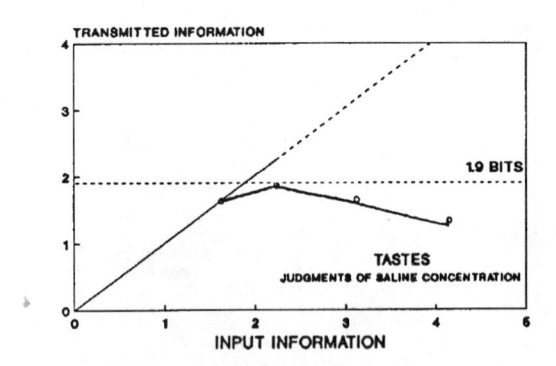

Fig. 3. Data from Beebe-Center, Rogers, and O'Connell (1) on the channel capacity for absolute judgments of saltiness.

different concentrations. The channel capacity is 1.9 bits, which is about four distinct concentrations. Thus taste intensities seem a little less distinctive than auditory stimuli, but again the order of magnitude is not far off.

On the other hand, the channel capacity for judgments of visual position seems to be significantly larger. Hake and Garner (8) asked observers to **interpolate** visually between two scale markers. Their results are shown in Fig. 4. They did the experiment in two ways. In one version they let the observer use any number between 0 and 100 to describe the position, although they presented stimuli at only 5, 10, 20, or 50 different positions. The results with this unlimited response technique are shown by the filled circles on the graph. In the other version the observers were limited in their responses to reporting just those stimulus values that were possible. That is to say, in the second version the number of different responses that the observer could make was exactly the same as the number of different stimuli that the experimenter might present. The results with this limited response technique are shown by the open circles on the graph. The two functions are so similar that it seems fair to conclude that the number of responses available to the observer had nothing to do with the channel capacity of 3.25 bits.

The Hake-Garner experiment has been repeated by Coonan and Klemmer. Although they have not yet published their results, they have given me permission to say that they obtained channel capacities ranging from 3.2 bits for very short exposures of the pointer position to 3.9 bits for longer exposures. These values are slightly higher than Hake and Garner's, so we must conclude that there are between 10 and 15 distinct positions along a linear interval. This is the largest channel capacity that has been measured for any **unidimensional** variable.

At the present time these four experiments on absolute judgments of simple, unidimensional stimuli are all that have appeared in the psychological journals. However, a great deal of work on other stimulus variables has not yet appeared in the journals. For example, Eriksen and Hake (6) have found that the channel capacity for judging the sizes of squares is 2.2 bits, or about five categories, under a wide range of experimental conditions. In a separate experiment Eriksen (5) found 2.8 bits for size, 3.1 bits for hue, and 2.3 bits for brightness. Geldard has measured the channel capacity for the skin by placing vibrators on the chest region. A good observer can identify about four intensities, about five durations, and about seven locations.

One of the most active groups in this area has been the Air Force Operational Applications Laboratory. Pollack has been kind enough to furnish me with the results of their measurements for several aspects of visual displays. They made measurements for area and for the curvature, length, and direction of lines. In one set of experiments they used a very short exposure of the stimulus — 1/40 second — and then they repeated the measurements with a 5-second exposure. For area they got 2.6 bits with the short exposure and 2.7 bits with the long exposure. For the length of a line they got about 2.6 bits with the short exposure and about 3.0 bits with the long exposure. Direction, or angle of inclination, gave 2.8 bits for the short exposure and 3.3 bits for the long exposure. Curvature was apparently harder to judge. When the length of the arc was constant, the result at the short exposure duration was 2.2 bits, but when the length of the chord was constant, the result was only 1.6 bits. This last value is the lowest that anyone has measured to date. I should add, however, that these values are apt to be slightly too low because the data from all subjects were pooled before the transmitted information was computed.

Now let us see where we are. First, the channel capacity does seem to be a valid notion for describing human observers. Second, the channel capacities

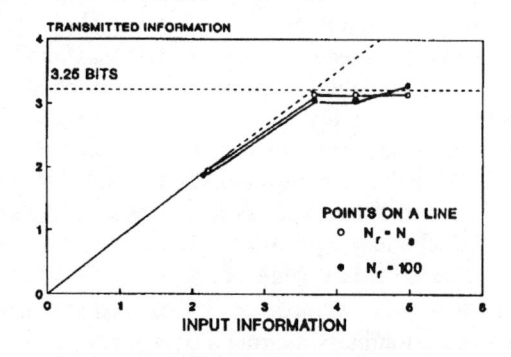

Fig. 4. Data from Hake and Garner (8) on the channel capacity for absolute judgments of the position of a pointer in a linear interval.

measured for these unidimensional variables range from 1.6 bits for curvature to 3.9 bits for positions in an interval. Although there is no question that the differences among the variables are real and meaningful, the more impressive fact to me is their considerable similarity. If I take the best estimates I can get of the channel capacities for all the stimulus variables I have mentioned, the mean is 2.6 bits and the standard deviation is only 0.6 bit. In terms of distinguishable alternatives, this mean corresponds to about 6.5 categories, one standard deviation includes from 4 to 10 categories, and the total range is from 3 to 15 categories. Considering the wide variety of different variables that have been studied, I find this to be a remarkably narrow range.

There seems to be some limitation built into us either by learning or by the design of our nervous systems, a design that keeps our channel capacities in this general range. On the basis of the present evidence it seems safe to say that we possess a finite and rather small capacity for making such unidimensional judgments and that this capacity does not vary a great deal from one simple sensory attribute to another.

ABSOLUTE JUDGMENTS OF MULTIDIMENSIONAL STIMULI

You may have noticed that I have been careful to say that this magical number seven applies to one-dimensional judgments. Everyday experience teaches us that we can identify accurately any one of several hundred faces, any one of several thousand words, any one of several thousand objects, etc. The story certainly would not be complete if we stopped at this point. We must have some understanding of why the one-dimensional variables we judge in the laboratory give results so far out of line with what we do constantly in our behavior outside the laboratory. A possible explanation lies in the number of independently variable attributes of the stimuli that are being judged. Objects, faces, words, and the like differ from one another in many ways, whereas the simple stimuli we have considered thus far differ from one another in only one respect.

Fortunately, there are a few data on what happens when we make absolute judgments of stimuli that differ from one another in several ways. Let us look first at the results Klemmer and Frick (13) have reported for the absolute judgment of the position of a dot in a square. In Fig. 5 we see their results. Now the channel capacity seems to have increased to 4.6 bits, which means that people can identify accurately any one of 24 positions in the square.

The position of a dot in a square is clearly a two-dimensional proposition. Both its horizontal and its

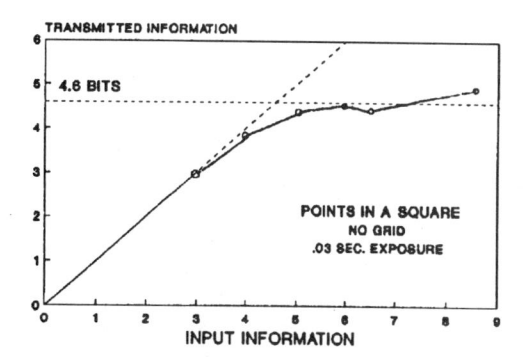

Fig. 5. Data from Klemmer and Frick (13) on the channel capacity for absolute judgments of the position of a dot in a square.

vertical position must be identified. Thus it seems natural to compare the 4.6-bit capacity for a square with the 3.25-bit capacity for the position of a point in an interval. The point in the square requires two judgments of the interval type. If we have a capacity of 3.25 bits for estimating intervals and we do this twice, we should get 6.5 bits as our capacity for locating points in a square. Adding the second independent dimension gives us an increase from 3.25 to 4.6, but it falls short of the perfect addition that would give 6.5 bits.

Another example is provided by Beebe-Center, Rogers, and O'Connell. When they asked people to identify both the saltiness and the sweetness of solutions containing various concentrations of salt and sucrose, they found that the channel capacity was 2.3 bits. Since the capacity for salt alone was 1.9, we might expect about 3.8 bits if the two aspects of the compound stimuli were judged independently. As with spatial locations, the second dimension adds a little to the capacity but not as much as it conceivably might.

A third example is provided by Pollack (18), who asked listeners to judge both the loudness and the pitch of pure tones. Since pitch gives 2.5 bits and loudness gives 2.3 bits, we might hope to get as much as 4.8 bits for pitch and loudness together. Pollack obtained 3.1 bits, which again indicates that the second dimension augments the channel capacity but not so much as it might.

A fourth example can be drawn from the work of Halsey and Chapanis (9) on confusions among colors of equal **luminance**. Although they did not analyze their results in informational terms, they estimate that there are about 11 to 15 identifiable colors, or, in our terms,

---

Interpolate. To estimate the values between two known values.
Unidimensional. Having only one dimension.
Luminance (loom-in-ants). The intensity of light from a given surface.

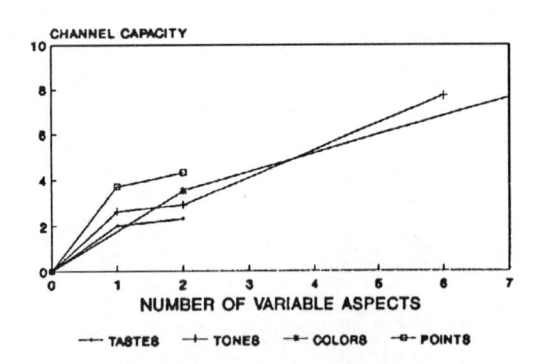

Fig. 6. The general form of the relation between channel capacity and the number of independently variable attributes of the stimuli.

about 3.6 bits. Since these colors varied in both **hue** and **saturation**, it is probably correct to regard this as a two-dimensional judgment. If we compare this with Eriksen's 3.1 bits for hue (which is a questionable comparison to draw), we again have something less than perfect addition when a second dimension is added.

It is still a long way, however, from these two-dimensional examples to the **multidimensional** stimuli provided by faces, words, etc. To fill this gap we have only one experiment, an auditory study done by Pollack and Ficks (19). They managed to get six different acoustic variables that they could change: frequency, intensity, rate of interruption, on-time fraction, total duration, and spatial location. Each one of these six variables could assume any one of five different values, so altogether there were 5^6, or 15,625 different tones that they could present. The listeners make a separate rating for each one of these six dimensions. Under these conditions the transmitted information was 7.2 bits, which corresponds to about 150 different categories that could be absolutely identified without error. Now we are beginning to get up into the range that ordinary experience would lead us to expect.

Suppose that we plot these data, fragmentary as they are, and make a guess about how the channel capacity changes with the dimensionality of the stimuli. The result is given in Fig. 6. In a moment of considerable daring I sketched the dotted line to indicate roughly the trend that the data seemed to be taking.

Clearly, the addition of independently variable attributes to the stimulus increases the channel capacity, but at a decreasing rate. It is interesting to note that the channel capacity is increased even when the several variables are not independent. Eriksen (5) reports that, when size, brightness, and hue all vary together in perfect correlation, the transmitted information is 4.1 bits as compared with an average of about 2.7 bits when these attributes are varied one at a time. By **confounding** three attributes, Eriksen increased the dimensionality of the input without increasing the amount of input information; the result was an increase in channel capacity of about the amount that the dotted function in Fig. 6 would lead us to expect.

The point seems to be that, as we add more variables to the display, we increase the total capacity, but we decrease the accuracy for any particular variable. In other words, we can make relatively crude judgments of several things simultaneously.

We might argue that in the course of evolution those organisms were most successful that were responsive to the widest range of stimulus energies in their environment. In order to survive in a constantly fluctuating world, it was better to have a little information about a lot of things than to have a lot of information about a small segment of the environment. If a compromise was necessary, the one we seem to have made is clearly the more adaptive.

Pollack and Fick's results are very strongly suggestive of an argument that linguists and phoneticians have been making for some time (11). According to the **linguistic** analysis of the sound of human speech, there are about eight or ten dimensions—the linguists call them *distinctive features*—that distinguish one **phoneme** from another. These distinctive features are usually **binary**, or at most **ternary**, in nature. For example, a binary distinction is made between vowels and consonants, a binary decision is made between oral and nasal consonants, a ternary decision is made among front, middle, and back phonemes, etc. This approach gives us quite a different picture of speech perception than we might otherwise obtain from our studies of the speech spectrum and of the ear's ability to discriminate relative differences among pure tones. I am personally much interested in this new approach (15), and I regret that there is not time to discuss it here.

It was probably with this linguistic theory in mind that Pollack and Ficks conducted a test on a set of tonal stimuli that varied in eight dimensions, but required only a binary decision on each dimension. With these tones they measured the transmitted information at 6.9 bits, or about 120 recognizable kinds of sounds. It is an intriguing question, as yet unexplored, whether one can go on adding dimensions indefinitely in this way.

In human speech there is clearly a limit to the number of dimensions that we use. In this instance, however, it is not known whether the limit is imposed by the nature of the perceptual machinery that must recognize the sounds or by the nature of the speech machinery that must produce them. Somebody will have to do the experiment to find out. There is a limit, however, at about eight or nine distinctive features in every language that has been studied, and so when we talk we must resort to still another trick for increasing our channel capacity. Language uses sequences of phonemes, so we make several judgments successively when we listen to words and sentences. That is to say, we use both simultaneous and successive discriminations in order to expand the rather rigid limits imposed by the inaccuracy of our absolute judgments of simple magnitudes.

These multidimensional judgments are strongly reminiscent of the abstraction experiment of Külpe (14). As you may remember, Külpe showed that observers report more accurately on an attribute for which they are set than on attributes for which they are not set. For example, Chapman (4) used three different attributes and compared the results obtained when the observers were instructed before the **tachistoscopic** presentation with the results obtained when they were not told until after the presentation which one of the three attributes was to be reported. When the instruction was given in advance, the judgments were more accurate. When the instruction was given afterwards, the subjects presumably had to judge all three attributes in order to report on any one of them and the accuracy was correspondingly lower. This is in complete accord with the results we have just been considering, where the accuracy of judgment on each attribute decreased as more dimensions were added. The point is probably obvious, but I shall make it anyhow, that the abstraction experiments did *not* demonstrate that people can judge only one attribute at a time. They merely showed what seems quite reasonable, that people are less accurate if they must judge more than one attribute simultaneously.

Subitizing

I cannot leave this general area without mentioning, however briefly, the experiments conducted at Mount Holyoke College on the discrimination of number (12). In experiments by Kaufman, Lord, Reese, and Vokmann random patterns of dots were flashed on a screen for 1/3 of a second. Anywhere from 1 to more than 200 dots could appear in the pattern. The subject's task was to report how many dots there were.

The first point to note is that on patterns containing up to five or six dots the subjects simply did not make errors. The performance on these small numbers of dots was so different from the performance with more dots that it was given a special name. Below seven the subjects were said to **subitize**; above seven they were said to *estimate*. This is, as you will recognize, what we once optimistically called "the span of attention."

This discontinuity at seven is, of course, suggestive. Is this the same basic process that limits our unidimensional judgments to about seven categories? The generalization is tempting, but not sound in my opinion. The data on number estimates have not been analyzed in informational terms; but on the basis of the published data I would guess that the subjects transmitted something more than four bits of information about the number of dots. Using the same arguments as before, we would conclude that there are about 20 or 30 distinguishable categories of numerousness. This is considerably more information than we would expect to get from a unidimensional display. It is, as a matter of fact, very much like a two-dimensional display. Although the dimensionality of the random dot patterns is not entirely clear, these results are in the same range as Klemmer and Frick's for their two-dimensional display of dots in a square. Perhaps the two dimensions of numerousness are area and density. When the subject can subitize, area and density may not be the significant variables, but when the subject must estimate perhaps they are significant. In any event, the comparison is not so simple as it might seem at first thought.

This is one of the ways in which the magical number seven has persecuted me. Here we have two closely related kinds of experiments, both of which point to the significance of the number seven as a limit on our capacities. And yet when we examine the matter more closely, there seems to be a reasonable suspicion that it is nothing more than a coincidence.

THE SPAN OF IMMEDIATE MEMORY

Let me summarize the situation in this way. There is a clear and definite limit to the accuracy with which we can identify absolutely the magnitude of a unidimen-

---

Hue (rhymes with "few"). The colors of the rainbow or of the visible spectrum.

Saturation (sat-your-RAY-shun). The intensity or richness of a color. Pink is a weak (desaturated) red.

Multidimensional. Having several dimensions.

Confounding. To confuse several things together, or be unable to distinguish among them.

Linguistic (lin-GWIS-tick). The scientific study of language.

Phoneme (FO-neem). The smallest unit of speech, such as "da" or "ba".

Binary. Consisting of two parts.

Ternary. Consisting of three parts.

Tachistoscopic (tah-KISS-tah-SCOPP-ick). A tachistoscope is an apparatus that lets you expose visual stimuli (such as letters, words, or numbers) for a fraction of a second.

Subitize (SOO-bit-tize.). To count precisely.

sional stimulus variable. I would propose to call this limit the *span of absolute judgment*, and I maintain that for unidimensional judgments this span is usually somewhere in the neighborhood of seven. We are not completely at the mercy of this limited span, however, because we have a variety of techniques for getting around it and increasing the accuracy of our judgments. The three most important of these devices are (*a*) to make relative rather than absolute judgments; or, if that is not possible, (*b*) to increase the number of dimensions along which the stimuli can differ; or (*c*) to arrange the task in such a way that we make a sequence of several absolute judgments in a row.

The study of relative judgments is one of the oldest topics in experimental psychology, and I will not pause to review it now. The second device, increasing the dimensionality, we have just considered. It seems that by adding more dimensions and requiring crude, binary, yes-no judgments on each attribute we can extend the span of absolute judgment from seven to at least 150. Judging from our everyday behavior, the limit is probably in the thousands, if indeed there is a limit. In my opinion, we cannot go on compounding dimensions indefinitely. I suspect that there is also a *span of perceptual dimensionality* and that this span is somewhere in the neighborhood of ten, but I must add at once that there is not objective evidence to support this suspicion. This is a question sadly needing experimental exploration.

Concerning the third device, the use of successive judgments, I have quite a bit to say because this device introduces memory as the handmaiden of discrimination. And, since **mnemonic** processes are at least as complex as are perceptual processes, we can anticipate that their interactions will not be easily disentangled.

Suppose that we start by simply extending slightly the experimental procedure that we have been using. Up to this point we have presented a single stimulus and asked the observer to name it immediately thereafter. We can extend this procedure by requiring the observer to withhold his response until we have given him several stimuli in succession. At the end of the sequence of stimuli he then makes his response. We still have the same sort of input-output situation that is required for the measurement of transmitted information. But now we have passed from an experiment on absolute judgment to what is traditionally called an experiment on immediate memory.

Before we look at any data on this topic I feel I must give you a word of warning to help you avoid some obvious associations that can be confusing. Everybody knows that there is a finite span of immediate memory and that for a lot of different kinds of test materials this span is about seven items in length. I have just shown you that there is a span of absolute judgment that can distinguish about seven categories and that there is a span of attention that will encompass about six objects at a glance. What is more natural than to think that all three of these spans are different aspects of a single underlying process? And that is a fundamental mistake, as I shall be at some pains to demonstrate. This mistake is one of the **malicious** persecutions that the magical number seven has subjected me to.

My mistake went something like this. We have seen that the invariant feature in the span of absolute judgment is the amount of information that the observer can transmit. There is a real operational similarity between the absolute judgment experiment and the immediate memory experiment. If immediate memory is like absolute judgment, then it should follow that the invariant feature in the span of immediate memory is also the amount of information that an observer can retain. If the amount of information in the span of immediate memory is a constant, then the span should be short when the individual items contain a lot of information and the span should be long when the items contain little information. For example, decimal digits are worth 3.3 bits apiece. We can recall about seven of them, for a total of 23 bits of information. Isolated English words are worth about 10 bits apiece. If the total amount of information is to remain constant at 23 bits, then we should be able to remember only two or three words chosen at random. In this way I generated a theory about how the span of immediate memory should vary as a function of the amount of information per item in the test materials.

The measurements of memory span in the literature are suggestive on this question, but not definitive. And so it was necessary to do the experiment to see. Hayes (10) tried it out with five different kinds of test materials: binary digits, decimal digits, letters of the alphabet, letters plus decimal digits, and with 1,000 monosyllabic words. The lists were read aloud at the rate of one item per second and the subjects had as much time as they needed to give their responses. A procedure described by Woodworth (20) was used to score the responses.

The results are shown by the filled circles in Fig. 7. Here the dotted line indicates what the span should have been if the amount of information in the span were constant. The solid curves represent the data. Hayes repeated the experiment using test vocabularies of different sizes but all containing only English monosyllables (open circles in Fig. 7). This more **homogeneous** test material did not change the picture significantly. With binary items the span is about nine and, although it drops to about five with monosyllabic English words, the difference is far less than the hypothesis of constant information would require.

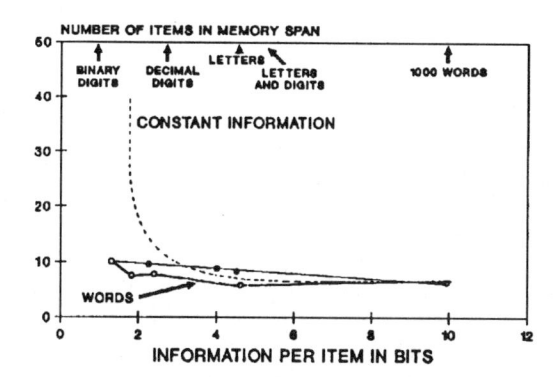

Fig. 7. Data from Hayes (10) on the span of immediate memory plotted as a function of the amount of information per item in the test materials.

There is nothing wrong with Hayes's experiment, because Pollack (16) repeated it much more elaborately and got essentially the same result. Pollack took pains to measure the amount of information transmitted and did not rely on the traditional procedure for scoring the responses. His results are plotted in Fig. 8. Here it is clear that the amount of information transmitted is not a constant, but increases almost linearly as the amount of information per item in the input is increased.

And so the outcome is perfectly clear. In spite of the coincidence that the magical number seven appears in both places, the span of absolute judgment and the span of immediate memory are quite different kinds of limitations that are imposed on our ability to process information. Absolute judgment is limited by the amount of information. Immediate memory is limited by the number of items. In order to capture this distinction in somewhat picturesque terms, I have fallen into the custom of distinguishing between *bits* of information and *chunks* of information. Then I can say that the number of bits of information is constant for absolute judgment and the number of chunks of information is constant for immediate memory. The span of immediate memory seems to be almost independent of the number of bits per chunk, at least over the range that has been examined to date.

The contrast of the terms *bit* and *chunk* also serves to highlight the fact that we are not very definite about what constitutes a chunk of information. For example, the memory span of five words that Hayes obtained when each word was drawn at random from a set of 1000 English monosyllables might just as appropriately have been called a memory span of 15 phonemes in it. Intuitively, it is clear that the subjects were recalling five words, not 15 phonemes, but the logical distinction is not immediately apparent. We are dealing here with a process of organizing or grouping the input into familiar units or chunks, and a great deal of learning has gone into the formation of these familiar units.

Recoding

In order to speak more precisely, therefore, we must recognize the importance of grouping or organizing the input sequence into units or chunks. Since the memory span is a fixed number of chunks, we can increase the number of bits of information that it contains simply by building larger and larger chunks, each chunk containing more information than before.

A man just beginning to learn radio-telegraphic code hears each **dit** and **dah** as a separate chunk. Soon he is able to organize these sounds into letters and then he can deal with the letters as chunks. Then the letters organize themselves as words, which are still larger chunks, and he begins to hear whole phrases. I do not mean that each step is a discrete process, or that plateaus must appear in his learning curve, for surely the levels of organization are achieved at different rates and overlap each other during the learning process. I am simply pointing to the obvious fact that the dits and dahs are organized by learning into patterns and that as these larger chunks emerge the amount of message that the operator can remember increases correspondingly.

> **Mnemonic** (knee-MON-ick). From the Greek word meaning "mindful." A mnemonic is any device or "trick" that helps you remember things.
>
> **Malicious** (ma-LISH-us). Behavior that is intented to harm others.
>
> **Homogeneous** (ho-moh-GEE-knee-us). From the Greek word meaning "same kind." Homogenized milk is made up of both milk and cream that have been mixed together to create a uniform mixture.
>
> **Dit, dah**. In the Morse used by telegraphers, the letters of the alphabet are represented by combinations of "dots" and "dashes." When speaking the code aloud, however, telegraphers usually substitute "dit" for "dot," and "dah" for "dash."

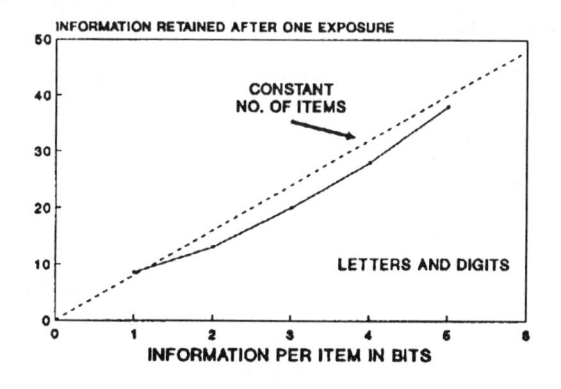

Fig. 8. Data from Pollack (16) on the amount of information retained after one presentation plotted as a function of the amount of information per item in the test materials.

TABLE 1
WAYS OF RECORDING SEQUENCES OF BINARY DIGITS

Binary Digits (Bits)	1 0 1 0 0 0 1 0 0 1 1 1 0 0 1 1 1 0

2:1	Chunks	10	10	00	10	01	11	00	11	10
	Recoding	2	2	0	2	1	3	0	3	2
3:1	Chunks	101	000		100	111		001	110	
	Recoding	5	0		4	7		1	6	
4:1	Chunks	1010		0010		0111		0011		10
	Recoding	10		2		7		3		
5:1	Chunks	10100			01001			11001		110
	Recoding	20			9			25		

In the terms I am proposing to use, the operator learns to increase the bits per chunk.

In the jargon of communication theory, this process would be called *recoding*. The input is given in a code that contains many chunks with few bits per chunk. The operator recodes the input into another code that contains fewer chunks with more bits per chunk. There are many ways to do this recoding, but probably the simplest is to group the input events, apply a new name to the group, and then remember the new name rather than the original input events.

Since I am convinced that this process is a very general and important one for psychology, I want to tell you about a demonstration experiment that should make perfectly explicit what I am talking about. This experiment was conducted by Sidney Smith and was reported by him before the Eastern Psychological Association in 1954.

Begin with the observed fact that people can repeat back eight decimal digits, but only nine binary digits. Since there is a large discrepancy in the amount of information recalled in these two cases, we suspect at once that a recoding procedure could be used to increase the span of immediate memory for binary digits. In Table 1 a method for grouping and renaming is illustrated. Along the top is a sequence of 18 binary digits, far more than any subject was able to recall after a single presentation. In the next line these same binary digits are grouped by pairs. Four possible pairs can occur: 00 is renamed 0, 01 is renamed 1, 10 is renamed 2, and 11 is renamed 3. That is to say, we recode from a base-two arithmetic to a base-four arithmetic. In the recoded sequence there are now just nine digits to remember, and this is almost within the span of immediate memory. In the next line the same sequence of binary digits is regrouped into chunks of three. There are eight possible sequences of three, so we give each sequence a new name between 0 and 7. Now we have recoded from a sequence of 18 binary digits into a sequence of 6 **octal** digits, and this is well within the span of immediate memory. In the last two lines the binary digits are grouped by fours and by fives and are given decimal-digit names from 0 to 15 and from 0 to 31.

It is reasonably obvious that this kind of recoding increases the bits per chunk, and packages the binary sequence into a form that can be retained within the span of immediate memory. So Smith assembled 20 subjects and measured their spans for binary and octal digits. The spans were 9 for binaries and 7 for octals. Then he gave each recoding scheme to five of the subjects. They studied the recoding until they said they understood it—for about 5 or 10 minutes. Then he tested their span for binary digits again while they tried to use the recoding schemes they had studied.

The recoding schemes increased their span for binary digits in every case. But the increase was not as large as we had expected on the basis of their span for octal digits. Since the discrepancy increased as the recoding ratio increased, we reasoned that the few minutes the subjects had spent learning the recoding schemes had not been sufficient. Apparently the translation from one code to the other must be almost automatic or the subject will lose part of the next group while he is trying to remember the translation of the last group.

Since the 4:1 and 5:1 ratios require considerable study, Smith decided to imitate Ebbinghaus and do the experiment on himself. With Germanic patience he

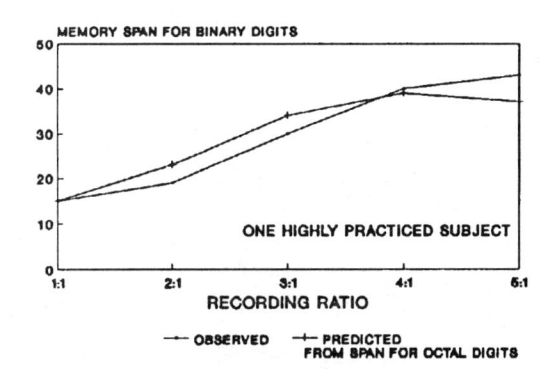

Fig. 9. The span of immediate memory for binary digits is plotted as a function of the recoding procedure used. The predicted function is obtained by multiplying the span for octals by 2, 3 and 2.3 for recoding into base 4, base 8, and base 10, respectively.

drilled himself on each recoding successively, and obtained the results shown in Fig. 9. Here the data follow along rather nicely with the results you would predict on the basis of his span for octal digits. He could remember 12 octal digits. With the 2:1 recoding, these 12 chunks were worth 24 binary digits. With the 3:1 recoding they were worth 36 binary digits. With the 4:1 and 5:1 recodings, they were worth about 40 binary digits.

It is a little dramatic to watch a person get 40 binary digits in a row and then repeat them back without error. However, if you think of this merely as a mnemonic trick for extending the memory span, you will miss the more important point that is implicit in nearly all such mnemonic devices. The point is that recoding is an extremely powerful weapon for increasing the amount of information that we can deal with. In one form or another we use recoding constantly in our daily behavior.

In my opinion the most customary kind of recoding that we do all the time is to translate into a verbal code. When there is a story or an argument or an idea that we want to remember, we usually try to rephrase it "in our own words." When we witness some event we want to remember, we make a verbal description of the event and then remember our verbalization. Upon recall we recreate by secondary elaboration the details that seem consistent with the particular verbal recoding we happen to have made. The well-known experiment by Carmichael, Hogan, and Walter (3) on the influence that names have on the recall of visual figures is one demonstration of the process.

The inaccuracy of the testimony of eyewitnesses is well known in legal psychology, but the distortions of testimony are not random—they follow naturally from the particular recoding that the witness used, and the particular recoding he used depends upon his whole life history. Our language is tremendously useful for repackaging material into a few chunks rich in information. I suspect that imagery is a form of recoding, too, but images seem much harder to get at operationally and to study experimentally than the more symbolic kinds of recoding.

It seems probable that even memorization can be studied in these terms. The process of memorizing may be simply the formation of chunks, or groups of items that go together, until there are few enough chunks so that we can recall all the items. The work by Bousfield and Cohen (2) on the occurrence of clustering in the recall of words is especially interesting in this respect.

SUMMARY

I have come to the end of the data that I wanted to present, so I would like now to make some summarizing remarks.

First, the span of absolute judgment and the span of immediate memory impose severe limitations on the amount of information that we are able to receive, process, and remember. By organizing the stimulus input simultaneously into several dimensions and successively into a sequence of chunks, we manage to break (or at least stretch) this informational bottleneck.

Second, the process of recoding is a very important one in human psychology and deserves much more explicit attention than it has received. In particular, the kind of linguistic recoding that people do seems to me to be the very lifeblood of the thought processes. Recoding procedures are a constant concern to clinicians, social psychologists, linguists, and anthropologists and yet, probably because recoding is less accessible to experimental manipulation than nonsense syllables or **T mazes**, the traditional experimental psychologist has contributed little or nothing to their analysis. Nevertheless, experimental techniques can be used, methods of recoding can be specified, behavioral indicants can be found. And I anticipate that we will find a very orderly set of relations describing what now seems an uncharted wilderness of individual differences.

Third, the concepts and measures provided by the theory of information provide a quantitative way of getting at some of these questions. The theory provides us with a yardstick for calibrating our stimulus materials and for measuring the performance of our subjects. In

---

Octal (OCK-tal). Having to do with the number 8.

T mazes. A maze in the shape of a capital T.

the interests of communication I have suppressed the technical details of information measurement and have tried to express the ideas in more familiar terms; I hope this paraphrase will not lead you to think they are not useful in research. Informational concepts have already proved valuable in the study of discrimination and of language; they promise a great deal in the study of learning and memory; and it has even been proposed that they can be useful in the study of concept formation. A lot of questions that seemed fruitless twenty or thirty years ago may now be worth another look. In fact, I feel that my story here must stop just as it begins to get really interesting.

And finally, what about the magical number seven? What about the seven wonders of the world, the seven seas, the seven deadly sins, the seven daughters of Atlas in the **Pleiades**, the seven ages of man, the seven levels of hell, the seven primary colors, the seven notes of the musical scale, and the seven days of the week? What about the seven-point rating scale, the seven categories for absolute judgment, the seven objects in the span of attention, and the seven digits in the span of immediate memory? For the present I propose to withhold judgment. Perhaps there is something deep and profound behind all these sevens, something just calling out for us to discover it. But I suspect that it is only a **pernicious**, **Pythagorean** coincidence.

FOOTNOTES

[1] Reprinted by permission of the author and the publisher from the *Psychological Review*, 1956, 63, 81-97. Copyright 1956 by the American Psychological Association.

2. This paper was first read as an Invited Address before the Eastern Psychological Association in Philadelphia on April 15, 1955. Preparation of the paper was supported by the Harvard Psycho-Acoustic Laboratory under Control N5ori-76 between Harvard University and the Office of Naval Research, U.S. Navy (Project NR142-201, Report PNR-174). Reproduction for any purpose of the U.S Government is permitted.

REFERENCES

1. BEEBE-CENTER, J.G., ROGERS, M.S., & O'CONNELL, D.N. Transmission of information about sucrose and saline solutions through the sense of taste. *J. Psychol.*, 1955, **39**, 157-160.
2. BOUSFIELD, W.A., & COHEN, B.H. The occurrence of clustering in the recall of randomly arranged words of different frequencies-of-usage. *J. gen. Psychol.*, 1955, **52**, 83-95.
3. CARMICHAEL, L., HOGAN, H.P., & WALTER, A.A. An experimental study of the effect of language on the reproduction of visually perceived form. *J. exp. Psychol.*, 1932, **15**, 73-86.
4. CHAPMAN, D.W. Relative effects of determinate and indeterminate *Aufgaben*. *Amer. J. Psychol.*, 1932, **44**, 163-174.
5. ERIKSEN, C.W. Multidimensional stimulus differences and accuracy of discrimination. *USAF, WADC Tech. Rep.*, 1954, No. 54-165.
6. ERIKSEN, C.W., & HAKE, H.W. Absolute judgments as a function of the stimulus range and the number of stimulus and response categories. *J. exp. Psychol.*, 1955, **49**, 323-332.
7. GARNER, W.R. An informational analysis of absolute judgments of loudness. *J. exp. Psychol.*, 1953, **46**, 373-380.
8. HAKE, H.W., & GARNER, W.R. The effect of presenting various numbers of discrete steps on scale reading accuracy. *J. exp. Psychol.*, 1951, **42**, 358-366.
9. HALSEY, R.M., AND CHAPANIS, A. Chromaticity-confusion contours in a complex viewing situation. *J. Opt. Soc. Amer.*, 1954, **44**, 442-454.
10. HAYES, J.R.M. Memory span for several vocabularies as a function of vocabulary size. In *Quarterly Progress Report*, Cambridge, Mass.: Acoustics Laboratory, Massachusetts Institute of Technology, Jan.-June, 1952.
11. JAKOBSON, R., FANT, C.G.M., & HALLE, M. *Preliminaries to speech analysis.* Cambridge, Mass.: Acoustics Laboratory, Massachusetts Institute of Technology, 1952. (Tech. Rep. No. 13.)
12. KAUFMAN, E.L., LORD, M.W., REESE, T.W., & VOLKMANN, J. The discrimination of visual number. *Amer. J. Psychol.*, 1949, **62**, 498-525.
13. KLEMMER, E.T., & FRICK, F.C. Assimilation of information from dot and matrix patterns. *J. exp. Psychol.*, 1953, **45**, 15-19.
14. Külpe, O. Versuche uber Abstraktion. *Ber. u. d. I Kongr. f. exper. Psychol.*, 1904, 56-68.
15. MILLER, G.A., & NICELY, P.E. An analysis of perceptual confusions among some English consonants. *J. Acoust. Soc. Amer.*, 1955, **27**, 338-352.
16. POLLACK, I. The assimilation of sequentially encoded information. *Amer. J. Psychol.*, 1953, **66**, 421-435.
17. POLLACK, I. The information of elementary auditory displays. *J. Acoust. Soc. Amer.*, 1952, **24**, 745-749.
18. POLLACK, I. The information of elementary auditory displays. II. *J. Acoust. Soc. Amer.*, 1953, **25**, 765-769.

19. POLLACK, I., & FICKS, L. Information of elementary multi-dimensional auditory displays. *J. Acoust. Soc. Amer.,* 1954, **26,** 155-158.
20. WOODWORTH, R.S. *Experimental psychology.* New York: Holt, 1938.

Pleiades (plee-ah-deez). A cluster of stars in the constellation Taurus. In Greek mythology they were the seven daughters of Atlas who turned into stars.

Pernicious (per-nish-us). Harmful or highly injurious.

Pythagorean (pie-thag-oh-REE-an). Pythagoras (pie-THAG-or-us) was a Greek philosopher and mathematician who believed that numbers had mystical properties.

CHAPTER 9

"The Information Available in Brief Visual Presentations"

George Sperling[1,2]

EDITORS' COMMENTS. One of the benefits that came about when some cognitive psychologists embraced the *information theory* approach is this: It prompted them to look at the processes of learning and memory in quite a new light. The study of human learning--that is, the acquisition, retention, and later reproduction of knowledge (or responses)--has a long and honored place in the field of experimental psychology. However, until the late 1950's, most researchers presumed that there was *a* memory "bank" of some kind in which stored items were filed. Thanks to articles such as this one by George Sperling, we now know that there are *many* memory banks, and that information flowing into the nervous system is both temporarily stored and processed at various stages during the input process.

Put simply, the information processing approach holds that sensory stimuli are "translated" into patterns of neural energy by the *sensory receptors*. The incoming information is held briefly (or "remembered") in *sensory registers*, one for each sensory modality. Initial "processing" occurs at this level, and consists primarily of "pattern recognition," or the detection of "unique features" of the input. This is the *sensory information stage* of input processing.

Next, *important information* about the input is transferred to *Short-term Memory*, or what is sometimes called *primary memory*. At this point, you become conscious of the input. After comparing the input with information filed away in long-term memory storage, you decide how to respond to the input.

Finally, if the input is important, you are likely to transfer it to *Long-term Memory*, which is sometimes called *secondary memory*.

Can your eyes actually "remember?" Oddly enough, yes, they can. You can prove this point to yourself if you wish. You and a friend should sit in a dark closet for half an hour or so--to let your eyes adapt to the darkness. Then you should stare directly into your friend's face as someone "pops" a flashbulb closeby. The light will be on for but a fraction of a second. But during that time, an image of your friend's face will be "painted" on your retina. Presuming you remain in complete darkness, this "ghostly image" will confront you for minutes afterwards, no matter where you turn your eyes. If you turn on the closet light, however, the "face image" will almost immediately fade as it is replaced by new visual inputs. (Sixty years ago, experimental psychologists referred to this phenomenon as "Swindell's Ghost.")

Under normal illumination--as Sperling notes--inputs held at the visual information stage of memory are similar to the frames of a motion picture film, where the input you are aware of right now is immediately supplanted by the next frame in the movie. However, if we present *just one frame at a time* under normal illumination, you can "recover" at least some of the information in that frame for a brief period thereafter.

Sperling's research is important for several reasons. First, it offered rather concrete proof that "sensory information storage" did, in fact, take place. Second, his work showed rather clearly how long inputs were actually held in this "memory storehouse," at least at the level of the retina.

We will comment further on the memory process in our introductions to the next several articles.

How much can be seen in a single brief exposure? This is an important problem because our normal mode of seeing greatly resembles a sequence of brief exposures. Erdmann and Dodge (1898) showed that in reading, for example, the eye assimilates information only in the brief pauses between its quick **saccadic** movements. The problem of what can be seen in one brief exposure, however, remains unsolved. The difficulty is that the simple expedient of instructing the observer of a single brief exposure to report what he has just seen is inadequate. When complex stimuli consisting of a number of letters are **tachistoscopically** presented, observers **enigmatically** insist that they have seen more than they can remember afterwards, that is, report afterwards.[3] The apparently simple question: "What did you see?" requires the observer to report both what he remembers and what he has forgotten.

The statement that *more is seen than can be remembered* implies two things. First, it implies a memory limit, that is, limit on the (memory) report. Such a limit on the number of items which can be given in the report following any brief stimulation has, in fact, been generally observed; it is called the span of attention, apprehension, or immediate memory (cf. Miller, 1956b). Second, *to see more than is remembered* implies that more information is available during, and perhaps for a short time after, the stimulus than can be reported. The considerations about available information are quite similar, whether the information is available for an hour (as it is in a book that is borrowed for an hour), or whether the information is available for only a fraction of a second (as in a stimulus which is exposed for only a fraction of a second). In either case it is quite probable that for a limited period of time more information will be available than can be reported. It is also true that initially, in both examples, the information is available to vision.

In order to circumvent the memory limitation in determining the information that becomes available following a brief exposure, it is obvious that the observer must not be required to give a report which exceeds his memory span. If the number of letters in the stimulus exceeds his memory span, then he cannot give a whole report of all the letters. Therefore, the observer must be required to give only a partial report of the stimulus contents. Partial reporting of available information is, of course, just what is required by ordinary schoolroom examinations and by other methods of sampling available information.

An examiner can determine, even in a short test, approximately how much the student knows. The length of the test is not so important as that the student not be told the test questions too far in advance. Similarly, an observer may be "tested" on what he has seen in a brief exposure of a complex visual stimulus. Such a test requires only a partial report. The specific instruction which indicates which part of the stimulus is to be reported is then given only after termination of the stimulus. On each trial the instruction, which calls for a specified part of the stimulus, is randomly chosen from a set of possible instructions which cover the whole stimulus. By repeating the interrogation (sampling) procedure many times, many different random samples can be obtained of an observer's performance on each of the various parts of the stimulus. The data obtained thereby make feasible the estimate of the total information that was available to the observer from which to draw his report on the average trial.

The time at which the instruction is given determines the time at which available information is sampled. By suitable coding, the instruction may be given at any time: before, during, or after the stimulus presentation. Not only the available information immediately following the termination of the stimulus, but a continuous function relating the amount of information available to the time of instruction may be obtained by such a procedure.

Many studies have been conducted in which observers were required to give partial reports, that is, to report only on one aspect or one location of the stimulus. In prior experiments, however, the instructions were often not randomly chosen, and the set of possible instructions did not systematically cover the stimulus. The notions of testing or sampling were not applied.[4] It is not surprising, therefore, that estimates have not been made of the total information available to the observer following a brief exposure of a complex stimulus. Furthermore, instructions have generally not been coded in such a way as to make it possible to control the precise time at which they were presented. Consequently, the **temporal** course of available information could not have been **quantitatively** studied. In the absence of precise data, experimenters have all too

---

Saccadic (sah-KAD-ick). Saccadic movements are the small rapid jerky movements your eye makes as it jumps from fixation on one point to another (as in reading).

Tachistoscopically (tah-kiss-tah-SCOP-ih-klee). The tachistoscope (tak-KISS-tah-scope) is a device used to present visual stimuli for very short durations (such as 0.1 sec.).

Enigmatically (ee-nig-MATT-ih-klee). From the Greek work meaning "to speak in riddles." To speak enigmatically is to speak in a puzzling or obscure manner.

Temporal (TEM-pore-al). Temporal refers to time.

Quantitatively (KWANT-ih-tate-iv-lee). Quantitative study involves the *measurement* of quantity or amount. Qualitative study involves the subjective, non-measureable aspects of human experience. Weight loss may be studied quantitatively, since you can measure how much a person weighs. The subjects' *feelings* about their weight loss would be studied qualitatively, primarily by asking the subjects what their feelings were.

frequently assumed that the time for which information is available to the observer corresponds exactly to the physical stimulus duration. Wundt (1899) understood this problem and convincingly argued that, for extremely short stimulus durations, the assumption that stimulus duration corresponded to the duration for which stimulus information was available was blatantly false, but he made no measurements of available information.

The following experiments were conducted to study quantitatively the information that becomes available to an observer following a brief exposure. Lettered stimuli were chosen because these contain a relatively large amount of information per item and because these are the kind of stimuli that have been used by most previous investigators. The first two experiments are essentially control experiments; they attempt to confirm that immediate-memory for letters is independent of the **parameters** of stimulation, that it is an individual characteristic. In the third experiment the number of letters available immediately after the extinction of the stimulus is determined by means of the sampling (partial report) procedure described above. The fourth experiment explores decay of available information with time. The fifth experiment examines some exposure parameters. In the sixth experiment a technique which fails to demonstrate a large amount of available information is investigated. The seventh experiment deals with the role of the historically important variable: order of report.

GENERAL METHOD

Apparatus. The experiments utilized a Gerbrands tachistoscope.[5] This is a two-field, mirror tachistoscope (Dodge, 1907b), with a mechanical timer. Viewing is binocular, at a distance of about 24 inches. Throughout the experiment, a dimly illuminated fixation field was always present.

The light source in the Gerbrands tachistoscope is a 4-watt fluorescent (daylight) bulb. Two such lamps operated in parallel light each field. The operation of the lamps is controlled by the microswitches, the steady-state light output of the lamp being directly proportional to the current. However, the phosphors used in coating the lamp continue to emit light for some time after the cessation of the current. This afterglow in the lamp follows an **exponential** decay function consisting of two parts: the first, a blue component, which accounts for about 40% of the energy, decays with a time constant which is a small fraction of a millisecond; the decay constant of the second, yellow, component was about 15 msec. in the lamp tested. Fig. 1 illustrates a 50-msec. light impulse on a linear intensity scale. The exposure time of 50 msec. was used in all experiments unless exposure time was itself a parameter. Preliminary experiments indicated that, with the presentations used, exposure duration was an unimportant parameter. Fifty msec. was sufficiently short so that eye movements during the exposure were rare, and it could conveniently be set with accuracy.

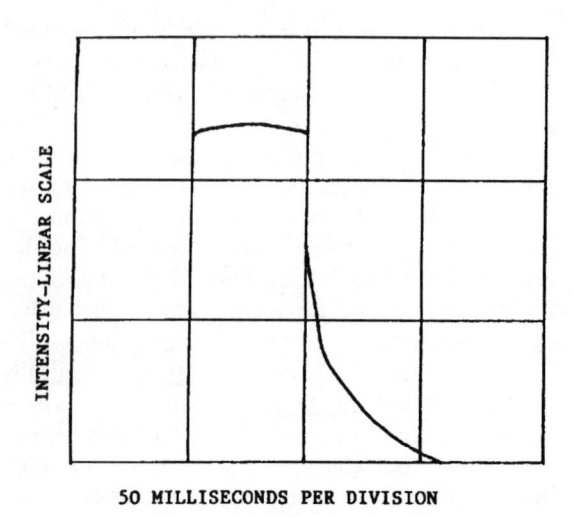

Fig. 1. A 50-millisecond light flash, such as was used in most of the experiments. (Redrawn from a photograph of an oscilloscope trace.)

Stimulus materials. The stimuli used in this experiment were lettered 5x8 cards viewed at a distance of 22 inches. The lettering was done with a Leroy No. 5 pen, producing capital letters about 0.45 inch high. Only the 21 consonants were used, to minimize the possibility of Ss interpreting the arrays as words. In a few sets of cards the letter Y was also omitted. In all, over 500 different stimulus cards were used.

There was very little learning of the stimulus materials either by the Ss or by the E. The only learning that was readily apparent was on several stimuli that had especially striking letter combinations. Except for the stimuli used for training, no S ever was required to report the same part of any stimulus more than two or three times, and never in the same session.

Figure 2 illustrates some typical arrays of letters. These arrays may be divided into several categories: (a) stimuli with

Fig. 2. Typical stimulus materials. Col. 1: 3, 5, 6, 6-massed. Col. 2: 3/3, 4/4, 3/3/3, 4/4/4 L&N.

3, 4, 5, 6, or 7 letters normally spaced on a single line; (b) stimuli with six letters closely spaced on a single line (6-massed); (c) stimuli having two rows of letters with three letters in each row (3/3), or two rows of four letters each (4/4); (d) stimuli having three rows of letters with three letters in each row (3/3/3). The stimulus information, calculated in **bits**, for some of the more complex stimuli is 26.4 bits (6-letters, 6-massed, 3/3), 35.1 bits (4/4), and 39.5 bits (3/3/3).

In addition to stimuli that contained only letters, some stimuli that contained both letters and numbers were used. These had eight (4/4 L&N, 35.7 bits) and twelve symbols (4/4/4 L&N, 53.6 bits), respectively, four in each row. Each row had two letters and two numbers--the positions being randomly chosen. The S was always given a sample stimulus before L&N stimuli were used and told of the constraint above. He was also told that O when it occurred was the number "zero" and was not considered a letter. Calculated with these constraints, the information in each row of four letters and numbers (17.9 bits) on such a card is nearly equal to the information in a row of four randomly chosen consonants (17.6 bits), even though there are different kinds of alternatives in each case.

Subjects. The nature of the experiments made it more economical to use small numbers of trained Ss rather than several large groups of untrained Ss. Four of the five Ss in the experiment were obtained through the student employment service. The fifth S (RNS) was a member of the faculty who was interested in the research. Twelve sessions were regularly scheduled for each S, three times weekly.

Instructions and trial procedures. S was instructed to look at the fixation cross until it was clearly in focus; then he pressed a button which initiated the presentation after a 0.5-sec. delay. This procedure constituted an approximate behavioral criterion of the degree of dark adaptation prior to the exposure, namely, the ability to focus on the dimly illuminated fixation cross.

Responses were recorded on a specially prepared response grid. A response grid appropriate to each stimulus was supplied. The response grid was placed on the table immediately below the tachistoscope, the room illumination being sufficient to write by. The Ss were instructed to fill in all the required squares on the response grid and to guess when they were not certain. The Ss were not permitted to fill in consecutive X's, but were required to guess "different letters." After a response, S slid the paper forward under a cover which covered his last response, leaving the next part of the response grid fully in view.

Series of 5 to 20 trials were grouped together without a change in conditions. Whenever conditions or stimulus types were changed, S was given two or three sample presentations with the new conditions or stimuli. Within a sequence of trials, S set his own rate of responding. The Ss (except ND) preferred rapid rates. In some conditions, the limiting rate was set by the E's limitations in changing stimuli and instruction tones. This was about three to four stimuli per minute.

Each of the first four and last two sessions began with and/or ended with a simple task: the reporting of all the letters in stimuli of 3, 4, 5, and 6 letters. This procedure was undertaken in addition to the usual runs with these stimuli to determine if there were appreciable learning effects in these tasks during the course of the experiment and if there was an accuracy decrement (fatigue) within individual sessions. Very little improvement was noted after the second session. This observation agrees with previous reports (Whipple, 1914). There was little difference between the beginning and end of sessions.

Scoring and tabulation of results. Every report of all Ss was scored both for total number of letters in the report which agreed with letters in the stimulus and for the number of letters reported in their correct positions. Since none of the procedures of the experiments had an effect on either of these scores independently of the other, only the second of these, *letters in the correct position*, is tabulated in the results. This score, which takes position into account, is less subject to guessing error,[6] and in some cases it is more readily interpreted than a score which does not take position into account. As the maximum correction for guessing would be about 0.4 letter for the 4/4/4 (12-letter) material--and considerably less for all other materials--no such correction is made in the treatment of the data. In general, data were not tabulated more accurately than 0.1 letter.

Data from the first and second sessions were not used if they fell below an Ss average performance on these tasks in subsequent sessions. This occurred for reports of five and of eight (4/4) letters for some Ss. A similar criterion applied in later sessions for tasks that were initiated later. In this case, the results of the first training session(s) are not incorporated in the total tabulation if they lie more than 0.5 letter from Ss average in subsequent sessions.

Experiment 1: Immediate-Memory

When an S is required to give a complete (whole) report of all the letters on a briefly exposed stimulus, he will generally not report all the letters correctly. The average number of letters which he does report correctly is usually called his *immediate-memory span or span of apprehension for that particular stimulus material under the stated observation conditions*. An expression such as immediate-memory span (Miller, 1956a) implies that the number of items reported by S remains invariant with changes in stimulating conditions. The present experiment seeks to determine to what extent the span of immediate-memory is independent of the number and spatial arrangement of letters, and of letters and numbers on stimulus cards. If this independence is demonstrated, then the qualification "for that particular stimulus material" may be dropped from

---

Parameters (pah-RAM-eh-ters). A parameter is any of a set of physical properties whose values determine the characteristics or behavior of something. How much of a given stimulus the experimenter asks the subject to report on would be one parameter of a study such as this one.

Exponential (ex-pohn-NEN-schull). When you write a² the 2 is an exponent. An exponential curve is one that typically increases (or decreases) at a rapid pace.

Bits. The smallest amount of information available. That amount of information required to reduce uncertainty by 50 percent.

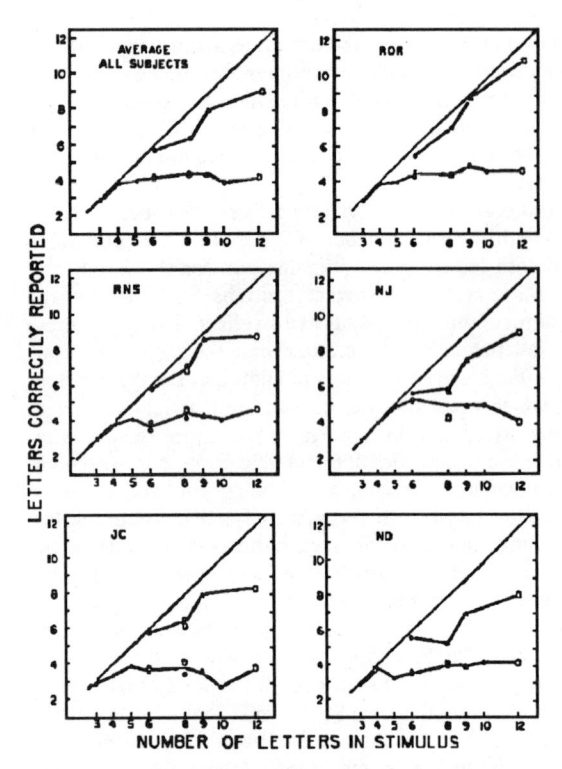

FIG. 3. "Channel capacity curves." Immediate-memory and letters available (output information) as functions of the number of stimulus letters (input information). Lower curves = immediate-memory (Exp. 1); upper curves = letters available immediately after termination of the stimulus; diagonal lines = maximum possible score (i.e., input = output). Code: × = letters on one line; + = 6-massed; o = 3/3, 4/4, 5/5; △ = 3/3/3; □ = 4/4 L&N, 4/4/4 L&N.

the term immediate-memory span when it is used in these experiments.

Procedure. Ss were instructed to write all the letters in the stimulus, guessing when they were not certain. All 12 types of stimulus materials were used. At least 15 trials were conducted with each kind of stimulus with each S. Each S was given at least 50 trials with the 3/3 (6-letter) stimuli which had yielded the highest memory span in preliminary experiments. The final run made with any kind of stimulus was always a test of immediate-memory. This procedure insured that Ss were tested for memory when they were maximally experienced with a stimulus.

Results. The lower curves in Fig. 3 represent the average number of letters correctly reported by each S for each material.[7] The most striking result is that immediate-memory is constant for each S, being nearly independent of the kind of stimulus used. The immediate-memory span for individual Ss ranges from approximately 3.8 for JC to approximately 5.2 for NJ with an average immediate-memory span for all Ss of about 4.3 letters. (The upper curves are discussed later.)

The constancy which is characteristic of individual immediate-memory curves of Fig. 3 also appears in the average curve for all Ss. For example, three kinds of stimuli were used that had six letters each: six letters normally spaced on one line, 6-massed, and 3/3-letters (see Fig. 2). When the data for all Ss are pooled, the scores for each of these three types of materials are practically the same: the range is 4.1-4.3 letters. The same constancy holds for stimuli containing eight symbols. The average number of letters correctly reported for each of the two different kinds of eight letter stimuli, 4/4, 4/4 L&N, is nearly the same: 4.4, 4.3, respectively.

Most Ss felt that stimuli containing both letters and numbers were more difficult than those containing letters only. Nevertheless, only NJ showed an objective deficit for the mixed material.

In conclusion, the average number of correct letters contained in an Ss whole report of the stimulus is approximately equal to the smaller of (a) the number of letters in the stimulus or (b) a numerical constant--the span of immediate-memory--which is different for each S. The use of the term immediate-memory span is therefore justified within the range of materials studied. This limit on the number of letters that can be correctly reported is an individual characteristic, but it is relatively similar for each of the five Ss of the study.

Experiment 2: Exposure Duration

The results of Experiment 1 showed that, regardless of material, Ss could not report more than an average of about 4.5 items per stimulus exposure. In order to determine whether this limitation was a peculiar characteristic of the short exposure duration (0.05 sec.), it was necessary to vary the exposure duration.

Procedure. As in the previous experiment, Ss were instructed to report all the letters in the stimulus. The stimuli were six letter cards (3/3). NJ, who was able to report more than five correct letters in Experiment I, was given 4/4 stimuli in order to make a possible increment in his accuracy of responding detectable. The Ss were given 10 trials in each of the four conditions, .015-, .050-, .150- (.200-), .500-sec. exposure duration, in the order above. In a later session, additional trials were conducted at .015-sec. exposure as a control for Experiment 5. These trials are averaged with the above data.

Results and discussion. Figure 4 illustrates the number of letters correctly reported as a function of the duration of exposure. The main result is that exposure duration, even over a wide range, is not an important parameter in determining the number of letters an S can

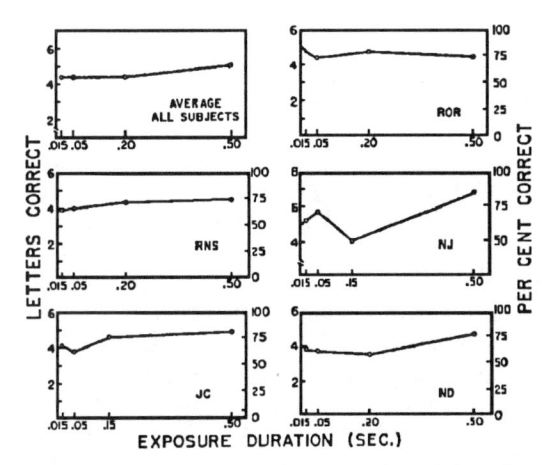

FIG. 4. Letters correctly reported as a function of exposure duration.

recall correctly. Both individually and as a group, Ss show no systematic changes in the number of letters correctly reported as the exposure duration was varied from 0.015 to 0.500 sec. The invariance of the number of letters reported as a function of exposure durations up to about 0.25 sec. for the kind of presentation used (dark pre- and post-exposure fields) has long been known (Schumann, 1904).

Experiment 3: Partial Report

Experiments 1 and 2 have demonstrated the span of immediate-memory as an invariant characteristic of each S. In Experiment 3 the principles of testing in a perceptual situation that were advanced in the introduction are applied in order to determine whether S has more information available than he can indicate in his limited immediate-memory report.

The S is presented with the stimulus as before, but he is required only to make a partial report. The length of this report is four letters or less, so as to lie within Ss immediate-memory span. The instruction that indicates which row of the stimulus is to be reported is coded in the form of a tone. The instruction tone is given after the visual presentation. The S does not know until he hears the tone which row is called for. This is therefore a procedure which samples the information that S has available after the termination of the visual stimulus.

Procedure. Initially, stimulus materials having only two lines were used, that is, 3/3 and 4/4. The S was told that a tone would be sounded, that this tone would come approximately simultaneously with the exposure, and that it would be either a high tone (2500 cps) or a low tone (250 cps). If it were a high tone, he was to write only the upper row of the stimulus; if a low tone, only the lower row. He was then shown a sample card of 3/3 letters and given several high and low tones. It was suggested that he keep his eyes fixated on the fixation point and be equally prepared for either tone. It would not be possible to outguess the E who would be using a random sequence of tones.

The tone duration was approximately 0.5 sec. The onset of the tone was controlled through the same microswitch that controlled the off-go of the light, with the completion of a connection from an **audio-oscillator** to the speaker. Intensity of the tone was adjusted so that the high (louder) tone was "loud but not uncomfortable."

In each of the first two sessions, each S received 30 training trials with each of the materials 3/3, 4/4. In subsequent sessions Ss were given series of 10 or more "test" trials. Later, a third, middle (650 cps) tone was introduced to correspond to the middle row of the 3/3/3 and 4/4/4 stimuli. The instructions and procedure were essentially the same as before.

In any given session, each tone might not occur with equal frequency for each type of stimulus. Over several sessions, usually two, this unequal frequency was balanced out so that an S had an exactly equal number of high, medium, and low tones for each material. If an S "misinterpreted" the tone and wrote the wrong row, he was asked to write what he could remember of the correct row. Only those letters which corresponded to the row indicated by the tone were considered.

Treatment of the Data. In the experiments considered in this section, S is never required to report the whole stimulus but only one line of a possible two or three lines. The simplest treatment is to plot the percentage of letters correct. This, in fact, will be done for all later comparisons. The present problem is to find a reasonable measure to enable comparison between the partial report and the immediate-memory data for the same stimuli. The measure, *percent correct*, does not describe the results of the immediate-memory experiments **parsimoniously**. In Experiment 1 it was shown that Ss report a constant number of letters, rather than a constant percentage of letters in the stimulus. The measure, *number of letters correct*, is inappropriate to the partial report data because the number of letters which S reports is limited by the E to at most three or four. The most reasonable procedure is to treat the partial report as a random sample of the letters which the S has available. Each partial report represents a

---

Audio-oscillator (aud-ih-oh OSS-sill-lay-tor). A device which produces sound at different tones and frequencies.

Parsimoniously (par-see-MOH-knee-us-lee). *Parsimoniously* means "to function in an efficient or economical manner."

typical sample of the number of letters S has available for report. For example, if an S is correct about 90% of the time when he is reporting three out of nine letters, then he is said to have 90% of the nine letters--about eight letters--available for partial report at the time the instruction tone is given.

In order to calculate the number of available letters, the average number of letters correct in the partial report is multiplied by the number of equiprobable (nonoverlapping), partial reports. If there are two tones and two rows, multiplication is by 2.0; if three, by 3.0. As before, only the number of correct letters in the correct position is considered.

Results. The development of the final, stable form of the behavior is relatively rapid for Ss giving partial reports. The average for all Ss after 30 trials (first session) with the 3/3 stimuli was 4.5; on the second day the average of 30 more trials was 5.1. On the third day Ss averaged 5.6 out of a possible six letters. Most of the improvement was due to just one S: ND who improved from 2.9 to 5.8 letters available. In the 3/3/3 stimulus training, all Ss reached their final value after the initial 40 trials on the first day of training. The considerable experience Ss had acquired with the partial reporting procedure at this time may account for the quick stabilization. NJ, whose score was 7.7 letters available on the first 20 trials, was given almost 150 additional trials in an unsuccessful attempt to raise this initial score.

In Fig. 3 the number of letters available as a function of the number of letters in the stimulus are graphed as the upper curves. For all stimuli and for all Ss, the available information calculated from the partial report is greater than that contained in the immediate-memory report. Moreover, from the divergence of the two curves it seems certain that, if still more complex stimuli were available, the amount of available information would continue to increase.

The estimate above is only a lower bound on the number of letters that Ss have available for report after the termination of the stimulus. An upper bound cannot be obtained from experiments utilizing partial reports, since it may always be argued that, with slightly changed conditions, an improved performance might result. Even the lower-bound measurement of the average available information, however, is twice as great as the immediate-memory span. The immediate-memory span for the 4/4/4 (12-letters and numbers) stimuli ranges from 3.9 to 4.7 symbols for the Ss, with an average of 4.3. Immediately after an exposure of the 4/4/4 stimulus material, the number of letters available to the Ss ranged from 8.1 (ND) to 11.0 (ROR), with an average of 9.1 letters available. This number of letters may be transformed into the bits of information represented by so many letters. For the 4/4/4 (12-letters and numbers) material, the average number of bits available, then, is 40.6, with a range from 36.2 to 49.1 (out of a possible 53.6 bits). These figures are considerably higher than the usual estimates. For example, in a recent review article Quastler (1956) writes: "All experimental studies agree that man can . . . assimilate less than 25 bits per glance" (p. 32). The data obtained in Experiment 3 not only exceed this maximum, but they contain no evidence that the information that became available to the Ss following the exposure represented a limit of "man" rather than a maximum determined by the limited information contained in the stimuli which were used.

Experiment 4: Decay of Available Information

Part 1: Development of Strategies of Observing

It was established in Experiment 3 that more information is available to the Ss immediately after termination of the stimulus than they could report. It remains to determine the fate of this surplus information, that is, the "forgetting curve." The partial report technique makes possible the sampling of the available information at the time the instruction signal is given. By delaying the instruction, therefore, decay of the available information as a function of time will be reflected as a corresponding decrease in the accuracy of the report.

Procedure. The principal modification from the preceding experiment is that the signal tone, which indicates to the S which row is to be reported, is given at various other times than merely "zero delay" following the stimulus off-go. The following times of indicator tone onset relative to the stimulus were explored: 0.05 sec. before stimulus onset (-.10 sec.) +0.0-, +0.15-, +0.30-, +0.50-, +1.0-sec. delays after stimulus off-go. The stimuli used were 3/3, 4/4.

The Ss were given five or more consecutive trials in each of the above conditions. These trials were always preceded by at least two samples in order to familiarize S with the exact time of onset. The particular delay of the instruction tone on any trial was thus fixed rather than chosen randomly. The advantages of this procedure are (a) optimal performance is most likely in each delay condition, if S is prepared for that precise condition (cf. Klemmer, 1957), (b) minimizing delay changes makes possible a higher rate of stimulus presentations. On the other hand, a random sequence of instruction tone delays would make it more likely that S was "doing the same thing" in each of the different delay conditions.

The sequence in which the different delay conditions followed each other was chosen either as that given

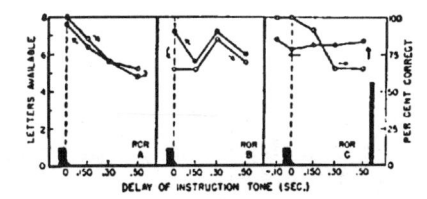

FIG. 5. Partial report of eight (4/4) letters, three consecutive sessions. Arrows indicate the sequence in which conditions followed within a session. The light flash is shown on same time scale at lower left of each figure. Bar at right indicates immediate-memory for this material. One subject (ROR).

above (ascending series of delay conditions) or in the reverse order (descending series). Within a session, a descending series always followed an ascending series and vice versa, irrespective of the stimulus materials used. At least two ascending and two descending series of delay conditions were run with each S and with each material after the initial training (Experiment 3) with that material. This number of trials insures that for each S there are at least 20 trials at each delay of the indicator tone.

Results and discussion. The development of the typical behavior is illustrated by the S, ROR, in Figs. 5a, b, c. Figure 5a shows ROR's performance in a single session, the first posttraining session. The upper and lower curves represent the ascending and descending series of tone instruction delays, respectively. The arrows indicate the order. Although each point is based upon only five trials, the curves are remarkably similar and regular. Clearly, most of the letters in excess of ROR's memory span are forgotten within about 0.25 sec. The rapid forgetting of these letters justifies calling this a short-term memory and accounts for the fact that it may easily be overlooked under less than optimal conditions.

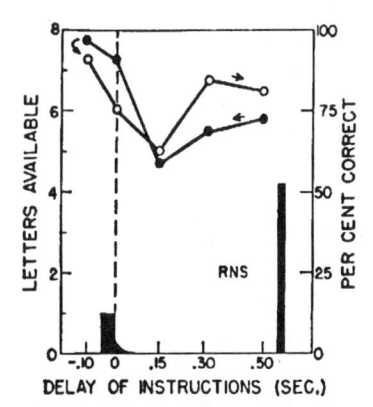

FIG. 6. Partial report of eight (4/4) letters, last of three sessions. Arrows indicate the sequence in which conditions followed within session. The light flash is shown on same time scale at lower left. Bar at right indicates immediate-memory for this material. (RNS)

In the following session (Fig. 5b) the descending series was given first. Here orderly behavior disintegrates. In the third session (Fig. 5c) two modifications were introduced: (a) the number of trials in each delay condition was increased to eight and (b) a new delay condition was given--namely, a signal tone coming 0.05 sec. before the stimulus onset. The curves are again regular, but they are obviously different for the ascending and descending series. For the session indicated in Fig 5c, an analysis of the errors by position shows that in the ascending series the errors are evenly split between the top and bottom rows of the stimulus; in the descending series, the top row is favored 3:1.

ROR's performance is analyzable in terms of two kinds of observing behavior (strategies) which the situation suggests. He may follow the instruction, given by E prior to training, that he pay equal attention to each row. In this case, errors are evenly distributed between rows. Or, he may try to anticipate the signal by guessing which instruction tone will be presented. In this case, S is differentially prepared to report one row. If the signal and Ss guess coincide, S reports accurately; if not, poorly. Such a guessing procedure would lead to the variability observed in Fig. 5b. On the other hand, S may prefer always to anticipate the same row--in the case of ROR (Fig. 5c, descending series), the top row. This would again allow reliable scores, provided only that there are an equal number of instruction signals calling for the top and bottom rows. **Concomitantly**, a differential accuracy of report for the two rows is observed. (ROR's preference for the top row is again prominent in Experiment 7, Figs. 10, 11.)

Equal attention responding is initially reinstated on the third day. The obvious change in procedure which is responsible is the introduction of a tone 0.05 sec. before the stimulus onset (-0.10 sec. "after" its termination). This signal is sufficiently in advance of the stimulus so that perfect responding is possible by looking at only the row indicated by the signal tone. ROR scores 100%, both in this condition and in the succeeding zero delay. The whole (ascending series) decay curve of Fig. 5c is highly similar to that of Fig. 5a. A run with 3/3 stimuli was interposed between the ascending and descending series shown in Fig. 5c. Since the guessing procedures were easily sufficient for a nearly perfect score with 3/3 materials, when the descending series of delay conditions was run, ROR continued guessing. While guessing was advantageous at the long delays; at the short delays it was a decided disadvantage.

Concomitantly (con-COM-ih-tant-lee). *Concomitantly* means "to accompany or be connected with."

Figure 6 illustrates the performances of RNS, a sophisticated observer. RNS described the two strategies (equal attention, guessing) to E. In accordance with the instructions to do as well as he could, RNS said that he switched from the first to the second strategy at delays longer than 0.15 sec. Thus in the three short delay conditions, RNS divided his errors almost evenly (19:21) between the favored (top) and the unfavored rows; in the two longer delays, errors were split 4:26. The dip in the curve indicates that RNS did not switch strategies quite as soon as he could have, for optimal performance. Such a dip is characteristically seen in experiments of this kind.

The other Ss exhibit similar curves.[8] These are not presented, as the main features have already been demonstrated by ROR and RNS. In summary, the method of delaying the instruction tone is a feasible one for determining the decay of the short-term memory contents, but experience with the difficult, long delays causes a considerable increase in the variability of Ss' performance which is carried over even to the short delay conditions. This has been attributed to Ss' change from an equal attention to a guessing strategy in observing the stimulus.[9]

Part 2: Final Level of Performance

The analysis of the preceding experiment has indicated that two distinct kinds of observing behavior develop when the instruction to report is delayed. The accuracy of report resulting from the first of these behaviors (equal attention) is correlated with the delay of the instruction tone; it is associated with the Ss initially giving equal attention to all parts of the stimulus. The accuracy of the other kind of report (guessing) is uncorrelated with the delay of the instruction; it is characterized by Ss' differential preparedness for some part of the stimulus (guessing). Equal attention observing is selected for further study here. The preceding experiment suggests three modifications that would tend to make equal attention observing more likely to occur, with a corresponding exclusion of guessing.

1. The use of stimuli with a larger number of letters, that is, 3/3/3 and 4/4/4. Differential attention to a constant small part of the stimulus is less likely to be reinforced, the larger the stimulus. The use of three tones instead of two diminishes the probability of guessing the correct tone.

2. Training with instruction tones that begin slightly before the onset of the stimulus. It is not necessary for S to guess in this situation since he can succeed by depending upon the instruction tone alone. This situation not only makes equal attention likely to occur, but differentially reinforces it when it does occur.

When delays of longer length are tested, priority should be given to an ascending series of delays so that S will, at the beginning of a particular delay sequence, have a high probability of entering with the desired observing behavior. This probability might be nearly 1.0 by interposing a series of trials on which the instruction is given in advance of, or immediately upon, termination of the stimulus and requiring that S perform perfectly on this task before he can continue to the particular delay being tested.[10] This tedious procedure was tried; but, as it did not have an appreciable effect upon the results, it was discontinued. The problem is that Ss learn to switch between the two modes of behavior in a small number of trials.

3. The E may be able to gain "verbal" control over Ss' modes of responding. Initially, however, even S cannot control his own behavior exactly. This suggests a limit to what E can do. For example, frequently Ss reported that, although they had tried to be equally prepared for each row, after some tones they realized that they had been selectively prepared for a particular row. This comment was made both when the tone and the row coincided and (more frequently) when they differed.

Some verbal control is, of course, possible. An instruction that was well understood was:

> You will see letters illuminated by a flash that quickly fades out. This is a visual test of your ability to read letters under these conditions, not a test of your memory. You will hear a tone during the flash or while it is fading which will indicate which letters you are to attempt to read. Do not read the card until you hear the tone, [etc.].

The instruction was changed at the midway point in the experiment. The S was no longer to do as well as he could by any means, but was limited to the procedure described above. Part 2 of this experiment, utilizing 9- and 12-letter stimuli, was carried out with the three modifications suggested above.

Results. The results for 3/3/3 and 4/4/4 letters and numbers are shown for each individual S in Figs. 7 and 8. The two **ordinates** are linearly related by the equation:

$$\% \text{ correct}/100 = \# \text{ letters in stimulus} = \text{letters available}$$

Each point is based on all the test trials in the delay condition. The points at zero delay of instructions for NJ and JC also include the training trials, as these Ss showed no subsequent improvement.

The data indicate that, for all Ss, the period of about one sec. is a critical one for the presentation of the

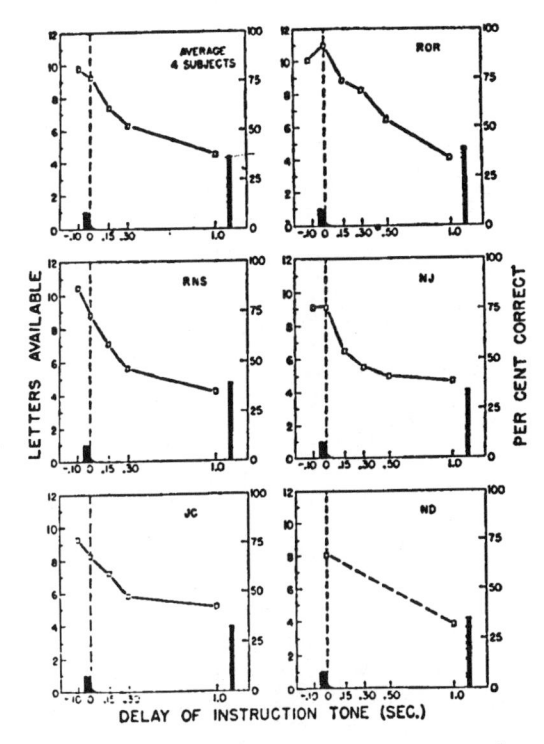

FIG. 7. Decay of available information: nine (3/3/3) letters. Light flash is shown on same time scale at lower left. Bar at right indicates immediate-memory for this material.

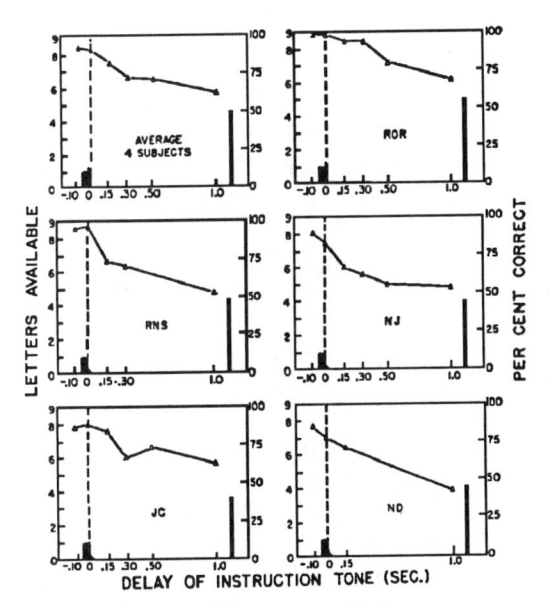

FIG. 8. Decay of available information: twelve (4/4/4) letters and numbers. Light flash is shown on same time scale at lower left. Bar at right indicates immediate-memory for this material.

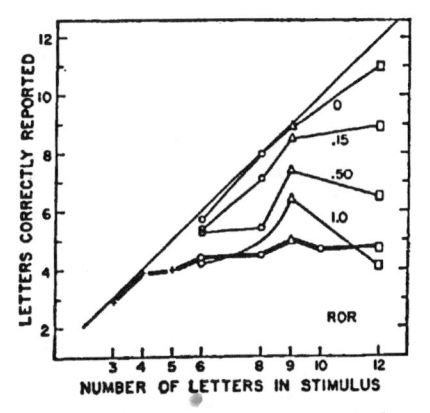

FIG. 9. Immediate-memory and available information. The parameter is the time at which available information is sampled (delay of instruction). Heavy line indicates immediate-memory for the same materials. One subject (ROR).

instruction to report. If Ss receive the instruction 0.05 sec. before the exposure, then they give accurate reports: 91% and 82% of the letters given in the report are correct for the 9- and 12-letter materials, respectively. These partial reports may be interpreted to indicate that the Ss have, on the average, 8.2 of 9 and 9.8 of 12 letters available. However, if the instruction is delayed until one sec. after the exposure, then the accuracy of the report drops 32% (to 69%) for the 9-letter stimuli, and 41% (to 38%) for the 12-letter stimuli. This substantial decline in accuracy brings the number of *letters available* very near to the number of letters that Ss give in immediate-memory (whole) reports.

The decay curves are similar and regular for each S and for the average of all Ss. Although individual differences are readily apparent, they are small relative to the effects of the delay of the instruction: For example, when an instruction was given with zero delay after the termination of the stimulus, the *least* accurate reports by any Ss are given by ND, who has 8.1 letters available immediately after the termination of the stimulus. With a one-sec. delay of instructions, the *most* accurate reports were given by JC, who has only 5.1 letters available at this time.

In Fig. 3, in which whole reports and partial reports were compared, only that particular partial report was considered in which the instruction tone followed the stimulus with zero delay. It is evident from this experiment that the zero delay instruction is unique only in that it is the earliest possible "after" instruction, but not because of any functional difference.

In Fig. 9, therefore, the 0.15-, 0.50-, and 1.00-sec. instruction delays are also plotted for one S, ROR. Data

Ordinates (OR-din-eights). The *ordinate* of a graph is the Y-axis.

for the six- (3/3) and eight- (4/4) letter stimuli are taken from the two ascending delay series with each material that yielded **monotonic** results. Figure 9 clearly highlights the significance of a precisely controlled coded instruction, given within a second of the stimulus off-go, for the comparison of partial and immediate-memory reports. One second after termination of the stimulus, the accuracy of ROR's partial reports is no longer very different from the accuracy of his whole reports.

Experiment 5: Some Exposure Parameters

In Experiment 3 it was shown that the number of letters reported correctly is almost independent of the exposure duration over a range from 15 to 500 msec. It is well known, however, that the relation between the accuracy of report and the exposure duration depends upon the pre- and post-exposure fields (Wundt, 1899).

In a technique developed in **Helmholtz's** laboratory (Baxt, 1871) the informational (stimulus) field is followed, after a variable delay, by a noninformational, homogeneous, bright post-exposure field. Using this method, Baxt showed that the number of reportable letters was a nearly linear function of the delay of the bright post-exposure field.[11]

Other combinations of pre- and post-exposure fields have also been tried (Dodge, 1907a). The usual tachistoscopic presentation utilizes gray pre- and post-exposure fields (Woodworth, 1938). Baxt's procedure, however, is the most disadvantageous for the observer. A similar procedure was therefore selected, in order to study whole and partial reports in a vastly different visual presentation from that of the previous experiments.

Procedure. 1. Ss were instructed to write all the letters of the stimulus; 3/3 stimuli were used. After several sample presentations of a stimulus card followed by a light post-exposure field, Ss were give a random sequence of normal (pre- and post-exposure fields dark) and Baxt (pre-exposure dark, post-exposure field light) trials. The Baxt trials do not correspond exactly to the presentation that Baxt used. In this experiment, the post-exposure field is the same intensity as the stimulus (informational) field, whereas Baxt usually used more intense post-exposure fields; also, the stimulus field always remains *on* until the onset of the post-exposure field, whereas Baxt used a fixed five-msec. duration for the stimulus field. The post-exposure field itself remains on for about one sec. The pre-exposure field is always dark, as in all the previous experiments. Two exposure durations, 0.015 and 0.050 sec., were tested.

TABLE 1
A COMPARISON OF RESPONSE ACCURACY WITH TWO DIFFERENT POST-EXPOSURE FIELDS

Subject	Exposure (sec.)	Normal	Baxt
RNS	(0.015)	3.9	2.5
	(0.050)	4.0	2.2
ROR	(0.015)	4.8	3.5
	(0.050)	4.4	2.8
ND	(0.015)	3.8	1.9
	(0.050)	3.7	2.3
NJ	(0.015)	5.1	2.4
	(0.050)	5.4	3.4
JC	(0.015)	4.1	2.7
	(0.050)	3.8	3.4
Mean	(0.015)	4.3	2.6
	(0.050)	4.3	2.8

Note.--Number of letters correctly reported. Whole report of six (3/3) letter stimuli. Normal = pre- and post-exposure fields dark; Baxt = pre-exposure field dark, post-exposure field white.

2. Three Ss were tested with Baxt presentation of a 3/3/3 stimulus at an exposure duration of 0.015 sec. The partial report procedure was used to determine the effects of the post-exposure field on the number of letters available.

3. The same three Ss were run as their own controls. The procedure was exactly the same as in Paragraph 2 above except that the post-exposure field was normal (dark).

Results. The complete results are given in Tables 1 and 2. In all tests, the Baxt procedure reduces the response accuracy of all Ss to about one-half of their normal score. This finding confirms the earlier studies. However, a linear relation between exposure duration and the number of letters reported was not observed. The failure to find a linear relation may be due to the previously mentioned differences between the presentations.

For RNS and ND, the number of letters available is nearly the same (about two) in the partial report of 9-letter stimuli as the whole report of 6-letter stimuli. The fact that in both procedures the number of letters given by Ss is the same suggests that a Baxt presentation reduces the number, or the length of time that letters are available, and that it does not directly affect the immediate-memory span.

ROR's partial reports of Baxt presentations are considerably more accurate than those of the other Ss, although they are not as accurate as his reports in control presentations. ROR seemed to show improve-

TABLE 2
A COMPARISON OF RESPONSE ACCURACY WITH TWO DIFFERENT POST-EXPOSURE FIELDS

Delay of Instruction (sec.):	0.0		0.15	
Exposure Duration (sec.):	0.015	0.05	0.015	0.05
Subject				
RNS (N)	8.0	8.7	5.4	6.6
(B)	2.0		2.2	
ROR (N)	8.6	8.9	8.3	8.5
(B)	6.3		5.4	
ND (N)	7.3	7.0	5.8	6.4
(B)	2.2		1.7	
Mean (N)	8.0	8.2	6.5	7.2
(B)	3.5		3.1	

Note.-- Number of letters available (fraction of letters correct in partial report X number of letters in stimulus). Stimuli: nine (3/3/3) letters. (N) = normal (pre- and post-exposure fields dark). (B) = Baxt (pre-exposure field dark, post-exposure field white).

ment on successive Baxt trials. JC, another S who seemed to show improvement, was given additional Baxt trials on which he continued to improve slowly. Unfortunately, it was unfeasible to determine the **asymptotic** performance of these two Ss. Whether the difference in performance between ROR, and RNS and ND is attributable to some overt response, such as squinting or blinking, was not determined.

Table 2 also enables the comparison of 0.015- and 0.050-sec. exposures of 3/3/3 stimuli. A decrease in exposure duration has only a slight effect on the number of letters available. This suggests, as in the immediate-memory experiments, that the duration of a tachistoscopic exposure is not as important a determinant of the number of letters available as the fields which follow the exposure.

Experiment 6: Letters and Numbers

In Experiment 3 partial reports were found to be uniformly more accurate than whole reports. In one case, stimuli of eight letters were used and only one row of four letters was reported. Designating the letters to be reported by their location is only one of a number of possible ways. In the following experiment, a quite similar set of stimuli is used; each stimulus has two letters and two numbers in each of the two rows. The partial report again consists of only four symbols, but these are designated either as letters or as numbers rather than by row. In addition, a number of controls which are also relevant to Experiment 3 are conducted.

Procedure. I. Training: The Ss were given practice trials with the instruction: "Write down only the numbers if you hear a short pip (tone 0.05-sec. duration) and only the letters if you hear the long tone (0.50-sec. duration)." The tones were then given with zero delay following the stimulus off-go. The stimuli were 4/4 L&N.

II. In the following session, tests were conducted with five different instructions:

1. Letters only--Instructions given well in advance of stimulus to write only the letters in the following card(s). (8 trials)

2. Numbers only--Write only the numbers in the following card(s). (8 trials)

3. Top only--Write only the top row in the following card(s). (4 trials)

4. Bottom only--write only the bottom row in the following card(s). (4 trials)

5. Instruction tone--Write either letters or numbers as indicated by tone. Tone onset 0.05 sec. before stimulus onset. (16 trials) ROR was also given additional trials at longer delay times.

Results. The results are illustrated in Table 3. For purposes of comparison, the number of correct letters

Monotonic (MON-oh-tahn-ick). A monotonic curve is one that never increases of decreases (as a function of any change in the independent variable).
Helmholtz (HELM-holts). Hermann Ludwig Ferdinand von Helmholtz was a German physicist who made important discoveries on the perception of visual and auditory stimuli in the late 1890's.
Asymptotic (ass-sim-TOT-ick, or A-sim-tot-ick). When a performance curve "levels off" and remains flat thereafter, we say it has "reached its asymptote" (ASS-sim-tote).

TABLE 3
COMPARISON OF FIVE PROCEDURES

Subject	Letters only	Numbers only	Average L&N	Instr. tone −0.10	Immediate-memory	One row only
RNS	5.0	4.5	4.8	4.3	4.6	7.3
ROR	6.5	6.5	6.5	6.3	4.5	7.3
ND	3.5	3.8	3.6	4.1	4.1	7.5
NJ	4.0	5.0	4.5	4.6	4.3	----
JC	3.3	4.0	3.6	3.4	4.1	8.0
Mean	4.5	4.8	4.6	4.5	4.3	----

Note.— Average letters and/or numbers available (fraction of letters—numbers—correct in partial report X number of symbols in stimulus). Stimuli: eight (4/4) letters and numbers.

is multiplied by two when an instruction was used which required S to report only four of the eight symbols of the stimulus. This includes instructions given well in advance of the stimulus. All measures, then, have 8.0 as the top score and are thus equivalent within a scale factor to percent correct measures. The range is 0-8 instead of 0-100. Scores which are based on partial reports are therefore directly comparable to the partial report scores (letters available) obtained in Experiments 3, 4, and 5.

When stimuli consist of letters and numbers, but Ss report only the letters or only the numbers, then the Ss' partial reports are only negligibly more accurate than their whole reports of the same stimuli. The average number of letters available (calculated from the partial report) is just 0.2 letter above the immediate-memory span for the same material. For practical purposes, the partial report score is the same score that Ss would obtain if they wrote all the letters and numbers they could (that is, gave a whole report) but were scored only for letters or only for numbers, independently by the experimenter. The partial report of letters only (or of numbers only) does not improve even when the instruction is given long in advance verbally instead of immediately before the exposure by a coded signal tone.

The estimate of the number of available letters and numbers which is obtained from the partial report of letters (or numbers) only is also the same as the estimate that would be obtained if, on each trial, Ss wrote only one row--either the top or the bottom --according to their whim. Reporting only one row of four letters and numbers is a task at which the Ss succeed with over 90% accuracy. Even if they are scored for the whole stimulus, by arbitrarily reporting only one row they would still achieve a score of almost 50% correct or almost four letters available. This is why no delay series were conducted. If Ss had ignored the instruction to write only the letters (or numbers) and had written only a single row on each trial, they would have shown less than a 0.5 letter decrement, no matter what the delay of the instruction.

Only ROR showed a substantial improvement when reporting only the numbers (or letters). He was the only S with whom it made sense to conduct a systematic delay series, although checks with other Ss confirmed this conclusion. Table 4 indicates that two extra symbols are available to ROR for report only when the tone is given before the stimulus, but not if it is given immediately after. It should be noted that the information in the instruction tone comes only after it has been on for 0.05 sec. At this time it either continues or is terminated. The actual "instruction" is thus given 0.05 sec. after the tone onset. ROR therefore requires that the *instruction* be given within 0.05 sec. of the stimulus termination if any benefit of the partial report procedure is to be retained.

TABLE 4
PARTIAL REPORTS OF LETTERS OR NUMBERS

Subj.	Prior Verbal Instr.	Delay of Instr. −0.10	Delay of Instr. 0.0	Tone (sec.) +0.25	Immediate memory
ROR	6.5	6.3	4.7	4.4	4.5

Note.— Average of symbols available (fraction of letters—numbers—correct in partial report X number of symbols in stimulus). Stimuli: eight (4/4) letters and numbers.

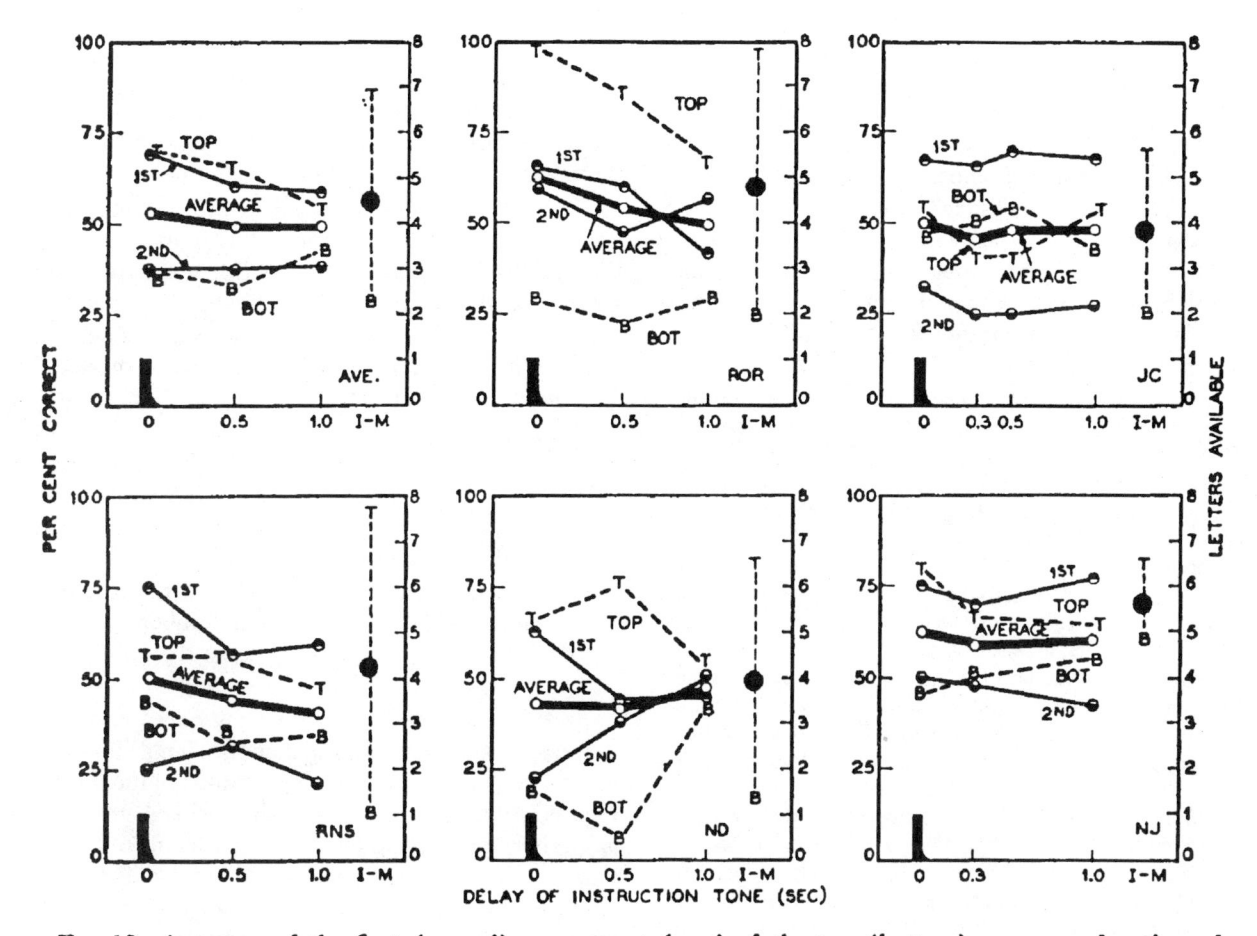

FIG. 10. Accuracy of the first (second) row reported and of the top (bottom) row as a function of the delay of the instruction to report one row first. Light flash is indicated at lower left; immediate-memory (I-M) at right.

Whether the Ss would have shown improvement with a large amount of additional training in the partial report of letters or numbers cannot be stated. Table 3 shows that, when Ss are required in advance to report only one row, this task is trivial. The substantial advantage of partial reports of rows (report by position) over partial reports of numbers or letters (report by category) when the instruction is given verbally long in advance of the exposure is retained even when the instruction is coded and given shortly after the exposure.

The failure in Experiment 6 to detect a substantial difference in accuracy between partial reports of only letters (or only numbers) and whole reports clearly illustrates that partial reports by position are more effective for studying the capacity of short-term information storage than partial reports by category.

Experiment 7: Order of Report

Interpretations of the effects of instructions upon the report following a single brief visual exposure have often been concerned with either the perceptual sensitizing effects of an instruction given before the exposure or with the importance of forgetting between the exposure and a post-exposure instruction to report. The decay curves of Experiment 4 include both of these effects. Previous studies, however, have usually assumed the order in which the various parts (aspects, dimensions, etc.) of the stimulus are reported to be the significant correlate of post-exposure forgetting. The possibility that information might be well retained even though not immediately reported has been mentioned (Broadbent, 1958), but experimental investigations of such an effect by an independent variation of the order of report by Wilcocks (1925), Lawrence and Laberge (1956), and Broadbent (1957a) have apparently shown otherwise. Broadbent (1957a) has also shown a case in which independent variation of the order of report did not reduce overall response accuracy.

In the present experiment, order of report is introduced as a purely "nuisance" variable for the S. The S is instructed to get as many letters correct as possible, but the E randomly manipulates the order in which they are to be reported. The experiment, is a survey of how Ss adapt to this kind of interference with the normal order of their report.

Procedure. The Ss were instructed to write the row indicated by the tone (high, low) first, then to write the other row. They were to try to get as many *total* letters correct as possible, it being of no importance in which particular row the correct letters might be. The instruction tone was given with 0.0-, .30- (or .50-), and 1.0-sec. delay after the termination of the stimulus.

Controls. In addition to the trials with a high or low tone, two sets of 8 (or 10) trials were given with a neutral, middle tone. The instruction was: "Write all the letters in any order you wish, but do not begin writing until you hear the tone." The tone was sounded with 0.0-sec. delay following termination of the stimulus and also with 1.0-sec. delay. It bears repeating here that Ss were not permitted just to mark X's but were required to guess various letters.

Results. Controls: The instruction which required Ss to wait for 1.0 sec. before beginning to write their answer was ignored by the Ss, since it was almost physically impossible to begin writing sooner. Consequently the two different controls-trials on which S was required to "wait" for 1.0 sec. and trials on which S could begin his report immediately-are grouped together. These data, which are almost exactly the same as the memory span data (Experiment 1), are presented on the far right in Fig. 10.

The Ss' responses on the control trials are analyzed in terms of the correlation between the location of letters on the stimulus and the accuracy of the report of these letters in the response. The symbols T and B above I-M in Fig. 10 represent the percentage of the letters of the top and of the bottom rows that Ss report correctly. The middle point is the average percentage of the letters of the top and bottom rows that were correctly reported by Ss. The middle point is therefore also the average percentage correct of all the letters that were reported. Figure 10 shows that all Ss report the top row of the stimulus more accurately than the bottom row, if they are not instructed with regard to the order in which they must report the rows.

The average accuracy with which Ss report the top and the bottom rows, when instructions to report one or the other of these rows are given with various delays after the exposure, is also illustrated in Fig. 10. The accuracy of reports of the top row decreases slightly as the delay of the instructions increases. In other respects, however, the data show no systematic changes in accuracy with changes in the delay of instructions. The data clearly indicate that the top row is generally reported more accurately than the bottom row although the instruction to report each row is given with equal frequency.

The same data may also be analyzed with regard to the accuracy of the row that must be reported first and the row that is reported last. All Ss except ROR are more accurate when they report the first row (the row called for by the instruction tone) than the second row. For most Ss, therefore, the order of report is correlated with the accuracy of report.

There is a slight tendency for the accuracy of report of the row which is reported first to decrease as the delay of the instructions increases. On the whole, however, the overall accuracy of report decreases slightly with the delay of the instruction to report one row first. The experimental interference with the normal order of report does not change the overall number of letters reported correctly by any S by more than about 0.5 letter.

In this task, unlike the preceding ones, individual differences are more striking than the similarities. The pooled data are highly untypical of three of the five Ss. Figure 11 was devised as a two-dimensional, graphical **analysis of variance** to compress the details of Fig. 10 into one figure.[12] Each coordinate represents the accuracy of one row of the report relative to the whole report. Thus the ordinate represents the number of letters that an individual S reports correctly in the top row of the stimulus (independently of order) divided by the total number of letters (both rows) that he reports correctly. Similarly, the **abscissa** represents the percentage of the total correct letters reported by S that are contained in his report of the first row. Since each coordinate is relative to Ss own accuracy, no point of the graph is inaccessible to S provided that, if necessary, he is willing to sacrifice some accuracy. Since the interference with Ss order of report in this experiment had only slight effects on the overall accuracy of Ss report, this method of presenting the data is justifiable.

From Fig. 11 it is immediately evident that, for example, 50% of the correct letters that JC reports are from the top row and, by implication, 50% are from the bottom row of the stimulus. More than 70% of the correct letters that JC reports are in the first row reported by him. ROR represents the converse, preferring to report the top row accurately, remaining indifferent to whether it is called for first or last. Other Ss lie between these extremes, each S maintaining approximately the same relative accuracy for the top and the first rows throughout the various delay conditions.

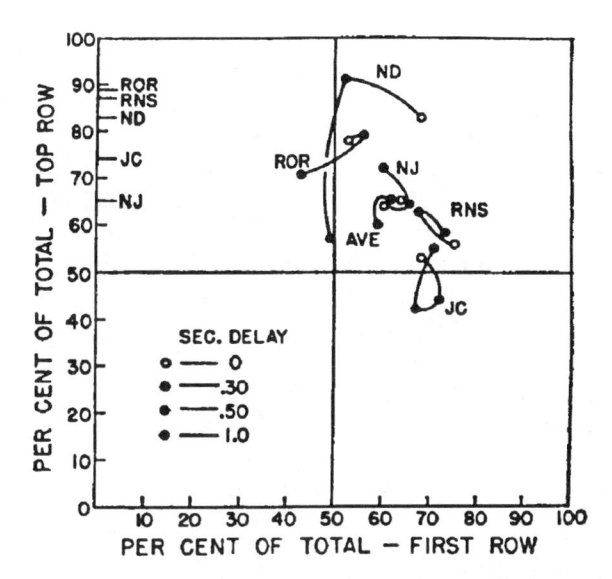

FIG. 11. Graphical analysis of position on stimulus vs. order of report as contributors to response accuracy. Each point represents the average of all trials of an *S* at a particular delay of instruction. The order in which the points are connected corresponds to the magnitude of the delays. Upper left: position preference in control (immediate-memory) report.

Each S, therefore, operates within a characteristic, limited area of the graph. ND is an exception. At zero delay of the instruction tone, both position and order account heavily for the correct letters reported by ND. At 0.5-sec. delay, ND ignored the order (preferring to concentrate on the top row), and at 1.0-sec. delay she lost her position (top row) preference as well. In these three conditions, the total number of letters correctly reported by ND remained approximately the same, within 0.5 letter of the control condition. At 1.0-sec. delay *neither position nor the order contribute to ND's accuracy of report*.

All Ss operate in the upper right quadrant of Fig. 11. This illustrates the finding that no S consistently reported the bottom row more accurately than the top, nor the last row better than the row first called for by the instruction tone. It does not, of course, indicate that Ss could not report the bottom row or the last row more accurately under other conditions. While Ss normally behave quite consistently, the data of ND show that they may try a number of different procedures. The instructions given the Ss prior to the experiment were not restrictive. No specific procedure for making a report was suggested to the Ss, because the purpose of the experiment was to find out how Ss respond when they are not given detailed instructions. With suitable instructions, training, and reinforcements, Ss could probably be induced to make most of the possible kinds of reports that can be diagrammed by Fig. 11. This remains an **empirical** problem.

The results obtained in this experiment support the conclusions that both a position preference and the order of report ordinarily correlate with the accuracy of response, but that probably *neither are necessary* conditions for response accuracy. Some Ss can relinquish the position preference and a favorable order of report with no appreciable decrement in accuracy. This finding is in opposition to Lawrence and Laberge's (1956) contention that accuracy is accounted for by the order of the report. Accuracy and order are often correlated, but if a favorable order of report is not *necessary* for accuracy, then it cannot be the cause of accuracy.

When S is give a signal indicating which row is to be reported first (Experiment 7), the accuracy of report of the row indicated by the signal (the first row reported) may be compared to the accuracy of the partial report (Experiment 3). The overt procedure on each trial is quite similar in Experiments 3 and 7. The only difference is that in order of report experiment, after the Ss have finished writing the row indicated by the signal, they must also write down the other row. In the partial report procedure they do not have to write the second row. The partial report and the order of report experiments also share a common dependent variable: the accuracy of report of the row indicated by the instruction signal.

In view of the similarity in procedure, it is surprising that the accuracy of this common datum should be so different in the two experiments. For example, when Ss give only the partial reports (the instruction signal being given immediately after termination of the stimulus), then they report 90% of the letters correctly in one row of 4/4 stimuli. When they are required to write the other row also, then they report only 69% of the first four letters correctly. Every S, individually, gives a more accurate partial report (Experiment 3) than a report of the first row--of two rows to be reported (Experiment 7). The consistent superiority of the partial report over the first half of a whole report prevails even when the instruction to report is delayed for 0.5 (or 0.3) sec. In all cases where data are available, each S reports a row of four letters more accurately when he does not have to write another row of four letters afterwards. That what Ss must write later should affect the accuracy of what

Analysis of variance. A statistical test used to determine whether the measured difference(s) between two groups of people are statistically significant.

Abscissa (ab-SIS-ah). The X-axis of a graph.

Empirical (em-PEER-ih-cal). To be "empirical" is to rely on data or experimentation rather than on theory or guess.

they write first must be explained--if we disregard **teleological** explanation--by the effect of prior instructions on the accuracy of the report. In other words, if order of report is effective in determining the accuracy of report, then this effect must be a function of instructions given prior to any report at all. For some Ss, no effect of order of report upon response accuracy was observed.

The two findings, that partial reports are uniformly more accurate than whole reports and that order of report may be uncorrelated with accuracy, contradict Lawrence and Laberge's conclusion that "partial" reports are essentially similar to "first" reports. In fact, the second finding (that in some circumstances order of report and accuracy of report are not correlated) provides a direct counterexample to their conclusion. Their different results may be in part due to the vastly different stimuli which they used. Lawrence and Laberge's entire stimuli each contained less information than two randomly chosen letters.

DISCUSSION

In all seven experiments, Ss were required to report the letters of briefly exposed lettered stimuli. Two kinds of reports were explored: *partial reports*, which required the Ss to report only a specified part of the stimulus, and *whole reports*, which required the Ss to report all the letters of the stimulus. Experiment 3 demonstrated that the accuracy of partial reports was consistently greater than the accuracy of whole reports. Another important difference between partial and whole reports is the correlation of accuracy with the delay of the instruction to report. This was shown in Experiment 4 in which the time delay of the instruction signal, which indicated the row of the stimulus to be reported, was varied. The accuracy of the partial report was found to be a sharply decreasing function of the time at which the instruction was given. If the instruction signal was delayed for one sec. after the exposure, the accuracy of the partial report was no longer very different from that of the whole report. In Experiment 7 it was shown that the accuracy of the whole report does not change as the time of the signal to report is varied-- over the same range of time--up to one sec. after the exposure.

The two kinds of report can also be considered in terms of the information (in these experiments, letters) which they indicate the S has available for report. In the whole report, the S reports all the information that he can. When he gives a partial report, the S may have additional available information that is not required for the report. A calculation of the information available to the Ss for their partial reports indicates that between two and three times more information is available for partial reports than for the whole reports. This discrepancy between the two kinds of report is short-lived. Information in excess of that indicated by the whole report was available to the Ss for only a fraction of a second following the exposure. At the end of this time, the accuracy of partial reports is no longer very different from that of whole reports.

The whole report has already been extensively studied by psychologists. The maximum number of items an individual can give in such a report is called his *span of immediate-memory*; whole reports are usually called *immediate-memory reports*. Experiments 1 and 2 extend the well-known conclusions that the span of immediate-memory is an individual characteristic and that it is constant over a wide range of stimuli and exposure conditions. Although, in immediate-memory experiments, items are conventionally presented sequentially, Experiments 1 and 2 illustrate that this is not necessary-that a simultaneous presentation may also give results characteristic of immediate-memory experiments.

The main problems to be considered here concern the partial-whole report discrepancy: (a) Why is the partial report more accurate than the whole report? (b) Why does the partial report retain this added accuracy only for a fraction of a second after the exposure?

The answers proposed are a systematic elaboration of an observation that is readily made by most viewers of the actual tachistoscopic presentation. They report that the stimulus field appears to be still readable at the time a tone is heard which follows the termination of the stimulus by 150 msec. In other words, the subjective image or sensation induced by the light flash outlasts the physical stimulus at least until the tone is heard. The stimulus information is thus "stored" for a fraction of a second as a persisting image of the objective stimulus. As the visual image fades, its legibility (information content) decreases, and consequently the accuracy of reports based upon it decreases.

There is other evidence, besides such **phenomenological** accounts, that suggests that information is available in the form of an image for a short time after extinction of the physical stimulus. In the first place, it is inconceivable that the observers should stop seeing the stimulus at exactly the moment the light is turned off. The rise and fall of sensation may be rapid, but they are not instantaneous. The question is not *whether* the observer continues to see the stimulus after the illumination is turned off, but for *how long* he continues to see the stimulus. A number of different kinds of psychophysical measurements of the rise and fall of sensation have been attempted. These estimates of the persistence of the visual sensation vary from a minimum of 0.05 sec. (Wundt, 1899) to almost one sec. (McDougall, 1904). The most representative estimates are in the neighborhood of 1/6 sec. (cf. Pieron, 1934), a figure that is in good agreement with the results.[13]

In Experiment 5 it was shown that the post-exposure field strongly influences the accuracy of both the partial and the whole report. This experiment indicates that the available information is sensitive to interference by *non-informational visual stimuli* which follow the exposure. The dependence of available information upon noninformational visual stimulation is just the dependence that would be expected of a visual image.

Finally, there are subtle aspects of the sequence of letters reported by an S which characterize the information that is available to him. In sequentially spoken letters, for example, there is a limit--two--on the number of letters that can be adjacent to any given letter. Different limits apply to a two-dimensional visual display. If information is stored in a form **topologically** similar to the stimulus, this may be detected by noting the sequential dependencies that limit successive responses to the stimulus.

Probably the kinds of sequential responding that would most clearly distinguish visual from auditory information storage would be (a) the ability of the S to read the rows of the visual stimulus backwards as well as forwards, or to report the columns or the diagonals, and (b) his inability to do an equivalent task when presented with the information sequentially. (All these procedures merely require the report of adjacent letters if the stimulus is two dimensional.) Unfortunately, these particular experiments were not conducted.

The foregoing experiments offer some relevant evidence. In contrast to spoken letters and numbers, which are most accurately recalled if they occur at the beginning or end of a sequence (Pollack, 1952),[14] no obvious gradients of accuracy were found in the foregoing experiments. The middle row actually tended to be slightly better reported than the other rows. Therefore, it is unlikely that the *entire* visual stimulus (12-letters and numbers) was transformed into an auditory (sequential) representation for storage. Such an entire transformation is also unlikely, though not impossible, because of the relatively small time between the stimulus exposure and the report.

An analysis of errors reveals numerous cases of errors that may be classified as "misreading" (for example, confusions between E and F, B and R) and as "mishearing" (for example, confusions between B and D, D and T--Miller & Nicely, 1955). Still other confusions (for example, C and G) are ambiguous. All of these types of errors occurred whenever errors occurred at all. The ubiquity of misreading and mishearing errors, taken at face value, suggests that both visual and auditory storage of information are always involved in both whole and partial reports. A non-quantitative error analysis is therefore not likely to shed much light on the question of visual imagery. The frequent mishearing errors suggest that the storage of letters, just prior to a written report, may share some of the characteristics of audition. Like the preceding analysis of the constraints upon successive responses, error analysis requires considerable research before it can be quantitatively applied to problems of imagery.

This then is the evidence--phenomenological reports, the effects of the post-exposure fields, the known facts of the persistence of sensation, and the detailed characteristics of the responses--that is consistent with the hypothesis that information is initially stored as a visual image and that the Ss can effectively utilize this information in their partial reports. In the present context, the term, visual image, is taken to mean that (a) the observer behaves as though the physical stimulus were still present when it is not (that is, after it has been removed) and that (b) his behavior in the absence of the stimulus remains a function of the same variables of visual stimulation as it is in its presence. The units of a visual image so defined are always those of an equivalent "objective image," the physical stimulus. It is as logical or illogical to compute the information contained in a visual image (as was done in Experiments 3 and 4) as it is to compute the information in a visual stimulus.

"Visual image" and "persistence of sensation" are terms suggested by the **asynchrony** between the time during which a stimulus is present and the time during which the observer behaves as though it were present. Although asynchrony is inevitable for short exposure durations, there is, of course, no need to use the term "visual image" in a description of this situation. One might, for example, refer simply to an "information storage" with the characteristics that were experimentally observed. This form of psychological isolationism does injustice to the vast amount of relevant researches.

Teleological (tee-lee-oh-LODGE-ih-kal). To be *teleological* is to assume that there is some "grand design" in nature which can be seen in all natural facts.

Phenomenological (fee-nom-ee-noh-LODGE-ih-kal). A phenomenon (fee-NOM-ee-non) is an event, a happening, an experience. A phenomenological report is the subject's report of his or her impressions of what happened.

Topologically (top-oh-LODGE-ih-kal). *Topology* (top-OLL-oh-gee) is the study of surfaces. If two things are "topologically similar," then their shapes or forms are much the same.

Asynchrony (A-sin-kron-ee). Two events are "synchronous" if they occur together, in rhythm. Two events are "asynchronous" if they occur out of phase, or out of rhythm.

Imagery that reputedly occurs long after the original stimulation (memory images, **eidetic** images, etc.) is of interest as well as imagery that occurs for only a few tenths of a second following stimulation. Whether the term "imagery" as it has been used here to describe the immediate effects of brief stimulation, is an appropriate term for the description of the lasting effects of stimulation is an empirical problem. It is hoped, however, that the principles and methods developed here will not be without relevance to these traditional problems.

Persistence of Vision and Afterimages

Between the short persistence of vision and the remembrance of a long-passed event, there is an intermediate situation, the afterimage, which requires consideration. In discussing afterimages, it will be useful to distinguish some phases of vision that normally follow an intense or prolonged stimulus. First, there is the "initial" (or primary, or original) "image" (or sensation, or impression, or perception, or response). Any combination of a term from the first and from the second of these groups may be used. The initial image is followed by a latent period during which nothing is seen and which may in turn be followed by a complex sequence of afterimages. Afterimages may be either positive or negative; almost any sequence is possible, but the initial image is almost always positive.[15] Some authors distinguish the initial image from a **positive afterimage** (for example, McDougall, 1904); others do not (for example, von Helmholtz, 1924-25). It is often implicit in such distinctions that the persistence of the initial image is due to a continued excitatory process, whereas afterimages arise from receptor fatigue. If there is no repeated waxing and waning of sensation, but merely a single rise and fall, one cannot distinguish two phases in the primary image, one corresponding to the "initial image" and the other to an identical "positive afterimage" of it.

Although it is difficult to prove that visual information is stored in the initial image, there can be no gainsaying that an afterimage may be a rich store of information. Positive or negative afterimages may carry many fine details, including details that were not visible at the time of stimulation (von Helmholtz, 1924-25). Afterimages generally last for at least several seconds, and following high energy stimulation they normally last for several minutes (Berry & Imus, 1935). The clarity of the details, of course, deteriorates with the passage of time. Since afterimages appear to move when the eye is moved, they usually have been considered retinal phenomena. Taken together, these facts imply that *there is a considerable capacity for visual information storage in the retina*. If the illumination of the stimulus cards used in the foregoing experiments had been sufficiently intense to blaze the letters upon the retina and thereby take maximum advantage of its information storage capacity, there could have been little doubt afterwards as to the nature or location of most of the available information. The stimulus presentations actually used, however, rarely elicited reports of afterimages; Ss usually reported seeing simply a single brief flash. The problem is therefore to determine the persistence of the image of the brief flash, or equivalently, the duration of seeing (the stimulus) or the persistence of vision (of the stimulus), rather than the duration of an afterimage. These terms are used to suggest that the S feels he is responding directly to the stimulus rather than to aftereffects of stimulation.

Psychologists have often carelessly assumed that the absence of discernible afterimages following a visual presentation was sufficient to insure that the duration of sensation will correspond to the duration of the physical stimulus, that is, that there is no persistence of vision at all. Wundt (1899) was one of the first to take vigorous exception to this naive view. Wundt's most compelling example was drawn from Weyer (1899). Weyer had found that two 40-microsecond light flashes had to be separated by 40 to 50 msec. in order for them to be seen as two distinct flashes; at smaller separations they were seen as a single flash. In the dark adapted eye, the minimum separable interval that consistently yielded reports of "two flashes" was 80 to 100 msec.

Wundt argued that the two flashes could not be seen as distinct until the sensation occasioned by the first flash had ceased. Thus, under optimum conditions, the minimum duration of the sensation of a short flash was at least 40 msec. which, in this case, was 1,000 times the stimulus duration. Wundt thought that, in order to determine the duration of a longer flash, one must merely add the 40 msec. of fade-out time to the actual physical light duration. While these details of Wundt's reasoning may be questioned, his main point, based on the example of the short flash, is indisputable: one does not directly control the time for which information is visually available simply by manipulating exposure duration. The experiments reported here provide a direct proof of this assertion.

An Application of the Results to Before and After Experiments

The previous experiments showed that more information is available to Ss for a few tenths of a second after the exposure than they can give in a complete report of what they have seen. It was suggested that the limit on the number of items in the memory report is a very general one, the span of immediate-memory, which is relatively independent of the nature of the stimulus. Evidence was offered that information in excess of the immediate-memory span is available to the S as a rapidly fading visual image of the stimulus. If more information is available to him than he can remember, the S must "choose" a part of it to remember. In doing so, he has chosen the part to forget. In Experiments 3 and 4, Ss exercised only locational choices, that is, portions of the stimulus were remembered only on the basis of their location. Locational choices are probably not the only effective choices that the S can make. During the short time that information is available to him, the S may process it in any way in which he normally handles information. Usually, what he does, or attempts to do, is determined by the instructions. The Ss (unobservable) response to the stimulus is probably the same whether the instruction to make this response is given before the stimulus presentation or after it; the difference between the two cases lies in the information that the response can draw upon. If the stimulus contains more information than the Ss immediate-memory span, and if the post-exposure instruction is delayed until the S has little of this extra information available, then a difference in the accuracy of the responses with prior- and post-exposure instructions will be observed. If the stimulus does not contain more information than can be coded for immediate-memory, or if the post-exposure instruction is given soon enough so that the S can utilize the still available information effectively, then only minor differences in the accuracy of responses with prior- and post-exposure instructions will be observed. If the stimulus is destitute of information (for example, a single, mutilated, dimly illuminated letter of the alphabet) then a host of other factors which are normally insignificant may become crucial. In this case, the "stimulus" itself may well be irrelevant (Goldiamond, 1957), and the effects of instruction given before or after the exposure must be predicted on some other basis.

There are some simple experiments in which it is known a priori that the effects of instructions given either before or after the exposure will be exactly the same. This degenerate situation can be illustrated by a stimulus which is exposed for one microsecond and with sufficient energy to be clearly visible. By suitable coding, the pre-exposure and post-exposure instructions can be separated by only two microseconds. The example serves to emphasize that what is implicitly referred to by "before and after" is not the exposure but something else: traditionally, the sensitization and/or forgetting that presumably occur in conjunction with the exposure. Thus, the theory that has been presented here merely gives an explicit statement of assumptions that have long been implicit.

Unobservable Responses and the Order of Report

The subjective response to the high signal tone is "looking up." Since eye movements cannot occur in time to change the retinal image with any of the presentations used (Diefendorf & Dodge, 1908) a successful looking-up must be described in terms of a shift in "attention." Nonetheless, such a shift in attention can be quantitatively studied by means of a stabilized retinal image (Pritchard, 1958) although Wundt (1912), who did not use this modern, technically difficult technique, was able to give many essential details. The reaction time for the attentional response, like the reaction time for more observable response, is greater than zero. Therefore, if the S is given an instruction before the presentation, he can prepare for, or sensitize himself to, the correct row of the stimulus even though there is not time enough for a useful eye movement. The response to an instruction which is given 0.05 sec. before the stimulus is probably the same as the response to a similar instruction that is given 0.1 sec. later, immediately after the exposure. The short time difference, 0.1 sec., accounts for the similar accuracy of responding in these two conditions.

Once his attention is directed to the appropriate row, the S still has to read the letters. This, too, takes time. Baxt's (1871) data indicate that the time required to read a letter is about 10 msec. Baxt's experiment, with some modifications, was repeated by the author, and similar results were obtained.[16]

How is all this relevant to the order of report? The order in which the letters are finally reported can be an important variable because of (a) purely temporal factors (letters that are reported first will be more accurately reported only because they are reported sooner after the exposure, the actual order of reporting the letters per se being relatively unimportant) or (b) interaction effects (the report of some letters is detrimental to the report of the remaining letters, that is, letters reported later suffer from **proactive interference** by the letters reported earlier).

Eidetic (eye-DET-ick). Having an eidetic image of something you've seen is like having an *exact* picture of that visual stimulus.

Positive afterimage. If you stare hard at a picture of a red rose on a yellow background for several seconds, then look at a blank (white) wall, you'll probably see a *negative afterimage* of the picture--that is, you'll see a green rose on a blue background. But if you glance at the same picture for less than a second, you may see a brief *positive* afterimage--that is, an image of the picture as it actually is.

Proactive interference. A disruption of memory. Proactive interference occurs when the information you are reading *now* interfers or limits your ability to remember something you learn immediately after this.

That purely temporal factors cannot be very important can be seen from the slope of the curves describing available information as a function of time. In the foregoing experiments, the amount of available information approached the immediate-memory span at about 0.5 to 1.0 sec. after the exposure; further decrements in available information as a function of time are slight. The report of the letters usually does not begin until 1.0-1.5 sec. after the exposure. The passage of time during the actual time that letters are being reported, therefore, cannot account for appreciable accuracy changes as a function of the order of report.

The second possible effect of order of report--the interfering effect of the letters reported first upon unreported letters--cannot be so readily discounted. Proactive interference would imply that partial reports are more accurate than whole reports by an amount dependent upon their relative lengths. The results of Experiment 4 tend to support this view. At delays of the instruction signal greater than 0.3 sec., partial reports of three letters (from stimuli of nine letters) indicate more available letters than do partial reports of four letters (from stimuli of twelve letters). On the other hand, in Experiment 7 one S, ROR, does not show decreased accuracy as a function of the length of his report. ROR is able to report eight letters as accurately when he begins his report with three or four incorrect letters as when he ends his report with three or four incorrect letters. Other Ss did not systematically attempt to report incorrect letters first. Had they been required to report incorrect letters first, they might well have been able to do so.

The choice of what part of the stimulus to attend to or of which letters to read is the choice of what fraction of the stimulus information to utilize. This choice can be made successfully only while the information is still available. The Ss prefer to report what they remember first, but this does not imply that they remember it because they report it first. It is difficult to disentangle the many factors that determine precisely what stimulus letters will appear in the response, but important choices of what information is to be recalled must occur while there is still something to choose from. Since the actual report begins only when there are available but a few letters in excess of the immediate-memory span, the order of report can at most play only the minor role of determining which of the few "excess" letters will be forgotten.[17]

The Questions of Generality and Repeatability

To what extent are the results obtained limited to the particular conditions of the foregoing experiments? The possibility that the actual physical fading of the light source is important to the availability of information can be rejected not only on prior grounds (see Apparatus) but also by the empirical findings. For example, in Fig. 9, the curve representing the number of letters available 0.15 sec. after exposure is quite similar to the 0.0-sec. delay curve. There is no visible energy emitted by the light source 0.15 sec. after its termination.

In the present case, the answer to the problem of repeatability of the results is made less speculative by three separate investigations that have since been conducted with similar techniques to those reported here.

The experiments have been repeated by the author[18] with a different tachistoscope, timer, and a light source that has only a negligible afterglow. All the main findings were reproducible.

Klemmer and Loftus (1958) confirmed the existence of a short-term, high information storage. They used a display consisting of four discrete line patterns, the S being required to report only one of these. The instruction was coded either as a signal light or verbally. Decay curves obtained when the instruction is delayed are similar to those reported above. A similar experiment has also been conducted by Averbach,[19] who used a television tachistoscope to present stimuli containing up to 16 letters. A pointer appeared above the letter to be reported. Initially, Ss had about twelve letters available for report, but the number decreased rapidly when the visual instruction was delayed.

It is usually technically more difficult to code instructions visually than acoustically. Although the principle of sampling in order to determine available information is common to both kinds of instructions, visually coded instructions differ in some interesting ways from acoustically coded instructions. For example, the time taken to "interpret"--or even to find--a visual instruction may well depend on its location relative to the fixation point. Moreover, there may be spatial interactions between the visual "instruction" and the symbols to be reported. On the other hand, prior to training, the task of interpreting a visual marker is easier for Ss than the equivalent task with an acoustically coded instruction. Ultimately, such differences are probably only of secondary importance since the two kinds of experiments agree quite well.

Three main findings emerge from the experiments reported here: a large amount of information becomes available to observers of a brief visual presentation, this information decays rapidly, the final level is approximately equal to the span of immediate-memory. Although the exact, quantitative aspects of information that becomes available following a brief exposure unquestionably depend upon the precise conditions of presentation, is seems fair to conclude that the main results can be duplicated even under vastly different circumstances in different laboratories.

SUMMARY AND CONCLUSIONS

When stimuli consisting of a number of items are shown briefly to an observer, only a limited number of the items can be correctly reported. This number defines the so-called "span of immediate-memory." The fact that observers commonly assert that they can *see* more than they can *report* suggests that memory sets a limit on a process that is otherwise rich in available information. In the present studies, a sampling procedure (partial report) was used to circumvent the limitation imposed by immediate-memory and thereby to show that at the time of exposure, and for a few tenths of a second thereafter, observers have two or three times as much information available as they can later report. The availability of this information declines rapidly, and within one second after the exposure the available information no longer exceeds the memory span.

Short-term information storage has been tentatively identified with the persistence of sensation that generally follows any brief, intense stimulation. In this case, the persistence is that of a rapidly fading, visual image of the stimulus. Evidence in support of this hypothesis of visual information storage was found in introspective accounts, in the type of dependence of the accuracy of partial reports upon the visual stimulation, and in an analysis of certain response characteristics. These and related problems were explored in a series of seven experiments.

An attempt was first made to show that the span of immediate-memory remains relatively invariant under a wide range of conditions. Five practiced observers were shown stimuli consisting of arrays of symbols that varied in number, arrangement, and composition (letters alone, or letters and numbers together). It was found (Experiments 1 and 2) that each observer was able to report only a limited number of symbols (for example, letters) correctly. For exposure durations from 15 to 500 msec., the average was slightly over four letters; stimuli having four or fewer letters were reported correctly nearly 100% of the time.

In order to circumvent the immediate-memory limit on the (whole) report of what has been seen, observers were required to report only a part--designated by location--of stimuli exposed for 50 msec. (partial report). The part to be reported, usually one out of three rows of letters, was small enough (three to four letters) to lie within the memory span. A tonal signal (high, middle, or low frequency) was used to indicate which of the rows was to be reported. The S did not know which signal to expect, and the indicator signal was not given until after the visual stimulus had been turned off. In this manner, the information available to the S was sampled immediately after termination of the stimulus.

Each observer, for each material tested (6, 8, 9, 12 symbols), gave partial reports that were more accurate than whole reports for the same material. For example, following the exposure of stimuli consisting of 12 symbols, 76% of the letters called for in the partial report were given correctly by the observers. This accuracy indicates that the total information available from which an observer can draw his partial report is about 9.1 letters (76% of 12 letters). This number of randomly chosen letters is equivalent to 40.6 bits of information, which is considerably more information than previous experimental estimates have suggested can become available in a brief exposure. Furthermore, it seems probable that the 40-bit information capacity observed in these experiments was limited by the small amount of information in the stimuli rather than by a capacity of the observers.

In order to determine how the available information decreases with time, the instruction signal, which indicated the row of the stimulus to be reported, was delayed by various amounts, up to 1-0 sec. (Experiment 4). The accuracy of the partial report was shown to be a sharply decreasing function of the delay in the instruction signal. Since, at a delay of 1.0 sec., the accuracy of the partial reports approached that of the whole reports, it follows that the information in excess of the immediate-memory span is available for less than a second. In contrast to the partial report, the accuracy of the whole report is not a function of the time at which the signal to report is given (Experiment 7).

The large amount of information in excess of the immediate-memory span, and the short time during which this information is available, suggests that it may be stored as a persistence of the sensation resulting from the visual stimulus. In order to explore further this possibility of visual information storage, some parameters of visual stimulation were studied. A decrease of the exposure duration from 50 to 15 msec. did not substantially affect the accuracy of partial reports (Experiment 5). On the other hand, the substitution of a white post-exposure field for the dark field ordinarily used greatly reduced the accuracy of both partial and whole reports. The ability of a homogeneous visual stimulus to affect the available information is evidence that the process depends on a persisting visual image of the stimulus.

Whether other kinds of partial reports give similar estimates of the amount of available information was examined by asking observers to report by category rather than by location. The observer reported numbers only (or the letters only) from stimuli consisting of both letters and numbers (Experiment 6). These partial reports were no more accurate than (whole) reports of all the letters and numbers. The ability of observers to give highly accurate partial reports of letters designated by location (Experiment 3), and their inability to give partial reports of comparable accuracy when the symbols to be reported are designated as either letters or numbers, clearly indicates that all kinds of partial reports are not equally suitable for demonstrating the ability of observers to retain large amounts of information for short time periods.

In the final study (Experiment 7), the order of report was systematically varied. Observers were instructed to get as many letters correct as possible, but the order in which they were to report the letters was not indicated until after the exposure. An instruction tone, following the exposure, indicated which of the two rows of letters on the stimulus was to be reported first. This interference with the normal order of report reduced only slightly the total number of letters that were reported correctly. As might be expected, the first row--the row indicated by the instruction tone--was reported more accurately than the second row (order effect). There was, however, a strong tendency for the top row to be reported more accurately than the bottom row (position effect). Although, as a group, the observers showed both effects, some failed to show either the order or the position effect, or both. The fact that, for some observers, order and position are not correlated with response accuracy suggests that order of report, and position, are not the major *causes* of, nor the necessary conditions for, response accuracy. The high accuracy of partial report observed in the experiments does not depend on the order of report or on the position of letters on the stimulus, but rather it is shown to depend on the ability of the observer to read a visual image that persists for a fraction of a second after the stimulus has been turned off.

FOOTNOTES

[1] Reprinted by permission of the author and the publisher from *Psychological Monographs*, 1960, 74, 1-29. Copyright 1960 by the American Psychological Association.

[2] This paper is a condensation of a doctoral thesis (Sperling, 1959). For further details, especially on methodology, and for individual data, the reader is referred to the original thesis. It is a pleasure to acknowledge my gratitude to George A. Miller and Roger N. Shepard whose support made this research possible and to E. B. Newman, J. Schwartzbaum and S. S. Stevens for their many helpful suggestions. Thanks are also due to Jerome S. Bruner for the use of his laboratory and his tachistoscope during his absence in the summer of 1957. This research was carried out under Contract AF 33(038) -14343 between Harvard University and the Operational Applications Laboratory, Air Force Cambridge Research Center, Air Research Development Command.

[3] Some representative examples are: Bridgin (1933), Cattell (1883), Chapman (1930), Dallenbach (1920), Erdmann and Dodge (1898), Glanville and Dallenbach (1929), Kulpe (1904), Schumann (1922), Wagner (1918), Whipple (1914), Wilcocks (1925), Woodworth (1938).

[4] The experiments referred to are (cf. Sperling, 1959): Kulpe (1904), Wilcocks (1925), Chapman (1932), Long, Henneman, and Reid (1953), Long and Lee (1953a), Long and Lee (1953b), Long, Reid, and Carvey (1954), Lawrence and Coles (1954), Adams (1955), Lawrence and Laberge (1956), Broadbent (1957a).

[5] Ralph Gerbrands company, 96 Ronald Road, Arlington 74, Massachusetts.

[6] If there are a large number of letters in the stimulus, the probability that these same letters will appear somewhere on the response grid, irrespective of position, becomes very high whether or not S has much information about the stimulus. In the limit, the correspondence approaches 100% provided only that the relative frequency of each letter in the response matches its relative frequency of occurrence in the stimulus pack. If the response is scored for both letter *and* position, then the percent guessing correction is independent of changes in stimulus size.

[7] See Sperling (1959) for tables giving the numerical values of all points appearing in this and in all other figures.

[8] See Sperling (1959) for tables containing individual averages of all trials for each S at each delay of instruction tone: 3/3, 4/4.

[9] Increase in variability (with consequent decrement in accuracy and/or speed) is not unusual after difficult conditions. For example, Cohen and Thomas (1957) in a clinically oriented study have reported an exactly analogous "hysteresis" phenomenon in a study of discriminative reaction time. Hysteresis refers to the fact that, when the difficulty of an experimental task is changed, the corresponding change in accuracy of response lags behind the change in task.

[10] It takes, on the average, a very large number of trials for S to get 10 consecutive perfect trials even if he has 6 or 7 of 9 letters available or knows with 2/3 probability what the tone will be. Success in this task within a reasonable time limit demands a level of excellence reached only with "equal attention" observing, as judged by the other criteria.

[11] This important method was described by Ladd (1899) and James (1890) in their textbooks, but it is no longer well known. Consequently it has been "rediscovered," most recently by Lindsley and Emmons (1958). Baxt (1871) intended that the

bright second field would interfere with the lingering image of the first (informational) field. Unfortunately, the effect depends in a complex way upon the intensity of the two fields. Derived time values must be used with caution. In some cases the Baxt technique may actually result in no loss of legibility, the second field producing a negative "afterimage" instead of merely interfering with the positive image (cf. Footnote 15).

[12]Figure 11 is based upon a suggestion by E. B. Newman. A statistical analysis of variance was not attempted since it would have had to be carried out separately on each S. There was not enough data to make this worthwhile, and Fig. 11 serves the same purpose.

[13]Measurements of the persistence of sensation have almost invariably used techniques which have at most questionable validity. Wundt's method depends upon masking, the effect of the persisting stimulus upon another stimulus. The masking power of a stimulus may be quite different from its visibility. McDougall's measurements, as well as those cited by Pieron, depend upon motion of a stimulus across the retina. Such measurements are undoubtedly influenced by the strong temporal and spatial interactions of the eye (Alpern, 1953). Schumann's ingenious application of the method of Baxt to the determination of persistence is probably the only experiment that utilizes pattern stimulation. The other methods have not been tried with pattern stimuli although there is, a priori, no good reason why they have not been. The possibility that the persistence of pattern information is quite different from persistence of "brightness" has not been investigated.

[14]Summarized in Luce (1956).

[15]Bidwell (1897) and Sperling (1960) describe conditions for seeing a negative "after-image without prior positive image." The method involves a presentation quite similar to that of Baxt (1871).

[16]Sperling, G. Unpublished experiments conducted at the Bell Telephone Laboratories, 1958.

[17]There are many ways in which proactive interference might occur. For example, if letters are stored sequentially prior to report (cf. Broadbent, 1957b), then the importance of order of report may lie in the agreement of the two sequences: storage and report.

[18]Sperling, G. Unpublished experiments conducted at the Bell Telephone Laboratories, 1958.

[19]Averbach, E. Unpublished experiments conducted at the Bell Telephone Laboratories, 1959.

REFERENCES

Adams, J. S. The relative effectiveness of pre- and post-stimulus setting as a function of stimulus uncertainty. Unpublished master's dissertation, Department of Psychology, University of North Carolina, 1955.

Alpern, M. Metacontrast. *J. Opt. Soc. Amer.*, 1953, **43**, 648-657.

Baxt, N. Uber die Zeit welche notig ist damit ein Gesichtseindruck zum Bewusstsein kommt und uber die Grosse (Extension) der bewussten Wahrnehmung beif einem Gesichtseindrucke von gegebener Dauer. *Pfluger's Arch. ges. Physiol.*, 1871, **4**, 325-336.

Berry, W., & Imus, H. Quantitative aspects of the flight of colors. *Amer. J. Psychol.*, 1935, **47**, 449-457.

Bidwell, S. On the negative after-images following brief retinal excitation. *Proc. Roy. Soc. Lond.*, 1897, **61**, 268-271.

Bridgin, R. L. A tachistoscopic study of the differentiation of perception. *Psychol. Monogr.*, 1933, **44**(1, Whole No. 197), 153-166.

Broadbent, D. E. Immediate memory and simultaneous stimuli. *Quart. J. exp. Psychol.*, 1957, **9**, 1-11. (a)

Broadbent, D. E. A mechanical model for human attention and memory. *Psychol. Rev.*, 1957, **64**, 205-215. (b)

Broadbent, D. E. *Perception and communication.* New York: Pergamon, 1958.

Cattell, J. McK. Uber die Tragheit der Netzhaut und des Sehcentrums. *Phil. Stud.*, 1883, **3**, 94-127.

Chapman, D. W. The comparative effects of determinate and indeterminate aufgaben. Unpublished doctor's dissertation, Harvard University, 1930.

Chapman, D. W. Relative effects of determinate and indeterminate Aufgaben. *Amer. J. Psychol.*, 1932, **44**, 163-174.

Cohen, L. D., & Thomas, D. R. Decision and motor components of reaction time as a function of anxiety level and task complexity. *Amer. Psychologist*, 1957, **12**, 420. (Abstract).

Dallenbach, K. M. Attributive vs. cognitive clearness. *J. exp. Psychol.*, 1920, **3**, 183-230.

Diefendorf, A. R., & Dodge, R. An experimental study of the ocular reations of the insane from photographic records. *Brain*, 1908, **31**, 451-489.

Dodge, R. An experimental study of visual fixation. *Psychol. Monogr.*, 1907, **8**(4, Whole No. 35). (a)

Dodge, R. An improved exposure apparatus. *Psychol. Bull.*, 1907, **4**, 10-13. (b)

Erdmann, B., & Dodge, R. *Psychologische Untersuchungen uber das Lesen auf experimenteller Grundlage.* Halle: Niemeyer, 1898.

Glanville, A. D., & Dallenbach, K. M. The range of attention. *Amer. J. Psychol.*, 1929, **41**, 207-236.

Goldiamond, I. Operant analysis of perceptual behavior. Paper read at Symposium on Experimental Analysis of Behavior, APA Annual Convention, 1957.

James, W. *The principles of psychology.* New York: Holt, 1890.

Klemmer, E. T. Simple reaction time as a function of time uncertainty. *J. exp. Psychol.*, 1957, **54**, 195-200.

Klemmer, E. T., & Loftus, J. P. *Numerals, nonsense forms, and information.* USAF Cambridge Research Center, Operational Applications Laboratory, Bolling Air Force Base, 1958. (Astia Doc. No. AD110063).

Kulpe, O. Versuche uber Abstraktion. In, *Bericht uber den erste Kongress fur experimentelle Psychologie.* Leipzig: Barth, 1904. Pp. 56-68.

Ladd, G. T. *Elements of physiological psychology: A treatise of the activities and nature of the mind.* New York: Scribner, 1889.

Lawrence, D. H., & Coles, G. R. Accuracy of recognition with alternatives before and after the stimulus. *J. exp. Psychol.,* 1954, **47,** 208-214.

Lawrence, D. H., & Laberge, D. L. Relationship between accuracy and order of reporting stimulus dimensions. *J. exp. Psychol.,* 1956, **51,** 12-18.

Lindsley, D. B., & Emmons, W. H. Perception time and evoked potentials. *Science,* 1958, **127,** 1061.

Long, E. R., Henneman, R. H., & Reid, L. S. Theoretical considerations and exploratory investigation of "set" as response restriction: The first of a series of reports on "set" as a determiner of perceptual responses. *USAF WADC tech. Rep., 1953,* No. 53-311.

Long, E. R., & Lee, W. A. The influence of specific stimulus cueing on location responses: The third of a series of reports on "set" as a determiner of perceptual responses. *USAF WADC tech. Rep.,* 1953, No. 53-314. (a)

Long, E. R., Lee, W. A. The role of spatial cuing as a response-limiter for location responses: The second of a series of reports on "set" as a determiner of perceptual responses. *USAF WADC tech. Rep.,* 1953, No. 53-312. (b)

Long, E. R., Reid, L. D., & Garvey, W. D. The role of stimulus ambiguity and degree of response restriction in the recognition of distorted letter patterns: The fourth of a series of reports on "set" as a determiner of perceptual responses. *USAF WADC tech. Rep.,* 1954, No. 54-147.

Luce, D. R. *A survey of the theory of selective information and some of its behavioral applications.* New York: Bureau of Applied Social Research, 1956.

McDougall, W. The sensations excited by a single momentary stimulation of the eye. *Brit. J. Psychol.,* 1904, **1,** 78-113.

Miller, G. A. Human memory and the storage of information. *IRE Trans. Information Theory,* 1956, **IT-2,** No. 3, 129-137. (a)

Miller, G. A. The magic number seven, plus or minus two: Some limits on our capacity for processing information. *Psychol. Rev.,* 1956, **63,** 81-97. (b)

Miller, G. A., & Nicely, P. E. An analysis of perceptual confusions among some English consonants. *J. Acoust. Soc. Amer.,* 1955, **27,** 338-352.

Pieron, H. L'evanouissement de la sensation lumineuse: Persistance indifferenciable et persistance totale. *Ann. psychol.,* 1934, **35,** 1-49.

Pollack, I. The assimilation of sequentially-encoded information. *Hum. Resources Res. Lab. MEMO Rep.,* 1952, No. 25.

Pritchard, R. M. Visual illusions viewed as stabilized retinal images. *Quart. J. exp. Psychol.,* 1958, **10,** 77-81.

Quastler, H. Studies of human channel capacity. In H. Quastler, *Three survey papers.* Urbana, Ill.: Control Systems Laboratory, Univer. Illinois, 1956. Pp. 13-33.

Schumann, F. Die Erkennung von Buchstaben und Worten bei momentaner Beleuchtigung. In, *Bericht uber den erste Kongress fur experimentelle Psychologie.* Leipzig: Barth, 1904. Pp. 34-40.

Schumann, F. The Erkennungsurteil. *Z. Psychol.,* 1922, **88,** 205-224.

Sperling, G. Information available in a brief visual presentation. Unpublished doctor's dissertation, Department of Psychology, Harvard University, 1959.

Sperling, G. Afterimage without prior image. *Science,* 1960, **131,** 1613-1614.

Von Helmholtz, H. *Treatise on physiological optics.* Vol. II. *The sensations of visions.* (Transl. from 3rd German ed.) Rochester, New York: Optical Society of America, 1924-25.

Wagner, J. Experimentelle Beitrage zur Psychologie des Lesens. *Z. Psychol.,* 1918, **80,** 1-75.

Weyer, E. M. The Zeitschwellen gleichartiger und disparater Sinneseindrucke. *Phil. Stud.,* 1899, **15,** 68-138.

Whipple, G. M. *Manual of physical and mental tests.* Vol. I. *Simpler processes.* Baltimore: Warwick & York, 1914.

Wilcocks, R. W. An examination of Kulpe's experiments on abstraction. *Amer. J. Psychol.,* 1925, **36,** 324-340.

Woodworth, R. S. *Experimental psychology.* New York: Holt, 1938.

Wundt, W. Zur Kritik tachistosckopischer Versuche. *Phil. Stud.* 1899, **15,** 287-317.

Wundt, W. *An introduction to psychology.* London: Allen & Unwin, 1912.

Classic Quotations from William James

False memories are by no means rare occurrences in most of us . . . The most frequent source of false memory is the accounts we give to others of our experiences. Such accounts we almost always make both more simple and more interesting than the truth. We quote what we should have said or done, rather than what we really said or did; and in the first telling we may be fully aware of the distinction. But ere long the fiction expels the reality from memory and reigns in its stead alone.

(*The Principles of Psychology* [1890], ch. 10.)

Memory requires more than mere dating of a fact in the past. It must be dated in *my* past. In other words, I must think that I directly experienced its occurrence. It must have that 'warmth and intimacy' . . . as characterizing all experiences 'appropriated' by the thinker as his own.

(*The Principles of Psychology* [1890], ch. 16.)

CHAPTER 10

"Short-Term Retention of Individual Verbal Items"

Lloyd R. Peterson and Margaret Jean Peterson[1,2]

> **EDITORS' COMMENTS.** In our comments at the start of the previous chapter, we noted that, according to the information processing approach, human memory has three stages: the Sensory Information Stage, Short-term Memory, and Long-term Memory. Sperling (Chapter 9) determined some of the variables that affect inputs as they are processed in the Sensory Information Stage. But what about Short-term Memory? What evidence led psychologists to the belief that inputs are typically held but a brief time in "primary memory," and then are either discarded (and lost forever) or converted into items filed in long-term storage?
>
> One of the research studies that first offered evidence for the existence of Short-term Memory is the present one by Peterson and Peterson. These researchers found that if they exposed their subjects to a nonsense syllable (such as XFG), then required the subjects to repeat the syllable a short time later on, what the subjects did during the "waiting period" greatly affected recall. Previous studies had shown that subjects do show some forgetting during a 10 second "wait period," but many subjects could recall the letters even 20 seconds afterward. However, the "wait periods" in these early studies were *empty*. That is, the subjects were not distracted in any fashion while waiting, and thus could *rehearse* the letters (by saying them silently, again and again) while waiting. When Peterson and Peterson required their subjects to "count backward by 3s" during the wait period, however, the subjects showed almost complete forgetting 18 seconds after being exposed to the test stimuli. Thus, preventing the subjects from "rehearsing" the test items prevented them from remembering the items. Evidence from this (and other studies) suggested that Short-term Memory of an input lasts perhaps seven seconds or so at the most. However, memory for each input is rapidly destroyed by each subsequent input to short-term storage. Psychologists sometimes refer to this as the "leaky bucket effect." That is, items enter short-term storage much as water enters the top of a leaky bucket; the items then are pushed lower and lower into the bucket as old items "leak out the bottom" and new inputs pour in at the top. The present view is that, as Miller noted, Short-term Memory has a "storage capacity" of seven items or so.
>
> There is another important aspect of Short-term Memory you should know about. A study of the *errors* made by subjects in Sperling-type experiments shows that the subjects mostly mis-remember letters that *have similar shapes*--they report an E when the stimulus letter was actually an F. In studies such as the one by Peterson and Peterson, though, subjects often report an E when the stimulus letter was a C or a Z. That is, they confuse letters that *sound alike*, rather than mistaking letters that *look alike*. Evidence of this sort suggests that, during the Sensory Information Stage, the receptors maintain *an exact copy* of the stimulus input. However, the input is often *translated into an auditory (or linguistic) form* during short-term storage. Indeed, it almost seems as if you "say the word (or letter) aloud," or "describe the stimulus in words," before the input is held in Short-term Memory.
>
> Now, what causes one item (but not another) to be transferred from temporary storage (Short-term Memory) to permanent storage (Long-term Memory)? We will cover that topic in our comments at the beginning of the next chapter. We will, however, give you one clue important to understanding the present article: Had Peterson and Peterson presented any one of their items in an unusual fashion--printed in red ink, for instance, when all the rest were in black--memory for that item would have increased dramatically.

It is apparent that the acquisition of verbal habits depends on the effects of a given occasion being carried over into later repetitions of the situation. Nevertheless, textbooks separate acquisition and retention into distinct categories. The limitation of discussions of retention to long-term characteristics is necessary in large part by the scarcity of data on the course of retention over intervals of the order of magnitude of the time elapsing between successive repetitions in an acquisition study. The presence of a retentive function within the acquisition process was postulated by Hull (1940) in his use of the **stimulus trace** to explain serial phenomena. Again, Underwood (1949) has suggested that forgetting occurs during the acquisition process. But these theoretical considerations have not led to empirical investigation. Hull (1952) quantified the stimulus trace on data concerned with the **CS-UCS interval** in **eyelid conditioning** and it is not obvious that the construct so quantified can be readily transferred to verbal learning. One objection is that a verbal stimulus produces a strong predictable response prior to the experimental session and this is not true of the originally neutral stimulus in eyelid conditioning.

Two studies have shown that the effects of verbal stimulation can decrease over intervals measured in seconds. Pillsbury and Sylvester (1940) found marked decrement with a list of items tested for recall 10 sec after a single presentation. However, it seems unlikely that this traditional presentation of a list and later testing for recall of the list will be useful in studying intervals near or shorter than the time necessary to present the list. Of more interest is a recent study by Brown (1958) in which among other conditions a single pair of **consonants** was tested after a 5-sec interval. **Decrement** was found at the one recall interval, but no systematic study of the course of retention over a variety of intervals was attempted.

EXPERIMENT I

The present investigation tests recall for individual items after several short intervals. An item is presented and tested without related items intervening. The initial study examines the course of retention after one brief presentation of the item.

Method

Subjects. The Ss were twenty-four students from introductory psychology courses at Indiana University. Participation in experiments was a course requirement.

Materials. The verbal items tested for recall were forty-eight **consonant syllables** with **Witmer association value** no greater than 33 per cent (Hilgard, 1951). Other materials were forty-eight three-digit numbers obtained from a table of random numbers. One of these was given to S after each presentation under instructions to count backward from the number. It was considered that continuous verbal activity during the time between presentation and signal for recall was desirable in order to minimize **rehearsal** behavior. The materials were selected to be categorically dissimilar and hence involve a minimum of **interference**.

Procedure. The S was seated at a table with E seated facing in the same direction on S's right. A black plywood screen shielded E from S. On the table in front of S were two small lights mounted on a black box. The general procedure was for E to spell a consonant syllable and immediately speak a three-digit number. The S then counted backward by three or four from this number. On flashing of a signal light S attempted to recall the consonant syllable. The E spoke in rhythm with a **metronome** clicking twice per second and S was

---

Stimulus trace. An early theory of memory held that, as a stimulus "moved through the nervous system," it "left a trace of itself behind," much as a river leaves a trace of itself when it cuts a riverbed out of the land it flows through. The more the stimulus "flowed" through the brain, the deeper (and stronger) the trace presumably became.

CS-UCS interval. The time between the onset of conditioning stimulus (sometimes called "conditioned stimulus") and the onset of the unconditional (or unconditioned) stimulus. If you ring a bell and then shock an animal in a conditioning experiment, the CS is the bell, the shock is the UCS, and the CS-UCS interval is the time between the onset of the bell and the onset of the shock. Clark Hull, an early learning theorist, believed that the optimal CS-UCS interval for most types of conditioning was about 0.5 sec.

Eyelid conditioning. A type of classical (Pavlovian) conditioning in which the UCS is a puff of air blown at the eyeball, and the UCR (unconditional response) is a blink.

Consonants (KON-soh-nants). All the letters of the alphabet that are not vowels, i.e., *b, c, d* and so forth.

Decrement (DECK-kree-ment). A decrease in performance.

Consonant syllables. Psychologists who study verbal learning often require their subjects to learn "nonsense syllables," such as *pak* or *qib*, that are not real words, but that are made up of both consonants and vowels. *Consonant syllables* are nonsense syllables made up entirely of consonants.

Witmer association value. Some nonsense syllables are easier to learn than others because the letters have become associated with each other. Thus, "thx" has a higher association value than does "zhx." Witmer has provided us with a list of which letters have high and low association values.

Rehearsal. If we show you the nonsense syllable "zhx" for one second, then ask you to recall it a minute later, you probably will be able to do so because you will keep "rehearsing" it while it's not visible. If we give you an unrelated task--such as counting backwards from 344 by threes--to perform during the minute's delay, you are far less likely to remember all three letters in the nonsense syllable.

Interference. "Counting backwards from 344 by threes" *interferes* with your ability to remember the nonsense syllable "zhx" in the above example. Many psychologists believe that most types of forgetting are due to interference, and not because the "memory trace" simply decays over time.

metronome (MET-troh-nome). A device that can be set to make a clicking sound at regular intervals. Musicians often use a metronome to help them learn to play a piece of music "in time."

```
SEC  0    1    2    3    4    5    6
     I    I    I    I    I    I    I
E    CHJ  506
                    506  503       CHJ
```

RECALL INTERVAL I ←--LATENCY--→ I

Figure 1. Sequence of events for a recall interval of 3 sec.

instructed to do likewise. The timing of these events is diagrammed in Figure 1. As E spoke the third digit, he pressed a button activating a Hunter interval timer. At the end of a preset interval the timer activated a red light and an electric clock. The light was the signal for recall. The clock ran until E heard S speak three letters, when E stopped the clock by depressing a key. This time between onset of the light and completion of a response will be referred to as a latency. It is to be distinguished from the interval from completion of the syllable by E to onset of the light, which will be referred to as the recall interval.

The instructions read to S were as follows: "Please sit against the back of your chair so that you are comfortable. You will not be shocked during this experiment. In front of you is a little black box. The top or green light is on now. This green light means that we are ready to begin a trial. I will speak some letters and then a number. You are to repeat the number immediately after I say it and begin counting backwards by 3s (4s) from that number in time with the ticking that you hear. I might say, ABC 309. Then you say, 309, 306, 303, etc., until the bottom or red light comes on. When you see this red light come on, stop counting immediately and say the letters that were given at the beginning of the trial. Remember to keep your eyes on the black box at all times. There will be a short rest period and then the green light will come on again and we will start a new trial." The E summarized what he had already said and then gave S two practice trials. During this practice S was corrected if he hesitated before starting to count, or if he failed to stop counting on signal, or if he in any other way deviated from the instructions.

Each S was tested eight times at each of the recall intervals, 3, 6, 9, 12, 15, and 18 sec. A given consonant syllable was used only once with each S. Each syllable occurred equally often over the group at each recall interval. A specific recall interval was represented once in each successive block of six presentations. The S counted backward by three on half of the trials and by four on the remaining trials. No two successive items contained letters in common. The time between signal for recall and the start of the next presentation was 15 sec.

Results and Discussion

Responses occurring any time during the 15-sec interval following signal for recall were recorded. In Figure 2 are plotted the proportions of correct recalls as **cumulative** functions of latency for each of the recall intervals. **Sign tests** were used to evaluate differences among the curves (Walker and Lev, 1953). At each latency differences among the 3-, 6-, 9-, and 18-sec recall interval curves are significant at the .005 level. For latencies of 6 sec and longer these differences are all significant at the 0.01 level. Note that the number correct with latency less than 2 sec does not constitute a majority of the total correct. These responses would not seem appropriately described as identification of the gradually weakening trace of a stimulus. There is a suggestion of an **oscillatory** characteristic in the events determining them.

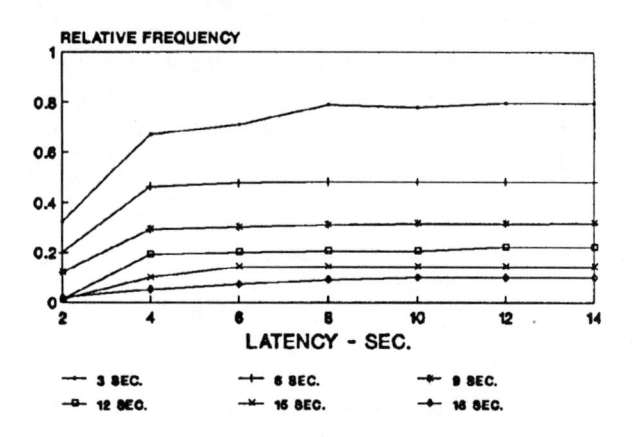

Figure 2. Correct recalls as cumulative functions of latency

The feasibility of an interpretation by a statistical model was explored by fitting to the data the **exponential** curve of Figure 3. The empirical points plotted here are proportions of correct responses with latencies shorter than 2.83 sec. Partition of the correct responses on the basis of latency is required by considerations developed in detail by Estes (1950). A given probability of response applies to an interval of time equal in length to the average time required for the response under consideration to occur. The mean latency of correct responses in the present experiment was 2.83 sec. Differences among the proportions of correct responses with latencies shorter than 2.83 sec were evaluated by sign tests. The difference between the 3- and 18-sec conditions was found to be significant at the 0.01 level. All differences among the 3-, 6-, 9-, 12-, and 18-sec conditions were significant at the 0.05 level.

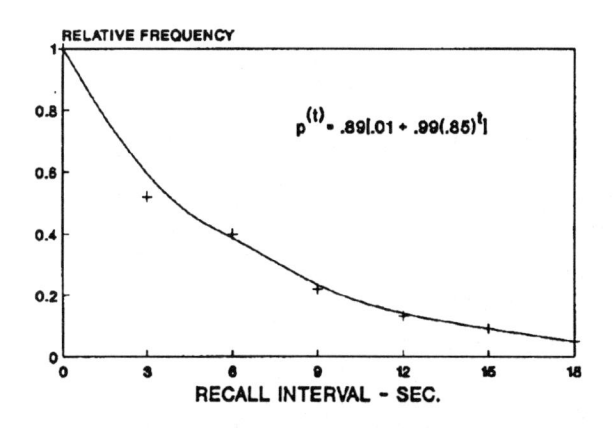

Figure 3. Correct recalls with latencies below 2.83 sec. as a function of recall interval

$p^{(t)} = .89[.01 + .99(.85)^t]$

The general equation of which the expression for the curve of Figure 3 is a specific instance is derived from the stimulus **fluctuation** model developed by Estes (1955). In applying the model to the present experiment it is assumed that the verbal stimulus produces a response in S which is conditioned to a set of elements contiguous with the response. The elements thus conditioned are a sample of a larger population of elements into which the conditioned elements disperse as time passes. The proportion of conditioned elements in the sample determining S's behavior thus decreases and with it the probability of the response. Since the fitted curve appears to do justice to the data, the observed decrement could arise from stimulus fluctuation.

The independence of successive presentations might be questioned in the light of finding that performance deteriorates as a function of previous learning (Underwood, 1957). The presence of **proactive interference** was tested by noting the correct responses within each successive block of twelve presentations. The short recall intervals were analysed separately from the long recall intervals in view of the possibility that **facilitation** might occur with the one and interference with the other. The proportions of correct responses for the combined 3- and 6-sec recall intervals were in order of occurrence 0.57, 0.66, 0.70, and 0.74. A sign test showed the difference between the first and last blocks to be significant at the 0.02 level. The proportions correct for the 15- and 18-sec recall intervals were 0.08, 0.15, 0.09, and 0.12. The gain from first to last blocks is not significant in this case. There is no evidence for proactive interference. There is an indication of improvement with practice.

EXPERIMENT II

The findings in Experiment I are compatible with the proposition that the after-effects of a single, brief, verbal stimulation can be interpreted as those of a trial of learning. It would be predicted from such an interpretation that probability of recall at a given recall interval should increase as a function of repetitions of the stimulation. Forgetting should proceed at differential rates for items with differing numbers of repetitions. Although this seems to be a reasonable prediction, there are those who would predict otherwise. Brown (1958), for instance, questions whether repetitions, as such, strengthen the "memory trace." He suggests that the effect of repetitions of a stimulus, or rehearsal, may be merely to postpone the onset of decay of the trace. If time is measured from the moment that the last stimulation ceased, then the forgetting curves should coincide in all cases, no matter how many occurrences of the stimulation have preceded the final occurrence. The second experiment was designed to obtain **empirical** evidence relevant to this problem.

Method

The Ss were forty-eight students from the source previously described. Half of the Ss were instructed to repeat the stimulus aloud in time with the metronome

---

Cumulative (QUEM-you-lah-tive). A cumulative curve (or mathematical function) is one that never decreases. Your age, for example, is cumulative, because you will never be younger than you are today. Your bank account, unfortunately, is not necessarily cumulative.

Sign tests. A fairly simple statistical measure used to determine whether two distributions are significantly different.

Oscillatory (OSS-sill-lah-tor-ee). The act of swinging back and forth, or up and down.

Exponential (ex-poh-NEN-shul). A curve that increases (or decreases) as a function of some exponent. In the expression a^2, for example, the "2" is an exponent.

Fluctuation (fluct-you-A-shun). The act of changing, or of shifting from one point to another. A traffic light, for instance, fluctuates among red, yellow, and green.

Proactive interference (PRO-act-tive). Literally, a stimulus input that occurs *now* which affects your ability to remember something you learn later on. Suppose, in an experiment, you are presented with the nonsense syllable "zhx" and asked to recall it a minute later. If a task you perform *before* learning the syllable affects later recall, you have experienced "proactive" interference. However, if a task you perform *after* learning the syllable (but before later recall) affects your performance, you have experienced *retroactive* interference with memory.

Facilitation (fass-sill-ih-TAY-shun). The opposite of interference. If a task you perform *now* improves your ability to remember a nonsense syllable you learn later, you have experienced proactive facilitation.

Empirical (em-PEER-ih-kal). Data-based, or measurable. As opposed to theoretical.

TABLE 1
PROPORTIONS OF ITEMS CORRECTLY RECALLED IN EXP. II

GROUP	Repetition Time (Sec.)	Recall Interval (Sec.)		
		3	9	18
Vocal	3	.80	.48	.34
	1	.68	.34	.21
	0	.60	.25	.14
Silent	3	.70	.39	.30
	1	.74	.35	.22
	0	.72	.38	.15

until stopped by E giving them a number from which S counted backward. The remaining Ss were not given instructions concerning use of the interval between E's presentation of the stimulus and his speaking the number from which to count backward. Both the "vocal" group and the "silent" group had equated intervals of time during which rehearsal inevitably occurred in the one case and could occur in the other case. Differences in frequency of recalls between the groups would indicate a failure of the uninstructed Ss to rehearse. The zero point marking the beginning of the recall interval for the silent group was set at the point at which E spoke the number from which S counted backward. This was also true for the vocal group.

The length of the rehearsal period was varied for Ss of both groups over three conditions. On a third of the presentations S was not given time for any repetitions. This condition was thus comparable to Experiment I, save that the only recall intervals used were 3, 9, and 18 sec. On another third of the presentations 1 sec elapsed during which S could repeat the stimulus. On another third of the presentations 3 sec elapsed, or sufficient time for three repetitions. Consonant syllables were varied as to the rehearsal interval in which they were used, so that each syllable occurred equally often in each condition over the group. However, a given syllable was never presented more than once to any S. The Ss were assigned in order of appearance to a randomized list of conditions. Six practice presentations were given during which corrections were made of departures from instructions. Other details follow the procedures of Experiment I.

Results and discussion

Table 1 shows the proportion of items recalled correctly. In the vocal group recall improved with repetition at each of the recall intervals tested. Conditions in the silent group were not consistently ordered. For purposes of statistical analysis the recall intervals were combined within each group. A sign test between numbers correct in the 0- and 3-repetition conditions of the vocal group showed the difference to be significant at the 0.01 level. The difference between the corresponding conditions of the silent group was not significant at the 0.05 level. Only under conditions where repetition of the stimulus was controlled by instructions did retention improve.

The obtained differences among the zero conditions of Experiment II and the 3-, 9-, and 18-sec recall intervals of Experiment I require some comment, since procedures were essentially the same. Since these are between-S comparisons, some differences would be predicted because of sampling variability. But another factor is probably involved. There were forty-eight presentations in Experiment I and only thirty-six in Experiment II. Since recall was found to improve over successive blocks of trials, a superiority in recall for Ss of Experiment I is reasonable. In the case of differences between the vocal and silent groups of Experiment II a statistical test is permissible, for Ss were assigned randomly to the two groups. **Wilcoxon's (1949) test for unpaired replicates**, as well as a **t test**, was used. Neither showed significance at the 0.05 level.

The 1- and 3-repetition conditions of the vocal group afforded an opportunity to obtain a measure of what recall would be at the zero interval in time. It was noted whether a syllable had been correctly repeated by S. Proportions correctly repeated were 0.90 for the 1-repetition condition and 0.88 for the 3-repetition condition. The chief source of error lay in the confusion of the letters "m" and "n". This source of error is not **confounded** with the repetition variable, for it is S who repeats and thus perpetuates his error. Further, individual items were **balanced** over the three conditions. There is no suggestion of any difference in responding among the repetition conditions at the beginning of the recall interval. These differences developed during the time that S was engaged in counting backward. A differential rate of forgetting seems indisputable.

The factors underlying the improvement in retention with repetition were investigated by means of an analysis of the status of elements within the individual items. The individual consonant syllable, like the nonsense syllable, may be regarded as presenting S with a serial learning task. Through repetitions unrelated components may develop serial dependencies until in the manner of familiar words they have become single units. The improved retention might then be attributed to increases in these serial dependencies. The analysis proceeded by ascertaining the dependent probabilities that letters would be correct given the event that the previous letter was correct. These dependent prob-

TABLE 2
DEPENDENT PROBABILITIES OF A LETTER BEING CORRECTLY RECALLED
IN THE VOCAL GROUP WHEN THE PRECEDING LETTER WAS CORRECT

Repetition Time (Sec.)	Recall Interval (Sec.)		
	3	9	18
3	.96	.85	.72
1	.90	.72	.57
0	.86	.64	.56

abilities are listed in Table 2. It is clear that with increasing repetitions the serial dependencies increase. Again combining recall intervals, a sign test between the zero condition and the three repetition condition is significant at the 0.01 level.

Learning is seen to take place within the items. But this finding does not eliminate the possibility that another kind of learning is proceeding concurrently. If only the correct occurrences of the first letters of syllables are considered, changes in retention apart from the serial dependencies can be assessed. The proportions of first letters recalled correctly for the 0-, 1-, and 3-repetition conditions were 0.60, 0.65, and 0.72, respectively. A sign test between the 0- and 3-repetition conditions was significant at the 0.05 level. It may tentatively be concluded that learning of a second kind took place.

The course of short-term verbal retention is seen to be related to learning processes. It would not appear to be strictly accurate to refer to retention after a brief presentation as a stimulus trace. Rather, it would seem appropriate to refer to it as the result of a trial of learning. However, in spite of possible objections to Hull's terminology the present investigation supports his general position that a short-term retentive factor is important for the analysis of verbal learning. The details of the role of retention in the acquisition process remain to be worked out.

SUMMARY

The investigation differed from traditional verbal retention studies in concerning itself with individual items instead of lists. Forgetting over intervals measured in seconds was found. The course of retention after a single presentation was related to a statistical model. Forgetting was found to progress at differential rates dependent on the amount of controlled rehearsal of the stimulus. A portion of the improvement in recall with repetitions was assigned to serial learning within the item, but a second kind of learning was also found.

It was concluded that short-term retention is an important, though neglected, aspect of the acquisition process.

FOOTNOTES

[1] Reprinted by permission of the authors and the publisher from the *Journal of Experimental Psychology*, 1959, **58**, 193-198. Copyright 1959 by the American Psychological Association.

[2] The initial stages of this investigation were facilitated by National Science Foundation Grant G-2596.

REFERENCES

BROWN, J. (1958). Some tests of the decay theory of immediate memory. *Quarterly Journal of Experimental Psychology*, 10, 12-21.

ESTES, W. K. (1950). Toward a statistical theory of learning. *Psychological Review*, 57, 94-107.

ESTES, W. K. (1955). Statistical theory of spontaneous recovery and regression. *Psychological Review*, 62, 145-154.

HILGARD, E. R. (1951). Methods and procedures in the study of learning. In S. S. Stevens (Ed.), *Handbook of Experimental Psychology*. Wiley.

HULL, C. L., HOVLAND, C. I., ROSS, R. T., HALL, M., PERKINS, D. T., and FITCH, F. B. (1940). *Mathematico-Deductive Theory of Rote Learning: A Study in Scientific Methodology*. Yale University Press.

HULL, C. L. (1952). *A Behavior System*. Yale University Press.

Wilcoxon's test for unpaired replicates (REP-lih-kates). A statistical device used for determining whether two sets of data are significantly different. *Replicate* means "repetition." Generally speaking, when scientists "replicate" (or repeat) an experiment, they prefer to have the same number of cases (or presentations) in both studies. Wilcoxon's test, however, can be used in those instances when there are unequal ("unpaired") presentations.

T-test. A statistical measure used to determine whether two sets of data are significantly different.

Confounded. Technically speaking, *confounded* means "confused." Two variables become confounded if you have designed your experiment so poorly that you cannot tell which one is responsible for your results.

Balanced. Suppose, in a given experiment you're running, you want your subjects to learn three nonsense syllables, one after the other. Let's assume the syllables are "baq," "zox," and "duj." In an unbalanced design, you might well present the syllables in the same order to all subjects. In a balanced design, however, you'd present some of the subjects with "baq, zox, duj." A second group of subjects would receive "baq, duj, zox," a third group would receive "zox, baq, duj," a fourth group would receive "zox, duj, baq," a fifth group would received "duj, baq, zox," while a sixth group would receive "duj, zox, baq." In this case, you have *balanced the order of presentation*, so your results won't be confounded by "order" variables.

PILLSBURY, W. B., and SYLVESTER, A. (1940). Retroactive and proactive inhibition in immediate memory. *Journal of Experimental Psychology,* 27, 532-545.

UNDERWOOD, B. J. (1949). *Experimental Psychology.* Appleton Century Crofts.

UNDERWOOD, B. J. (1957). Interference and forgetting. *Psychological Review,* 64, 49-60.

WALKER, H., and LEV, J. (1953). *Statistical Inference.* Holt.

WILCOXON, F. (1949). *Some Rapid Approximate Statistical Procedures.* American Cyanamid Co.

Classic Quotations from William James

As we take, in fact, a general view of the wonderful stream of our consciousness, what strikes us first is this different pace of its parts. Like a bird's life, it seems to be made of an alternation of flights and perchings.
(*The Principles of Psychology* [1890], ch. 9.)

As the brain changes are continuous, so do all these consciousnesses melt into each other like dissolving views. Properly they are but one protracted consciousness, one unbroken stream.
(*The Principles of Psychology* [1890], ch. 9.)

CHAPTER 11

"Levels of Processing: A Framework for Memory Research"

Fergus I.M. Craik and Robert S. Lockhart[1,2]

EDITORS' COMMENTS. According to the information processing viewpoint, stimulus inputs are held briefly in "sensory storage," during which time they are briefly *processed* in order to determine their "critical features" (such as pattern, novelty, and so forth). Trivial aspects of the stimulus are suppressed (or somehow "forgotten"); important aspects of the stimulus, however, are then *translated* into acoustic (or linguistic) terms as the input moves into "short-term storage." Again, the input is *processed* in some fashion by the brain (or mind) while in primary (or short-term) memory. Usually this "processing" consists of *evaluating the importance* of the stimulus input, often by comparing it with past inputs (stored in permanent memory). At this point, a response of some kind may occur. At this point, too, if the input is somehow "significant," it may be recorded in long-term storage. Otherwise, the input is forgotten.

As intuitively logical as the information processing approach may be, it has certain flaws, many of which are pointed out by Craik and Lockhart in this article. These authors prefer the notion that you remember some inputs (and forget others) depending on the *depth* (or intensity) of processing that the input receives in the brain (mind). What Craik and Lockhart are saying, in effect, is that the more *important* an input is to you, personally--the more it catches your attention, or the more the input prompts you to think about its meaning--the more likely it is that you will store the input away in long-term storage.

The importance of the Craik and Lockhart article is that it (and others like it) led learning theorists to re-examine the information processing approach. However, on inspection, there are just as many problems associated with the "levels of processing" viewpoint as with the more classical approach. For example, Craik and Lockhart have considerable difficulty in explaining *before the fact* why some inputs receive "deep processing," while other inputs don't. It is one thing to say that if you "pay attention" to an input, or if it is "highly significant" to you, you will tend to remember it. But *why* you "pay attention" to the input (or why it is "highly significant") is something Craik and Lockhart are less than clear about.

In truth, recent research by psychologist Katherine Nelson and her colleagues may provide answers.[3] Nelson has found that young children create "scripts," or generalized sets of expectancies, about most situations. They then tend to remember *departures from the scripts* far better than they remember specific situations. For example, have you ever asked a child, "What did you do in school today?" The youngster is quite likely to tell you, "Nothing," a response most adults find particularly frustrating. What the child is really saying, according to Katherine Nelson, is that "Nothing occurred that wasn't part of the daily routine." (You can get around this problem by asking the child to tell you what happened the first few minutes at school, what occurred at recess, and so forth. The child is then likely to describe the "daily script," and might well mention minor variations that occurred on that particular day.)

Presuming that adults tend to "create scripts" as do children, it seems likely that we, too, are more likely to remember inputs that are *departures from the normal* than inputs which merely "confirm our expectancies." Thus, one of the main functions of long-term storage may be that of *creating expectancies*. This viewpoint has the benefit of combining perceptual theory with learning theory, for perceptual psychologists have long insisted that the major innate motivation most organisms have is that of *reducing uncertainty*.

We still must answer the question "Once an item is stored in Long-term Memory, how do you retrieve it?" We will leave you uncertain about the answer, though, until our comments at the start of the next chapter.

Abstract. This paper briefly reviews the evidence for multistore theories of memory and points out some difficulties with the approach. An alternative framework for human memory research is then outlined in terms of depth or levels of processing. Some current data and arguments are reexamined in the light of this alternative framework and implications for further research considered.

Over the past decade, models of human memory have been dominated by the concept of **stores** and the transfer of information among them. One major criterion for distinguishing between stores has been their different retention characteristics. The temporal properties of stored information have, thus, played a dual role: Besides constituting the basic phenomenon to be explained, they have also been used to generate the **theoretical constructs** in terms of which the explanation is formulated. The apparent circularity has been avoided by the specification of additional properties of the stores (such as their capacity and **coding characteristics**) thereby characterizing them independently of the phenomena to be explained. The constructs, thus formulated, have been used to account for data across a variety of **paradigms** and experimental conditions. The essential concept underlying such explanations is that of information being transferred from one store to another, and the store-to-store transfer models may be distinguished, at least in terms of emphasis, from explanations which associate different retention characteristics with qualitative changes in the memory code.

In the present paper we will do three things: (a) examine the reasons for proposing multistore models, (b) question their adequacy, and (c) propose an alternative framework in terms of **levels of processing**. We will argue that the memory trace can be understood as a byproduct of perceptual analysis and that trace persistence is a positive function of the depth to which the stimulus has been analyzed. Stimuli may also be retained over short intervals by continued processing at a constant depth. These views offer a new way to interpret existing data and provide a heuristic framework for further research.

MULTISTORE MODELS

The Case in Favor

When man is viewed as a processor of information (Miller, 1956; Broadbent, 1958), it seems necessary to postulate holding mechanisms or memory stores at various points in the system. For example, on the basis of his **dichotic** listening studies, Broadbent (1958) proposed that information must be held transiently before entering the limited-capacity processing channel. Items could be held over the short term by recycling them, after perception, through the same **transient** storage system. From there, information could be transferred into and retained in a more permanent long-term store. Broadbent's ideas have been developed and extended by Waugh and Norman (1965), Peterson (1966), and Atkinson and Shiffrin (1968). According to the modal model (Murdock, 1967), it is now widely accepted that memory can be classified into three levels of storage: sensory stores, short-term memory (STM) and long-term memory (LTM). Since there has been some ambiguity in the usage of terms in this area, we shall follow the convention of using STM and LTM to refer to experimental situations, and the terms "short-term store" (STS) and "long-term store" (LTS) to refer to the two relevant storage systems.

Stores. A "memory store" is some part of the brain (or mind) where memories are "held in storage."

Theoretical constructs (KON-strucks). In an experiment, an *independent variable* is some part of the experiment that is controlled by the experimenter, such as the stimulus that the experimenter presents to the subject. A *dependent variable* is some aspect of the experiment that depends on (or is affected by) the independent variable, such as the subject's response to the stimulus presented by the experimenter. A *theoretical construct* is a made-up ("constructed") explanation for the observed relationship between the independent and dependent variables. For example, suppose you present a subject named Mary with a kitten and Mary reacts by smiling and petting the animal. The kitten is an independent variable. It is "independent" because you (not Mary) determine when to present it. The kitten is a "variable" because you could have shown Mary a snake instead. "Smiling at and petting the kitten" is the dependent variable. The reaction is "dependent" because it was made in response to the independent variable (the kitten), and it is "variable" because Mary might have sneezed or run away from the animal instead. Why did Mary react as she did? If you assume that Mary "loves small animals," you have *constructed a theory* that explains the relationship between the "sight of a kitten" (the independent variable) and "smiling and petting" the dependent variable. *Love, in this instance, is a theoretical construct.*

Coding characteristics. Many psychologists believe that your brain stores the memory of a stimulus input according to the physical or psychological characteristics of the input. For example, if you see a frog, you might "code" this input in memory according to such characteristics as "green," "small," "four-legged," and "animal," among other things.

Paradigms (PAIR-ih-dimes). "Models," or "plans of attack."

Levels of processing. A model of memory which holds that the ability to remember is dependent on how deeply (or extensively) we process incoming information. The deeper the information is processed, the more "coding characteristics" it probably has and the better we remember it.

Dichotic (dy-KOTT-tick). An experiment involving "dichotic" listening typically involves having the subject wear earphones, and then presenting *different* auditory stimulation to each ear.

Transient (TRANS-see-ent). *Transient* means "to pass through quickly." Fifty years ago, hotels used to advertise for "Transients," meaning they rented rooms to people who didn't expect to stay very long.

TABLE 1
Commonly Accepted Differences Between the Three Stages of Verbal Memory (See Text for Sources)

Feature	Sensory registers	Short-term store	Long-term store
Entry of information	Preattentive	Requires attention	Rehearsal
Maintenance of information	Not possible	Continued attention Rehearsal	Repetition Organization
Format of information	Literal copy of input	Phonemic Probably visual Possibly semantic	Largely semantic Some auditory and visual
Capacity	Large	Small	No known limit
Information loss	Decay	Displacement Possibly decay	Possibly no loss Loss of accessibility or discriminability by interference
Trace duration	1/4-2 Seconds	Up to 30 seconds	Minutes to years
Retrieval	Readout	Probably automatic Items in consciousness Temporal/phonemic cues	Retrieval cues Possibly search process

Stimuli can be entered into the sensory stores regardless of whether or not the subject is paying attention to that source; that is, sensory stores are "**preattentive**" (Neisser, 1967). The input is represented in a rather literal form and can be overwritten by further inputs in the same **modality** (Neisser, 1967; Crowder & Morton, 1969). Further features which distinguish the sensory registers from later stores are the modality-specific nature and moderately large capacity of sensory stores and the transience of their contents.

Attention to the material in a sensory register is equivalent to reading it out and transferring it to STS. Here, verbal items are coded in some **phonemic** fashion (Shulman, 1971) or in **auditory-verbal-linguistic** terms (Atkinson & Shiffrin, 1968). The STS is further distinguished from sensory memories by virtue of its limited capacity (Miller, 1956; Broadbent, 1958), by the finding that information is lost principally by a process of displacement (Waugh & Norman, 1965), and by the slower rate of forgetting from STS: 5-20 seconds as opposed to the $1/4$-2-second estimates for sensory storage. While most research has concentrated on verbal STS, there is evidence that more literal "representational" information may also be held over the short term (Posner, 1967), although the relationship between such modality-specific stores and the verbal STS has not been made clear.

The distinctions between STS and LTS are well-documented. Whereas STS has a limited capacity, LTS has no known limit; verbal items are usually coded phonemically in STS but largely in terms of their **semantic** features in LTS (Baddeley, 1966); forgetting from STS is complete within 30 seconds or less while forgetting from LTS is either very slow or the material is not forgotten at all (Shiffrin & Atkinson, 1969). In the free-recall paradigm, it is generally believed that the last few items are retrieved from STS and prior items are retrieved from LTS; it is now known that several variables affect one of these retrieval components without affecting the other (Glanzer, 1972). Further persuasive evidence for the STS/LTS dichotomy comes from clinical studies (Milner, 1970; Warrington, 1971). The distinguishing features of the three storage levels are summarized in Table 1.

The attractiveness of the "box" approach is not difficult to understand. Such multistore models are apparently specific and concrete; information flows in well-regulated paths between stores whose characteristics have intuitive appeal; their properties may be elicited by experiment and described either behaviorally or mathematically. All that remains, it seems, is to specify the properties of each component more precisely and to work out the transfer functions more accurately.

Despite all these points in their favor, when the evidence for multistore models is examined in greater detail, the stores become less tangible. One warning sign is the progressively greater part played by "control processes" in more recent formulations (for example, Atkinson & Shiffrin, 1971). In the next section we consider the adequacy of multistore notions more critically.

The Case Against

The multistore approach has not been without its general critics (Melton, 1963; Murdock, 1972). Other workers have objected to certain aspects of the formulation. For example, Tulving and Patterson (1968) argued against the notion of information being transferred from one store to another. Similarly, Shallice and Warrington (1970) presented evidence against the idea that information must necessarily "pass through" STS to enter LTS.

In our view, the criteria listed in the previous section do not provide satisfactory grounds for distinguishing between separate stores. The adequacy of the evidence will be considered with reference to the concepts of capacity, coding, and finally, the retention function itself.

Capacity

Although limited capacity has been a major feature of the information flow approach, and especially a feature of STS in multistore models, the exact nature of the capacity limitation is somewhat obscure. In particular, it has been unclear whether the limitation is one of processing capacity, storage capacity, or is meant to apply to some interaction between the two. In terms of the computer analogy on which information flow models are based, the issue is whether the limitation refers to the storage capacity of a memory register or to the rate at which the processor can perform certain operations. The notion of a limited-capacity channel (Broadbent, 1958) appears to emphasize the second interpretation while later models of memory, such as that of Waugh and Norman (1965), appear to favor the storage interpretation. Both interpretations are present in Miller (1956) but the relationship between the two is not explicitly worked out.

Attempts to measure the capacity of STS have leant towards the storage interpretation, and considered number of items to be the appropriate scale of measurement. Such attempts have provided quite a range of values. For example, recent estimates of primary memory size (Baddeley, 1970; Murdock, 1972) have yielded values between two and four words. However, measures of memory span (which have been said to reflect the limited capacity of the STM box) are typically between five and nine items, depending on whether the items in question are words, letters or digits (Crannell & Parrish, 1957). Finally, if the words in a span test form a sentence, young subjects can accurately reproduce strings of up to 20 words (Craik & Masani, 1969). Thus, if capacity is a critical feature of STM operation, a box model has to account for this very wide range of capacity estimates.

The most widely accepted explanation of this variation is that capacity is limited in terms of chunks, and that few or many items can be recoded into a chunk depending on the meaningfulness of the material. Apart from the difficulty of defining a chunk independently from its memorial consequences, this view entails a rather flexible notion of STS as a storage compartment which can accept a variety of codes from simple physical features to complex semantic ones.

From the standpoint of the present paper, the concept of capacity is to be understood in terms of a limitation on processing; limitations of storage are held to be a direct consequence of this more fundamental limitation.

Coding

Working with verbal material, Conrad (1964) and Baddeley (1966) provided one plausible basis for distinguishing STS and LTS. They concluded that information in STS was coded acoustically and that coding was predominantly semantic in LTS. Further research has blurred this distinction, however. First, it has been shown that STS coding can be either acoustic or articulatory (Levy, 1971; Peterson & Johnson, 1971). Second, recent papers by Kroll and his colleagues (Kroll *et al.,* 1970) have demonstrated that even with verbal material, STS can sometimes be visual. Apparently STS can accept a variety of physical codes.

Can STS also hold semantic information? The persistence of contradictory evidence suggests either that the question has been inappropriately formulated or

Preattentive. In information theory terms, a stimulus input which is stored briefly at the receptor level is said to be at the "preattentive" level. For instance, if we flash a brilliant picture of someone's face directly at your eyes, your retina will maintain a bright image of the face for a few seconds even if you don't choose to pay attention to the image itself.

Modality (moh-DAL-ih-tee). A *modality* is a "way of doing something," or a "processing channel." Vision is one sensory modality; hearing is a different sensory modality.

Phonemic (foh-NEEM-ick). Phonemes are the smallest units of speech, such as "da" or "ba."

Auditory-verbal-linguistic (lin-GWISS-tic). Many psychologists believe that, as you read, the words you see are stored as *exact visual images* at the receptor level ("sensory information storage"), but that you almost immediately translate the visual images into "verbal inputs" or "spoken language" before you store the words in Short- or Long-term memory. If you "hear a little voice" inside your mind saying these words silently as you read them, you have coded the words in "auditory-verbal-linguistic" fashion.

Semantic. Having to do with the meaning of language.

that the answer depends on the paradigm used. When traditional STM paradigms are considered, the answer seems to be "no" (Kintsch & Buschke, 1969; Craik & Levy, 1970), although Shulman (1970, 1972) has recently presented persuasive evidence in favor of a semantic STS. While type of coding may originally have seemed a good basis for the distinction between short-term and long-term memory, the distinction no longer appears satisfactory. A defender of the multistore notion might argue that STS coding is flexible, but this position removes an important characteristic by which one store is distinguished from another.

We will argue that the coding question is more appropriately formulated in terms of the processing demands imposed by the experimental paradigm and the material to be remembered. In some paradigms and with certain material, acoustic coding may be either adequate or all that is possible. In other circumstances processing to a semantic level may be both possible and advantageous.

Forgetting Characteristics

If memory stores are to be distinguished in terms of their forgetting characteristics, a minimal requirement would seem to be that the retention function should be invariant across different paradigms and experimental conditions. While this invariance has not been rigorously tested, there are cases where it clearly breaks down. We will give two examples. First, in the finite-state models of **paired-associate** learning, the state commonly identified as STS shows forgetting characteristics which are different from those established for STS in other paradigms (Kintsch, 1970, p. 206). In the former case, STS retention extends over as many as 20 intervening items while in the free-recall and probe paradigms (Waugh & Norman, 1965), STS information is lost much more rapidly. As a second example, the durability of the memory trace for visual stimuli appears to depend on the material and the paradigm. According to Neisser (1967), the **icon** lasts 1 second or less, Posner (1969) and his colleagues have found evidence for visual persistence of up to 1.5 seconds, while other recent studies by Murdock (1971), Phillips and Baddeley (1971) and by Kroll *et al.* (1970) have yielded estimates of 6, 10, and 25 seconds, respectively. Estimates are even longer in recognition memory for pictures (Shepard, 1967; Haber, 1970). Given that we recognize pictures, faces, tunes, and voices after long periods of time, it is clear that we have long-term memory for relatively literal nonverbal information. Thus, it is difficult to draw a line between "sensory memory" and "representational" or "pictorial" memory.

We will argue that retention depends upon such aspects of the paradigm as study time, amount of material presented and mode of test; also upon the extent to which the subject has developed systems to analyze and enrich particular types of stimuli; that is, the familiarity, compatibility, and meaningfulness of the material.

Although we believe that the multistore formulation is unsatisfactory in terms of its capacity, coding, and forgetting characteristics, obviously there are some basic findings which any model must accommodate. It seems certain that stimuli are encoded in different ways within the memory system: A word may be encoded at various times in terms of its visual, phonemic, or semantic features, its verbal associates, or an image. Differently encoded representations apparently persist for different lengths of time. The phenomenon of limited capacity at some points in the system seems real enough and, thus, should also be taken into consideration. Finally, the roles of perceptual, attentional, and rehearsal processes should also be noted.

One way of coping with the kinds of inconsistencies we have described is to postulate additional stores (see, Morton, 1970; Sperling, 1970). However, we think it is more useful to focus on the encoding operations themselves and to consider the proposal that rates of forgetting are a function of the type and depth of encoding. This view is developed in the next section.

LEVELS OF PROCESSING

Many theorists now agree that perception involves the rapid analysis of stimuli at a number of levels or stages (Selfridge & Neisser, 1960; Treisman, 1964; Sutherland, 1968). Preliminary stages are concerned with the analysis of such physical or sensory features as lines, angles, brightness, pitch, and loudness, while later stages are more concerned with matching the input against stored abstractions from past learning; that is, later stages are concerned with pattern recognition and the extraction of meaning. This conception of a series or hierarchy of processing stages is often referred to as "depth of processing" where greater "depth" implies a greater degree of semantic or cognitive analysis. After the stimulus has been recognized, it may undergo further processing by enrichment or elaboration. For example, after a word is recognized, it may trigger associations, images or stories on the basis of the subject's past experience with the word. Such "elaboration coding" (Tulving & Madigan, 1970) is not restricted to verbal material. We would argue that similar levels of processing exist in the perceptual analysis of sounds, sights, smells and so on. Analysis proceeds through a series of sensory stages to levels associated with matching or pattern recognition and finally to semantic-associative stages of stimulus enrichment.

One of the results of this perceptual analysis is the **memory trace**. Such features of the trace as its coding characteristics and its persistence thus arise essentially as byproducts of perceptual processing (Morton, 1970). Specifically, we suggest that trace persistence is a function of depth of analysis, with deeper levels of analysis associated with more elaborate, longer lasting, and stronger traces. Since the organism is normally concerned only with the extraction of meaning from the stimuli, it is advantageous to store the products of such deep analyses, but there is usually no need to store the products of preliminary analyses. It is perfectly possible to draw a box around early analyses and call it sensory memory and a box around intermediate analyses called short-term memory, but that procedure both oversimplifies matters and evades the more significant issues.

Although certain analytic operations must precede others, much recent evidence suggests that we perceive at meaningful, deeper levels before we perceive the results of logically prior analyses (Macnamara, 1972; Savin & Bever, 1970). Further elaborative coding does not exist in a hierarchy of necessary steps and this seems especially true of later processing stages. In this sense, "spread" of encoding might be a more accurate description, but the term "depth" will be retained as it conveys the flavor of our argument.

Highly familiar, meaningful stimuli are compatible, by definition, with existing cognitive structures. Such stimuli (for example, pictures and sentences) will be processed to a deep level more rapidly than less meaningful stimuli and will be well-retained. Thus, speed of analysis does not necessarily predict retention. Retention is a function of depth, and various factors, such as the amount of attention devoted to a stimulus, its compatibility with the analyzing structures, and the processing time available, will determine the depth to which it is processed.

Thus, we prefer to think of memory tied to levels of perceptual processing. Although these levels may be grouped into stages (sensory analyses, pattern recognition, and stimulus elaboration, for example), processing levels may be more usefully envisaged as a **continuum** of analysis. Thus, memory, too, is viewed as a continuum from the transient products of sensory analyses to the highly durable products of semantic-associative operations. However, superimposed on this basic memory system there is a second way in which stimuli can be retained—by recirculating information at one level of processing. In our view, such descriptions as "continued attention to certain aspects of the stimulus," "keeping the items in consciousness," "holding the items in the rehearsal buffer," and "retention of the items in primary memory" all refer to the same concept of maintaining information at one level of processing. To preserve some measure of continuity with existing terminology, we will use the term primary memory (PM) to refer to this operation, although it should be noted that our usage is more restricted than the usual one.

We endorse Moray's (1967) notion of a limited-capacity central processor which may be deployed in a number of different ways. If this processing capacity is used to maintain information at one level, the phenomena of short-term memory will appear. The processor itself is neutral with regard to coding characteristics: The observed PM code will depend on the processing modality within which the processor is operating. Further, while limited capacity is a function of the processor itself, the number of items held will depend upon the level at which the processor is operating. At deeper levels the subject can make greater use of learned rules and past knowledge; thus, material can be more efficiently handled and more can be retained. There is apparently great variability in the ease with which information at different levels can be maintained in PM. Some types of information (for example, phonemic features of words) are particularly easy to maintain while the maintenance of others (such as early visual analyses—the "icon") is apparently impossible.

The essential feature of PM retention is that aspects of the material are still being processed or attended to. Our notion of PM is, thus, synonymous with that of James (1890) in that PM items are still in consciousness. When attention is diverted from the item, information will be lost at the rate appropriate to its level of processing—slower rates for deeper levels. While PM retention is, thus, equivalent to continued processing, this type of

---

Paired-associate. In many verbal learning studies, the subject is given two lists of common words (or nonsense syllables). The subject's task typically is to *associate* each item on the first list with a particular item on the second list. For example, "dog" and "sky" might be the first pair of words, while "tag" and "box" might be the second pair. At some later time, after the subject has learned to associate each pair of items, the subject is presented with the first member of each word-pair and must reproduce the correct second word. Thus, if given "dog," the subject must respond "sky," not "box."

Icon (EYE-kon). From the Greek word meaning "a visual representation or image." An icon is an image.

Memory trace. Some psychologists assume that a stimulus input leaves a "trace" of itself somewhere in the brain, much as running your finger through a snowbank leaves a groove that "traces out" where your finger has been.

Continuum (kon-TIN-you-um). Something absolutely continuous or uninterrupted, such as the number system (1, 2, 3 . . .), or some set of data that has no "holes" in it.

processing merely prolongs an item's high accessibility without leading to formation of a more permanent memory trace. This Type I processing, that is, repetition of analyses which have already been carried out, may be contrasted with Type II processing which involves deeper analysis of the stimulus. Only this second type of rehearsal should lead to improved memory performance. To the extent that the subject utilizes Type II processing, memory will improve with total study time, but when he engages in Type I processing, the "total time hypothesis" (see Cooper & Pantle, 1967) will break down. Stoff and Eagle (1971) have reported findings in line with this suggestion.

To summarize, it is suggested that the memory trace is better described in terms of depth of processing or degree of stimulus elaboration. Deeper analysis leads to a more persistent trace. While information may be held in PM, such maintenance will not in itself improve subsequent retention; when attention is diverted, information is lost at a rate which depends essentially on the level of analysis.

EXISTING DATA REEXAMINED

Incidental Learning

When memory traces are viewed as the product of a particular form of processing, much of the incidental learning literature acquires a new significance. There are several reviews of this literature (Postman, 1964; McLaughlin, 1965), and we will make no attempt to be comprehensive. An important characteristic of the **incidental learning paradigm** is that the subject processes the material in a way compatible with or determined by the orienting task. The comparison of retention across different orienting tasks, therefore, provides a relatively pure measure of the memorial consequences of different processing activities. According to the view of the present paper, and in agreement with Postman (1964), the instruction to learn facilitates performance only insofar as it leads the subject to process the material in a manner which is more effective than the processing induced by the orienting task in the incidental condition. Thus, it is possible, that with an appropriate orienting task and an inappropriate intentional strategy, learning under incidental conditions could be superior to that under intentional conditions.

From the point of view of this paper, then, the interesting thing to do is to systematically study retention following different orienting tasks within the incidental condition, rather than to compare incidental with intentional learning. Under incidental conditions, the experimenter has a control over the processing the subject applies to the material that he does not have when the subject is merely instructed to learn and uses an unknown coding strategy.

We will consider several examples which illustrate this point. Tresselt and Mayzner (1960) tested free recall after incidental learning under three different orienting tasks: crossing out vowels, copying the words, and judging the degree to which the word was an instance of the concept "economic." Under the last condition, the number of words recalled was four times higher than that of the first and twice that of the second condition. Similar results using the free-recall paradigm have been obtained by Hyde and Jenkins (1969), and Johnston and Jenkins (1971). The experiments by Jenkins and his colleagues showed that with lists of highly associated word pairs, free recall and organization resulting from an orienting task which required the use of the word as a semantic unit, was equivalent to that of an intentional control group with no incidental task, but both were substantially superior to an incidental group whose task involved treating the word structurally (checking for certain letters or estimating the number of letters in the word). These results are consistent with those of Mandler (1967) who showed that incidental learning during categorization of words yielded a similar recall level to that of a group who performed the same activity but who knew that their recall would be tested.

Experiments involving the incidental learning of sentences (Bobrow & Bower, 1969; Rosenberg & Schiller, 1971) have shown that recall after an orienting task that required processing the sentence to a semantic level was substantially superior to recall of words from equivalently exposed sentences which were processed nonsemantically.

Schulman (1971) had subjects scan a list of words for targets defined either structurally (such as words containing the letter A) or semantically (such as words denoting living things). After the scanning task, subjects were given an unexpected test of recognition memory. Performance in the semantically defined target conditions was significantly better than that in the structurally defined conditions although scanning time per word was approximately the same in most cases.

These results support the general conclusion that memory performance is a positive function of the level of processing required by the orienting task. However, beyond a certain stage, the form of processing which will prove optimal depends on the retrieval or trace utilization requirements of the subsequent memory test. There is clear evidence in the incidental learning literature that the relative value of different orienting tasks is not the same for all tests of memory.

This conclusion is supported by comparisons of the differential effects of orienting tasks on recognition and recall. Eagle and Leiter (1964) found that whereas free recall in an unhindered intentional condition was superior to that of an incidental group and to a second intentional group who had also to perform the orienting task, these latter two conditions showed superior recognition performance. Such a result poses no difficulty provided it is assumed that optimal processing does not take the same form for both memory tests. In the Eagle and Leiter (1964) experiment, the orienting task, while almost certainly involving some degree of semantic analysis, might have served to prevent the kind of elaborative processing necessary for later access to the stored information. On the other hand, such elaborative coding might hinder subsequent discrimination between target words and the associatively related distractors used in this experiment. Results consistent with this kind of analysis have also been reported by Dornbush and Winnick (1967) and Estes and DaPolito (1967).

While the orienting tasks used by Wicker and Bernstein (1969) in their study of incidental paired-associate learning all required analysis to a semantic level, they did not facilitate subsequent performance to the same degree. When the orienting task involved the production of mediating responses, performance was equal to that of unhindered intentional learning and superior to when the orienting task was rating words for pleasantness. In single-trial free recall, this latter orienting task produces performance equal to that of intentional learning (Hyde & Jenkins, 1969). Identical orienting tasks do not seem to have equivalent effects across different paradigms. The interaction between initial encoding and subsequent retrieval operations is worth emphasizing. Although the distinction between availability and accessibility (Tulving & Pearlstone, 1966) is a useful one, the effectiveness of a retrieval cue depends on its compatibility with the item's initial encoding or, more generally, the extent to which the retrieval situation reinstates the learning context.

Selective Attention and Sensory Storage

Moray (1959) showed that words presented to the nonattended channel in a dichotic listening test were not recognized in a later memory test. Similarly, Neisser (1964) has shown that nontarget items in a visual search task left no recognizable trace. Thus, if stimuli are only partially analyzed, or processed only to peripheral levels, their record in memory is extremely fleeting. This point was neatly demonstrated by Treisman (1964). When the same prose passage was played to both ears dichotically, but staggered in time with the unattended ear leading, the lag between messages had to be reduced to 1.5 seconds before the subject realized that the messages were identical. When the attended (<u>shadowed</u>) ear was leading, however, subjects noticed the similarity at a mean lag of 4.5 seconds. Thus, although the subjects were not trying to remember the material in either case, the further processing necessitated by shadowing was sufficient to treble the durability of the memory trace. Treisman also found that meaningfulness of the material (reversed speech versus normal speech, and random words versus prose) affected the lag necessary for recognition, but only when the attended channel was leading. If the message was rejected after early analyses, meaningfulness played no part; but when the message was attended, more meaningful material could be processed further and was, thus, retained longer. The three estimates of memory persistence in these experiments (1.5 seconds for all nonattended material, 3 seconds for attended reversed speech and attended strings of random words, and 5 seconds for attended prose) can be attributed to the functioning of different stores, but it is more reasonable, in our view, to postulate that persistence is a function of processing level.

While further studies will not be reviewed in such detail, it may be noted that the findings and conclusions of many other workers in the area of sensory memory can also be accommodated in the present framework. Neisser (1967, p. 33) concluded that "longer exposures lead to longer-lasting icons." Studies by Norman (1969), Glucksberg and Cowen (1970), and Peterson and Kroener (1964) may all be interpreted as showing that nonattended verbal material is lost within a few seconds.

Massaro (1970) suggested that memory for an item is directly related to the amount of perceptual processing of the item, a statement which is obviously in line with the present proposals, although his later arguments (Massaro, 1972), that echoic memory inevitably lasts only 250 milliseconds, are probably overgeneralizations. Shaffer and Shiffrin concluded from an experiment on picture recognition that "it might prove more fruitful to consider the more parsimonious view that there is just a single short-term visual memory. This

<u>Incidental learning paradigm</u> (PAIR-ah-dime). A type of experiment on verbal learning used to determine whether a subject learned more about a given task situation than the subject was required to learn. For instance, suppose you were given a page from this book and asked to cross out all the vowels as quickly as possible without paying attention to the words themselves. Once you finish, however, the experimenter removes the page from sight and asks you to describe the *meaning* of the material you read. Since you weren't required to pay attention to the words themselves, any learning you showed would be "incidental."

<u>Shadowed</u>. In most dichotic learning situations, the subject hears different auditory inputs in each ear. If the subject is told to "pay attention" to the inputs to the right ear, we say that the subject is *shadowing* those inputs, or following them as closely as your shadow follows you on a sunny day.

short-term visual memory would decay quickly when the information content of the visual field was high and more slowly when the information content was greatly reduced" (Shaffer & Shiffrin, 1972, p. 295). Plainly this view is similar to our own, although we would argue that the continuum extends to long-term retention as well. We would also suggest that it is processing level, rather than information content, which determines the rate of decay.

The STS/LTS Distinction

The phenomenon of a limited-capacity holding mechanism in memory (Miller, 1956; Broadbent, 1958) is handled in the present framework by assuming that a flexible central processor can be deployed to one of several levels in one of several encoding dimensions, and that this central processor can only deal with a limited number of items at a given time. That is, items are kept in consciousness or in primary memory by continuing to rehearse them at a fixed level of processing. The nature of the items will depend upon the encoding dimension and the level within that dimension. At deeper levels the subject can make more use of learned cognitive structures so that the item will become more complex and semantic. The depth at which primary memory operates will depend both upon the usefulness to the subject of continuing to process at that level and also upon the **amenability** of the material to deeper processing. Thus, if the subject's task is merely to reproduce a few words seconds after hearing them, he need not hold them at a level deeper than phonemic analysis. If the words form a meaningful sentence, however, they are compatible with deeper learned structures and larger units may be dealt with. It seems that primary memory deals at any level with units or "chunks" rather than with information (see Kintsch, 1970, pp. 175-181). That is, we rehearse a sound, a letter, a word, an idea, or an image in the same way that we perceive objects and not constellations of attributes.

As pointed out earlier, a common distinction between memory stores is their different coding characteristics; STS is said to be predominantly acoustic (or articulatory) while LTS is largely semantic. According to the present argument, acoustic errors will predominate only insofar as analysis has not proceeded to a semantic level. There are at least three sources of the failure of processing to reach this level: the nature of the material, limited available processing capacity, and task demands. Much of the data on acoustic confusions in short-term memory is based on material such as letters and digits which have relatively little semantic content. The nature of this material itself tends to constrain processing to a structural level of analysis and it should be no surprise, therefore, that errors of a structural nature result. Such errors can also occur with meaningful material if processing capacity is diverted to an irrelevant task (Eagle & Ortoff, 1967).

A further set of results relevant to the STS/LTS distinction are those that show that, in free recall, variables such as presentation rate and word frequency affect long-term but not short-term retention (Glanzer, 1972). Our interpretation of these findings is that increasing presentation rate, or using unfamiliar words, inhibits or prevents processing to those levels necessary to support long-term retention, but does not affect coding operations of the kind that are adequate for short-term retention. It follows from this interpretation that diverting processing capacity as in the Eagle and Ortoff (1967) experiments should result in a greater decrement in long-term than in short-term retention and, indeed, there is good evidence that such is the case (Murdock, 1965; Silverstein & Glanzer, 1971).

Conversely, manipulations that influence processing at a structural level should have transitory, but no long-term, effects. Modality differences (Murdock, 1966) provide a clear example. Finally, long-term recall should be facilitated by manipulations which induce deeper or more elaborative processing. We suggest that the encoding variability hypothesis as it has been used to account for the spacing effect in free recall (Madigan, 1969; Melton, 1970) is to be understood in these terms.

The Serial Position Curve

Serial-position effects have been a major source of evidence for the STS/LTS distinction (see Broadbent, 1971, pp. 354-361; Kintsch, 1970, pp. 153-162). In free recall, the recency effect is held to reflect output from STS while previous items are retrieved from LTS (Glanzer & Cunitz, 1966). Several theoretical accounts of the primacy effect have been given, but perhaps the most plausible is that initial items receive more rehearsals and are, thus, better registered in LTS (Atkinson & Shiffrin, 1968; Bruce & Papay, 1970). We agree with these conclusions. Since the subject knows he must stop attending to initial items in order to perceive and rehearse subsequent items, he subjects these first items to Type II processing; that is, deeper semantic processing. Final list items can survive on phonemic encoding, however, which gives rise to excellent immediate recall (since they are still being processed in primary memory) but is wiped out by the necessity to process interpolated material. In fact, if terminal items have been less deeply processed than initial items, the levels of processing formulation would predict that in a subsequent recall attempt, final items should be recalled least well of all list items. The finding of negative recency (Craik, 1970) supports this prediction. An alternative explanation of negative recency could be that recency items were rehearsed fewer times than earlier items (Rundus, 1971). However, recent studies by Jacoby and Bartz (1972), Watkins (1972), and Craik (1972) have shown that it is the type rather than the amount of processing which determines the subsequent recall of the last few items in a list.

In serial recall, subjects must retain the first few items so that they can at least commence their recall correctly. The greatly enhanced primacy effect is thus probably attributable, in part at least, to primary-memory retention. The degree to which subjects also encode initial items at a deeper level is likely to depend on the material and the task. Using a relatively slow (2.5 seconds) presentation rate and words as visually presented stimuli, Palmer and Ornstein (1971) found that an interpolated task only partially eliminated the primacy effect. However, Baddeley (1968) presented digits auditorily at a 1-second rate and found that primacy was entirely eliminated by the necessity to perform a further task.

Repetition and Rehearsal Effects

One suggestion in the present formulation is that Type I processing does nothing to enhance memory for the stimulus; once attention is diverted, the trace is lost at the rate appropriate to its deepest analyzed level. Thus, the concept of processing has been split into Type I or same-level processing and Type II processing which involves further, deeper analysis of the stimulus and leads to a more durable trace. Similarly, the effects of repeated presentation depend on whether the repeated stimulus is merely processed to the same level or encoded differently on its further presentations. There is evidence, both in audition (Moray, 1959; Norman, 1969), and in vision (Turvey, 1967), that repetition of an item encoded only at a sensory level, does not lead to an improvement in memory performance.

Tulving (1966) has also shown that repetition without intention to learn does not facilitate learning. Tulving's explanation of the absence of learning in terms of inter-item organization cannot easily be distinguished from an explanation in terms of levels of processing. Similarly, Glanzer and Meinzer (1967) have shown that overt repetition of items in free recall is a less effective strategy than that normally used by subjects. Although both Waugh and Norman (1965) and Atkinson and Shiffrin (1968) have suggested that rehearsal has the dual function of maintaining information in primary memory and transferring it to secondary memory, the experiments by Tulving (1966) and by Glanzer and Meinzer (1967) show that this is not necessarily so. Thus, whether rehearsal strengthens the trace or merely postpones forgetting depends on what the subject is doing with his rehearsal. Only deeper processing will lead to an improvement in memory.

CONCLUDING COMMENTS

Our account of memory in terms of levels of processing has much in common with a number of other recent formulations. Cermak (1972), for example, has outlined a theoretical framework very similar to our own. Perceptually oriented attribute-encoding theories such as those of Bower (1967) and Norman and Rumelhart (1970) have a close affinity with the present approach as does that of Posner (1969), who advocates stages of processing with different characteristics associated with each stage.

If the memory trace is viewed as the byproduct of perceptual analysis, an important goal of future research will be to specify the memorial consequences of various types of perceptual operations. We have suggested the comparison of orienting tasks within the incidental learning paradigm as one method by which the experimenter can have more direct control over the encoding operations that subjects perform. Since deeper analysis will usually involve longer processing time, it will be extremely important to disentangle such variables as study time and amount of effort from depth as such. For example, time may be a correlate of memory to the extent that time is necessary for processing to some level, but it is possible that further time

---

Amenability (a-men-ah-BILL-it-tee, or sometimes a-meen-ah-BILL-it-tee). To be "amenable" is to be easy to please. Amenable *information* is that which is easily understood.

Serial-position effects. If you are given a list of words to learn, and then are tested a minute or so later to see how many you recall, you probably will remember the first items on the list slightly better than you remember the final items on the list—and you will probably recall items in the middle of the list worst of all. Put more simply, the *position* of the item in the *series* of words affects how well you can remember it. Recent studies[3] suggest that the serial position effect occurs only under certain conditions, namely, when when the interval between learning and testing is of moderate duration. Suppose you are given a single, brief exposure to each word on a four-word list. If you are tested immediately afterwards, you probably will recall items at the end of the list better than those in the middle, and recall items in the middle of the list better than those at the beginning (the "recency" effect, since you remember best the items you learned most recently). If you are tested 100 seconds after seeing the words, you will recall the items at the first of the list better than those in the middle, and those items in the middle better than those at the end of the list (the "primacy" effect, since you remember best those items you learned first). Only if you are tested 10-20 seconds after the single, brief exposure will you remember items at *both* the beginning and the end of the list better than those in the middle.

spent in merely recycling the information after this optimal level will not predict trace durability.

Our approach does not constitute a theory of memory. Rather, it provides a conceptual framework — a set of orienting attitudes — within which memory research might proceed. While multistore models have played a useful role, we suggest that they are often taken too literally and that more fruitful questions are generated by the present formulation. Our position is obviously speculative and far from complete. We have looked at memory purely from the input or encoding end; no attempt has been made to specify either how items are differentiated from one another, are grouped together and organized, or how they are retrieved from the system. While our position does not imply any specific view of these processes, it does provide an appropriate framework within which they can be understood.

FOOTNOTES

[1] Reprinted by permission of the authors and the publisher from the *Journal of Verbal Learning and Verbal Behavior*, 1972, 11, 671-684. Copyright 1972 by Academic Press.

[2] This research was supported by Grants A8261 and A0355 from the National Research Council of Canada to the first and second author, respectively. We thank our colleagues who read a preliminary version of the paper and made many helpful suggestions.

[3] Nelson, K., et al. (1986). *Event knowledge: Structure and function in development.* Hillsdale, NJ: Erlbaum.

[4] Wright, A.A., et al. (1985). Memory processing of serial lists by pigeons, monkeys, and people. *Science,* 229, 287-289.

REFERENCES

ATKINSON, R. C., & SHIFFRIN, R. M. Human memory: A proposed system and its control processes. In K. W. Spence and J. T. Spence (Eds.) *The psychology of learning and motivation: Advances in research and theory,* Vol. II. New York: Academic Press, 1968. Pp. 89-195.

ATKINSON, R. C., & SHIFFRIN, R. M. The control of short-term memory. *Scientific American,* 1971, 224, 82-89.

BADDELEY, A. D. Short-term memory for word sequences as a function of acoustic, semantic, and formal similarity. *Quarterly Journal of Experimental Psychology,* 1966, 18, 362-365.

BADDELEY, A. D. How does acoustic similarity influence short-term memory? *Quarterly Journal of Experimental Psychology,* 1968, 20, 249-264.

BADDELEY, A. D. Estimating the short-term component in free recall. *British Journal of Psychology,* 1970, 61, 13-15.

BOBROW, S. A., & BOWER, G. H. Comprehension and recall of sentences. *Journal of Experimental Psychology,* 1969, 80, 455-461.

BOWER, G. H. A multicomponent theory of the memory trace. In K. W. Spence and J. T. Spence (Eds.) *The psychology of learning and motivation: Advances in research and theory,* Vol. 1. New York: Academic Press, 1967. Pp. 230-325.

BROADBENT, D. E. *Perception and communication.* New York: Pergamon Press, 1958.

BROADBENT, D. E. *Decision and stress.* New York: Academic Press, 1971.

BRUCE, D., & PAPAY, J. P. Primacy effect in single-trial free recall. *Journal of Verbal Learning and Verbal Behavior,* 1970, 9, 473-486.

CERMAK, L. S. *Human memory. Research and theory.* New York: Ronald, 1972.

CONRAD, R. Acoustic confusions in immediate memory. *British Journal of Psychology,* 1964, 55, 75-84.

COOPER, E. H., & PANTLE, A. J. The total-time hypothesis in verbal learning. *Psychological Bulletin,* 1967, 68, 221-234.

CRAIK, F. I. M. The fate of primary memory items in free recall. *Journal of Verbal Learning and Verbal Behavior,* 1970, 9, 143-148.

CRAIK, F.I.M. A 'levels of analysis' view of memory. Paper presented at the 2nd Erindale Symposium on Communication and Affect, March, 1972.

CRAIK, F. I. M., & LEVY, B. A. Semantic and acoustic information in primary memory. *Journal of Experimental Psychology,* 1970, 86, 77-82.

CRAIK, F. I. M., & MASANI, P. A. Age and intelligence differences in coding and retrieval of word lists. *British Journal of Psychology,* 1969, 60, 315-319.

CRANNELL, C. W., & PARRISH, J. M. A comparison of immediate memory span for digits, letters, and words. *Journal of Psychology,* 1957, 44, 319-327.

CROWDER, R. G., & MORTON, J. Precategorical acoustic storage. *Perception and Psychophysics,* 1969, 5, 365-373.

DORNBUSH, R. L., & WINNICK, W. A. Short-term intentional and incidental learning. *Journal of Experimental Psychology,* 1967, 73, 608-611.

EAGLE, M., & LEITER, E. Recall and recognition in intentional and incidental learning. *Journal of Experimental Psychology,* 1964, 68, 58-63.

EAGLE, M., & ORTOFF, E. The effect of level of attention upon "phonetic" recognition errors. *Journal of Verbal Learning and Verbal Behavior,* 1967, 6, 226-231.

ESTES, W. K., & DaPOLITO, F. Independent variation of information storage and retrieval processes in paired-associate learning. *Journal of Experimental Psychology,* 1967, 75, 18-26.

GLANZER, M. Storage mechanisms in recall. In G. H. Bower (Ed.) *The psychology of learning and motivation: Advances in research and theory.* Vol. 5. New York: Academic Press, 1972. Pp. 129-193.

GLANZER, M., & CUNITZ, A. R. Two storage mechanisms in free recall. *Journal of Verbal Learning and Verbal Behavior,* 1966, **5,** 351-360.

GLANZER, M., & MEINZER, A. The effects of intralist activity on free recall. *Journal of Verbal Learning and Verbal Behavior,* 1967, **6,** 928-935.

GLUCKSBERG, S., & COWEN, G. N. Memory for nonattended auditory material. *Cognitive Psychology,* 1970, **1,** 149-156.

HABER, R. N. How we remember what we see. *Scientific American,* 1970, **222,** 104-112.

HYDE, T. S., & JENKINS, J. J. The differential effects of incidental tasks on the organization of recall of a list of highly associated words. *Journal of Experimental Psychology,* 1969, **82,** 472-481.

JACOBY, L. L., & BARTZ, W. H. Encoding processes and the negative recency effect. *Journal of Verbal Learning and Verbal Behavior,* 1972, **11,** 561-565.

JAMES, W. *Principles of psychology.* New York: Holt, 1890.

JOHNSTON, C. D., & JENKINS, J. J. Two more incidental tasks that differentially affect associative clustering in recall. *Journal of Experimental Psychology,* 1971, **89,** 92-95.

KINTSCH, W. *Learning, memory, and conceptual processes.* New York: Wiley, 1970.

KINTSCH, W., & BUSCHKE, H. Homophones and synonyms in short-term memory. *Journal of Experimental Psychology,* 1969, **80,** 403-407.

KROLL, N. E. A., PARKS, T., PARKINSON, S. R., BIEBER, S.L., & JOHNSON, A. L. Short-term memory while shadowing. Recall of visually and aurally presented letters. *Journal of Experimental Psychology,* 1970, **85,** 220-224.

LEVY, B. A. Role of articulation in auditory and visual short-term memory. *Journal of Verbal Learning and Verbal Behavior,* 1971, **10,** 123-132.

MACNAMARA, J. Cognitive basis of language learning in infants. *Psychological Review,* 1972, **79,** 1-13.

MADIGAN, S. A. Intraserial repetition and coding processes in free recall. *Journal of Verbal Learning and Verbal Behavior,* 1969, **8,** 828-835.

MANDLER, G. Organization and Memory. In K. W. Spence and J. T. Spence (Eds.) *The psychology of learning and motivation: Advances in research and theory,* Vol. 1. New York: Academic Press, 1967, Pp. 328-372.

MASSARO, W. Perceptual processes and forgetting in memory tasks. *Psychological Review,* 1970, **77,** 557-567.

MASSARO, D. W. Preperceptual images, processing time, and perceptual units in auditory perception. *Psychological Review,* 1972, **79,** 124-145.

McLAUGHLIN, B. "Intentional" and "incidental" learning in human subjects: The role of instructions to learn and motivation. *Psychological Bulletin,* 1965, **63,** 359-376.

MELTON, A. W. Implications of short-term memory for a general theory of memory. *Journal of Verbal Learning and Verbal Behavior,* 1963, **2,** 1-21.

MELTON, A. W. The situation with respect to the spacing of repetitions and memory. *Journal of Verbal Learning and Verbal Behavior,* 1970, **9,** 596-606.

MILLER, G. A. The magical number seven, plus or minus two: Some limits on our capacity for processing information. *Psychological Review,* 1956, **63,** 81-97.

MILNER, B. Memory and the medial temporal regions of the brain. In K. H. Pribram and D. E. Broadbent (Eds.) *Biology of memory.* New York: Academic Press, 1970. Pp. 29-50.

MORAY, N. Attention in dichotic listening: Affective cues and the influence of instructions. *Quarterly Journal of Experimental Psychology,* 1959, **9,** 56-60.

MORAY, N. Where is capacity limited? A survey and a model. In A. Sanders (Ed.) *Attention and performance.* Amsterdam: North-Holland, 1967.

MORTON, J. A functional model of memory. In D. A. Norman (Ed.) *Models of human memory.* New York: Academic Press, 1970. Pp. 203-254.

MURDOCK, B. B., JR. Effects of a subsidiary task on short-term memory. *British Journal of Psychology,* 1965, **56,** 413-419.

MURDOCK, B. B., JR. Visual and auditory stores in short-term memory. *Quarterly Journal of Experimental Psychology,* 1966, **18,** 206-211.

MURDOCK, B. B., JR. Recent developments in short-term memory. *British Journal of Psychology,* 1967, **58,** 421-433.

MURDOCK, B. B., JR. Four channel effects in short-term memory. *Psychonomic Science,* 1971, **24,** 197-198.

MURDOCK, B. B., JR. Short-term memory. In G. H. Bower (Ed.) *Psychology of learning and motivation,* Vol. 5. New York: Academic Press, 1972. Pp. 67-127.

NEISSER, U. Visual search. *Scientific American,* 1964, **210,** 94-102.

NEISSER, U. *Cognitive psychology.* New York: Appleton-Century-Crofts, 1967.

NORMAN, D. A. Memory while shadowing. *Quarterly Journal of Experimental Psychology,* 1969, **21,** 85-93.

NORMAN, D. A., & RUMELHART, D. E. A system for perception and memory. In D. A. Norman (Ed.) *Models of human memory.* New York: Academic Press, 1970. Pp 21-64.

PALMER, S. E., & ORNSTEIN, P. A. Role of rehearsal strategy in serial probed recall. *Journal of Experimental Psychology,* 1971, **88,** 60-66.

PETERSON, L. R. Short-term verbal memory and learning. *Psychological Review,* 1966, **73,** 193-207.

PETERSON, L. R., & JOHNSON, S. T. Some effects of minimizing articulation on short-term retention. *Journal of Verbal Learning and Verbal Behavior,* 1971, **10,** 346-354.

PETERSON, L. R., & KROENER, S. Dichotic stimulation and retention. *Journal of Experimental Psychology,* 1964, **68,** 125-130.

PHILLIPS, W. A., & BADDELEY, A. D. Reaction time and short-term visual memory. *Psychonomic Science,* 1971, **22,** 73-74.

POSNER, M. I. Short-term memory systems in human information processing. *Acta Psychologica*, 1967, **27**, 267-284.

POSNER, M. I. Abstraction and the process of recognition. In G. H. Bower and J. T. Spence (Eds.) *The psychology of learning and motivation: Advances in research and theory*, Vol. III. New York: McGraw-Hill, 1969. Pp. 152-179.

POSTMAN, L. Short-term memory and incidental learning. In A. W. Melton (Ed.) *Categories of human learning*. New York: Academic Press, 1964. Pp. 145-201.

ROSENBERG, S., & SCHILLER, W. J. Semantic coding and incidental sentence recall. *Journal of Experimental Psychology*, 1971, **90**, 345-346.

RUNDUS, D. Analysis of rehearsal processes in free recall. *Journal of Experimental Psychology*, 1971, **89**, 63-77.

SAVIN, H. B., & BEVER, T. G. The nonperceptual reality of the phoneme. *Journal of Verbal Learning and Verbal Behavior*, 1970, **9**, 295-302.

SCHULMAN, A. I. Recognition memory for targets from a scanned word list. *British Journal of Psychology*, 1971, **62**, 335-346.

SELFRIDGE, O. G., & NEISSER, U. Pattern recognition by machine. *Scientific American*, 1960, **203**, 60-68.

SHAFFER, W. O., & SHIFFRIN, R. M. Rehearsal and storage of visual information. *Journal of Experimental Psychology*, 1972, **92**, 292-296.

SHALLICE, T., & WARRINGTON, E. K. Independent functioning of verbal memory stores: A neuropsychological study. *Quarterly Journal of Experimental Psychology*, 1970, **22**, 261-273.

SHEPARD, R. N. Recognition memory for words, sentences, and pictures. *Journal of Verbal Learning and Verbal Behavior*, 1967, **6**, 156-163.

SHIFFRIN, R. M., & ATKINSON, R. C. Storage and retrieval processes in long-term memory. *Psychological Review*, 1967, **76**, 179-193.

SHULMAN, H. G. Encoding and retention of semantic and phonemic information in short-term memory. *Journal of Verbal Learning and Verbal Behavior*, 1970, **9**, 499-508.

SHULMAN, H. G. Similarity effects in short-term memory. *Psychological Bulletin*, 1971, **75**, 399-415.

SHULMAN, H. G. Semantic confusion errors in short-term memory. *Journal of Verbal Learning and Verbal Behavior*, 1972, **11**, 221-227.

SILVERSTEIN, C., & GLANZER, M. Concurrent task in free recall: Differential effects of LTS and STS. *Psychonomic Science*, 1971, **22**, 367-368.

SPERLING, G. Short-term memory, long-term memory, and scanning in the processing of visual information. In A. Young and D. B. Lindsley (Eds.) *Early experience and visual information processing in perceptual and reading disorders*. Washington: National Academy of Sciences, 1970. Pp. 198-215.

STOFF, M., & EAGLE, M. N. The relationship among reported strategies, presentation rate, and verbal ability and their effects on free recall learning. *Journal of Experimental Psychology*, 1971, **87**, 423-428.

SUTHERLAND, N. S. Outlines of a theory of visual pattern recognition in animals and man. *Proceedings of the Royal Society. Series B*, 1968, **171**, 297-317.

TREISMAN, A. Monitoring and storage of irrelevant messages in selective attention. *Journal of Verbal Learning and Verbal Behavior*, 1964, **3**, 449-459.

TRESSELT, M. E., & MAYZNER, M. S. A study of incidental learning. *Journal of Psychology*, 1960, **50**, 339-347.

TULVING, E. Subjective organization and effects of repetition in multi-trial free-recall learning. *Journal of Verbal Learning and Verbal Behavior*, 1966, **5**, 193-197.

TULVING, E., & MADIGAN, S. A. Memory and verbal learning. *Annual Review of Psychology*, 1970, **21**, 437-484.

TULVING, E., & PATTERSON, R. D. Functional units and retrieval processes in free recall. *Journal of Experimental Psychology*, 1968, **77**, 239-248.

TULVING, E., & PEARLSTONE, Z. Availability versus accessibility of information in memory for words. *Journal of Verbal Learning and Verbal Behavior*, 1966, **5**, 381-391.

TURVEY, M. T. Repetition and the preperceptual information store. *Journal of Experimental Psychology*, 1967, **74**, 289-293.

WARRINGTON, E. K. Neurological disorders of memory. *British Medical Bulletin*, 1971, **27** 243-247.

WATKINS, M. J. The characteristics and functions of primary memory. Unpublished Ph.D. thesis, University of London, 1972.

WAUGH, N. C., & NORMAN, D. A. Primary memory. *Psychological Review*, 1965, **72**, 89-104.

WICKER, F. W., & BERNSTEIN, A. L. Association value and orienting task in incidental and intentional paired-associate learning. *Journal of Experimental Psychology*, 1969, **81**, 308-311.

Classic Quotations from William James

We have thus... not memory so much as memories... We can *set* our memory as it were to retain things for a certain time, and then let them depart.
  (*The Principles of Psychology* [1890], ch. 16.)

The *attention* which we lend to an experience is proportional to its vivid or interesting character; and it is a notorious fact that what interests us most vividly at the time is, other things equal, what we remember best. An impression may be so exciting emotionally as almost to leave a *scar* upon the cerebral tissues.
  (*The Principles of Psychology* [1890], ch. 16.)

A thing is important if anyone *think* it important.
  (*The Principles of Psychology* [1890], ch. 28 note.)

CHAPTER 12

"The 'Tip of the Tongue' Phenomenon"

Roger Brown and David McNeill[1]

EDITORS' COMMENTS. If we assume that you file inputs away in long-term storage primarily because they are important to you (see previous chapter), we are left with the following question: *Where* and *how* are your memories stored? Truthfully, we don't entirely know the answer to that question. But we have gotten many clues to what we might call "the memory mystery" from two types of studies. First, some people lose the ability to *recall* certain types of items from Long-term Memory when they suffer brain damage. Research on those unfortunate individuals who experience strokes (or other insults to the brain) suggests that memories of *words*, at least, are stored in the temporal lobes of the brain--those areas on both sides of the cerebral hemispheres just above the ears. Patients with temporal lobe damage often show a type of memory disorder called *aphasia*, or an impairment in the ability to use or remember language. Second, even normal individuals such as yourself occasionally have difficulties recalling a given item--a condition sometimes called "tip of the tongue" aphasia.

Studies of aphasic patients--and of the "tip of the tongue" aphasia--indicate that you tend to file items away in permanent memory in terms of several rather specific categories. According to Harold Goodglass, there are eight major memory categories.[2] Let's look briefly at these categories as we try to figure out how you might recall the word "horse" when someone shows you a picture of this animal: (1) *Identity*. This is the word or item itself. As you try to recall "horse," therefore, the first thing you'd look for in your "menal file cards" is this precise term. (2) *Class*. Horses are animals, so some of your memories of horses would be filed under the general class they belong to. (3) *Attributes*. Some horses are big, others small; some horses are black, while others are brown. Your memories of horses will usually include the sensory attributes of the various horses you've encountered. (4) *Context*. You expect to encounter horses in barns, at racetracks, or on farms, not in your bathroom or inside the microwave oven. Thus, a cue to the word *horse* would be "ranch," but not "wash basin." (5) *Function*. Horses are for riding; thus memories of horses might well be coded as "transportation" (or "objects to bet on"), not as "objects to type letters on." (6) *Sensory associations*. Horses have unique smells, and make unique sounds. The word "neigh" is associated with horses, but not the word "oink." (7) *Clangs and visual patterns*. The word "horse" rhymes with "force," has five letters, is just one syllable long, and begins with an "h." All these attributes of the word are *code items* in long-term storage. (8) *Reproductive memory*. Along with the word itself, your Long-term Memory contains information about how to *say* the word, how to *write* (or *type*) it, and even how to *draw a picture* of the animal.

Evidence supporting the importance of these eight memory categories can be found in this (and other research) by Roger Brown and David McNeill. But as it happens, you can test the validity of their findings by examining your own behavior the next time you experience difficulties trying to recall a word. Do you ask yourself, "What letter does it begin with?" If so, you're hunting for a Category 7 clue. And if, during an examination, you recall that a term you need to answer a test question appeared on the upper right-hand side of the page in your textbook, you're hunting for a Category 4 clue. The better you understand this article, therefore, and the more you learn about how your memory works, the better your test scores should become!

Abstract. The "tip of the tongue" (TOT) phenomenon is a state in which one cannot quite recall a familiar word but can recall words of similar form and meaning. Several hundred such states were precipitated by reading to Ss the definitions of English words of low frequency and asking them to try to recall the words. It was demonstrated that while in the TOT state, and before recall occurred, Ss had knowledge of some of the letters in the missing word, the number of syllables in it, and the location of the primary stress. The nearer S was to successful recall the more accurate the information he possessed. The recall of parts of words and attributes of words is termed "generic recall." The interpretation offered for generic recall involves the assumption that users of a language possess the mental equivalent of a dictionary. The features that figure in generic recall may be entered in the dictionary sooner than other features and so, perhaps, are wired into a more elaborate associative network. These more easily retrieved features of low-frequency words may be the features to which we chiefly attend in word-perception. The features favored by attention, especially the beginnings and endings of words, appear to carry more information than the features that are not favored, in particular the middles of words.

William James wrote, in 1893: "Suppose we try to recall a forgotten name. The state of our consciousness is peculiar. There is a gap therein; but no mere gap. It is a gap that is intensely active. A sort of **wraith** of the name is in it, beckoning us in a given direction, making us at moments tingle with the sense of our closeness and then letting us sink back without the longed-for term. If wrong names are proposed to us, this singularly definite gap acts immediately so as to negate them. They do not fit into its mould. And the gap of one word does not feel like the gap of another, all empty of content as both might seem necessarily to be when described as gaps" (p. 251).

The "tip of the tongue" (TOT) state involves a failure to recall a word of which one has knowledge. The evidence of knowledge is either an eventually successful recall or else an act of recognition that occurs, without additional training, when recall has failed. The class of cases defined by the conjunction of knowledge and a failure of recall is a large one. The TOT state, which James described, seems to be a small subclass in which recall is felt to be imminent.

For several months we watched for TOT states in ourselves. Unable to recall the name of the street on which a relative lives, one of us thought of *Congress* and *Corinth* and *Concord* and then looked up the address and learned that it was *Cornish*. The words that had come to mind have certain properties in common with the word that had been sought (the "target word"): all four begin with *Co*; all are two-syllable words; all put the primary stress on the first syllable. After this experience we began putting direct questions to ourselves when we fell into the TOT state, questions as to the number of syllables in the target word, its initial letter, etc.

Woodworth (1934), before us, made a record of data for naturally occurring TOT states and Wenzl (1932, 1936) did the same for German words. Their results are similar to those we obtained and consistent with the following preliminary characterization. When complete recall of a word is not presently possible but is felt to be imminent, one can often correctly recall the general type of the word; **generic** recall may succeed when particular recall fails. There seem to be two common varieties of *generic* recall. (a) Sometimes a part of the target word is recalled, a letter or two, a syllable, or **affix.** Partial recall is necessarily also *generic* since the class of words defined by the possession of any *part* of the target word will include words other than the target. (b) Sometimes the abstract form of the target is recalled, perhaps the fact that it was a two-syllable sequence with the primary stress on the first syllable. The whole word is represented in *abstract form recall* but not on the letter-by-letter level that constitutes its identity. The recall of an abstract form is also necessarily *generic*, since any such form defines a class of words extending beyond the target.

Wenzl and Woodworth had worked with small collections of data for naturally occurring TOT states. These data were, for the most part, provided by the investigators; were collected in an unsystematic fashion; and were analyzed in an impressionistic nonquantitative way. It seemed to us that such data left the facts of generic recall in doubt. An occasional correspondence between a retrieved word and a target word with respect to number of syllables, stress pattern or initial letter is, after all, to be expcted by chance. Several months of "self-observation and asking-our-friends" yielded fewer than a dozen good cases and we realized that an improved method of data collection was essential.

We thought it might pay to "prospect" for TOT states by reading to **S** definitions of uncommon English words and asking him to supply the words. The procedure was given a preliminary test with nine Ss who were

---

Wraith (rhymes with "faith"). A ghost, or a shadow-like object.

Generic (jen-AIR-ick). A general class of objects.

Affix (AFF-icks). A fixed set of letters that is added to either the front or the end of words. If added to the beginning of a word, the affix is called a *prefix*. For example, *hemi* is a prefix that means "half," as in "hemisphere." If the affix is added to the end of the word, it is called a "suffix." Both "ing" and "tion" are suffixes.

S. An abbreviation for "the subject."

individually interviewed for 2 hrs each.[3] In 57 instances an S was, in fact, "seized" by a TOT state. The signs of it were unmistakable; he would appear to be in mild torment, something like the brink of a sneeze, and if he found the word his relief was considerable. While searching for the target S told us all the words that came to his mind. He volunteered the information that some of them resembled the target in sound but not in meaning; others he was sure were similar in meaning but not in sound. The **E** intruded on S's agony with two questions: (a) How many syllables has the target word? (b) What is its first letter? Answers to the first question were correct in 47% of all cases and answers to the second question were correct in 51% of the cases. These outcomes encouraged us to believe that generic recall was real and to devise a group procedure that would further speed up the rate of data collection.

METHOD

Subjects

Fifty-six Harvard and Radcliffe undergraduates participated in one of three evening sessions; each session was 2 hrs long. The Ss were volunteers from a large General Education Course and were paid for their time.

Word List

The list consisted of 49 words which, according to the Thorndike-Lorge *Word Book* (1952), occur at least once per four million words but not so often as once per one million words The level is suggested by these examples: **apse**, **nepotism**, **cloaca**, **ambergris**, and **sampan**. We thought the words used were likely to be in the passive or recognition vocabularies of our Ss but not in their active recall vocabularies. There were 6 words of 1 syllable; 19 of 2 syllables; 20 of 3 syllables; 4 of 4 syllables. For each word we used a definition from *The American College Dictionary* (Barnhart, 1948) edited so as to contain no words that closely resembled the one being defined.

Response Sheet

The response sheet was laid off in vertical columns headed as follows:

Intended word (+ *One I was thinking of*).
             (- *Not*).
Number of syllables (1-5).
Initial letter.

Words of similar sound.   (1. Closest in sound)
                                (2. Middle   )
                                (3. Farthest in Sound)

Words of similar meaning.

Word you had in mind if not intended word.

Procedure

We instructed Ss to the following effect.

In this experiment we are concerned with that state of mind in which a person is unable to think of a word that he is certain he knows, the state of mind in which a word seems to be on the tip of one's tongue. Our technique for precipitating such states is, in general, to read definitions of uncommon words and ask the subject to recall the word.

(1) We will first read the definition of a low-frequency word.

(2) If you should happen to know the word at once, or think you do, or, if you should simply not know it, then there is nothing further for you to do at the moment. Just wait.

(3) If you are unable to think of the word but feel sure that you know it and that it is on the verge of coming back to you then you are in a TOT state and should begin at once to fill in the columns of the response sheet.

(4) After reading each definition we will ask whether anyone is in the TOT state. Anyone who is in that state should raise his hand. The rest of us will then wait until those in the TOT state have written on the answer sheet all the information they are able to provide.

(5) When everyone who has been in the TOT state has signalled us to proceed, we will read the target word. At this time, everyone is to write the word in the leftmost column of the response sheet. Those of you who have known the word since first its definition was read are asked not to write it until this point. Those of you who simply did not know the word or who had thought of a different word will write now the word we read. For those of you who have been in the TOT state two eventualities are possible. The word read may strike you as definitely the word you have been seeking. In that case please write ' + ' after the word, as the instructions at the head of the column direct. The other possibility is that you will not be sure whether the word read is the one you have been seeking or, indeed, you may be sure that it is not. In this case you are asked to write the sign '-' after the word. Sometimes when the word read out is not the one you have been seeking, your actual target may come to mind. In this case, in addition to the minus

sign in the leftmost column, please write the actual target word in the rightmost column.

(6) Now we come to the column entries themselves. The first two entries, the guess as to the number of syllables and the initial letter, are required. The remaining entries should be filled out if possible. When you are in a TOT state, words that are related to the target word do almost always come to mind. List them as they come, but separate words which you think resemble the target in sound from words which you think resemble the target in meaning.

(7) When you have finished all your entries, but before you signal us to read the intended target word, look again at the words you have listed as "Words of similar sound." If possible, rank these, as the instructions at the head of the column direct, in terms of the degree of their seeming resemblance to the target. This must be done without knowledge of what the target actually is.

(8) The search procedure of a person in the TOT state will sometimes serve to retrieve the missing word before he has finished filling in the columns and before we read out the word. When this happens please mark the place where it happens with the words "Got it" and *do not provide any more data.*

RESULTS

Classes of Data

There were 360 instances, across all words and all Ss, in which a TOT state was signalled. Of this total, 233 were positive TOTs. A positive TOT is one for which the target word is known and, consequently, one for which the data obtained can be scored as accurate or inaccurate. In those cases where the target was not the word intended but some other word which S finally recalled and wrote in the rightmost column his data were checked against that word, his effective target. A negative TOT is one for which the S judged the word read out not to have been his target and, in addition, one in which S proved unable to recall his own functional target.

The data provided by S while he searched for the target word are of two kinds: explicit guesses as to the number of syllables in the target and the initial letter of the target; words that came to mind while he searched for the target. The words that came to mind were classified by S into 224 words similar in sound to the target (hereafter called "SS" words) and 95 words similar in meaning to the target (hereafter called "SM" words). The S's information about the number of syllables in, and the initial letter of the target may be inferred from correspondences between the target and his SS words as well as directly discovered from his **explicit** guesses. For his knowledge of the stress pattern of the target and of letters in the target, other than the initial letter, we must rely on the SS words alone since explicit guesses were not required.

To convey a sense of the SS and SM words we offer the following examples. When the target was sampan the SS words (not all of them real words) included: *Saipan, Siam, Cheyenne, sarong, sanching,* and *sympoon.* The SM words were: *barge, houseboat,* and *junk.* When the target was **caduceus** the SS words included: *Casadesus, Aeschelus, cephalus,* and *leucosis.* The SM words were: *fasces, Hippocrates, lictor,* and *snake.* The spelling in all cases is S's own.

We will, in this report, use the SM words to provide baseline data against which to evaluate the accuracy of the explicit guesses and of the SS words. The SM words are words produced under the spell of the positive TOT state but judged by S to resemble the target in meaning rather than sound. We are quite sure that the SM words are somewhat more like the target than would be a collection of words produced by Ss with no knowledge of the target. However, the SM words make a better comparative baseline than any other data we collected.

General Problems of Analysis

The data present problems of analysis that are not common in psychology. To begin with, the words of the list did not reliably precipitate TOT states. Of the original 49 words, all but **zither** succeeded at least once; the range was from one success to nine. The Ss made actual targets of 51 words not on the original list and all but five of these were pursued by one S only. Clearly none of the 100 words came even close to precipitating a TOT state in all 56 Ss. Furthermore, the Ss varied in their susceptibility to TOT states. There were nine who

---

E. An abbreviation for "the experimenter."

Apse (aps). A part of a building (such as a church) that projects out from the walls and usually is semicircular in shape; the area behind the altar in a church.

Nepotism (KNEE-oh-tism). The act of hiring your own relatives simply because they're related to you.

Cloaca (KLOH-ah-kah). A sewer.

Ambergris (AM-ber-gris). A waxy substance, often used in perfumes, believed to originate in the intestines of the sperm whale.

Sampan (SAM-pan). A type of boat found in the Orient.

Explicit (EX-pliss-it). Something that is open, or visible. As opposed to *implicit*, which means "hidden, or assumed."

Caduceus (ka-DUCE-ee-us). The symbol of the medical profession — a staff with two wings at the top, and with two snakes wrapped around the staff.

Zither (ZITH-er). A stringed instrument, usually having 30 to 40 strings, played with a pick.

experienced none at all in a 2-hr period; the largest number experienced in such a period by one S was eight. In our data, then, the entries for one word will not usually involve the same Ss or even the same number of Ss as the entries for another word. The entries for one S need not involve the same words or even the same number of words as the entries for another S. Consequently for the tests we shall want to make there are no significance tests that we can be sure are appropriate.

In statistical theory our problem is called the "fragmentary data problem."[4] The best thing to do with fragmentary data is to report them very fully and analyze them in several different ways. Our detailed knowledge of these data suggests that the problems are not serious for, while there is some variation in the pull of words and the susceptibility of Ss, there is not much variation in the quality of the data. The character of the material recalled is much the same from word to word and S to S.

Table 1
Actual Numbers of Syllables and Guessed
Numbers for all TOTs in the Main Experiment

	Guessed Numbers					No guess	Mode	Mean
	1	2	3	4	5			
Actual Numbers 1	9	7	1	0	0	0	1	1.53
2	2	55	22	2	1	5	2	2.33
3	3	19	61	10	1	5	3	2.86
4	0	2	12	6	2	3	3	3.36
5	0	0	3	0	1	1	3	3.50

Number of Syllables

As the main item of evidence that S in a TOT state can recall with significant success the number of syllables in a target word he has not yet found we offer Table 1. The entries on the diagonal are instances in which guesses were correct. The order of the means of the explicit guesses is the same as the order of the actual numbers of syllables in the target words. The **rank order correlation** between the two is 1.0 and such a correlation is **significant** with a $p = .001$ (**one-tailed**) even when only five items are correlated. The **modes** of the guesses correspond exactly with the actual numbers of syllables, for the values one through three; for words of four and five syllables the modes continue to be three.

When all TOTs are combined, the contributions to the total effects of individual Ss and of individual words are unequal. We have made an analysis in which each word counts but once. This was accomplished by calculating the mean of the guesses made by all Ss for whom a particular word precipitated a TOT state and taking that mean as the score for that word. The new means calculated with all words equally weighted were, in order: 1.62; 2.30; 2.80; 3.33; and 3.50. These values are close to those of Table 1 and **rho** with the actual numbers of syllables continues to be 1.0.

We also made an analysis in which each S counts but once. This was done by calculating the mean of an S's guesses for all words of one syllable, the mean for all words of two syllables, etc. In comparing the means of guesses for words of different length one can only use those Ss who made at least one guess for each actual length to be compared. In the present data only words of two syllables and three syllables precipitated enough TOTs to yield a substantial number of such matched scores. There were 21 Ss who made guesses for both two-syllable and three-syllable words. The simplest way to evaluate the significance of the differences in these guesses is with the **Sign Test**. In only 6 of 21 matched scores was the mean guess for words of two syllables larger than the mean for words of three syllables. The difference is significant with a $p = .039$ (one-tailed). For actual words that were only one syllable apart in length, Ss were able to make a significant distinction in the correct direction when the words themselves could not be called to mind.

The 224 SS words and the 95 SM words provide supporting evidence. Words of similar sound (SS) had the same number of syllables as the target in 48% of all cases. This value is close to the 57% that were correct for explicit guesses in the main experiment and still closer to the 47% correct already reported for the pretest. The SM words provide a clear contrast; only 20% matched the number of syllables in the target. We conclude that S in a positive TOT state has a significant ability to recall correctly the number of syllables in the word he is trying to retrieve.

In Table 1 it can be seen that the modes of guesses exactly correspond with the actual numbers of syllables in target words for the values one through three. For still longer target words (four and five syllables) the means of guesses continue to rise but the modes stay at the value three. Words of more than three syllables are rare in English and the generic entry for such words may be the same as for words of three syllables; something like "three or more" may be used for all long words.

Initial Letter

Over all positive TOTs, the initial letter of the word S was seeking was correctly guessed 57% of the time.

The pretest result was 51% correct. The results from the main experiment were analyzed with each word counting just once by entering a word's score as "correct" whenever the most common guess or the only guess was in fact correct; 62% of words were, by this reckoning, correctly guessed. The SS words had initial letters matching the initial letters of the target words in 49% of all cases. We do not know the chance level of success for this performance but with 26 letters and many words that began with uncommon letters the level must be low. Probably the results for the SM words are better than chance and yet the outcome for these words was only 8% matches.

We did an analysis of the SS and SM words, with each S counting just once. There were 26 Ss who had at least one such word. For each S we calculated the proportion of SS words matching the target in initial letter and the same proportion for SM words. For 21 Ss the proportions were not tied and in all but 3 cases the larger value was that of the SS words. The difference is significant by Sign Test with $p = .001$ (one-tailed).

The evidence for significantly accurate generic recall of inital letters is even stronger than for syllables. The absolute levels of success are similar but the chance baseline must be much lower for letters than for syllables because the possibilities are more numerous.

Table 2
Syllables Receiving Primary Stress in Target Words and SS Words

		Target words	
		1st syllable	2nd syllable
SS Words	1st Syllable	25	6
	2nd syllable	6	12

Syllabic Stress

We did not ask S to guess the stress pattern of the target word but the SS words provide relevant data. The test was limited to the syllabic location of the primary or heaviest stress for which *The American College Dictionary* was our authority. The number of SS words that could be used was limited by three considerations. (a) Words of one syllable had to be excluded because there was no possibility of variation. (b) Stress locations could only be matched if the SS word had the same number of syllables as the target, and so only such matching words could be used. (c) Invented words and foreign words could not be used because they do not appear in the dictionary. Only 49 SS words remained.

As it happened all of the target words involved (whatever their length) placed the primary stress on either the first or the second syllable. It was possible, therefore, to make a 2 X 2 table for the 49 pairs of target and SS words which would reveal the correspondences and noncorrespondences. As can be seen in Table 2 the SS words tended to stress the same syllable as the target words. The X^2 for this table is 10.96 and that value is significant with $p < .001$. However, the data do not meet the independence requirement, so we cannot be sure that the matching tendency is significant. There were not enough data to permit any other analyses, and so we are left suspecting that S in a TOT state has knowledge of the stress pattern of the target, but we are not sure of it.

Letters in Various Positions

We did not require explicit guesses for letters in positions other than the first, but the SS words provide

Rank order correlation. Suppose you want to see if there is any connection between the height and weight of the members of a football team. You would weight each player and measure his height. Then you could *rank* each player according to both variables. You might find that player A was both the tallest and heaviest of the team members, while player B was second tallest but third heaviest. After you had gathered your data, you might use a statistical test called a "rank order correlation" to determine if there was a significant (or non-chance) relationship between the players' height and weight. A perfect correlation is +1.0. However, if weight were *negatively* correlated with height, you'd get a correlation of -1.0. A correlation of 0 (or close to it) means there is little connection between the two variables

Significant. In statistics, we use the term *significant* to imply that the results of a study probably didn't occur by chance. Generally speaking, if the probability (p) is 0.05 or less (usually written as $p < .05$, or $p = .05$), we assume that the results were not due to chance and thus are significant.

One-tailed. Consider a bell-shaped distribution, which has a peak in the middle (the mean), and two "tails" spreading off from the peak. Normally, when you test for significance, you use a "two-tailed test" because you don't know whether your results will lie above or below the mean. However, if you predict that the results must be (let's say) *above* the mean, you may use a "one-tailed test" instead. Since you are more likely to get significant results using a one-tailed test, most experimenters prefer to use one whenever they legitimately can.

Modes. There are three "measures of central tendency" frequently used in statistics. The *mean* is the mathematical average of a distribution of scores. The *median* is the score in the exact middle of the distribution. The *mode* is the most frequent score in the distribution. In a perfect "bell-shaped curve," the mean, median, and mode are the same.

Rho (roh). A type of correlation coefficient. A rho of 1.0 indicates that the variables involved are perfectly correlated.

Sign Test. A statistical device for determining whether two sets of data are significantly different.

X^2. A statistical test for determining whether two sets of data are significantly different.

relevant data. The test was limited to the following positions: first, second, third, third-last, second-last, and last. A target word must have at least six letters in order to provide data on the six positions; it might have any number of letters larger than six and still provide data for the six (relatively defined) positions. Accordingly we included the data for all target words having six or more letters.

Figure 1 displays the percentages of letters in each of six positions of SS words which matched the letters in the same positions of the corresponding targets. For comparison purposes these data are also provided for SM words. The SS curve is at all points above the SM curve; the two are closest together at the third-last position. The values for the last three positions of the

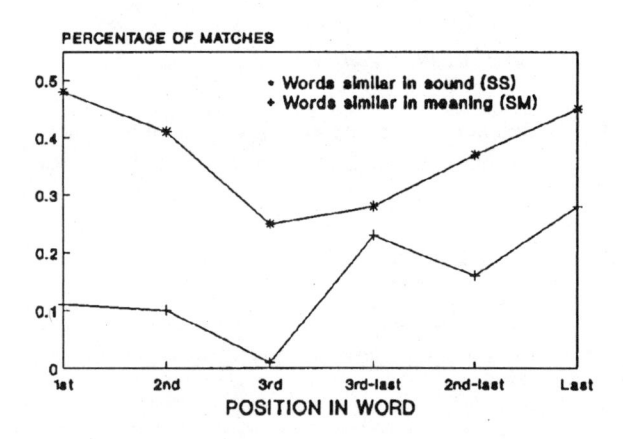

Figure 1. Percentages of letter matches between target words and SS words for six serial positions.

SS curve quite closely match the values for the first three positions. The values for the last three positions of the SM curve, on the other hand, are well above the values for the first three positions. Consequently the *relative* superiority of the SS curve is greater in the first three positions.

The letter-position data were also analyzed in such a way as to count each target word just once, assigning each position in the target a single score representing the proportion of matches across all Ss for that position in that word. The order of the SS and SM points is preserved in this finer analysis. We did Sign Tests comparing the SS and SM values for each of the six positions. As Fig. 1 would suggest the SS values for the first three positions all exceeded the SM values with *p*s less than .01 (one-tailed). The SS values for the final two positions exceeded the SM values with *p*s less than .05 (one-tailed). The SS values for the third-last position were greater than the SN values but not significantly so.

The cause of the upswing in the final three positions of the SM curve may be some difference in the distribution of information in early and late positions of English words. Probably there is less variety in the later positions. In any case the fact that the SS curve lies above the SM curve for the last three positions indicates that S in a TOT state has knowledge of the target in addition to his knowledge of English word structure.

Chunking of Suffixes

The request to S that he guess the initial letter of the target occasionally elicited a response of more than one letter; e.g., *ex* in the case of *extort* and *con* in the case of *convene*. This result suggested that some letter (or **phoneme**) sequences are stored as single entries having been "chunked" by long experience. We made only one test for chunking and that involved three-letter suffixes.

It did not often happen that an S produced an SS word that matched the target with respect to all of its three last letters. The question asked of the data was whether such three-letter matches occurred more often when the letters constituted an English suffix than when they did not. In order to determine which of the target words terminated in such a suffix, we entered *The American College Dictionary* with final trigrams. If there was an entry describing a **suffix** appropriate to the grammatical and **semantic** properties of the target we considered the trigram to be a suffix. There were 20 words that terminated in a suffix, including *fawning, unctuous,* and *philatelist*.

Of 93 SS words produced in response to a target terminating in a suffix, 30 matched the target in their final three letters. Of 130 SS words supplied in response to a target that did not terminate in a suffix only 5 matched the target in their final three letters. The data were also analyzed in a way that counts each S just once and uses only Ss who produced SS words in response to both kinds of target. A Sign Test was made of the difference between matches of suffixes and matches of endings that were not suffixes; the former were more common with $p = .059$ (one-tailed). A comparable Sign Test for SM words was very far from significance. We conclude that suffix-chunking probably plays a role in generic recall.

Proximity to the Target and Quality of Information

There were three varieties of positive TOT states: (1) Cases in which S *recognized* the word read by E as the word he had been seeking; (2) Cases in which S *recalled* the intended word before it was read out; (3) Cases in which S *recalled* the word he had been seeking before E read the intended word and the recalled word was not the same as the word read. Since S in a TOT state of either type 2 or type 3 reached the target before the intended word was read and S in a TOT state of type 1 did not, the TOTs of the second and third types may be considered "nearer" the target than TOTs of the first type. We have no basis for ordering types 2 and 3 relative to one another. We predicted that Ss in the two kinds of TOT state that ended in recall (types 2 and 3) would produce more accurate information about the target than Ss in the TOT state that ended in recognition (type 1).

The prediction was tested on the explicit guesses of initial letters since these were the most complete and sensitive data. There were 138 guesses from Ss in a type 1 state and 58 of these, or 42%, were correct. There were 36 guesses from Ss in a type 2 state and, of these, 20, or 56%, were correct. There were 59 guesses from Ss in a type 3 state and of these 39, or 66%, were correct. We also analyzed the results in such a way as to count each word only once. The percentages correct were: for type 1, 50%; type 2, 62%; type 3, 63%. Finally, we performed an analysis counting each S just once but averaging together type 2 and type 3 results in order to bring a maximum number of Ss into the comparison. The combining action is justified since both type 2 and type 3 were states ending in recall. A Sign Test of the differences showed that guesses were more accurate in the states that ended in recall than in the states that ended in recognition; one-tailed $p < .01$. Supplementary analyses with SS and SM words confirmed these results. We conclude that when S is nearer his target his generic recall is more accurate than when he is farther from the target.

Special interest attaches to the results from type 2 TOTs. In the method of our experiment there is nothing to guarantee that when S said he recognized a word he had really done so. Perhaps when E read out a word, S could not help thinking that that was the word he had in mind. We ourselves do not believe anything of the sort happened. The single fact that most Ss claimed fewer than five positive TOTs in a 2-hr period argues against any such effect. Still it is reassuring to have the 36 type 2 cases in which S recalled the intended word *before* it was read. The fact that 56% of the guesses of initial letters made in type 2 states were correct is hard-core evidence of generic recall. It may be worth adding that 65% of the guesses of the number of syllables for type 2 cases were correct.

Judgments of the Proximity of SS Words

The several comparisons we have made of SS and SM words demonstrate that when recall is imminent S can distinguish among the words that come to mind those that resemble the target in form from those that do not resemble the target in form. There is a second kind of evidence which shows that S can tell when he is "getting close" (or "warm").

In 15 instances Ss rated two or more SS words for comparative similarity to the target. Our analysis contrasts those rated "most similar" (1) with those rated next most similar (2). Since there were very few words rated (3) we attempted no analysis of them. Similarity points were given for all the features of a word that have now been demonstrated to play a part in generic recall– with the single exception of stress. Stress had to be disregarded because some of the words were invented and their stress patterns were unknown.

The problem was to compare pairs of SS words, rated 1 and 2, for overall similarity to the target. We determined whether each member matched the target in number of syllables. If one did and the other did not, then a single similarity point was assigned the word that matched. For each word, we counted, beginning with the initial letter, the number of consecutive letters in common with the target. The word having the longer sequence that matched the target earned one similarity point. An exactly comparable procedure was followed for sequences starting from the final letter. In sum, each word in a pair could receive from zero to three similarity points.

We made Sign Tests comparing the total scores for words rated most like the target (1) and words rated next most like the target (2). This test was only slightly inappropriate since only two target words occurred twice in the set of 15 and only one S repeated in the set. Ten of 12 differences were in the predicted direction and the one-tailed $p = .019$. It is of some interest that similarity points awarded on the basis of letters in the middle of the words did not even go in the right direction. Figure 1 has already indicated that they also do not figure in Ss' judgments of the comparative similarity to the target of pairs of SS words. Our conclusion is that S at a given distance from the target can accurately judge which of two words that come to mind is more like the

<u>Phoneme</u> (FOH-neem). The smallest unit of speech, such as "da" or "ba.
<u>Suffix</u> (SUFF-icks). An "ending" that is common to many words, such as "ing" or "tion."
<u>Semantic</u> (see-MAN-tick). Semantics is the study of the *meaning* of words.

target and that he does so in terms of the features of words that appear in generic recall.

Conclusions

When complete recall of a word has not occurred but is felt to be imminent there is likely to be accurate generic recall. Generic recall of the *abstract form* variety is evidenced by S's knowledge of the number of syllables in the target and of the location of the primary stress. Generic recall of the *partial* variety is evidenced by S's knowledge of letters in the target word. This knowledge shows a bowed **serial-position effect** since it is better for the ends of a word than for the middle and somewhat better for beginning positions than for final positions. The accuracy of generic recall is greater when S is near the target (complete recall is imminent) than when S is far from the target. A person experiencing generic recall is able to judge the relative similarity to the target of words that occur to him and these judgments are based on the features of words that figure in partial and abstract form recall.

DISCUSSION

The facts of generic recall are relevant to theories of speech perception, reading, the understanding of sentences, and the organization of memory. We have not worked out all the implications. In this section we first attempt a model of the TOT process and then try to account for the existence of generic memory.

A Model of the Process

Let us suppose (with Katz and Fodor, 1963, and many others) that our long-term memory for words and definitions is organized into the functional equivalent of a dictionary. In real dictionaries, those that are books, entries are ordered alphabetically and bound in place. Such an arrangement is too simple and too inflexible to serve as a model for a mental dictionary. We will suppose that words are entered on **keysort cards** instead of pages and that the cards are punched for various features of the words entered. With real cards, paper ones, it is possible to retrieve from the total deck any subset punched for a common feature by putting a metal rod through the proper hole. We will suppose that there is in the mind some speedier equivalent of this retrieval technique.

The model will be described in terms of a single example: When the target word was *sextant*, Ss heard the definition: "A navigational instrument used in measuring angular distances, especially the altitude of sun, moon, and stars at sea." This definition precipitated a TOT state in 9 Ss of the total 56. The SM words included: *astrolabe, compass, dividers*, and *protractor*. The SS words included: *secant, sextet*, and *sexton*.

The problem begins with a definition rather than a word and so S must enter his dictionary backwards, or in a way that would be backwards and quite impossible for the dictionary that is a book. It is not impossible with keysort cards, providing we suppose that the cards are punched for some set of semantic features. Perhaps these are the semantic "markers" that Katz and Fodor (1963) postulate in their account of the comprehension of sentences. We will imagine that it is somehow possible to extract from the definition a set of markers and that these are, in the present case: "navigation, instrument, having to do with geometry." Metal rods thrust into the holes for each of these features might fish up such a collection of entries as: *astrolabe, compass, dividers*, and *protractor*. This first retrieval, which is in response to the definition, must be semantically based and it will not, therefore, account for the appearance of such SS words as *sextet* and *sexton*.

There are four major kinds of outcome of the first retrieval and these outcomes correspond with the four main things that happen to Ss in the TOT experiment. We will assume that a definition of each word retrieved is entered on its card and that it is possible to check the input definition against those on the cards. The first possible outcome is that *sextant* is retrieved along with *compass* and *astrolabe* and the others and that the definitions are specific enough so that the one entered for *sextant* registers as matching the input and all the others as not-matching. This is the case of correct recall; S has found a word that matches the definition and it is the intended word. The second possibility is that *sextant* is not among the words retrieved and, in addition, the definitions entered for those retrieved are so imprecise that one of them (the definition for *compass*, for example) registers as matching the input. In this case S thinks he has found the target though he really has not. The third possibility is that *sextant* is not among the words retrieved, but the definitions entered for those retrieved are specific enough so that none of them will register a match with the input. In this case, S does not know the word and realizes the fact. The above three outcomes are the common ones and none of them represents a TOT state.

In the TOT case the first retrieval must include a card with the definition of *sextant* entered on it but with the word itself incompletely entered. The card might, for instance, have the following information about the word: two-syllables, initial s, final t. The entry would be a punchcard equivalent of S__T. Perhaps an incomplete entry of this sort is James's "singularly definite gap" and the basis for generic recall.

The S with a correct definition, matching the input, and an incomplete word entry will know that he knows the word, will feel that he almost has it, that it is on the tip of his tongue. If he is asked to guess the number of syllables and the initial letter he should, in the case we have imagined, be able to do so. He should also be able to produce SS words. The features that appear in the incomplete entry (two-syllables, initial s, and final t) can be used as the basis for a second retrieval. The subset of cards defined by the intersection of all three features would include cards for *secant* and *sextet*. If one feature were not used then *sexton* would be added to the set.

Which of the facts about the TOT state can now be accounted for? We know that Ss were able, when they had not recalled a target, to distinguish between words resembling the target in sound (SS words) and words resembling the target in meaning only (SM words). The basis for this distinction in the model would seem to be the distinction between the first and second retrievals. Membership in the first subset retrieved defines SM words and membership in the second subset defines SS words.

We know that when S had produced several SS words but had not recalled the target he could sometimes accurately rank-order the SS words for similarity to the target. The model offers an account of this ranking performance. If the incomplete entry for *sextant* includes three features of the word then SS words having only one or two of these features (e.g., *sexton*) should be judged less similar to the target than SS words having all three of them (e.g., *secant*).

When an SS word has all of the features of the incomplete entry (as do *secant* and *sextet* in our example) what prevents its being mistaken for the target? Why did not the S who produced sextet think that the word was "right?" Because of the definitions. The forms meet all the requirements of the incomplete entry but the definitions do not match.

The TOT state often ended in recognition; i.e., S failed to recall the word but when E read out *sextant* S recognized it as the word he had been seeking. The model accounts for this outcome as follows. Suppose that there is only the incomplete entry S__T in memory, plus the definition. The E now says (in effect) that there exists a word *sextant* which has the definition in question. The word *sextant* then satisfies all the data points available to S; it has the right number of syllables, the right initial letter, the right final letter, and it is said to have the right definition. The result is recognition.

The proposed account has some testable implications. Suppose that E were to read out, when recall failed, not the correct word sextant but an invented word like *sekrant* or *saktint* which satisfies the incomplete entry as well as does *sextant* itself. If S had nothing but the incomplete entry and E's testimony to guide him then he should "recognize" the invented words just as he recognizes *sextant*.

The account we have given does not accord with intuition. Our intuitive notion of recognition is that the features which could not be called were actually in storage but less accessible than the features that were recalled. To stay with our example, intuition suggests that the features of *sextant* that could not be recalled, the letters between the first and the last, were entered on the card but were less "legible" than the recalled features. We might imagine them printed in small letters and faintly. When, however, the E reads out the word sextant, then S can make out the less legible parts of his entry and, since the total entry matches E's word, S recognizes it. This sort of recognition should be "tighter" than the one described previously. *Sekrant* and *saktint* would be rejected.

We did not try the effect of invented words and we do not know how they would have been received but among the outcomes of the actual experiment there is one that strongly favors the faint-entry theory. Subjects in a TOT state, after all, sometimes recalled the target word without any prompting. The incomplete entry theory does not admit of such a possibility. If we suppose that the entry is not S__T but something more like S*ex tan*T (with the italicized lower-case letters representing the faint-entry section) we must still explain how

---

Serial-position effect. If you are given a list of words to learn, and then are tested a minute or so later to see how many you recall, you probably will remember the first items on the list slightly better than you remember the final items on the list—and you will probably recall items in the middle of the list worst of all. Put more simply, the *position* of the item in the *series* of words affects how well you can remember it. Recent studies suggest that the serial position effect occurs only under certain conditions, namely, when the interval between learning and testing is of moderate duration. Suppose you are given a single, brief exposure to each word on a four-word list. If you are tested immediately afterward, you probably will recall items at the end of the list better than those in the middle, and recall items in the middle of the list better than those at the beginning (the "recency" effect, since you remember best the items you learned most recently). If you are tested 100 seconds after seeing the words, you will recall the items at the first of the list better than those in the middle, and those items in the middle better than those at the end of the list (the "primacy" effect, since you remember best those items you learned first). Only if you are tested 10-20 seconds after the single, brief exposure will you remember items at *both* the beginning and the end of the list better than those in the middle.

Keysort cards. In the 1960's, data gathered during an experiment were recorded by punching holes in cards about the size of a business envelope. The cards could be "sorted" in various ways by a machine that would select only those cards with holes in certain positions—or sorted manually by sticking an ice pick (or similar tool) through the holes.

it happens that the faintly entered, and at first inaccessible, middle letters are made accessible in the case of recall.

Perhaps it works something like this. The features that are first recalled operate as we have suggested, to retrieve a set of SS words. Whenever an SS word (such as *secant*) includes middle letters that are matched in the faintly entered section of the target then those faintly entered letters become accessible. The match brings out the missing parts the way heat brings out anything written in lemon juice. In other words, when *secant* is retrieved the target entry grows from, S*ex tan*T to SE*x tA*NT. The retrieval of *sextet* brings out the remaining letters and S recalls the complete word—*sextant*.

It is now possible to explain the one as yet unexplained outcome of the TOT experiment. Subjects whose state ended in recall had, before they found the target, more correct information about it than did Ss whose state ended in recognition. More correct information means fewer features to be brought out by duplication in SS words and so should mean a greater likelihood that all essential features will be brought out in a short period of time.

All of the above assumes that each word is entered in memory just once, on a single card. There is another possibility. Suppose that there are entries for *sextant* on several different cards. They might all be incomplete, but at different points, or, some might be incomplete and one or more of them complete. The several cards would be punched for different semantic markers and perhaps for different associations so that the entry recovered would vary with the rule of retrieval. With this conception we do not require the notion of faint entry. The difference between features commonly recalled, such as the first and last letters, and features that are recalled with difficulty or perhaps only recognized, can be rendered in another way. The more accessible features are entered on more cards or else the cards on which they appear are punched for more markers; in effect, they are wired into a more extended associative net.

The Reason for Generic Recall

In adult minds words are stored in both visual and auditory terms and between the two there are complicated rules of translation. Generic recall involves letters (or phonemes), affixes, syllables, and stress location. In this section we will discuss only letters (legible forms) and will attempt to explain a single effect—the serial-position effect in the recall of letters. It is not clear how far the explanation can be extended.

In brief overview this is the argument. The design of the English language is such that one word is usually distinguished from all others in a more-than-minimal way, i.e., by more than a single letter in a single position. It is consequently *possible* to recognize words when one has not stored the complete letter sequence. The evidence is that we do not store the complete sequence if we do not have to. We begin by attending chiefly to initial and final letters and storing these. The order of attention and of storage favors the ends of words because the ends carry more information than the middles. An incomplete entry will serve for recognition, but if words are to be produced (or recalled) they must be stored in full. For most words, then, it is eventually necessary to attend to the middle letters. Since end letters have been attended to from the first they should always be more clearly entered or more elaborately connected than middle letters. When recall is required of words that are not very familiar to S, as it was in our experiment, the end letters should often be accessible when the middle are not.

In building pronounceable sequences the English language, like all other languages, utilizes only a small fraction of its **combinatorial** possibilities (Hockett, 1958). If a language used all possible sequences of phonemes (or letters) its words could be shorter, but they would be much more vulnerable to misconstruction. A change of any single letter would result in reception of a different word. As matters are actually arranged, most changes result in no word at all; for example: *textant, sixtant, sektant*. Our words are highly redundant and fairly indestructible.

Underwood (1963) has made a distinction for the learning of nonsense syllables between the "nominal" stimulus which is the syllable presented and the "functional" stimulus which is the set of characteristics of the syllable actually used to cue the response. Underwood reviews evidence showing that college students learning paired-associates do not learn any more of a stimulus trigram than they have to. If, for instance, each of a set of stimulus trigrams has a different initial letter, then Ss are not likely to learn letters other than the first, since they do not need them.

Feigenbaum (1963) has written a computer program (EPAM) which simulates the selective-attention aspect of verbal learning as well as many other aspects. "... EPAM has a *noticing order for letters of syllables*, which prescribes at any moment a letter-scanning sequence for the matching process. Because it is observed that subjects generally consider end letters before middle letters, the noticing order is initialized as follows: first letter, third letter, second letter" (p. 304). We believe that the differential recall of letters in various positions, revealed in Fig. 1 of this paper, is to be explained by the operation in the perception of real words of a rule very much like Feigenbaum's.

Feigenbaum's EPAM is so written as to make it possible for the noticing rule to be changed by experience. If the middle position were consistently the position that differentiated syllables, the computer would learn to look there first. We suggest that the human tendency to look first at the beginning of a word, then at the end and finally the middle has "grown" in response to the distribution of information in words. Miller and Friedman (1957) asked English speakers to guess letters for various open positions in segments of English text that were 5, 7, or 11 characters long. The percentages of correct first guesses show a very clear serial-position effect for segments of all three lengths. Success was lowest in the early positions, next lowest in the final positions, and at a maximum in the middle positions. Therefore, information was greatest at the start of a word, next greatest at the end, and least in the middle. Attention needs to be turned where information is, to the parts of the word that cannot be guessed. The Miller and Friedman segments did not necessarily break at word boundaries but their discovery that the middle positions of continuous text are more easily guessed than the ends applies to words.

Is there any evidence that speakers of English do attend first to the ends of English words? There is no evidence that the eye fixations of adult readers consistently favor particular parts of words (Woodworth and Schlosberg, 1954). However, it is not eye fixation that we have in mind. A considerable stretch of text can be taken in from a single fixation point. We are suggesting that there is selection within this stretch, selection accomplished centrally; perhaps by a mechanism like Broadbent's (1958) "biased filter."

Bruner and O'Dowd (1958) studied word perception with __tachistoscopic__ exposures too brief to permit more than one fixation. In each word presented there was a single reversal of two letters and the S knew this. His task was to identify the *actual* English word responding as quickly as possible. When the *actual* word was AVIATION, Ss were presented with one of the following: VAIATION, AVITAION, AVIATINO. Identification of the actual word as AVIATION was best when S saw AVITAION, next best when he saw AVIATINO, and most difficult when he saw VAIATION. In general, a reversal of the two initial letters made identification most difficult, reversal of the last two letters made it somewhat less difficult, reversal in the middle made least difficulty. This is what should happen if words are first scanned initially, then finally, then medially. But the scanning cannot be a matter of eye movements; it must be more central.

Selective attention to the ends of words should lead to the entry of these parts into the mental dictionary, in advance of the middle parts. However, we ordinarily need to know more than the ends of words. Underwood has pointed out (1963), in connection with paired-associate learning, that while partial knowledge may be enough for a stimulus syllable which need only be recognized it will not suffice for a response item which must be produced. The case is similar for natural language. In order to speak one must know all of a word. However, the words of the present study were low-frequency words, words likely to be in the passive or recognition vocabularies of the college-student Ss but not in their active vocabularies; stimulus items, in effect, rather than response items. If knowledge of the parts of new words begins at the ends and moves toward the middle we might expect a word like *numismatics*, which was on our list, to be still registered as NUM__ICS. Reduced entries of this sort would in many contexts serve to retrieve the definition.

The argument is reinforced by a well-known effect in spelling. Jensen (1962) has analyzed thousands of spelling errors for words of 7, 9, or 11 letters made by children in the eighth and tenth grades and by junior college freshmen. A striking serial-position effect appears in all his sets of data such that errors are most common in the middle of the word, next most common at the end, and least common at the start. These results are as they should be if the order of attention and entry of information is first, last, and then, middle. Jensen's results show us what happens when children are forced to produce words that are still on the recognition level. His results remind us of those bluebooks in which students who are uncertain of the spelling of a word write the first and last letters with great clarity and fill in the middle with indecipherable squiggles. That is what should happen when a word that can be only partially recalled must be produced in its entirety. End letters and a stretch of squiggles may, however, be quite adequate for recognition purposes. In the TOT experiment we have perhaps placed adult Ss in a situation comparable to that created for children by Jensen's spelling tests.

There are two points to clarify and the argument is finished. The Ss in our experiment were college students, and so in order to obtain words on the margin of knowledge we had to use words that are very infrequent

__Combinatorial__ (com-bin-ah-TORR-ee-al). The various ways in which some set of items can be combined. For instance, the numbers "1, 2, 3" can be combined in six ways: 1, 2, 3; 1, 3, 2; 2, 1, 3; 2, 3, 1; 3, 2, 1; and 3, 1, 2.

__Tachistoscopic__ (tah-kiss-toh-SCOPP-ick). A tachistoscope is a device for presenting visual stimuli for a fraction of a second.

in English as a whole. It is not our thought, however, that the TOT phenomenon occurs only with rare words. The absolute location of the margin of word knowledge is a function of S's age and education, and so with other Ss we would expect to obtain TOT states for words more frequent in English. Finally the need to produce (or recall) a word is not the only factor that is likely to encourage registration of its middle letters. The amount of detail needed to specify a word uniquely must increase with the total number of words known, the number from which any one is to be distinguished. Consequently the growth of vocabulary, as well as the need to recall, should have some power to force attention into the middle of a word.

FOOTNOTES

[1] Reprinted by permission of the authors and the publisher from the *Journal of Verbal Learning and Verbal Behavior*, 1966, **5**, 325-337. Copyright 1966 by Academic Press.

[2] Goodglass, H. (1980). Disorders of naming following brain injury. *American Scientist*, **68**, 647-655.

[3] We wish to thank Mr. Charles Hollen for doing the pretest interviews.

[4] We wish to thank Professor Frederick Mosteller for discussing the fragmentary data problem with us.

REFERENCES

BARNHART, C. L. (Ed.) *The American college dictionary.* New York: Harper, 1948.

BROADBENT, D. E. *Perception and communication.* New York: Macmillan, 1938.

BRUNER, J. S., AND O'DOWD, D. A note on the informativeness of words. *Language and Speech,* 1958, **1,** 98-101.

FEIGENBAUM, E. A. The simulation of verbal learning behavior. In E. A. Feigenbaum and J. Feldman (Eds.) *Computers and thought.* New York: McGraw-Hill, 1963. Pp. 297-309.

HOCKETT, C. F. *A course in modern linguistics.* New York: Macmillan, 1958.

JAMES, M. *The principles of psychology,* Vol. 1. New York: Holt, 1893.

JENSEN, A. R. Spelling errors and the serial-position effect. *J. educ. Psychol.,* 1962, **53,** 105-109.

KATZ, J. J., and FODOR, J. A. The structure of a semantic theory. *Language,* 1963, **39,** 170-210.

MILLER, G. A., and FRIEDMAN, ELIZABETH A. The reconstruction of mutilated English texts. *Inform. Control,* 1957, **1,** 38-55.

THORNDIKE, E. L., AND LORGE, I. *The teacher's word book of 30,000 words.* New York: Columbia Univer., 1952.

UNDERWOOD, B. J. Stimulus selection in verbal learning. In C. N. Cofer and B. S. Musgrave (Eds.) *Verbal behavior and learning: problems and processes.* New York: McGraw-Hill, 1963. Pp. 33-48.

WENZIL, A. Empirische und theoretische Beitrage zur Erinnerungsarbeit bei erschwerter Wortfindung. *Arch. ges. Psychol.,* 1932, **85,** 181-218.

WENZIL, A. Empirische und theoretische Beitrage zur Erinnerungsarbeit bei erschwerter Wortfindung. *Arch. ges. Psychol.,* 1936, 97, 294-318.

WOODWORTH, R. S. *Psychology.* (3rd ed.) New York: Holt, 1934.

WOODWORTH, R. S., AND SCHLOSBERG, H. *Experimental psychology.* (Rev. ed). New York: Holt, 1954.

Classic Quotations from William James

Nothing so fatiguing as the eternal hanging on of an uncompleted task.
    (Letter to Carl Stumpf, January 1, 1886.)

All improvement of memory consists, then, in the improvement of one's habitual methods of recording facts.
    (*The Principles of Psychology* [1890], ch. 16.)

A thing forgotten on one day will be remembered on the next. Something we have made the most strenuous efforts to recall, but all in vain, will, soon after we have given up the attempt, saunter into the mind, as Emerson somewhere says, as innocently as if it had never been sent for. Experiences of bygone date will revive after years of absolute oblivion, often as the result of some cerebral disease or accident which seems to develop latent paths of association, as the photographer's fluid develops the picture sleeping in the . . . film.
    (*The Principles of Psychology* [1890], ch. 16.)

CHAPTER 13

*"The Brain as a Dream State Generator:
An Activation-Synthesis Hypothesis of the Dream Process"*

J.A. Hobson and R.W. McCarley[1,2,3]

EDITORS' COMMENTS. Sleep researchers spend much of their time trying to solve three major problems: (1) Why do we sleep? (2) Why do we dream? and (3) What controls the *content* of our dreams? Let's begin by looking briefly at all three of these issues.

Why do we sleep? This question may strike you as being silly, if not downright stupid. "We sleep in order to restore our bodies," you may respond. Yet, study after study has shown that *physical* restoration of your body tissue (and processes) takes place just as rapidly when you lie down and rest (while staying awake) as when you lie down and lose consciousness (as you do while sleeping). What, then, does *unconsciousness* add to the restorative process? To be truthful, we aren't yet sure. We do know that you *must* sleep, but we still don't know why.

Why do we dream? The answer to the question "Why do we sleep?" may well lie in the fact that you *dream* when asleep, but not when you're "just resting." If we deprive you of dream sleep for several days, your physical performance and mental acuity both tend to deteriorate. You also tend to "catch up" on dreaming when given the chance. Apparently dreaming is necessary both for physiological and psychological health. Why that should be the case, though, we can't really say.

What controls the content of our dreams? At an international meeting of dream researchers--held at about the time the Hobson and McCarley article was published--eight of the world's best-known dream researchers couldn't reach any agreement on this issue. The best-known answer probably was provided by Sigmund Freud, who believed that the conscious ego relaxes during sleep, thus allowing the unconscious id to "gratify its primitive wishes" by expressing them as dreams. (The preconscious "censor" disguises the true meaning of the dream, however, to make it more acceptable to the ego.) There is little in the way of scientific data to support this "mentalistic, psychoanalytic viewpoint," though.

In this article, Hobson and McCarley give their (body-oriented) answers to the three major questions posed above. According to these dream researchers, certain lower centers of your brain become activated when you sleep as a natural consequence of your biological rhythms. Your dreams, according to Hobson and McCarley, are the "narrative" that your cortex makes up to explain the random neural firings that arise in the lower centers of the brain while you sleep.

Hobson and McCarley's article is important because these authors were among the first to pull together all the known data on what actually happens--at a neurophysiological level--when you dream. (A more up-to-date account of their position appears in Hobson's book, *The Dreaming Brain*, published in 1988 by Basic Books, Inc.) As clever as this theory is, however, it seems to beg the question of *why* your mind "constructs" the type of narrative that it does. Put simply, Hobson and McCarley tell us *how* dreaming occurs. But it will probably take a more "mentalistic" theory to explain *why* you dream the sometimes weird things that you dream.

One final point: This article is filled with technical terms and medical jargon, and thus is "a difficult read." If you wish to master any scientific field, however, you must first learn the vocabulary used by experts in that field. To help you along in this regard, we have provided you with the definitions of 85 terms. Good luck!

Abstract. Recent research in the neurobiology of dreaming sleep provides new evidence for possible structural and functional substrates of formal aspects of the dream process. The data suggest that dreaming sleep is physiologically determined and shaped by a brain stem neuronal mechanism that can be modeled physiologically and mathematically. Formal features of the generator processes with strong implications for dream theory include periodicity and automaticity of forebrain activation, suggesting a preprogrammed neural basis for dream mentation in sleep; intense and sporadic activation of brain stem sensorimotor circuits including reticular, oculomotor, and vestibular neurons, possibly determining spatiotemporal aspects of dream imagery; and shifts in transmitter ratios, possibly accounting for dream amnesia. The authors suggest that the automatically activated forebrain synthesizes the dream by comparing information generated in specific brain stem circuits with information stored in memory.

Since the turn of the century, dream theory has been dominated by the psychoanalytic hypothesis that dreaming is a reactive process designed to protect consciousness and sleep from the disruptive effect of unconscious wishes that are released in sleep (1). Thus dreaming has been viewed as a psychodynamically determined state, and the distinctive formal features of dream content have been interpreted as manifestations of a defensive transformation of the unconscious wishes found unacceptable to consciousness by a hypothetical **censor**. A critical **tenet** of this wish fulfillment-disguise theory is that the transformation of the unconscious wish by the censor disguises or degrades the **ideational** information in forming the dream imagery. We were surprised to discover the origins of the major tenets of psychoanalytic dream theory in the neurophysiology of 1890 and have specified the transformations made by Freud in an earlier, related article (2). In detailing the neurophysiological origins of psychoanalytic dream theory, the concept of mind-body **isomorphism**, denoting similarity of form between psychological and physiological events, was seen as an explicit premise of Freud's thought.

Sharing Freud's conviction that mind-body isomorphism is a valid approach, we will now review modern neurophysiological evidence that we believe permits and necessitates important revisions in psychoanalytic dream theory. The activation-synthesis hypothesis that we will begin to develop in this paper asserts that many formal aspects of the dream experience may be the obligatory and relatively undistorted psychological concomitant of the regularly recurring and physiologically determined brain state called "dreaming sleep." It ascribes particular formal features of the dream experience to the particular organizational features of the brain during that state of sleep. More specifically, the theory details the mechanisms by which the brain becomes periodically activated during sleep and specifies the means by which both sensory input and motor output are simultaneously blocked, so as to account for the maintenance of sleep in the face of strong central activation of the brain. The occurrence and character of dreaming are seen as both determined and shaped by these physiological processes.

The most important tenet of the activation-synthesis hypothesis is that during dreaming the activated brain generates its own information by a **pontine** brain stem neuronal mechanism, which will be described in detail. We hypothesize that this internally generated sensorimotor information, which is partially random and partially specific, is then compared with stored sensorimotor data in the synthesis of dream content. The functional significance of the brain activation and the synthesis of **endogenous** information in dreaming sleep is not known, but we suggest that state-dependent learning is at least as likely a result of dreaming as is tension reduction or sleep maintenance.

While we believe that the two processes emphasized in this paper—activation and synthesis—are major and important advances in dream theory, we wish to state explicitly and comment on some of the things that our theory does not attempt to do. The activation-synthesis hypothesis does not exclude possible defensive distortions of the value-free sensorimotor dream stimuli, but

---

Censor. According to Freud, dreams are the "royal road to understanding what goes on in the unconscious mind." Freud believed that, when you are awake, your *ego* blocks out (suppresses) unacceptable thoughts and emotions generated by your *id*. However, when you are asleep, your ego no longer functions effectively; thus the *id* would be able to "sneak" its frightening images past the *ego* were it not for the actions of the *censor*, which is a part of your preconscious mind and thus functions when you are unconscious. The *censor* satisfies both the *ego* and the *id* by "disguising" or "transforming" the *id's* unacceptable desires into images more acceptable to the *ego*. Much of psychoanalytic treatment consists of *interpreting* dreams to discover the unconscious wishes the *censor* was trying to disguise. Given his views, it's understandable that Freud called dreams "the royal road" to comprehending the unconscious.

Tenet (TEN-et). A principle or belief generally held to be true.

Ideational (id-ee-A-shun-al). Consisting of, or referring to, the content of thoughts or ideas.

Isomorphism (eye-so-MORF-ism). Two things are "isomorphic" (eye-so-MORF-ic) if they exist in one-to-one correspondence. If you believe that for each mental experience there must exist a corresponding physiological activity in the brain, you believe that there is an "isomorphism" between the mind and brain.

Pontine (PON-teen). The *pons* is a neural structure in the brain stem that lies between the spinal cord and the main part of the brain. The "pontine brain stem" is the region of the stem containing the pons.

Endogenous (en-DODGE-en-ous). Stimuli generated inside the body. As opposed to exogenous (see below).

it does deny the primacy of any such process in attempting to explain formal aspects of dream content or the fundamental **impetus** to dreaming itself. The idea that dreams reveal wishes is also beyond the direct reach of our new theory, but some specific alternatives to this interpretation of several classic dream situations can be advanced.

TABLE 1
Electrographic Criteria for Behavioral State Determination

State	Electro-myogram	EEG	Electro-oculogram
Waking	+	Low voltage, fast	+
Sleep Synchronized	+	High voltage, slow	-
Desynchronized	-	Low voltage, fast	+

The new theory cannot yet account for the emotional aspects of the dream experience, but we assume that they are produced by the activation of brain regions subserving **affect** in parallel with the activation of the better known sensorimotor pathways. Finally, the new theory does not deny meaning to dreams, but it does suggest 1) a more direct route to their acquisition than **anamnesis** via free association, since dream origins are in basic physiological processes and not in disguised wishes, 2) a less complex approach to their interpretation than conversion from **manifest** to latent content, since unusual aspects of dreams are not seen as disguises but as results of the way the brain and mind function during sleep, and 3) a broader view of their use in therapy than that provided by the transference frame of reference, since dreams are not to be interpreted as the product of disguised unconscious (transference) wishes. Dreams offer a royal road to the mind and brain in a behavioral state, with different operating rules and principles than during waking and with the possibility of clinically useful insights from the product of these differences. These points are discussed in the last section of this paper and elsewhere (3).

WHAT IS A DREAM?

A dream may be defined as a mental experience, occurring in sleep, which is characterized by **hallucinoid** imagery, predominantly visual and often vivid; by bizarre elements due to such **spatiotemporal** distortions as condensation, discontinuity, and acceleration; and by a delusional acceptance of these phenomena as "real" at the time that they occur. Strong emotion may or may not be associated with these distinctive formal properties of the dream, and subsequent recall of these mental events is almost invariably poor unless an immediate arousal from sleep occurs.

That this technical jargon describes a universal human experience seems certain, since the five key points in this definition are easily elicited from both naive and sophisticated individuals when they are asked to characterize their dreams. We leave aside the question of whether other less vivid and nonperceptual forms of mental activity during sleep should also be called "dreams" and confine ourselves here to the psychophysiology of the hallucinoid type of dream. In doing so, we not only simplify the immediate task at hand but may also gain insight into the mechanisms underlying the most **florid** symptoms of psychopathology. We mean, of course, the hallucinations and delusions of the psychotic experience, which have so often invited comparison with the dream as we have defined it here.

WHAT IS THE STATE OF THE BRAIN DURING DREAMING SLEEP?

The **physiological substrate** of the dream experience is the CNS in one of its three principal operating states: waking (W), synchronized sleep (S), and desynchronized sleep (D). These states can be reliably and objectively differentiated by recording the **EEG**, the **electromyogram** (EMG), and the **electrooculogram** (see table 1). Hallucinoid dreaming in man occurs predominantly during the periodically recurrent phase of sleep characterized by EEG **desynchronization**, EMG suppression, and **REMs** (4). We call this kind of sleep "D" (meaning desynchronized but also conveniently denoting dreaming).

In the systems analysis terms used in Figure 1, this D brain state is characterized by the following "sensorimotor" properties: activation of the brain; relative exclusion of external input; generation of some internal input, which the activated forebrain then processes as information; and blocking of motor output, except for the **oculomotor** pathway. In this model the substrate of emotion is considered to be a part of the forebrain; it will not be further distinguished here because we have no specific physiological evidence as to how this part of the system might work in any brain state. Memory is not shown but is considered to be a differentiated function of the brain that operates during the D state, such that output from long-term storage is facilitated but input to long-term storage is blocked. A highly specific hypothesis about dream amnesia has previously been derived (5) from the same evidence that we will now

FIGURE 1
Systems Model of Dream State Generation

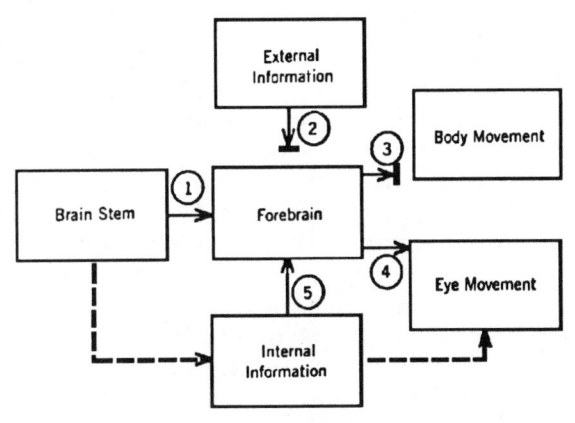

Processes Accounted for:
1. Activation of forebrain
2. Blockade of exteroceptive input
3. Blockade of motor output
4. Oculomotor activation
5. Provision of forebrain with internally generated information

FIGURE 2
Physiological Model of Dream State Generation Using the Sagittal Section of the Cat Brain and Showing the Bulbar (BRF), Pontine (PRF), and Midbrain (MRF) Divisions of the Reticular Formation

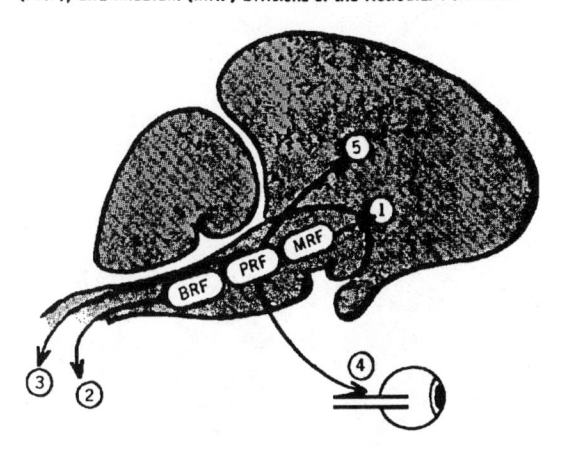

Processes Accounted for:
1. Activation of forebrain
2. Blockade of exteroceptive input
3. Blockade of motor output
4. Oculomotor activation
5. Provision of forebrain with internally generated information

review in our attempt to account for the general sensorimotor aspects of the dream process.

ELECTROPHYSIOLOGY OF THE BRAIN DURING THE DREAM STATE

The three major electrographic features of the D state are of obvious relevance to our attempt to answer the following three questions about the organization of the brain in the dream state.

How is the forebrain activated in the D state? Since EEG desynchronization also characterizes waking, similar mechanisms of "activation" may be involved in both instances. Physiological evidence suggests that this is so: the <u>reticular formation</u> of the <u>anterior</u> brain stem is at least as active in D sleep as it is in the waking state (see Figure 2).

How is motor output blocked in the D state? Physiological evidence clearly shows that the profound EMG suppression of D sleep is a consequence of the direct inhibition of spinal cord motoneurons (6). As a

---

<u>Impetus</u> (IM-pee-tus). A driving force.

<u>Affect</u> (AFF-fect). The psychological aspects of an emotion. However, some writers use the term "affect" interchangeably with "emotion."

<u>Anamnesis</u> (an-am-KNEE-sis). A fancy term for "memory" or "remembering."

<u>Manifest</u> (MAN-ih-fest). Something out in the open, or visible, as opposed to something that is "latent," or hidden.

<u>Hallucinoid</u> (hal-LOO-sin-noid). Having the appearance or form of a hallucination.

<u>Spatiotemporal</u> (SPAY-she-oh-TEMP-or-al). Literally, "space-time."

<u>Florid</u> (FLOOR-id). Fullblown or flowery. Florid symptoms are those that are exaggerated or highly noticeable.

<u>Physiological substrate</u> (SUB-straight). *Substrate* means "foundation." The term "physiological substrate of the dream experience" refers to the neural and biochemical activity that takes place when you dream.

<u>EEG, Electromyogram, Electrooculogram</u>. The EEG, or electroencephalogram (e-leck-tro-en-SEFF-ah-low-gram), is a device for measuring electrical activity in the brain. The electromyogram (e-leck-tro-MY-oh-gram) is a device for measuring electrical activity in the nerves that control the major muscles. The electrooculogram (e-leck-tro-OCK-you-low-gram) is a device for measuring electrical activity in the muscles that control the eyes.

<u>Desynchronization</u> (de-sin-kron-ih-ZAY-shun). On a calm day, the waves on an ocean are *synchronized* (SIN-kron-ized), which is to say that they follow one another at the same pace. In deep sleep, your brain waves are synchronized. When you begin to dream, however, your brain waves become desynchronized, in that they no longer show a regular pattern.

<u>REMs</u>. Abbreviation for "rapid eye movements." When you dream, your eyes move about rapidly, almost as if you were watching what you were dreaming about.

<u>Oculomotor</u> (OCK-you-low-moh-tor). The oculomotor pathway is that set of nerves which run from the brain to the muscles in the eye.

<u>Reticular formation</u> (rhee-TICK-you-lar). The reticular formation screens incoming sensory information for "significance" and alerts the higher centers of the brain that important information is to arrive at the cortex by way of some sensory nerve.

<u>Anterior</u> (AN-teer-ih-or). The front side of something.

consequence, any organized motor patterns that might be generated during the intense brain activation of D sleep cannot be expressed.

That organized movement patterns are in fact generated, but not expressed, in normal D sleep is dramatically demonstrated by cats with lesions of the **anterodorsal** pontine brain stem (7). The animals show all of the major manifestations of D sleep except the **atonia**; instead of the fine twitches of the digits and the limb jerks that are normally present in D, these cats display complex motor behaviors including repetitive paw movements and well-coordinated attack and defense sequences that have no apparent relationship to the environment.

How is sensory imagery generated in the D state? In waking, a **corollary** discharge of the oculomotor system has been shown to suppress visual transmission during **saccadic** eye movements, possibly contributing to the stability of the visual field during that state (8). The same mechanisms might underlie the hallucinoid dream imagery by inhibiting and exciting neurons of the **lateral geniculate body** (9) and the visual cortex (10) during D sleep, when retinal input is reduced and unformed.

The possibility that oculomotor impulses trigger visual imagery is particularly intriguing in view of the demonstrated quantitative correlation between eye movement intensity and dream intensity (11). More specific correlations have also been reported to relate eye movement direction to orientation of the hallucinated gaze in dreams (12). This finding has been interpreted as indicative of "scanning" the visual field — implying cortical control of the eye movements in dreaming sleep. An alternative, although not exclusive, hypothesis is that the oculomotor activity is generated at the brain stem level and that the cortex is then provided with **feed-forward** information about the eye movements. According to this view, we are not so much scanning dream imagery with our D sleep eye movements as we are synthesizing the visual imagery appropriate to them. We will return to the implications of this intriguing possibility in discussing the generation of eye movements in dreaming sleep, but we wish to stress here the general significance of this clue to the identity of an "internal information generator" operating at the brain stem level in the dreaming sleep state.

The eye-movement-related inhibition of sensory relays (13), as well as the possible **occlusion** of **exogenous** inputs by internally generated excitation, may also contribute to the maintenance of sleep in the face of strong central activation of the brain. In this sense the dream process is seen as having a sleep maintenance mechanism built into its physiological substrate rather than a sleep guardian function operating at the psychological level.

A firm general conclusion can be reached at this point: the desynchronized phase of sleep is the physiological substrate of hallucinoid dreaming, as defined. This conclusion is of profound significance to psychophysiology, since we can now reliably and objectively characterize and measure many aspects of the brain when it is in the dream state. For example, one feature that emerges from the psychophysiological study of dreaming and one that was not at all evident from **introspective**, psychoanalytically oriented research, is that the brain enters the dream state at regular intervals during sleep and stays in that state for appreciable and predictable lengths of time. One clear implication of this finding is that dreaming is an automatically preprogrammed brain event and not a response to exogenous (day residue) or endogenous (visceral) stimuli. A second implication is that the dream state generator mechanism is periodic, that is, the dream state generator is a neurobiological clock (14). Since the length of the sleep cycle and, by inference, the frequency of dreaming, is a function of body size within and across mammalian species (15), the system controlling the

FIGURE 3
The Anatomy of the Pontine Brain Stem*

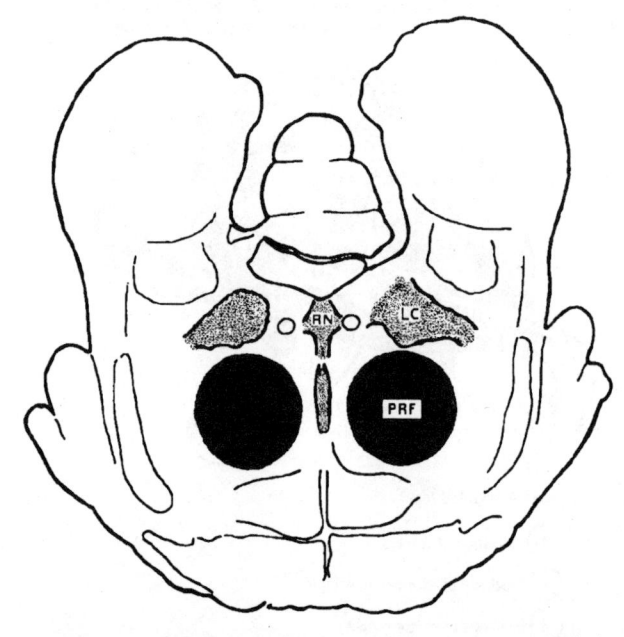

*On this frontal section of the cat brain stem, the cells that are selectively activated are in the paramedian reticular formation (PRF) (giganto cellular tegmental field), while the cells that are selectively inactivated lie more dorsally (in the region of the locus coeruleus [LC]) and medially (in the region of the raphe nuclei [RN]). Compare this with figure 5, which summarizes the neurophysiology and shows the anatomy in a sagittal section.

length of the period must have a structural substrate. Thus we must account for size-related periodicity with our model of the dream state generator.

AN ANIMAL MODEL OF THE BRAIN DURING THE DREAM STATE

We said that the length of the sleep cycle varies "across species." Does that mean that nonhuman animals dream? Unfortunately we cannot know, but we are willing to assert that if they do so, it is when their brains are in the D sleep state. Because we have no direct evidence of any significant difference between the brain state of man and the brain state of other mammals in D sleep, we therefore feel justified in asserting that the brain state of our experimental animal, the cat, constitutes a reasonable subject for our study of the brain as a dream process generator, whether or not cats dream. This assertion seems justified since we are restricting our attention here to formal aspects of the dream experience; our experimental model need not dream or even possess "consciousness" to be useful as a source of physiological information. If we accept this argument and use the definition of dreaming offered above, then the presence of D sleep in cats (16) offers nothing less than an animal model in which to study the neurophysiological basis of a hallucinoid mental process in man. Such a model is as important in experimental psychiatry as it is rare. Let us now turn to the biological data upon which our sketches of the brain as a dream state generator are based.

LOCALIZATION OF THE POWER SUPPLY OR TRIGGER ZONE OF THE DREAM STATE GENERATOR

Lesion, stimulation, and recording studies pioneered by Jouvet (17) have strongly implicated the pontine brain stem as critical to the generation of the desynchronized sleep phase (see Figure 3 for a summary of the neuroanatomy of this region). Important findings supporting this hypothesis include the following.

Large lesions of the pontine reticular formation prevent the occurrence of desynchronized sleep for several weeks in cats (17). This suggests that the pontine reticular formation may be the site of an executive or triggering mechanism for desynchronized sleep. **Prepontine** transections and forebrain **ablation** have no effect upon periodicity or duration of the skeletal, muscular, and oculomotor manifestations of D sleep (17).

The data indicate that the trigger, the power supply and the clock are pontine.

The pontine brain stem is thus implicated as the site of both the trigger and the clock. The periodicity of the D sleep clock in **poikilothermic** pontine cats lengthens as temperature declines, indicating orthodox metabolic mediation of the cycle, in contrast to the temperature independence of circadian rhythms. If we assume that the physiological substrate of consciousness is in the forebrain, these facts completely eliminate any possible contribution of ideas (or their neural substrate) to the primary driving force of the dream process.

Small lesions of the **dorsal** pontine brain stem, in the region of the **locus coeruleus** (LC), may eliminate the atonia but no other aspects of desynchronized sleep (7). This suggests that inhibition of muscle tone is somehow dependent upon the integrity of the LC. The elaborate motor behavior that characterizes the D sleep of cats with LC lesions has been described as "pseudohallucinatory" (7). Whether or not one accepts the sensory implications of that designation, the importance of motor inhibition in quelling the effects of central excitation during the dream state is clear.

Anterodorsal (AN-teer-oh-DOOR-sal). The "front face" of the rear portion of something.

Atonia (a-TONE-ee-ah). "To have tone" is to be in harmony. *Atonia* is a condition in which the muscles lack "tone," or coordinated activity.

Corollary (CORE-oh-lair-ee). A corollary activity is something that naturally accompanies or parallels some primary activity.

Saccadic (sack-CAD-ick). When you read the words on this page, your eyes don't move smoothly across each line. Rather, they jump rapidly (and rather jerkily) from one spot to another. You fixate briefly at each spot; then your eyes make a saccadic (jerky) movement to the next fixation point. Vision is typically suppressed during the saccadic movement itself.

Lateral geniculate body (jen-NICK-you-late). A part of the thalamus which processes visual information.

Feed-forward. Feedback is information about what has already occurred. Feed-forward is information about what *should* occur in the future.

Occlusion (ock-CLUE-shun). To occlude (ock-CLOOD) something is to shut it out.

Exogenous (ex-ODGE-ee-nous). Something that originates outside the body.

Introspective (in-troh-SPECK-tive). When you "look inward" at your own mental activities you are introspecting.

Prepontine (PREE-pon-teen). Prepontine transections are surgical cuts that are made in tissue in front of the pons.

Ablation (ab-BLAY-shun). To *ablate* is the same thing as to remove by surgery.

Poikilothermic (poy-kill-oh-THERM-ick). Your body temperature typically is stable whether the outside temperature is high or low. Animals, such as frogs, whose body temperatures vary according to the environment they are in are said to be poikilothermic.

Dorsal (DOOR-sal). The rear (posterior) portion of anything, but particularly of an animal or a part of an animal.

Locus coeruleus (LOW-cuss sair-REW-lee-us, or kair-RULE-ee-us). The Latin words for "blue spot." A small area in the brain stem does, indeed, have a bluish look to it.

This finding has an important bearing on mechanisms of dream paralysis and suggests that in the classic chase dream, the dreamer who has trouble fleeing from a pursuer is as much accurately reading the activated state of his motor pattern generator and the paralyzed state of his spinal neurons as he is "wishing" to be caught. This dream experience is so universal and the feeling of constrained motor action so impressive as to make its physiological basis in the descending inhibition of motoneurons seem to us inescapable. Conversely, this reasonable and adequate explanation of the **paradox** of the chase dream makes its interpretation as wish fulfillment less compelling. Other implications of the D sleep activation of various motor system pattern generators for movements and dream plots have been discussed elsewhere (3).

The **vestibular system**, as classically established, integrates head position and movement with eye position and posture. Pompeiano and Morrison (18) showed that lesions of the vestibular nuclei interfered with the bursts of REM but not with the isolated eye movements of D. This finding suggested that the vestibular system contributed to the elaboration and rhythmicity of the eye movements but that the eye movement generator was extravestibular. Magherini and associates (19) found that systemic injections of the **anticholinesterase** agent **physostigmine** produced rhythmic eye movements in **decerebrate** cats, suggesting that the eye movement generator may be **cholinergic**. Thus the central, automatic activation during sleep of the vestibular system may provide a substrate for endogenously generated, specific information about body position and movement. Flying dreams may thus be a logical, direct, and unsymbolic way of synthesizing information generated endogenously by the vestibular system in D sleep. In view of this reasonable and direct explanation, it seems gratuitous to "interpret" the sensual flying dream as sexual.

In accord with the isomorphism principle, the degree of neuronal activation in brain systems should parallel the frequency and intensity of dreams to these systems (3), and the predominance of visual sensorimotor activity in both brain and mind supports this notion. Symbol formation and the often bizarre **juxtaposition** of sensations in the dream may be a reflection of the heightened degree of simultaneous activation of multiple sensory channels in dreaming as compared with waking (3).

Long-term electrical stimulation of the pontine brain stem results in the earlier appearance of sleep episodes and in increases in the absolute amounts of desynchronized sleep, but it does not affect the periodicity of its occurrence (20). By implication, the delivery of electrical energy accomplishes what most psychological and behavioral treatments fail to achieve: an increase in the duration of dreaming sleep. Testing the assumption that the generator neurons are **cholinoceptive**, our laboratory team has recently established that injection of the cholinergic agent **carbachol** into the pontine reticular formation produces prolonged enhancement of D-like sleep behavior (21). In man the **parenteral** injection of the anticholinesterase agent physostigmine potentiates D sleep, and the pharmacologically induced episodes are associated with hallucinoid dreaming (22). The time of occurrence and duration of dreams may thus be chemically determined.

In summary, these results support the hypothesis that the pontine brain stem is the generator zone for the D sleep state. The trigger mechanism for the whole system, including the eye movement generator, may be cholinoceptive and the executive zones are probably in the reticular formation. The LC is involved, possibly in a permissive or reciprocal way, and is especially important in **mediating** spinal reflex inhibition. Together, these two regions may constitute the clock. We will have more to say about the hypothesis of reciprocal interaction between them later in this paper.

FIGURE 4
Mechanisms of Sleep Paralysis*

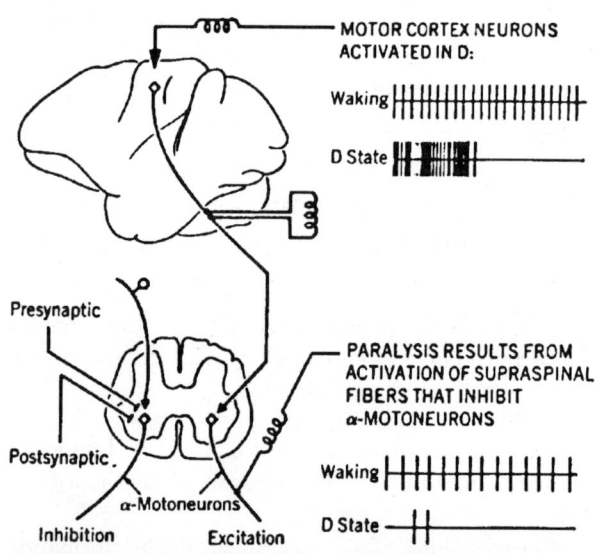

*The upper part of the figure illustrates the intense activation in D sleep of antidromically identified pyramidal tract neurons of the motor cortex. Note the relatively regular discharge in waking (W) and the clustering of discharges in D sleep in these models of 3-second epochs of microelectrode recordings (vertical lines indicate discharges). The lower portion of the figure shows the inhibitory events of D at the spinal cord level that largely prevent alpha motoneuron discharge and consequent muscle excitation, despite the activation of excitatory (arrow) pyramidal tract fibers. Both presynaptic and postsynaptic inhibition (bars) are present in D (sketched on the left side of the cord section). Absence of this inhibition in W allows alpha motoneuron discharge in response to excitation from pyramidal tract fibers (17).

Although the brain stem mechanisms mediating atonia remain obscure, it is clear from the work of Pompeiano (6) that both **monosynaptic** and **polysynaptic** spinal reflexes are tonically inhibited during D sleep (see Figure 4). In addition, during the bursts of REM, there is a descending **presynaptic** inhibition of the most rapidly conducting (group 1a) spinal afferent endings. Both presynaptic and postsynaptic inhibition appear to be of brain stem origin. **Phasic** presynaptic inhibition has also been shown to occur in sensory relays elsewhere in the brain during D sleep (6). Thus motor output is tonically damped throughout D and sensory input is phasically damped in concert with the REM bursts. In other words, we are not only paralyzed during our dreams, but the degree to which we are paralyzed fluctuates in concert with the intensity of the internally generated information and the degree to which we suppress exogenous input.

On the basis of this evidence, the systems terminology used earlier (see Figure 1) can be tentatively translated into the anatomical and physiological terms of Figure 2; and the activation-synthesis hypothesis dreaming can be stated as follows: during D sleep, cholinergic mechanism in the reticular formation of the pontine brain stem is periodically activated. The consequences of this activation are as follows:

1. The forebrain is tonically activated, probably via the midbrain reticular formation that is also responsible for its activation during waking. Thus the forebrain is made ready to process information.

2. The spinal reflexes are tonically inhibited, possibly via the bulbar reticular formation and LC; thus motor outflow is blocked despite high levels of activity in the brain, including the **motor cortex**.

3. The oculomotor and vestibular systems are phasically activated by the pontine reticular formation so as to produce eye movements. This circuitry, in its entirety, is an internal information source or generator that provides the forebrain with spatially specific but temporally disorganized information about eye velocity, relative position, and direction of movement. Information may similarly be derived from the brain stem generators of patterned motor activity.

4. At the same time that internal information feedback is being generated by the activation of various motor systems, **exteroceptive** input to sensory systems is phasically blocked. This may intensify the relative impact of the endogenous inputs to the brain, accounting for the intensity of dream imagery and preventing sleep disruption by the externally generated excitation.

This working sketch of the dream state generator, based on the classical localizing methods of experimental neurology, is intriguing but unsatisfying in that it fails to specify the mechanisms by which the pontine generator is turned on, kept active for a time, and then shut off. Further, it does not say anything about the mechanism of periodicity. To provide details about the anatomy and physiology of the periodic trigger

Paradox (PAIR-ah-docks). A statement that seemingly is self-contradictory, yet also seemingly is true.

Vestibular system (vess-TIB-you-lar). Several small organs in the inner ear that detect movement of the body and/or head.

Anticholinesterase (AN-tie-KOH-linn-EST-ter-ace). This article contains the names of many complex chemicals found in the brain. All these chemicals can affect the behavior of individual neurons as well as the behavior of individual organisms. Since we know far more about these chemicals now than when this article was published, there is little sense in defining them in terms of what scientists knew in 1977. There also is little need for you to know much about these chemicals unless you plan to do research on brain chemistry. Briefly put, though, any chemical whose name ends in "ase" is a destructive agent. For example, DNA-ase is a chemical that breaks up DNA molecules. Thus, cholinesterase is a chemical that breaks up choline esters, while anticholinesterase is a chemical that inhibits the action of cholinesterase.

Physostigmine (FY-so-STIG-meen). A complex chemical that inhibits the action of anticholinesterase.

Decerebrate (dee-SAIR-ee-brait). An animal that has had its cerebrum(s) removed, usually by surgery.

Cholinergic (KOH-leen-ER-jick). The suffix (SUFF-icks) *ergic* means "works like." The phrase in the text "suggesting that the eye movement generator may be cholinergic" means that the authors believe that eye movements during sleep are set off by a neurotransmitter called "acetylcholine," or by some similar transmitter.

Juxtaposition (JUCKS-tah-poh-SISH-shun). To juxtapose (JUCKS-tah-pose) two objects is to place them side by side.

Cholinoceptive (KOH-leen-oh-SEP-tive). A neuron that is "receptive to (or can be stimulated by) a neurotransmitter containing choline."

Carbachol (KAR-bah-koll). A chemical that is a cholinergic agent.

Parenteral (pair-ENT-er-al). The medical term *enteral* means "intestine." The term *par* means "by way of." A parenteral injection is one that goes into the area of the intestine.

Mediating (ME-dee-eight-ting). To mediate something, you bring it about by means of some intermediary agent.

Monosynaptic, Polysynaptic (MAHN-oh-sin-APT-tick; POL-ee-sin-APT-tick). The synapse (SIN-aps) is the junction point between two neurons. Some reflexes cross but a single synapse as they occur, and thus are monosynaptic. Other more complex reflexes involve several synapses, and thus are polysynaptic.

Presynaptic (PREE-sin-apt-tick). Consider two neurons, A and B, that make synapse with each other such that when A fires, it can cause B to fire as well by releasing transmitters at the A-B synapse. There are two major ways to prevent A from causing B to fire. The first, called presynaptic inhibition, involves preventing A from releasing transmitters into the A-B synapse. The second, called postsynaptic inhibition, involves preventing B from *responding* to the transmitters that A releases.

Phasic (FAY-sick). Phasic inhibition is that which is synchronous (or wave-like).

Motor cortex. The rear (posterior) portion of the frontal lobe contains the motor cortex, so-called because electrical stimulation to this part of the brain causes muscular contractions in various parts of the body.

Exteroceptive (EX-teer-oh-SEP-tive). Stimulation from outside (exterior to) the body.

FIGURE 5
Cellular Neurophysiology of Dream State Generation*

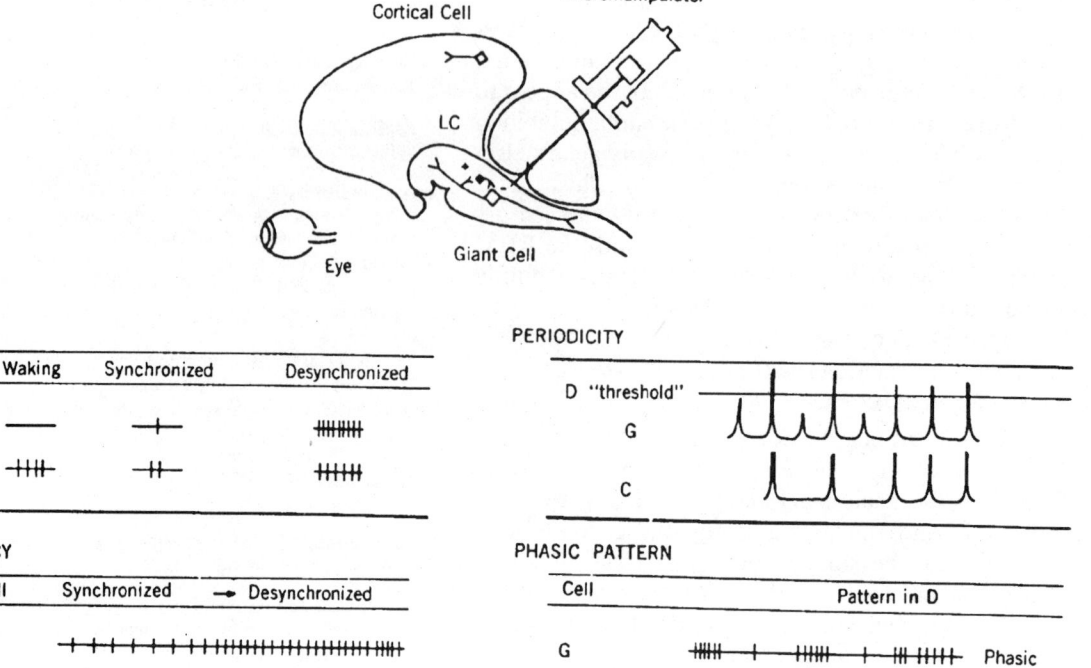

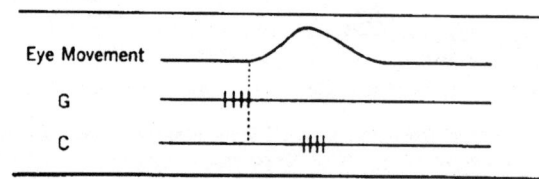

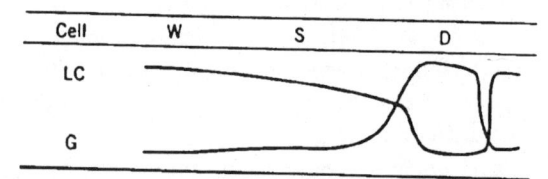

*The cell recordings are made from hydraulically driven microelectrodes that can be stereotaxically directed at neurons in the cat brain during natural sleep. Two classes of brain stem neurons are represented by the reticular giant cell (G in the physiological models) and the LC cell; the synaptic interactions suggested are detailed in figure 8. A cortical cell is also shown.

The results of the cell recording experiments are shown in six models representing the criteria used to quantify discharge properties: selectivity—giant cells concentrate their discharge in D to a greater extent than cerebral cortical or other brain stem neurons; tonic latency—giant cells show rate increases that precede those of cortical neurons during the S to D transition; phasic latency—giant cells fire before the REMs of D, while cortical neurons fire after them; periodicity—peaks in the giant cell activation curves are periodic and the higher peaks are associated with D sleep episodes and peaks of cortical activity; phasic pattern—giant cells show a higher degree of clustered firing in D than do other neurons; and reciprocal interaction—the rate curves of giant cells and LC cells are reciprocal over the sleep cycle.

mechanisms of the generator process, we will now turn our attention to the neuronal level of analysis. In doing so, we also come full circle in our reaffirmation of isomorphism since it was the neuron that Freud recognized as the physical unit of the nervous system on which he based his dream theory (2).

HISTOLOGICAL FEATURES OF RELEVANCE TO THE PERIODIC TRIGGERING OF THE DREAMING SLEEP STATE GENERATOR

Several structural details of the pontine brain stem are notable as possible elements of a D sleep control device with rhythmic properties (see Figure 3 for an illustration of the anatomy discussed).

In his discussion of the histology of the pontine brain stem, **Cajal** (23) emphasized three points:

1. The **paramedian** reticular giant cells, with their **rostral** and **caudal** axonal projections, are admirably suited to serve as output elements of the generator; when excited they could influence many other cells. The work of Brodal (24) and the Scheibels (25) shows that the spinal cord and thalamus receive projections from these elements. Although they are relatively few in number, conservative estimates of their post-synaptic domain indicate that each directly projects to nine million (9×10^6) postsynaptic neurons. Thus the 3,000 pontine reticular giant cells in the cat might make many billions of synapses (2.9×10^{10}). Since the giant cells also project to other brain stem nuclei and have recurrent axons to themselves, mutual interaction with **raphe**-type elements (see below) and self-reexcitation are both possible. These two features could be used to create excitability variability, with powerful consequences for the whole nervous system.

2. The raphe neurons of the midline are ideally situated and connected to regulate excitability of paramedian elements, and they also have extensive projections to other brain regions. The discovery that these cells concentrate the **biogenic amine serotonin** (26) gives this regulatory hypothesis an attractive corollary: these cells might regulate excitability of their postsynaptic neurons via specific transmitter substances. Another brain stem cell group, in the locus coeruleus, has been shown to concentrate the amine **norepinephrine** (26). There are thus at least two neuronal candidates for a level setting role, and both are probably inhibitory. Since the giant cells are excitatory (and probably cholinergic; see below), a substrate for reciprocal interaction is established.

3. Cajal (23) suggested that input to the central reticular core might be via small **stellate cells** in the lateral zone. This input channel, which we now know to be more diffuse than was originally suspected, could be used to abort or damp the core oscillator at critical ambient stimulus levels. This is an important feature, since adaptation depends on the capacity to interrupt the cycle and not to incorporate all exogenous stimuli into the dream plot.

CELLULAR ACTIVITY IN THE PONTINE BRAIN STEM DURING THE SLEEP CYCLE

A direct experimental approach to the question of D state control has been made with cats by recording from individual neurons in many parts of the brain as the sleep cycle normally evolved. In this experimental paradigm, the frequency and pattern of extracellular **action potentials**, which are the signal units of nerve cells, are taken as indices of a cell's excitability; the influence of a recorded neuron upon other cells and that neuron's own control mechanism may also be inferred from the data. This method has the advantage of being relatively physiological since it does little to alter or damage the properties of the system under study.

When cats are kept active at night, they will sleep under the necessary conditions of restraint during the daytime. The microelectrodes can then be **stereotaxically** directed at the brain stem and individual cell activity recorded for as long as 20 hours, allowing many successive sleep cycles to be studied (see Figure 5).

Cajal (kah-HAHL). A noted Spanish scientist who lived at the turn of the century and who made enormous contributions to the understanding of neurophysiology.

Paramedian (PAIR-ah-MEED-ee-an). The term *para* means "along side of." A "paramedic" is someone who works along with (or assists) a medical doctor. Paramedian cells are those that lie just to the side of the middle (or median) of the reticular formation.

Rostral (ROSS-trahl). The front end or "nose area of an organism (or part of an organism)."

Caudal (CAWD-al). The tail end of something.

Raphe (rhymes with "safe"). A *raphe* is the "seamless union of two objects lying side by side." Raphe-type elements are those that lie immediately on either side of the dividing line between two objects.

Biogenic amine serotonin (BY-oh-JENN-ick a-MEEN sair-oh-TONE-inn). The term *biogenic* means "produced by a living organism." Serotonin is an amine (that is, contains ammonia) that acts as a neurotransmitter.

Norepinephrine (NOR-epp-ee-NEFF-rin). Another name for noradrenalin(e); an arousal hormone.

Stellate cells (STEL-ate). *Stellate* means "star-shaped."

Action potentials. When a neuron "fires," a wave of electrochemical activity sweeps down the cell from the dendrites to the axon. This wave is called an "action potential."

Stereotaxically (stair-ee-oh-TAX-ih-kal-ly). When neuroscientists insert an electrode into the brain of an animal, they use a stereotaxic device to make sure the tip of the electrode is correctly positioned in all three dimensions. Roughly speaking, *stereotaxic* means "controlled movement in three dimensions."

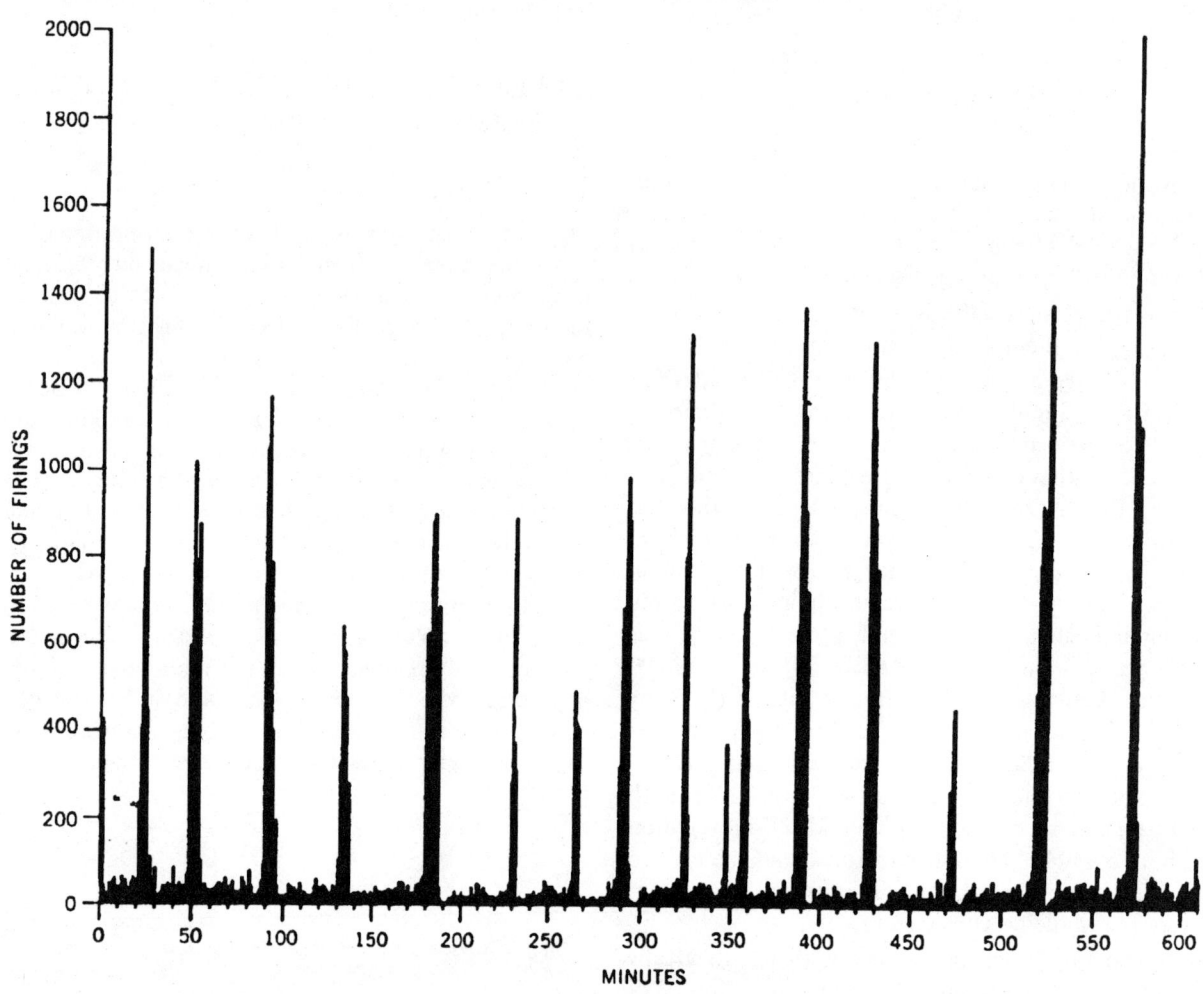

FIGURE 6
Discharge Activity of a Giant Cell Neuron Recorded over Multiple Sleep-Waking Cycles*

*Each peak corresponds to a desynchronized sleep episode, and a regular trend of discharge activity over a cycle is observable: a peak in desynchronized sleep; a rapid decline at the end of the desynchronized sleep episode; a trough, often associated with waking; a slow rise (in synchronized sleep and preceding all electrographic signs of desynchronized sleep); and an explosive acceleration at the onset of desynchronized sleep. Note also the extreme modulation of activity and the periodicity (30).
Reprinted by permission from *Science*, volume 189, pages 58–60, July 4, 1975. Copyright 1975 by the American Association for the Advancement of Science.

The pontine brain stem control hypothesis has been tested in three ways at the level of single cells.

Selectivity criterion: which cells change rate most in D? We guessed that cells which showed pronounced alterations in discharge rate over the sleep cycle were more likely to be playing a controlling role than those showing minimal change. We further assumed that those cells having peaks of activity in phase with the D phase of the cycle were more likely to be specifically and actively involved in dreaming sleep state control than those with multiple peaks. We found that the giant cells of the pontine **tegmentum** concentrated their discharge in the D phase of sleep to a greater extent than any other group of neurons (27). They became our prime candidate for a generator function.

Tonic latency criterion: which cells change rate first in D onset? If the cells with positive discharge selectivity were driving the dreaming sleep phase of the sleep cycle, then their rates would be expected to increase in advance of the behavioral state change. Such phase leads might well be longer than those of the follower neurons under the control of the giant cells. The giant cells, when recorded over entire sleep cycles and through repeated sleep cycles, were found to change rate continuously (28). Significant rate increases occurred *as long as 5 minutes* before a desynchronized sleep phase. When the 2 minutes just prior to desynchronized sleep onset were studied, a rate increase in a pool of giant cells was observed 10 seconds

FIGURE 7
Temporal Clustering of Extracullularly Recorded Discharges of Cat Giant Cell Neurons During D Sleep*

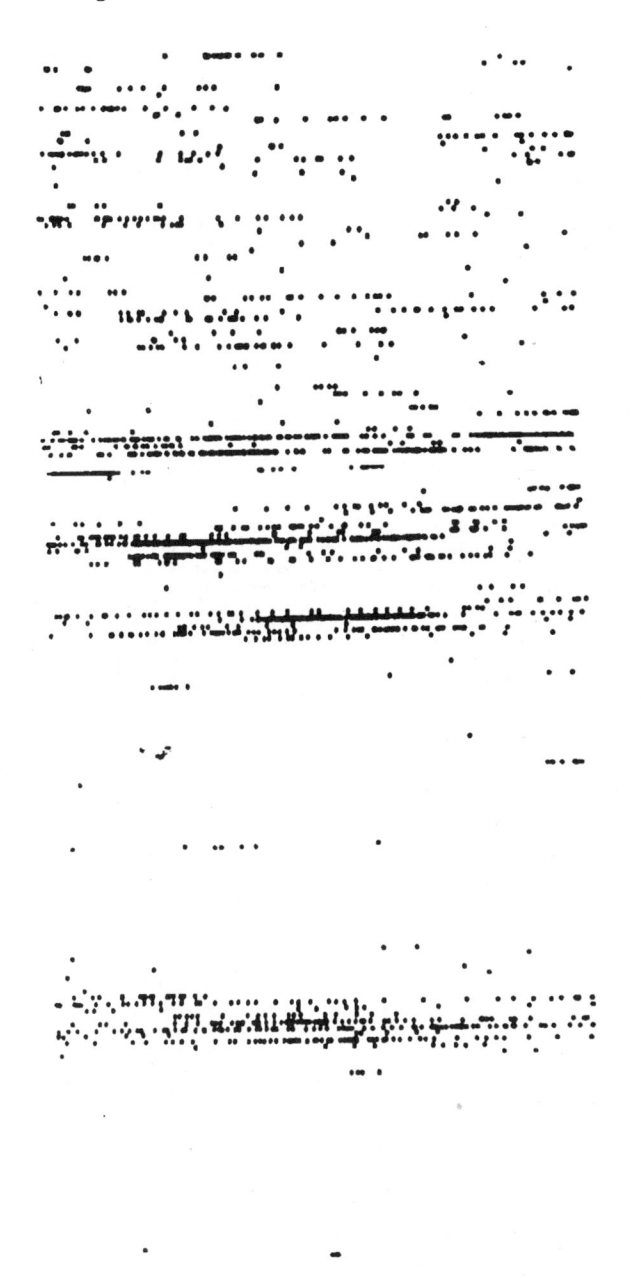

*Each discharge is represented by a dot; the time sequences runs from left to right and top to bottom, with each line 1 second in duration. The figure encompasses about 200 seconds of D sleep activity. Clustering is visible as closely spaced dots and, over longer durations, as "bands" of activity, some of which appear to occur rhythmically. Note the various durations of clusters and the presence of shorter duration clusters of activity within longer duration clusters. Clusters are delimited by periods of relatively inactivity. Such sequences of glial cell neuronal activity are temporally associated with runs of eye movements and ponto-geniculo-occipital waves, and similar sequences of executive neuron discharges may represent the neuronal substrate of dream sequences in man (Hobson and McCarley, unpublished data).

before a similar increase in a pool of cerebral cortical neurons.

The rapidly accelerating limb of the giant cell activity curves at D sleep phase onset indicated that this was a time of maximal excitability change in this pool of neurons. The goodness of fit of the data by an **exponential** curve indicated that reexcitation within the pool might be superimposed upon disinhibition from without. The positive tonic latency indicated that the activation of the forebrain might be a consequence of activation of the brain stem but that the converse could not be the case.

Phasic latency criterion: which cells fire before eye movements of D? Because of the proximity and direct projections to oculomotor neurons from giant cells, we tested the possibility that they might be generating the REMs so characteristic of the desynchronized phase of sleep by determining the time of occurrence of short-term rate increases by the giant cells in relation to eye movement onset. On the average, such rate increases were more prominent and anticipated eye movement by longer intervals than other brain stem neurons (29). Rate increases by presumed follower elements (in the **posterolateral** cerebral cortex) *followed* the eye movements by many milliseconds. It could therefore be concluded that the eye movements might be initiated by giant cells but could not be generated by cortical neurons. This finding practically wrecks the scanning hypothesis and strongly favors the idea that visual cortical events are determined by events in the oculomotor brain stem.

At this point we felt justified in concluding that the giant cells of the pontine tegmentum were critical output elements in a sleep cycle control mechanism. More particularly, we proposed that they might be generator elements for some of the tonic and phasic excitatory events in the desynchronized sleep phase of the cycles: most important to the activation-synthesis hypothesis of dreaming are the determination of EEG desynchronization (activation of the forebrain) and REMs (provision of forebrain with internally generated information). At the very least, we felt that we had found an important avenue to understanding sleep cycle control, since we could now examine the properties and possible mechanisms of giant cell excitability regulation. In this regard there are three additional points worthy of emphasis.

Tegmentum (teg-MENT-tum). Outer covering.
Exponential (ex-pohn-NEN-shull). When you write "a^2," the "2" is an exponent. An exponential curve is one that typically increases (or decreases) at a rapid pace.
Posterolateral. The visual cortex lies on the posterior surface of the brain. The term *lateral* means "side."

FIGURE 8
Reciprocal Interaction Model of Generator Process*

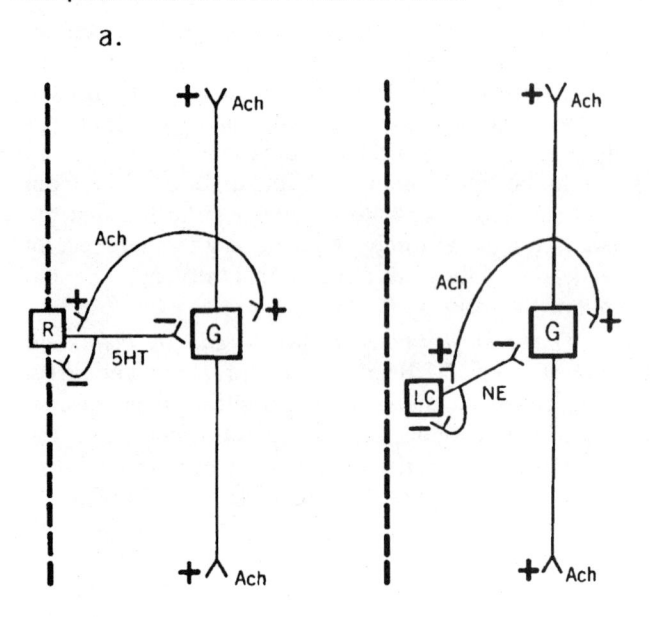

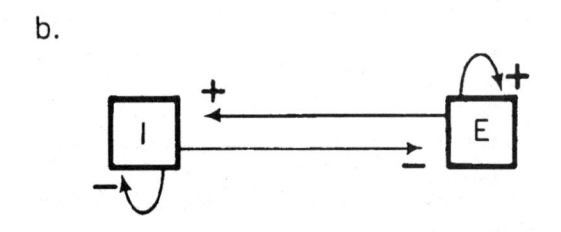

a.

b.

*Physiological models used to organize and interpret results of pharmacological experiments on desynchronized sleep. The G cells are seen as executive elements; they excite with and are excited by acetylcholine (Ach). They interact reciprocally with two aminergic cell groups, the LC and raphe (R), which utilize norepinephrine (NE) and serotonin (5HT) respectively. Both amines are hypothesized to be inhibitory to the G cells. D sleep will therefore be enhanced by increasing G cell excitability, and this can occur by either adding cholinergic drive or subtracting aminergic inhibition. Conversely, D sleep will be suppressed by subtracting cholinergic drive or by adding aminergic inhibition.
Formal reduction of the elements in the top portion of the figure yields the general model of reciprocal interaction, of inhibitory (I,-) and excitatory (E, +) populations, each of which contains a self-loop as well as a projection to the other set. The resulting oscillation of activity in the two sets can be mathematically described by the Lotka-Volterra equations.

Periodicity criterion. Long-term recordings of giant cells revealed peaks of activity in phase with each full-blown desynchronized sleep episode (30) (see Figure 6). Less prominent peaks were associated with abortive episodes and were rarely seen with no electrographic evidence of desynchronized sleep. **Spectral analysis** of these long-term data confirmed the impression of powerful periodicity in the discharge peaks, indicting that 1) sleep cycles are periodic, 2) underlying cell activity is probably even more so, and by definition, 3)

FIGURE 9
Time Course of Giant Cell Activity over the Sleep Cycle*

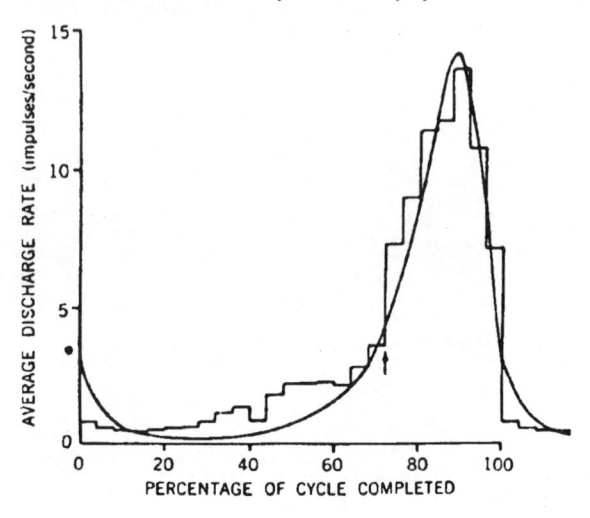

*The histogram shows the average discharge level (impulses/second) of a giant cell neuron over 12 sleep-waking cycles, each normalized to constant duration. The cycle begins and ends with the end of a desynchronized sleep period. The arrow indicates the average time of D sleep onset. The smooth curve is derived from a mathematical model of sleep cycle control and shows a good fit to the experimental data. The probability of obtaining dream-like mentation reports might be expected to show the same trajectory as these curves (30). Reprinted by permission from *Science*, volume 189, pages 58-60, July 4, 1975. Copyright 1975 by the American Association for the Advancement of Science.

cell excitability is under the control of a neurobiological clock. The possible mechanisms of excitability control are thus of great interest.

Phasic pattern criterion. The pattern of giant cell discharge within each D sleep episode indicated that classical pacemaker mechanisms are *not* involved in giant cell excitability regulation (31). Regular **interspike intervals** were exceptional, indicating that the rate increases were not caused by endogenous membrane depolarizations. The tendency, rather, was for giant cells to discharge in intermittent, prolonged clusters of irregularly distributed spikes as if the cells were responding to excitatory postsynaptic potentials from other neurons (see Figure 7). In our view, a likely source of much of this input, especially as the longer clusters developed, was other giant cells. Once other neurons were excited, feedback from them is to be expected. It also seemed likely that the clusters of giant cell discharge were causally related to the eye movement bursts of the D sleep phase.

Reciprocal interaction criterion. If giant cell excitability change is not an intrinsic property of the giant cells, what other cell group might regulate it and in what way might that regulation be effected? Since all indices showed giant cells to discharge first in relation to both the tonic and phasic events of desynchronized sleep, we considered the possible contribution of inhibitory neurons. Since interneurons do not appear to exist in the giant cell fields, such cells should be discrete from but proximal to the giant cell. To be effective, projections should be abundant and should have inhibitory transmitter action upon the giant cells. Reciprocal rate changes during the sleep cycle are to be expected if such cells exist. We have discovered just such changes in a small number of unidentified cells in the region of the posterior locus coeruleus and the **nucleus subcoeruleus** (32). Not only is discharge concentration of these elements quantitatively inverse to those of the giant cells in the phases of the cycle, but their decelerating rate curve is the approximate mirror image of that of the giant cells at desynchronized sleep onset as seen in part C. We called such cells "D-off" cells to contrast their activity curves with those of the giant cells, prototypes of the "D-on" species of neurons. We do not know if the "D-off" cells are **catecholaminergic** but their location and discharge properties make this possible.

McGinty and associates (33) have found similar reciprocal rate changes in the dorsal raphe nucleus (DRN) neurons and we have recently confirmed this finding. The low regular rates of discharge by these cells in waking suggest a level-setting or pacemaker function. Their location and discharge properties are the same as those cells thought to be **serotonergic** on the basis of pharmacological experiments (34). Since both the LC and DRN are adjacent to and project to giant cells, and since giant cells receive abundant serotonergic and catecholaminergic endings, we thought that the mutual interconnections of these D-on and D-off cells could form a substrate for reciprocal interaction which regulated sleep cycle oscillation (30).

A MODEL FOR A BRAIN STEM SLEEP CYCLE OSCILLATOR

Restricting attention to within-sleep changes, we constructed a physiological model that bears a striking resemblance to the **a priori schema** derived from Cajal (see Figure 8, top portion). Most of the connections have been demonstrated but many of the synaptic assumptions are as yet unproven physiologically. In addition to being explanatory, the model suggests experiments, particularly those employing pharmacological methods, the results of which will lead to its future modification. Since the LC, DRM, and giant cell groups are chemically differentiated, we deduced that their action and interaction may involve specific neurotransmitters.

In preliminary tests of the model, we have found that microinjection of the **cholinomimetic** substance carbachol into the giant cell zone not only gives more potent desynchronized sleep phase enhancement than injections into the adjacent tegmental fields but simultaneously activates giant cells. The results also indicate that an opposite effect is obtained at locus coeruleus sites (as if an inhibitory cell group were being activated). We have not yet tested this last hypothesis directly, but the LC cells do resume firing before the end of D sleep. We assume that as FTG excitation declines and LC inhibition grows, the cycle ends. In the decerebrate cat, physostigmine-induced D episodes are associated with activation of neurons in the giant cell and suppression of firing by cells in the LC and DRN (35).

The physiological model can be reduced to a simple unit susceptible to mathematical analysis (see Figure 8, bottom portion). Cell group E (giant cell) and cell group I (raphe and/or LC) are assumed to be mutually interconnected; cell group E is excitatory to itself and to group I, which inhibits itself and group E. Growth of activity in one group occurs at the expense of growth in the other, and vice versa. As such the cell groups are analogous to two populations, prey and predator, whose interaction can be described by a set of nonlinear differential equations, the Lotka-Volterra equations (30). As shown in Figure 9, the time course of activity of cell group E closely resembles that predicted by these equations. It is now possible to plot the activity curves of cell group I and compare the actual data with the curves predicted by the model. The phase lag between the reciprocal cycles remains to be explained and the previously noted fact that cycle length is proportional to brain size suggests that a distance factor may be at work. The distance between the two cell fields could be such a factor through its determination of protein transport time. Assuming an average LC-FTG internuclear distance of 2.5 mm and a fast protein transport time of 96 mm/day, a period length of about 35 minutes is predicted for the cat. This figure is within limits normal for that species. Another possible substrate for the long,

---

Spectral analysis (SPECK-tral). A spectral analysis is an method of searching for regularities across the entire spectrum of brain waves.

Interspike intervals. During slow-wave sleep, spikes of neural excitation often occur in rather regular fashion. The interspike interval is the time between spikes.

Nucleus subcoeruleus (NEW-klee-us sub-sair-REW-le-us). A tiny center just below the "blue spot."

Catecholaminergic (kat-eh-kohl-a-meen-ER-jick). Catecholamines are a general class of neural transmitters that include adrenalin and noradrenalin. To say something is catecholaminergic means that it can be stimulated by catecholamines.

Serotonergic (sair-oh-tone-ER-jick). Capable of being stimulated by serotonin.

A priori schema (a pri-OR-eye SCHEME-ah). A schema is a plan or model. *A priori* means "an assumption or plan made before the fact."

Cholinomimetic (koh-leen-oh-me-MET-tick). Something that mimics or acts like choline.

FIGURE 10
Two Models of the Dream Process*

PSYCHOANALYTIC MODEL

| UNCONSCIOUS | → | EGO | → CENSOR | SLEEP | WAKING |
| Repressed wishes strive constantly and actively for discharge. | | Wishes to sleep, withdraws cathexes. Day residue stirs up unconscious wish threatening to disrupt sleep and invade consciousness. | PRECONSCIOUS ········· | → | |

DREAM WORK
Disguises dream thoughts via displacement, symbol formation, pictorialization, condensation, and so forth.

→ LATENT CONTENT
→ REPORT MANIFEST CONTENT

ACTIVATION-SYNTHESIS MODEL

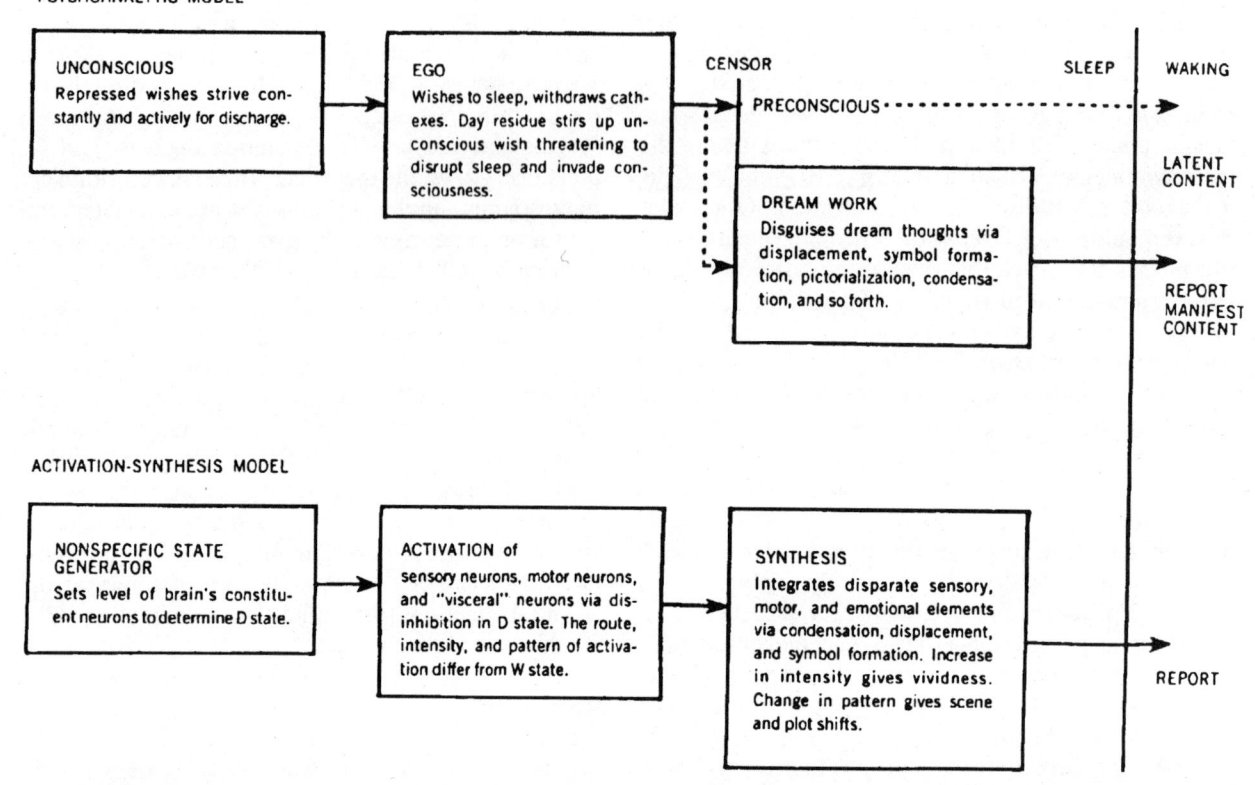

| NONSPECIFIC STATE GENERATOR | → | ACTIVATION of | → | SYNTHESIS |
| Sets level of brain's constituent neurons to determine D state. | | sensory neurons, motor neurons, and "visceral" neurons via disinhibition in D state. The route, intensity, and pattern of activation differ from W state. | | Integrates disparate sensory, motor, and emotional elements via condensation, displacement, and symbol formation. Increase in intensity gives vividness. Change in pattern gives scene and plot shifts. |

→ REPORT

*In the psychoanalytic model the motive force of the process is the dynamically repressed unconscious wish that is released from control in sleep. The dream thoughts that emerge threaten consciousness and sleep; they are deterred by the censor. The "dream work" transforms the unconscious wish by the processes that are listed. The product, or manifest content, that becomes conscious thus contains only disguised elements of the original (latent) dream thoughts. The activation-synthesis model is designed to contrast activation-synthesis theory with the guardian-censorship theory illustrated in the top portion of this figure. The motive force of the process is seen to be nonspecific neural energy or excitation hypothesized to arise from a nonspecific generator. This excitation affects the component systems of the forebrain represented in the upper box: sensory systems generate scene frames, structural fragments, and qualitative features; cognitive systems generate ideas that may be conscious (day residue thoughts) or unconscious (instinctually determined); emotion is also generated at this first stage. The dream report, easily obtainable if a state change to waking occurs, is seen as an accurate reflection of the integrated product of disparate, internally generated elements.

size-dependent time constant of the cycle is the recently discovered class of long-duration postsynaptic transmitter actions (36) that may be mediated by second messengers such as <u>cyclic AMP</u> (37). Since the cyclic <u>nucleotides</u> activate <u>protein kinases</u>, the metabolic activity of the neuron, including the synthesis of neurotransmitters, can be linked to and entrained by membrane events.

An important point is that the mathematical model parallels, but is not identical to, the physiological model. This means that even if the specific assumptions about physiological interaction are incorrect, the mathematical model may be viable and useful in another system—for example, the coupling of the <u>circadian and ultradian oscillators</u> (14) or, at another level of analysis, in a molecular system. This is particularly important to keep in mind since it is also at the molecular level that time constant elements necessary to explain the long periodicity of the sleep-dream cycle may be found.

PSYCHOLOGICAL IMPLICATIONS OF THE CELLULAR NEUROPHYSIOLOGY OF DREAM SLEEP GENERATION

Hallucinoid dreaming is regarded as the psychological concomitant of D sleep. Brain activity in the D state has been analyzed to account for activation of the forebrain, occlusion of sensory input, blockade of motor output at the spinal cord level, and the generation of information within the system. The evidence that the pontine brain stem contains a clock-trigger mechanism that contributes to activation of the forebrain, occlusion of sensory input, and the generation of internal information has been reviewed. The periodicity of the triggering mechanism is hypothesized to be a function of reciprocal interaction of reciprocally connected chemically coded cell groups in the pontine brain stem.

The psychological implications of this model, which we call the activation-synthesis hypothesis of the dream process (schematically represented in Figure 10), contrast sharply with many tenets of the dream theory provided by psychoanalysis (also represented in Figure 10) in the following ways:

1. *The primary motivating force for dreaming* is not psychological but physiological since the time of occurrence and duration of dreaming sleep are quite constant, suggesting a preprogrammed, neurally determined genesis. In fact, the neural mechanisms involved can now be precisely specified. This conclusion does not, of course, mean that dreams are not also psychological events; nor does it imply that they are without psychological meaning or function. But it does imply that the process is much more basic than the psychodynamically determined, **evanescent**, "guardian of sleep" process that Freud had imagined it to be; and it casts serious doubt upon the exclusively psychological significance attached to both the occurrence and quality of dreams.

2. *Specific stimuli for the dream imagery* appear to arise **intracerebrally**, but from the pontine brain stem and not in cognitive areas of the cerebrum. These stimuli, whose generation appears to depend upon a largely random or reflex process, may provide spatially specific information which can be used in constructing dream imagery; but the unusual intensity, intermittency, and velocity of the eye movements may also contribute to features of the dream experience which are formally bizarre and have been interpreted as defensive by psychoanalysis. Thus such features as scene shifts, time compression, personal condensations, splitting, and symbol formation may be directly isomorphic with the state of the nervous system during dreaming sleep. In other words, the forebrain may be making the best of a bad job in producing even partially coherent dream imagery from the relatively noisy signals sent up to it from the brain stem.

The dream process is thus seen as having its origin in sensorimotor systems with little or no primary ideational, **volitional**, or emotional content. This concept is markedly different from that of the "dream thoughts" or wishes seen by Freud as the primary stimulus for the dream. The sensorimotor stimuli are viewed as possibly providing a frame into which ideational, volitional, or emotional content may be projected to form the integrated dream image, but this frame is itself conflict free. Thus both the major energetic drive for the dream process and the specific primary stimulus of the dream content are **genotypically** determined and therefore conflict free in the specifically psychodynamic sense of the term.

3. *The elaboration of the brain stem stimulus* by the perceptual, conceptual, and emotional structures of the forebrain is viewed as primarily a synthetic constructive process, rather than a distorting one as Freud presumed. Best fits to the relative **inchoate** and incomplete data provided by the primary stimuli are called up from memory, the access to which is facilitated during dreaming sleep. The brain, in the dreaming sleep state, is thus likened to a computer searching its addresses for key words. Rather than indicating a need for disguise, this fitting of phenotypic experiential data to genotypic stimuli is seen as the major basis of the "bizarre" formal qualities of dream **mentation**. There is, therefore, no need to postulate either a censor or an information degrading process working at the censor's behest. The dream content elaborated by the forebrain may include conflictually charged memories, but even this aspect of dream construction is seen as synthetic and transparent rather than degradative and opaque.

4. *With respect to the forgetting of dreams*, the normally poor recall is seen principally to reflect a state-dependent amnesia, since a carefully effected state change, to waking, may produce abundant recall even of highly charged dream material. There is thus no need to invoke repression to account for the forgetting of dreams. This hypothesis is appealingly economical, and in the light of the reciprocal interaction hypothesis dream amnesia can now be modeled in a testable way as the result of a different balance between cholinergic

---

Cyclic AMP. A chemical that regulates neural metabolism and function.

Nucleotides (NEW-klee-oh-tides). One of the basic building blocks in DNA and RNA.

Protein kinases (PRO-teen KIGH-nay-zes). Chemicals that affect cyclic AMP.

Circadian and ultradian oscillators (seer-KADE-ih-an and ULL-tra-DEE-an OSS-sill-a-tors). The body has various biological rhythms or "clocks" that operate on regular schedules. However, these "clocks" oscillate or vary slightly from time to time. The term *circa* means "about a day," meaning that the clock involved runs on (approximately) a 24-hour schedule. The term *ultradian* means "beyond a day." Evanescent (ev-an-ESS-ent). Transient, or not lasting very long.

Intracerebrally (in-trah-sair-REE-bra-lee). Something that occurs "inside the cerebrum," or "inside the brain."

Volitional (voh-LISH-un-al). *Volition* means "voluntary control."

Genotypically (jean-oh-TIP-ih-kal-lee). Something that is typical of, or determined by, a given set of genes.

Inchoate (INkoh-ate). Imperfectly formed.

Mentation (men-TAY-shun). Thinking, or some other form of mental activity.

and aminergic neuronal activity and the resulting effects on second messengers and macromolecules (5). Among its other surprising gifts to psychophysiology, dreaming sleep may thus also provide a biological model for the study of memory, and a functional role for dreaming sleep in promoting some aspect of the learning process is suggested.

SUMMARY AND CONCLUSIONS

Assuming that isomorphism, or identity of form, must characterize the simultaneous physiological and psychological events during dreaming, we have reviewed the general and cellular neurophysiology of dreaming sleep in search of new ways of accounting for some of the formal aspects of dream psychology. We have noted that the occurrence of dreaming depends upon the periodic activation of the forebrain during sleep. We have hypothesized that the activated forebrain synthesizes the dreams by fitting experiential data to information endogenously and automatically generated by reticular, vestibular, and oculomotor neurons in the pontine brain stem. A specific physiological and mathematical model of the pontine generator, based upon single cell recording studies in cats, is described: the model **posits** reciprocal interaction between inhibitory aminergic (level-setting) and excitatory cholinergic (generator) neurons.

Some of the "bizarre" formal features of the dream may directly reflect the properties of the brain stem neuronal generator mechanism. The physiological features of the generator mechanisms and their corresponding psychological implications include the following: the automaticity and periodicity of activation indicate a metabolically determined, conflict-free energetics of the dream process; the random but specific nature of the generator signals could provide abnormally sequenced and shaped, but spatiotemporally specific, frames for dream imagery; and the clustering of runs of generator signals might constitute time-marks for dream subplots and scene changes. Further, the activation by generator neurons of diffuse postsynaptic forebrain elements in multiple parallel channels might account for the disparate sensory, motor, and emotional elements that contribute to the "bizarreness" of dreams; the suppression of motor output and sensory input simultaneous with central activation of both sensory and motor patterns could assure the maintenance of sleep in the face of massive central excitation of the brain; and the change in the ratio of neurotransmitters affecting forebrain neurons might account for dream amnesia and indicate a state-dependent alteration of **neural plasticity**, with implications for the learning process.

FOOTNOTES

[1] Reprinted by permission of the authors and the publisher from the *American Journal of Psychiatry*, 1977, **134**, 1335-1348. Copyright 1977, the American Psychiatric Association.

[2] Dr. Allen Hobson is Professor of Psychiatry, Harvard Medical School, and Director, Laboratory of Neurophysiology, Massachusetts Mental Health Center. He is the author of *The Dreaming Brain* (Basic Books, New York, 1988), a book which further develops the theory first presented here.

[3] Based on the text of the Sandoz Lecture presented by Dr. Hobson at the University of Edinburgh, April 23, 1975. The research described herein was supported by Alcohol, Drug Abuse, and Mental Health Administration grant MH-13923 from the National Institute of Mental Health and by the Milton Fund of Harvard University. The authors wish to express their appreciation to Drs. John Nemiah and John Nelson for their helpful comments on the manuscript.

REFERENCES

1. Freud S: The interpretation of dreams (1900), in *The Complete Psychological Works*, standard ed, vols 4 and 5. Translated and edited by Strachey J. London, Hogarth Press, 1966
2. McCarley RW, Hobson JA: The neurobiological origins of psychoanalytic dream theory. *Am J Psychiatry* **134**:1211-1221, 1977
3. McCarley RW: Mind-body isomorphism and the study of dreams, in *Advances in Sleep Research*, vol 6. Edited by Fishbein W. New York, Spectrum (in press)
4. Dement W, Kleitman N: The relation of eye movements during sleep to dream activity: an objective method for the study of dreaming. *J Exp Psychol* **53**:89-97, 1957
5. Hobson JA: The reciprocal interaction model of sleep cycle control: implication for PGO wave generation and dream amnesia, in *Sleep and Memory*. Edited by Drucker, Colin R, & McGaugh J. New York, Academic Press, 1977, pp 159-183
6. Pompeiano O: The neurophysiological mechanisms of the postural and motor events during desynchronized sleep. *Res Publ Assoc Res Nerv Ment Dis* **45**:351-423, 1967
7. Jouvet M, Delorme F: Locus coeruleus et sommeil paradoxol. *Soc Biol* **159**:895, 1965
8. Volkman F: Vision during voluntary saccadic eye movements. *J Opt Soc Am* **52**:571-578, 1962
9. Bizzi E: Discharge pattern of single geniculate neurons during the rapid eye movements of sleep. *J Neurophysiol* **29**:1087-1095, 1966
10. Evarts EV: Activity of individual cerebral neurons during sleep and arousal. *Res Publ Assoc Res Nerv Ment Dis* **45**:319-337, 1967
11. Hobson JA, Goldfrank F, Snyder F: Sleep and respiration. *J Psychiatr Res* **3**:79-90, 1965

12. Roffwarg HP, Dement WC, Muzio JN, et al: Dream imagery: relationship to rapid eye movements of sleep. *Arch Gen Psychiatry* 7:235-258, 1962
13. Pompeiano O: Sensory inhibition during motor activity in sleep, in *Neurophysiological Basis of Normal and Abnormal Motor Activities*. Edited by Yahr MD, Purpura DP. New York, Raven Press, 1967, pp. 323-375
14. Hobson JA: The sleep-dream cycle, a neurobiological rhythm, in *Pathobiology Annual*. Edited by Ioachim H. New York, Appleton-Century Crofts, 1975, pp 369-403
15. Zepelin H, Rechtschaffen A: Mammalian sleep, longevity and energy metabolism. *Brain Behav Evol* 10:425-470, 1974
16. Dement W: The occurrence of low-voltage fast electroencephlogram patterns during behavioral sleep in the cat. *Electroencephalogr Clin Neurophysiol* 10:291-296, 1958
17. Jouvet M: Recherches sur les structures nerveuses et les mecanismes responsables des differentes phases du sommeil physiologique. *Arch Ital Biol* 100:125-206, 1962
18. Pompeiano O, Morrison AR: Vestibular influences during sleep. 1. Abolition of the rapid eye movements of desynchronized sleep following vestibular lesions. *Arch Ital Biol* 103:569-595, 1965
19. Magherini PC, Pompeiano O, Thoden U: Cholinergic mechanisms related to REM sleep. 1. Rhythmic activity of the vestibular-oculomotor system induced by an anticholinesterase in the decerebrate cat. *Arch Ital Biol* 110:234-259, 1972
20. Frederickson CJ, Hobson JA: Electrical stimulation of the brain stem and subsequent sleep. *Arch Ital Biol* 108:564-576, 1970
21. Amatruda TT, Black DA, McKenna TM, et al: Sleep cycle control and cholinergic mechanisms: differential effects of carbachol at pontine brain stem sites. *Brain Res* 98:501-515, 1975
22. Sitaram N, Wyatt RJ, Dawson S, et al: REM sleep induction by physostigmine infusion during sleep. *Science* 191:1281-1283, 1976
23. Cajal R: *Histologie du System Nerveux*, vol 1. Madrid. Consejo Superior de Investigaciones Cientificas, 1952
24. Brodal A: *The Reticular Formation of the Brain Stem. Anatomical Aspects and Functional Correlations*. Edinburgh, Oliver Boyd, 1957
25. Scheibel ME, Scheibel AB: Anatomical basis of attention mechanisms in vertebrate brains, in *The Neurosciences: A Study Program*. Edited by Quarton GC, Melnechuk T, Schmitt FO. New York, Rockefeller University Press, 1967, pp 577-602
26. Dahlstrom A, Fuxe K: Evidence for the existence of monoamine-containing neurons in the central nervous system. I. Demonstration of monoamines in the cell bodies of brain stem neurons. *Acta Physiol Scand* 62:1-55, 1964
27. Hobson JA, McCarley RW, Pivik RT, et al: Selective firing by cat pontine brain stem neurons in desynchronized sleep. *J Neurophysiol* 37:497-511, 1974
28. Hobson JA, McCarley RW, Freedman R, et al: Time course of discharge rate changes by cat pontine brain stem neurons during the sleep cycle. *J Neurophysiol* 37:1297-1309, 1974
29. Pivik RT, McCarley RW, Hobson JA: Eye movement-associated discharge in brain stem neurons during desynchronized sleep. *Brain Res* 121:59-76, 1977
30. McCarley RW, Hobson JA: Neuronal excitability modulation over the sleep cycle: a structural and mathematical model. *Science* 189:58-60, 1975
31. McCarley RW, Hobson JA: Discharge patterns of cat pontine brain stem neurons during desynchronized sleep. *J Neurophysiol* 38:751-766, 1975
32. Hobson JA, McCarley RW, Wyzinski PW: Sleep cycle oscillation: reciprocal discharge by two brainstem neuronal groups. *Science* 189:55-58, 1975
33. McGinty DJ, Harper RM, Fairbanks MK: 5 HNT-containing neurons: unit activity in behaving cats, in *Serotonin and Behavior*. Edited by Barchas J, Usdin E. New York, Academic Press, 1973, pp 267-279
34. Aghajanian GK, Foote WE, and Sheard MH: Action of psychogenic drugs on single midbrain raphe neurons. *J Pharmacol Exp Ther* 171:178-187, 1970
35. Pompeiano O, Hoshino K: Central control of posture: reciprocal discharge by two pontine neuronal groups leading to supression of decerebrate rigidity. *Brain Res* 116:131-138, 1976.
36. Libet B: Generation of slow inhibitory and excitatory post-synaptic potentials. *Fed Proc* 29:1945-1955, 1970
37. Bloom FE: Role of cyclic nucleotides in central synaptic function. *Rev Physiol Biochem Pharmacol* 74:1-103, 1975.

Posits (PAH-sits). Assumes.

Neural plasticity (plas-TISS-ih-tee). *Plasticity* means "changeable." Presumably, during learning, the neurons change their functions (or perhaps even their structures).

CHAPTER 14

"The 'Visual Cliff'"

Eleanor J. Gibson and Richard D. Walk[1]

EDITORS' COMMENTS. The *mind-body problem* is one of the two major controversies in psychology. The *nature-nurture problem* is the other. And, as you might guess, these two "grand theoretical battles" are closely linked.

How much of what you are today was determined by your genes? Were you born to be the person you are, no matter what sort of environment you grew up in? That is, are you little different from a plant whose pattern of growth and flowering is "programmed" into the DNA? If so, then all that your early environment could do was to hasten or retard the unfolding of your innate tendencies. (This is, of course, a very strong "body" position.) On the other hand, if at birth your mind was little more than a "blank tablet on which experience writes," as the British philosopher John Locke put it many years ago, then the way you were *nurtured* (rather than your genes) was the most important force shaping you into the unique person that you are today. Generally speaking, "nurturists" such as Locke tend to emphasize the importance of mental (rather than physical) activities as determinants of human behavior.

In the field of perception, the "naturist" position is perhaps best represented by James Gibson and his wife, Eleanor. Some 40 years ago, James Gibson suggested that your brain is "hard-wired" to *see the world as it really is*. Put more technically, he stated that *sensory inputs impose order on your mind*. He believed that psychologists could explain almost all perceptual experiences in terms of information to be found in the stimulus itself. Therefore, Gibson said, we should study *external stimuli*, not "internal processes." As far as perception is concerned, Gibson didn't ask what goes on "inside your head." Instead, he asked "what kind of stimulus world is your head inside of?"

Eleanor Gibson has had as distinguished a career in psychology as did her husband. One day, several years ago, she found herself eating a picnic meal on the rim of the Grand Canyon. Looking straight down into that deep river bed, she began to worry about the safety of the children playing around her. Would a very young child be able to perceive the enormous drop-off at the edge of the cliff? Or would the child go toddling right over the edge if no adult were around to restrain the child? Once Gibson had returned to her laboratory at Cornell University, she attempted to answer both these questions. And to do so, she and Richard Walk designed an artificial *visual cliff* on which they could test infants safely.

Although in this article Gibson and Walk report evidence strongly favoring the "naturist" position, in subsequent research Gibson (and others) have found that there are great individual differences between infants in their response to the visual cliff. Some babies seem to be *visually oriented*. These infants recoil with fear from the sight of the cliff. Others tend to be *touch oriented*. These youngsters apparently trust their skin senses more than their eyes, and crawl right out on the glass covering the cliff as long as it offers firm support. Thus, the issue of whether infants are born with an innate fear of heights is far from settled. Gibson and Walk were, however, among the first to show that *some important aspects* of visual development were genetically determined.

We will have more to say about the *nature-nurture* problem in our comments on the next chapter, when we discuss which aspects of *intelligence* seem to be inherited, and which are learned.

(Reprinted with permission. Copyright © 1960 by Scientific American, Inc. All Rights reserved.)

Human infants at the creeping and toddling stage are notoriously prone to falls from more or less high places. They must be kept from going over the brink by side panels on their cribs, gates on stairways and the vigilance of adults. As their muscular coordination matures they begin to avoid such accidents on their own. Common sense might suggest that the child learns to recognize falling-off places by experience--that is, by falling and hurting himself. But is experience really the teacher? Or is the ability to perceive and avoid a brink part of the child's original endowment?

Answers to these questions will throw light on the genesis of space perception in general. Height perception is a special case of distance perception: information in the light reaching the eye provides stimuli that can be utilized for the discrimination both of depth and of receding distance on the level. At what stage of development can an animal respond effectively to these stimuli? Does the onset of such response vary with animals of different species and **habitats**?

At Cornell University we have been investigating these problems by means of a simple experimental setup that we call a visual cliff. The cliff is a simulated one and hence makes it possible not only to control the optical and other stimuli (auditory and tactual, for instance) but also to protect the experimental subjects. It consists of a board laid across a large sheet of heavy glass which is supported a foot or more above the floor. On one side of the board a sheet of patterned material is placed flush against the undersurface of the glass, giving the glass the appearance as well as the substance of solidity. On the other side a sheet of the same material is laid upon the floor; this side of the board thus becomes the visual cliff.

We tested 38 infants ranging in age from six months to 14 months on the visual cliff. Each child was placed upon the center board, and his mother called him to her from the cliff side and the shallow side successively. All of the 27 infants who moved off the board crawled out on the shallow side at least once; only three of them crept off the brink onto the glass suspended above the pattern on the floor. Many of the infants crawled away from the mother when she called to them from the cliff side; others cried when she stood there, because they could not come to her without crossing an apparent **chasm**. The experiment thus demonstrated that most human infants can discriminate depth as soon as they can crawl.

The behavior of the children in this situation gave clear evidence of their dependence on vision. Often they would peer down through the glass on the deep side and then back away. Others would pat the glass with their hands, yet despite this tactual assurance of solidity would refuse to cross. It was equally clear that their perception of depth had matured more rapidly than had their locomotor abilities. Many supported themselves on the glass over the deep side as they maneuvered awkwardly on the board; some even backed out onto the glass as they started toward the mother on the shallow side. Were it not for the glass some of the children would have fallen off the board. Evidently infants should not be left close to a brink, no matter how well they may discriminate depth.

This experiment does not prove that the human infant's perception and avoidance of the cliff are innate. Such an interpretation is supported, however, by the experiments with nonhuman infants. On the visual cliff we have observed the behavior of chicks, turtles, rats, lambs, kids, pigs, kittens and dogs. These animals showed various reactions, each of which proved to be characteristic of their species. In each case the reaction is plainly related to the role of vision in the survival of the species, and the varied patterns of behavior suggest something about the role of vision in evolution.

In the chick, for example, depth perception manifests itself with special rapidity. At an age of less than 24 hours the chick can be tested on the visual cliff. It never makes a "mistake" and always hops off the board on the shallow side. Without doubt this finding is related to the fact that the chick, unlike many other young birds, must scratch for itself a few hours after it is hatched.

Kids and lambs, like chicks, can be tested on the visual cliff as soon as they can stand. The response of these animals is equally predictable. No goat or lamb ever stepped onto the glass of the deep side, even at one day of age. When one of these animals was placed upon the glass on the deep side, it displayed characteristic **stereotyped** behavior. It would refuse to put its feet down and would back up into a posture of defense, its front legs rigid and its hind legs limp. In this state of immobility it could be pushed forward across the glass until its head and field of vision crossed the edge of the surrounding solid surface, whereupon it would relax and spring forward upon the surface.

At the Cornell Behavior Farm a group of experimenters has carried these experiments with kids and goats a step further. They fixed the patterned material to a sheet of plywood and were thus able to adjust the "depth" of the deep side. With the pattern

Habitat (HAB-ih-tat). A habitat is a place where a plant or animal species naturally lives and grows.

Chasm (KAZ-um). A deep opening such as a valley, gorge or canyon.

Stereotype. A stereotype is a fixed or unconscious way of responding to some person or object.

Child's depth perception is tested on the visual cliff. The apparatus consists of a board laid across a sheet of heavy glass, with a patterned material directly beneath the glass on one side and several feet below it on the other. Placed on the center board (*top left*), the child crawls to its mother across the "shallow" side (*top right*). Called from the "deep" side, he pats the glass (*bottom left*), but despite this tactual evidence that the "cliff" is in fact a solid surface he refuses to cross over to the mother (*bottom right*).

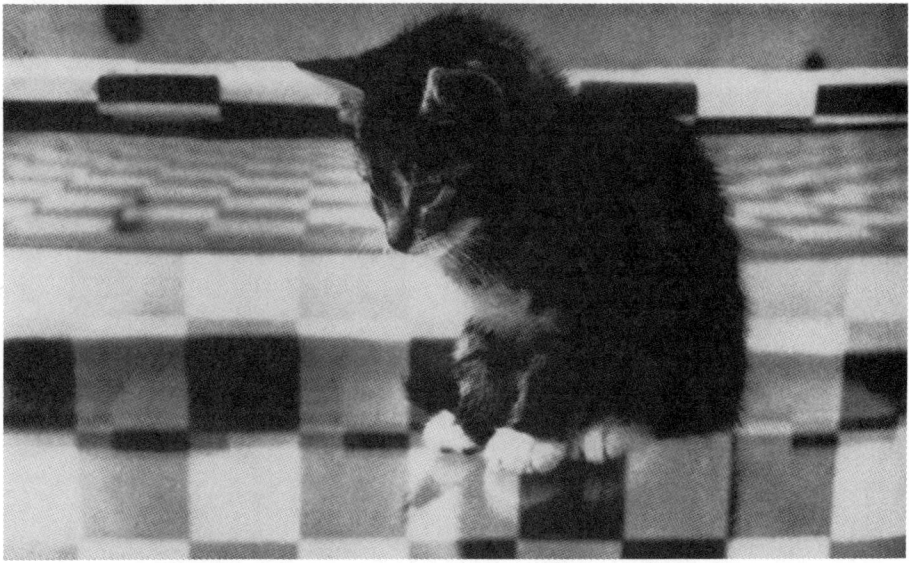

Kitten's depth perception also manifests itself at an early age. Though the animal displays no alarm on the shallow side (*top*), it "feezes" when placed on the glass over the deep side (*bottom*); in some cases it will crawl aimlessly backward in a circle.

held immediately beneath the glass, the animal would move about the glass freely. With the optical floor dropped more than a foot below the glass, the animal would immediately freeze into its defensive posture. Despite repeated experience of the tactual solidity of the glass, the animals never learned to function without optical support. Their sense of security or danger continued to depend upon the visual cues that give them their perception of depth.

The rat, in contrast, does not depend predominantly upon visual cues. Its nocturnal habits lead it to seek food largely by smell, when moving about in the dark, it responds to tactual cues from the stiff whiskers (<u>vibrissae</u>) on its snout. Hooded rats tested on the visual cliff show little preference for the shallow side so long as they can feel the glass with their vibrissae. Placed upon the

<u>Vibrissae</u> (vy-BRISS-ee). The stiff hairs that grow around the nose or on other parts of the face of many mammals.

glass over the deep side, they move about normally. But when we raise the center board several inches, so that the glass is out of reach of their whiskers, they evince good visual depth-discrimination: 95 to 100 per cent of them descend on the shallow side.

Cats, like rats, are nocturnal animals, sensitive to tactual cues from their vibrissae. But the cat, as a predator, must rely more strongly on its sight. Kittens proved to have excellent depth-discrimination.
At four weeks--about the earliest age that a kitten can move about with any facility--they invariably choose the shallow side of the cliff. On the glass over the deep side, they either freeze or circle aimlessly backward until they reach the center board [*see Figures on previous page*].

The animals that showed the poorest performance in our series were the turtles. The late Robert M. Yerkes of Harvard University found in 1904 that aquatic turtles have somewhat poorer depth-discrimination than land turtles. On the visual cliff one might expect an aquatic turtle to respond to the reflections from the glass as it might to water and so prefer the deep side. They showed no such preference: 76 per cent of the aquatic turtles

Goats show depth perception at an age of only one day. A kid walks freely on the shallow side (*top*); on the deep side (*middle*) it leaps the "chasm" to safety (*bottom*).

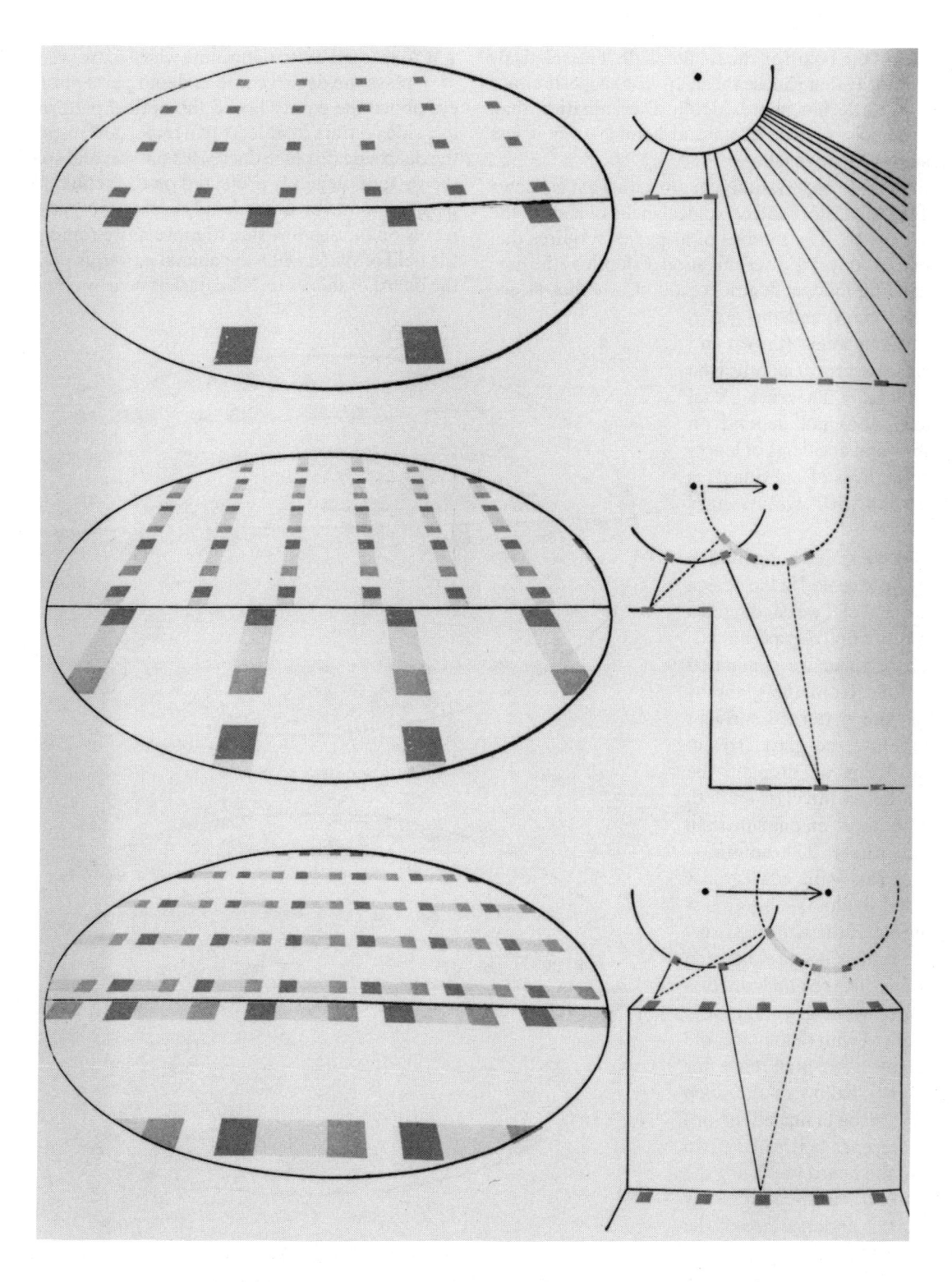

Two types of visual depth-cue are diagrammed schematically on this page. Ellipses approximate the visual vield of an animal standing near the edge of the cliff and looking toward it; diagrams at right give the geometrical explanation of differences in the fields. The spacing of the pattern elements (*solid color*) decreases sharply beyond the edge of the cliff (*top*). The optical motion (*shaded color*) of the elements as the animal moves forward (*center*) or sideways (*bottom*) show a similar drop-off.

crawled off the board on the shallow side. The relatively large minority that choose the deep side suggests either that this turtle has poorer depth-discrimination than other animals, or that its natural habitat gives it less occasion to "fear" a fall.

All of these observations square with what is known about the life history and ecological niche of each of the animals tested. The survival of a species requires that its members develop discrimination of depth by the time they take up independent locomotion, whether at one day (the chick and the goat), three to four weeks (the rat and the cat) or six to 10 months (the human infant). That such a vital capacity does not depend on possibly fatal accidents of learning in the lives of individuals is consistent with evolutionary theory.

To make sure that no hidden bias was concealed in the design of the visual cliff we conducted a number of control experiments. In one of them we eliminated reflections from the glass by lighting the patterned surfaces from below the glass (to accomplish this we dropped the pattern below the glass on both sides, but more on one side than on the other). The animals--hooded rats--still consistently chose the shallow side. As a test of the role of the patterned surface we replaced it on either side of the centerboard with a homogeneous gray surface. Confronted with this choice, the rats showed no preference for either the shallow or the deep side. We also eliminated the optical difference between the two sides of the board by placing the patterned surface directly against the undersurface of the glass on each side. The rats then descended without preference to either side. When we lowered the pattern 10 inches below the glass on each side, they stayed on the board.

We set out next to determine which of two visual cues plays the decisive role in depth perception. To an eye above the center board the optical pattern on the two sides differs in at least two important respects. On the deep side distance decreases the size and spacing of the pattern elements projected on the retina. "**Motion parallax**," on the other hand, causes the pattern elements on the shallow side to move more rapidly across the field of vision when the animal moves its position on the board or moves its head, just as nearby objects seen

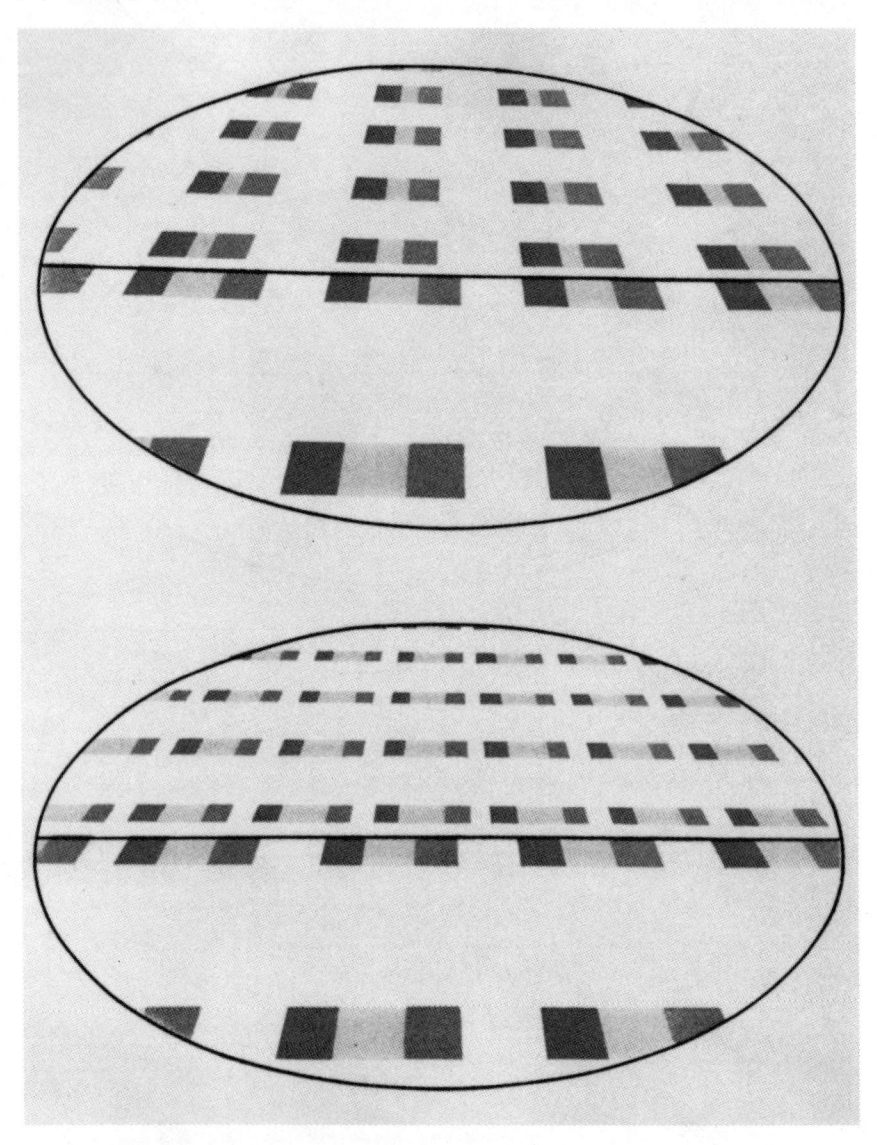

Separation of visual cues is shown in these diagrams. Pattern density is held constant (*top*) by using a larger pattern on the low side of the cliff; the drop in optical motion (motion parallax) remains. Motion parallax is equalized (*bottom*) by placing patterns at same level; the smaller pattern on one side preserves difference in spacing.

from a moving car appear to pass by more quickly than distant ones [see Figures on previous page]. To eliminate the potential distance cue provided by pattern density we increased the size and spacing of the pattern elements on the deep side in proportion to its distance from the eye. With only the cue of motion parallax to guide them, adult rats still preferred the shallow side, though not so strongly as in the standard experiment. Infant rats chose the shallow side nearly 100 per cent of the time under both conditions, as did day-old chicks. Evidently both species can discriminate depth by differential motion alone, with no aid from texture density and probably little help from other cues. The perception of distance by binocular parallax, which doubtless plays an important part in human behavior, would not seem to have a significant role, for example, in the depth perception of chicks and rats.

To eliminate the cue of motion parallax we placed the patterned material directly against the glass on either side of the board but used smaller and more densely spaced pattern-elements on the cliff side. Both young and adult hooded rats preferred the side with the larger pattern, which evidently "signified" a nearer surface. Day-old chicks, however, showed no preference for the larger patern. It may be that learning plays some part in the preference exhibited by the rats, since the young rats were tested at a somewhat older age than the chicks. This supposition is supported by the results of our experiments with animals reared in the dark.

The effects of early experience and of such deprivations as dark-rearing represent important clues to the relative roles of maturation and learning in animal behavior. The first experiments along this line were performed by K. S. Lashley and James T. Russell at the University of Chicago in 1934. They tested light-reared and dark-reared rats on a "**jumping stand**" from which they induced animals to leap toward a platform placed at varying distances. Upon finding that both groups of animals jumped with a force closely correlated with distance, they concluded that depth perception in rats is innate. Other investigators have pointed out, however, that the dark-reared rats required a certain amount of "pretraining" in the light before they could be made to jump. Since the visual-cliff technique requires no pretraining, we employed it to test groups of light-reared and dark-reared hooded rats. At the age of 90 days both groups showed the same preference for the shallow side of the apparatus, confirming Lashley's and Russell's conclusion.

Recalling our findings in the young rat, we then took up the question of whether the dark-reared rats relied upon motion parallax or upon contrast in texture density to discriminate depth. When the animals were confronted with the visual cliff, cued only by motion parallax, they preferred the shallow side, as had the light-reared animals. When the choice was cued by pattern density, however, they departed from the pattern of the normal animals and showed no significant preference. The behavior of dark-reared rats thus resembles that of the day-old chicks, which also lack visual experience. It seems likely, therefore, that of the two cues only motion parallax is an innate cue for depth discrimination. Responses to differential pattern-density may be learned later.

One cannot automatically extrapolate these results to other species. But experiments with dark-reared kittens indicate that in these animals, too, depth perception matures independently of trial and error learning. In the kitten, however, light is necessary for normal visual maturation. Kittens reared in the dark to the age of 27 days at first crawled or fell off the center board equally often on the deep and shallow sides. Placed upon the glass over the deep side, they did not back in a circle like normal kittens but showed the same behavior that they had exhibited on the shallow side. Other investigators have observed equivalent behavior in dark-reared kittens; they bump into obstacles, lack normal eye movement and appear to "stare" straight ahead. These difficulties pass after a few days in the light. We accordingly tested the kittens every day. By the end of a week they were performing in every respect like normal kittens. They showed the same unanimous preference for the shallow side. Placed upon the glass over the deep side, they balked and circled backward to a visually secure surface. Repeated descents to the deep side, and placement upon the glass during their "blind" period, had not taught them that the deep side was "safe." Instead they avoided it more and more consistently. The initial blindness of dark-reared kittens makes them ideal subjects for studying the maturation of depth perception. With further study it should be possible to determine which cues they respond to first and what kinds of visual experience accelerate or retard the process of maturation.

Motion parallax (PAIR-al-ax). When you are riding in a car, objects close to the car seem to be moving in the opposite direction to the one you're going in, and distant objects appear to be moving (backward) much more slowly than do near objects. This difference in apparent movement is called "motion parallax."

Jumping stand. A platform used in animal experiments. The animal sits atop the tiny platform (which is supported by a thin pole) and faces a wall with holes (or small "doors") cut into the wall. The holes are typically covered with stimulus cards. The animal must jump toward one of the stimulus cards. If it picks the correct stimulus, the card falls over when hit and the animal falls into a small chamber that contains food as a reward. If the animal jumps at the incorrect stimulus, the card is locked and the animal falls into a net beneath the wall and thus is punished for its mistake. If the animal refuses to jump, it is given mild punishment (often electric shock) until it does.

Importance of pattern in depth perception is shown in these photographs. Of two patterns set at the same depth, normal rats almost invariably preferred the larger (*top row and bottom left*), presumably because it "signified" a nearer and therefore safer surface. Confronted with two patternless surfaces set at different depths, the animals displayed no preference (*bottom right*).

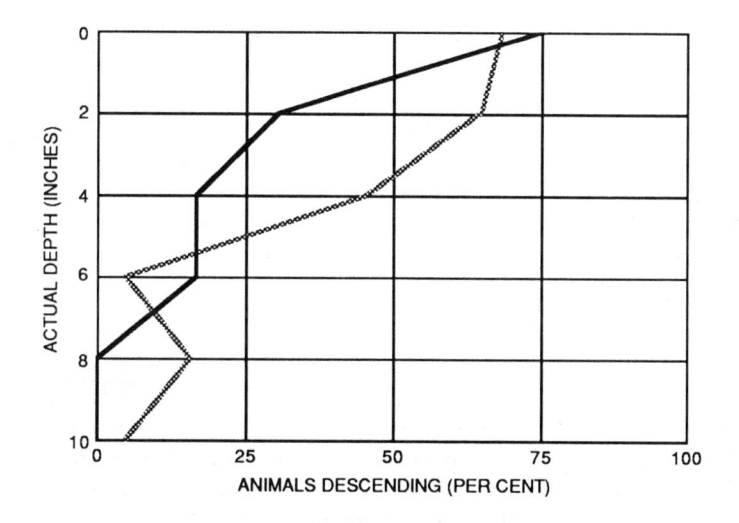

Control experiment measured the effect on rats of reflections on the glass of the apparatus. The percentage of animals leaving the center board decreased with increasing depth in much the same way, whether glass was present (*top curve*) or not (*bottom curve*).

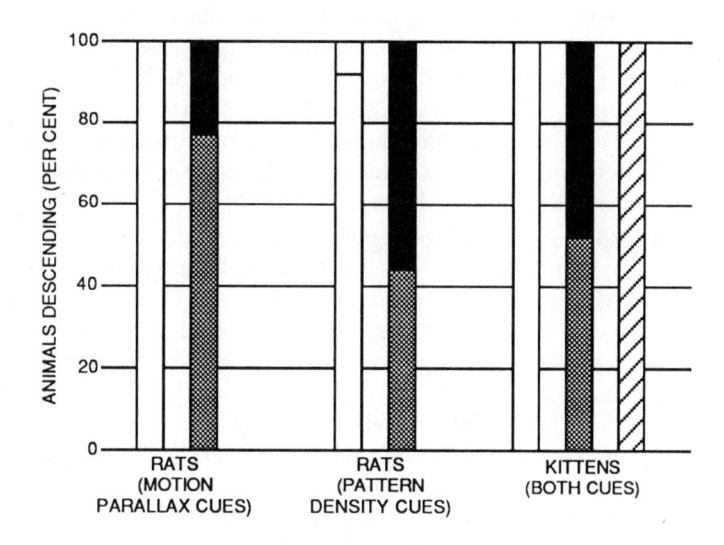

Dark-rearing experiments reveal the order in which different depth-cues are utilized as animals mature. Animals reared in the light (*open bars*) all strongly preferred the shallow side (*light gray*) to the deep side (*darker gray*). Dark-reared rats (*solid bars*), utilizing motion parallax alone, still preferred the shallow side; pattern density alone elicited no preference. Dark-reared kittens also showed no preference, because of temporary blindness. After seven days in the light all of them chose the shallow side (*hatched bar*).

From our first few years of work with the visual cliff we are ready to venture the rather broad conclusion that a seeing animal will be able to discriminate depth when its locomotion is adequate, even when locomotion begins at birth. But many experiments remain to be done, especially on the role of different cues and on the effects of different kinds of early visual experience.

FOOTNOTES

[1] Reprinted by permission from *Scientific American*, 1960, 202, 64-71.

CHAPTER 15

"IQ Test Performance of Black Children Adopted by White Families"

Sandra Scarr and R.A. Weinberg[1,2]

> **EDITORS' COMMENTS.** Nature, or Nurture? As far as *intelligence* is concerned, the conservative viewpoint has always been that this aspect of the human personality is primarily inherited: "Like father, like son"; "Blood will tell"; "An apple never falls very far from the tree."
>
> Indeed, this "naturist" viewpoint has long been used as political justification for segregation of the races, for denying human rights to certain ethnic groups, and even for slavery. But what kinds of *scientific* evidence can the naturists muster in order to bolster their views on the heritability of intelligence? In 1969, Arthur Jensen published an article in the *Harvard Educational Review* entitled "How much can we boost I.Q. and scholastic achievement?" In this 123-page paper, Jensen cites study after study showing that (in the US) blacks typically score about 15 points lower on intelligence tests than do whites. Blacks also score somewhat lower on these tests than do other disadvantaged groups, such as Hispanics and American Indians. This point, in and of itself, seems to be true. However, the *interpretation* that one gives to these data is open to question. Jensen--a strong believer in the "native superiority of the white race"--holds that the only acceptable explanation for the data is that blacks are *genetically inferior* to whites, at least as far as intelligence is concerned. Most other psychologists disagree--not with the data, but with the interpretation.
>
> For example, in 1986, R.D. Bock and Elsie Moore published their study of the "cognitive development" of 12,000 Americans between the ages of 15 and 23.[3] Bock and Moore found, as did Jensen, that blacks do score lower than whites on many tests of intelligence or cognitive development. However, these authors conclude that the differences are *not* due to *genetic endowment*. First of all, they note that the sorts of questions asked on intelligence tests are strongly biased toward the performance that middle-class, well-educated white parents expect of their own children. Youngsters reared in other cultures, where the emphasis might well be on learning rather different sorts of cognitive and behavioral skills, might not be expected to perform as well as do middle-class white children. Furthermore, we know from many research studies that intelligence tests scores are enhanced if the child is reared in a "culturally-stimulating environment" rather than in deprived circumstances. After reviewing all the data, Bock and Moore conclude that
>
> > A more satisfactory explanation [for overall group performance differences on the tests] is simply that the communities represented . . . maintain, for historical reasons, different norms, standards, and expectations concerning performance within the family, in school, and in other institutions that shape children's behavior. Young people adapt to these norms and apply their talents and energies accordingly.
>
> If Bock and Moore are right, then we might expect that black infants who were adopted into *either* black or white middle-class homes would have significantly higher intelligence test scores than would black infants reared by their natural parents in deprived circumstances. And as Sandra Scarr and Richard Weinberg report in this article, that indeed turns out to be the case.
>
> There are at least two important conclusions we can draw from this article: First, intelligence test scores are strongly influenced by environmental factors. And second, children who are given intellectual stimulation early in life do better in school than do children reared in unstimulating circumstances. We do not as yet know how much we can "boost IQ and raise academic performance" by improving a child's early environment. And doubtless certain aspects of what we call "intelligence" are affected by inheritance. However, the scientific data simply do not support Jensen's conclusion that one ethnic or racial group is "genetically superior" to any other ethnic or racial group.

ABSTRACT: The poor performance of black children on IQ tests and in school has been hypothesized to arise from (a) genetic racial differences or (b) cultural environmental disadvantages. To separate genetic factors from rearing conditions, 130 black/interracial children adopted by advantaged white families were studied. The socially classified black adoptees, whose natural parents were educationally average, scored above the IQ and the school achievement mean of the white population. Biological children of the adoptive parents scored even higher. Genetic and environmental determinants of differences among the black/interracial adoptees were largely confounded. The high IQ scores of the socially classified black adoptees indicate malleability for IQ under rearing conditions that are relevant to the tests and the schools.

It is well known that black children reared by their own families achieve IQ scores that average about a **standard deviation** (15 points) below whites (Jensen, 1973; Loehlin, Lindzey, & Spuhler, 1975). This finding is at the heart of a continuing controversy in the educational arena. Recent studies (Cleary, Humphreys, Kendrick, & Wesman, 1975) confirm the hypothesis that low IQ scores predict poor school performance, regardless of race. Thus, more black children than white children fail to achieve academically and to earn the credentials required by higher occupational status, with its concomitant social prestige and economic security (Husen, 1974; Jencks, 1972).

In an attempt to remedy the alarming rate of school failure, compensatory educational programs, which were directed particularly at black children, were introduced in the 1960s. At the same time, but for different reasons, a more intensive intervention began: the adoption of black children by white families. Whereas compensatory educational programs involve the child for a few hours per day, transracial adoption alters the entire social ecology of the child. Parents, siblings, home, peers, school, neighborhood, and community--the child's rearing environment--are transformed by adoption.

The existence of transracial families offers much to the scientific study of **social milieus** and intellectual performance (Grow & Shapiro, 1974; Loehlin et al., 1975). Transracial adoption is the human analog of the cross-fostering design, commonly used in animal behavior genetics research (e.g., Manosevitz, Lindzey, Thiessen, 1969). The study of transracial adoption can yield estimates of biological and **sociocultural** effects on the IQ test performance of cross-fostered children.

The results of a transracial or cross-fostering study require careful interpretation. Black children reared in white homes are socially labeled as black and therefore may suffer racial discrimination. Because of the unmeasured effects of racism, poor IQ test performance by black children in white homes cannot be uncritically interpreted as a result of genetic limitations. In addition, equal performance by black and other adoptees cannot be interpreted as an indication of the *same* range of reaction for all groups. Again, the unknown effects of racism may inhibit the intellectual development of the black adoptees. However, equally high IQs for black and other adoptees would imply that IQ performance is considerably malleable.

Upper-middle-class white families have an excellent reputation for rearing children who perform well on IQ tests and in school. When such families adopt white children, the adoptees have been found to score above average on IQ tests, but not as highly as the biological offspring of the same and similar families (Burks, 1928; Freeman, Holzinger, & Mitchell, 1928; Leahy, 1935; Munsinger, 1975b; Skodak & Skeels, 1949). How do the IQ test scores of black children adopted by white families compare to the scores of both white adoptees and the biological children of these parents?

If black children have genetically limited intellectual potential, as some have claimed (Jensen, 1973; Shockley, 1971, 1972), their IQ performance will fall below that of other children reared in white upper-middle-class homes. On the other hand, if black children have a range of reaction similar to other adoptees, their IQ scores should have a similar distribution. The concept, range of reaction, refers to the fact that **genotypes** do not usually specify a single **phenotype.** Rather, genotypes specify a range of phenotypic responses that the organism can make to a variety of environmental conditions.

This is an investigation of the IQ test performance of black and interracial black children adopted by white families in Minnesota. The present study is part of a larger investigation of the psychosocial functioning of transracial adoptive families. Intellectual, personality,

---

Standard deviation (dee-vee-A-shun). The standard deviation is a mathematical way of figuring out how much a test score deviates from the mean, median, or mode (usually the mean). The standard deviation thus gives you a precise way of measuring how significantly your own score on a test varies or departs from the norm.

Social milieus (mill-YEWS). Social environments, or social backgrounds.

Sociocultural (soh-see-oh-CULT-your-al). Most psychologists believe that intelligence is a product of two variables, what the person inherits from his or her genes ("nature") and what the person learns from her or his social milieu ("nurture.")

Genotypes (GEE-noh-types). The genetic characteristics of an organism such as innate skin color. Your children won't inherit your suntan, but they will inherit your basic skin color.

Phenotype (FEE-noh-types). The visible characteristics of an organism, such as a suntan or a broken bone, that are produced by interaction of the organism with

and attitudinal tests were administered to the parents and all children over the age of 4 years. Extensive interviews were conducted with the parents, and ratings of the home environment were made.

Minnesota has been in the forefront of interracial adoption. Although the black population of the state is small (.9% in 1970), there were too many black and interracial children available for adoption and too few black families to absorb them. Minority group children--black, American Indian, Korean, and Vietnamese--have consequently been adopted by white families in large numbers. Furthermore, in recent years, many nonwhite children have been adopted from other states.

The climate for interracial adoption changed dramatically in the late 1950s and early 1960s because of the efforts of public and private agencies and the pioneering white adoptive parents. Several agency and parent organizations were formed to promote the adoption of black and interracial black children. The most influential, continuing organization is the Open Door Society of Minnesota, formed in 1966 by adoptive parents of socially classified black children. The founding president of the Open Door Society is a leading columnist on one of the Minneapolis daily newspapers who frequently writes about his multiracial family. The intellectual and social climate of Minnesota is generally conducive to liberal and humanitarian movements such as interracial adoption.

GOALS OF THE STUDY

We posed five major questions in the study:

1. What is the estimated reaction range for IQ scores of black/interracial children reared in typical black environments or in white adoptive homes?

2. Do interracial children (with one black and one white parent) perform at higher levels on IQ tests than do children with two black parents; that is, does the degree of white ancestry affect IQ scores?

3. How do the IQ scores of socially classified black children reared in white homes compare to those of other adopted children and biological white children within the same families; that is, do different racial groups, when exposed to similar environments, have similar distributions of IQ scores?

4. How well do socially classified black children reared in white families perform in school?

5. How accurately can we predict the IQ test performance of adopted children from the educational characteristics of their natural parents, from the educational, intellectual, and other characteristics of their adoptive homes, and from their placement histories?

THE FAMILIES

The 101 participating families were recruited through the Newsletter of the Open Door Society and by letters from the State Department of Public Welfare Adoption Unit to families with black adopted children, 4 years of age and older, who were adopted throughout the state of Minnesota through Lutheran Social Service and Children's Home Society. These agencies have placed the majority of black and interracial children in the state. We were unable to ascertain how many transracial adoptive families learned about the study from the Newsletter, because the mailing list of about 300 includes agencies, social workers, and interested citizens. In addition, we do not know how many of these families were also contacted by the State Department of Public Welfare. The support of the Open Door Society was important, however, in affirming the legitimacy of the study.

The State Department of Public Welfare mailed 228 letters to tranracial adoptive families. In some cases a family received more than one letter if they had adopted more than one child. Table 1 describes the results of the

TABLE 1
Recruitment of Families

Method	n
Department of Public Welfare letters	
Not eligible to participate	46[a]
Unknown	
Letter undelivered	43
No response	41
Eligible	
Not participating	
In another study	3
Don't approve of study	2
Child appears white	3
Personal reasons	3
No reason given	3
Live too far away	10
Yes, but changed their minds	6
Participating	68
Total letters sent	228
Open Door Society	
Not eligible to participate	19[a]
Eligible	
Not participating	
Live too far away	4
Yes, but changed their minds	1
Participating	33
Total responses	57

[a]Most because their black children were under 4 years of age.

TABLE 2
Out-of-State Origins of the Adopted Children

Origin	n
Other adopted	
Korea	7
Vietnam	1
Canada (Indian)	5
Ecuador (Indian)	2
Black and interracial adopted	
Illinois	4
Iowa	1
Kentucky	9
Massachusettes	11
New York	3
North Dakota	1
Ohio	2
Texas	2
Utah	1
Washington	2
Wisconsin	16
White adopted	
Massachusettes	1
Total	68

mailing. Of the 136 families known to be eligible for participation in the study, 74% did participate.

The 101 participating families included 321 children 4 years of age or older: 145 biological children (81 males, 64 females) and 176 adopted children (101 males, 75 females), of whom 130 are socially classified as black and 25 as white. The remaining 21 included Asian, North American Indian, and Latin American Indian children.

All of the adopted children were unrelated to the adoptive parents. Adopted children reared in the same home were unrelated, with the exception of four sibling pairs and one triad adopted by the same families.

The sample of families live within a 150-mile radius of the Twin Cities (Minneapolis-St. Paul) metropolitan area. Although nearly all of the children were adopted in Minnesota, 68 were born outside of the state. Through interstate cooperation, the child placement agencies arranged for the adoption of many nonwhite children from other states. Table 2 gives the out-of-state origins of the sample.

PROCEDURES

Most of the information was obtained directly from members of the adoptive families. Some additional data on the natural parents and the children's preadoption history were obtained by State Department of Public Welfare personnel from the adoption records. Achievement and aptitude test scores were supplied by school districts for all of the school-aged children to whom such tests had been administered.

The IQ Assessment

Both parents and all children in the family over 4 years of age were administered an age-appropriate IQ test as part of an extensive battery of intellectual, personality, attitudinal, and demographic measures. Children under 4 years of age were excluded because IQ tests are less predictive of later IQ at younger ages. By 4, the correlation of IQ with adolescent scores is about .7. The tests were administered in the family home during two visits by a team of trained testers. The examiners were all graduate students who had completed at least a year-long course in **psychoeducational** assessment and who had participated in a training session on assessment for this study. Among the 21 examiners were 6 males and 15 females, including 2 blacks. Testers were assigned randomly to members of the family.

Both parents and all children 16 years of age and older were administered the **Wechsler Adult Intelligence Scale** (WAIS; Wechsler, 1955). Children between 8 and 15 were given the Wechsler Intelligence Scale for Children (WISC; Wechsler, 1949), and children between 4 and 7 were administered the **Stanford-Binet Intelligence Scale** Form L-M (Terman & Merrill, 1972).

All scoring of protocols and computations of IQ scores were done by a graduate student with extensive experience in administering and scoring IQ measures. This student had no contact with the families and with the examiners except to clarify questionable responses. In no case was the scorer aware of the child's race or adoptive status.

The Adoption Records

The Director of the Adoption Unit, State Department of Public Welfare, abstracted the following information from the records of the adopted children and their families:

Psychoeducational. Psychoeducational assessment is that which involves learning how to give tests for such psychological characteristics as *intelligence* that are important educational variables.
Wechsler Adult Intelligence Scale (WECKS-ler). Abbreviated WAIS. A popular intelligence test that is administered individually by asking questions to a subject, as opposed to a group test which is almost always a pen-and-paper test given to large numbers of people simultaneously.
Stanford-Binet Intelligence Scale (bee-nay). An early intelligence test which, like the WAIS, is individually administered. The Stanford-Binet was developed by Louis Terman at Stanford, and was based on the work of Alfred Binet, a Frenchman who developed the first real intelligence test.

TABLE 3
Demographic Characteristics of the Adoptive and Natural Parents

Characteristic	n	M	SD	Range
Income				
Adoptive	100	$15,000–17,500	$5,000	$5,000–<$35,000
Education				
Adoptive father	101	16.9	3.0	9–22
Adoptive mother	101	15.1	2.2	12–21
Natural father	46	12.1	2.0	8–17
Natural mother[a]	135	12.0	2.2	6–18
Age				
Adoptive fathers[b]	100	37.3	6.7	28–59
Adoptive mothers[b]	100	35.5	5.8	26–53
Natural fathers[c]	55	26.3	6.6	16–44
Natural mothers[c]	150	21.6	5.3	12–40

[a] If the 40 students are excluded, the mean is the same.
[b] Current.
[c] At birth of child.

1. The child: (a) birthdate; (b) number and dates of preadoption placements, unless the child was in the adoptive home at 2 months of age; (c) evaluation of the quality of preadoption placements, rated by the authors on a scale of 1 poor to 3 good; 4 = placement only in the adoptive home; (d) date of placement in adoptive home.

2. The natural parents: (a) age at birth of child; (b) educational level at birth of child as an estimate of intellectual functioning, since IQ scores were not available; (c) occupation of mother; (d) race.

The race of the two natural parents was used to classify their child's race. If a child had one or two black parents, he was considered socially black.

Family Demographics

As part of the interview portion of the testing session, each parent was asked his or her birthdate, last school grade completed, occupation and whether it was full time or part time, range of income, and date of marriage. Occupations were coded for prestige using the scale developed from the National Opinion Research Center (NORC) survey (Reiss, 1961).

The School Data

With parental consent, forms requesting recent aptitude and achievement test scores were mailed to the schools of all school-aged children participating in the study; 100% of the forms were returned. Because school districts use a variety of tests,[4] comparable scores were combined across tests. For aptitude tests, a total score was generated. For achievement tests, a vocabulary, a composite reading, and an arithmetic score were used.

RESULTS

Since the major focus of the study was to estimate the level of IQ performance of the black adoptees and to account for that performance level, the nature and quality of the children's adoptive experience were examined.

Family Characteristics

The adoptive families who participated in the study can be characterized as highly educated and above average in occupational status and income. Table 3 is a summary of selected demographic characteristics of the adoptive and natural parents.

The educational level of the adoptive parents exceeded that of the adopted children's natural parents by 4-5 years. The typical occupations of the adoptive fathers were clergyman, engineer, and teacher. Nearly half (46.5%) of the adoptive mothers were employed at least part time, typically as teachers, nurses, and secretaries. The mean educational level of the natural parents was high school graduation, which is close to the median for that age cohort of the general population. Actually, the black mothers had one year less education than the black females in their age group (25-44). Fathers of the early-adopted black children had slightly more. Table 4 shows the average educational level of the white mothers of interracial black children, the black mothers, and the black fathers, compared to local and regional norms. (Because there were only two white fathers of interracial children, they have been omitted from the table.) In contrast, the mean educational level of the adoptive parents was atypically high. Typical occupations of the natural mothers were office workers, nurse's aides, and students. Insufficient information was available on the occupations of the natural fathers.

TABLE 4
Educational Levels of the Natural Parents of Adopted Children, Compared to Their Populations

	Natural parents of the adopted children	Natural parents of the early-adopted children	North Central region	Minneapolis–St. Paul[a]
Black mothers	10.8	10.8	11.9	12.0
White mothers of interracial children	12.4	12.6	12.5	12.5
Black fathers	12.3	12.6	12.0	12.0

Note. Levels given in years.
[a] Men or women, aged 25-44 years.

TABLE 5
The Adopted Children

	All adopted (n = 176)	White (n = 25)	Black/interracial (n = 130)	Asian/Indian (n = 21)
Preadoption				
Number of placements[a]				
M	1.06	.77	1.02	1.57
SD	1.04	1.24	.93	1.12
Range	0-6	0-4	0-6	0-4
Quality of placements[a,b]				
M	3.17	3.46	3.18	2.50
SD	.63	.84	.50	.73
Range	1-4	1-4	2-4	1-4
Adoptive placement				
Age of placement[c]				
M	22.48	19.04	17.97	60.71
SD	34.20	32.80	24.70	56.90
Range	0-189	0-94	0-124	1-189
Time in adoptive home[c]				
M	64.70	104.20	57.25	63.81
SD	33.50	39.30	25.50	38.20
Range	8-199	22-187	8-199	9-137
Current age[c]				
M	87.18	123.24	74.22	124.52
SD	40.80	48.00	29.60	44.40
Range	48-257	69-257	48-201	52-218

[a] Information available for 156 children: 22 white; 120 black/interracial; 14 Asian/Indian
[b] Quality of placement was rated 1=poor to 3=good; 4=placed when less than 2 months old.
[c] In months.

Preadoptive Experience

Table 5 includes two measures of the children's preadoptive placements: number and quality. The information is presented for all adoptees and by race.

Forty-four children were placed in their adoptive homes by 2 months of age and were considered to have had no previous placements. The remaining adopted children had from one to six previous placements. Black children had a smaller number of preadoption placements, and the quality of their placements was better than that of the Asian/Indian adoptees. Fewer black children were in institutions or were removed from homes for neglect or abuse, and more were in agency foster homes.

Only 18 of the 176 adopted children had ever lived with their biological parents: 7 of the Asian/Indian adoptees, for an average of 85 months; 3 of the white children, for an average of 28 months; and 8 of the black children, for an average of 36 months.

The Adoptive Experience

As shown in Table 5, the average age of placement in the adoptive homes was 22 months, but the median age of placement was 6 months. One hundred and eleven children, including 99 black and interracial adoptees, were placed in their adoptive homes during the first year of life. The Asian and Indian children were placed significantly later than either white or black children. The socially classified black children, however, had lived with their adoptive families for fewer years than the others, particularly than the white adoptees. Also shown in Table 5, black and interracial children were currently younger, on the average, than the others.

TABLE 6
WAIS IQ Scores of Adoptive Parents

	Mother				Father			
WAIS	n	M	SD	Range	n	M	SD	Range
Verbal	100	118.3	10.4	92-144	99	120.7	10.6	92-140
Performance	99	115.9	11.4	86-143	99	118.2	10.9	91-149
Full Scale	99	118.2	10.1	96-143	99	120.8	10.0	93-140

IQ Scores of Adoptive Parents

As indicated in Table 6, the mean WAIS IQ scores of the adoptive parents were in the high average to superior range of intellectual functioning. The distribution of scores extends from the low average to the very superior, with considerable restriction of range. The scores were congruent with the very high educational level of the group.

IQ Scores of the Natural Children of the Adoptive Parents

The mean IQ scores of the natural children of the adoptive families were in the high average to superior range of intellectual functioning. As expected from **polygenic theory**, when both parents have high IQ scores, there is less regression toward the population mean than under conditions of random mating. Table 7 gives the Stanford-Binet, WISC, and WAIS results for the natural children. Only the Wechsler scores had a restricted range. With tests combined, the total IQ score of the natural children averaged 116.7 with a standard deviation of 14.0.

Polygenic theory (POL-ee-JEN-ick). *Polygenic* means "determined by many genes." Some traits, such as eye color, are determined by a single gene. Other traits, such as intelligence, seem so complex that most scientists theorized that they are determined by a set or group of related genes.

TABLE 7
IQ Scores of the Natural Children of the Adoptive Parents

| | Total |||| Males |||| Females ||||
Scale	n	M	SD	Range	n	M	SD	Range	n	M	SD	Range
Stanford-Binet	48	113.8	16.7	81–148	26	111.6	16.5	81–148	22	116.3	16.9	88–140
WISC												
Verbal	82	113.5	13.1	84–147	50	114.0	12.8	89–147	32	112.8	13.6	84–144
Performance	82	119.5	14.9	68–147	50	120.5	12.5	82–143	32	117.8	18.1	68–147
Full Scale	82	117.9	12.7	87–150	50	118.5	10.8	96–145	32	117.0	15.3	87–150
WAIS												
Verbal	14	117.5	11.0	100–139	5	121.6	13.9	103–139	9	115.2	9.2	100–125
Performance	14	117.7	10.8	103–137	5	121.8	14.6	104–137	9	115.4	8.1	103–125
Full Scale	14	118.9	11.2	101–141	5	123.0	14.9	104–141	9	116.6	8.6	101–126

Note. WISC= Wechsler Intelligence Scale for Children. WAIS= Wechsler Adult Intelligence Scale.

The IQ Scores of Adopted Children

The mean IQ scores of the adopted children were in the average range. As shown in Table 8, the scores on the three IQ tests, although for children at different age levels, were highly comparable. The adopted children did not perform as well as either the adoptive parents or their biological children.

For all of the groups of children, the Stanford-Binet (1972 norms) yielded a slightly lower mean score than did the WISC or WAIS. Had the 1960 Stanford-Binet norms been used, the average IQ scores of the children would have been 7 points higher.

IQ Scores of Adopted Children by Race

Although adopted children of various ages were administered different tests, their performance was sufficiently comparable that we could combine the IQ scores across the three tests. Table 9 gives the mean IQ scores by race.

Although all groups had comparable ranges and were performing within the average range of intellectual functioning, the black and interracial children scored, on the average, between the white and Asian/Indian adopted groups. The scores of the socially classified black and white groups were significantly above the mean of the general population. The Asian/Indian adopted children scored exactly at the population mean. The means of the three groups of adopted children differ significantly ($p < .005$). The children adopted during the first year of life scored higher than those adopted after the first year. The average score for the 111 early-adopted group was an IQ of 111; for the 65 later adoptees, the mean IQ score was 97.5.

For those who hypothesize that blacks have lower IQ scores than whites because of their African ancestry, we compared socially classified black children with one versus two black natural parents. On the average,

TABLE 8
IQ Scores of Adopted Children

| | Total |||| Males |||| Females ||||
Scale	n	M	SD	Range	n	M	SD	Range	n	M	SD	Range
Stanford-Binet	122	106.5	13.9	68–144	69	107.1	12.6	80–144	53	105.6	15.5	68–136
WISC												
Verbal	48	101.2	15.6	66–142	30	101.9	14.4	71–139	18	100.2	17.9	66–142
Performance	48	109.7	17.7	62–143	30	111.0	18.3	62–143	18	107.5	17.0	80–142
Full Scale	48	105.8	16.1	64–140	30	106.9	15.8	64–140	18	104.1	16.8	80–133
WAIS												
Verbal	6	98.3	7.0	86–107	3	95.3	8.7	86–107	3	101.3	2.1	99–103
Performance	6	113.5	6.5	107–119	3	113.0	4.9	107–119	3	114.0	9.5	108–125
Full Scale	6	105.2	6.3	94–113	3	102.7	7.8	94–113	3	107.7	2.9	106–111

Note. WISC= Wechsler Intelligence Scale for Children. WAIS= Wechsler Adult Intelligence Scale.

TABLE 9
IQ Scores for Adopted Children by Race, with Tests Combined

Children	n	M	SD	Range
All adopted				
Black and interracial	130	106.3	13.9	68–144
White	25	111.5	16.1	62–143
Asian/Indian	21	99.9	13.3	66–129
Early-adopted				
Black and interracial	99	110.4	11.2	86–136
White	9	116.8	13.4	99–138
Asian/Indian[a]				

[a] Only 3 cases.

children with two black parents have a higher degree of African ancestry than those with one black and one white parent. Table 10 compares the IQ scores, placement histories, and natural-parent education of children with one or two black parents. Socially classified black children with one parent of unknown, Asian, Indian, or other racial background have been eliminated from this analysis.

The 29 children with two black parents achieved a mean IQ score of 96.8. The 68 with only one black parent scored on the average 109.0. It is essential to note, however, that the groups also differed significantly ($p < .05$) in their placement histories and natural mother's education. Children with two black parents were significantly older at adoption, had been in the adoptive home a shorter time, and had experienced a greater number of preadoption placements. The natural parents of the black/black group also averaged a year less of education than those of the black/white group, which suggests an average difference between the groups in intellectual ability. There were also significant differences between the adoptive families of black/black and black/white children in father's education and mother's IQ. One can see in Table 10 that the children with two black parents had poorer histories and had natural and adoptive parents with lower educational levels and abilities. It will be shown in the section on IQ variance that these characteristics largely account for the IQ differences between black children with one or two black parents.

Expectancy Effect

It is possible, though not likely, that the adoptive parents' belief about the child's racial background could influence the child's intellectual development. If parents expected interracial children to score higher than children with two black parents, there could be an expectancy effect. Twelve interracial children were believed by their adoptive parents to be black/black. Only two black/black children were believed to be interracial, and they have been omitted from the analysis.

Interracial children believed to be the offspring of two black parents scored on the average at the same level as interracial children correctly classified by their adoptive parents. The mean IQ score of 43 correctly identified interracial children was 108.4 ($SD = 12.6$). The average IQ score of 12 interracial children believed to be black/black was 108.6 ($SD = 10.2$). There was no evidence for an expectancy effect.

The Criticism of Self-Selection

Self-selection has been used to criticize the above-average IQ scores obtained in other adoption studies.

TABLE 10
Comparison of Adopted Children with One or Two Black Natural Parents

Variable	Black/black n	M	SD	Range	Black/white[a] n	M	SD	Range
IQ	29	96.8	12.8	80–130	68	109.0	11.5	86–136
Age at adoption[b]	29	32.3	33.1	1–124	68	8.9	11.2	0–52
Time in home[b]	29	42.2	14.3	8–120	68	60.6	17.4	33–199
Quality of placement	27	2.9	.4	2–4	64	3.3	.5	3–4
Number of placements	27	1.2	.7	0–3	64	.8	.9	0–6
Natural mother's education	22	10.9	1.9	6–14	66	12.4	1.8	7–18
Natural father's education	15	12.1	1.4	10–16	20	12.5	2.2	8–17
Adoptive father's education	29	16.5	2.7	12–21	68	17.2	2.8	12–21
Adoptive mother's education	29	14.9	2.3	12–20	68	15.3	2.0	11–20
Adoptive father's IQ	29	119.5	10.3	106–137	66	121.4	10.1	93–140
Adoptive mother's IQ	28	116.4	7.5	100–129	68	119.2	10.5	96–143

[a] 66 black fathers, 2 black mothers.
[b] In months.

TABLE 11
School Achievement Test Scores of Black/Interracial Adopted and Natural Children: Mean National Percentiles

Test	M %ile	SD	n
Black adoptees			
Vocabulary	57.2	29.1	20
Reading	55.0	28.6	24
Mathematics	55.2	29.9	19
Aptitude (IQ)	108.8	5.9	5
Natural children			
Vocabulary	73.1	11.7	48
Reading	74.5	25.8	77
Mathematics	71.3	22.6	69
Aptitude (IQ)	119.6	11.7	39

Munsinger (1975a) noted that obviously retarded and damaged infants are not likely to be adopted, a fact which raises the mean IQ of adoptees above the population average. This bias is slight, however: If all infants with eventual IQ scores of less than 60 (at most 3% of children) were eliminated from the adoption pool, the mean IQ of adoptees would be raised by only 1 IQ point.

Another bias could be the self-selection of families whose children appear normal in intelligence and school work. The range of IQ scores in this study **contraindicates** a strong bias in this regard, because 15 of the 176 adopted children have IQ scores of 85 and below. Furthermore, since 74% of those families known to be eligible did participate and the average IQ of all adoptees was 106, the average IQ of children in the 26% of the families who did not participate would have to be unreasonably low to explain mean results. If we consider the sample to be composed entirely of interracial children, with white adoptees offsetting those with two black parents, their average IQ should fall between those of black and white children in the region.

To lower the average adoptee's IQ to a hypothetical average of 95 for interracial children, the nonparticipants would have to have IQ scores that average 64, or in the retarded range. This is highly unlikely for any sample of adopted children.

School Achievement

The IQ assessments of the present study should bear a meaningful relationship to school achievement. Slightly above average IQ test performance should predict to slightly above average school achievement. The school data are also important because they come from many different school districts and are uncon-

TABLE 12
Correlations of Natural Parent Characteristics, Child's Adoptive Experience, Adoptive Family Characteristics, and Child's IQ Scores for Black/Interracial Children

	1	2	3	4	5	6	7	8	9	10	11	12	13
Natural parent characteristics													
1. Natural mother's race (117)													
2. Natural mother's education (107)[a]	−.36												
3. Natural father's education (37)	−.19	.27											
Adoptive experience													
4. Age at placement (130)	.36	−.34	−.27										
5. Time in home (130)	−.45	.27	.37	−.31									
6. Number of placements (112)	.22	−.17	−.31	.50	−.21								
7. Quality of placements (112)	−.30	.26	.17	−.37	.15	−.65							
Adoptive family characteristics													
8. Adoptive mother's education (130)	−.10	.22	.12	−.10	.12	−.13	.02						
9. Adoptive father's education (130)	−.13	.26	.25	−.27	.26	−.14	.04	.56					
10. Adoptive father's occupation (129)	.01	.07	.04	.00	.09	.01	−.05	.31	.29				
11. Family income (129)	.08	.16	−.06	.16	.12	−.04	−.06	.31	.04	.45			
12. Adoptive father's IQ (127)	−.01	.12	.33	−.19	.06	−.33	.08	.26	.47	.18	−.07		
13. Adoptive mother's IQ (128)	−.18	.09	.29	−.01	.26	−.05	−.05	.53	.30	.21	.27	.21	
Child's IQ													
14. Black adoptees (130)	−.41	.31	.45	−.36	.30	−.36	.38	.22	.34	−.01	−.00	.18	.17

Note. Total N=130. Numbers in parentheses are ns.
[a] Students included.

taminated by any biases that may have inadvertently influenced testing in our study. Most importantly, they represent a "real-life" criterion of intellectual achievement.

Table 11 gives the mean national percentile scores for vocabulary, reading, and mathematics achievement, and a total aptitude score expressed in IQ form, for the socially classified black adopted and natural children of the adoptive families. Although the sample sizes were rather small, the black children in school were performing slightly above the national norms on standard scholastic achievement tests, just as their IQ scores would predict. The average IQ of the children with achievement test scores was 104.9. The mean aptitude scores of the 5 black adoptees who had been given school-administered group IQ tests were quite close to their average scores on the WISC and Stanford-Binet. The correlation between aptitude and individual IQ scores could not be calculated because of small sample size.

The natural children of the adoptive parents scored higher than the adopted children on scholastic achievement tests, as predicted by their individual IQ test scores. Furthermore, their group-tested IQ performance was also very close to their average IQ as assessed in this study with individual tests. The correlation between the individual and group test scores of the 39 natural children was 78 ($p < .001$).

SOURCES OF VARIANCE IN BLACK ADOPTEES' IQ SCORES

The possible effects of the adoptive experience and of natural and adoptive family variables on IQ scores were explored in correlational and regression analyses. To account both for the differences between black/black and black/white children and for the above-average performance of the black adopted children on the IQ tests, we intercorrelated their natural parents' education, natural mother's race, their adoptive experience, adoptive family characteristics, and IQ scores. We were particularly concerned about the confounding of racial variables with preadoptive and adoptive family variables that could affect the children's IQ performance. Selective placement of the children of better educated (presumably brighter) natural mothers with better educated adoptive families--a situation that creates genotype-environment correlations--also needed to be examined. The correlation matrix is presented in Table 12.[5]

Natural Parents and the Child's Adoptive Experience

The educational and racial characteristics of the natural mothers of the adopted children had a great deal to do with when and by whom the children were adopted. Less well educated mothers, who were more often black, had children who were placed later for adoption, had spent less time in the adoptive homes, and were adopted by families with lower educational and income levels. The same pattern held for natural fathers' education. (Since all but two of the known natural fathers were black, father's race was omitted from the analysis.)

The black children's IQ scores were significantly correlated with the same placement and adoptive family variables. Children who were adopted earlier, who had spent more years in the adoptive homes, who had fewer preadoptive placements, and who had better quality placements had higher IQ scores. In addition, adopted black and interracial children who had better educated and higher-IQ adoptive parents had higher IQs. Thus, there was an important confounding of the characteristics of the natural parents, the preadoption experience, and the adoptive family, all of which affected the level of the black/interracial children's intellectual functioning.

Selective Placement

Selective placement further confuses the sources of variance in the black children's intellectual functioning. As Table 12 indicates, the natural mother's educational level is correlated with the adoptive parents' educational level, between .22 and .26, suggesting that the adoption agencies practiced selective placement, based on the educational information they had available. The correlations of natural mother's education and adoptive parents' IQ scores are not as high (.09 and .12), presumably because the agencies did not have the IQ data available. Selective placement increases the similarity between natural parents and their (adopted) children and between the adoptive family and their adopted children.

The biological and social factors, many of which separately and together can affect IQ scores, were largely confounded in the sample of black and interracial adoptees. Therefore, we did not attempt to estimate point values for the genetic and environmental

---

Contraindicates (KON-trah-IN-dih-kates). To *contraindicate* something is to make it "inadvisable."

TABLE 13

Two-Step Multiple Regression of Biological and Adoptive Family Variables on the IQ Scores of Black/Interracial Children, Adoptive Variables First

Step	Multiple R	R^2	R^2 change	Simple r	p <
1. Social variables					
Adoptive mother's education	.22	.05	.05	.22	.001
Quality of placements	.44	.19	.14	.38	
Adoptive father's IQ	.45	.20	.01	.18	
Adoptive father's occupation	.46	.21	.00	-.01	
Family income	.46	.21	.00	-.00	
Adoptive mother's IQ	.46	.21	.01	.17	
Age at placement	.53	.28	.07	-.36	
Adoptive father's education	.56	.31	.03	.34	
Number of placements	.56	.31	.00	-.36	
Time in home	.56	.31	.00	.30	
2. Biological variables					
Natural mother's education[a]	.57	.32	.01	.31	.001
Natural mother's race	.59	.35	.03	-.41	

[a]Students included; natural mother's education entered first to leave residual variance for race.

contributions to IQ differences. Instead, we decided to present two regression analyses.

When the *biological* variables were put into the regression first, we could find out how much of the remaining variance would be accounted for by the social variables. When the *social* variables were put into the regression equation first, we could determine how much of the remaining variance would be determined by the biological variables. Tables 13 and 14 present the two regression analyses (see Footnote 4).

In Table 13, the social variables, including placement and adoptive family measures, were stepped in first. The natural family data, called biological variables, were entered second into the regression equation. In Table 14, the biological variables were entered first, the social variables second. Both steps were statistically significant in both tables.

When the social variables were entered first, they accounted for 31% of the total variance in the IQ scores of socially classified black adopted children. The biological variables added 4% of the variance without natural father's education and 11% with father's education. (Because the sample of black children with natural father information was small, $n = 37$, a separate regression including only those children was done. The results for the other variables were very similar, and father's education accounted for an additional 7% of the total IQ variance.)

When the biological variables were entered into the regression analysis first, natural mother's education and race accounted for 20% of the variance in the black children's IQ scores. (Natural father's education added 11%, but the sample size was too small to include in the full analysis.) The social variables, stepped in second, added 15% of the IQ variance.

It is impossible to distinguish the effects of the separate social and biological variables, because 24.5 of the 35% of the variance accounted for was shared by the so-called biological and social variables. Using part correlations, we found that natural mother's race and adopted father's education each contributed 3% to the variance of the socially classified black adoptee's IQ scores, and the quality of the children's preadoptive placements contributed 2%. The remaining 1.4% of the unique variance was contributed almost equally by the other "biological" and "social" variables.

In the case of natural mother's race, it is unwarranted to conclude that race stands solely for genetic differences between the races. In this sample, natural mother's race was correlated with many measured social variables; it is conceivably correlated with other *unmeasured* social variables. Race does make a small contribution to the socially classified black children's IQ variance, independent of the other measures, but not necessarily independent of other environmental variables.

Another consideration in the interpretation of the regression analyses is the restricted range of variation in adoptive family characteristics. Parental education, IQ scores, income, occupational status, and other un-

TABLE 14

Two-Step Multiple Regression of Biological and Adoptive Family Variables on the IQ Scores of Black/Interracial Children, Biological Variables First

Step	Multiple R^2	R^2	R^2 change	Simple r	p<
1. Biological variables					
Natural mother's education[a]	.31	.09	.09	.31	.001
Natural mother's race	.44	.20	.10	-.41	
2. Social variables					
Adoptive father's occupation	.44	.20	.00	-.01	.001
Adoptive father's IQ	.47	.22	.03	.18	
Adoptive mother's IQ	.48	.23	.01	.17	
Quality of placements	.54	.29	.06	.38	
Adoptive father's education	.58	.34	.05	.34	
Family income	.58	.34	.00	-.00	
Adoptive mother's education	.58	.34	.00	.22	
Number of placements	.59	.35	.01	-.36	
Age at placement	.59	.35	.00	-.36	
Time in home	.59	.35	.00	.30	

[a]Students included; natural mother's education entered first to leave residual variance for race.

measured family variables, such as child-rearing practices, varied over half or less of their normal range in the general population. Thus, the adoptive family variables accounted for less of the IQ variance among black and interracial adoptees than they would in a more varied adoptive population. The importance of the social variables is very likely to be underestimated.

DISCUSSION

This study attempted to answer five questions about the impact of transracial adoption on the IQ performance of black and interracial children adopted into white homes. The first question focused on the reaction range of IQ scores within the black population. Would socially classified black children reared in economically advantaged white homes score above those reared in black environments?

The average IQ score of black and interracial children, adopted by advantaged white families, was found to be 106. Early-adopted black and interracial children performed at an even higher level. This mean represents an increase of 1 standard deviation above the average IQ of 90 usually achieved by black children reared in their own homes in the North Central region (Kaufman & Doppelt, in press). Furthermore, in the Minneapolis public school district, the average performance of 4th-grade children on the Gates-MacGinitee vocabulary test at a school with 87% black and interracial enrollment in 1973 was about the 21st national percentile, which translates to an IQ equivalent of about 90.

Since 68 of the 130 black children were known to have one white parent and only 29 were known to have had two black parents (the remainder were of other mixed or unknown parentage), it may seem misleading to compare the adoptees to black children in the general population. Even if all of the black children were interracial offspring, however, a strong genetic hypothesis should not predict that they would score well above the white population average. Nor should they score as highly as white adoptees. In fact, the black and interracial children of this sample scored as highly on IQ tests as did white adoptees in previous studies with large samples (Burks, 1928; Leahy, 1935).

In other words, the range of reaction of socially classified black children's IQ scores from average (black) to advantaged (white) environments is at least 1 standard deviation. Conservatively, if we consider only the adopted children with two black parents (and late and less favorable adoptive experiences), the IQ reaction range is at least 10 points between these environments. If we consider the early-adopted group, the IQ range may be as large as 20 points. The level of school achievements among the black and interracial adoptees is further evidence of their above-average performance on standard intellectual measures.

The dramatic increase in the IQ mean and the additional finding that placement and adoptive family characteristics account for a major portion of the IQ differences among the socially classified black children strongly suggest that the IQ scores of these children are environmentally malleable.

One reason for the substantial increase in test performance of the black and interracial adoptees is that their rearing environments are culturally relevant to the tests and to the school. Amid the IQ controversy, some have argued that standardized measures are inappropriate for children whose cultural background is different from that of the tests. While the rejection of IQ tests as predictors of academic success, on the basis of their cultural bias, is untenable (Jensen, 1974), we believe that the tests and the schools share a common culture to which black children are not as fully acculturated as are white children. However, the socially classified black children in this study have been fully exposed to the culture of the tests and the school, although they are still socially defined as black.

IQ Comparisons Within the Black Group

The second question concerned a comparison of the IQ scores of children whose parents were both black with black children of interracial parentage. The interracial children scored about 12 points higher than those with two black parents, but this difference was associated with large differences in maternal education and preplacement history. The part correlations suggested that variation in the race of mothers accounted for 3% of the children's IQ variance, but even this percentage of variance probably includes some additional and unmeasured environmental differences between the groups.

For example, black mothers are known to be at greater risk than white mothers for nutritional deficiencies, maternal death, infant mortality, and other reproductive casualties (Scarr-Salapatek & Williams, 1973). The prematurity rate among black mothers is more than double that of whites. These **antenatal** risks are often found to be associated with long-term developmental problems among the children. The interracial children, all but two of whom have white mothers, were less likely to have suffered any of these problems.

Comparisons of Black/Interracial, Asian/Indian, and Natural Children of the Adoptive Families

The third question asked for comparisons among the IQ scores of black/interracial, Asian/Indian adoptees, and the biological children of the adoptive families. There were significant differences in IQ scores among the groups. The socially classified black children scored on the average between the white and Asian/Indian adoptees, but these results were confounded with placement variables. Among the early adoptees, there were too few white and Asian/Indian children to make meaningful comparisons. The black/interracial early adoptees, however, performed at IQ 110, on the average.

Compared to adopted children in previous studies, the average IQ of 110 for the 99 early-adopted black/interracial children compares well with the 112.6 reported by Leahy (1935, p. 285) for white adoptees in professional families.

The above-average IQ level of adopted children, reported in all adoption studies, reflects both their better-than-average environments and the elimination of severely retarded children from the pool of potential adoptees. Although Munsinger's (1975a) review concluded that adoptive family environments have little or no impact on the intellectual development of adoptees, past studies have not adequately tested this hypothesis. Because children who are selected for adoption are not grossly defective, their predicted IQ level is slightly above that of the general population. In this study, however, the adopted *black/interracial* children could not have been predicted to have average IQ scores above the mean of the *white* population unless adoptive family environments have considerable impact.

The biological children of the adoptive families scored above the average of the black/interracial early adoptees. Not only have the biological children been in their families since birth, but their natural parents are considerably brighter than those of the adopted children, regardless of race.

School Achievement

A fourth question focused on the school achievement of the black/interracial adoptees and the biological children in the adoptive families. Black/interracial adoptees were found to score slightly above average on school-administered achievement and aptitude tests, as predicted by their IQ scores. The natural children of the adoptive families scored higher than the socially classified black adoptees on school achievement measures, a finding which is congruent with their higher IQ scores. The school achievement data provided validation for our IQ assessment.

Genetic and Environmental Sources of IQ Variance

The final question posed by the study dealt with the relative contributions of biological and social environmental measures to IQ differences among the socially classified black children. The placement variables, adoptive family characteristics, and genetic background all contributed to the IQ differences among the black/interracial adoptees. Because the social and biological variables were confounded, it is very difficult to make a clear comparison. Although this study has an unusual sample of children, we propose that genetic and social variables are usually confounded in families. Indeed, we suspect that genotype-environment correlations are the rule and that they account for a sizable portion of the IQ variance in the general population.

In making any comparison between biological and social variables, we must be concerned about the quality of those measures. Although the adoptive family variables are only indices of the qualities of the environment that have an impact on children, the natural parent data are even more limited. It would have been advantageous to have comparable IQ scores for the natural parents, rather than educational levels, although the latter correlate about .7 with IQ in the general population (Jencks, 1972).

Because the social variables accounted for a substantial portion of the IQ variance among black/interracial adoptees, it is likely that IQ performance is malleable within the range of existing environments. If all black chilren had environments such as those provided by the adoptive families in this study, we would predict that their IQ scores would be 10-20 points higher than the scores are under current rearing conditions.

Social Implications of the Study

Given the above-average IQ scores of black/interracial children adopted transracially, it may seem that we are endorsing the adoption of black children by white families as a social policy. There is no question that adoption constitutes a massive intervention, as noted earlier, and that it has a favorable impact on IQ scores. However, there is good reason why transracial adoption is not a **panacea** for low IQ scores among black children. Only an infinitesimally small proportion of black children will ever be available for adoption, and of those, many will and *should be* adopted by black families.

What we do endorse is that *if* higher IQ scores are considered important for educational and occupational success, then there is need for social action that will provide black children with home environments that facilitate the acquisition of intellectual skills tapped by IQ measures. Although there has been some research describing the immediate environments of middle-, working-, and lower-class homes (Hess & Shipman, 1965; Kohn, 1959; White & Watts, 1973), there is still a need to investigate how families, such as these transracial adoptive families, constitute an ecological system in which IQ skills are developed. The physical environment, the amount and quality of parent-child interaction, the parents' attitudes and practices in child rearing, the neighborhood and community settings of the family, and the larger social contexts of employment, economic security, and cultural values must all be considered in describing the parameters of family effects.

Educational interventions alone are unlikely to have the effects reported here for adoption. Schools, as presently constituted, cannot have the far-reaching, intensive impact of the family and home.

Our emphasis on IQ scores in this study is not an endorsement of IQ as the ultimate human value. Although important for functioning in middle-class educational environments, IQ tests do not sample a huge spectrum of human characteristics that are requisite for social adjustment. Empathy, sociability, and altruism, to name a few, are important human attributes that are not guaranteed by a high IQ. Furthermore, successful adaptation within ethnic subgroups may be less dependent on the intellectual skills tapped by IQ measures than is adaptation in middle-class white settings.

This study was not designed to address the social issues we have just highlighted. Rather, it was intended to examine the effects of cross-fostering on the IQ scores of black/interracial children. The major questions of the study concerned the relative effects of genetic background and social environment on IQ levels and variations among socially classified black children. The major findings of the study support the view that the social environment plays a dominant role in determining the average IQ level of black children and that both social and genetic variables contribute to individual variation among them.

Antenatal (ANT-tee-NAY-tal). *Ante* means "before," while *natal* means "birth."
Panacea (pan-ah-SEE-ah). A *panacea* is a "cure all," or a "solution to everything."

FOOTNOTES

[1] Reprinted by permission of the authors and the publisher from the *American Psychologist*, 1976, *31*, 726-739. Copyright 1976 by the American Psychological Association.

[2] The present study was supported by the Grant Foundation and the National Institute of Child Health and Human Development (HD-08016). This study was conducted with the full collaboration of the Minnesota State Department of Public Welfare, Adoption Unit, directed by Ruth Weidell and assisted by Marjorie Flowers. Their help was invaluable. The additional support of the Open Door Society, Lutheran Social Service, and The Children's Home Society, all of Minnesota, facilitated the study. We are very grateful for the assistance of Louise Carter-Saltzman, Harold Grotevant, Margaret Getman, Marsha Sargrad, Patricia Webber, Joanne Bergman, William Thompson, and Carol Nelson.

[3] Bock, R. D., & Moore, E. G. J. (1986). *Advantage and disadvantage: A profile of American youth*. Hillsdale, NJ: Erlbaum.

[4] Eight aptitude and 11 achievement tests were used by the various school districts. A list is available from the authors.

[5] The age of the child and the race and sex of the examiner are omitted from the tables because they are uncorrelated with the children's IQ scores (rs = .01, .06, and .01, respectively). In the correlation and regression analyses (Tables 12-14), natural mothers who were students at the time of the child's birth were included. Of the 107 mothers of black children for whom we had educational data, 34 were students in high school or college. Since the mean educational level of the natural mothers, with and without the students, was the same and since the correlation of natural mother's education and child's IQ was higher when students were included, we decided to present the tables based on the larger ns.

REFERENCES

Burks, B. S. The relative influence of nature and nurture upon mental development; a comparative study of foster parent-foster child resemblance and true parent-true child resemblance. *Yearbook of the National Society for the Study of Education*, 1928, *27*, 219-316.

Cleary, T. A., Humphreys, L. G., Kendrick, S. A., & Wesman, A. Educational uses of tests with disadvantaged students. *American Psychologist*, 1975, *30*, 15-41.

Freeman, F. N., Holzinger, K. J., & Mitchell, B. C. The influence of environment on the intelligence, school achievement and conduct of foster children. *Yearbook of the National Society for the Study of Education*, 1928, *27*, 101-217.

Grow, L. J., & Shapiro, D. *Black children-white parents*. New York: Child Welfare League of America, 1974.

Hess, R. D., & Shipman, V. C. Early experience and the socialization of cognitive modes in children. *Child Development*, 1965, *36*, 869-886.

Husen, T. *Talent, equality, and meritocracy*. The Hague: Martinue Nijhoff, 1974.

Jencks, C. *Inequality: A reassessment of the effects of family and schooling in America*. New York: Basic Books, 1972.

Jensen, A. R. *Educability and group differences*. New York: Basic Books, 1973.

Jensen, A. R. How biased are culture-loaded tests? *Genetic Psychology Monographs*, 1974, *90*, 185-244.

Kaufman, A. S., & Doppelt, J. E. Analysis of WISC-R standardization data in terms of the stratification variables. *Child Development*, in press.

Kohn, M. L. Social class and the exercise of parental authority. *American Sociological Review*, 1959, *24*, 352-366.

Leahy, A. M. Nature-nurture and intelligence. *Genetic Psychology Monographs*, 1935, *17*, 237-307.

Loehlin, J., Lindzey, G., & Spuhler, J. N. *Race differences in intelligence*. San Francisco, Calif.: Freeman, 1975.

Manosevitz, M., Lindzey, G., & Thiessen, D. *Behavioral genetics: Method and research*. New York: Appleton-Century-Crofts, 1969.

Munsinger, H. The adopted child's IQ: A critical review. *Psychological Bulletin*, 1975, *82*, 623-659. (a)

Munsinger, H. Children's resemblance to their biological and adopting parents in two ethnic groups. *Behavior Genetics*, 1975, *5*, 239-254. (b)

Reiss, A. J., Jr. *Occupations and social status*. New York: Free Press, 1961.

Scarr-Salapatek, S., & Williams, M. L. The effects of early stimulation on low-birth-weight infants. *Child Development*, 1973, *44*, 94-101.

Shockley, W. Morals, mathematics, and the moral obligation to diagnose the origin of Negro IQ deficits. *Review of Educational Research*, 1971, *41*, 369-377.

Shockley, W. Dysgenics, geneticity, raciology: A challenge to the intellectual responsibility of educators. *Phi Delta Kappan*, 1972, *53*, 297-307).

Skodak, M., & Skeels, H. M. A final follow-up study of one hundred children. *The Journal of Genetic Psychology*, 1949, *75*, 85-125.

Terman, L. M., & Merrill, M. *Stanford-Binet Intelligence Scale*. Boston, Mass.: Houghton Mifflin, 1972.

Wechsler, D. *Wechsler Intelligence Scale for Children*. New York: Psychological Corporation, 1949.

Wechsler, D. *Wechsler Adult Intelligence Scale*. New York: Psychological Corporation, 1955.

White, B. L., & Watts, J. C. *Experience and environment*. Englewood Cliffs, N.J.: Prentice-Hall, 1973.

Classic Quotations from William James

Truth *happens* to an idea. It *becomes* true, is *made* true by events. Its verity is in fact an event, a process; the process namely of its verifying itself, its veri-*fication*. Its validity is the process of its valid-*ation*.
(Pragmatism [1907], Lecture 6.)

Real culture lives by sympathies and admirations, not by dislikes and disdains; under all misleading wrappings it pounces unerringly upon the human core.
(Memories and Studies [1911].)

CHAPTER 16

"Imitation of Film-Mediated Aggressive Models"

Albert Bandura, Dorothea Ross, and Sheila A. Ross[1,2,3]

EDITORS' COMMENTS. As we noted in our comments at the beginning of the article by Tolman and Honzik (Chapter 3), one of the longest-running battles in experimental psychology has been fought between the "pure" behaviorists (who believe that organisms merely respond to environmental stimuli in a "pre-programmed" manner), and the "cognitive" psychologists (who hold that most behavior is determined by *internal* variables and thus is the result of individual choice). As we mentioned earlier, the behaviorist viewpoint dominated psychology during the first part of this century, but by the 1960's, the cognitive position had come back into fashion again.

Always, of course, there were those scientists who stood somewhere in the middle of this battle royal, trying hard to *combine* some of the best elements of both extreme viewpoints. One such person is Albert Bandura who, aware of the weaknesses (as well as the strengths) of behaviorism and cognitive psychology, helped develop what is now called *social learning theory*. Behaviorists--such as E.L. Thorndike and B.F. Skinner--insisted that responses were learned because they were *directly reinforced*. Bandura wisely noted that people often learn by *observing the actions of others*. For example, if you see someone put a quarter in a slot machine and win $1,000, you are more likely to put a quarter in the machine yourself than if you hadn't witnessed the *consequences* of the other person's actions. You are also more likely to avoid making a response if you see someone else make that response and then get punished for doing so. Behaviorists have tremendous difficulty explaining this type of "observational learning," because your behaviors actually change *without direct reinforcement*. How can a new behavior be learned, the stimulus-response theorists asked, when the organism not only never responded itself, but also wasn't rewarded in any (non-cognitive) fashion? But many cognitively-oriented theorists were just as troubled because social learning theory emphasizes the *interaction* between the organism and its environment, while cognitive psychologists tend to view behavior as being primarily under the influence of such internal factors as "traits," "personality," "attitudes," and "thought patterns."

Bandura's position is *cognitive* because he assumes that you are capable of "thinking" about what you should do next, and then acting on your decisions. However, his social learning theory is also *behavioral* because he assumes you are guided by observing the *direct reinforcement* others receive as well as by the positive or negative feedback you personally receive.

Social learning theory is now one of the dominant positions within the field of psychology. The present paper helped bring the theory to prominence by demonstrating one of its central beliefs: Children do tend to imitate the actions of various models they encounter in their social environment. However, the article was important (and controversial) for other reasons, as well. To begin with, it offered evidence that children who watch violence in films (or on television) are more likely to engage in aggressive behaviors themselves. Needless to say, the entertainment industry was not exactly thrilled by Bandura's findings. But the article was also influential because it was an early attack on *trait theory*: There simply was little or no significant correlation between (1) the ratings the subjects' received on such traits as "aggressiveness" and (2) how the subjects actually behaved. As Bandura had predicted, it was the complex *interaction* among traits, social environment, and prior experience that determined how the subjects would respond.

Abstract. In a test of the hypothesis that exposure of children to film-mediated aggressive models would increase the probability of Ss' aggression to subsequent frustration, 1 group of experimental Ss observed real-life aggressive models, a 2nd observed these same models portraying aggression on film, while a 3rd group viewed a film depicting an aggressive cartoon character. Following the exposure treatment, Ss were mildly frustrated and tested for the amount of imitative and nonimitative aggression in a different experimental setting. The overall results provide evidence for both the facilitating and the modeling influence of film-mediated aggressive stimulation. In addition, the findings reveal that the effects of such exposure are to some extent a function of the sex of the model, sex of the child, and the reality cues of the model.

Most of the research on the possible effects of film-mediated stimulation upon subsequent aggressive behavior has focused primarily on the **drive reducing** function of fantasy. While the experimental evidence for the **catharsis** or drive reduction theory is **equivocal** (Albert, 1957; Berkowitz, 1962; Emery, 1959; Feshbach, 1955, 1958; Kenny, 1952; Lovaas, 1961; Siegel, 1956), the modeling influence of pictorial stimuli has received little research attention.

A recent incident (San Fransisco Chronicle, 1961) in which a boy was seriously knifed during a re-enactment of a switchblade knife fight the boys had seen the previous evening on a televised rerun of the James Dean movie, *Rebel Without a Cause,* is a dramatic illustration of the possible imitative influence of film stimulation. Indeed, **anecdotal** data suggest that portrayal of aggression through pictorial media may be more influential in shaping the form aggression will take when a person is instigated on later occasions, than in altering the level of instigation to aggression.

In an earlier experiment (Bandura & Huston, 1961), it was shown that children readily imitated aggressive behavior exhibited by a model in the presence of the model. A succeeding investigation (Bandura, Ross, & Ross, 1961), demonstrated that children exposed to aggressive models generalized aggressive responses to a new setting in which the model was absent. The present study sought to determine the extent to which film-mediated aggressive models may serve as an important source of imitative behavior.

Aggressive models can be ordered on a reality-fictional stimulus dimension with real-life models located at the reality end of the continuum, nonhuman cartoon characters at the fictional end, and films portraying human models occupying an intermediate position. It was predicted, on the basis of saliency and similarity of cues, that the more remote the model was from reality, the weaker would be the tendency for subjects to imitate the behavior of the model.

Of the various interpretations of imitative learning, the sensory feedback theory of imitation recently proposed by Mowrer (1960) is elaborated in greatest detail. According to this theory, if certain responses have been repeatedly positively reinforced, **proprioceptive** stimuli associated with these responses acquire secondary reinforcing properties and thus the individual is predisposed to perform the behavior for the positive feedback. Similarly, if responses have been **negatively reinforced**, response correlated stimuli acquire the capacity to arouse anxiety which, in turn, inhibit the occurrence of the **negatively valenced** behavior. On the basis of these considerations, it was predicted subjects who manifest high aggression anxiety would perform significantly less imitative and nonimitative aggression than subjects who display little anxiety over aggression. Since aggression is generally considered female inappropriate behavior, and therefore

---

Drive reducing. Many learning/motivation theorists believe that the onset of a "basic need," such as the need for food, creates a *drive state*, in this case, that of "hunger." Food is said to be "reinforcing" because it *reduces the hunger drive*. Some theorists also hold that *thinking about food* or having *fantasies about eating* can also reduce the hunger drive.

Catharsis (kah-THAR-sis). Freud believed that the body/mind built up libidinal (psychic) energy that had to be released in some fashion or another. Catharsis is the release of pent-up libidinal energy.

Equivocal (ee-QUIV-ih-kal). Debatable; not proven.

Anecdotal (an-eck-DOAT-al). An anecdote is a story, or a report given by someone who supposedly witnessed an event. As opposed to *empirical* data, which are gathered in a controlled fashion, as in a laboratory experiment.

Proprioceptive (proh-pee-oh-SEPP-tive). Internal stimuli; informational inputs arising from the muscles, glands, skin, organs, and so forth.

Negatively reinforced. To *reinforce* something means to "strengthen" it. When you *reinforce* a given response, you "strengthen" it or, to be more precise, you increase the probability that the response will occur again. There are two types of reinforcement, *positive* and *negative*. Both types *strengthen* responses. Positive reinforcement is associated with the *onset* of a "pleasurable" event, while negative reinforcement is associated with the *offset* of an "unpleasant" event. Food is both positively and negatively reinforcing: It tastes good (the onset of pleasure) and it reduces hunger (the offset of an unpleasant drive). *Punishment*, on the other hand, suppresses responding--which is to say that it temporarily reduces the probability that a response will occur again in the near future. Punishment is associated with the *onset* of an "unpleasant" event or the *offset* of a "pleasant" event. *Negative reinforcement is the exact opposite of punishment!* The authors misuse the term in this article, apparently thinking that negative reinforcement means the same thing as punishment, *which it does not,* and many other psychologists have (sadly enough) imitated this mistake. Since the *correct* definition of "negative reinforcement" is an item that often appears on the Graduate Record Exam, it would surely pay you to remember that *negative reinforcement is not punishment.*

Negatively valenced (VAY-lenced). As used by many social psychologists, the term *negatively valenced* refers to behavior that is inappropriate, antisocial, or likely to lead to punishment.

likely to be negatively reinforced in girls (Sears, Maccoby, & Levin, 1957), it was also predicted that male subjects would be more imitative of aggression than females.

To the extent that observation of adults displaying aggression conveys a certain degree of permissiveness for aggressive behavior, it may be assumed that such exposure not only facilitates the learning of new aggressive responses but also weakens competing inhibitory responses in subjects and thereby increases the probability of occurrence of previously learned patterns of aggression. It was predicted, therefore, that subjects who observed aggressive models would display significantly more aggression when subsequently frustrated than subjects who were equally frustrated but who had no prior exposure to models exhibiting aggression.

METHOD

Subjects

The subjects were 48 boys and 48 girls enrolled in the Stanford University Nursery School. They ranged in age from 35 to 69 months, with a mean age of 52 months.

Two adults, a male and a female, served in the role of models both in the real-life and the human film-aggression condition, and one female experimenter conducted the study for all 96 children.

General Procedure

Subjects were divided into three experimental groups and one control group of 24 subjects each. One group of experimental subjects observed real-life aggressive models, a second group observed these same models portraying aggression on film, while a third group viewed a film depicting an aggressive cartoon character. The experimental groups were further subdivided into male and female subjects so that half the subjects in the two conditions involving human models were exposed to same-sex models, while the remaining subjects viewed models of the opposite sex.

Following the exposure experience, subjects were tested for the amount of imitative and nonimitative aggression in a different experimental setting in the absence of the models.

The control group subjects had no exposure to the aggressive models and were tested only in the generalization situation.

Subjects in the experimental and control groups were matched individually on the basis of ratings of their aggressive behavior in social interactions in the nursery school. The experimenter and a nursery school teacher rated the subjects on four five-point rating scales which measured the extent to which subjects displayed physical aggression, verbal aggression, aggression toward inanimate objects, and aggression inhibition. The later scale, which dealt with the subjects' tendency to inhibit aggressive reactions in the face of high instigation, provided the measure of aggression anxiety. Seventy-one percent of the subjects were rated independently by both judges so as to permit an assessment of interrater agreement. The reliability of the composite aggression score, estimated by means of the Pearson product-moment correlation, was .80.

Data for subjects in the real-life aggression condition and in the control group were collected as part of a previous experiment (Bandura et al., 1961). Since the procedure is described in detail in the earlier report, only a brief description of it will be presented here.

Experimental Conditions

Subjects in the Real-Life Aggressive condition were brought individually by the experimenter to the experimental room and the model, who was in the hallway outside the room, was invited by the experimenter to come and join in the game. The subject was then escorted to one corner of the room and seated at a small table which contained potato prints, multicolor picture stickers, and colored paper. After demonstrating how the subject could design pictures with the materials provided, the experimenter escorted the model to the opposite corner of the room which contained a small table and chair, a tinker toy set, a mallet, and a 5-foot inflated Bobo doll. The experimenter explained that this was the model's play area and after the model was seated, the experimenter left the experimental room.

The model began the session by assembling the tinker toys but after approximately a minute had elapsed, the model turned to the Bobo doll and spent the remainder of the period aggressing toward it with highly novel responses which are unlikely to be performed by children independently of the observation of the model's behavior. Thus, in addition to punching the Bobo doll, the model exhibited the following distinctive aggressive acts which were to be scored as imitative responses:

The model sat on the Bobo doll and punched it repeatedly in the nose.

The model then raised the Bobo doll and **pommeled** it on the head with a mallet.

Following the mallet aggression, the model tossed the doll up in the air aggressively and kicked it about the room. This sequence of physically aggressive acts was repeated approximately three times interspersed with verbally aggressive responses such as, "Sock him in the nose...," "Hit him down ...," "Throw him in the air ...," "Kick him ...," and "Pow."

Subjects in the Human Film-Aggression condition were brought by the experimenter to the semidarkened experimental room, introduced to the picture materials, and informed that while the subjects worked on potato prints, a movie would be shown on a screen, positioned approximately 6 feet from the subject's table. The movie projector was located in a distant corner of the room and was screened from the subject's view by large wooden panels.

The color movie and a tape recording of the sound track was begun by a male projectionist as soon as the experimenter left the experimental room and was shown for a duration of

10 minutes. The models in the film presentation were the same adult males and females who participated in the Real-Life condition of the experiment. Similarly, the aggressive behavior they portrayed in the film was identical with their real-life performance.

For subjects in the Cartoon Film-Aggression condition, after seating the subject at the table with the picture construction material, the experimenter walked over to a television console approximately 3 feet in front of the subject's table, remarked, "I guess I'll turn on the color TV," and ostensibly tuned in a cartoon program. The experimenter then left the experimental room. The cartoon was shown on a glass lens screen in the television set by means of a rear projection arrangement screened from the subject's view by large panels.

The sequence of aggressive acts in the cartoon was performed by the female model costumed as a black cat similar to the many cartoon cats. In order to heighten the level of irreality of the cartoon, the floor area was covered with artificial grass and the walls forming the backdrop were adorned with brightly colored trees, birds, and butterflies creating a fantasyland setting. The cartoon began with a close-up of a stage on which the curtains were slowly drawn revealing a picture of a cartoon cat along with the title, *Herman the Cat*. The remainder of the film showed the cat pommeling the Bobo doll on the head with a mallet, sitting on the doll and punching it in the nose, tossing the doll in the air, and kicking it about the room in a manner identical with the performance in the other experimental conditions except that the cat's movements were characteristically feline. To induce further a cartoon set, the program was introduced and concluded with appropriate cartoon music, and the cat's verbal aggression was repeated in a high-pitched, animated voice.

In both film conditions, at the conclusion of the movie the experimenter entered the room and then escorted the subject to the test room.

Aggression Instigation

In order to differentiate clearly the exposure and test situations subjects were tested for the amount of imitative learning in a different experimental room which was set off from the main nursery school building.

The degree to which a child has learned aggressive patterns of behavior through imitation becomes most evident when the child is instigated to aggression on later occasions. Thus, for example, the effects of viewing the movie, *Rebel Without a Cause*, were not evident until the boys were instigated to aggression on the following day, at which time they re-enacted the televised switchblade knife fight in considerable detail. For this reason, the children in the experiment, both those in the control group, and those who were exposed to the aggressive models, were mildly frustrated before they were brought to the test room.

Following the exposure experience, the experimenter brought the subject to an anteroom which contained a varied array of highly attractive toys. The experimenter explained that the toys were for the subjects to play with, but, as soon as the subject became sufficiently involved with the play material, the experimenter remarked that these were her very best toys, that she did not let just anyone play with them, and that she had decided to reserve these toys for some other children. However, the subject could play with any of the toys in the next room. The experimenter and the subject then entered the adjoining experimental room.

It was necessary for the experimenter to remain in the room during the experimental session; otherwise, a number of the children would either refuse to remain alone or would leave before the termination of the session. In order to minimize any influence her presence might have on the subject's behavior, the experimenter remained as inconspicuous as possible by busying herself with paper work at a desk in the far corner of the room and avoiding any interaction with the child.

Test for Delayed Imitation

The experimental room contained a variety of toys, some of which could be used in imitative or nonimitative aggression, and others which tended to elicit predominantly nonaggressive forms of behavior. The aggressive toys included a 3-foot Bobo doll, a mallet and peg board, two dart guns, and a tether ball with a face painted on it which hung from the ceiling. The nonaggressive toys, on the other hand, included a tea set, crayons and coloring paper, a ball, two dolls, three bears, cars and trucks, and plastic farm animals.

In order to eliminate any variation in behavior due to mere placement of the toys in the room, the play material was arranged in a fixed order for each of the sessions.

The subject spent 20 minutes in the experimental room during which time his behavior was rated in terms of predetermined response categories by judges who observed the session through a one-way mirror in an adjoining observation room. The 20-minute session was divided in 5-second intervals by means of an electric interval timer, thus yielding a total number of 240 response units for each subject.

The male model scored the experimental sessions for all subjects. In order to provide an estimate of interjudge agreement, the performances of 40% of the subjects were scored independently by a second observer. The responses scored involved highly specific concrete classes of behavior, and yielded high interscorer reliabilities, the product-moment coefficients being in the .90s.

Response Measures

The following response measures were obtained:

Imitative aggression. This category included acts of striking the Bobo doll with the mallet, sitting on the doll and punching it in the nose, kicking the doll, tossing it in the air, and verbally aggressive responses, "Sock him," "Hit him down," "Kick him," "throw him in the air," and "Pow."

Partially imitative responses. A number of subjects imitated the essential components of the model's behavior but did not perform the complete act, or they directed the imitative aggressive response to some object other than the Bobo

Pommeled (PUM-meld). To *pommel* something means "to hit it with a rapid series of blows."

doll. Two responses of this type were scored and were interpreted as partially imitative behavior:

Mallet aggression. The subject strikes objects other than the Bobo doll aggressively with the mallet.

Sits on Bobo doll. The subject lays the Bobo doll on its side and sits on it, but does not aggress toward it.

Nonimitative aggression. This category included acts of punching, slapping, or pushing the doll, physically aggressive acts directed toward objects other than the Bobo doll, and any hostile remarks except for these in the verbal imitation category; for example, "Shoot the Bobo," "Cut him," "Stupid ball," "Knock over people," "Horses fighting, biting."

Aggressive gun play. The subjects shoots darts or aims the guns and fires imaginary shots at objects in the room.

Ratings were also made of the number of behavior units in which subjects played nonaggressively or sat quietly and did not play with any of the material at all.

RESULTS

The mean imitative and nonimitative aggression scores for subjects in the various experimental and control groups are presented in Table 1.

Since the distributions of scores departed from normality and the assumption of **homogeneity of variance** could not be made for most of the measures, the Freidman two-way **analysis of variance** by ranks was employed for testing the significance of the obtained differences.

Total Aggression

The mean total aggression scores for subjects in the real-life, human film, cartoon film, and the control groups are 83, 92, 99, and 54, respectively. The results of the analysis of variance performed on these scores reveal that the main effect of treatment conditions is significant ($Xr^2 = 9.06$, $p < .05$), confirming the prediction that exposure of subjects to aggressive models increases the probability that subjects will respond aggressively when instigated on later occasions. Further analyses of pairs of scores by means of the Wilcoxon matched-pairs signed-ranks test show that subjects who viewed the real-life models and the film-mediated models do not differ from each other in total aggressiveness but all three experimental groups expressed significantly more aggressive behavior than the control subjects (Table 2).

TABLE 1
MEAN AGGRESSION SCORES FOR SUBGROUPS OF EXPERIMENTAL AND CONTROL SUBJECTS

Response category	Real-life aggressive F Model	Real-life aggressive M Model	Human film-aggressive F Model	Human film-aggressive M Model	Cartoon film-aggressive	Control group
Total aggression						
Girls	65.8	57.3	87.0	79.5	80.9	36.4
Boys	76.8	131.8	114.5	85.0	117.2	72.2
Imitative aggression						
Girls	19.2	9.2	10.0	8.0	7.8	1.8
Boys	18.4	38.4	34.3	13.3	16.2	3.9
Mallet aggression						
Girls	17.2	18.7	49.2	19.5	36.8	13.1
Boys	15.5	28.8	20.5	16.3	12.5	13.5
Sits on Bobo doll[a]						
Girls	10.4	5.6	10.3	4.5	15.3	3.3
Boys	1.3	0.7	7.7	0.0	5.6	0.6
Nonimitative aggression						
Girls	27.6	24.9	24.0	34.3	27.5	17.8
Boys	35.5	48.6	46.8	31.8	71.8	40.4
Aggressive gun play						
Girls	1.8	4.5	3.8	17.6	8.8	3.7
Boys	7.3	15.9	12.8	23.7	16.6	14.3

[a] This response category was not included in the total aggression score.

TABLE 2
SIGNIFICANCE OF THE DIFFERENCES BETWEEN EXPERIMENTAL AND CONTROL GROUPS
IN THE EXPRESSION OF AGGRESSION

Response category	Xr^2	p	Live vs. Film p	Live vs. Cartoon p	Film vs. Cartoon p	Live vs. Control p	Film vs. Control p	Cartoon vs. Control p
Total aggression	9.06	<.05	ns	ns	ns	<.01	<.01	<.005
Imitative aggression	23.88	<.001	ns	<.05	ns	<.001	<.001	<.005
Partial imitation								
Mallet aggression	7.36	.10>p>.05						
Sits on Bobo doll	8.05	<.05	ns	ns	ns	ns	<.05	<.005
Nonimitative aggression	7.28	.10>p>.05						
Aggressive gun play	8.06	<.05	<.01[b]	ns	ns	ns	<.05	ns

[a] The probability values are based on the Wilcoxon test.
[b] This probability value is based on a two-tailed test of significance.

Imitative Aggressive Responses

The Freidman analysis reveals that exposure of subjects to aggressive models is also a highly effective method for shaping subjects' aggressive responses (Xr^2 = 23.88, p <.001). Comparisons of treatment conditions by the Wilcoxon test reveal that subjects who observed the real-life models and the film-mediated models, relative to subjects in the control group, performed considerably more imitative physical and verbal aggression (Table 2).

Illustrations of the extent to which some of the subjects became virtually "carbon copies" of their models in aggressive behavior are presented in Figure 1. The top frame shows the female model performing the four novel aggressive responses; the lower frames depict a male and a female subject reproducing the behavior of the female model they had observed earlier on film.

The prediction that imitation is positively related to the reality cues of the model was only partially supported. While subjects who observed the real-life aggressive models exhibited significantly more imitative aggression than subjects who viewed the cartoon model, no significant differences were found between the live and film, and the film and cartoon conditions, nor did the three experimental groups differ significantly in total aggression or in the performances of partially imitative behavior (Table 2). Indeed, the available data suggest that, of the three experimental conditions, exposure to humans on film portraying aggression was the most influential in eliciting and shaping aggressive behavior. Subjects in this condition, in relation to the control subjects, exhibited more total aggression, more imitative aggression, more partially imitative behavior, such as sitting on the Bobo doll and mallet aggression, and they engaged in significantly more aggressive gun play. In addition, they performed significantly more aggressive gun play than did subjects who were exposed to the real-life aggressive models (Table 2).

Influence of Sex of Model and Sex of Child

In order to determine the influence of sex of model and sex of child on the expression of imitative and nonimitative aggression, the data from the experimental groups were combined and the significance of the differences between groups was assessed by t tests for uncorrelated means. In statistical comparisons involving relatively **skewed** distributions of scores the Mann-Whitney U test was employed.

Sex of subjects had a highly significant effect on both the learning and the performance of aggression. Boys, in relation to girls, exhibited significantly more total aggression (t = 2.69, p <.01), more imitative aggression (t = 2.82, p <.005), more aggressive gun play (z = 3.38, p <.001), and more nonimitative aggressive behavior (t = 2.98, p <.005). Girls, on the other hand, were more inclined than boys to sit on the Bobo doll but refrained from punching it (z = 3.47, p <.001).

The analyses also disclosed some influences of the sex of the model. Subjects exposed to the male model, as compared to the female model, expressed significantly more aggressive gun play (z = 2.83, p <.005). The most marked differences in aggressive gun play (U = 9.5, p <.001), however, were found between girls exposed to the female model (M = 2.9) and males who observed the male model (M = 19.8). Although the overall model difference in partially imitative behavior, Sits on Bobo, was not significant, Sex X Model subgroup

---

Homogeneity of variance (hoh-moh-gee-KNEE-it-tee). To use certain statistical tests in order to determine if two distributions of scores are significantly different, you must assume that the *variability* of the scores is the same (i.e., homogeneous) for both distributions.

Analysis of variance. A statistical device for determining whether two distributions are significantly different.

Skewed. Some distributions are "bell-shaped," which is to say that the right half of the curve is more-or-less a mirror-image of the left. However, if the distribution is *skewed*, one half extends much farther out on the X-axis than does the other.

Fig. 1. Photographs from the film, *Social Learning of Aggression through Imitation of Aggressive Models.*

comparisons yielded some interesting results. Boys who observed the aggressive female model, for example, were more likely to sit on the Bobo doll without punching it than boys who viewed the male model ($U = 33$, $p < .05$). Girls reproduced the nonaggressive component of the male model's aggressive pattern of behavior (i.e., sat on the doll without punching it) with considerably higher frequency than did boys who observed the same model ($U = 21.5$, $p < .02$). The highest incidence of partially imitative responses was yielded by the group of girls who viewed the aggressive female model ($M = 10.4$), and the lowest values by the boys who were exposed to the male model ($M = 0.3$). This difference was significant beyond the .05 significance level. These findings, along with the sex of child and sex of model differences reported in the preceding sections, provide further support for the view that the influence of models in promoting social learning is determined, in part, by the sex appropriateness of the model's behavior (Bandura et al., 1961).

Aggressive Predisposition and Imitation

Since the correlations between ratings of aggression and the measures of imitative and total aggressive behavior, calculated separately for boys and girls in each of the experimental conditions, did not differ significantly, the data were combined. The correlational analyses performed on these pooled data failed to yield any significant relationships between ratings of aggression anxiety, frequency of aggressive behavior, and the experimental aggression measures. In fact, the array means suggested nonlinear regressions although the departures from linearity were not of sufficient magnitude to be statistically significant.

DISCUSSION

The results of the present study provide strong evidence that exposure to filmed aggression heightens aggressive reactions in children. Subjects who viewed the aggressive human and cartoon models on film exhibited nearly twice as much aggression than did subjects in the control group who were not exposed to the aggressive film content.

In the experimental design typically employed for testing the possible cathartic function of **vicarious** aggression, subjects are first frustrated, then provided with an opportunity to view an aggressive film following which their overt or fantasy aggression is measured. While this procedure yields some information on the immediate influence of film-mediated aggression, the full effects of such exposure may not be revealed until subjects are instigated to aggression on a later occasion. Thus, the present study, and one recently reported by Lovaas (1961), both utilizing a design in which subjects first observed filmed aggression and then were frustrated, clearly reveal that observation of models portraying aggression on film substantially increases rather than decreases the probability of aggressive reactions to subsequent frustrations.

Filmed aggression, not only facilitated the expression of aggression, but also effectively shaped the form of the subjects' aggressive behavior. The finding that children modeled their behavior to some extent after the film characters suggests that pictorial mass media, particularly television, may serve as an important source of social behavior. In fact, a possible generalization of responses originally learned in the television situation to the experimental film may account for the significantly greater amount of aggressive gun play displayed by subjects in the film condition as compared to subjects in the real-life and control groups. It is unfortunate that the qualitative features of the gun behavior were not scored since subjects in the film condition, unlike those in the other two groups, developed interesting elaborations in gun play (for example, stalking the imaginary opponent, quick drawing, and rapid firing), characteristic of the Western gun fighter.

The view that the social learning of aggression through exposure to aggressive film content is confined to deviant children (Schramm, Lyle, & Parker, 1961), finds little support in our data. The children who participated in the experiment are by no means a deviant sample, nevertheless, 88% of the subjects in the Real-Life and in the Human Film condition, and 79% of the subjects in the Cartoon Film condition, exhibited varying degrees of imitative aggression. In assessing the possible influence of televised stimulation on viewers' behavior, however, it is important to distinguish between learning and overt performance. Although the results of the present experiment demonstrate that the vast majority of children *learn* patterns of social behavior through pictorial stimulation, nevertheless, informal observation suggests that children do not, as a rule, *perform* indiscriminately the behavior of televised characters, even those they regard as highly attractive models. The replies of parents whose children participated in the present study to an open-end questionnaire item concerning their handling of imitative behavior suggest that this may be in part a function of negative reinforcement, as most parents were quick to discourage their children's overt imitation of television characters by prohibiting certain programs or by labeling the imitative behavior in a disapproving manner. From our knowledge of the effects of punishment on behavior, the responses in question would be expected to retain their original strength and could reappear on later occasions in the presence of appropriate eliciting stimuli, particularly if instigation is high, the instruments for aggression are available, and the threat of noxious consequences is reduced.

The absence of any relationships between ratings of the children's predisposition to aggression and their aggressive behavior in the experimental setting may simply reflect the inadequacy of the predictor measures. It may be pointed out, however, that the reliability of the ratings was relatively high. While this does not assure validity of the measures, it does at least indicate there was consistency in the raters' estimates of the children's aggressive tendencies.

A second, and perhaps more probable, explanation is that proprioceptive feedback alone is not sufficient to account for response inhibition or facilitation. For example, the proprioceptive cues arising from hitting responses directed toward parents and toward peers may differ little, if any; nevertheless, tendencies to aggress toward parents are apt to be strongly inhibited while peer aggression may be readily expressed (Bandura, 1960; Bandura & Walters, 1959). In most social interaction sequences, proprioceptive cues make up only a small part of the total stimulus complex and, therefore, it is necessary to take into consideration additional stimulus components, for the most part external, which probably serve as important discriminative cues for the expression of aggression. Consequently, prediction of the occurrence or inhibition of specific classes of responses would be expected to depend upon the presence of a certain pattern of proprioceptive or

Vicarious (vy-CARE-ih-us). If your boss criticizes you, and you want to kick him/her (but can't because you'll be fired) so you kick the cat instead, you have *vicariously* kicked your boss. More precisely, *vicarious* means "substitute."

introceptive stimulation together with relevant **discriminative external stimuli**.

According to this line of reasoning, failure to obtain the expected positive relationships between the measures of aggression may be due primarily to the fact that permissiveness for aggression, conveyed by situational cues in the form of aggressive film content and play material, was sufficient to override the influence of internal stimuli generated by the commission of aggressive responses. If, in fact, the behavior of young children, as compared to that of adults, is less likely to be under internal stimulus control, one might expect environmental cues to play a relatively important role in eliciting or inhibiting aggressive behavior.

A question may be raised as to whether the aggressive acts studied in the present experiment constitute "genuine" aggressive responses. Aggression is typically defined as behavior, the goal or intent of which is injury to a person, or destruction of an object (Bandura & Walters, 1959; Dollard, Doob, Miller, Mowrer, & Sears, 1939; Sears, Maccoby, & Levin, 1957). Since intentionality is not a property of behavior but primarily an inference concerning antecedent events, the categorization of an act as "aggressive" involves a consideration of both stimulus and mediating or terminal response events.

According to a social learning theory of aggression recently proposed by Bandura and Walters (in press), most of the responses utilized to hurt or to injure others (for example, striking, kicking, and other responses of high magnitude), are probably learned for prosocial purposes under nonfrustration conditions. Since frustration generally elicits responses of high magnitude, the latter classes of responses, once acquired, may be called out in social interactions for the purpose of injuring others. On the basis of this theory it would be predicted that the aggressive responses acquired imitatively, while not necessarily mediating aggressive goals in the experimental situation, would be utilized to serve such purposes in other social settings with higher frequency by children in the experimental conditions than by children in the control group.

The present study involved primarily vicarious or **empathic** learning (Mowrer, 1960) in that subjects acquired a relatively complex repertoire of aggressive responses by the mere sight of a model's behavior. It has been generally assumed that the necessary conditions for the occurrence of such learning is that the model perform certain responses followed by positive reinforcement to the model (Hill, 1960; Mowrer, 1960). According to this theory, to the extent that the observer experiences the model's reinforcement vicariously, the observer will be prone to reproduce the model's behavior. While there is some evidence from experiments involving both human (Lewis & Duncan, 1958; McBrearty, Marston, & Kanfer, 1961; Sechrest, 1961) and animal subjects (Darby & Riopelle, 1959; Warden, Fjeld, & Koch, 1940), that vicarious reinforcement may in fact increase the probability of the behavior in question, it is apparent from the results of the experiment reported in this paper that a good deal of human imitative learning can occur without any reinforcers delivered either to the model or to the observer. In order to test systematically the influence of vicarious reinforcement on imitation, however, a study is planned in which the degree of imitative learning will be compared in situations in which the model's behavior is paired with reinforcement with those in which the model's responses go unrewarded.

FOOTNOTES

[1] This investigation was supported in part by Research Grants M-4398 and M-5162 from the National Institute of Health, United States Public Health Service, and the Lewis S. Haas Child Development Research Fund, Stanford University.

The authors are indebted to David J. Hicks for his generous assistance with the photography and to John Steinbruner who assisted with various phases of this study.

[2] This research was carried out while the junior author was the recipient of an American Association of University Women International Fellowship for postdoctoral research.

[3] Reprinted by permission of the authors and the publisher from the *Journal of Abnormal and Social Psychology*, 1963, **66**, 3-11. Copyright 1963 by the American Psychological Association.

REFERENCES

Albert, R.S. The role of mass media and the effect of aggressive film content upon children's aggressive responses and identification choices. *Genet. psychol. Monogr.*, 1957, 55, 221-285.

Bandura, A. Relationship of family patterns to child behavior disorders. Progress Report, 1960, Stanford University, Project No. M-1734, United States Public Health Service.

Bandura, A., & Huston, Aletha C. Identification as a process of incidental learning. *J. abnorm. soc. Psychol.*, 1961, 63, 311-318.

Bandura, A., Ross, Dorothea, & Ross, Sheila A. Transmission of aggression through imitation of aggressive models. *J. abnorm. soc. Psychol.*, 1961, *63*, 575-582.

Bandura, A., & Walters, R.H. *Adolescent aggression*. New York: Ronald, 1959.

Bandura, A., & Walters, R.H. *The social learning of deviant behavior: A behavioristic approach to socialization*. New York: Holt, Rinehart, & Winston, in press.

Berkowitz, L. *Aggression: A social psychological analysis*. New York: McGraw-Hill, 1962.

Darby, C.L., & Riopelle, A.J. Observational learning in the Rhesus monkey. *J. comp. physiol. Psychol.*, 1959, 52, 94-98.

Dollard, J., Doob, L.W., Miller, N.E., Mowrer, O.H., & Sears, R.R. *Frustration and aggression*. New Haven: Yale University Press, 1939.

Emery, F.E. Psychological effects of the Western film: A study in television viewing: II. The experimental study. *Hum. Relat.*, 1959, 12, 215-232.

Feshbach, S. The drive-reducing function of fantasy behavior. *J. abnorm. soc. Psychol.*, 1955, 50, 3-11.

Feshbach, S. The stimulating versus cathartic effects of a vicarious aggressive activity. Paper read at the Eastern Psychological Association, 1958.

Hill, W.F. Learning theory and the acquisition of values. *Psychol. Rev.*, 1960, 67, 317-331.

Kenny, D.T. An experimental test of the catharsis theory of aggression. Unpublished doctoral dissertation, University of Washington, 1952.

Lewis, D.J., & Duncan, C.P. Vicarious experience and partial reinforcement. *J. abnorm. soc. Psychol.*, 1958, 57, 321-326.

Lovaas, O.J. Effect of exposure to symbolic aggression on aggressive behavior. *Child Develpm.*, 1961, 32, 37-44.

McBrearty, J.F., Marston, A.R., & Kanfer, F.H. Conditioning a verbal operant in a group setting: Direct vs. vicarious reinforcement. *Amer. Psychologist*, 1961, 16, 425. (Abstract)

Mowrer, O.H. *Learning theory and the symbolic processes*. New York: Wiley, 1960.

San Fransisco Chronicle. James Dean knifing in South City. *San Fransisco Chron.*, March 1, 1961, 6.

Schramm, W., Lyle, J., & Parker, E.B. *Television in the lives of our children*. Stanford: Stanford Univer. Press, 1961.

Sears, R.R., Maccoby, Eleanor, E., & Levin, H. *Patterns of child rearing*. Evanston: Row, Peterson, 1957.

Sechrest, L. Vicarious reinforcement of responses. *Amer. Psychologist*, 1961, 16, 356. (Abstract)

Siegel, Alberta E. Film-mediated fantasy aggression and strength of aggressive drive. *Child Develpm.*, 1956, 27, 365-378.

Warden, C.J., Fjeld, H.A., & Koch, A.M. Imitative behavior in cebus and Rhesus monkeys. *J. genet. Psychol.*, 1040, 56, 311-322..

Discriminative external stimuli (dis-KRIM-ih-nah-tiv). In S-R learning theories, stimuli become *bonded* to or *associated* with responses, usually because the S-R connection has been reinforced. When learning occurs, therefore, the occurrence of the S(timulus) automatically elicits or calls forth the R(esponse). For example, if you turn on a light and then shock an animal, it will soon start to cringe as soon at the light comes on, *before* the onset of the light. In Skinner's Operant Conditioning theory, however, the organism learns that if it happens to *emit* (or "produce") a response when a certain stimulus is present, it will be reinforced. For instance, if a rat learns that pressing a bar will yield food *only* when a light above the bar is lit, the light will soon become a "discriminative external stimulus." In this case, the light does not *elicit* the bar-press response, but rather informs the animal that reinforcement is available if the animal happens to press the bar.

Empathetic (em-pah-THET-ic). Empathy (EM-pah-the) is the ability to experience (or participate in) someone else's emotions or ideas.

CHAPTER 17

"On Predicting Some of the People Some of the Time: The Search for Cross-situational Consistencies in Behavior"

Daryl J. Bem and Andrea Allen[1]

EDITORS' COMMENTS. "Why do you do the things that you do?" Human beings have probably been asking this question ever since human beings *began* asking questions. And, in a sense, all of psychology can be seen as an attempt to find an answer to this puzzling query.

One of the early, not-so-scientific explanations for human behavior probably was "People act as they do because that's the way people *are*." Put in more technical terms, we might assume that you behave as you do because you were born with (or acquired early in life) certain *traits* or *pre-dispositions* that encourage you to respond to a wide variety of situations in a consistent fashion. Do you make it a practice to help other people whenever you can? If so, we might say that you possess the trait of "helpfulness," or of "consideration for others," or even of "nurturance." If you found a wallet on the street and returned it to its owner, we might well assume you possess the trait of *honesty*. And if we could make a list of *all* of your "main traits," then surely we would wind up with a fairly accurate description of your personality.

Or would we?

Maybe not, for there is basic flaw or two in the trait approach. First, it tends to be circular. You *are* honest because you possess the *trait* of honesty. And how do we know you possess this trait? Because you *are* honest. Second, there are precious few "pre-dispositions" that apply *across all situations*. You might return a wallet containing $5, but what if you found one containing $500,000? And would your actions change if you were starving, or your mother needed an operation you couldn't afford, or if you were absolutely certain that no one would ever discover you had the money?

Despite its flaws, the "trait concept" is pervasive, not merely in personality theory but in language itself. More than 50 years ago, Gordon Allport and H.S. Odbert made a list of 18,000 English words, each of which was actually a *trait description* (Allport & Odbert, 1936). You can't even *think* of some other person, Allport claimed, without generating a whole list of "trait words" that you associate with that individual. Little wonder, then, that "traits" are such an important part of most personality theories.

However, despite the thousands of articles published on the topic, the "trait concept" really doesn't have all that much *scientific* evidence to support it. Indeed, as personality theorist Walter Mischel stated 20 years ago, "With the possible exception of intelligence, highly generalized behavioral consistencies have not been demonstrated, and the concept of personal traits as broad response predispositions is thus untenable" (Mischel, 1968). Mischel notes that, when looked at *objectively*, much of the "consistency" in human behavior seems to be a function of the *situation the person is in*, and not of the individual's personality. However, while we have 18,000 terms to describe *internal traits*, we don't really have many terms to describe *situations*--much less terms to describe the *interaction* between person and situation. Why this lack of terminology? Apparently, despite all the data, most of us continue to prefer to attribute the *causes* of human behavior to personality factors inside the individual.

Which is the more important determinant of your actions, the *structure of your personality* (that is, your traits), or the *situation you find yourself in*? In truth, as Daryl J. Bem and Andrea Allen point out in this article, you can't ignore either. For surely it is the *interaction* between personality factors *and* the present situation that determines why you do the things you do.

*The historically recurring controversy over the existence of cross-situational consistencies in behavior is sustained by the discrepancy between our intuitions, which affirm their existence, and the research literature, which does not. It is argued that the **nomothetic** assumptions of the traditional research paradigm are incorrect and that by adopting some of the **idiographic** assumptions employed by our intuitions, higher cross-situational correlation coefficients can be obtained. A study is reported which shows that it is possible to identify on a priori grounds those individuals who will be cross-situationally consistent and those who will not, and it is concluded that not only must personality assessment attend to situations — as has been recently urged — but to persons as well.*

Our persistent belief in personality traits, the stubborn assumption that there are pervasive cross-situational consistencies in an individual's behavior, is, quite literally, one of our most ancient convictions:

Penuriousness is economy carried beyond all measure. A Penurious Man is one who goes to a debtor to ask for his half-obol [about 1 cent] interest before the end of the month. At a dinner where expenses are shared, he counts the number of cups each person drinks, and he makes a smaller **libation to Artemis** than anyone. . . . If his wife drops a copper, he moves furniture, beds, chests and hunts in the curtains. . . . [P]enurious men have hair cut short and do not put on their shoes until mid-day; and when they take their cloak to the **fuller** they urge him to use plenty of earth so that it will not be spotted so soon [Theophrastus (372-287 B.C.), quoted in Allport, 1937, p. 57].

If this bit of historical personality theorizing has a contemporary ring, it is, in part, because the same underlying assumption of cross-situational consistency is still with us. It is most explicit in trait and type theories of personality, but some variant of it can be discerned in nearly all contemporary formulations. Even **psychodynamic** theories, which are uniquely competent in dealing with **phenotypic** inconsistencies in behavior, do so precisely by postulating an underlying **genotypic** consistency in the personality which rationalizes the apparent contradictions. Our intuitions are even more persuaded. For them the assumption of cross-situational consistency is virtually synonymous with the concept of personality itself. There are few other beliefs about human behavior which are as compellingly self-evident.

But like many other assumptions, the consistency assumption did not fare well during the depression years, when three separate studies with very similar methodologies began to raise serious doubts about its validity. The earliest and best known challenge issued from the extensive multivolume *Studies in the Nature of Character* by Hartshorne and May (1928, 1929; Hartshorne, May & Shuttleworth, 1930), who found so little consistency among diverse measures of "moral character" in a group of children that they concluded that such traits as deception, helpfulness, cooperativeness, persistence and self-control are "groups of specific habits rather than general traits." Foreshadowing findings which emerged from hundreds of later studies on scores of personality traits, Hartshorne and May reported that the average intercorrelation of the 23 tests used to construct a "total character score" was a modest +.30.

During the same years as the Hartshorne-May inquiry, a less well known but equally troublesome study on **extroversion-introversion** was published by Theodore Newcomb (1929), who explicitly set out to test the consistency assumption. He kept daily behavioral records on 51 boys at a summer camp for several weeks, recording behaviors in 30 different situations. The behaviors were conceptually organized into 10 separate traits (e.g., **volubility** versus **taciturnity**, ascendancy versus submission, etc.) which in turn collectively defined the two personality types of extrovert and introvert.

At the level of specific behaviors, Newcomb found little or no consistency from one situation to another. At the level of trait consistency, the intercorrelations among behaviors composing a given trait averaged only .14, almost identical to the figure obtained from a ran-

---

Nomothetic (noh-moh-THET-ick). The nomothetic approach to explaining human behavior is based on the belief that certain scientific laws or principles can explain the actions of all people in all situations. The focus here is on the search for similarities among all people rather than on individual differences.

Idiographic (id-ee-oh-GRAFF-ic). Idiographic assumptions are those that explain human behavior in terms of consistencies *within the individual* rather than on consistent laws that apply *across individuals*. The focus here is on individual differences rather than on human similarities.

Penuriousness (penn-YOUR-ee-us-ness). The state of being extremely stingy or frugal with money.

Libation to Artemis (lie-BAY-shun to ART-tee-mis). A drink (libation) or toast offered to the Greek goddess of the moon.

Fuller. In ancient Greece, fullers (or "cleaners") rubbed dirt into clothes to absorb stains.

Psychodynamic. That area of psychology concerned with mental or emotional processes developing in early childhood and the effects these processes have on behavior and mental states.

Phenotypic. The visible characteristics of an organism, such as a suntan or a broken bone.

Genotypic. The genetic characteristics of an organism, such as innate skin color. Your children won't inherit your suntan, but they will inherit your basic skin color.

Extroversion-introversion. Many psychologists believe that all humans can be placed on a scale that runs from *extrovert* ("outgoing") to *introvert* ("socially withdrawn").

Volubility (vol-you-BILL-it-tee). The characteristic of talking a lot.

Taciturnity (tass-ih-TURN-ih-tee). The characteristic of not talking very much, or of not talking at all.

domly selected set of behaviors. And finally, there was only a slight tendency for traits to be related to one another as expected by their extrovert-introvert classification.

The third study is in some ways the most damaging of all since it investigated punctuality, a trait one would expect to be much more homogeneous than "moral character" or extroversion-introversion. In this study, Dudycha (1936) made 15,360 observations on over 300 college students, recording each student's time of arrival at 8:00 a.m. classes, **commons**, appointments, extracurricular activities, vesper services, and entertainments. The mean cross-situational correlation turned out to be +.19, with the highest correlation—between punctuality at entertainments and at commons—reaching .44.

These three studies are virtually unique in that the investigators actually observed behavior **in vivo** across several situations, a devotion to duty practically unknown in today's literature on the same topic. Meanwhile, the pencil-paper attempts to predict behavior from a trait conception of personality were faring no better, leading Lehmann and Witty (1934) to conclude a review of the literature by saying that "over and over, a battery of tests designed to measure traits such as persistence, or aggressiveness, or honesty, yields results so unreliable and undependable... that one is led to question the actual existence of the general traits [p. 490]."

At the same time that the belief in cross-situational consistency was suffering these empirical blows, stimulus-response behaviorism was providing the theoretical argument for the counter belief in the situational specificity of behavior. And with psychologists like Gordon Allport (1937) and Ross Stagner (1937) willing to defend modified trait conceptions of personality against this onslaught, the controversy was a lively one for nearly a decade before receding into the background just prior to World War II (Sanford, 1970).

All of this leads one to appreciate the sense of **déjà vu** that must currently be affecting psychology's elder statesmen now that the "consistency problem" has suddenly been rediscovered (e.g., Alker, 1972; Allport, 1966; Argyle & Little, 1972; Averill, 1973; D. Bem, 1972; Bowers, 1973; Campus, 1974; Endler, 1973a, 1973b; Endler & Hunt, 1968; Harre & Secord, 1972; Mischel, 1968, 1969, 1973a, 1973b; Moos, 1969; Peterson, 1968; Stagner, 1973; Vale & Vale, 1969; Vernon, 1964; Wachtel, 1973; Wallach & Leggett, 1972).

The major figure in this current round of debate appears to be Walter Mischel (1968), who, after reviewing both past and current research, concludes that the predictive utility of a trait-based approach to personality still remains undemonstrated and that situational specificity of behavior appears to be the rule rather than the exception. Although other contemporary authors have drawn similar conclusions (e.g., Peterson, 1968; Vernon, 1964), it is Mischel who has provoked the most controversy by arguing that the commonly observed +.30 ceiling on cross-situational correlation coefficients probably reflects true behavioral variability rather than imperfect methodology. Since this constitutes a fundamental conceptual challenge, the controversy is one again filling journal pages after a 30-year intermission.

And the stubborn **dilemma** which sustains this conflict and accounts for its durability still remains unsolved: The sharp discrepancy between our intuitions, which tell us that individuals do in fact display pervasive cross-situational consistencies in their behavior, and the vast **empirical** literature, which tells us that they do not. Intuitions or research? One of them must be wrong.

ERRORS OF INTUITION AND THE NOMOTHETIC FALLACY OF THE RESEARCH PARADIGM

There are many persuasive reasons for believing that it is our intuitions which are in error (Jones & Nisbett, 1971; Mischel, 1968). First, for example, we hold "implicit personality theories," preconceived notions of what traits and behaviors go with what other traits and behaviors. (See Schneider, 1973, for a recent review.) This leads us not only to generalize beyond our observations and fill in the missing data with "consistent" data of our own manufacture, (e.g., Passini & Norman, 1966) but also to "see" positive correlations which are, in fact, not there (e.g., Chapman & Chapman, 1969; Newcomb, 1929). Moreover, we are biased toward "primacy" effects (e.g., Jones & Goethals, 1971); once we have formed an initial impression of a person, we will perceive inconsistent information about him as more consistent than it deserves to be, assimilating it to our initial judgment.

Second, recent research in attribution theory (e.g., Jones & Davis, 1965; Jones & Harris, 1967; Jones & Nisbett, 1971; Kelley, 1967) has demonstrated that we tend to overestimate the degree to which behavior is caused by traits of the individual and underestimate the degree to which it is caused by external factors. We are therefore willing to generalize about his behavior, **extrapolating** it to other, unobserved settings in which the situational forces might be quite different.

Third, the set of situations in which we observe most individuals is probably more limited than we realize, both in extent and representativeness. For example, our own presence can frequently evoke a consistent mode of responding in another person (e.g., Kelley & Stahelski, 1970). Accordingly, we are systematically excluded from observing a whole host of situations across which our acquaintances' behaviors are likely to be more variable than they are across the situations in which we do observe them.

Fourth, we probably misconstrue or overgeneralize some of the consistencies which are present. For example, Mischel's (1968) review reveals that the evidence for temporal consistency in behavior is often quite respectable; an individual's behavior is often consistent from one time to another if the situations are similar. Our intuitions may well go from this demonstrable temporal consistency to an unwarranted cross-situational consistency. Moreover, some features of behavior do show cross-situational consistency, such as intellectual ability, cognitive styles, expressive behaviors and, of course, simple physical appearance. To the extent that these behaviors or cues serve to anchor our inferences about other aspects of behavior—via our implicit personality theories—we will again overgeneralize the degree of cross-situational consistency actually present.

Finally, our language entices us to think of human behavior in trait terms. As Allport and Odbert (1936) reported, there are about 18,000 trait or traitlike terms in our language, nearly five percent of the entire **lexicon**. In contrast, we have an impoverished and awkward vocabulary for labeling situations.

These, then, are a sample of reasons for thinking that, in the matter of cross-situational consistency, intuitions are wrong, and the research is right. We, however, do not believe it. Despite the compelling impact of these arguments, we still believe that intuitions capture reality more faithfully than does the research. In particular, we believe that there is a basic error in drawing inferences about cross-situational consistency from the traditional research literature in personality, an error which was identified nearly 40 years ago by Gordon Allport (1937). The **fallacy** resides in the fact that this entire research tradition is predicated upon nomothetic rather than idiographic assumptions about the nature of individual differences. Thus nearly all of the research is based on some variant of the nomothetic assumption that a particular trait dimension or set of trait dimensions is universally applicable to all persons and that individual differences are to be identified with different locations on those dimensions. For example, the Hartshorne-May study (1928) assumed that an honesty-dishonesty dimension could be used to characterize all of the children in the sample and that the differences among the children could be specified in terms of their *degree* of honesty. A more elaborate version of the same nomothetic assumption can be found in **factor-analytic formulations** which assume that there is a universal factor structure of personality and that individual differences are to be specified by different points in the factor **n-space**.

In contrast, Allport's idiographic view emphasized that individuals differ not only in the ways in which traits are related to one another in each person but that they differ also in terms of which traits are even relevant. Thus in commenting upon the fact that Hartshorne and May found lying and cheating to be essentially uncorrelated ($r = .13$), Allport noted that one child may lie because he is afraid of hurting the feelings of the teacher, whereas another may steal pennies in order to buy social acceptance from his peers. For neither of these two children do the behaviors of lying and cheating constitute items on a scale called "honesty," a concept which exists in the head of the investigator, not in the behavior of the children. Accordingly, the low correlations "prove only that children are not consistent *in*

Commons. In England during the Middle Ages, when "knighthood was in flower," the knights ate their meals with the nobility, in the main dining room. The servants, or "common folk," were fed at a common table in or near the kitchen. We now use the term "commons" to refer to any building which contains a dining hall.

In vivo (in VEE-voh). Literally, "in real life," or within the living envionrment of the person or animal. An "in vivo" experiment is one that involves living subjects tested in their normal environment. An "in vitro" (VEE-troh) experiment is one that is a simulation of real life, or that takes place in a test tube or laboratory situation rather than in the real world.

Déjà vu (day-zha-voo). The feeling that you have previously experienced what you are presently experiencing.

Dilemma (die-LEMM-ah). A dilemma is a problem with two equally-painful solutions, or with no real solution at all.

Empirical (em-PEER-ih-kal). Data-based, as opposed to theoretical. To depend on facts rather than on theory or feelings.

Extrapolating (ex-TRAP-poh-lay-ting). To generalize from one set of data to another, or to forecast the future on the basis of the present and/or past. If I say, "Guess which number is coming next: 1, 2, 3, 4, 5...?" and you respond "6," you have *extrapolated* your answer from the data given you.

Lexicon. From the Greek word meaning "speech." A lexicon is the total number of words in a given language.

Fallacy (FAL-ah-see). A false idea or mistaken belief.

Factor-analytic formulations (form-you-LAY-shuns). Factor analysis is a statistical device that presumably lets you discover the "underlying factors" that account for correlations or other relationships between variables. Your grade point average is highly correlated with the score that you get on an intelligence test. But a high GPA doesn't *cause* a high IQ, or vice versa. Rather, the underlying factor of *intelligence* presumably accounts for both your grades and your IQ. Factor analysis is one way of trying to determine what basic traits account for a variety of related behaviors.

N-space. Ordinary space has three dimensions, and thus is a 3-dimensional space. Factor analysis yields an n-dimensional space, for each factor is presumed to be a separate dimension. If factor analysis of a given set of data turns up five underlying factors, then you have a 5-dimensional space.

the same way, not that they are inconsistent with *themselves* (1937, p. 250)." To put the same objection in slightly different terms, the research will yield the conclusion that a sample of individuals is inconsistent to the degree that their behaviors do not sort into the equivalence class which the investigator imposes by his choice of behaviors and situations to sample.

But there is more. Even if an entire sample of individuals does share the investigator's partitioning of behaviors into the same equivalence class, there is a still more stringent requirement of consistency imposed by the traditional research paradigm: scalability.[2] That is, the sample of individuals must all rank order the "difficulty levels" of the behaviors in the same way.

Consider, for example, the "friendliness" of the second author [Andrea Allen]. She is very friendly to undergraduates in her office, moderately outgoing in a small seminar, and somewhat reserved before a large class. If we can agree that all of these behaviors belong in a common equivalence class labeled "friendliness," she will be judged to be moderately friendly on this trait dimension. She "passes" the "easy" item, has some difficulty with a "harder" item, and "flunks" the "most difficult" item. Note that we do not judge her to be inconsistent any more than we judge a student to be inconsistent when he solves an addition problem but fails a calculus item. We do not do so because their behavior conforms to our *a priori* ordering of the items in terms of their difficulty levels: their behavior "scales" in the Guttman sense (Scott, 1968; Stouffer, Guttman, Suchman, Lazarsfeld, Star, & Clausen, 1950).

But now consider the "friendliness" of the first author [Daryl J. Bem]. He, too, passes one item and flunks one item. He is rather formal with undergraduates who appear in his office, moderately outgoing in a small seminar, and open, personable, and friendly before a sea of 300 faces in introductory psychology. But somehow his behavior does not seem describable in terms of the same underlying dimension. He appears not "moderately friendly," but "blatantly inconsistent." And this is because his behaviors do not conform to the a priori Guttman scale which we have implicitly imposed on this equivalence class of behaviors. He passes hard items but flunks easy items.

Now reconsider the traditional research study in which a sample of individuals is assessed on some trait across two or more situations. To the extent that individuals in the sample scale the behaviors differently from one another—as the first and second authors do on "friendliness"—their rankings relative to one another will change from one situation to another. The second author will rank first in friendliness in the office encounter; the first author will rank first in the large lecture hall. Under such circumstances, the cross-situational correlation coefficients will plummet toward zero. Only to the extent that all of the individuals in the sample scale the behaviors in the same way will the cross-situational correlations be high.

In summary, then, the traditional trait-based research study will yield evidence of cross-situational consistency only if the individuals in the research sample agree with the investigator's a priori claim that the sampled behaviors and situations belong in a common equivalence class *and* only if the individuals agree among themselves on how to scale those behaviors and situations. The fallacy to which Gordon Allport originally called attention thus becomes clear. The traditional verdict of inconsistency is in no way an inference about individuals; it is a statement about a disagreement between an investigator and a group of individuals and/or a disagreement among the individuals within the group. This fallacy is a direct consequence of the traditional nomothetic assumptions about individual differences. (See a related line of argument by Baldwin, 1946, and McClelland, 1951.)

In contrast to the empirical research, our intuitions operate on idiographic rather than nomothetic assumptions. When we are asked to characterize a friend, we do not invoke some a priori set of fixed dimensions which we apply to everyone. Rather, we permit ourselves to select a small subset of traits which strike us as pertinent and to discard as irrelevant the other 17,993 trait terms in the lexicon. Moreover, we try to compose trait descriptions which conform to the individual's own partitioning of equivalence classes. If John always does his schoolwork early, is meticulous about his personal appearance, and is always punctual, it may well occur to us to describe him as conscientious. But if he is always conscientious about his schoolwork, being negligent in these other areas, we may well describe him as a totally dedicated student, one who has time for little else. The important point is that we are not likely to characterize him as someone who is inconsistently conscientious. That is, we do not first impose a trait term (e.g., conscientious) and then modify it by describing the instances which fail to fall into that equivalence class. Rather, we attempt first to organize his behaviors into rational sets and only then to label them.

We are, moreover, somewhat sensitive to the scaling criterion. We will describe the second author as moderately friendly rather than inconsistent because we recognize the underlying Guttman scale to which her behavior conforms. But when we encounter the first author, whose behavior does not scale according to the recognized "friendliness" dimension, we will typically try to repartition his behaviors before accepting a verdict of inconsistency. Thus the first author is, perhaps, a moderately aloof chap who is a great stage performer. That is, we attempt to construct a new set of equivalence classes which better "capture" the individual's personality. Note also that this intuitive process automatically **finesses** the problem of situational specificity by embracing in a common equivalence class only those behaviors and situations which cohere for the individual, thereby excluding a priori any maverick behaviors and situations. The trait description is thus fractionated, expanded, contracted, and modified until a best fit of greatest generality and parsimony is achieved. It is only when we fail to discover a set of rationally-scaled equivalence classes which conform to the individual's behavior that a judgment of "inconsistency" is finally rendered. This is the essence of the idiographic approach to personality.

We are not here denying the well-documented biases and illusions which plague our intuitions, nor do we claim that the more formalized idiographic procedures used by clinicians have a better track record in terms of predictive utility than nomothetic ones; they do not (Mischel, 1968). But in terms of the underlying logic and fidelity to reality, we believe that our intuitions are right; the research, wrong.

IDIOGRAPHIC ASSESSMENT AND NOMOTHETIC SCIENCE

The problem with concluding that an idiographic approach represents the path to truth, however, has always been that one is never sure what to do next. To the extent that one accepts psychology's goal as the construction of general nomothetic principles, the idiographic approach appears a scientific dead end, a capitulation to the man-in-the-street view that a science of psychology is impossible because "everybody is different from everybody else." It is this pessimism which seems largely responsible for the fact that the field's respect and admiration for Gordon Allport has never been translated into research programs based upon his conception of personality (cf. Sanford, 1970). Interestingly, the approach of behaviorism has probably discouraged the study of personality differences for much the same reason. To the extent that an individual's behavioral **repertoire** faithfully reflects the idiosyncratic vagaries of his past reinforcement history, searching for some rational nomothetic basis of personality organization would not appear to be a very hopeful enterprise. As Mischel (1968) notes—not pessimistically, however—the approach of social behavior theory does not

> label the individual with generalized trait terms and stereotypes... Behavioral assessment involves an exploration of the unique or idiographic aspects of the single case, perhaps to a greater extent than any other approach. Social behavior theory recognizes the individuality of each person and of each unique situation [p. 190].

But the impasse is not insurmountable. The use of idiographic assessment procedures did not appear to deter Freud from formulating nomothetic principles of personality organization. Similarly, albeit more modestly, Mischel (1973b) has recently proposed a set of nomothetic principles within the idiographic assumptions of social behavior theory. A third example is provided by George Kelly's (1955) psychology of personal constructs and its associated idiographic assessment procedure, the **Role Repertory Test**. In fact, it is Kelly's approach which best exemplifies the spirit behind the present arguments. Thus Kelly permits the individual to generate his own traitlike descriptors ("constructs") for characterizing himself and his social world and to determine which behaviors and situations are to be embraced by those descriptors, that is, to determine what Kelly has termed the individual's "range of convenience" for the construct. Note that such an approach could reveal, for example, that an individual who regards himself as extremely conscientious might not consider his casual attitude toward personal hygiene as pertinent to that trait. The fact that the investigator's concept or equivalence class of conscientiousness might include personal hygiene within it is not relevant.

The basic point here is simply that there is no inherent conflict between an idiographic approach to assessment and a nomothetic science of personality, whether one opts for a psychoanalytic orientation, a social learning viewpoint, or a systematization of everyman's trait theory.

Guttman scale (GUT-man). There are a number of different scales, or measuring instruments, used in psychological research. Some scales have precise units of measurement, such as weight: 2 pounds is precisely twice as much as 1 pound, and 400 pounds is twice the weight of 200 pounds. A Guttman scale (developed by Louis Guttman) is used when what you are measuring is much less precise than is weight. For example, suppose you rate two people, John and Mary, on a seven-point rating scale that runs from 1 ("very, very unfriendly") to 4 ("neither friendly nor unfriendly") to 7 ("very, very friendly"). You give John a score of 3 ("somewhat unfriendly") and Mary a score of 6 ("very friendly"). You know that Mary is *more* friendly than John is, but is she three times as friendly, or five times as friendly? You can't tell, because the intervals between the points on the Guttman scale aren't precise.

Finesses (fin-NESS-es). A term first used in bridge (and other card games) to describe a way of avoiding losing a trick. In daily speech, to "finesse" a problem is to by-pass it in some fashion (often by ignoring it).

Repertoire (rep-pur-twar). A list of skills or capabilities.

Role Repertory Test (REP-per-tor-ee). A psychological test that attempts to determine how many roles a subject is capable of playing.

It should be clear, however, that idiographic assessment only permits one to predict certain behaviors across certain situations for certain people but not beyond that. Consequently, a conflict does arise if an investigator refuses to relinquish the power to decide which behaviors of which people are to be studied in which situations; the logic of idiographic assessment requires that the individual himself must be given this power, whereas the particular concerns of the investigator may require these decisions to be fixed parameters.

Consider, for example, the researcher who wishes to study, say, need for achievement in a particular setting in a particular population. No matter how persuasive he finds our arguments for the merits of idiographic assessment, he is simply not interested in studying a different set of personality variables in each individual. But, on the other hand, our arguments imply that need for achievement may not even *be* a trait dimension which usefully characterizes many of the individuals in the sample. As his low validity coefficients will attest, those individuals will contribute only noise to his investigation. The dilemma is real. If our arguments here are sound, one simply cannot, in principle, ever do any better than predicting some of the people some of the time. It is an idiographic fact of life.

Our advice to such an investigator, then, follows directly: Find those people. Separate those individuals who are cross-situationally consistent on the trait dimension and throw the others out, for by definition, only the behavior of consistent individuals can be meaningfully characterized by the investigator's construct; only their behaviors can be partitioned into the equivalence class under investigation. Perhaps a statistical metaphor will make this proposal seem less illegitimate: Unless an individual's variance on a particular trait dimension is small, it makes no sense to attach psychological significance to his mean on that dimension.

We submit that even this token gesture toward a more idiographic assessment has its rewards. First of all, one may obtain valuable knowledge about the trait dimension itself; it could be useful (as well as humbling) to discover why, which, and how many individuals fail to share the investigator's partitioning of the world into his favorite equivalence class. But perhaps even better, we believe that the rewards for this small idiographic commitment can even be paid in the sacred coin of the realm: bigger correlation coefficients! The following demonstration illustrates the point.

A PRIORI ASSESSMENT OF CROSS-SITUATIONAL CONSISTENCY[3]

Our purpose in this study was to test whether or not individuals can be divided on the basis of self-report into those who are cross-situationally consistent on a particular trait and those who are not. Our hypothesis is straightforward: Individuals who identify themselves as consistent on a particular trait dimension will in fact be more consistent cross-situationally than those who identify themselves as highly variable. In population terms, the cross-situational correlation coefficients of the self-identified low-variability group should be significantly higher than the coefficients of the high-variability group. In order to add a bit more persuasive elegance to the study, we tested this hypothesis twice on the same population of subjects using two **orthogonal** personality traits, friendliness and conscientiousness.

Method

As part of a questionnaire entitled the Cross-Situation Behavior Survey (CSBS), all students in Stanford's introductory psychology course were asked to assess themselves on several trait dimensions, including friendliness and conscientiousness. On each dimension, the individual was asked to rate both his overall level and his variability. For example, on the friendliness dimension, he was asked, "In general, how friendly and outgoing are you?" and "How much do you vary from one situation to another in how friendly and outgoing you are?" Parallel pairs of questions were asked about conscientiousness and other traits. Responses were obtained on a seven-point scale which ranged from "not at all" to "extremely." It will be noted that these questions thus permit the individual to employ his own concept of the trait dimension, to average across the situations he sees as pertinent and to ignore situations he sees as irrelevant. Accordingly, these global self-ratings will be successful in predicting behavior only to the extent that the individual's definition of a trait dimension coincides with the definition we will necessarily be imposing by our selection of situations to sample.

Using the same seven-point response scale, we also obtained each individual's self-ratings on specific behavior-situation items for each trait. For example, the CSBS included a 24-item scale which assessed the trait of friendliness in specific situations (e.g., "When in a store, how likely are you to strike up a conversation with a sales clerk?") and a 23-item conscientiousness scale (e.g., "How carefully do you double-check your term papers for typing and spelling errors?"). Thus if the global self-ratings can be seen as reflecting the individual's own definitions of the trait dimensions, then these CSBS scales can be viewed as reflecting the investigators' conception of these dimensions. The **internal reliabilities (coefficient alpha)** of the two trait scales were .91 and .84 for

TABLE 1
INTERCORRELATIONS AMONG THE SIX FRIENDLINESS VARIABLES FOR LOW- AND HIGH-VARIABILITY SUBJECTS

Low \ High	Self-report	Mother's report	Father's report	Peer's report	Group discussion	Spontaneous friendliness	All variables
1. Self-report							
2. Mother's Report	.61 / .52						
3. Father's Report	.48 / .24	.75 / .28					
4. Peer's Report	.62 / .56	.71 / .40	.50 / .34				
5. Group Discussion	.52 / .59	.34 / .41	.50 / .13	.45 / .39			
6. Spontaneous Friendliness	.61 / −.06	.46 / −.18	.69 / −.20	.39 / .09	.73 / .30		
MEAN CORRELATIONS	.57 / .39	.59 / .30	.60 / .16	.54 / .37	.52 / .37	.59 / .01	.57 / .27

friendliness and conscientiousness, respectively, and the correlation between them was +.13.

Cross-situational Assessment. From the introductory psychology course, 32 male and 32 female students were recruited as subjects. In addition to the initial testing session in which all students participated, the subjects were seen on three separate occasions, and they also signed release forms giving us permission to obtain ratings on them from their parents and one of their close peers, usually a roommate. From these various sessions, the following six friendliness variables and seven conscientiousness variables were derived.

Friendliness: (1) Self-report; (2) Mother's Report (3) Father's Report (4) Peer's Report: Each of these four judges provided us with an independent assessment of the individual's friendliness by rating him on the global friendliness item and the 24-item CSBS friendliness scale. For each judge, these two measures were combined into a single score. *(5) Group Discussion:* Each individual was observed as he participated in a group discussion with three other subjects of the same sex. A measure of each individual's friendliness in the group was derived from the frequency and duration of his vocalizations and the group's postdiscussion rating of his friendliness. *(6) Spontaneous Friendliness:* Each individual was observed as he waited in a waiting room with an experimental confederate, and a measure of spontaneous friendliness was derived from his latency in initiating conversation.

Conscientiousness: (1) Self-Report; (2) Mother's Report; (3) Father's Report; (4) Peer's Report: As with friendliness, each of these four judges provided us with an independent assessment of the individual's conscientiousness by rating him on the global conscientiousness item and the 23-item CSBS conscientiousness scale. *(5) Returning Evaluations:* During the quarter, each individual received four evaluation forms by mail as part of an ongoing assessment of the introductory psychology course. Each form asked him to evaluate one of the course lectures and to return the form anonymously prior to the subsequent class period. (The forms for our subjects were numerically coded.) Measures of his promptness in returning each of the four forms were combined into a single index. *(6) Course Readings:* Each of the course evaluation

---

Validity coefficients (val-ID-it-tee koh-ee-FISH-ents). A validity coefficient reflects how well a test measures what it is intended to measure.

Orthogonal (or-THOG-oh-nal). Uncorrelated, or at right angles.

Internal reliabilities (coefficient alpha). The alpha coefficient of a scale (or psychological test) tells you how internally consistent the scale is.

TABLE 2
CORRELATIONS BETWEEN EYSENCK'S EXTRAVERSION-
INTROVERSION SCALE AND SIX FRIENDLINESS
VARIABLES AS A FUNCTION OF
SELF-RATED VARIABILITY

Extraversion versus:	Self-rated variability	
	Low	High
Self-Report	.77	.65
Mother's Report	.54	.37
Father's Report	.26	.24
Peer's Report	.71	.41
Group Discussion	.34	.18
Spontaneous Friendliness	.25	-.12
Mean correlation[a]	.51	.31
Mean correlation (omitting self-report)[b]	.44	.22

[a] Correlated t=3.96, p<.01, one-tailed test.
[b] Correlated t=3.22, p<.025, one-tailed test.

forms described above asked the individual to check off the course readings he had been able to complete up to that time, providing us with four separate reports of his conscientiousness in school work. *(7) Neatness:* The neatness and cleanliness of each individual's hair and clothing were rated on two separate occasions by three independent judges and his living quarters were rated on nine aspects of neatness during a surprise visit paid during the last week of the quarter. These several observations were combined into an overall neatness score.

Finally, it should be noted that experimental assistants and observers were all blind with respect to the individual's scores on the trait dimensions, and no observer made more than one observation for each trait on the same individual.

Results

The first step in the analysis of results was to classify each individual on a priori grounds as a low-variability or a high-variability subject in a way that would not be confounded with his actual position on the trait dimension. Accordingly, for each trait, a subject was first classified into one of seven subgroups on the basis of his response to the question "In general, how friendly and outgoing [conscientious] are you?". Then, on the basis of his response to the question "How much do you vary from one situation to another in how friendly and outgoing [conscientious] you are?", he was designated as a low-variability or a high-variability subject, respectively, depending upon whether he was below or above the median among the same-sex subjects at the same point on the trait scale. Thus low and high variability were redefined at each of the seven points on the global trait scale in order to **partial out** any relationship between an individual's self-rated variability and his self-rated position on the trait dimension.

In order to assess each individual's cross-situational consistency for each trait, we converted each of the 13 variables to a standard T score with a mean of 50 and a **standard deviation** of 10 across the 64 subjects. We then calculated each individual's standard deviation across the six friendliness variables and across the seven conscientiousness variables. These two standard deviations thus reflect the individual's cross-situational variability on friendliness and conscientiousness, respectively; the larger the standard deviation, the more variable he is across situations.

Friendliness. With respect to friendliness dimension, our hypothesis was confirmed. Individuals who indicate that they do not vary much from one situation to another do, in fact, display significantly less variability across situations than do those who say they do vary (6.42 versus 7.90; $t = 2.34$, $p < .02$, one-tailed test). Moreover, an individual's self-rated friendliness per se is not related to his cross-situational variability; in particular, individuals in the lowest, middle, and highest thirds of the distribution on the self-rated friendliness scale did not differ from one another in their cross-situational variability, $F(2, 61) = 1.10$, **ns**.

Table 1 shows how the differential cross-situational consistency of low- and high-variability individuals translates into cross-situational predictability in correlational terms. The intercorrelations of the six variables for the 32 low-variability subjects are shown above the diagonal; intercorrelations for the 32 high variability subjects, below the diagonal. The bottom row of Table 1 serves to summarize the **matrix** by showing the mean correlation between the column variable and the remaining five variables for the two groups separately.[4]

As Table 1 shows, 13 of the 15 intercorrelations are higher for low-variability subjects than they are for high-variability subjects, six of them significantly so ($p < .05$, one-tailed test). The mean intercorrelation among all the variables is +.57 for the low-variability group and +.27 for the high-variability group. Note also that the predicted effect is quite general across different pairs of situations. For example, Mother's Report and Father's Report, two measurements that one would expect to be highly similar and "contaminated" by one another, show a correlation of +.75 for the low-variability group but only +.28 for the high-variability group ($p < .005$, one-tailed test); similarly, Group Discussion and Spontaneous Friendliness, the two methodologically independent behavioral observations, show a correlation of +.73 for the low-variability group but only +.30 for the high-variability group ($p < .009$, one-tailed test). Thus, not only have our expectations been confirmed, but the magic +.30 barrier appears to have been penetrated.

TABLE 3
INTERCORRELATIONS AMONG THE SEVEN CONSCIENTIOUSNESS VARIABLES
FOR LOW- AND HIGH-VARIABILITY SUBJECTS

Low \ High	Self-report	Mother's report	Father's report	Peer's report	Returning evaluations	Course readings	Neatness	All Variables
1. Self Report								
2. Mother's Report	.47 / .27							
3. Father's Report	.31 / .23	.83 / .46						
4. Peer's Report	.44 / .25	.50 / .04	.38 / .49					
5. Returning Evaluations	.43 / -.12	.60 / .03	.42 / .10	.49 / .11				
6. Course Readings	.40 / -.07	.20 / -.31	.31 / -.24	.61 / -.16	-.01 / .18			
7. Neatness	.31 / .55	.13 / .39	.11 / .43	.23 / .45	-.01 / -.14	-.11 / -.61		
Mean correlations	.40 / .20	.50 / .15	.43 / .26	.45 / .21	.33 / .03	.25 / -.22	.12 / .19	.36 / .12
Mean corr. (omitting Neatness)	.41 / .11	.56 / .10	.49 / .22	.49 / .16	.40 / .06	.32 / -.12	----	.45 / .09

It will be noted that the "moderating variable" in this analysis, the variable which separates the population into groups which are differentially predictable, is the individual's response to the single question "How much do you vary from one situation to another in how friendly and outgoing you are?" To see whether such an item could enhance the utility of a standard personality inventory as well, we computed the correlations between the six friendliness variables and the extraversion-introversion scale of the Eysenck Personality Inventory (Eysenck & Eysenck, 1968), which all of our subjects had taken at the initial testing session. Using the same criterion for low and high variability as before, Table 2 displays the correlations for the two groups separately. It is seen that the extraversion-introversion scale of the

Partial out. A statistical technique in which the effects of a certain variable are removed from study.

Standard deviation. The standard deviation is a mathematical way of figuring out how much a test score deviates from the mean, median, or mode (usually the mean). Generally speaking, a test score must be two standard deviations (or more) above or below the mean to be considered a significant departure from the mean. On most intelligence tests, the standard deviation is about 16 points. If you score 110 on such a test, and the mean is 100 points, you are not significantly brighter than the average person because your score is less than one standard deviation from the mean. If you score 135, however, your score is more than two standard deviations above the mean, and we presume you thus are significantly brighter than the average person is.

ns. Abbreviation for "not significant," that is, a result that probably was due to chance.

Matrix (MAY-tricks). A matrix of scores is a set of scores that can be presented in rows and columns in rectangular form. Most "tables" that display data in journal articles are set up in matrix form.

Eysenck Personality Inventory does indeed have greater predictive utility for self-identified low-variability subjects than for high-variability subjects ($t = 3.96, p < .01$). Moreover, the effect remains significant even if the methodologically similar Self-Report variable is removed from the analysis ($t = 3.22, p < .025$).

Conscientiousness. As we noted earlier, the global self-rating items used to classify our subjects permit the individual to utilize his own definition of the trait, to implicitly average across behaviors he regards as pertinent and to ignore all others. As we pointed out, this seemed likely to yield our predicted results only to the extent that the subjects' trait definitions coincided with our own. For the trait of friendliness, an adequate commonality of definition was achieved. For example, the correlation between the individual's global self-rating of his friendliness and his mean score on our CSBS friendliness items was +.84. The corresponding correlation for the conscientiousness trait, however, was significantly lower, $r = .62$; $Z_{difference} = 2.74, p < .006$, two-tailed test, implying that the trait term "conscientiousness" is more likely to denote different equivalence classes of behaviors for different individuals than is the trait term "friendliness." Not unexpectedly, then, we were not able to replicate the friendliness findings for the conscientiousness trait when we employed our subjects' global self-ratings as the classification variables.

Accordingly, we turned to *our* definition of conscientiousness as the basis for subject classification, designating each individual as low or high variability as a function of his variance on the CSBS conscientiousness scale. In particular, we calculated each individual's variance across the 23 conscientiousness items and divided it by his variance across all 86 items of the questionnaire. This <u>ipsatized</u> variance index not only corrects for the individual's tendency to respond consistently or inconsistently to CSBS items irrespective of their content, but it also has a more conceptual interpretation as well. It reflects the degree to which an individual "extracts" the particular trait-scale items from the total pool of items and "clusters" them into an equivalence class. Statistically the ipsatized variance is like an inverted <u>F ratio</u>, representing the ratio of two variances which assumes a value of zero if the individual responds identically to each item on the trait scale and a value of one if he does not "cluster" the items on a trait scale at all.[5]

Subjects were first formed into matched pairs on the basis of their CSBS conscientiousness scores, and then each individual was classified as low or high variability, respectively, depending upon whether his ipsatized variance was lower or higher than that of his matched partner. It will be recognized that this again serves to partial out any relationship between the individual's variability and his location on the trait dimension. As before, the individual's cross-situational variability is assessed by his standard deviation across the several situations.

With this method of classification, the results confirm our hypothesis, paralleling exactly our findings for the friendliness dimension. Thus low-variability subjects were significantly less variable across situations than high-variability subjects (7.46 versus 8.89, correlated $t = 2.80, p < .005$, one-tailed test). And again, an individual's standing on the trait itself was not related to his cross-situational variability; individuals in different thirds of the distribution on the CSBS conscientiousness scale did not differ from one another in their cross-situational variability $F(2,61) < 1, ns$.[6]

Table 3 translates the differential cross-situational consistency of low- and high-variability individuals into correlational terms. As before, correlations for the 32-low variability subjects are found above the diagonal, the 32 high-variability subjects, below the diagonal.

It is seen in Table 3 that 15 of the 21 intercorrelations are higher for low-variability subjects than they are for high-variability subjects, with 9 of them significantly so ($p < .05$, one-tailed test). As the summary rows of the table reveal, only the Neatness variable fails to conform to our hypothesis accounting for all but two of the reversals in the matrix. The bottom row of the table shows the mean intercorrelations obtained when this variable is omitted.

But it is precisely the Neatness variable which illustrates the main point of this article. As an inspection of the correlation matrix reveals, it is only we, the investigators, who think that school-related conscientiousness (Returning Evaluations and Course Readings) and personal neatness ought to belong in the same equivalence class. Our subjects do not. Our low-variability subjects find them to be orthogonal (-.01 and 0.11), and our high-variability subjects apparently have time to do their schoolwork *or* to keep things neat and clean, but not both ($r = -.61$).

The judgments by self, parents, and peers are also interesting in this regard. An inspection of the correlations in the matrix reveals that judges of low-variability subjects appear to be responding to both kinds of conscientiousness almost equally, with some bias toward greater attention to school-related conscientiousness. But judges of high-variability subjects seem to be ignoring school-related conscientiousness and responding primarily to the inversely-related personal neatness. It is this latter pattern which causes the Neatness variable to violate our hypothesis that low-variability subjects would have the higher correlations.

The moral of all this, of course, is that we need to move even further toward idiographic assessment. In this demonstration, we have relinquished the presumption that all traits are relevant to all people but stubbornly retained the right to dictate which behaviors and situations shall constitute the trait itself. When an investigator is willing to release this degree of freedom as well, his validity coefficients will reward him with an appropriate increment in magnitude. In the present study, for example, we might have asked the subjects to rate the several CSBS items for their relevance to the various trait dimensions. In this way, we might have discovered *a priori* those subjects who do not share our personal delusion that the conscientious person does his schoolwork and attends to his personal neatness.

PREDICTIVE UTILITY OF TRAITS AND SITUATIONS

We have argued in this article that it is not possible, in principle, to do any better than predicting some of the people some of the time. Furthermore, our arguments would seem to imply that an investigator must simply abandon the highly variable individual since the trait under investigation has no predictive utility for him. But this is not always true. As Mischel (1968, 1973b) has persuasively argued, variability is not synonymous with either **capriciousness** or unpredictability. Indeed, an individual's cross-situational variability may well be the mark of a highly refined "discriminative facility" (Mischel, 1973b), the ability to respond appropriately to subtle changes in situational contingencies. Although such an individual cannot be predicted from a knowledge of his standing on a personality trait, he may be precisely the individual who is most predictable from a knowledge of the situation. In short, if some of the people can be predicted some of the time from personality traits, then some of the people can be predicted some of the time from situational variables.

This point is nicely illustrated in recent work on sex roles by S. Bem (1974, in press). Whereas previous research in this area has been concerned either with the sex-typed masculine males and feminine females or, occasionally, with the sex-reversed feminine males and masculine females, S. Bem has constructed a sex-role inventory which permits her to identify "**androgynous**" individuals as well, individuals who attribute both masculine and feminine characteristics to themselves in about equal amounts without regard for their sex-role connotations. Thus, with respect to either of the two trait terms masculinity or femininity, androgynous individuals are the "high variability" subjects; neither trait has predictive utility for them. And as hypothesized, Bem finds that androgynous individuals of both sexes vary their behavior cross-situationally so that they are able to "do well" at both masculine and feminine tasks and behaviors, whereas sex-typed individuals do not do well in situations or settings which call for behaviors incongruent with their self-described sex roles. For example, only the androgynous subjects showed both "masculine" independence in an Asch conformity experiment as well as "feminine" nurturance when given the opportunity to play with a baby kitten (S. Bem, in press). There are, in short, some occasions when one can predict some of the high-variability people some of the time.

It should be clear from this discussion that the position we have argued in this article cannot be characterized as opposing either side of the debate between those who believe that behavior is consistent across situations and those who believe that behavior is situationally specific. The shift to idiographic assumptions about the nature of individual differences dissolves this false **dichotomy** and permits one to believe in both propositions. As noted early in this article, the actual **cleavage** is between nomothetic and idiographic criteria for consistency and inconsistency.

Similarly, it should be clear that we have not been arguing an "anti-Mischel" position. Both Mischel and we agree that the nomothetic assumptions of the traditional approach in personality virtually guarantee a +.30 ceiling on validity coefficients and, hence, that trait-based approaches predicated on such assumptions will continue to fail the test of predictive utility. Mischel and we agree that only an idiographic approach can break through this predictive barrier. Mischel and we agree that the classification of situations must be an integral part of any assessment procedure; moreover, we agree that such classification will have to be in terms of the individual's own **phenomenology**, not the investigator's (Mischel, 1973b), a suggestion that is bound to increase further the déjà vu of any psychologist

---

Ipsatized (IP-sah-tized). When you "ipsatize" variance scores, you use a statistical device that allows you to combine the scores to yield a single number between 1 and 0.

F ratio. A statistic used to represent the magnitude of difference between two sets of scores.

Capriciousness (cap-PREE-shush-ness). The tendency to change suddenly or unpredictably.

Androgynous (an-DRODGE-ih-nous). Having the characteristics or nature of both male and female.

Dichotomy (die-KOT-oh-mee). A division into two mutually exclusive, or contradictory, groups.

Cleavage (KLEE-vage). To cleave something is to split it into two parts.

Phenomenology (fee-nom-ee-NOL-oh-gee). The study of human consciousness.

old enough to remember Kurt Lewin (1935). It is true that Mischel and we have chosen different conceptual languages in which to express these points, and future divergences will surely emerge as a consequence, but the two formulations are far more similar in their basic assumptions than their formal appearances would suggest.

The failure of traditional assessment procedures and the belief that person-situation interactions will account for most of the psychologically interesting variance in behavior have led several recent writers to emphasize that personality assessment must begin to attend seriously to situations. We agree. We have merely chosen to emphasize the perfectly symmetric, but perhaps more subtle, point that personality assessment must also begin to attend seriously to persons.

FOOTNOTES

[1] Reprinted by permission of the authors and the publisher from *Psychological Review*, 1974, **81**, 506-520. Copyright 1974 by the American Psychological Association.

[2] We are indebted to Stanford colleague Lee Ross for bringing this point to our attention.

[3] We are grateful to many people for help in executing this study, particularly to Fred Bart Astor who served as overall supervisor and research assistant and to Margaret Bond who transformed raw observations into meaningful data. For their multiple roles as trained observers, experimental confederates, and general research assistants, we are grateful to John Backes, Margaret Bond, Kathleen Chiappori, Tom Deremigio, Gowen Roper, Jeremy Rosenblum, and Ann Scholey. Above all, however, we are grateful to our subjects, who were genuine partners in this research effort. In return for their cooperation, we attempted to keep them as fully informed of our procedures and rationale as the design would permit.

[4] All calculations and analyses involving correlation coefficients are actually performed on their Z-transforms.

[5] In 1961, Berdie used an intraindividual variance measure as a moderating variable for predicting mathematical aptitude. (See also Campus, 1974, and Fiske and Rice, 1955.)

[6] We believe that, like conscientiousness, most traits would not attain the degree of definitional consensus between subject and investigator displayed by the friendliness trait. Accordingly, we believe that the ipsatized variance index, rather than the single item self-rating of variability, will prove to be the more promising candidate for the moderating variable in any future work. Moreover, the ipsatized variance index can be calculated for any set of questionnaire items the investigator chooses even when the layman has no trait term for labeling the potential equivalence class so defined.

REFERENCES

Alker, H. A. Is personality situationally specific or intrapsychically consistent? *Journal of Personality*, 1972, **40**, 1-16.

Allport, G. W. *Personality: A psychological interpretation*. New York: Holt, 1937.

Allport, G. W. Traits revisited. *American Psychologist*, 1966, **21**, 1-10.

Allport, G. W., & Odbert, H. S. Trait-names: A psycholexical study. *Psychological Monographs*, 1936, **47**(1, Whole No. 211).

Argyle, M., & Little, B. R. Do personality traits apply to social behavior? *Journal for the Theory of Social Behaviour*, 1972, **2**, 1-35.

Averill, J. R. The dis-position of psychological dispositions. *Journal of Experimental Research in Personality*, 1973, **6**, 275-282.

Baldwin, A. L. The study of individual personality by means of the intraindividual correlation. *Journal of Personality*, 1946, **14**, 151-168.

Bem, D. J. Constructing cross-situational consistencies in behavior: Some thoughts on Alker's critique of Mischel. *Journal of Personality*, 1972, **40**, 17-26.

Bem, S. L. The measurement of psychological androgyny. *Journal of Consulting and Clinical Psychology*, 1974, **42**, 155-162.

Bem, S. L. Sex-role adaptability: One consequence of psychological androgyny. *Journal of Personality and Social Psychology*, in press.

Berdie, R. F. Intra-individual variability and predictability. *Educational and Psychological Measurement*, 1961, **21**, 663-676.

Bowers, K. S. Situationism in psychology: An analysis and a critique. *Psychological Review*, 1973, **80**, 307-336.

Campus, N. Transituational consistency as a dimension of personality. *Journal of Personality and Social Psychology*, 1974, **29**, 593-600.

Chapman, L. J., & Chapman, J. P. Illusory correlations as an obstacle to the use of valid psycho-diagnostic signs. *Journal of Abnormal Psychology*, 1969, **74**, 271-280.

Dudycha, G. J. An objective study of punctuality in relation to personality and achievement. *Archives of Psychology*, 1936, **204**, 1-319.

Endler, N. S. The case for person-situation interactions. Paper presented at the meeting of the American Psychological Association, Montreal, August 1973. (a)

Endler, N. S. The person versus the situation--A pseudo issue? A response to Alker. *Journal of Personality*, 1973, **41**, 287-303. (b)

Endler, N. S., & Hunt, J. McV. S-R inventories of hostility and comparisons of the proportions of variance from persons, responses, and situations for hostility and anxiousness. *Journal of Personality and Social Psychology*, 1968, **9**, 309-315.

Eysenck, H. J., & Eysenck, S. B. G. *Manual for the Eysenck Personality Inventory*. San Diego: Educational and Industrial Testing Service, 1968.

Fiske, D. W., & Rice, L. Intra-individual response variability. *Psychological Bulletin,* 1955, **52,** 217-250.

Harre, R., & Secord, P. F. *The explanation of social behavior.* Oxford: Basil, Blackwell, & Mott, 1972.

Hartshorne, H., & May, M. A. *Studies in the nature of character.* Vol. 1. *Studies in deceit.* New York: Macmillan, 1928.

Hartshorne, H., & May, M. A. *Studies in the nature of character.* Vol. 2. *Studies in service and self-control.* New York: Macmillan, 1929.

Hartshorne, H., May, M. A., & Shuttleworth, F. K. *Studies in the nature of character.* Vol. 3. *Studies in the organization of character.* New York: Macmillan, 1930.

Jones, E. E., & Davis, K. E. From acts to dispositions: The attribution process in person perception. In L. Berkowitz (Ed.), *Advances in experimental social psychology.* Vol. 2. New York: Academic Press, 1965.

Jones, E. E., & Goethals, G. R. *Order effects in impression formation: Attribution context and the nature of the entity.* New York: General Learning Press, 1971.

Jones, E. E., & Harris, V. A. The attribution of attitudes. *Journal of Experimental Social Psychology,* 1967, **3,** 1-24.

Jones, E. E., & Nisbett, R. E. *The actor and observer: Divergent perceptions of the causes of behavior.* New York: General Learning Press, 1971.

Kelley, H. H. Attribution theory in social psychology. In D. Levine (Ed.), *Nebraska Symposium on Motivation: 1967.* Lincoln: University of Nebraska Press, 1967.

Kelley, H. H., & Stahelski, A. J. Social interaction basis of cooperators' and competitors' beliefs about others. *Journal of Personality and Social Psychology,* 1970, **16,** 66-91.

Kelly, G. A. *The psychology of personal constructs.* New York: Norton, 1955, 2 vols.

Lehmann, H. C., & Witty, P. A. Faculty psychology and personality traits. *American Journal of Psychology,* 1934, **44,** 490.

Lewin, K. *A dynamic theory of personality.* New York: McGraw-Hill, 1935.

McClelland, D. C. *Personality.* New York: William Sloane Associates, 1951.

Mischel, W. *Personality and assessment.* New York: Wiley, 1968.

Mischel, W. Continuity and change in personality. *American Psychologist,* 1969, **24,** 1012-1018.

Mischel, W. On the empirical dilemmas of psychodynamic approaches: Issues and alternatives. *Journal of Abnormal Psychology,* 1973, **82,** 335-344. (a)

Mischel, W. Toward a cognitive social learning reconceptualization of personality. *Psychological Review,* 1973, 80, 252-283. (b)

Moos, R. H. Sources of variance in responses to questionnaires and in behavior. *Journal of Abnormal Psychology,* 1969, **74,** 405-412.

Newcomb, T. M. *Consistency of certain extrovert-introvert behavior patterns in 51 problem boys.* New York: Columbia University, Teachers College, Bureau of Publications, 1929.

Passini, F. T., & Norman, W. T. A universal conception of personality structure? *Journal of Personality and Social Psychology,* 1966, **4,** 44-49.

Peterson, D. R. *The clinical study of social behavior.* New York: Appleton-Century-Crofts, 1968.

Sanford, N. *Issues in personality theory.* San Francisco: Jossey-Bass, 1970.

Schneider, D. J. Implicit personality theory: A review. *Psychological Bulletin,* 1973, **79,** 294-309.

Scott, W. A. Attitude measurement. In G. Lindzey & E. Aronson (Eds.), *The handbook of social psychology.* Vol. 2. Menlo Park, Calif.: Addison-Wesley, 1968.

Stagner, R. *Psychology of personality.* New York: McGraw-Hill, 1937.

Stagner, R. Traits are relevant logical and empirical analysis. Paper presented at the meeting of the American Psychological Association, Montreal, August 1973.

Stouffer, S. A., Guttman, L., Suchman, E. A., Lazarsfeld, P. F., Star, S. A., & Clausen, J. A. *Studies in social psychology in World War II.* Vol. 4. *Measurement and prediction.* Princeton: Princeton University Press, 1950.

Vale, J. R., & Vale, G. R. Individual difference and general laws in psychology: A reconciliation. *American Psychologist,* 1969, **24,** 1093-1108.

Vernon P. E. *Personality assessment: A critical survey.* New York: Wiley, 1964.

Wachtel, P. Psychodynamics, behavior therapy, and the implacable experimenter: An inquiry into the consistency of personality. *Journal of Abnormal Psychology,* 1973, **82,** 324-334.

Wallach, M. A., & Leggett, M. I. Testing the hypothesis that a person will be consistent: Stylistic consistency versus situational specificity in size of children's drawing. *Journal of Personality,* 1972, **40,** 309-330.

CHAPTER 18

"The Social Readjustment Rating Scale"

Thomas H. Holmes and Richard H. Rahe[1,2]

EDITORS' COMMENTS. There is almost nothing in the entire field of psychology more fashionable today than the study of "stress," particularly its effects on human health and behavior. And little wonder this is the case, since stress has been implicated as a contributing factor in a wide variety of diseases, from AIDS to heart attacks. Also, many psychologists believe that stress is one of the causal factors in most types of mental disorders, from depression to schizophrenia.

Given the wide-spread blaming of stress as "the symptom of our times," it may surprise you to learn that the whole concept of stress is fairly new. It was only 50 years or so ago that Canadian researcher Hans Selye (SELL-ye) described the physiological reactions that occur during a stress reaction, and thereby made the concept of "stress" popular in the field of psychosomatic medicine. (Obviously people *experienced* stress prior to that time; they merely didn't have a neat term to describe what their bodily reactions were.) Selye said there were three stages of the stress reaction. (1) An *alarm reaction*, in which your mind and body go into a state of shock. Your temperature and blood pressure drop, your tissues swell with fluid, and your ability to think clearly is affected. (2) A *stage of resistance*, during which your body begins to repair the damage suffered during shock. And (3) a *stage of exhaustion* that occurs if the stress continues for too long or is too severe.

Given all the bad press that stress has gotten of late, it may also surprise you to learn that even Hans Selye believed that there was "good stress" as well as bad. Selye called it *eustress*, and believed that moderate levels of eustress were necessary for survival. According to Selye, a life that was totally "stress free" would probably be a rather short one.

Selye assumed that a given stressor would affect almost everyone in the same fashion. And early research by Thomas Holmes and Richard Rahe--reported in this article--seemed to support Selye's position. Holmes and Rahe interviewed and checked the medical histories of thousands of people. They found (as you will see) a significant correlation between *major events* in these people's lives and their *physical condition* in the following year or two. Recent research, however, suggests that the "major events" which Holmes and Rahe described account for less than 15 percent of the stress that people typically report. Also, there is tremendous variability in how various situations affect different people. Men and women, for instance, are stressed by quite a different set of "major events".[3] Then, too, the situations described as "most traumatic" by Holmes and Rahe are not particularly relevant for the very young or the very old.[4] Furthermore, people living in small towns and on farms apparently experience more stress--or react to it less effectively--than do individuals living in urban areas.[5] And most important of all, perhaps, is the fact that many people can handle the stress associated with life's "major events," but have problems adjusting to the "little hassles" that bedevil all of us daily.[4]

In psychology, therefore, stress research has begun to focus more on how people *appraise* stressful situations than on the actual events which supposedly *cause* stress. For your *perception* of what happens to you often determines how well you will *adjust* to stress.

Nonetheless, we must give Holmes and Rahe credit for helping focus our attention on how important the social environment is in determining both physical and mental health.

In previous studies (1) it has been established that a cluster of social events requiring change in ongoing life adjustment is significantly associated with the time of illness onset. Similarly, the relationship of what has been called "life stress," "emotional stress," "object loss," etc. and illness onset has been demonstrated by other investigations (2-13). It has been **adduced** from these studies that this clustering of social or life events achieves **etiologic** significance as a necessary but not sufficient cause of illness and accounts in part for the time of onset of disease.

Methodologically, the interview or questionnaire technique used in these studies has yielded only the *number* and *types* of events making up the cluster. Some estimates of the magnitude of these events is now required to bring greater precision to this area of research and to provide a quantitative basis for new **epidemiological** studies of diseases. This report defines a method which achieves this requisite.

METHOD

A sample of convenience composed of 394 subjects completed the paper and pencil test (Table 1). (See Table 2 for characteristics of the sample.) The items were the 43 life events **empirically** derived from clinical experience. The following written instructions were given to each subject who completed the Social Readjustment Rating Questionnaire (SRRQ).

(A) Social readjustment includes the amount and duration of change in one's accustomed pattern of life resulting from various life events. As defined, social readjustment measures the intensity and length of time necessary to accommodate to a life event, *regardless of the desirability of this event*.

(B) You are asked to rate a series of life events as to their relative degrees of necessary readjustment. In scoring, *use all of your experience* in arriving at your answer. This means personal experience where it applies as well as what you have learned to be the case for others. Some persons accommodate to change more readily than others; some persons adjust with particular ease or difficulty to only certain events. Therefore, strive to give your opinion of the average degree of readjustment necessary for each event rather than the extreme.

(C) The mechanics of rating are these: Event 1, Marriage, has been given an arbitrary value of 500. As you complete each of the remaining events think to yourself, "Is this event indicative of more or less readjustment than marriage?" "Would the readjustment take longer or shorter to accomplish?" If you decide the readjustment is more intense and proacted, then choose a *proportionally larger* number and place it in the blank directly opposite the event in the column marked "VALUES." If you decided the event represents less and shorter readjustment than marriage then indicate how much less by placing a *proportionally smaller* number in the opposite blank. (If an event requires intense readjustment over a short time span, it may approximate in value an event requiring less intense readjustment over a long period of time.) If the event is equal in social readjustment to marriage, record the number 500 opposite the event.

The order in which the items were presented is shown in Table 1.

RESULTS

The Social Readjustment Rating Scale (SRRS) is shown in Table 3. This table contains the magnitude of the life events which is derived when the mean score, divided by 10, of each item for the entire sample is calculated and arranged in rank order. That consensus is high concerning the relative order and magnitude of the means of items is demonstrated by the high **coefficients of correlation** (Pearson's r) between the discrete groups contained in the sample. Table 2 reveals that all the coefficients of correlations are above 0.90 with the exception of that between white and Negro which was 0.82. Kendall's **coefficient of concordance** (W) for the 394 individuals was 0.477, significant at $p = < 0.0005$.

DISCUSSION

Placed in historical perspective, this research evolved from the **chrysalis** of Psychobiology generated by Adolph Meyer (14). His invention of the 'life chart,' a device for organizing the medical data as a dynamic biography, provided a unique method for demonstrating his schema of the relationship of biological, psychological, and sociological phenomena to the processes of health and disease in man. The importance of many of the life events used in this research was emphasized by Meyer: "... changes of habitat, of school

---

Adduced (ad-DEWSD). To *adduce* something is to "reason it out," or to "conclude it is true from looking at the facts of the matter."

Etiologic (ee-tee-oh-LODGE-ick). Etiology is the study of *causes*, particularly the causes of various diseases or disorders. *Etiologic* significance means "causal" significance.

Epidemiological (ep-pee-dee-mee-oh-LODGE-ih-kal). Epidemiology is that branch of medicine which studies the incidence, distribution, and control of a given disease in a given population.

Empirically (em-PEER-ih-kal-lee). To be "empirical" is to be guided by data and evidence rather than by theory or presupposition.

Coefficients of correlation (koh-ih-FISH-ents). A coefficient of correlation is a statistical device that tells you how similar two sets of data are. Pearson's r is one type of coefficient of correlation, but there are many other types.

Coefficient of concordance (kon-KOR-dance). Similar to a coefficient of correlation.

Chrysalis (KRIS-sah-liss). In biology, a chrysalis is a stage of development in the life of a butterfly, when it is completely covered with a protective coating. More broadly speaking, a chrysalis is one of the early stages of the development of *anything*.

TABLE 1. SOCIAL READJUSTMENT RATING QUESTIONNAIRE

	Events	Values
1.	Marriage	500
2.	Troubles with the boss	--
3.	Detention in jail or other institution	--
4.	Death of spouse	--
5.	Major change in sleeping habits (a lot more or a lot less sleep, or a change in part of day when asleep)	--
6.	Death of a close family member	--
7.	Major change in eating habits (a lot more or a lot less food intake, or very different meal hours or surroundings)	--
8.	Foreclosure on a mortgage or loan	--
9.	Revision of personal habits (dress, manners, associations, etc.)	--
10.	Death of a close friend	--
11.	Minor violations of the law (e.g., traffic tickets, jay walking, disturbing the peace, etc.)	--
12.	Outstanding personal achievement	--
13.	Pregnancy	--
14.	Major change in the health or behavior of a family member	--
15.	Sexual difficulties	--
16.	In-law troubles	--
17.	Major change in number of family get-togethers (e.g., a lot more or a lot less than usual)	--
18.	Major change in financial state (e.g., a lot worse off or a lot better than usual)	--
19.	Gaining a new family member (e.g., through birth, adoption, oldster moving in, etc.)	--
20.	Change in residence	--
21.	Son or daughter leaving home (e.g., marriage, attending college, etc.)	--
22.	Marital separation from mate	--
23.	Major change in church activities (e.g., a lot more or a lot less than usual)	--
24.	Marital reconciliation with mate	--
25.	Being fired from work	--
26.	Divorce	--
27.	Changing to a different line of work	--
28.	Major change in number of arguments with spouse (e.g., either a lot more or a lot less than usual regarding childrearing, personal habits, etc.)	--
29.	Major change in responsibilities at work (e.g., promotion, demotion, lateral transfer)	--
30.	Wife beginning or ceasing work outside the home	--
31.	Major change in working hours or conditions	--
32.	Major change in usual type and/or amount of recreation	--
33.	Taking on a mortgage greater than $10,000 (e.g., purchasing a home, business, etc.)	--
34.	Taking on a mortgage or loan less than $10,000 (e.g., purchasing a car, TV, freezer, etc.)	--
35.	Major personal injury or illness	--
36.	Major business readjustment (e.g., merger, reorganization, bankruptcy, etc.)	--
37.	Major change in social activities ((e.g., clubs, dancing, movies, visiting, etc.)	--
38.	Major change in living conditions (e.g., building a new home, remodeling, deterioration of home or neighborhood)	--
39.	Retirement from work	--
40.	Vacation	--
41.	Christmas	--
42.	Changing to a new school	--
43.	Beginning or ceasing formal schooling	--

TABLE 2. PEARSON'S COEFFICIENT OF CORRELATION BETWEEN DESCRETE GROUPS IN THE SAMPLE

Group	No. in group	vs.	Group	No. in group	Coefficient of correlation
Male	179	vs.	Female	215	0.965
Single	171	vs.	Married	223	0.960
Age < 30	206	vs.	Age 30-60	137	0.958
Age < 30	206	vs.	Age > 60	51	0.923
Age 30-60	137	vs.	Age > 60	51	0.965
1st Generation	19	vs.	2nd Generation	69	0.908
1st Generation	19	vs.	3rd Generation	306	0.929
2nd Generation	69	vs.	3rd Generation	306	0.975
< College	182	vs.	4 Years of College	212	0.967
Lower Class	71	vs.	Middle Class	323	0.928
White	363	vs.	Negro	19	0.820
White	363	vs.	Oriental	12	0.940
Protestant	241	vs.	Catholic	42	0.913
Protestant	241	vs.	Jewish	19	0.971
Protestant	241	vs.	Other religion	45	0.948
Protestant	241	vs.	No religious preference	47	0.926

entrance, graduations or changes or failures; the various jobs, the dates of possibly important births and deaths in the family, and other fundamentally important environmental influences" (14).

More recently, in Harold G. Wolff's laboratory,[6] the concepts of Pavlov, Freud, Cannon, and Skinner were incorporated in the Meyerian schema. The research resulting from this synthesis adduced powerful evidence that 'stressful' life events, by evoking psychophysiologic reactions, played an important causative role in the natural history of many diseases (15-19). Again, many of the life events denoted 'stressful' were those enumerated by Meyers and in Table 1 of this report.

Beginning in this laboratory in 1949, the life chart device has been used systematically in over 5000 patients to study the quality and quantity of life events empirically observed to cluster at the time of disease onset. Inspection of Table 1 reveals that each item derived from this experience is unique. There are 2 categories of items: those indicative of the life style of the individual, and those indicative of occurrences involving the individual. Evolving mostly from ordinary, but some from extraordinary, social and interpersonal transactions, these events pertain to major areas of dynamic significance in the social structure of the American way of life. These include family **constellation**, marriage, occupation, economics, residence, group and peer relationships, education, religion, recreation and health.

During the developmental phase of this research the interview technique was used to assess the meaning of the events for the individual. As expected, the psychological significance and emotions varied widely with the patient. Also it will be noted that only some of the events are negative or 'stressful' in the conventional sense, i.e., are socially undesirable. Many are socially desirable and consonant with the American values of achievement, success, materialism, practicality, efficiency, future orientation, conformism and self-reliance.

There was identified, however, one theme common to all these life events. The occurrence of each usually evoked or was associated with some adaptive or coping behavior on the part of the involved individual. Thus, each item has been constructed to contain life events whose **advent** is either indicative of or requires a significant change in the ongoing life pattern of the individual. The emphasis is on change from the existing steady state and not on psychological meaning, emotion, or social desirability.

The method for assigning a magnitude to the items was developed for use in Psychophysics—the study of the psychological perception of the quality, quantity, magnitude, intensity of physical **phenomena**. This subjective assessment of the observer plotted against the physical dimension being perceived (length of objects, intensity of sound, brightness of light, number of objects, etc.) provides a reliable delineation of man's ability to quantify certain of his experiences (20). In this research, the assumption was made that participants in the contemporary American way of life could utilize this innate psychological capacity for making quantitative judgments about psychosocial phenomena as well as psychophysical phenomena (21, 22). The data generated by this investigation appear to justify the assumption. Although some of the discrete subgroups do assign a different order and magnitude to the items,

TABLE 3. SOCIAL READJUSTMENT RATING SCALE

Rank	Life event	Mean value
1.	Death of spouse	100
2.	Divorce	73
3.	Marital separation	65
4.	Jail term	63
5.	Death of close family member	63
6.	Personal injury or illness	53
7.	Marriage	50
8.	Fired at work	47
9.	Marital reconciliation	45
10.	Retirement	45
11.	Change in health of family member	44
12.	Pregnancy	40
13.	Sex difficulties	39
14.	Gain of new family member	39
15.	Business readjustment	39
16.	Change in financial state	38
17.	Death of close friend	37
18.	Change to different line of work	36
19.	Change in number of arguments with spouse	35
20.	Mortgage over $10,000	31
21.	Foreclosure of mortgage or loan	30
22.	Change in responsibilities at work	29
23.	Son or daughter leaving home	29
24.	Trouble with in-laws	29
25.	Outstanding personal achievement	28
26.	Wife begin or stop work	26
27.	Begin or end school	26
28.	Change in living conditions	25
29.	Revision of personal habits	24
30.	Trouble with boss	23
31.	Change in work hours or conditions	20
32.	Change in residence	20
33.	Change in schools	20
34.	Change in recreation	19
35.	Change in church activities	19
36.	Change in social activities	18
37.	Mortgage or loan less than $10,000	17
38.	Change in sleeping habits	16
39.	Change in number of family get-togethers	15
40.	Change in eating habits	15
41.	Vacation	13
42.	Christmas	12
43.	Minor violations of the law	11

it is the degree of similarity between the population within the sample that is impressive. The high degree of consensus also suggests a universal agreement between groups and among individuals about the significance of the life events under study that transcends differences in age, sex, marital status, education, social class, generation American, religion and race.

The method used in this research, when applied to psychophysical phenomena, generates a **ratio scale**. A discussion of whether or not the magnitudes assigned to the items in Table 3 actually constitute a ratio scale is beyond the intent of this report (21, 22). However, this issue will be dealt with in a subsequent report (23).

FOOTNOTES

[1] Reprinted by permission of the authors and the publisher from the *Journal of Psychosomatic Research*, 1967, 11, 213-218. Copyright 1967, Pergamon Press.

[2] This investigation was supported in part by Public Health Service Undergraduate Training in Psychiatry Grant No. 5-T2-MH-5939-13 and Undergraduate Training in Human Behavior Grant No. 5-T2-MH-7871-03 from the National Institute of Mental Health; O'Donnell Psychiatric Research Fund; and The Scottish Rite Committee for Research in Schizophrenia.

[3] Baruch, G.K., Biener, L., & Barnett, R.C. (1987). Women and gender in research on work and family stress. *American Psychologist*, 42, 130-136.

[4] Lazarus, R.S., & Folkman, S. (1984). *Stress, appraisal, and coping.* New York: Springer.

[5] Page, J. (1984). Rural stress. *Science 84*, 5(2), 104-105.

[6] Harold G. Wolff, M.D. (1898-1962) was Anne Parrish Tizell Professor of Medicine (Neurology), Cornell University Medical College and the New York Hospital.

REFERENCES

1. Rahe, R. M., Meyer, M., Smith, M., Kjaer, G., and Holmes, T. H. Social stress and illness onset. *J. Psychosom. Res.* 8, 35 (1964).
2. Graham, D. T. and Stevenson, I. Disease as response to life stress. In *The Psychological Basis of Medical Practice* (H. I. Lief, V. F. Lief, and N. R. Lief, Eds.) Harper & Row, New York (1963).
3. Greene, W. A., Jr., Psychological factors and reticulo-endothelial disease-I. Preliminary observations on a group of males with lymphomas and leukemias. *Psychosom. Med.* 16, 220 (1954).
4. Greene, W. A., Jr., Young, L. E. and Swisher, S. N. Psychological factors and reticulo-endothelial disease-II. Observations on a group of women with lymphomas and leukemias. *Psychosom. Med.* 18, 284 (1956).
5. Greene, W. A., Jr., and Miller, G. Psychological factors and reticulo-endothelial disease-IV. Observations on a group of children and adolescents with leukemia; an interpretation of disease development in terms of the mother-child unit. *Psychosom. Med.* 20, 124 (1958).
6. Weiss, E., Dlin, B., Rollin, H. R., Fischer, H. K. and Bepler, C. R. Emotional factors in coronary occulsion. *A.M.A. Archs. Internal Med.* 99, 628 (1957).
7. Fischer, H. K., Dlin, B., Winters, W., Hagner, S. and Weiss, E. Time patterns and emotional factors related to the onset of coronary occulsion. (Abstract) *Psychosom. Med.* 24, 516 (1962).
8. Kissen, D. M. Specific psychological factors in pulmonary tuberculosis. *Hlth Bull. Edinburgh* 14, 44 (1956).
9. Kissen, D. M. Some psychological aspects of pulmonary tuberculosis. *Int. J. Soc. Psychiat.* 3, 252 (1958).
10. Hawkins, N. G., Davies, R. and Holmes, T. H. Evidence of psycholosocial factors in the development of pulmonary tuberculosis. *Am. Rev. Tuberc. Pulmon. Dis.* 75, 5 (1957).
11. Smith, M. Psychogenic factors in skin disease, Medical Thesis, University of Washington, Seattle (1962).
12. Rahe, R. H. and Holmes, T. H. Social psychologic and psychophysiologic aspects of inguinal hernia. *J. Psychosom. Res.* 8, 487 (1965).
13. Kjaer, G. Some psychosomatic aspects of pregnancy with particular reference to nausea and vomiting. Medical Thesis, University of Washington, Seattle (1959).
14. Lief, A. (Ed.) *The Commonsense Psychiatry of Dr. Adolf Meyer,* McGraw-Hill, New York (1948).
15. Wolff, H. G., Wolff, S., and Hare, C. C. (Eds.) *Life Stress and Bodily Disease,* Res. Publs. Ass. Res. Nerv. Ment. Dis. Vol. 29. Williams & Wilkins, Baltimore (1950).
16. Holmes, T. H., Goodell, H., Wolf, S., and Wolff, H. G. *The Nose. An Experimental Study of Reactions Within the Nose in Human Subjects During Varying Life Experiences*, Charles C. Thomas, Springfield, Illinois (1950).
17. Wolff, S. *The Stomach*, Oxford University Press, New York (1965).
18. Wolf, S., Cardon, P. V., Shepard, E. M., and Wolff, H. G. *Life Stress and Essential Hypertension*, Williams & Wilkins, Baltimore (1955).
19. Grace, W. J., Wolf, S., and Wolff, H. G. *The Human Colon*, Paul B. Hoeber, New York (1951).

Constellation (kon-stel-LAY-shun). In social psychology (or psychiatry), the "family constellation" is a drawing, usually with one or both parents at the center, showing how all the family members are attached to each other, or the "power structure" of the family.

Advent (ADD-vent). The beginning or onset of something.

Phenomena (fee-NOM-ih-nah). Plural of *phenomenon*. A phenomenon is some event that you are conscious of, something that you become aware of.

Ratio scale. Scientists who construct measuring devices, such as the one described in this article, often wish to prove that the scores yielded by their tests are very precise. A weight scale is a "ratio scale" because the *ratio* between 2 pounds and 4 pounds is exactly the same as that between 6 pounds and 12 pounds. Thus, a weight scale is very precise. The Holmes and Rahe scale goes from 0 to 100. If the scale were a true ratio scale, then the stress associated with an event that has a score of 100 ("death of spouse") would be exactly twice that of an event with a score of 50 ("marriage").

20. Stevens, S. S. and Galanter, E. H. Ratio scales and category scales for a dozen perseptual continua. *J. Exp. Psychol.* **54**, 377 (1957).
21. Sellin, T. and Wolfgang, M. E. *The Measurement of Delinquency*, John Wiley, New York (1964).
22. Stevens, S. S. A metric for the social consensus. *Science* **151**, 530 (1966).
23. Masuda, M. and Holmes, T. H. This issue, p. 219.

Classic Quotations from William James

The philosophy which is so important in each of us is not a technical matter; it is our more or less dumb sense of what life honestly and deeply means. It is only partly got from books; it is our individual way of just seeing and feeling the total push and pressure of the cosmos.
(*Pragmatism* [1907], Lecture 1.)

No particular results then, so far, but only an attitude of orientation, is what the pragmatic method means. The attitude of looking away from first things, principles, "categories," supposed necessities; and of looking toward last things, fruits, consequences, facts.
(*Pragmatism* [1907], Lecture 2.)

CHAPTER 19

"Effects of Group Pressure Upon the Modification and Distortion of Judgments"

S.E. Asch[1]

EDITORS' COMMENTS. Solomon Asch was one of the very first social psychologists to *prove scientifically* how influential the opinions of others are on the behavior of the normal individual. His way of doing so was simple: He hired "confederates" (sometimes called "stooges") to give false reports in an experimental situation to see how those reports influenced the judgments of "naive" subjects (sometimes called "critical" subjects). The answer is "quite a lot," although the size of the effect depends on many factors.

To give you a feel for what the Asch study was like, let's suppose you volunteer to be a subject in a study such as this one. You arrive at the laboratory at a certain time, only to find that 16 other subjects (all "stooges," although you wouldn't know that at the start) are waiting for you to arrive. The experimenter then asks all of you to make judgments about the lengths of lines, and since you were the last to arrive, you'd give your judgments last. In the first few trials, the other 16 report just what you saw. However, they soon begin giving judgments that are "outrageous" from your point of view. Since you report *after* all 16 of them had given their judgments, how would you react? Would you continue to "call 'em as you saw 'em"? Or would you "yield" to the majority opinion at least some of the time? When asked about this matter *before* actually participating, most students claim they would maintain their independence. In truth, if the conditions are strong enough, most students end up yielding on at least *some* of the trials.

There are several important findings reported in this study that have been replicated many times since by other investigators: (1) Most "critical subjects" report feeling tremendous stress in this situation, whether they yield or remain independent. (2) The vaguer the instructions, and the more difficult the task, the more likely it is that the "critical subject" will yield. (3) The more unanimous the "stooges" are in their reports, the stronger the pressure becomes on the "critical subject" to yield to the majority.

You should also note that, when Asch pitted 16 "critical subjects" against one "stooge" (who reported last), the "critical subjects" poked considerable fun at the "stooge," trying their best to force this "jerk" to fall into line with the rest of the group. (*You'd* never do such a cruel thing, would you?) However, when Asch matched 16 "critical subjects" against 3 "stooges," the critical subjects didn't joke nearly as much. These results give us important information about the methods groups use to *maintain discipline* among their members.

We must also point out that subsequent studies (by Asch and many other investigators) suggest that there isn't really a "yielding personality type" as such. Rather, almost anyone will yield if the pressures are great enough, particularly if the person is *rewarded* for doing so on frequent occasions; and almost anyone will resist group pressures in some situations, particularly if the person has been *positive reinforced* for doing so in the past.

Finally, we should note that the general public has tended to ignore (or even deny the importance of) this study, just as the public has (generally speaking) rejected the findings of Milgram and most other experimenters who have demonstrated what a strong influence the social environment has on human behavior. The question then becomes, will you "yield" to the opinion of the general public in this matter? Or will you accept Asch's findings as being valid, and then begin to look at how your own thoughts and actions are influenced by your own reference groups? Only you can answer those questions!

INTRODUCTION

We shall here describe in summary form the conception and first findings of a program of investigation into the conditions of independence and submission to **group pressure**. This program is based on a series of earlier studies conducted by the writer while a Fellow of the John Simon Guggenheim Memorial Foundation. The earlier experiments and the theoretical issues which prompted them are discussed in a forthcoming work by the writer on social psychology.

Our immediate object was to study the social and personal conditions that induce individuals to resist or to yield to group pressures when the latter are perceived to be *contrary to fact*. The issues which this problem raises are of obvious consequence for society; it can be of decisive importance whether or not a group will, under certain conditions, submit to existing pressures. Equally direct are the consequences for individuals and our understanding of them, since it is a decisive fact about a person whether he possesses the freedom to act independently, or whether he characteristically submits to group pressures.

The problem under investigation requires the direct observation of certain basic processes in the interaction between individuals, and between individuals and groups. To clarify these seems necessary if we are to make fundamental advances in the understanding of the formation and reorganization of attitudes, of the functioning of public opinion, and of the operation of **propaganda**. Today we do not possess an adequate theory of these central psycho-social processes. **Empirical** investigation has been predominantly controlled by general propositions concerning group influence which have as a rule been assumed but not tested. With few exceptions investigation has relied upon descriptive formulations concerning the operation of suggestion and prestige, the inadequacy of which is becoming increasingly obvious, and upon **schematic** applications of stimulus-response theory.

The bibliography lists articles representative of the current theoretical and empirical situation. Basic to the current approach has been the **axiom** that group pressures characteristically induce psychological changes *arbitrarily*, in far-reaching disregard of the material properties of the given conditions. This mode of thinking has almost exclusively stressed the slavish submission of individuals to group forces, has neglected to inquire into their possibilities for independence and for productive relations with the human environment, and has virtually denied the capacity of men under certain conditions to rise above group passion and prejudice. It was our aim to contribute to a clarification of these questions, important both for theory and for their human implications, by means of direct observation of the effects of groups upon the decisions and evaluations of individuals.

THE EXPERIMENT AND FIRST RESULTS

To this end we developed an experimental technique which has served as the basis for the present series of studies. We employed the procedure of placing an individual in a relation of radical conflict with all the other members of a group, of measuring its effect upon him in **quantitative** terms, and of describing its psychological consequences. A group of eight individuals was instructed to judge a series of simple, clearly structured perceptual relations--to match the length of a given line with one of three unequal lines. Each member of the group announced his judgments publicly. In the midst of this monotonous "test" one individual found himself suddenly contradicted by the entire group, and this contradiction was repeated again and again in the course of the experiment. The group in question had, with the exception of one member, previously met with the experimenter and received instructions to respond at certain points with wrong--and unanimous--judgments. The errors of the majority were large (ranging between 0.5" and 1.75") and of an order not encountered under control conditions. The outstanding person--the critical subject--whom we had placed in the position of a *minority of one* in the midst of a *unanimous majority*--was the object of investigation. He faced, possibly for the first time in his life, a situation in which a group unanimously contradicted the evidence of his senses.

Group pressure. This term refers to the influence our reference or peer group has on our attitudes and behavior. Group pressure is felt by an individual when he or she expresses an opinion too far from the reference group norm, and is pressured by the other members to fall back into line.

Propaganda (prop-ah-GAN-dah). From the Latin word meaning "to create offspring." You "propagate" plants when you plant seeds. You propagate ideas when you try to convinve people to believe in them.

Empirical (em-PEER-ih-kal). To be "empirical" is to rely on data or experimentation rather than on theory or guess.

Schematic (ski-MAT-ick). A drawing or plan that attempts to explain a complex operation in "bare bones" (outline) fashion and thus misses the rich detail of the operation as it occurs in real life.

Axiom (ak-SEE-um). An "axiom" is a proposition or belief widely regarded as the self-evident truth.

Quantitative (KWANT-ih-tate-ive). Quantitative study involves the "measurement" of quantity or amount. As opposed to *qualitative* study, which involves the subjective, non-measureable aspects of human experience. Measuring what people actually *do* is "quantative." Asking people what they *feel* about their behaviors is "qualitative."

TABLE 1
Lengths of Standard and Comparison Lines

Trials	Length of Standard Line (in inches)	Comparison Lines (in inches) 1	2	3	Correct Response	Group Response	Majority Error (in inches)
1	10	8.75	10	8	2	2	
2	2	2	1	1.50	1	1	
3	3	3.75	4.25	3	3	1*	+0.75
4	5	5	4	6.50	1	2*	-1.0
5	4	3	5	4	3	3	
6	3	3.75	4.25	3	3	2*	+1.25
7	8	6.25	8	6.75	2	3*	-1.25
8	5	5	4	6.50	1	3*	+1.50
9	8	6.25	8	6.75	2	1*	-1.25
10	10	8.75	10	8	2	2	
11	2	2	1	1.50	1	1	
12	3	3.75	4.25	3	3	1*	+0.75
13	5	5	4	6.50	1	2*	-1.0
14	4	3	5	4	3	3	
15	3	3.75	4.25	3	3	2*	+1.25
16	8	6.25	8	6.75	2	3*	-1.25
17	5	5	4	6.50	1	3*	+1.50
18	8	6.25	8	6.75	2	1*	-1.75

*Starred figures designate the erroneous estimates by the majority.

This procedure was the starting point of the investigation and the point of departure for the study of further problems. Its main features were the following: (1) The critical subject was submitted to two contradictory and irreconcilable forces--the evidence of his own experience of an utterly clear perceptual fact and the unanimous evidence of a group of equals. (2) Both forces were part of the immediate situation; the majority was concretely present, surrounding the subject physically. (3) The critical subject, who was requested together with all others to state his judgments publicly, was obliged to declare himself and to take a definite stand vis-a-vis the group. (4) The situation possessed a self-contained character. The critical subject could not avoid or evade the dilemma by reference to conditions external to the experimental situation. (It may be mentioned at this point that the forces generated by the given conditions acted so quickly upon the critical subjects that instances of suspicion were rare.)

The technique employed permitted a simple quantitative measure of the "majority effect" in terms of the frequency of errors in the direction of the distorted estimates of the majority. At the same time we were concerned from the start to obtain evidence of the ways in which the subjects perceived the group, to establish whether they became doubtful, whether they were tempted to join the majority. Most important, it was our object to establish the grounds of the subject's independence of yielding--whether, for example, the yielding subject was aware of the effect of the majority upon him, whether he abandoned his judgment deliberately or compulsively. To this end we constructed a comprehensive set of questions which served as the basis of an individual interview immediately following the experimental period. Toward the conclusion of the interview each subject was informed fully of the purpose of the experiment, of his role and of that of the majority. The reactions to the disclosure of the purpose of the experiment became in fact an integral part of the pro-

TABLE 2
Distribution of Errors in Experimental and Control Groups

Number of Critical Errors	Critical Group* (N = 50) F	Control Group (N = 37) F
0	13	35
1	4	1
2	5	1
3	6	
4	3	
5	4	
6	1	
7	2	
8	5	
9	3	
10	3	
11	1	
12	0	
Total	50	37
Mean	3.84	0.08

* All errors in the critical group were in the direction of the majority estimates.

cedure. We may state here that the information derived from the interview became an indispensable source of evidence and insight into the psychological structure of the experimental situation, and in particular, of the nature of the individual differences. Also, it is not justified or advisable to allow the subject to leave without giving him a full explanation of the experimental conditions. The experimenter has a responsibility to the subject to clarify his doubts and to state the reasons for placing him in the experimental situation. When this is done most subjects react with interest and many express gratification at having lived through a striking situation which has some bearing on wider human issues.

Both the members of the majority and the critical subjects were male college students. We shall report the results for a total of fifty critical subjects in this experiment. In Table 1 we summarize the successive comparison trials and the majority estimates.

The quantitative results are clear and unambiguous.

1. There was a marked movement toward the majority. One-third of all the estimates in the critical group were errors identical with or in the direction of the distorted estimates of the majority. The significance of this finding becomes clear in the light of the virtual absence of errors in control groups the members of which recorded their estimates in writing. The relevant data of the critical and control groups are summarized in Table 2.

2. At the same time the effect of the majority was far from complete. The preponderance of estimates in the critical group (68 per cent) was correct despite the pressure of the majority.

3. We found evidence of extreme individual differences. There were in the critical group subjects who remained independent without exception, and there were those who went nearly all the time with the majority. (The maximum possible number of errors was 12, while the actual range of errors was 0-11.) One-fourth of the critical subjects was completely independent; at the other extreme, one-third of the group displaced the estimates toward the majority in one-half or more of the trials.

The differences between the critical subjects in their reactions to the given conditions were equally striking.

There were subjects who remained completely confident throughout. At the other extreme were those who became disoriented, doubt-ridden, and experienced a powerful impulse not to appear different from the majority.

For purposes of illustration we include a brief description of one independent and one yielding subject.

Independent. After a few trials he appeared puzzled, hesitant. He announced all disagreeing answers in the form of "Three, sir; two, sir"; not so with the unanimous answers. At trial 4 he answered immediately after the first member of the group, shook his head, blinked, and whispered to his neighbor: "Can't help it, that's one." His later answers came in a whispered voice, accompanied by a deprecating smile. At one point he grinned embarrassedly, and whispered explosively to his neighbor: "I always disagree--darn it!" During the questioning, this subject's constant refrain was: "I called them as I saw them, sir." He insisted that his estimates were right without, however, committing himself as to whether the others were wrong, remarking that "that's the way I see them and that's the way they see them." If he had to make a practical decision under similar circumstances, he declared, "I would follow my own view, though part of my reason would tell me that I might be wrong." Immediately following the experiment the majority engaged this subject in a brief discussion. When they pressed him to say whether the entire group was wrong and he alone right, he turned upon them defiantly, exclaiming: "You're *probably* right, but you may be wrong!" To the disclosure of the experiment this subject reacted with the statement that he felt "exultant and relieved," adding, "I do not deny that at times I had the feeling: 'to heck with it, I'll go along with the rest.'"

Yielding. This subject went with the majority in 11 out of 12 trials. He appeared nervous and somewhat confused, but he did not attempt to evade discussion; on the contrary, he was helpful and tried to answer to the best of his ability. He opened the discussion with the statement: "If I'd been the first I probably would have responded differently"; this was his way of stating that he had adopted the majority estimates. The primary factor in his case was loss of confidence. He perceived the majority as a decided group, acting without hesitation: "If they had been doubtful I probably would have changed, but they answered with such confidence." Certain of his errors, he explained, were due to the doubtful nature of the comparisons; in such instances he went with the majority. When the object of the experiment was explained, the subject volunteered: "I suspected about the middle--but tried to push it out of my mind." It is of interest that his suspicion was not able to restore his confidence and diminish the power of the majority. Equally striking is his report that he assumed the experiment to involve an "illusion" to which the others, but not he, were subject. This assumption too did not help to free him; on the contrary, he acted as if his divergence from the majority was a sign of defect. The principal impression this subject produced was of one so caught up by immediate difficulties that he lost clear reasons for his actions, and could make no reasonable decisions.

A FIRST ANALYSIS OF INDIVIDUAL DIFFERENCES

On the basis of the interview data described earlier, we undertook to differentiate and describe the major forms of reaction to the experimental situation, which we shall now briefly summarize.

Among the *independent* subjects we distinguished the following main categories: (1) Independence based on *confidence* in one's perception and experience. The most striking characteristic of these subjects is the vigor with which they withstand the group opposition. Though they are sensitive to the group, and experience the conflict, they show a resilience in coping with it, which is expressed in their continuing reliance on their perception and the effectiveness with which they shake off the oppressive group opposition.

(2) Quite different are those subjects who are independent and *withdrawn*. These do not react in a spontaneously emotional way, but rather on the basis of explicit principles concerning the necessity of being an individual.

(3) A third group of independent subjects manifest considerable tension and *doubt,* but adhere to their judgments on the basis of a felt necessity to deal adequately with the task.

The following were the main categories of reaction among the *yielding* subjects, or those who went with the majority during one-half or more of the trials.

(1) *Distortion of perception* under the stress of group pressure. In this category belong a very few subjects who yield completely, but are not aware that their estimates have been displaced or distorted by the majority. These subjects report that they came to perceive the majority estimates as correct.

(2) *Distortion of judgment.* Most submitting subjects belong to this category. The factor of greatest importance in this group is a decision the subjects reach that their perceptions are inaccurate, and that those of the majority are correct. These subjects suffer from primary doubt and lack of confidence; on this basis they feel a strong tendency to join the majority.

(3) *Distortion of action.* The subjects in this group do not suffer a modification of perception nor do they conclude that they are wrong. They yield because of an overmastering need not to appear different from or inferior to others, because of an inability to tolerate the appearance of defectiveness in the eyes of the group. These subjects suppress their observations and voice the majority position with awareness of what they are doing.

The results are sufficient to establish that independence and yielding are not psychologically homogeneous, that submission to group pressure (and freedom from pressure) can be the result of different psychological conditions. It should also be noted that the categories described above, being based exclusively on the subjects' reactions to the experimental conditions, are descriptive, not presuming to explain why a given individual responded in one way rather than another. The further exploration of the basis for the individual differences is a separate task upon which we are now at work.

EXPERIMENTAL VARIATIONS

The results described are clearly a joint function of two broadly different sets of conditions. They are determined first by the specific external conditions, by the particular character of the relation between social evidence and one's own experience. Second, the presence of pronounced individual differences points to the important role of personal factors, of factors connected with the individual's character structure. We reasoned that there are group conditions which would produce independence in all subjects, and that there probably are group conditions which would induce intensified yielding in many, though not in all. Accordingly we followed the procedure of *experimental variation,* systematically altering the quality of social evidence by means of systematic variation of group conditions. Secondly, we deemed it reasonable to assume that behavior under the experimental social pressure is significantly related to certain basic, relatively permanent characteristics of the individual. The investigation has moved in both of these directions. Because the study of the character-qualities which may be functionally connected with independence and yielding is still in progress, we shall limit the present account to a sketch of the representative experimental variations.

THE EFFECT OF NONUNANIMOUS MAJORITIES

Evidence obtained from the basic experiment suggested that the condition of being exposed *alone* to the opposition of a "compact majority" may have played a decisive role in determining the course and strength of the effects observed. Accordingly we undertook to investigate in a series of successive variations the effects of *nonunanimous* majorities. The technical problem of altering the uniformity of a majority is, in terms of our procedure, relatively simple. In most instances we merely directed one or more members of the instructed group to deviate from the majority in prescribed ways. It is obvious that we cannot hope to compare the performance of the same individual in two situations on the assumption that they remain independent of one another. At best we can investigate the effect of an earlier upon a later experimental condition. The comparison of different experimental situations therefore requires the use of different but comparable groups of critical subjects. This is the procedure we have followed. In the variations to be described we have maintained the conditions of the basic experiment (*e.g.,* the sex of the subjects, the size of the majority, the content of the task, and so on) save for the specific factor that was varied. The following were some of the variations we studied:

1. *The presence of a "true partner."* (a) In the midst of the majority were *two* naive, critical subjects. The subjects were separated spatially, being seated in the fourth and eighth positions, respectively. Each therefore heard his judgment confirmed by one other person (provided the other person remained independent), one prior to, the other subsequently to announcing his own judgment. In addition, each experienced a break in the unanimity of the majority. There were six pairs of critical subjects. (b) In a further variation the "partner" to the critical subject was a member of the group who had been instructed to respond correctly throughout. This procedure permits the exact control of the partner's responses. The partner was always seated in the fourth position; he therefore announced his estimates in each case before the critical subject.

The results clearly demonstrate that a disturbance of the unanimity of the majority markedly increased the independence of the critical subjects. The frequency of pro-majority errors dropped to 10.4 per cent of the total number of estimates in variation (a), and to 5.5 per cent in variation (b). These results are to be compared with the frequency of yielding to the unanimous majorities in the basic experiment, which was 32 percent of the total number of estimates. It is clear that the presence in the field of *one other* individual who responded correctly was sufficient to deplete the power of the majority, and in some cases to destroy it. This finding is all the more striking in the light of other variations which demonstrate the effect of even small minorities provided they are unanimous. Indeed, we have been able to show that a unanimous majority of three is, under

---

Deprecating (DEP-pre-kate-ing). Expressing mild or regretful disapproval. A deprecating statement is a "put-down."

Homogeneous (ho-moh-GEE-knee-us). From the Greek word meaning "same kind." The more alike members of a group are, the more homogeneous the group is.

the given conditions, far more effective than a majority of eight containing one dissenter. That critical subjects will under these conditions free themselves of a majority of seven and join forces with one other person in the minority is, we believe, a result significant for theory. It points to a fundamental psychological difference between the condition of being alone and having a minimum of human support. It further demonstrates that the effects obtained are not the result of a summation of influences proceeding from each member of the group; it is necessary to conceive the results as being relationally determined.

2. *Withdrawal of a "true partner."* What will be the effect of providing the critical subject with a partner who responds correctly and then withdrawing him? The critical subject started with a partner who responded correctly. The partner was a member of the majority who had been instructed to respond correctly and to "desert" to the majority in the middle of the experiment. This procedure permits the observation of the same subject in the course of transition from one condition to another. The withdrawal of the partner produced a powerful and unexpected result. We had assumed that the critical subject, having gone through the experience of opposing the majority with a minimum of support, would maintain his independence when alone. Contrary to this expectation, we found that the experience of having had and then lost a partner restored the majority effect to its full force, the proportion of errors rising to 28.5 per cent of all judgments, in contrast to the preceding level of 5.5 per cent. Further experimentation is needed to establish whether the critical subjects were responding to the sheer fact of being alone, or to the fact that the partner abandoned them.

3. *Late arrival of a "true partner."* The critical subject started as a minority of one in the midst of a unanimous majority. Toward the conclusion of the experiment one member of the majority "broke" away and began announcing correct estimates. This procedure, which reverses the order of conditions of the preceding experiment, permits the observation of the transition from being alone to being a member of a pair against a majority. It is obvious that those critical subjects who were independent when alone would continue to be so when joined by another partner. The variation is therefore of significance primarily for those subjects who yielded during the first phase of the experiment. The appearance of the late partner exerts a freeing effect, reducing the level to 8.7 per cent. Those who had previously yielded also became markedly more independent, but not completely so, continuing to yield more than previously independent subjects. The reports of the subjects do not cast much light on the factors responsible for the result. It is our impression that having once committed himself to yielding, the individual finds it difficult and painful to change his direction. To do so is tantamount to a public admission that he has not acted rightly. He therefore follows the precarious course he has already chosen in order to maintain an outward semblance of consistency and conviction.

4. *The presence of a "compromise partner."* The majority was consistently extremist, always matching the standard with the most unequal line. One instructed subject (who, as in the other variations, preceded the critical subject) also responded incorrectly, but his estimates were always intermediate between the truth and the majority position. The critical subject therefore faced an extremist majority whose unanimity was broken by one more moderately erring person. Under these conditions the frequency of errors was reduced but not significantly. However, the lack of unanimity determined in a strikingly consistent way the *direction* of the errors. The preponderance of the errors, 75.7 per cent of the total, was moderate, whereas in a parallel experiment in which the majority was unanimously extremist (*i.e.*, with the "compromise" partner excluded), the incidence of moderate errors was reduced to 42 per cent of the total. As might be expected, in a unanimously moderate majority, the errors of the critical subjects were without exception moderate.

THE ROLE OF MAJORITY SIZE

To gain further understanding of the majority effect, we varied the size of the majority in several different variations. The majorities, which were in each case unanimous, consisted of 16, 8, 4, 3, and 2 persons, respectively. In addition, we studied the limited case in which the critical subject was opposed by one instructed subject. Table 3 contains the means and the range of errors under each condition.

TABLE 3

Errors of Critical Subjects with Unanimous Majorities of Different Size

Size of Majority	Control	1	2	3	4	8	16
N	37	10	15	10	10	50	12
Mean # of Errors	0.08	0.33	1.53	4.0	4.20	3.84	3.75
Range of Errors	0 - 2	0 - 1	0 - 5	1 - 12	0 - 11	0 - 11	0 - 10

With the opposition reduced to one, the majority effect all but disappeared. When the opposition proceeded from a group of two, it produced a measurable though small distortion, the errors being 12.8 per cent of the total number of estimates. The effect appeared in full force with a majority of three. Larger majorities of four, eight, and sixteen did not produce effects greater than a majority of three.

The effect of a majority is often silent, revealing little of its operation to the subject, and often hiding it from the experimenter. To examine the range of effects it is capable of inducing, decisive variations of conditions are necessary. An indication of one effect is furnished by the following variation in which the conditions of the basic experiment were simply reversed. Here the majority, consisting of a group of sixteen, was naive; in the midst of it we placed a single individual who responded wrongly according to instructions. Under these conditions the members of the naive majority reacted to the lone dissenter with amusement and disdain. Contagious laughter spread through the group at the droll minority of one. Of significance is the fact that the members lack awareness that they draw their strength from the majority, and that their reactions would change radically if they faced the dissenter individually. In fact, the attitude of derision in the majority turns to seriousness and increased respect as soon as the minority is increased to three. These observations demonstrate the role of social support as a source of power and stability, in contrast to the preceding investigations which stressed the effects of withdrawal of social support, or to be more exact, the effects of social opposition. Both aspects must be explicitly considered in a unified formulation of the effects of group conditions on the formation and change of judgments.

THE ROLE OF THE STIMULUS-SITUATION

It is obviously not possible to divorce the quality and course of the group forces which act upon the individual from the specific stimulus-conditions. Of necessity the structure of the situation molds the group forces and determines their direction as well as their strength. Indeed, this was the reason that we took pains in the investigations described above to center the issue between the individual and the group around an elementary and fundamental matter of fact. And there can be no doubt that the resulting reactions were directly a function of the contradiction between the objectively grasped relations and the majority position.

These general considerations are sufficient to establish the need of varying the stimulus-conditions and of observing their effect on the resulting group forces. We are at present conducting a series of investigations in which certain aspects of the stimulus-situation are systematically altered.

One of the dimensions we are examining is the magnitude of discrepancies above the threshold. Our technique permits an easy variation of this factor, since we can increase or decrease at will the deviation of the majority from the given objective conditions. Hitherto we have studied the effect of a relatively moderate range of discrepancies. Within the limits of our procedure we find that different magnitudes of discrepancy produce approximately the same amount of yielding. However, the quality of yielding alters: as the majority becomes more extreme, there occurs a significant increase in the frequency of "compromise" errors. Further experiments are planned in which the discrepancies in question will be extremely large and small.

We have also varied systematically the structural clarity of the task, including in separate variations judgments based on mental standards. In agreement with other investigators, we find that the majority effect grows stronger as the situation diminishes in clarity. Concurrently, however, the disturbance of the subjects and the conflict-quality of the situation decrease markedly. We consider it of significance that the majority achieves its most pronounced effect when it acts most painlessly.

SUMMARY

We have investigated the effects upon individuals of majority opinions when the latter were seen to be in a direction contrary to fact. By means of a simple technique we produced a radical divergence between a majority and a minority, and observed the ways in which individuals coped with the resulting difficulty. Despite the stress of the given conditions, a substantial proportion of individuals retained their independence throughout. At the same time a substantial minority yielded, modifying their judgments in accordance with the majority. Independence and yielding are a joint function of the following major factors: (1) The character of the stimulus situation. Variations in structural clarity have a decisive effect: with diminishing clarity of the stimulus-conditions the majority effect increases. (2) The character of the group forces. Individuals are highly sensitive to the structural qualities of group opposition. In particular, we demonstrated the great importance of the factor of unanimity. Also, the majority effect is a function of the size of group opposition. (3) The character of the individual. There were wide, and indeed, striking differences among individuals within the same experimental situation. The hypothesis was proposed that these are functionally dependent on relatively enduring character differences, in particular those pertaining to the person's social relations.

FOOTNOTES

[1] Reprinted by permission of the author and the publisher from an article in K.S. Guetzkow (Ed.), *Groups, leadership, and men*. Pittsburgh: Carnegie Press, 1951. Copyright 1951 by Carnegie Press.

BIBLIOGRAPHY

Asch, S.E. Studies in the principles of judgments and attitudes: II. Determination of judgments by group and by ego-standards. *J. soc. Psychol.,* 1940, **12,** 433-465.

Asch, S.E. The doctrine of suggestion, prestige and imitation in social psychology. *Psychol. Rev.,* 1948, **55,** 250-276.

Asch, S.E., Block, H., and Hertzman, M. Studies in the principles of judgments and attitudes. I. Two basic principles of judgment. *J. Psychol.,* 1938, **5,** 219-251.

Coffin, E.E. Some conditions of suggestion and suggestibility: A study of certain attitudinal and situational factors influencing the process of suggestion. *Psychol. Monogr.,* 1941, **53,** No. 4.

Lewis, H.B. Studies in the principles of judgments and attitudes: IV. The operation of prestige suggestion. *J. soc. Psychol.,* 1941, **14,** 229-256.

Lorge, I. Prestige, suggestion, and attitudes. *J. soc. Psychol.,* 1936, **7,** 386-402.

Miller, N.E. and Dollard, J. *Social Learning and Imitation*. New Haven: Yale Universtiy Press, 1941.

Moore, H.T. The comparative influence of majority and expert opinion. *Amer. J. Psychol.,* 1921, **32,** 16-20.

Sherif, M. A study of some social factors in perception. *Arch. Psychol.,* N.Y., 1935, No. 187.

Thorndike, E.L. *The Psychology of Wants, Interests, and Attitudes*. New York: D. Appleton-Century Company, Inc., 1935.

Classic Quotations from William James

The concrete man has but one interest--to be right. That to him is the art of all arts, and all means are fair which help him to it.
          (*The Sentiment of Rationality* [1882].)

Genius . . . means little more than the faculty of perceiving in an unhabitual way.
          (*The Principles of Psychology* [1890], ch. 19.)

An act has no ethical quality whatever unless it be chosen out of several all equally possible.
          (*The Principles of Psychology* [1890], ch. 9.)

CHAPTER 20

"Behavioral Study of Obedience"

Stanley Milgram[1,2]

> **EDITORS' COMMENTS.** Few articles in the history of psychology caused as much public commotion on publication as did this study by Stanley Milgram. As you read the article, you'll understand why.
>
> Milgram recruited "normal" subjects to act as "teachers" in an experiment. Each subject sat in front of a very impressive piece of equipment that *supposedly* was a powerful shock generator. In fact, the machine was a fake, and *no* electrical shock was used in the experiment. However, the subjects were not aware this was the case. They were told to "shock" another person (called the "learner") every time that person made a mistake while trying to learn a long list of words. (The "learner," who was sitting in another room, supposedly was another subject, but actually was Milgram's confederate.) The switches on the shock generator were labeled in series, from "slight shock (15 volts)" to "Danger: Severe shock (375 volts)" to "XXX (450 volts)." The more mistakes the "learner" made, the higher the shock level the "teacher" was supposed to deliver.
>
> At the start of each session, the "learner" made few errors and hence got low-level shock. But as the session continued, the confederate deliberately made more frequent errors, and the more severe the shock level became. When the shock level reached 300 volts, the "learner" suddenly pounded on the wall in protest and then *stopped responding entirely*, as if he had suffered an attack of some kind. However, the experimenter (dressed in an impressive-looking white lab coat) said in a very stern voice, "Whether the learner likes it or not, you *must go on*."
>
> Now, what would *you* have done if you were the "teacher" in this situation. Would you continue to adminster higher and higher levels of "shock" to someone who might have fainted (or might even have died)? Or would you have quit? Most college students asked this question insist they would have stopped. But in fact, in the Milgram study, 65 percent of the subjects continued to the very end--to "XXX (450 volts)." The subjects sweated, moaned, protested vigorously, and even got sick. However, as Milgram puts it so eloquently, "Yet they obeyed."
>
> Publication of Milgram's findings brought a storm of protest. Some social scientists protested that Milgram's use of *deception* was immoral and might have been "personally damaging" to the subjects when they discovered they had been *tricked* into doing things they admitted they shouldn't have done. In response, the American Psychological Association banned the "unwarranted use of deception" in similar research. However, there is no evidence that the subjects in this (and similar) experiments were "damaged" in any way--and they might well have discovered something important about human behavior from the experience: That in a culture where "obedience to authority" is typically considered a virtue and hence highly rewarded, we shouldn't be surprised when people do, indeed, "obey."
>
> The general public seems to have protested against Milgram's research because his results were unacceptable to them. Indeed, most of the protesters "attributed" Milgram's findings to "flaws" in the personalities of the individual subjects he used. "Nice people"--that is, the protesters themselves--surely wouldn't have done such terrible things. In truth, though, what Milgram showed was that much of human behavior--including some dreadful actions indeed--are the result of the *social situation*, not of "innate traits or pre-dispositions."
>
> Despite Milgram's research--and dozens of similar studies that gave essentially the same results--you probably won't be convinced that *you* would have done as most of Milgram's subjects did. But as you read this disturbing article, you might wish to keep repeating Milgram's observation to yourself again and again: *And yet they obeyed*.

This article describes a procedure for the study of destructive obedience in the laboratory. It consists of ordering a naive S to administer increasingly more severe punishment to a victim in the context of a learning experiment. Punishment is administered by means of a shock generator with 30 graded switches ranging from Slight Shock to Danger: Severe Shock. The victim is a confederate of the E. The primary dependent variable is the maximum shock the S is willing to administer before he refuses to continue further. 26 Ss obeyed the experimental commands fully, and administered the highest shock on the generator. 14 Ss broke off the experiment at some point after the victim protested and refused to provide further answers. The procedure created extreme levels of nervous tension in some Ss. Profuse sweating, trembling, and stuttering were typical expressions of this emotional disturbance. One unexpected sign of tension--yet to be explained--was the regular occurrence of nervous laughter, which in some Ss developed into uncontrollable seizures. The variety of interesting behavioral dynamics observed in the experiment, the reality of the situation for the Ss, and the possibility of parametric variation within the framework of the procedure, point to the fruitfulness of further study.

Obedience is as basic an element in the structure of social life as one can point to. Some system of authority is a requirement of all communal living, and it is only the man dwelling in isolation who is not forced to respond, through defiance or submission, to the commands of others. Obedience, as a determinant of behavior, is of particular relevance to our time. It has been reliably established that from 1933-45 millions of innocent persons were systematically slaughtered on command. Gas chambers were built, death camps were guarded, daily quotas of corpses were produced with the same efficiency as the manufacture of appliances. These inhumane policies may have originated in the mind of a single person, but they could only be carried out on a massive scale if a very large number of persons obeyed orders.

Obedience is the psychological mechanism that links individual action to political purpose. It is the dispositional cement that binds men to systems of authority. Facts of recent history and observation in daily life suggest that for many persons obedience may be a deeply ingrained behavior tendency, indeed, a **prepotent** impulse overriding training in ethics, sympathy, and moral conduct. C. P. Snow (1961) points to its importance when he writes:

> When you think of the long and gloomy history of man, you will find more hideous crimes have been committed in the name of obedience than have ever been committed in the name of rebellion. If you doubt that, read William Shirer's "Rise and Fall of the Third Reich." The German Officer Corps were brought up in the most rigorous code of obedience . . . in the name of obedience they were party to, and assisted in, the most wicked large scale actions in the history of the world [p. 24].

While the particular form of obedience dealt with in the present study has its **antecedents** in these episodes, it must not be thought all obedience entails acts of aggression against others. Obedience serves numerous productive functions. Indeed, the very life of society is predicated on its existence. Obedience may be **ennobling** and educative and refer to acts of charity and kindness, as well as to destruction.

General Procedure

A procedure was devised which seems useful as a tool for studying obedience (Milgram, 1961). It consists of ordering a naive subject to administer electric shock to a victim. A simulated shock generator is used, with 30 clearly marked voltage levels that range from 15 to 450 volts. The instrument bears verbal designations that range from Slight Shock to Danger: Severe Shock. The responses of the victim, who is a trained **confederate** of the experimenter, are standardized. The orders to administer shocks are given to the naive subject in the context of a "learning experiment" **ostensibly** set up to study the effects of punishment on memory. As the experiment proceeds the naive subject is commanded to administer increasingly more intense shocks to the victim, even to the point of reaching the level marked Danger: Severe Shock. Internal resistances become stronger, and at a certain point the subject refuses to go on with the experiment. Behavior prior to this rupture is considered "obedience," in that the subject complies with the commands of the experimenter. The point of rupture is the act of disobedience. A quantitative value is assigned to the subject's performance based on the maximum intensity shock he is willing to administer before he refuses to participate further. Thus for any particular subject and for any particular experimental condition the degree of obedience may be specified with

---

Prepotent (pre-POH-tent). Something that has exceptional power or influence.

Antecedents (an-teh-SEED-ents). An antecedent is a preceding event, something that comes *before*.

Ennobling (en-NOH-bling). You "ennoble" something when you improve it, or make it better.

Confederate. A confederate in an experiment is an associate of the experimenter, someone who follows an exact script rather than reacting in an unplanned fashion. Typically, the "naive" subject--the person actually being tested--doesn't realize that the confederate is actually part of the experiment.

Ostensibly (oss-TEN-sib-blee). *Ostensible* means "apparent," such as an experiment that looks like what it is.

a numerical value. The **crux** of the study is to systematically vary the factors believed to alter the degree of obedience to the experimental commands.

The technique allows the important variables to be manipulated at several points in the experiment. One may vary aspects of the source of command, content and form of command, **instrumentalities** for its execution, target object, general social setting, etc. The problem therefore, is not one of designing increasingly more numerous experimental conditions, but of selecting those that best illuminate the *process* of obedience from the **sociopsychological** standpoint.

Related Studies

The inquiry bears an important relation to philosophic analyses of obedience and authority (Arendt, 1958; Friedrich, 1958; Weber, 1947), an early experimental study of obedience by Frank (1944), studies in "authoritarianism" (Adorno, Frendel-Brunswik, Levinson, & Sanford, 1950; Rokeach, 1961), and a recent series of analytic and empirical studies in social power (Cartwright, 1959). It owes much to the long concern with *suggestion* in social psychology, both in its normal forms (e.g., Binet, 1900) and in its clinical manifestations (Charcot, 1881). But it derives, in the first instance, from direct observation of a social fact; the individual who is commanded by a legitimate authority ordinarily obeys. Obedience comes easily and often. It is a **ubiquitous** and indispensable feature of social life.

METHOD

Subjects

The subjects were 40 males between the ages of 20 and 50, drawn from New Haven and the surrounding communities. Subjects were obtained from a newspaper advertisement and direct mail solicitation. Those who responded to the appeal believed they were to participate in a study of memory and learning at Yale University. A wide range of occupations is represented in the sample. Typical subjects were postal clerks, high school teachers, salesmen, engineers, and laborers. Subjects ranged in educational level from one who had

TABLE 1

DISTRIBUTION OF AGE AND OCCUPATIONAL TYPES IN THE EXPERIMENT

Occupations	20-29 years (n)	30-39 years (n)	40-50 years (n)	Percentage of total (Occupations)
Workers, skilled & unskilled	4	5	6	37.5
Sales, business, & white collar	3	6	7	40.0
Professional	1	5	3	22.5
Percentage of total (Age)	20	40	40	

Note.–Total N=40.

not finished elementary school, to those who had doctorate and other professional degrees. They were paid $4.50 for their participation in the experiment. However, subjects were told that payment was simply for coming to the laboratory, and that the money was theirs no matter what happened after they arrived. Table 1 shows the proportion of age and occupational types assigned to the experimental condition.

Personnel and Locale

The experiment was conducted on the grounds of Yale University in the elegant interaction laboratory. (This detail is relevant to the perceived legitimacy of the experiment. In further variations, the experiment was dissociated from the university, with consequences for performance.) The role of experimenter was played by a 31 year old high school teacher of biology. His manner was impassive, and his appearance somewhat stern throughout the experiment. He was dressed in a gray technician's coat. The victim was played by a 47 year old accountant, trained for the role; he was of Irish-American stock, whom most observers found mild-mannered and likable.

Procedure

One naive subject and one victim (an accomplice) performed in each experiment. A pretext had to be devised that would justify the administration of electric shock by the naive subject. This was effectively accomplished by the cover story. After a general introduction on the presumed relation between punishment and learning, subjects were told:

> But actually, we know *very little* about the effect of punishment on learning, because almost no truly scientific studies have been made of it in human beings.
>
> For instance, we don't know how *much* punishment is best for learning--and we don't know how much difference it makes as to who is giving the punishment, whether an

adult learns best from a younger or an older person than himself--or many things of that sort.

So in this study we are bringing together a number of adults of different occupations and ages. And we're asking some of them to be teachers and some of them to be learners.

We want to find out just what effect different people have on each other as teachers and learners, and also what effect *punishment* will have on learning in this situation.

Therefore, I'm going to ask one of you to be the teacher here tonight and the other one to be the learner.

Does either of you have a preference?

Subjects then drew slips of paper from a hat to determine who would be the teacher and who would be the learner in the experiment. The drawing was rigged so that the naive subject was always the teacher and the accomplice always the learner. (Both slips contained the word "Teacher.") Immediately after the drawing, the teacher and learner were taken to an adjacent room and the learner was strapped into an "electric chair" apparatus.

The experimenter explained that the straps were to prevent excessive movement while the learner was being shocked. The effect was to make it impossible for him to escape from the situation. An **electrode** was attached to the learner's wrist, and electrode paste was applied to "avoid blisters and burns." Subjects were told that the electrode was attached to the shock generator in the adjoining room.

In order to improve credibility the experimenter declared, in response to a question by the learner: "Although the shocks can be extremely painful, they cause no permanent tissue damage."

Learning task. The lesson administered by the subject was a **paired-associate** learning task. The subject read a series of word pairs to the learner, and then read the first word of the pair along with four terms. The learner was to indicate which of the four terms had originally been paired with the first word. He communicated his answer by pressing one of four switches in front of him, which in turn lit up one of four numbered quadrants in an answer-box located atop the shock generator.

Shock generator. The instrument panel consists of 30 lever switches set in a horizontal line. Each switch is clearly labeled with a voltage designation that ranges from 15 to 450 volts. There is a 15-volt increment from one switch to the next going from left to right. In addition, the following verbal designations are clearly indicated for groups of four switches going from left to right: Slight Shock, Moderate Shock, Strong Shock, Very Strong Shock, Intense Shock, Extreme Intensity Shock, Danger: Severe Shock. (Two switches after this last designation are simply marked XXX.)

Upon depressing a switch: a pilot light corresponding to each switch is illuminated in bright red; an electric buzzing is heard; an electric blue light, labeled "voltage energizer," flashes; the dial on the voltage meter swings to the right; various relay clicks are sounded.

The upper left-hand corner of the generator is labeled Shock Generator, Type ZLB, Dyson Instrument Company, Waltham, Mass. Output 15 Volts-450 Volts.

Details of the instrument were carefully handled to insure an appearance of authenticity. The panel was engraved by precision industrial engravers, and all components were of high quality. No subject in the experiment suspected that the instrument was merely a simulated shock generator.[3]

Sample shock. Each naive subject is given a sample shock on the shock generator, prior to beginning his run as teacher. This shock is always 45 volts, and is applied by pressing the third switch of the generator. The shock is applied to the wrist of the naive subject, and has its source in a 45-volt battery wired into the generator. This further convinces the subject of the authenticity of the generator.

Shock instructions. The subject is told to administer a shock to the learner each time he gives a wrong response. Moreover--and this is the key command--the subject is instructed to "move one level higher on the shock generator each time the learner flashes a wrong answer." He is also instructed to announce the voltage level before administering a shock. This serves to continually remind subjects of the increasing intensity of shocks administered to the learner.

Preliminary and regular run. Pretests revealed that the procedure of reading words and administering

---

Crux (kruks). The key to solving a puzzling or difficult problem.

Instrumentalities (in-strew-men-TAL-ih-tees). The instruments or items needed to carry out an experiment. In the present experiment, the shock machine is an instrument for carrying out the study.

Sociopsychological. The "social psychological" point of view. The belief that factors in the social environment (such as learned values or attitudes, or the setting in which the event occurs) interact with internal factors (such as personality traits) to produce a given behavior.

Ubiquitous (you-BICK-quit-us). Being everywhere; something that you constantly encounter.

Electrode (ee-LEK-trode). A device used to detect electrical activity in the body, or to administer electric shock to an organism.

Paired-associate. A learning technique in which the subject is required to "pair" words in one list with words in a second list. Later, when the first word in the "pair" is given to the subject, he or she must recall what the "associated" word was.

shocks requires some practice before it can be handled smoothly. Therefore, immediately preceding the regular run, the teacher is given a preliminary series of 10 words to read to the learner. There are 3 neutral words in the practice series (i.e., words that the learner answers correctly), so that shocks are administered for 7 of the words, with the maximum shock at 105 volts (moderate shock). Almost all subjects master the procedure by the time the preliminary run is over.

Subjects are then presented with a second list, and are told that the procedure is the same as for the first list; the experimenter adds, however:

> When you get to the bottom of the list, repeat it over again, and continue giving shocks, until the learner has learned all the pairs correctly.

The experimenter instructs the subject to

> start from 15 volts and increase the shock level one step each time the learner gives a wrong answer.

Feedback from the victim. In all conditions the learner gives a predetermined set of responses to the word pair test, based on a schedule of approximately three wrong answers to one correct answer. In the present experimental condition no vocal response or other sign of protest is heard from the learner until Shock Level 300 is reached. When the 300-volt shock is administered, the learner pounds on the wall of the room in which his is bound to the electric chair. The pounding can be heard by the subject. From this point on, the learner's answers no longer appear on the four-way panel.

At this juncture, subjects ordinarily turn to the experimenter for guidance. The experimenter instructs the subject to treat the absence of a response as a wrong answer, and to shock the subject according to the usual schedule. He advises the subjects to allow 5-10 seconds before considering no response as a wrong answer, and to increase the shock level one step each time the learner fails to respond correctly. The learner's pounding is repeated after the 315-volt shock is administered; afterwards he is not heard from, nor do his answers reappear on the four-way signal box.

Experimenter feedback. At various points in the experiment the subject may turn to the experimenter for advice on whether he should continue to administer shocks. Or he may indicate that he does not wish to go on. It was important to standardize the experimenter's responses to these inquiries and reactions.

If the subject indicated his unwillingness to go on, the experimenter responded with a sequence of "prods," using as many as necessary to bring the subject into line.

Prod 1: Please continue, *or* Please go on.

Prod 2: The experiment requires that you continue.

Prod 3: It is absolutely essential that you continue.

Prod 4: You have no other choice, you *must* go on.

The prods were always made in sequence: Only if Prod 1 had been unsuccessful, could Prod 2 be used. If the subject refused to obey the experimenter after Prod 4, the experiment was terminated. The experimenter's tone of voice was at all times firm, but not impolite. The sequence was begun anew on each occasion that the subject **balked** or showed reluctance to follow orders.

Special prods. If the subject asked if the learner was liable to suffer permanent physical injury, the experimenter said:

> Although the shocks may be painful, there is no permanent tissue damage, so please go on. [Followed by Prods 2, 3, and 4 if necessary.]

If the subject said that the learner did not want to go on, the experimenter replied:

> Whether the learner likes it or not, you must go on until he has learned all the word pairs correctly. So please go on. [Followed by Prods 2, 3 and 4 if necessary.]

Dependent Measures

The primary **dependent measure** for any subject is the maximum shock he administers before he refuses to go any further. In principle this may vary from 0 (for a subject who refuses to administer even the first shock) to 30 (for a subject who administers the highest shock on the generator). A subject who breaks off the experiment at any point prior to administering the thirtieth shock level is termed a *defiant* subject. One who complies with experimental commands fully, and proceeds to administer all shock levels commanded, is termed an *obedient* subject.

Further records. With few exceptions, experimental sessions were recorded on magnetic tape. Occasional photographs were taken through one-way mirrors. Notes were kept on any unusual behavior occurring during the course of the experiments. On occasion, additional observers were directed to write objective descriptions of the subjects' behavior. The latency and duration of shocks were measured by accurate timing devices.

Interview and dehoax. Following the experiment, subjects were interviewed; open-ended questions, projective measures, and attitude scales were employed. After the interview, procedures were undertaken to assure that the subjects would leave the laboratory in a state of well being. A friendly reconciliation was arranged between the subject and the victim, and an effort was made to reduce any tensions that arose as a result of the experiment.

RESULTS

Preliminary Notions

Before giving an account of the experimental results, it is instructive to consider how persons predict others will perform when commanded to administer powerful shocks to another person. Fourteen Yale seniors, all psychology majors, were provided with a detailed description of the experimental situation. They were asked to reflect carefully on it, and to predict the behavior of 100 hypothetical subjects. More specifically, they were instructed to plot the distribution of obedience of "100 Americans of diverse occupations, and ranging in age from 20 to 50 years," who were placed in the experimental situation.

There was considerable agreement among the respondents on the expected behavior of hypothetical subjects. All respondents predicted that only an insignificant minority would go through to the end of the shock series. (The estimates ranged from 0 to 3%; i.e., the most "pessimistic" member of the class predicted that of 100 persons, 3 would continue through to the most potent shock available on the shock generator--450 volts.) The class mean was 1.2%. The question was also posed informally to colleagues of the author, and the most general feeling was that few if any subjects would go beyond the designation Very Strong Shock.

Result of Experiment 1

Subjects accept situation. With few exceptions subjects were convinced of the reality of the experimental situation, that they were administering shocks to another person, and the most potent shocks were extremely painful. In the post-experimental interview subjects were asked: "How painful to the learner were the last few shocks that you administered to him?" Subjects were instructed to indicate their answers on a printed 14-point scale ranging from "Not at all painful" to "Extremely painful." The modal response was 14 (Extremely painful) with the mean at 13.42.

Signs of extreme tension. Many subjects showed signs of nervousness in the experimental situation, and especially upon administering the more powerful shocks. In a large number of cases the degree of tension reached extremes that are rarely seen in sociopsychological laboratory studies. Subjects were observed to sweat, tremble, stutter, bite their lips, groan, and dig their fingernails into their flesh. These were characteristic rather than exceptional responses to the experiment.

One sign of tension was the regular occurrence of nervous laughing fits. Fourteen of the 40 subjects showed definite signs of nervous laughter and smiling. The laughter seemed entirely out of place, even bizarre. Full-blown, uncontrollable seizures were observed for 3 subjects. On one occasion we observed a seizure so violently convulsive that it was necessary to call a halt to the experiment. The subject, a 46-year-old encyclopedia salesman, was seriously embarrassed by his untoward and uncontrollable behavior. In the post-experimental interviews subjects took pains to point out that they were not sadistic types, and that the laughter did not mean they enjoyed shocking the victim.

Distribution of scores. It had been conjectured that persons would not, in general, agree to administer shocks beyond the level designated as Very Strong Shock. The distribution of maximum shocks for this experiment is shown in Table 2. The obtained distribution of scores deviates radically from the prediction.

Upon command of the experimenter, each of the 40 subjects went beyond the expected breakoff point. No subject stopped prior to administering Shock Level 20. (At this level--300 volts--the victim kicks on the wall and no longer provides answers to the teacher's multiple-choice questions.)

Of the 40 subjects, 5 refused to obey the experimental commands beyond the 300-volt level. Four more subjects administered one further shock, and then refused to go on. Two broke off at the 330-volt level, and 1 each at 345, 360, and 375 volts. Thus a total of 14 subjects defied the experimenter. It is instructive to reprint their remarks at the point of defiance, as transcribed from the tape recordings:

[0124] I think he's trying to communicate, he's knocking. . . .Well it's not fair to shock the guy. . . . these are terrific volts. I don't think this is very humane. . . . Oh, I can't go on with this; no, this isn't right. It's a hell of an experiment. The guy is suffering in there. No, I don't want to go on. This is crazy. [Subject refused to administer more shocks.]

[0123] He's banging in there. I'm gonna chicken out. I'd like to continue, but I can't do that to a man. . . . I'm

---

Balked. To show reluctance or stop short of doing something.

Dependent measures. Dependent measures are those which result from running the study. The number of pounds lost on a diet is the dependent measure of the effects of the diet, because the weight loss typically depends on which diet the subject follows.

TABLE 2
DISTRIBUTION OF BREAKOFF POINTS

Verbal designation and voltage indication	Number of subjects for whom this was maximum shock
Slight Shock	
15	0
30	0
45	0
60	0
Moderate Shock	
75	0
90	0
105	0
120	0
Strong Shock	
135	0
150	0
165	0
180	0
Very Strong Shock	
195	0
210	0
225	0
240	0
Intense Shock	
255	0
270	0
285	0
300	5
Extreme Intensity Shock	
315	4
330	2
345	1
360	1
Danger: Severe Shock	
375	1
390	0
405	0
420	0
XXX	
435	0
450	26

sorry I can't do that to a man. I'll hurt his heart. You take your check.... No really, I couldn't do it.

These subjects were frequently in a highly agitated and even angered state. Sometimes, verbal protest was at a minimum, and the subject simply got up from his chair in front of the shock generator, and indicated that he wished to leave the laboratory.

Of the 40 subjects, 26 obeyed the orders of the experimenter to the end, proceeding to punish the victim until they reached the most potent shock available on the shock generator. At that point, the experimenter called a halt to the session. (The maximum shock is labeled 450 volts, and is two steps beyond the designation: Danger: Severe Shock.) Although obedient subjects continued to administer shocks beyond the 300-volt level, and displayed fears similar to those who defied the experimenter; yet they obeyed.

After the maximum shocks had been delivered, and the experimenter called a halt to the proceedings, many obedient subjects heaved sighs of relief, mopped their brows, rubbed their fingers over their eyes, or nervously fumbled cigarettes. Some shook their heads, apparently in regret. Some subjects had remained calm throughout the experiment, and displayed only minimal signs of tension from beginning to end.

DISCUSSION

The experiment yielded two findings that were surprising. The first finding concerns the sheer strength of obedient tendencies manifested in this situation. Subjects have learned from childhood that it is a fundamental breach of moral conduct to hurt another person against his will. Yet, 26 subjects abandon this tenet in following the instructions of an authority who has no special powers to enforce his commands. To disobey would bring no material loss to the subject; no punishment would ensue. It is clear from the remarks and outward behaviour of many participants that in punishing the victim they are often acting against their own values. Subjects often expressed deep disapproval of shocking a man in the face of his objections, and others denounced it as stupid and senseless. Yet the majority complied with the experimental commands. This outcome was surprising from two perspectives: first, from the standpoint of predictions made in the questionnaire described earlier. (Here, however, it is possible that the remoteness of the respondents from the actual situation, and the difficulty of conveying to them the concrete details of the experiment, could account for the serious underestimation of obedience.)

But the results were also unexpected to persons who observed the experiment in progress, through one-way mirrors. Observers often uttered expressions of disbelief upon seeing a subject administer more powerful shocks to the victim. These persons had a full acquaintance with the details of the situation, and yet systematically underestimated the amount of obedience that subjects would display.

The second unanticipated effect was the extraordinary tension generated by the procedures. One might suppose that a subject would simply break off or continue as his conscience dictated. Yet, this is very far from what happened. There were striking reactions of tension and emotional strain. One observer related:

> I observed a mature and initially poised businessman enter the laboratory smiling and confident. Within 20 minutes he was reduced to a twitching, stuttering wreck, who was rapidly approaching a point of nervous collapse. He constantly pulled on his earlobe, and twisted his hands. At one point he pushed his fist into his forehead and muttered:"Oh God, let's stop it."And yet he continued to respond to every word of the experimenter, and obeyed to the end.

Any understanding of the phenomenon of obedience must rest on an analysis of the particular conditions in which it occurs. The following features of the experiment go some distance in explaining the high amount of obedience observed in the situation.

1. The experiment is sponsored by and takes place on the grounds of an institution of unimpeachable reputation, Yale University. It may be reasonably presumed that the personnel are competent and reputable. The importance of this background authority is now being studied by conducting a series of experiments outside of New Haven, and without any visible ties to the university.

2. The experiment is, on the face of it, designed to attain a worthy purpose--advancement of knowledge about learning and memory. Obedience occurs not as an end in itself, but as an instrumental element in a situation that the subject construes as significant, and meaningful. He may not be able to see its full significance, but he may properly assume that the experimenter does.

3. The subject perceives that the victim has voluntarily submitted to the authority system of the experimenter. He is not (at first) an unwilling captive impressed for involuntary service. He has taken the trouble to come to the laboratory presumably to aid the experimental research. That he later becomes an involuntary subject does not alter the fact that, initially, he consented to participate without qualification. Thus he had in some degree incurred an obligation toward the experimenter.

4. The subject, too, has entered the experiment voluntarily, and perceives himself under obligation to aid the experimenter. He has made a commitment, and to disrupt the experiment is a repudiation of this initial promise of aid.

5. Certain features of the procedure strengthen the subject's sense of obligation to the experimenter. For one, he has been paid for coming to the laboratory. In part this is canceled out by the experimenter's statement that:

> Of course, as in all experiments, the money is yours simply for coming to the laboratory. From this point on, no matter what happens, the money is yours.[4]

6. From the subject's standpoint, the fact that he is the teacher and the other man the learner is purely a chance consequence (it is determined by drawing lots) and he, the subject, ran the same risk as the other man in being assigned the role of learner. Since the assignment of positions in the experiment was achieved by fair means, the learner is deprived of any basis of complaint on this count. (A similar situation obtains in Army units, in which--in the absence of volunteers--a particularly dangerous mission may be assigned by drawing lots, and the unlucky soldier is expected to bear his misfortune with sportsmanship.)

7. There is, at best, ambiguity with regard to the **prerogatives** of a psychologist and the corresponding rights of his subject. There is a vagueness of expectation concerning what a psychologist may require of his subject, and when he is overstepping acceptable limits. Moreover, the experiment occurs in a closed setting, and thus provides no opportunity for the subject to remove these ambiguities by discussion with others. There are few standards that seem directly applicable to the situation, which is a novel one for most subjects.

8. The subjects are assured that the shocks administered to the subject are "painful but not dangerous." Thus they assume that the discomfort caused the victim is momentary, while the scientific gains resulting from the experiment are enduring.

9. Through Shock Level 20 the victim continues to provide answers on the signal box. The subject may construe this as a sign that the victim is still willing to "play the game." It is only after Shock Level 20 that the victim repudiates the rules completely, refusing to answer further.

These features help to explain the high amount of obedience obtained in this experiment. Many of the arguments raised need not remain matters of speculation, but can be reduced to testable propositions to be confirmed or disproved by further experiments.[5]

The following features of the experiment concern the nature of the conflict which the subject faces.

10. The subject is placed in a position in which he must respond to the competing demands of two per-

---

Prerogatives (pre-ROG-ah-tives). The special rights or exclusive powers of a certain person. For instance, only the president (in the US) has the prerogative of vetoing legislation passed by the Congress.

sons: the experimenter and the victim. The conflict must be resolved by meeting the demands of one or the other; satisfaction of the victim and the experimenter are mutually exclusive. Moreover, the resolution must take the form of a highly visible action, that of continuing to shock the victim or breaking off the experiment. Thus the subject is forced into a public conflict that does not permit any completely satisfactory solution.

11. While the demands of the experimenter carry the weight of scientific authority, the demands of the victim spring from his personal experience of pain and suffering. The two claims need not be regarded as equally pressing and legitimate. The experimenter seeks an abstract scientific datum; the victim cries out for relief from physical suffering caused by the subject's actions.

12. The experiment gives the subject little time for reflection. The conflict comes on rapidly. It is only minutes after the subject has been seated before the shock generator that the victim begins his protests. Moreover, the subject perceives that he has gone through but two-thirds of the shock levels at the time the subject's first protests are heard. Thus he understands that the conflict will have a persistent aspect to it, and may well become more intense as increasingly more powerful shocks are required. The rapidity with which the conflict descends on the subject, and his realization that is is predictably recurrent may well be sources of tension to him.

13. At a more general level, the conflict stems from the opposition of two deeply ingrained behavior dispositions: first, the disposition not to harm other people, and second, the tendency to obey those whom we perceive to be legitimate authorities.

FOOTNOTES

[1] Reprinted by permission of the author and the publisher from *Journal of Abnormal and Social Psychology*, 1963, **67**, 371-378. Copyright 1963 by the American Psychological Association.

[2] This research was supported by a grant (NSF G-17916) from the National Science Foundation. Exploratory studies conducted in 1960 were supported by a grant from the Higgins Fund at Yale University. The research assistance of Alan C. Elms and John Wayland is gratefully acknowledged.

[3] A related technique, making use of a shock generator, was reported by Buss (1961) for the study of aggression in the laboratory. Despite the considerable similarity of technical detail in the experimental procedures, both investigators proceeded in ignorance of the other's work. Milgram provided plans and a photograph of his shock generator, experimental procedure, and first results in a report to the National Science Foundation in January 1961. This report received only limited circulation. Buss reported his procedure 6 months later, but to a wider audience. Subsequently, technical information and reports were exchanged. The present article was first received in the Editor's office on December 27, 1961; it was resubmitted with deletions on July 27, 1962.

[4] Forty-three subjects, undergraduates at Yale University, were run in the experiment without payment. The results are very similar to those obtained with paid subjects.

[5] A series of recently completed experiments employing the obedience paradigm is reported in Milgram (1964).

REFERENCES

ADORNO, T., FRENKEL-BRUNSWIK, ELSE, LEVINSON, D.J., & SANFORD, R.N. *The authoritarian personality*. New York: Harper, 1950.

ARENDT, H. What was authority? In C.J. Friedrich (Ed.), *Authority*. Cambridge: Harvard Univer. Press, 1958. Pp. 81-112.

BINET, A. *La suggestibilité*. Paris: Schleicher, 1900.

BUSS, A.H. *The psychology of aggression*. New York: Wiley, 1961.

CARTWRIGHT, S. (Ed.) *Studies in social power*. Ann Arbor: University of Michigan Institute for Social Research, 1959.

CHARCOT, J.M. *Oeuvres complètes*. Paris: Bureaux du Progrès Médical, 1881.

FRANK, J.D. Experimental studies of personal pressure and resistance. *J. gen. Psychol.*, 1944, 30, 23-64.

FRIEDRICH, C.J. (Ed.) *Authority*. Cambridge: Harvard Univer. Press, 1958.

MILGRAM, S. Dynamics of obedience. Washington: National Science Foundation, 25 January 1961 (Mimeo).

MILGRAM, S. Some conditions of obedience and disobedience to authority. *Hum. Relat.*, 1964, in press.

ROKEACH, M. Authority, authoritarianism, and conformity. In I.A. Berg & B.M. Bass (Eds.), *Conformity and deviation*. New York: Harper, 1961. Pp. 230-257.

SNOW, C.P. Either-or. *Progressive*, 1961(Feb.), 24.

WEBER, M. *The theory of social and economic organization*. Oxford: Oxford Univ. Press, 1947.

Classic Quotations from William James

An unlearned carpenter of my acquaintance once said in my hearing: "There is very little difference between one man and another; but what little there is, is very important." This distinction seems to me to go to the heart of the matter.
(The Will to Believe [1897].)

There is but one unconditional commandment, which is that we should seek incessantly, with fear and trembling, so to vote and to act as to bring about the very largest total universe of good which we can see.
(The Will to Believe [1897].)

CHAPTER 21

"Cognitive Consequences of Forced Compliance"

Leon Festinger and James M. Carlsmith[1,2]

> **EDITORS' COMMENTS.** Over the years, Stanford psychologist Leon Festinger has conducted a series of intriguing experiments on what happens when people's *actions* come into conflict with their *attitudes* or *values*. In one of his first studies, Festinger worked with H.W. Riecken and Stanley Schachter. During the early 1950's, these social scientists made extensive observations of a "doomsday group" whose leader had predicted the world would end on a certain day. As the fatal day approached, the members of the group became more and more excited and tried to convince others to repent and join their group in order to "save their souls." When "doomsday" arrived, the members of the group gathered together to await final judgment and to pray for deliverance. To their amazement, the day passed, and so did several other days, and the world continued to speed along on its merry way. And how did the leader of the "doomsday group" respond to the failure of her predictions? Apparently, by finding a "rational excuse" for what actually had happened. Several days after the date the world was supposed to end, she told members of her clan that "God had spoken to her, and had spared the world in answer to the group's prayers." The group members then reacted with great joy. Rather than rejecting their leader for being wrong in her predictions, they accepted her more warmly and believed even more firmly in her prophecies.[3] The "failed prophecy" study led Festinger to hypothesize that whenever people are put in situations where their actions are in conflict with their values or attitudes, they experience *cognitive dissonance*. That is, whenever we do something we think we shouldn't have, we face the problem of explaining our actions to ourselves. Festinger stated we are usually highly motivated to reduce cognitive dissonance when it occurs, and we do so chiefly by changing our *beliefs* or attitudes to make them agree with our *actual behaviors*--and then we go right on behaving the way we always had.
>
> The study reprinted here--with J.M. Carlsmith--was perhaps the first *laboratory* experiment to give strong support to the theory of cognitive dissonance. Since then, hundreds of other researchers have confirmed the basic outlines of Festinger's approach. However, we now know that many types of people don't experience much "dissonance." For example, Hungarian psychologist Csaba Szabo found that subjects who tended to be "manipulators" showed little or no dissonance (and changed their attitudes very little) when paid to write essays opposed to their normal views. Subjects who weren't "manipulators," however, tended to experience "high dissonance" and changed their attitudes a significant amount.[4]
>
> Festinger's concept of cognitive dissonance is, in many ways, similar to French psychologist Jean Piaget's notion of *dis-equilibrium*. Piaget believed that when children experience an event whose outcome is *contrary to their expectations*, their cognitive structures are disrupted until they can find some explanation for this unpredicted occurrence. Piaget thought that the "urge to achieve cognitive equilibrium" was the major motivating force behind cognitive development in children.
>
> We now know that neither "cognitive dissonance" nor "dis-equilibrium" is the single dominant force underlying attitude change or cognitive development. Rather, it is the continual *interplay* between the person's genetic endowment, past history, and present environment that determines what people think and how they act. However, the Festinger and Carlsmith article is a "classic," not only because of the hundreds of similar studies it engendered, but also because it prompted experimenters to look at the considerable difference between *attitude change* and *behavior change*.

What happens to a person's private opinion if he is forced to do or say something contrary to that opinion? Only recently has there been any experimental work related to this question. Two studies reported by Janis and King (1954; 1956) clearly showed that, at least under some conditions, the private opinion changes so as to bring it into closer correspondence with the overt behavior the person was forced to perform. Specifically, they showed that if a person is forced to improvise a speech supporting a point of view with which he disagrees, his private opinion moves toward the position advocated in the speech. The observed opinion change is greater than for persons who only hear the speech or for persons who read a prepared speech with emphasis solely on **elocution** and manner of delivery. The authors of these two studies explain their results namely in terms of mental rehearsal and thinking up new arguments. In this way, they propose, the person who is forced to improvise a speech convinces himself. They present some evidence, which is not altogether conclusive, in support of this explanation. We will have more to say concerning this explanation in discussing the results of our experiment.

Kelman (1953) tried to pursue the matter further. He reasoned that if the person is induced to make an overt statement contrary to his private opinion by the offer of some reward, then the greater the reward offered, the greater should be the subsequent opinion change. His data, however, did not support this idea. He found, rather, that a large reward produced less subsequent opinion change than did a smaller reward. Actually, this finding by Kelman is consistent with the theory we will outline below but, for a number of reasons, is not conclusive. One of the major weaknesses of the data is that not all subjects in the experiment made an overt statement contrary to their private opinion in order to obtain the offered reward. What is more, as one might expect, the percentage of subjects who complied increased as the size of the offered reward increased. Thus, with self-selection of who did and who did not make the required overt statement and with varying percentages of subjects in the different conditions who did make the required statement, no interpretation of the data can be unequivocal.

Recently, Festinger (1957) proposed a theory concerning **cognitive dissonance** from which come a number of derivations about opinion change following forced compliance. Since these derivations are stated in detail by Festinger (1957, Ch. 4), we will here give only a brief outline of the reasoning.

Let us consider a person who privately holds opinion "X" but has, as a result of pressure brought to bear on him, publicly stated that he believes "not X."

1. This person has two cognitions which, psychologically, do not fit together: one of these is the knowledge that he believes "X," the other the knowledge that he has publicly stated that he believes "not X." If no factors other than his private opinion are considered, it would follow, at least in our culture, that if he believes "X" he would publicly state "X." Hence, his cognition of his private belief is dissonant with his cognition concerning his actual public statement.

2. Similarly, the knowledge that he has said "not X," is consonant with (does fit together with) those cognitive elements corresponding to the reasons, pressures, promises of rewards and/or threats of punishment which induced him to say "not X."

3. In evaluating the total magnitude of dissonance, one must take account of both dissonances and consonances. Let us think of the sum of all the dissonances involving some particular cognition as "D" and the sum of all the consonances as "C." Then we might think of the total magnitude of dissonance as being a function of "D" divided by "D" plus "C."

Let us then see what can be said about the total magnitude of dissonance in a person created by the knowledge that he said "not X" and really believes "X." With everything else held constant, this total-magnitude of dissonance would decrease as the number and importance of the pressures which induced him to say "not X" increased.

Thus, if the overt behavior was brought about by, say, offers of reward or threats of punishment, the magnitude of dissonance is maximal if these promised rewards or threatened punishments were just barely sufficient to induce the person to say "not X." From this point on, as the promised rewards or threatened punishment become larger, the magnitude of dissonance becomes smaller.

4. One way in which the dissonance can be reduced is for the person to change his private opinion so as to bring it into correspondence with what he has said. One would consequently expect to observe such opinion change after a person has been forced or induced to say something contrary to his private opinion. Furthermore, since the pressure to reduce dissonance will be a function of the magnitude of the dissonance, the observed

---

Elocution (el-oh-KEW-shun). The art of effective public speaking.

Cognitive dissonance (DISS-oh-nance). *Dissonance* means "a lack of agreement." If you hold two thoughts, attitudes, or beliefs that contradict one another, you will often experience "cognitive dissonance." In Festinger's original theory, he stated that you have an innate tendency to reduce such dissonance, and that this tendency is one of your major motives in life. In fact, Jean Piaget said much the same thing, although Piaget and Festinger don't agree on what the most likely way of reducing dissonance typically is.

opinion change should be greatest when the pressure used to **elicit** the overt behavior is just sufficient to do it.

The present experiment was designed to test this derivation under controlled, laboratory conditions. In the experiment we varied the amount of reward used to force persons to make a statement contrary to their private views. The prediction [from 3 and 4 above] is that the larger the reward given to the subject, the smaller will be the subsequent opinion change.

PROCEDURE

Seventy-one male students in the introductory psychology course at Stanford University were used in the experiment. In this course, students are required to spend a certain number of hours as subjects (Ss) in experiments. They choose among the available experiments by signing their names on a sheet posted on the bulletin board which states the nature of the experiment. The present experiment was listed as a two-hour experiment dealing with "Measures of Performance."

During the first week of the course, when the requirement of serving in experiments was announced and explained to the students, the instructor also told them about a study that the psychology department was conducting. He explained that, since they were required to serve in experiments, the department was conducting a study to evaluate these experiments in order to be able to improve them in the future. They were told that a sample of students would be interviewed after having served as Ss. They were urged to cooperate in these interviews by being completely frank and honest. The importance of this announcement will become clear shortly. It enabled us to measure the opinions of our S's in a context not directly connected with our experiment and in which we could reasonably expect frank and honest expressions of opinions.

When the S arrived for the experiment on "Measures of Performance" he had to wait for a few minutes in the secretary's office. The experimenter (E) then came in, introduced himself to the S and, together, they walked into the laboratory room where the E said:

> This experiment usually takes a little over an hour but, of course, we had to schedule it for two hours. Since we have that extra time, the introductory psychology people asked if they could interview some of our subjects. [Offhand and conversationally.] Did they announce that in class? I gather that they're interviewing some people who have been in experiments. I don't know much about it. Anyhow, they may want to interview you when you're through here.

With no further introduction or explanation the S was shown the first task, which involved putting 12 spools onto a tray, emptying the tray, refilling it with spools, and so on. He was told to use one hand and to work at his own speed. He did this for one-half hour. The E then removed the tray and spools and placed in front of the S a board containing 48 square pegs. His task was to turn each peg a quarter turn clockwise, then another quarter turn, and so on. He was told again to use one hand and to work at his own speed. The S worked at this task for another half hour.

While the S was working on these tasks, the E sat, with a stop watch in his hand, busily making notations on a sheet of paper. He did so in order to make it convincing that this was what the E was interested in and that these tasks, and how the S worked on them, was the total experiment. From our point of view the experiment had hardly started. The hour which the S spent working on the repetitive, monotonous tasks was intended to provide, for each S uniformly, an experience about which he would have a somewhat negative opinion.

After the half hour on the second task was over, the E conspicuously set the stop watch back to zero, put it away, pushed his chair back, lit a cigarette, and said:

> O.K. Well, that's all we have in the experiment itself. I'd like to explain what this has been all about so you'll have some idea of why you were doing this. [E pauses.] Well, the way the experiment is set up is this. There are actually two groups in the experiment. In one, the group you were in, we bring the subject in and give him essentially no introduction to the experiment. That is, all we tell him is what he needs to know in order to do the tasks, and he has no idea of what the experiment is all about, or what it's going to be like, or anything like that. But in the other group, we have a student that we've hired that works for us regularly, and what I do is take him into the next room where the subject is waiting--the same room you were waiting in before--and I introduce him as if he had just finished being a subject in the experiment. That is, I say: "This is so-and-so, who's just finished the experiment, and I've asked him to tell you a little of what it's about before you start." The fellow who works for us then, in conversation with the next subject, makes these points: [The E then produced a sheet headed "For Group B" which had written on it: It was very enjoyable, I had a lot of fun, I enjoyed myself, it was very interesting, it was intriguing, it was exciting. The E showed this to the S and then proceeded with his false explanation of the purpose of the experiment.] Now, of course, we have this student do this, because if the experimenter does it, it doesn't look as realistic, and what we're interested in doing is comparing how these two groups do on the experiment--the one with this previous expectation about the experiment, and the other, like yourself, with essentially none.

Up to this point the procedure was identical for Ss in all conditions. From this point on they diverged somewhat. Three conditions were run, Control, One Dollar, and Twenty Dollars, as follows:

Control Condition

The E continued:

Is that fairly clear? [Pause.] Look, that fellow [looks at watch] I was telling you about from the introductory psychology class said he would get here a couple of minutes from now. Would you mind waiting to see if he wants to talk to you? Fine. Why don't we go into the other room to wait? [The E left the S in the secretary's office for four minutes. He then returned and said:] O.K. Let's check and see if he does want to talk to you.

One and Twenty Dollar Conditions

The E continued:

Is that fairly clear how it is set up and what we're trying to do? [Pause.] Now, I also have a sort of strange thing to ask you. The thing is this. [Long pause, some confusion and uncertainty in the following, with a degree of embarrassment on the part of the E. The manner of the E contrasted strongly with the preceding unhesitant and assured false explanation of the experiment. The point was to make it seem to the S that this was the first time the E had done this and that he felt unsure of himself.] The fellow who normally does this for us couldn't do it today--he just phoned in, and something or other came up for him--so we've been looking around for someone that we could hire to do it for us. You see, we've got another subject waiting [looks at watch] who is supposed to be in that other condition. Now Professor ---, who is in charge of this experiment, suggested that perhaps we could take a chance on your doing it for us. I'll tell you what we had in mind: the thing is, if you could do it for us now, then of course you would know how to do it, and if something like this should ever come up again, that is, the regular fellow couldn't make it, and we had a subject scheduled, it would be very reassuring to us to know that we had somebody else we could call on who knew how to do it. So, if you would be willing to do this for us, we'd like to hire you to do it now and then be on call in the future, if something like this should ever happen again. We can pay you a dollar (twenty dollars) for doing this for us, that is, for doing it now and then being on call. Do you think you could do that for us?

If the S hesitated, the E said things like, "It will only take a few minutes," "The regular person is pretty reliable; this is the first time he has missed," or "If we needed you we could phone you a day or two in advance; if you couldn't make it, of course, we wouldn't expect you to come." After the S agreed to do it, the E gave him the previously mentioned sheet of paper headed "For Group B" and asked him to read it through again. The E then paid the S one dollar (twenty dollars), made out a hand-written receipt form, and asked the S to sign it. He then said:

O.K., the way we'll do it is this. As I said, the next subject should be here by now. I think the next one is a girl. I'll take you into the next room and introduce you to her, saying that you've just finished the experiment and that we've asked you to tell her a little about it. And what we want you to do is just sit down and get into a conversation with her and try to get across the points on that sheet of paper. I'll leave you alone and come back after a couple of minutes. O.K.?

The E then took the S into the secretary's office where he had previously waited and where the next S was waiting. (The secretary had left the office.) He introduced the girl and the S to one another saying that the S had just finished the experiment and would tell her something about it. He then left saying he would return in a couple of minutes. The girl, an undergraduate hired for this role, said little until the S made some positive remarks about the experiment and then said that she was surprised because a friend of hers had taken the experiment the week before and had told her that it was boring and that she ought to try to get out of it. Most Ss responded by saying something like "Oh, no, it's really very interesting. I'm sure you'll enjoy it." The girl, after this listened quietly, accepting and agreeing to everything the S told her. The discussion between the S and the girl was recorded on a hidden tape recorder.

After two minutes the E returned, asked the girl to go into the experimental room, thanked the S for talking to the girl, wrote down his phone number to continue the fiction that we might call on him again in the future and then said: "Look, could we check and see if that fellow from introductory psychology wants to talk to you?"

From this point on, the procedure for all three conditions was once more identical. As the E and the S started to walk to the office where the interviewer was, the E said: "Thanks very much for working on those tasks for us. I hope you did enjoy it. Most of our subjects tell us afterward that they found it quite interesting. You get a chance to see how you react to the tasks and so forth." This short persuasive communication was made in all conditions in exactly the same way. The reason for doing it, theoretically, was to make it easier for anyone

---

Elicit (ee-LISS-it). The smell of bacon frying typically *elicits* a mouth-watering response, whether you wish to salivate or not. An "elicited" response is one that is pulled out of you automatically. However, you can also "emit" (or make) many responses voluntarily.

who wanted to persuade himself that the tasks had been, indeed, enjoyable.

When they arrived at the interviewer's office, the E asked the interviewer whether or not he wanted to talk to the S. The interviewer said yes, the E shook hands with the S, said good-bye, and left. The interviewer, of course, was always kept in complete ignorance of which condition the S was in. The interview consisted of four questions, on each of which the S was first encouraged to talk about the matter and was then asked to rate his opinion or reaction on an 11-point scale. The questions are as follows:

1. Were the tasks interesting and enjoyable? In what way? In what way were they not? Would you rate how you feel about them on a scale from -5 to +5 where -5 means they were extremely dull and boring, +5 means they were extremely interesting and enjoyable, and zero means they were neutral, neither interesting nor uninteresting.

2. Did the experiment give you an opportunity to learn about your own ability to perform these tasks? In what way? In what way not? Would you rate how you feel about this on a scale from 0 to 10 where 0 means you learned nothing and 10 means you learned a great deal.

3. From what you know about the experiment and the tasks involved in it, would you say the experiment was measuring anything important? That is, do you think the results may have scientific value? In what way? In what way not? Would you rate your opinion on this matter on a scale from 0 to 10 where 0 means the results have no scientific value or importance and 10 means they have a great deal of value and importance.

4. Would you have any desire to participate in another similar experiment? Why? Why not? Would you rate your desire to participate in a similar experiment again on a scale from -5 to +5, where -5 means you would definitely dislike to participate, +5 means you would definitely like to participate, and 0 means you have no particular feeling about it one way or the other.

As may be seen, the questions varied in how directly relevant they were to what the S had told the girl. This point will be discussed further in connection with the results.

At the close of the interview the S was asked what he thought the experiment was about and, following this, was asked directly whether or not he was suspicious of anything and, if so, what he was suspicious of. When the interview was over, the interviewer brought the S back to the experimental room where the E was waiting together with the girl who had posed as the waiting S. (In the control condition, of course, the girl was not there.) The true purpose of the experiment was then explained to the S in detail, and the reasons for each of the various steps in the experiment were explained carefully in relation to the true purpose. All experimental Ss in both One Dollar and Twenty Dollar conditions were asked, after this explanation, to return the money they had been given. All Ss, without exception, were quite willing to return the money.

The data from 11 of the 71 Ss in the experiment had to be discarded for the following reasons:

1. Five Ss (three in the One Dollar and two in the Twenty Dollar condition) indicated in the interview that they were suspicious about having been paid to tell the girl the experiment was fun and suspected that that was the real purpose of the experiment.

2. Two Ss (both in the One Dollar condition) told the girl that they had been hired, that the experiment was really boring but they were supposed to say it was fun.

3. Three Ss (one in the One Dollar and two in the Twenty Dollar condition) refused to take the money and refused to be hired.

4. One S (in the One Dollar condition), immediately after having talked to the girl, demanded her phone number saying he would call her and explain things, and also told the E he wanted to wait until she was finished so he could tell her about it.

These 11 Ss were, of course, run through the total experiment anyhow and the experiment was explained to them afterwards. Their data, however, are not included in the analysis.

Summary of Design

There remain, for analysis, 20 Ss in each of the three conditions. Let us review these briefly: 1. *Control condition*. These Ss were treated identically in all respects to the Ss in the experimental conditions, except that they were never asked to, and never did, tell the waiting girl that the experimental tasks were enjoyable and lots of fun. 2. *One Dollar condition*. These Ss were hired for one dollar to tell a waiting S that tasks, which were really rather dull and boring, were interesting, enjoyable, and lots of fun. 3. *Twenty Dollar condition*. These Ss were hired for twenty dollars to do the same thing.

RESULTS

The major results of the experiment are summarized in Table 1 which lists, separately for each of the three experimental conditions, the average rating which the Ss gave at the end of each question on the interview. We will discuss each of the questions on the interview separately, because they were intended to measure different things. One other point before we proceed to examine the data. In all the comparisons, the Control condition should be regarded as a baseline from which to evaluate the results in the other two conditions. The Control condition gives us, essentially, the reactions of Ss to the tasks and their opinions about the experiment as falsely explained to them, without the experimental introduction of dissonance. The data from the other conditions may be viewed, in a sense, as changes from this baseline.

How Enjoyable the Tasks Were

The average ratings on this question, presented in the first row of figures in Table 1, are the results most important to the experiment. These results are the ones most directly relevant to the specific dissonance which was experimentally created. It will be recalled that the tasks were purposely arranged to be rather boring and monotonous. And, indeed, in the Control condition the average rating was -.45, somewhat on the negative side of the neutral point.

TABLE 1
AVERAGE RATINGS ON INTERVIEW QUESTIONS
FOR EACH CONDITION

Question on Interview	Experimental Condition		
	Control (N = 20)	One Dollar (N = 20)	20 Dollars (N = 20)
How enjoyable tasks were (rated from -5 to +5)	-.45	+1.35	-.05
How much they learned (rated from 0 to 10)	3.08	2.80	3.15
Scientific importance (rated from 0 to 10)	5.60	6.45	5.18
Participate in similar exper. (rated from -5 to +5)	-.62	+1.20	-.25

In the other two conditions, however, the Ss told someone that these tasks were interesting and enjoyable. The resulting dissonance could, of course, most directly be reduced by persuading themselves that the tasks were, indeed, interesting and enjoyable. In the One Dollar condition, since the magnitude of dissonance was high, the pressure to reduce this dissonance would also be high. In this condition, the average rating was +1.35, considerably on the positive side and significantly different from the Control condition at the .02 level[5] ($t = 2.48$).

In the Twenty Dollar condition, where less dissonance was created experimentally because of the greater importance of the consonant relations, there is correspondingly less evidence of dissonance reduction. The average rating in this condition is only -.05, slightly and not significantly higher than the Control condition. The difference between the One Dollar and Twenty Dollar conditions is significant at the .03 level ($t = 2.22$). In short, when an S was induced, by offer of reward, to say something contrary to his private opinion, this private opinion tended to change so as to correspond more closely with what he had said. The greater the reward offered (beyond what was necessary to elicit the behavior) the smaller was the effect.

Desire to Participate in a Similar Experiment

The results from this question are shown in the last row of Table 1. This question is less directly related to the dissonance that was experimentally created for the Ss. Certainly, the more interesting and enjoyable they felt the tasks were, the greater would be their desire to participate in a similar experiment. But other factors would enter also. Hence, one would expect the results on this question to be very similar to the results on "how enjoyable the tasks were" but weaker. Actually, the result, as may be seen in the table, are in exactly the same direction, and the magnitude of the mean differences is fully as large as on the first question. The variability is greater, however, and the differences do not yield high levels of statistical significance. The difference between the One Dollar condition (+1.20) and the Control condition (-.62) is significant at the .08 level ($t = 1.78$). The difference between the One Dollar condition and the Twenty Dollar condition (-.25) reaches only the .15 level of significance ($t = 1.46$).

The Scientific Importance of the Experiment

This question was included because there was a chance that differences might emerge. There are, after all, other ways in which the experimentally created dissonance could be reduced. For example, one way would be for the S to magnify for himself the value of the reward he obtained. This, however, was unlikely in this experiment because money was used for the reward and it is undoubtedly difficult to convince oneself that one dollar is more than it really is. There is another possible way, however. The Ss were given a very good reason, in addition to being paid, for saying what they did to the waiting girl. The Ss were told it was necessary for the experiment. The dissonance could, consequently, be reduced by magnifying the importance of this cognition. The more scientifically important they considered the experiment to be, the less was the total magnitude of dissonance. It is possible, then, that the results on this question, shown in the third row of figures in Table 1, might reflect dissonance reduction.

The results are weakly in line with what one would expect if the dissonance were somewhat reduced in this manner. The One Dollar condition is higher than the other two. The difference between the One and Twenty Dollar conditions reaches the .08 level of significance on a two-tailed test ($t = 1.79$). The difference between the One Dollar and Control conditions is not impressive at all ($t = 1.21$). The result that the Twenty Dollar condition is actually lower than the Control condition is undoubtedly a matter of chance ($t = 0.58$).

How Much They Learned from the Experiment

The results on this question are shown in the second row of figures in Table 1. The question was included because, as far as we could see, it had nothing to do with the dissonance that was experimentally created and could not be used for dissonance reduction. One would then expect no differences at all among the three conditions. We felt it was important to show that the effect was not a completely general one but was specific to the content of the dissonance which was created. As can be readily seen in Table 1, there are only negligible differences among conditions. The highest t value for any of these differences is only 0.48.

DISCUSSION OF A POSSIBLE ALTERNATIVE EXPLANATION

We mentioned in the introduction that Janis and King (1954; 1956) in explaining their findings, proposed an explanation in terms of the self-convincing effect of mental rehearsal and thinking up new arguments by the person who had to improvise a speech. Kelman (1953), in the previously mentioned study, in attempting to explain the unexpected finding that the persons who complied in the moderate reward condition changed their opinion more than in the high reward condition, also proposed the same kind of explanation. If the results of our experiment are to be taken as strong **corroboration** of the theory of cognitive dissonance, this possible alternative explanation must be dealt with.

Specifically, as applied to our results, this alternative explanation would maintain that perhaps, for some reason, the Ss in the One Dollar condition worked harder at telling the waiting girl that the tasks were fun and enjoyable. That is, in the One Dollar condition they may have rehearsed it more mentally, thought up more ways of saying it, may have said it more convincingly, and so on. Why this might have been the case is, of course, not immediately apparent. One might expect that, in the Twenty Dollar condition, having been paid more, they would try to do a better job of it than in the One Dollar condition. But nevertheless, the possibility exists that the Ss in the One Dollar condition may have improvised more.

TABLE 2
AVERAGE RATINGS OF DISCUSSION BETWEEN SUBJECT AND GIRL

Dimension Rated	Condition		
	1 Dollar	20 Dollars	Value of t
Content before remark by girl (rated from 0 to 5)	2.26	2.62	1.08
Content after remark by girl (rated from 0 to 5)	1.63	1.75	0.11
Over-all content (rated from 0 to 5)	1.89	2.19	1.08
Persuasiveness and conviction (rated from 0 to 10)	4.79	5.50	0.99
Time spent on topic (rated from 0 to 10)	6.74	8.19	1.80

Because of the desirability of investigating this possible alternative explanation, we recorded on a tape recorder the conversation between each S and the girl. These recordings were transcribed and then rated, by two independent raters, on five dimensions. The ratings were, of course done in ignorance of which condition each S was in. The reliabilities of these ratings, that is, the correlations between the two independent raters, ranged from .61 to .88, with an average reliability of .71. The five ratings were:

1. The content of what the S said *before* the girl made the remark that her friend told her it was boring. The stronger the S's positive statements about the tasks, and the more ways in which he said they were interesting and enjoyable, the higher the rating.

2. The content of what the S said after the girl made the above-mentioned remark. This was rated in the same way as for the content before the remark.

3. A similar rating of the over-all content of what the S said.

4. A rating of how persuasive and convincing the S was in what he said and the way in which he said it.

5. A rating of the amount of time in the discussion that the S spent discussing the tasks as opposed to going off into irrelevant things.

The mean ratings for the One Dollar and Twenty Dollar conditions, averaging the ratings of the two independent raters, are presented in Table 2. It is clear from examining the table that, in all cases, the Twenty Dollar condition is slightly higher. The differences are small, however, and only on the rating of "amount of time" does the difference between the two conditions even approach significance. We are certainly justified in concluding that the Ss in the One Dollar condition did not improvise more nor act more convincingly. Hence, the alternative explanation discussed above cannot account for the findings.

SUMMARY

Recently, Festinger (1957) has proposed a theory concerning cognitive dissonance. Two derivations from this theory are tested here. These are:

1. If a person is induced to do or say something which is contrary to his private opinion, there will be a tendency for him to change his opinion so as to bring it into correspondence with what he has done or said.

2. The larger the pressure used to elicit the overt behavior (beyond the minimum needed to elicit it) the weaker will be the above mentioned tendency.

A laboratory experiment was designed to test these derivations. Subjects were subjected to a boring experience and then paid to tell someone that the experience had been interesting and enjoyable. The amount of money paid the subject was varied. The private opinions of the subjects concerning the experiences were then determined.

The results strongly corroborate the theory that was tested.

FOOTNOTES

[1] Reprinted by permission of the authors and the publisher from the *Journal of Abnormal and Social Psychology*, 1959, **58**, 203-210. Copyright 1959 by the American Psychological Association.

[2] The experiment reported here was done as part of a program of research supported by a grant from the National Science Foundation to the senior author. We wish to thank Leonard Hommel, Judson Mills, and Robert Terwilliger for their help in designing and carrying out the experiment. We would also like to acknowledge the help of Ruth Smith and Marilyn M. Miller.

[3] Festinger, L., Riecken, H., & Schachter, S. (1956). *When prophecy fails*. Minneapolis: University of Minnesota Press.

[4] Szabo, C. (1985). Effect of role-play on attitude change. *Magyar Pszichologiai Szemle*, **42**, 495-507.

[5] All statistical tests referred to in this paper are two-tailed.

REFERENCES

FESTINGER, L. *A theory of cognitive dissonance*. Evanston, Ill: Row, Peterson, 1957.

JANIS, I. L., & KING, B. T. The influence of role-playing on opinion change. *J. abnorm. soc. Psychol.*, 1954, 49, 211-218.

KELMAN, H. Attitude change as a function of response restriction. *Hum. Relat.*, 1953, 6, 185-214.

KING, B. T., & JANIS, I. L. Comparison of the effectiveness of improvised versus non-improvised role-playing in producing opinion changes. *Hum. Relat.*, 1956, 9, 177-186.

Corroboration (cor-ROB-or-a-shun). To "corroborate" something is to offer support for it.

CHAPTER 22

"The Effects of Psychotherapy: An Evaluation"

Hans J. Eysenck[1]

> **EDITORS' COMMENTS.** There has long been a serious split in psychology--and in most other sciences, as well--between those individuals interested in *gathering* facts and those individuals interested in *applying* the facts to real-life situations. In psychology, the split is most noticeable between the "experimentalists" and the "clinicians" (or "psychotherapists"). The clinicians often accuse the laboratory scientists of "being more interested in training rats than in helping people," while the experimentalists often accuse the psychotherapists of being "little more than witch doctors."
>
> Hans Eysenck is an experimental psychologist who has conducted much of his research in clinical settings. After receiving his doctorate, he took a position in a mental hospital and soon began trying to evaluate whether various forms of psychotherapy actually "worked". Eysenck's superior--a die-hard clinician--thought that this was a ridiculous venture, since "everyone knew that therapy was effective." When Eysenck's preliminary data suggested otherwise, his superior threatened to fire him if he published his findings. Eysenck waited a few years, until his career was secure, and then (in 1952) published this article.
>
> To say the least, Eysenck's findings (that the "more intensive the therapy, the worse the results") caused a furor. The psychoanalysts, in particular, attacked him viciously. And little wonder they did so, since Eysenck's data suggested that psychoanalytic therapy produced significantly worse "cure rates" than did giving the patient no therapy at all! However, even the "less intensive" types of therapy didn't fare very well in Eysenck's study, since patients given *any* form of "talk therapy" had recovery rates that were about the same as (or slightly lower than) those of patients given no psychological treatment whatsoever.
>
> Part of the problem of evaluating the effects of psychotherapy lies, of course, in the definition of "cure rate." For, as Laurence Grimm pointed out in 1981, "There simply is no universally accepted set of measures to define the effectiveness of treatment and little agreement on what aspects of the client's behavior are most critical to change".[2] Generally speaking, therapists who trust *their impressions* of improvement in their own patients tend to report much higher "cure rates" than do experimentalists who insist that the results of treatment must be "objective and measurable."
>
> Despite the criticism that this article engendered, Eysenck's data have stood the test of time fairly well. Several subsequent studies have shown that the measurable "cure rate" for psychoanalysis is about 45 percent,[3] while the "cure rate" for most other types of "talk therapy" is about 70 percent.[4] The one exception to Eysenck's original data is this: Most experts now that believe the "cure rate" for patients given *no treatment at all* is about 50 percent, not the 72 percent Eysenck reports.[5]
>
> Eysenck's 1952 article is a "classic" for many reasons. First, it forced clinical psychologists to pay more attention to the *actual* results of their efforts. And second, by doing so, it encouraged many clinicians to look at what *really* was occurring during therapeutic sessions, rather than relying almost entirely on their subjective impressions. Finally, thanks in large part to Eysenck, we now know that psychotherapy *does* indeed help people--although not as much (nor as frequently) as we once thought was the case.

The recommendation of the Committee on training in Clinical Psychology of the American Psychological Association regarding the training of clinical psychologists in the field of psychotherapy has been criticized by the writer in a series of papers [10, 11, 12]. Of the arguments presented in favor of the policy advocated by the Committee, the most cogent one is perhaps that which refers to the social need for the skills possessed by the psychotherapist. In view of the importance of the issues involved, it seemed worth while to examine the evidence relating to the actual effects of **psychotherapy**, in an attempt to seek clarification on a point of fact.

BASE LINE AND UNIT OF MEASUREMENT

In the only previous attempt to carry out such an evaluation, Landis has pointed out that "before any sort of measurement can be made, it is necessary to establish a base line and a common unit of measure. The only unit of measure available is the report made by the physician stating that the patient has recovered, is much improved, is improved or unimproved. This unit is probably as satisfactory as any type of human subjective judgment, partaking of both the good and bad points of such judgments" [26, p. 156.] For a unit Landis suggests "that of expressing therapeutic results in terms of the number of patients recovered or improved per 100 cases admitted to the hospital." As an alternative, he suggests "the statement of therapeutic outcome for some given group of patients during some stated interval of time."

Landis realized quite clearly that in order to evaluate the effectiveness of any form of therapy, data from a **control group** of nontreated patients would be required in order to compare the effects of therapy with the spontaneous remission rate. In the absence of anything better, he used the **amelioration** rate in state mental hospitals for patients diagnosed under the heading of "neuroses." As he points out:

> There are several objections to the use of the consolidated amelioration rate . . . of the . . . state hospitals. . . . as a base rate for spontaneous recovery. The fact that **psychoneurotic** cases are not usually committed to state hospitals unless in a very bad condition; the relatively small number of voluntary patients in the group; the fact that such patients do get some degree of psychotherapy especially in the reception hospitals; and the probably quite different economic, educational, and social status of the state Hospital group compared to the patients reported from each of the other hospitals--all argue against the acceptance of [this] figure . . . as a truly satisfactory base line, but in the absence of any other better figure this must serve [26, p. 168].

Actually the various figures quoted by Landis agree very well. The percentage of neurotic patients discharged annually as recovered or improved from New York state hospitals is 70 (for the years 1925-1934); for the United States as a whole it is 68 (for the years 1926 to 1933). The percentage of neurotics discharged as recovered or improved within one year of admission is 66 for the United States (1933) and 68 for New York (1914). The consolidated amelioration rate of New York state hospitals, 1917-1934, is 72 per cent. As this is the figure chosen by Landis, we may accept it in preference to the other very similar ones quoted. By and large, we may thus say that of severe neurotics receiving in the main custodial care, and very little if any psychotherapy, over two-thirds recovered or improved to a considerable extent. "Although this is not, strictly speaking, a basic figure for 'spontaneous' recovery, still any therapeutic method must show an appreciably greater size than this to be seriously considered" [26, p. 160].

Another estimate of the required "base line" is provided by Denker:

> Five hundred consecutive disability claims due to psychoneurosis, treated by general practitioners throughout the country, and not by accredited specialists or **sanatoria**, were reviewed. All types of neurosis were included, and no attempt made to differentiate the **neurasthenic**, anxiety, compulsive, hysteric, or other states, but

---

Psychotherapy. Psychological, as opposed to medical or behavioral, treatment. Most forms of psychotherapy are designed to "cure" a patient of his or her mental/emotional/behavioral problems, usually by talking with the patient until the patient "gains insight" or understanding of what the "underlying difficulties" really are. The patient then is expected to use this knowledge to "cure" herself or himself of the problem. In behavior therapy, however, the focus is on *changing behaviors* rather than on *achieving insight*. There are, at present, at least 250 different types of psychotherapy, all of which (with the possible exception of psychoanalysis) have about the same cure rate. Recent studies suggest that psychoanalysis typically has a lower overall cure rather than do other forms of "talk therapy," while behavioral treatment often does a better job of achieving *measurable* improvement (particularly in terms of improved performance on the job and in interpersonal situations).

Control group. A control group is a group of subjects in an experiment who do not receive any treatment, or who receive "placebos or "false treatment." If you wanted to see whether a new drug "cured headaches," you probably would use at least three groups of subjects: The experimental group would get the new drug, the first control group would get a "placebo," or sugar pill, while the second control group would receive no medication at all. If the subjects in the experimental group reported significantly greater relief than did the subjects in either control group, you could confidently state that the new drug "worked." The choice of proper control groups lies at the heart of good experimental design.

Amelioration (a-meel-ih-or-A-shun). Literally, "to make better."

Psychoneurotic (SIGH-koh-new-ROT-tick). An older name for "neurotic," a diagnosis given to people who suffer from a mild mental disorder.

Sanatoria (san-ah-TOR-ee-ah). An old name for "hospitals," or institutions where things were kept as "sanitary" (clean and germ-free) as possible.

Neurasthenic (new-rass-THEN-ick). An old diagnostic category that included people who had trouble relating to other people, or who suffered from constant fatigue, depression, headaches, and other stress-related symptoms.

Table 1
Summary of Reports of the Results of Psychotherapy

	N	Cured; Much Improved	Improved	Slightly Improved	Not Improved; died; left treatment	% Cured; much improved; improved
(A) Psychoanalytic						
1. Fenichel [13, pp. 28-40]	484	104	84	99	197	39
2. Kessel & Hyman [24]	34	16	5	4	9	62
3. Jones [22, pp.12-14]	59	20	8	28	3	47
4. Alexander [1, pp. 30-43]	141	28	42	23	48	50
5. Knight [25]	42	8	20	7	7	67
All cases	760	335		425		44%
(B) Eclectic						
1. Huddleson [20]	200	19	74	80	27	46
2. Matz [30]	775	10	310	310	145	41
3. Maudsley Hospital Report (1931)	1721	288	900		533	69
4. Maudsley Hospital Report (1931)	1711	371	765	575		64
5. Neustattter [32]	46	9	14	8	15	50
6. Luff & Garrod [27]	500	140	135	26	199	55
7. Luff & Garrod [27]	210	38	84	54	34	68
8. Ross [34]	1089	547	306		236	77
9. Yaskin [40]	100	29	29		42	58
10. Curran [7]	83	51			32	61
11. Masserman & Carmichael [29]	50	7	20	5	18	54
12. Carmichael & Masserman [4]	77	16	25	14	22	53
13. Schilder [35]	35	11	11	6	7	63
14. Malinton & Wall [16]	100	32	34	17	17	66
15. Mamilton et al. [15]	100	48	5	17	32	51
16. Landis [26]	119	40	47		32	73
17. Inst. Med. Psych. (quoted Neustatter)	270	58	132	55	25	70
18. Wilder [39]	54	3	24	16	11	50
19. Miles et al. [31]	53	13	18	13	9	58
All cases	7293	4661		2632		64%

the greatest care was taken to eliminate the true **psychotic** or organic lesions which in the early stages of illness so often simulate neurosis. These cases were taken consecutively from the files of the Equitable Life Assurance Society of the United States, were from all parts of the country, and all had been ill of a neurosis for at least three months before claims were submitted. They, therefore, could be fairly called severe, since they had been totally disabled for at least a three months' period, and rendered unable to carry on with any occupation for remuneration or profit for at least that time [9, p. 2164].

These patients were regularly seen and treated by their own physicians with **sedatives**, tonics, suggestion, and reassurance, but in no case was any attempt made at anything but this most superficial type of "psychotherapy" which has always been the stock-in-trade of the general practitioner. Repeated statements, every three months or so by their physicians, as well as independent investigations by the insurance company, confirmed the fact that these people actually were not engaged in productive work during the period of their illness. During their disablement, these cases received disability benefits. As Denker points out, "It is appreciated that this fact of disability income may have actually prolonged the total period of disability and acted as a barrier to incentive for recovery. One would, therefore, not expect the therapeutic results in such a group of cases to be as favorable as in other groups where the economic factor might act as an important spur in helping the sick patient adjust to his neurotic conflict and illness" [9, p. 2165].

The cases were all followed up for at least a five-year period, and often as long as ten years after the period of disability had begun. The criteria of "recovery" used by Denker were as follows: (a) return to work, and ability to carry on well in economic adjustments for at least a five-year period; (b) complaint of no further or very slight difficulties; (c) making of successful social adjustments. Using these criteria, which are very similar to those usually used by psychiatrists, Denker found that 45 per cent of the patients recovered after one year, another 27 per cent after two years, making 72 per cent in all. Another 10 per cent, 5 per cent, and 4 per cent recovered during the third, fourth, and fifth years, respectively, making a total of 90 per cent recoveries after five years.

This sample contrasts in many ways with that used by Landis. The cases on which Denker reports were probably not quite as severe as those summarized by Landis: they were all voluntary, nonhospitalized patients, and came from a much higher socioeconomic stratum. The majority of Denker's patients were clerical workers, executives, teachers, and professional men. In spite of these differences the recovery figures for the two samples are almost identical. The most suitable figure to choose from those given by Denker is probably that for the two-year recovery rate, as follow-up studies seldom go beyond two years and the higher figures for three-, four-, and five-year follow-up would overestimate the efficiency of this "base line" procedure. Using, therefore, the two-year recovery figure of 72 per cent, we find that Denker's figure agrees exactly with that given by Landis. We may, therefore, conclude with some confidence that our estimate of some two-thirds of severe neurotics showing recovery or considerable improvement without the benefit of systematic psychotherapy is not likely to be very far out.

EFFECTS OF PSYCHOTHERAPY

We may now turn to the effects of psychotherapeutic treatment. The results of nineteen studies reported in the literature, covering over seven thousand cases, and dealing with both psychoanalytic and **eclectic** types of treatment, are quoted in detail in Table 1. An attempt has been made to report results under the four headings: (a) Cured, or much improved, (b) Improved; (c) Slightly improved; (d) Not improved, died, discontinued treatment, etc. It was usually easy to reduce additional categories given by some writers to these basic four; some writers give only two or three categories, and in those cases it was, of course, impossible to subdivide further, and the figures for combined categories are given.[6] A slight degree of subjectivity inevitably enters into this procedure, but it is doubtful if it has caused much distortion. A somewhat greater degree of subjectivity is probably implied in the writer's judgment as to which disorders and diagnoses should be considered to fall under the heading of "neurosis." Schizophrenic, manic-depressive, and paranoid states have been excluded; organ neuroses, psychopathic states, and character disturbances have been included. The number of cases where there was genuine doubt is probably too small to make much change in the final figures, regardless of how they are allocated.

A number of studies have been excluded because of such factors as excessive inadequacy of follow-up, partial duplication of cases with others included in our table, failure to indicate type of treatment used, and other reasons which made the results useless from our point of view. Papers thus rejected are those by Thorley & Craske [37], Bennett and Semrad [2], H. I. Harris [19], Hardcastle [17], A. Harris [18], Jacobson and Wright [21], Friess and Nelson [14], Comroe [5], Wenger [38], Orbison [33], Coon and Raymond [6], Denker [8], and Bond and Braceland [3]. Their inclusion would not have altered our conclusions to any considerable degree, although, as Miles *et al.* point out: "When the various studies are compared in terms of thoroughness, careful planning, strictness of criteria and objectivity, there is often an inverse correlation between these factors and the percentage of successful results reported" [31, p. 88].

Certain difficulties have arisen from the inability of some writers to make their column figures agree with their totals, or to calculate percentages accurately. Again, the writer has exercised his judgment as to which figures to accept. In certain cases, writers have given figures of cases where there was a recurrence of the disorder after apparent cure or improvement, without indicating how many patients were affected in these two groups respectively. All recurrences of this kind have been subtracted from the "cured" and "improved" totals, taking half from each. The total number of cases involved in all these adjustments is quite small. Another investigator making all decisions exactly in the opposite direction to the present writer's would hardly alter the final percentage figures by more than 1 or 2 per cent.

We may now turn to the figures as presented. Patients treated by means of psychoanalysis improve to the extent of 44 per cent; patients treated eclectically improve to the extent of 64 per cent; patients treated only custodially or by general practitioners improve to the extent of 72 per cent. There thus appears to be an inverse correlation between recovery and psychotherapy; the more psychotherapy, the smaller the recovery rate. This conclusion requires certain qualifications.

In our tabulation of psychoanalytic results, we have

Psychotic (sigh-KOT-ick). A very severe form of "mental disorder" which often requires hospitalization.

Sedatives (SED-ah-tives). Sedatives are those drugs which slow down or inhibit neural activity to the point of putting a person to sleep.

Eclectic (ek-KLECK-tick). From the Greek word meaning "to gather." To be eclectic is to "gather" or select the best aspects of several different theories or methods.

classed those who stopped treatment together with those not improved. This appears to be reasonable; a patient who fails to finish his treatment, and is not improved, is surely a therapeutic failure. The same rule has been followed with the data summarized under "eclectic" treatment, except when the patient who did not finish treatment was definitely classified as "improved" by the therapist. However, in view of the peculiarities of Freudian procedures it may appear to some readers to be more just to class those cases separately, and deal only with the percentage of completed treatments which are successful. Approximately one-third of the psychoanalytic patients listed broke off treatment, so that the percentage of successful treatments of patients who finished their course must be put at approximately 66 per cent. It would appear, then, that when we discount the risk the patient runs of stopping treatment altogether, his chances of improvement under psychoanalysis are approximately equal to his chances of improvement under eclectic treatment, and slightly worse than his chances under a general practitioner or custodial treatment.

Two further points require clarification: (a) Are patients in our "control" groups (Landis and Denker) as seriously ill as those in our "experimental" groups? (b) Are standards of recovery perhaps less stringent in our "control" than in our "experimental" groups? It is difficult to answer these questions definitely, in view of the great divergence of opinion between psychiatrists. From a close scrutiny of the literature it appears that the "control" patients were probably at least as seriously ill as the "experimental" patients, and possibly more so. As regards standards of recovery, those in Denker's study are as stringent as most of those used by psychoanalysts and eclectic psychiatrists, but those used by the State Hospitals whose figures Landis quotes are very probably more lenient. In the absence of agreed standards of severity of illness, or of extent of recovery, it is not possible to go further.

In general, certain conclusions are possible from these data. They fail to prove that psychotherapy, Freudian or otherwise, facilitates the recovery of neurotic patients. They show that roughly two-thirds of a group of neurotic patients will recover or improve to a marked extent within about two years of the onset of their illness, whether they are treated by means of psychotherapy or not. This figure appears to be remarkably stable from one investigation to another, regardless of type of patient treated, standard of recovery employed, or method of therapy used. From the point of view of the neurotic, these figures are encouraging; from the of view of the psychotherapist, they can hardly be called very favorable to his claims.

The figures quoted do not necessarily disprove the possibility of therapeutic effectiveness. There are obvious shortcomings in any actuarial comparison and these shortcomings are particularly serious when there is so little agreement among psychiatrists relating even to the most fundamental concepts and definitions. Definite proof would require a special investigation, carefully planned and methodologically more adequate than these *ad hoc* comparisons. But even the much more modest conclusions that the figures fail to show any favorable effects of psychotherapy should give pause to those who would wish to give an important part in the training of clinical psychologists to a skill the existence and effectiveness of which is still unsupported by any scientifically acceptable evidence.

These results and conclusions will no doubt contradict the strong feeling of usefulness and therapeutic success which many psychiatrists and clinical psychologists hold. While it is true that subjective feelings of this type have no place in science, they are likely to prevent an easy acceptance of the general argument presented here. This contradiction between objective fact and subjective certainty has been remarked on in other connections by Kelly and Fiske, who found that "One aspect of our findings is most disconcerting to us: the inverse relationship between the confidence of staff members at the time of making a prediction and the measured validity of that prediction. Why is it, for example, that our staff members tended to make their best predictions at a time when they subjectively felt relatively unacquainted with the candidate, when they had constructed no systematic picture of his personality structure? Or conversely, why is it that with increasing confidence in clinical judgment ... we find decreasing validities of predictions?" [23, p. 406].

In the absence of agreement between fact and belief, there is urgent need for a decrease in the strength of belief, and for an increase in the number of facts available. Until such facts as may be discovered in a process of rigorous analysis support the prevalent belief in therapeutic effectiveness of psychological treatment, it seems premature to insist on the inclusion of training in such treatment in the curriculum of the clinical psychologist.

SUMMARY

A survey was made of reports on the improvement of neurotic patients after psychotherapy, and the results compared with the best available estimates of recovery without benefit of such therapy. The figures fail to support the hypothesis that psychotherapy facilitates recovery from neurotic disorder. In view of the many difficulties attending such actuarial comparisons, no further conclusions could be derived from the data whose shortcomings highlight the necessity of properly planned and executed experimental studies into this important field.

FOOTNOTES

[1] Reprinted by permission of the author and the publisher from the *Journal of Consulting Psychology*, 1952, **16**, 319-324. Copyright 1952 by the American Psychological Association. H.J. Eysenck is Professor Emeritus, Institute of Psychiatry, University of London.

[2] Grimm, L.G. (1981). Catholic views on the long-term effects of psychotherapy. *Contemporary Psychology*, **26**, 750-752.

[3] Garfield, S.L. (1983). Effectiveness of psychotherapy: The perennial controversy. *Professional Psychology*, **14**, 35-43.

[4] Stiles, W.B., Shapiero, D.A., & Elliott, R. (1986). Are all psychotherapies equivalent? *American Psychologist*, **41**, 165-180.

[5] DeLeon, P.H., VandenBos, G.R., & Cummings, N.A. (1983). Psychotherapy--Is it safe, effective, and appropriate? The beginning of an evolutionary dialogue. *American Psychologist*, **38**, 907-911.

[6] In one or two cases where patients who improved or improved slightly were combined by the original author, the total figure has been divided equally between the two categories.

REFERENCES

1. Alexander, F. *Five year report of the Chicago Institute for Psychoanalysis.* 1932-1937.
2. Bennett, A. E., & Semrad, E. V. Common errors in diagnosis and treatment of the psychoneurotic patients a study of 100 case histories. *Nebr. med. J.*, 1936, **21**, 90-92.
3. Bond, E. D., & Braceland, F. J. Prognosis in mental disease. *Amer. J. Psychiat.*, 1937, **94**, 263-274.
4. Carmichael, H. T., & Masserman, T. H. Results of treatment in a psychiatric outpatients' department. *J. Amer. med. Ass.*, 1939, **113**, 2292-2298.
5. Comroe, B. I. Follow-up study of 100 patients diagnosed as "neurosis." *J. nerv. ment. Dis.*, 1936, **83**, 679-684.
6. Coon, G. P., & Raymond., A. A review of the psychoneuroses at Stockbridge. Stockbridge, Mass.: Austen Riggs Foundation, Inc., 1940.
7. Curran, D. The problem of assessing psychiatric treatment. *Lancet*, 1937, **II**, 1005-1009.
8. Denker, P. G. Prognosis and life expectancy in the psychoneuroses. *Proc. Ass. Life Insur. med. Dir. Amer.*, 1937, **24**, 179.
9. Denker, R. Results of treatment of psychoneuroses by the general practitioner. A follow-up study of 500 cases. *N. Y. State J. Med.*, 1946, **46**, 2164-2166.
10. Eysenck, H. J. Training in clinical psychology: an English point of view. *Amer. Psychologist*, 1949, **4**, 173-176.
11. Eysenck, H. J. The relation between medicine and psychology in England. In W. Dennis (Ed.), *Current trends in the relation of psychology and medicine.* Pittsburgh: Univer. of Pittsburgh Press, 1950.
12. Eysenck, H. J. Function and training of the clinical psychologist. *J. ment. Sci.*, 1950, **96**, 1-16.
13. Fenichel, O. *Ten years of the Berlin Psychoanalysis Institute.* 1920-1930.
14. Friess, C., & Nelson, M. J. Psychoneurotics five years later. *Amer. J. ment. Sci.*, 1942, **203**, 539-558.
15. Hamilton, D. M., Vanney, I. H., & Wall, T. H. Hospital treatment of patients with psychoneurotic disorder. *Amer. J. Psychiat.*, 1942, **99**, 243-247.
16. Hamilton, D. M., & Wall, T. H. Hospital treatment of patients with psychoneurotic disorder. *Amer. J. Psychiat.*, 1941, **98**, 551-557.
17. Hardcastle, D. H. A follow-up study of one hundred cases made for the Department of Psychological Medicine, Guy's Hospital. *J. ment. Sci.*, 1934, **90**, 536-549.
18. Harris, A. The prognosis of anxiety states. *Brit. med. J.*, 1938, **2**, 649-654.
19. Harris, H. I. Efficient psychotherapy for the large outpatient clinic. *New England J. Med.*, 1939, **221**, 1-5.
20. Huddleson, J. H. Psychotherapy in 200 cases of psychoneurosis. *Mil. Surgeon*, 1927, **60**, 161-170.
21. Jacobson, J. R., & Wright, K. W. Review of a year of group psychotherapy. *Psychiat. Quart.*, 1942, **16**, 744-764.
22. Jones, E. *Decennial report of the London Clinic of Psychoanalysis.* 1926-1936.
23. Kelly, E. L., & Fiske, D. W. The prediction of success in the VA training program in clinical psychology. *Amer. Psychologist*, 1950, **5**, 395-406.
24. Kessel, L., & Hyman, H. T. The value of psychoanalysis as a therapeutic procedure. *J. Amer. med. Ass.*, 1933, **101**, 1612-1615.
25. Knight, R. O. Evaluation of the results of psychoanalytic therapy. *Amer. J. Psychiat.*, 1941, **98**, 434-446.
26. Landis, C. Statistical evaluation of psychotherapeutic methods. In S. E. Hinsie (Ed.), *Concepts and problems of psychotherapy.* London: Heineman, 1938. Pp. 155-165.
27. Luff, M. C., & Garrod, M. The after-results of psychotherapy in 500 adult cases. *Brit. med. J.*, 1935, **2**, 54-59.
28. Mapother, E. Discussion. *Brit. J. med. Psychol.*, 1927, **7**, 57.
29. Masserman, T. H., & Carmichael, H. T. Diagnosis and prognosis in psychiatry. *J. ment. Sci.*, 1938, **84**, 893-946.
30. Matz, P. B. Outcome of hospital treatment of ex-service patients with nervous and mental disease in the U. S. Veteran's Bureau. *U.S. Vet. Bur. med. Bull.*, 1929, **5**, 829-842.
31. Miles, H. H. W., Barrabee, E. L., & Finesinger, J. E. Evaluation of psychotherapy. *Psychosom. Med.*, 1951, **13**, 83-105.
32. Neustatter, W. L. The results of fifty cases treated by psychotherapy. *Lancet*, 1935, **I**, 796-799.
33. Orbison, T. J. The psychoneuroses: psychasthenia, neurasthenia and hysteria, with special reference to a certain

method of treatment. *Calif. west. Med.,* 1925, **23,** 1132-1136.
34. Ross, T. A. *An enquiry into prognosis in the neuroses.* London: Cambridge Univer. Press, 1936.
35. Schilder, P. Results and problems of group psychotherapy in severe neuroses. *Ment. Hyg. N. Y.,* 1939, **23,** 87-98.
36. Skottowe, I., & Lockwood, M. R. The fate of 150 psychiatric outpatients. *J. ment. Sci.,* 1935, **81,** 502-508.
37. Thorley, A. S., & Craske, N. Comparison and estimate of group and individual method of treatment. *Brit. med. J.,* 1950, **1,** 97-100.
38. Wenger, P. Uber weitere Ergebnisse der Psychotherapie in Rahmen einer Medizinischen Poliklinik. *Wien. med. Wschr.,* 1934, **84,** 320-325.
39. Wilder, J. Facts and figures on psychotherapy. *J. clin. Psychopath.,* 1945, **7,** 311-347.
40. Yaskin, J. C. The psychoneuroses and neuroses. A review of 100 cases with special reference to treatment and results. *Amer. J. Psychiat.,* 1936, **93,** 107-125.

Classic Quotations from William James

The deadliest enemies of nations are not their foreign foes; they always dwell within their borders. And from these internal enemies civilization is always in need of being saved. The nation blessed above all nations is she in whom the civic genius of the people does the saving day by day, by acts without external picturesqueness; by speaking, writing, voting reasonably; by smiting corruption swiftly; by good temper between parties; by the people knowing true men when they see them, and preferring them as leaders to rabit partisans or empty quacks.

(*Memories and Studies* [1911].)

CHAPTER 23

"On Being Sane in Insane Places"

David L. Rosenhan[1]

> **EDITORS' COMMENTS.** Suppose, as part of a project in a psychology class, you went to a nearby mental hospital and tried to "con" the authorities into admitting you as a patient. Do you think you'd succeed? Or do you think that you could "fake" symptoms of mental illness so readily that you could fool the psychiatrist who examined you?
>
> Prior to the publication of David L. Rosenhan's classic article, almost all psychologists assumed that the "screening process" would automatically weed out all *pseudopatients* at a mental hospital. After all, if we can't tell the difference between someone who is *really* insane and someone who is merely *faking* insanity, how good can psychiatric diagnoses be? Alas, when Rosenhan had perfectly normal individuals apply to a number of mental hospitals, *every one of the subjects* was not only admitted, but was also diagnosed as suffering from a *major psychosis*.
>
> Once admitted, the pseudopatients had to find some way of getting out of the mental hospital. And *that* turned out to be surprisingly difficult, as you will see. But think about it--if hospital personnel can't differentiate between normals and insane people on admission, how could they possibly tell the difference *inside* the hospital? (In defense of mental health personnel, we might note that their tradition is to admit almost anyone to a mental hospital who asks to enter. As one expert put it, "Life inside an asylum is so unpleasant that only someone who really was crazy would ever ask for admission.")
>
> Rosenhan's article is important for many reasons. To begin with, he reminds us (as so many others have) that we always judge people *in context*. Behaviors that are perfectly normal in one situation are seen as being highly abnormal in a different context. However, we tend to *perceive* people's actions as being determined entirely by *internal* variables, not by the situation they find themselves in. Second, Rosenhan's data clearly show that, once we attach a "social label" to an individual, we tend thereafter to respond to the *label*, not to the person. We then *distort* anything the person does so that their actions presumably "fit the label." Third, Rosenhan's observation (see note 11) that many of the real patients began imitating the behaviors of the pseudopatients gave a strong boost to behavior therapy. And finally, this article gives ample demonstration that the diagnostic categories used in psychiatry are "less than exact" (to be charitable about the matter). For, in truth, the patients themselves were better than the hospital personnel at judging who was "insane" and who was "normal."
>
> As you might well imagine, Rosenhan received a barrage of biting criticism from the mental health establishment once his article appeared in print. Not all the response was negative, however, and it was because of articles such as this one that--during the mid-1970's--a movement began to move patients out of mental hospitals and back to the community. Sadly enough, society offered little "outpatient" assistance to these discharged patients, and many of them ended up as "street people." Rosenhan suggests that the best way to get most of these people off the streets--and out of the hospitals--is to teach them the mental and behavioral skills they need in order to survive in "normal" circumstances. However, as long as we continue to insist that all abnormal behavior is a result of "mental illness," we are not likely to give much thought to helping people learn the survival skills they need to stay off the streets (and out of mental hospitals). And as long as we continue to maintain that actions are determined almost entirely by factors inside the individual--such as genes and personality traits--instead of by the *interaction* between the person and his or her environment, we are not likely to profit from Rosenhan's findings.

If sanity and insanity exist, how shall we know them?

The question is neither **capricious** nor itself insane. However much we may be personally convinced that we can tell the normal from the abnormal, the evidence is simply not compelling. It is commonplace, for example, to read about murder trials wherein eminent psychiatrists for the defense are contradicted by equally eminent psychiatrists for the prosecution on the matter of the defendant's sanity. More generally, there are a great deal of conflicting data on the reliability, utility, and meaning of such terms as "sanity," "insanity," "mental illness," and "schizophrenia" (1). Finally, as early as 1934, **Benedict** suggested that normality and abnormality are not universal (2). What is viewed as normal in one culture may be seen as quite **aberrant** in another. Thus, notions of normality and abnormality may not be quite as accurate as people believe they are.

To raise questions regarding normality and abnormality is in no way to question the fact that some behaviors are deviant or odd. Murder is deviant. So, too, are hallucinations. Nor does raising such questions deny the existence of the personal anguish that is often associated with "mental illness." Anxiety and depression exist. Psychological suffering exists. But normality and abnormality, sanity and insanity, and the diagnoses that flow from them may be less **substantive** than many believe them to be.

At its heart, the question of whether the sane can be distinguished from the insane (and whether degrees of insanity can be distinguished from each other) is a simple matter: do the salient characteristics that lead to diagnoses reside in the patients themselves or in the environments and contexts in which observers find them? From **Bleuler**, through **Kretchmer**, through the formulators of the recently revised *Diagnostic and Statistical Manual* of the American Psychiatric Association, the belief has been strong that patients present symptoms, that those symptoms can be categorized, and, implicitly, that sane are distinguishable from the insane. More recently, however, this belief has been questioned. Based in part on theoretical and anthropological considerations, but also on philosophical, legal, and therapeutic ones, the view has grown that psychological categorization of mental illness is useless at best and downright harmful, misleading, and **pejorative** at worst. Psychiatric diagnoses, in this view, are in the minds of the observers and are not valid summaries of characteristics displayed by the observed (3-5).

Gains can be made in deciding which of these is more nearly accurate by getting normal people (that is, people who do not, and have never suffered, symptoms of serious psychiatric disorders) admitted to psychiatric hospitals and then determining whether they were discovered to be sane and, if so, how. If the sanity of such **pseudopatients** were always detected, there would be **prima facie** evidence that a sane individual can be distinguished from the insane context in which he is found. Normality (and presumably abnormality) is distinct enough that it can be recognized wherever it occurs, for it is carried within the person. If, on the other hand, the sanity of the pseudopatients were never discovered, serious difficulties would arise for those who support traditional modes of psychiatric diagnosis. Given that the hospital staff was not incompetent, that the pseudopatient had been behaving as sanely as he had been outside of the hospital, and that it had never been previously suggested that he belonged in a psychiatric hospital, such an unlikely outcome would support the view that psychiatric diagnosis betrays little about the patient but much about the environment in which an observer finds him.

This article describes such an experiment. Eight sane people gained secret admission to 12 different hospitals (6). There diagnostic experiences constitute the data of the first part of this article; the remainder is devoted to a description of their experiences in psychiatric institutions. Too few psychiatrists and psychologists, even those who have worked in such hospitals, know what the experience is like. They rarely talk about it with former patients, perhaps because they distrust information coming from the previously insane. Those who have worked in psychiatric hospitals are likely to have adapted so thoroughly to the settings that they are insensitive to the impact of that experience. And while there have been occasional reports of researchers who submitted themselves to psychiatric hospitalization (7), these researchers have commonly remained in the hospitals for short periods of time, often

---

Capricious (cap-PREE-shus). Impulsive, or arbitrary.

Benedict. Ruth Benedict was an anthropologist who believed that what was "normal" in one culture might well be viewed as abnormal in another.

Aberrant (AB-er-ant). Unusual, or deviant.

Substantive (SUB-stan-tive). Having substance; something based on reality rather than theory.

Bleuler (BLEW-ler). A Swiss psychiatrist who was an early supporter of Sigmund Freud and psychoanalysis, Eugen Bleuler was one of the first to describe the mental disorder we now call "schizophrenia."

Kretchmer (KRETCH-mer). Ernst Kretchmer, an early psychiatrist, believed that "body type" determined personality.

Pejorative (peh-JOR-ah-tive). To make worse.

Pseudopatients (SOO-doh-PAY-shunts). Literally, "false patients, or "pretend patients."

Prima facie (PREE-mah FAH-she). A Latin phrase (used primarily in legal situations) that means that something appears true "on the face of it."

with the knowledge of the hospital staff. It is difficult to know the extent to which they were treated like patients or like research colleagues. Nevertheless, their reports about the inside of the psychiatric hospital have been valuable. This article extends those efforts.

PSEUDOPATIENTS AND THEIR SETTINGS

The eight pseudopatients were a varied group. One was a psychology graduate student in his 20's. The remaining seven were older and "established." Among them were three psychologists, a **pediatrician**, a psychiatrist, a painter, and a housewife. Three pseudopatients were women, five were men. All of them employed pseudonyms lest their alleged diagnoses embarrass them later. Those who were in mental health professions alleged another occupation in order to avoid the special attentions that might be accorded by staff, as a matter of courtesy or caution, to ailing colleagues (8). With the exception of myself (I was the first pseudopatient and my presence was known to the hospital administrator and chief psychologist and, so far as I can tell, to them alone), the presence of pseudopatients and the nature of the research program was not known to the hospital staffs (9).

The settings were similarly varied. In order to generalize the findings, admission into a variety of hospitals was sought. The 12 hospitals in the sample were located in five different states on the East and West coasts. Some were old and shabby. Some were quite new. Some were research-oriented, others not. Some had good staff-patient ratios, others were quite understaffed. Only one was a strictly private hospital. All of the others were supported by state or federal funds or, in one instance, by university funds.

After calling the hospital for an appointment, the pseudopatient arrived at the admissions office complaining that he had been hearing voices. Asked what the voices said, he replied that they were often unclear, but as far as he could tell "empty," "hollow," and "thud." The voices were unfamiliar and were of the same sex as the pseudopatient. The choice of these symptoms was occasioned by their apparent similarity to **existential** symptoms. Such symptoms are alleged to arise from painful concerns about the perceived meaninglessness of one's life. It is as if the hallucinating person were saying, "My life is empty and hollow." The choice of these symptoms was also determined by the *absence* of a single report of existential psychoses in the literature.

Beyond alleging the symptoms and falsifying name, vocation, and employment, no further alterations of person, history, or circumstances were made. The significant events of the pseudopatient's life history were presented as they had actually occurred. Relationships with parents and siblings, with spouse and children, with people at work and in school, consistent with the aforementioned exceptions, were described as they were or had been. Frustrations and upsets were described along with joys and satisfactions. These facts are important to remember. If anything, they strongly biased the subsequent results in favor of detecting sanity, since none of their histories or current behaviors were seriously pathological in any way.

Immediately upon admission to the psychiatric ward, the pseudopatient ceased simulating *any* symptoms of abnormality. In some cases, there was a brief period of mild nervousness and anxiety, since none of the pseudopatients really believed that they would be admitted so easily. Indeed, their shared fear was that they would be immediately exposed as frauds and greatly embarrassed. Moreover, many of them had never visited a psychiatric ward; even those who had, nevertheless had some genuine fears about what might happen to them. Their nervousness, then, was quite appropriate to the novelty of the hospital setting, and it abated rapidly.

Apart from that short-lived nervousness, the pseudopatient behaved on the ward as he behaved "normally." The pseudopatient spoke to patients and staff as he might ordinarily. Because there is uncommonly little to do on a psychiatric ward, he attempted to engage others in conversation. When asked by staff how he was feeling, he indicated that he was fine, that he no longer experienced symptoms. He responded to instructions from attendants, to calls for medication (which was not swallowed), and to dining-hall instructions. Beyond such activities as were available to him on the admissions ward, he spent his time writing down his observations about the ward, its patients, and the staff. Initially these notes were written "secretly," but as it soon became clear that no one much cared, they were subsequently written on standard tablets of paper in such public places as the day room. No secret was made of these activities.

The pseudopatient, very much as a true psychiatric patient, entered a hospital with no foreknowledge of when he would be discharged. Each was told that he would have to get out by his own devices, essentially by convincing the staff that he was sane. The psychological stresses with hospitalization were considerable, and all but one of the pseudopatients desired to be discharged almost immediately after being admitted. They were, therefore, motivated not only to behave sanely, but to be **paragons** of cooperation. That their behavior was in no way disruptive is confirmed by nursing reports, which have been obtained on most of the patients. These reports uniformly indicate that the patients were "friendly," "cooperative," and "exhibited no abnormal indications."

THE NORMAL ARE NOT DETECTABLY SANE

Despite their public "show" of sanity, the pseudopatients were never detected. Admitted, except in one case, with the diagnosis of schizophrenia (*10*), each was discharged with a diagnosis of schizophrenia "in remission." The label "in remission" should in no way be dismissed as a formality, for at no time during hospitalization had any question been raised about any pseudopatient's simulation. Nor are there any indications in the hospital records that the pseudopatient's status was suspect. Rather, the evidence is strong that, once labeled schizophrenic, the pseudopatient was stuck with that label. If the pseudopatient was to be discharged, he must naturally be "in remission"; but he was not sane, nor in the institution's view, had he ever been sane.

The uniform failure to recognize sanity cannot be attributed to the quality of the hospitals, for, although there were considerable variations among them, several are considered excellent. Nor can it be alleged that there was simply not enough time to observe the pseudopatients. Length of hospitalization ranged from 7 to 52 days, with an average 19 days. The pseudopatients were not, in fact, carefully observed, but this failure clearly speaks more to traditions within psychiatric hospitals than to lack of opportunity.

Finally, it cannot be said that the failure to recognize the pseudopatients' sanity was due to the fact that they were not behaving sanely. While there was clearly some tension present in all of them, their daily visitors could detect no serious behavioral consequences—nor, indeed, could other patients. It was quite common for the patients to "detect" the pseudopatients' sanity. During the first three hospitalizations, when accurate counts were kept, 35 of a total of 118 patients on the admissions ward voiced their suspicions, some vigorously. "You're not crazy. You're a journalist, or a professor [referring to the continual note-taking]. You're checking up on the hospital." While most of the patients were reassured by the pseudopatient's insistence that he had been sick before he came in but was fine now, some continued to believe that the pseudopatient was sane throughout his hospitalization (*11*). The fact that the patients often recognized normality when staff did not raises important questions.

Failure to detect sanity during the course of hospitalization may be due to the fact that physicians operate with a strong bias toward what statisticians call the type 2 error (*5*). This is to say that physicians are more inclined to call a healthy person sick (a false positive, type 2) than a sick person healthy (a false negative, type 1). The reasons for this are not hard to find: it is clearly more dangerous to misdiagnose illness than health. Better to err on the side of caution, to suspect illness even among the healthy.

But what holds for medicine does not hold equally well for psychiatry. Medical illnesses, while unfortunate, are not commonly pejorative. Psychiatric diagnoses, on the contrary, carry with them personal, legal, and social **stigmas** (*12*). It was therefore important to see whether the tendency toward diagnosing the sane insane could be reversed. The following experiment was arranged at a research and teaching hospital whose staff had heard these findings but doubted that such an error could occur in their hospital. The staff was informed that at some time during the following 3 months, one or more pseudopatients would attempt to be admitted into the psychiatric hospital. Each staff member was asked to rate each patient who presented himself at admissions or on the ward according to the likelihood that the patient was a pseudopatient. A 10 point scale was used, with a 1 and 2 reflecting high confidence that the patient was a pseudopatient.

Judgments were obtained on 193 patients who were admitted for psychiatric treatment. All staff who had had sustained contact with or primary responsibility for the patient—attendants, nurses, psychiatrists, physicians, psychologists—were asked to make judgments. Forty-one patients were alleged, with high confidence, to be pseudopatients by at least one member of the staff. Twenty-three were considered suspect by at least one psychiatrist. Nineteen were suspected by one psychiatrist *and* one other staff member. Actually, no genuine pseudopatient (at least from my group) presented himself during this period.

The experiment is instructive. It indicates that the tendency to designate sane people as insane can be reversed when the stakes (in this case, prestige and diagnostic **acumen**) are high. But what can be said of the 19 people who were suspected of being "sane" by

---

Pediatrician (pee-dee-ah-TRISH-shun). A medical doctor who specializes in treating children.
Existential (EX-is-TENT-shull). Existentialism is a recent philosophy that holds people are responsible for what happens to them, and that realizing this fact tends to isolate one individual from another and fill the individual with dread.
Paragons (PAIR-ah-gons). Models.
Stigmas (STIG-mahs). Marks of shame.
Acumen (ACK-you-men). Keeness and depth of perception.

one psychiatrist and another staff member? Were these people truly "sane," or was it rather the case that in the course of avoiding the type 2 error the staff tended to make more errors of the first sort—calling the crazy "sane?" There is no way of knowing. But one thing is certain: any diagnostic process that lends itself so readily to massive errors of this sort cannot be a very reliable one.

THE STICKINESS OF PSYCHODIAGNOSTIC LABELS

Beyond the tendency to call the healthy sick—a tendency that accounts better for diagnostic behavior on admission than it does for such behavior after a lengthy period of exposure—the data speak to the massive role of labeling in psychiatric assessment. Having once been labeled schizophrenic, there is nothing the pseudopatient can do to overcome the tag. The tag profoundly colors others' perceptions of him and his behavior.

From one viewpoint, these data are hardly surprising, for it has long been known that elements are given meaning by the context in which they occur. Gestalt psychology made this point vigorously, and Asch (*13*) demonstrated that there are "central" personality traits (such as "warm" versus "cold") which are so powerful that they markedly color the meaning of other information in forming an impression of a given personality (*14*). "Insane," "schizophrenic," "manic-depressive," and "crazy" are probably among the most powerful of such central traits. Once a person is designated abnormal, all of his other behaviors and characteristics are colored by that label. Indeed, that label is so powerful that many of the pseudopatients' normal behaviors were overlooked entirely or profoundly misinterpreted. Some examples may clarify this issue.

Earlier I indicated that there were no changes in the pseudopatient's personal history and current status beyond those of name, employment, and, where necessary, vocation. Otherwise, a **veridical** description of personal history and circumstances was offered. Those circumstances were not psychotic. How were they made consonant with the diagnosis of psychosis? Or were those diagnoses modified in such a way as to bring them into accord with the circumstances of the pseudopatient's life, as described by him?

As far as I can determine, diagnoses were in no way affected by the relative health of the circumstances of a pseudopatient's life. Rather, the reverse occurred: the perception of his circumstances was shaped entirely by the diagnosis. A clear example of such translation is found in the case of a pseudopatient who had had a close relationship with his mother but was rather remote from his father during his early childhood. During adolescence and beyond, however, his father became a close friend, while his relationship with his mother cooled. His present relationship with his wife was characteristically close and warm. Apart from occasional angry exchanges, friction was minimal. The children had rarely been spanked. Surely there is nothing especially pathological about such a history. Indeed, many readers may see a similar pattern in their own experiences, with no markedly **deleterious** consequences. Observe, however, how such a history was translated in the psychopathological context, this from the case summary prepared after the patient was discharged.

> This white 39-year-old male... manifests a long history of considerable **ambivalence** in close relationships, which begins in early childhood. A warm relationship with his mother cools during his adolescence. A distant relationship to his father is described as becoming very intense. **Affective** stability is absent. His attempts to control emotionality with his wife and children are punctuated by angry outbursts and, in the case of the children, spankings. And while he says that he has several good friends, one senses considerable ambivalence embedded in those relationships also.

The facts of the case were unintentionally distorted by the staff to achieve consistency with a popular theory of the dynamics of a schizophrenic reaction (*15*). Nothing of an ambivalent nature had been described in relations with parents, spouse, or friends. To the extent that ambivalence could be inferred, it was probably not greater than is found in all human relationships. It is true the pseudopatient's relationships with his parents changed over time, but in the ordinary context that would hardly be remarkable—indeed, it might very well be expected. Clearly, the meaning ascribed to his verbalizations (that is, ambivalence, affective instability) was determined by the diagnosis: schizophrenia. An entirely different meaning would have been ascribed if it were known that the man was "normal."

All pseudopatients took extensive notes publicly. Under ordinary circumstances, such behavior would have raised questions in the minds of observers, as, in fact, it did among patients. Indeed, it seemed so certain that the notes would elicit suspicion that elaborate precautions were taken to remove them from the ward each day. But the precautions proved needless. The closest any staff member came to questioning these notes occurred when one pseudopatient asked his physician what kind of medication he was receiving and began to write down the response. "You needn't write it," he was told gently. "If you have trouble remembering, just ask me again."

If no questions were asked of the pseudopatients, how was their writing interpreted? Nursing records for three patients indicate that the writing was seen as an aspect of their pathological behavior. "Patient engages in writing behavior" was the daily nursing comment on one of the pseudopatients who was never questioned about his writing. Given that the patient is in the hospital, he must be psychologically disturbed. And given that he is disturbed, continuous writing must be a behavioral manifestation of that disturbance, perhaps a subset of the compulsive behaviors that are sometimes correlated with schizophrenia.

One tacit characteristic of psychiatric diagnosis is that it locates the sources of aberration within the individual and only rarely within the complex of stimuli that surrounds him. Consequently, behaviors that are stimulated by the environment are commonly misattributed to the patient's disorder. For example, one kindly nurse found a pseudopatient pacing the long hospital corridors. "Nervous, Mr. X?" she asked. "No, bored," he said.

The notes kept by pseudopatients are full of patient behaviors that were misinterpreted by well-intentioned staff. Often enough, a patient would go "berserk" because he had, wittingly or unwittingly been mistreated by, say, an attendant. A nurse coming upon the scene would rarely inquire even cursorily into the environmental stimuli of the patient's behavior. Rather, she assumed that his upset derived from his pathology, not from his present interactions with other staff members. Occasionally, the staff might assume that the patient's family (especially when they had recently visited) or other patients had stimulated the outburst. But never were the staff found to assume that one of themselves or the structure of the hospital had anything to do with a patient's behavior. One psychiatrist pointed to a group of patients who were sitting outside the cafeteria entrance half an hour before lunchtime. To a group of young residents he indicated that such behavior was characteristic of the oral-acquisitive nature of the syndrome. It seemed not to occur to him that there were very few things to anticipate in a psychiatric hospital besides eating.

A psychiatric label has a life and an influence of its own. Once the impression has been formed that the patient is schizophrenic, the expectation is that he will continue to be schizophrenic. When a sufficient amount of time has passed, during which the patient has done nothing bizarre, he is considered to be in remission and available for discharge. But the label endures beyond discharge, with the unconfirmed expectation that he will behave as a schizophrenic again. Such labels, conferred by mental health professionals, are as influential on the patient as they are on his relatives and friends, and it should not surprise anyone that the diagnosis acts on all of them as a self-fulfilling prophecy. Eventually, the patient himself accepts the diagnosis, with all of its surplus meanings and expectations, and behaves accordingly (5).

The inferences to be made from these matters are quite simple. Much as Zigler and Phillips have demonstrated that there is enormous overlap in the symptoms presented by patients who have been variously diagnosed (16), so there is enormous overlap in the behaviors of the sane and the insane. The sane are not "sane" all of the time. We lose our tempers "for no good reason." We are occasionally depressed or anxious, again for no good reason. And we may find it difficult to get along with one or another person—again for no reason that we can specify. Similarly, the insane are not always insane. Indeed, it was the impression of the pseudopatients while living with them that they were sane for long periods of time—that the bizarre behaviors upon which their diagnoses were allegedly predicated constituted only a small fraction of their total behavior. If it makes no sense to label ourselves permanently depressed on the basis of an occasional depression, then it takes better evidence than is presently available to label all patients insane or schizophrenic on the basis of bizarre behaviors or cognitions. It seems more useful, as Mischel (17) has pointed out, to limit our discussions to *behaviors*, the stimuli that provoke them, and their correlates.

It is not known why powerful impressions of personality traits, such as "crazy" or "insane" arise. Conceivably, when the origins of and stimuli that give rise to a behavior are remote or unknown, or when the behavior strikes us as immutable, trait labels regarding the *behaver* arise. When, on the other hand, the origins and stimuli are known and available, discourse is limited to the behavior itself. Thus, I may hallucinate because I am sleeping, or I may hallucinate because I have ingested a peculiar drug. These are termed sleep-induced hallucinations, or dreams, and drug-induced hallucinations, respectively. But when the stimuli to my hallucinations are unknown, that is called craziness, or schizophrenia—as if that inference were somehow as illuminating as the others.

Veridical (vair-RID-ih-kal). True, or genuine.

Deleterious (dell-eh-TEER-ih-ous). Something is deleterious if it has a harmful effect.

Ambivalence (am-BIV-ah-lence). Uncertainty, or swinging from one position to the opposite.

Affective (af-FECK-tive). Emotional.

THE EXPERIENCE OF PSYCHIATRIC HOSPITALIZATION

The term "mental illness" is of recent origin. It was coined by people who were humane in their inclinations and who wanted very much to raise the station of (and the public's sympathies toward) the psychologically disturbed from that of witches and "crazies" to one that was akin to the physically ill. And they were at least partially successful, for the treatment of the mentally ill *has* improved considerably over the years. But while treatment has improved, it is doubtful that people really regard the mentally ill in the same way that they view the physically ill. A broken leg is something one recovers from, but mental illness allegedly endures forever (*18*). A broken leg does not threaten the observer, but a crazy schizophrenic? There is by now a host of evidence that attitudes toward the mentally ill are characterized by fear, hostility, aloofness, suspicion, and dread (*19*). The mentally ill are society's lepers.

That such attitudes infect the general population is perhaps not surprising, only upsetting. But that they affect the professionals—attendants, nurses, physicians, psychologists, and social workers—who treat and deal with the mentally ill is more disconcerting, both because such attitudes are self-evidently pernicious and because they are unwitting. Most mental health professionals would insist that they are sympathetic toward the mentally ill, that they are neither avoidant nor hostile. But it is more likely that an exquisite ambivalence characterizes their relations with psychiatric patients, such that their avowed impulses are only part of their entire attitude. Negative attitudes are there too and can easily be detected. Such attitudes should not surprise us. They are the natural offspring of the labels patients wear and the places in which they are found.

Consider the structure of the typical psychiatric hospital. Staff and patients are strictly segregated. Staff have their own living space, including their dining facilities, bathrooms, and assembly places. The glassed quarters that contain the professional staff, which the pseudopatients came to call "the cage," sit out on every dayroom. The staff emerge primarily for caretaking purposes—to give medication, to conduct a therapy or group meeting, to instruct or reprimand a patient. Otherwise, staff keep to themselves, almost as if the disorder that afflicts their charges is somehow catching.

So much is patient-staff segregation the rule that, for four public hospitals in which an attempt was made to measure the degree to which staff and patients mingle, it was necessary to use "time out of the staff cage" as the operational measure. While it was not the case that all time spent out of the cage was spent mingling with patients (attendants, for example, would occasionally emerge to watch television in the dayroom), it was the only way in which one could gather reliable data on time for measuring.

The average amount of time spent by attendants outside of the cage was 11.3 percent (range 3 to 52 percent). This figure does not represent only time spent mingling with patients, but also includes time spent on such chores as folding laundry, supervising patients while they shave, directing ward clean-up, and sending patients to off-ward activities. It was the relatively rare attendant who spent time talking with patients or playing games with them. It proved impossible to obtain a "percent mingling time" for nurses, since the amount of time they spent out of the cage was too brief. Rather, we counted instances of emergence from the cage. On the average, daytime nurses emerged from the cage 11.5 times per shift, including instances when they left the ward entirely (range, 4 to 39 times). Late afternoon and night nurses were even less available, emerging on the average 9.4 times per shift (range, 4 to 41 times). Data on early morning nurses, who arrived usually after midnight and departed at 8 a.m. are not available because patients were asleep during most of this period.

Physicians, especially psychiatrists were even less available. They were rarely seen on the wards. Quite commonly, they could be seen only when they arrived and departed, with the remaining time being spent in their offices or in the cage. On the average, physicians emerged on the ward 6.7 times per day (range, 1 to 17 times). It proved difficult to make an accurate estimate in this regard, since physicians often maintained hours that allowed them to come and go at different times.

The hierarchical organization of the psychiatric hospital has been commented on before (*20*), but the latent meaning of that kind of organization is worth noting again. Those with the most power have least to do with patients, and those with the least power are most involved with them. Recall, however, that the acquisition of role-appropriate behaviors occurs mainly through the observation of others, with the most powerful having the most influence. Consequently, it is understandable that attendants not only spend more time with patients than do any other members of the staff—that is required by their station in the hierarchy—but also, insofar as they learn from their superiors' behavior, spend as little time with patients as they can. Attendants are seen mainly in the cage, which is where the models, the action, and the power are.

I turn now to a different set of studies, these dealing with staff response to patient-initiated contact. It has long been known that the amount of time a person

Table 1

Self-initiated contact by pseudopatients with psychiatrists and nurses and attendants, compared to contact with other groups.

Contact	Psychiatric hospitals		University campus (nonmedical)	University medical center		
				Physicians		
	(1)	(2)	(3)	(4)	(5)	(6)
	Psychiatriasts	Nurses and attendants	Faculty	"Looking for a psychiatrist"	"Looking for an internist"	No additional comment
Responses:						
Moves on, head averted (%)	71	88	0	0	0	0
Makes eye contact (%)	23	10	0	11	0	0
Pauses and chats (%)	2	2	0	11	0	10
Stops and talks (%)	4	0.5	100	78	100	90
Mean number of questions answered (out of 6)	*	*	6	3.8	4.8	4.5
Respondents (No.)	13	47	14	18	15	10
Attempts (No.)	185	1283	14	18	15	10

*Not Applicable

spends with you can be an index of your significance to him. If he initiates and maintains eye contact, there is reason to believe that he is considering your requests and needs. If he pauses to chat or actually stops and talks, there is added reason to infer that he is individuating you. In four hospitals, the pseudopatient approached the staff member with a request which took the following form: "Pardon me, Mr. [or Dr. or Mrs.] X, could you tell me when I will be eligible for grounds privileges?" (or "... when I will be presented at the staff meeting?" or "... when I am likely to be discharged?"). While the content varied according to the appropriateness of the target and the pseudopatient's (apparent) current needs the form was always a courteous and relevant request for information. Care was taken never to approach a particular member of the staff more than once a day, lest the staff member become suspicious or irritated. In examining these data, remember that the behavior of the pseudopatients was neither bizarre nor disruptive. Once could indeed engage in good conversation with them.

The data for these experiments are shown in Table 1, separately for physicians (column 1), and for nurses and attendants (column 2). Minor differences between these four institutions were overwhelmed by the degree to which staff avoided continuing contacts that patients had initiated. By far, their most common response consisted of either a brief response to the question, offered while they were "on the move" and with head averted, or no response at all.

The encounter frequently took the following bizarre form: (pseudopatient) "Pardon me, Dr. X. Could you tell me when I am eligible for grounds privileges?" (physician) "Good morning, Dave. How are you today?" (Moves off without waiting for a response.)

It is instructive to compare these data with data recently obtained at Stanford University. It has been alleged that large and eminent universities are characterized by faculty who are so busy that they have no time for students. For this comparison, a young lady approached individual faculty members who seemed to be walking purposefully to some meeting or teaching engagement and asked them the following six questions.

1) Pardon me, could you direct me to Encina Hall? (at the medical school: ... to the Clinical Research Center?).

2) Do you know where Fish Annex is? (there is no Fish Annex at Stanford).

3) Do you teach here?.

4) How does one apply for admission to the college? (at the medical school: ... to the medical school?).

5) Is it difficult to get in?

6) Is there financial aid?

Without exception, as can be seen in Table 1 (column 3), all of the questions were answered. No matter how rushed they were, all respondents not only maintained eye contact, but stopped to talk. Indeed, many of the respondents went out of their way to direct or take the questioner to the office she was seeking, to try to locate "Fish Annex," or to discuss with her the possibilities of being admitted to the university.

Similar data, also shown in Table 1 (columns 4, 5, and 6) were obtained in the hospital. Here too, the young lady came prepared with six questions. After the first questions, however, she remarked to 18 of her respondents (column 4), "I'm looking for a psychiatrist," and to 15 others (column 5), "I'm looking for an internist." Ten other respondents received no inserted comment (column 6). The general degree of cooperative responses is considerably higher for these university groups than it was for pseudopatients in psychiatric hospitals. Even so, differences are apparent within the medical school setting. Once having indicated that she was looking for a psychiatrist, the degree of cooperation elicited was less than when she sought an internist.

POWERLESSNESS AND DEPERSONALIZATION

Eye contact and verbal contact reflect concern and individuation; their absence, avoidance and depersonalization. The data I have presented do not do justice to the rich daily encounters that grew up around matters of depersonalization and avoidance. I have records of patients who were beaten by staff for the sin of having initiated verbal contact. During my own experience, for example, one patient was beaten in the presence of other patients for having approached an attendant and told him, "I like you." Occasionally, punishment meted out to patients for misdemeanors seemed so excessive that it could not be justified by the most radical interpretations of psychiatric canon. Nevertheless, they appeared to go unquestioned. Tempers were often short. A patient who had not heard a call for medication would be roundly <u>excoriated</u>, and the morning attendants would often wake patients with, "Come on, you m – – – f – – -s, get out of bed!"

Neither anecdotal nor "hard" data can convey the overwhelming sense of powerlessness which invades the individual as he is continually exposed to the depersonalization of the psychiatric hospital. It hardly matters *which* psychiatric hospital – the excellent public ones and the very plush private hospital were better than the rural and shabby ones in this regard, but, again, the features that psychiatric hospitals had in common overwhelmed by far their apparent differences.

Powerlessness was evident everywhere. The patient is deprived of his legal rights by dint of his psychiatric commitment (21). He is shorn of credibility by virtue of his psychiatric label. His freedom of movement is restricted. He cannot initiate contact with the staff, but may only respond to such overtures as they make. Personal privacy is minimal. Patient quarters and possessions can be entered and examined by any staff member, for whatever reason. His personal history and anguish is available to any staff member (often including the "grey lady" and "candy striper" volunteer) who chooses to read his folder, regardless of their therapeutic relationship to him. His personal hygiene and waste evacuation are often monitored. The water closets may have no doors.

At times, depersonalization reached such proportions that the pseudopatients had the sense that they were invisible, or at least unworthy of account. Upon being admitted, I and other pseudopatients took the initial physical examinations in a semipublic room, where staff members went about their own business as if we were not there.

On the ward, attendants delivered verbal and occasionally serious physical abuse to patients in the presence of other observing patients, some of whom (the pseudopatients) were writing it all down. Abusive behavior, on the other hand, terminated quite abruptly when other staff members were known to be coming. Staff are credible witnesses. Patients are not.

A nurse unbuttoned her uniform to adjust her brassiere in the presence of an entire ward of viewing men. One did not have the sense that she was being seductive. Rather, she didn't notice us. A group of staff persons might point to a patient in the dayroom and discuss him animatedly, as if he were not there.

One illuminating instance of depersonalization and invisibility occurred with regard to medications. All told, the pseudopatients were administered nearly 2100 pills, including Elavil, Stelazine, Compazine, and Thorazine, to name but a few.[2] (That such a variety of medications should have been administered to patients presenting identical symptoms is itself worthy of note.) Only two were swallowed. The rest were either pocketed or deposited in the toilet. The pseudopatients were not alone in this. Although I have no precise records on how many patients rejected their medications, the pseudopatients frequently found the medications of other patients in the toilet before they deposited their own. As long as they were cooperative, their behavior and the pseudopatients' own in this matter, as in other important matters, went unnoticed throughout.

Reactions to such depersonalization among pseudopatients were intense. Although they had come to the hospital as participant observers and were fully aware that they did not "belong," they nevertheless found themselves caught up in and fighting the process of depersonalization. Some examples: a graduate student in psychology asked his wife to bring his textbooks to the hospital so he could "catch up on his homework"—this despite the elaborate precautions taken to conceal his professional association. The same student, who had trained for quite some time to get into the hospital, and who had looked forward to the experience, "remembered" some drag races that he had wanted to see on the weekend and insisted that he be discharged by that time. Another pseudopatient attempted to romance with a nurse. Subsequently, he informed the staff that he was applying for admission to graduate school in psychology and was very likely to be admitted, since a graduate professor was one of his regular hospital visitors. The same person began to engage in psychotherapy with other patients—all of this as a way of becoming a person in an impersonal environment.

THE SOURCES OF DEPERSONALIZATION

What are the origins of depersonalization? I have already mentioned two. First are attitudes held by all of us toward the mentally ill—including those who treat them—attitudes characterized by fear, distrust, and horrible expectations on the one hand, and benevolent intentions on the other. Our ambivalence leads, in this instance as in others, to avoidance.

Second, and not entirely separate, the **hierarchical** structure of the psychiatric hospital facilitates depersonalization. Those who are at the top have least to do with patients, and their behavior inspires the rest of the staff. Average daily contact with psychiatrists, psychologists, residents, and physicians combined ranged from 3.9 to 25.1 minutes, with an overall mean of 6.8 (six pseudopatients over a total of 129 days of hospitalization). Included in this average are time spent in the admissions interview, ward meetings in the presence of a senior staff member, group and individual psychotherapy contacts, case presentation conferences, and discharge meetings. Clearly, patients do not spend much time in interpersonal contact with doctoral staff. And doctoral staff serve as models for nurses and attendants.

There are probably other sources. Psychiatric installations are presently in serious financial straits. Staff shortages are pervasive, staff time at a premium. Something has to give, and that something is patient contact. Yet, while financial stresses are realities, too much can be made of them. I have the impression that the psychological forces that result in depersonalization are much stronger than the fiscal ones and that the addition of more staff would not correspondingly improve patient care in this regard. The incidence of staff meetings and the enormous amount of record-keeping on the patients, for example, have not been as substantially reduced as has patient contact. Priorities exist, even during hard times. Patient contact is not a significant priority in the traditional psychiatric hospital, and fiscal pressures do not account for this. Avoidance and depersonalization may.

Heavy reliance upon **psychotropic** medication tacitly contributes to depersonalization by convincing staff that treatment is indeed being conducted and that further patient contact may not be necessary. Even here, however, caution needs to be exercised in understanding the role of psychotropic drugs. If patients were powerful rather than powerless, if they were viewed as interesting individuals rather than diagnostic entities, if they were socially significant rather than social **lepers**, if their anguish truly and wholly compelled our sympathies and concerns, would we not *seek* contact with them, despite the availability of medications? Perhaps for the pleasure of it all?

THE CONSEQUENCES OF LABELING AND DEPERSONALIZATION

Whenever the ratio of what is known to what needs to be known approaches zero, we tend to invent "knowledge" and assume that we understand more than we actually do. We seem unable to acknowledge that we simply don't know. The needs for diagnosis and remediation of behavioral and emotional problems are enormous. But rather than acknowledge that we are just embarking on understanding, we continue to label patients "schizophrenic," "manic-depressive," and "insane," as if in those words we had captured the essence of understanding. The facts of the matter are that we have known for a long time that diagnoses are often not useful or reliable, but we have nevertheless continued to use them. We now know that we cannot distinguish

---

Excoriated (ex-KOR-ih-ated). To *excoriate* someone is to give them strong or vicious criticism.

Hierarchical (HIGH-er-ARK-ih-kal). Arranged in order, from top to bottom or from highest to lowest.

Psychotropic (SIGH-koh-TROP-ick). Something that acts on the mind rather than on the body.

Lepers (LEP-ers). People who suffer from leprosy (LEP-proh-see), a disfiguring disease. In olden days, lepers were segregated into isolated colonies where they couldn't transmit this unfortunate disease to others.

insanity from sanity. It is depressing to consider how that information will be used.

Not merely depressing, but frightening. How many people, one wonders, are sane but not recognized as such in our psychiatric institutions? How many have been needlessly stripped of their privileges of citizenship, from the right to vote and drive to that of handling their own accounts? How many have **feigned** insanity in order to avoid the criminal consequences of their behavior, and conversely, how many would rather stand trial than live interminably in a psychiatric hospital—but are wrongly thought to be mentally ill? How many have been stigmatized by well-intentioned, but nevertheless erroneous, diagnoses? On the last point, recall again that a "type 2 error" in psychiatric diagnosis does not have the same consequences it does in medical diagnosis. A diagnosis of cancer that has been found to be in error is cause for celebration. But psychiatric diagnoses are rarely found to be in error. The label sticks, a mark of inadequacy forever.

Finally, how many patients might be "sane" outside the psychiatric hospital but seem insane in it—not because craziness resides in them, as it were, but because they are responding to a bizarre setting, one that may be unique to institutions which harbor **nether** people? Goffman (4) calls the process of socialization to such institutions "**mortification**"—an apt metaphor that includes the processes of depersonalization that have been described here. And while it is impossible to know whether the pseudopatients's responses to these processes are characteristic of all inmates—they were, after all, not real patients—it is difficult to believe that these processes of socialization to a psychiatric hospital provide useful attitudes or habits of response for living in the "real world."

SUMMARY AND CONCLUSIONS

It is clear that we cannot distinguish the sane from the insane in psychiatric hospitals. The hospital itself imposes a special environment in which the meanings of behavior can easily be misunderstood. The consequences to patients hospitalized in such an environment—the powerlessness, depersonalization, segregation, mortification, and self-labeling—seem undoubtedly countertherapeutic.

I do not, even now, understand this problem well enough to perceive solutions. But two matters seem to have some promise. The first concerns the proliferation of community mental health facilities, of crisis intervention centers, of the human potential movement, and of behavior therapies that, for all of their own problems, tend to avoid psychiatric labels, to focus on specific problems and behaviors, and to retain the individual in a relatively nonpejorative environment. Clearly, to the extent that we refrain from sending the distressed to insane places, our impressions of them are less likely to be distorted. (The risk of distorted perceptions, it seems to me, is always present, since we are much more sensitive to an individual's behaviors and verbalizations than we are to the subtle contextual stimuli that often promoted them. At issue here is a matter of magnitude. And, as I have shown, the magnitude of distortion is exceedingly high in the extreme context that is a psychiatric hospital.)

The second matter that might prove promising speaks to the need to increase the sensitivity of mental health workers and researchers to the *Catch 22* position of psychiatric patients. Simply reading materials in this area will be of help to some such workers and researchers. For others, directly experiencing the impact of psychiatric hospitalization will be of enormous use. Clearly, further research into the social psychology of such total institutions will both facilitate treatment and deepen understanding.

I and other pseudopatients in the psychiatric setting had distinctly negative reactions. We do not pretend to describe the subjective experiences of true patients. Theirs may be different from ours, particularly with the passage of time and the necessary process of adaptation to one's environment. But we can and do speak to the relatively more objective indices of treatment within the hospital. It could be a mistake, and a very unfortunate one, to consider that what happened to us derived from malice or stupidity on the part of the staff. Quite the contrary, our overwhelming impression of them was of people who really cared, who were committed and who were uncommonly intelligent. Where they failed, as they sometimes did painfully, it would be more accurate to attribute those failures to the environment in which they, too, found themselves than to personal **callousness**. Their perceptions and behavior were controlled by the situation, rather than being motivated by a malicious disposition. In a more **benign** environment, one that was less attached to global diagnosis, their behaviors and judgments might have been more benign and effective.

FOOTNOTES

[1]Reprinted by permission of the author and publisher from *Science,* 1973, **179,** 250-258. Copyright 1973 by the American Association for the Advancement of Science.

²Elavil (EL-ah-vil) is an upper, while Stelazine (STELL-ah-zine), Compazine (COMP-ah-zine), and Thorazine (THOR-ah-zine) are major tranquilizers and antipsychotic drugs.

REFERENCES AND NOTES

1. P. Ash., *J. Abnorm. Soc. Psychol.* **44**, 272 (1949); A.T. Beck, *Amer. J. Psychiat.* **119**, 210 (1962); A. T. Boisen, *Psychiatry* **2**, 233 (1938); N. Kreitman, *J. Ment. Sci.* **107**, 876 (1961): N. Kreitman, P. Sainsbury, J. Morrisey, J. Towers, J. Scrivener, *ibid.*, p. 887; H.O. Schmitt and C.P. Fonda, *J. Abnorm. Soc. Psychol.* **53**, 262 (1956); W. Seeman, *J. Nerv. Ment. Dis.* **118**, 541 (1953). For an analysis of these artifacts and summaries of the disputes, see J. Zubin, *Annu. Rev. Psychol.* **18**, 373 (1967); L. Phillips and J.G. Dragums, *ibid.*, **22** 447 (1971).
2. R. Benedict, *J. Gen. Psychol.* **10**, 59 (1934).
3. See in this regard H. Becker, *Outsiders: Studies in the Sociology of Deviance* (Free Press, New York, 1963); B. M. Braginsky, D. D. Braginsky, K. Ring, *Methods of Madness: The Mental Hospital as a Last Resort* (Holt, Rinehart & Winston, New York, 1969); G.M. Crocetti and P.V. Lemkau, *American Sociol. Rev.* **30**, 577 (1965); E. Goffman, *Behavior in Public Places* (Free Press, New York, 1964); R. D. Laing, *The Divided Self; A Study of Sanity and Madness* (Quadrangle, Chicago, 1960); D. L. Phillips, *Amer. Sociol. Rev.* **28**, 963 (1963); T. R. Sarbin, *Psychol. Today* **6**, 18 (1972); E. Schur, *Amer. J. Sociol.* **75**, 309 (1969); T. Szasz, *Law, Liberty and Psychiatry* (Macmillan, New York, 1963); *The Myth of Mental Illness: Foundations of a Theory of Mental Illness* (Hoeber Harper, New York, 1963). For a critique of some of these views, see W. R. Gove, *Amer. Sociol. Rev.* **35**, 873 (1970).
4. E. Goffman, *Asylums* (Doubleday, Garden City, N.Y., 1963).
5. T. J. Scheff, *Being Mentally Ill: A Sociological Theory* (Aldine, Chicago, 1966).
6. Data from a ninth pseudopatient are not incorporated in this report because, although his sanity went undetected, he falsified aspects of his personal history, including his marital status and parental relationships. His experimental behaviors therefore were not identical to those of the other pseudopatients.
7. A. Barry, *Bellevue Is a State of Mind* (Harcourt Brace Jovanovich, New York, 1971); I. Belknap, *Human Problems of a State Mental Hospital* (McGraw-Hill, New York, 1956); W. Caudill, F. C. Redlich, H.R. Gilmore, E.B. Brody, *Amer. J. Orthopsychiat.* **22**, 314 (1952); A.R. Goldman, R.H. Bohr, T.A. Steinberg, *Prof. Psychol.* **1**, 427 (1970); unauthored, *Roche Report* I (No. 13), 8 (1971).
8. Beyond the personal difficulties that the pseudopatient is likely to experience in the hospital, there are legal and social ones that, combined, require considerable attention before entry. For example, once admitted to a psychiatric institution, it is difficult, if not impossible, to be discharged on short notice, state law to the contrary notwithstanding. I was not sensitive to these difficulties at the outset of the project, nor to the personal and situational emergencies that can arise, but later a writ of habeas corpus was prepared for each of the entering pseudopatients and an attorney was kept "on call during every hospitalization. I am grateful to John Kaplan and Robert Bartels for legal advice and assistance in these matters.
9. However distasteful such concealment is, it was a necessary first step to examining these questions. Without concealment, there would have been no way to know how valid these experiences were; nor was there any way of knowing whether whatever detections occurred were a tribute to the diagnostic acumen of the staff or to the hospital's rumor network. Obviously, since my concerns are general ones that cut across individual hospitals and staffs, I have respected their anonymity and have eliminated clues that might lead to their identification.
10. Interestingly, of the 12 admissions, 11 were diagnosed as schizophrenic and one, with identical symptomatology, as manic-depressive psychosis. This diagnosis has a more favorable prognosis, and it was given by the only private hospital in our sample. On the relations between social class and psychiatric diagnosis, see A. deB. Hollingshead and F.C. Redlich, *Social Class and Mental Illness: A Community Study* (Wiley, New York, 1958).
11. It is possible, of course, that patients have quite broad latitudes in diagnosis and therefore are inclined to call many people sane, even those whose behavior is patently aberrant. However, although we have no hard data on this matter, it was our distinct impression that this was not the case. In many instances, patients not only singled us out for attention, but came to imitate our behaviors and styles.
12. J. Cumming and E. Cumming, *Community Ment. Health* **1**, 135 (1965); A. Farina and K. Ring, *J. Abnorm. Psychol.* **70**, 47 (1965); H.E. Freeman and O.G. Simmons, *The Mental Patient Comes Home* (Wiley, New York, 1963); W.J. Johannsen, *Ment. Hygiene* **53**, 218 (1969); A.S. Linsky, *Soc. Psychiat.* **5**, 166 (1970).
13. S.E. Asch, *J. Abnorm. Soc. Psychol.* **41**, 258 (1946); *Social Psychology* (Prentice-Hall, New York, 1952).
14. See also I.N. Mensh and J. Wishner, *J. Personality* **16**, 188 (1947); J. Wishner, *Psychol. Rev.* **67**, 96 (1960); J.S. Bruner and R. Tagiuri, in *Handbook of Social Psychology*, G. Lindzey, Ed. (Addison-Wesley, Cambridge, Mass., 1954, vol. 2, pp 634-654; J.S. Bruner, D. Shapiro, R. Tagiuri, in *Person Perception and Interpersonal Behavior*, R. Tagirui and L. Petrillo, Eds. (Stanford Univ. Press, Stanford, Calif., 1958), pp. 277-288.
15. For an example of a similar self-fulfilling prophecy, in this instance dealing with the central trait of intelligence, see R.

Feigned (rhymes with "rained"). Pretended.

Nether (NETH-er). Lower. The official name for Holland is "The Netherlands," meaning "The Lowlands."

Mortification (mor-tif-ih-KAY-shun). Self-inflicted pain or shame.

Callousness (KAL-us-ness). A "callous" is a hardened lump of tissue (such as skin). The *corpus callosum*--the bridge of neural tissue which connects the two hemispheres of the brain--gets its name from its "hardened appearance."

Benign (bee-NINE). Something that is comfortable, or not dangerous. A benign tumor is one that isn't life-threatening.

Rosenthal and L. Jacobson, *Pygmalion in the Classroom* (Holt, Rinehart & Winston, New York, 1969).
16. E. Zigler and L. Phillips, *J. Abnorm. Soc. Psychol.* **63**, 69 (1961). See also R. K. Freudenberg and J.P. Robertson, *A.M.A. Arch. Neurol. Psychiatr.* **76**, 14 (1956).
17. W. Mischel, *Personality and Assessment* (Wiley, New York, 1968).
18. The most recent and unfortunate instance of this tenet is that of Senator Thomas Eagleton.
19. T.R. Sarbin and J.C. Mancuso, *J. Clin. Consult. Psychol.* **35**, 159 (1970); T.R. Sarbin, *ibid.* **31**, 447 (1967).
20. A.H. Stanton and M.S. Schwartz, *The Mental Hospital: A Study of Institutional Participation in Psychiatric Illness and Treatment* (Basic, New York, 1954).
21. D.B. Wexler and S.E. Scoville, *Ariz. Law Rev.* **13**, 1 (1971).
22. I thank W. Mischel, E. Orne, and M.S. Rosenhan for comments on an earlier draft of this manuscript.